D1544540

Blood and Politics

blood
AND
politics

The History of the White Nationalist Movement
from the Margins to the Mainstream

Leonard Zeskind

Farrar Straus Giroux • New York

Farrar, Straus and Giroux
18 West 18th Street, New York 10011

Distributed in Canada by Douglas & McIntyre Ltd.
Printed in the United States of America
First edition, 2009

Library of Congress Cataloging-in-Publication Data
Zeskind, Leonard.
    Blood and politics : the history of the white nationalist movement
from the margins to the mainstream / Leonard Zeskind.—1st ed.
        p.   cm.
    Includes bibliographical references and index.
    ISBN-13: 978-0-374-10903-5 (hardcover : alk. paper)
    ISBN-10: 0-374-10903-6 (hardcover : alk. paper)
    1. White supremacy movements—United States—History.
2. Nationalism—United States—History.   3. Whites—Race identity—United
States.   4. Whites—United States—Politics and government.   5. Racism—
United States—History.   6. United States—Race relations.   7. United
States—Ethnic relations.   8. United States—Politics and government—
1945–1989.   9. United States—Politics and government—1989–   I. Title.

E184.A1Z47   2009
305.800973—dc22

                                                            2008046131

Designed by Debbie Glasserman

www.fsgbooks.com

1   3   5   7   9   10   8   6   4   2

For Carol

CONTENTS

PREFACE

As the last century ended and the year 2000 began, my hometown newspaper, *The Kansas City Star*, asked me to write a short guest opinion piece predicting the course of the new century. It was part of a journalistic time capsule, an editor said, and would likely be read a hundred years hence. The same had been done by the newspaper's forebearers on January 1, 1901, when men considered "prominent" in Kansas City wrote short pieces about the future. A bit nervous about prognosticating in general, particularly in fewer than five hundred words, I asked the editor to send, as a guide, copies of the articles written one hundred years prior.

Each had been penned by a religious, civic, political, or economic captain of the city. A great hopefulness pervaded their expectations of scientific and industrial advances. In this regard, these city fathers (and they were all fathers) reflected the optimistic spirit of the age. Edward Bellamy's *Looking Backward* was then immensely popular, for example, as one of almost fifty utopian novels published during that period.[1] One of the most fascinating aspects of these turn-of-the-century opinion pieces is that several predicted a happy future in explicitly racist terms. Not that they didn't worry about challenges to white supremacy's permanence. The city's "leading lawyer" feared that "the yellow peril threatens the world with untold disaster." One preacher fretted that the Fourteenth Amendment, which constitutionally guaranteed the rights of citizenship to black people, had been a "capital blunder." But a more prominent Baptist minister prophesied a noble century to come, including the end of war and the uplift of the poor, all under "the growing supremacy of the Anglo-Saxon."[2] In this regard also, the city's sires reflected the spirit of the nation's elites at that time. University deans then taught that humanity could be improved through eugenics, the supposed science of selective "up breeding."[3] The Supreme Court had recently ruled that "separate" was equal, and newspapers uncritically published accounts steeped in these and related ideas.

The twentieth century did not end as it had begun. Science and technology, as predicted, did reach new heights. They split the atom, took us to the moon, and created a global cyberspace communications system. They could have also provided food to every hungry soul on the planet— but they didn't. Instead, scientific advances fed an unending series of wars, genocides, and man-made disasters. And the ethic of Aryan supremacy, so prevalent a hundred years earlier, (temporarily) buried itself beneath the mountains of human ash produced by Hitler's crematories. After World War Two, Europeans ceded legal sovereignty over Africa, Asia, and Latin America to their noticeably more darkly hued (former) subjects, even as the strains of four centuries of colonial exploitation were not erased. And in Kansas City, the newspaper-for-the-future included opinions by four women and three persons of color, including the city's first black mayor.

My contribution to that time capsule stemmed directly from the subject under consideration here. I predicted a mid-twenty-first century conflict within the United States as white people became a minority in a nation of minorities and were no longer able to preserve a system of white privilege through majority-rule winner-take-all democracy. As the century wore on, I wrote, white nationalists would push toward instituting new forms of racial apartheid and other antidemocratic measures. The outcome in the year 2100, I argued, would depend on what we learned today about white supremacy and white nationalism.[4] This book does not pretend to predict prospective events, but it is not simply an account of the past either. While it is a history focused on the last decades of the twentieth century and the first years of the twenty-first, it is my intention that it serve as part of a prolegomenon to the future discussion of racial egalitarianism and democracy. My hope is that it will provide the reader a view of the contemporary white nationalist movement that is both comprehensive and instructive. Though it takes into account organizations, individuals, and events such as the Ku Klux Klan, David Duke, and the Oklahoma City bombing—things ascribed more to memory at this point than daily life—the objective is to demonstrate that this movement, driven by a vision well within the mainsprings of American life, is already self-consciously pitching itself toward the future. Perhaps when white nationalism's next iteration emerges, our country will better understand it.

. . .

My own route to this book spans more than a quarter of a century. In the late 1970s, when I first began studying the subject, I worked in steel fabrication shops reading blueprints and welding together beer truck drop frames, parts for rock quarry conveyor systems, and pieces of car plant assembly lines. As a grassroots activist, who traced my own involvements back to anti–Vietnam War protests and support for black freedom movements, I was both surprised and concerned by a renewal of Ku Klux Klan and neo-Nazi violence in the South. I had once believed "the Klan" to be a thing of the past. But I was wrong. Assaults in Mississippi in 1978, shots aimed at civil rights leaders in Alabama, and the murder of five communists in North Carolina in 1979 were the most overt proof. When a coalition of religious, civil rights, and leftist organizations called for a march to protest racist violence in Greensboro on February 1, 1980—the twentieth anniversary of the historic lunch counter sit-ins—I took time off from my job and drove south from Kansas City. More than ten thousand paraded that day, in an uplifting and inspiring demonstration of human solidarity.

Convinced by the history of the early civil rights movement that small groups of determined individuals could influence and change the world around them, I believed that racists could turn the wheels of history as well as antiracists could. If I believed that losing a day's pay to march against Klan violence could help repair the world, I also began to see how white supremacists holding meetings, distributing literature, and shooting at people could tear that same world apart. During those years I thought less about immediate government and public policy toward the racist upsurge and more about the cumulative impact it was having on civil society, the voluntary institutions upon which this country's cultural and social life is founded. Like a chain of unfiltered smokestacks, white supremacists were poisoning the political atmosphere, as well as spilling blood upon the earth. It has been these concerns that have remained with me over the decades since.

With the eager curiosity of an initiate, I began by investigating this problem in depth. I read racist and anti-Semitic booklets and periodicals, kept newspaper clippings, and began a primitive filing system. When events allowed, I attended meetings and rallies—a survivalist expo where guns mixed with religion, a small Klan rally populated by men wearing swastikas, and a Posse Comitatus gathering where Aryan organizers drew in distraught farmers. Sometimes I would stand to the side and formally take notes and photos. Sometimes I would just blend in. Often I would strike up a conversation and get to know the person next to me. At one tax protest event, an engaging Arizonan attended and played the bagpipes. Shortly thereafter I discovered that he was a state leader in Aryan Nations, one of the most violence-prone groups. It became obvious to me that many of these racists and anti-Semites were otherwise just ordinary folks.

I started writing and speaking about what I had learned and with a few colleagues published several issues of a small-circulation magazine. Soon my own contributions were noticed by others. When a particularly nasty strain of anti-Semitism began mutating through the Midwest, local Jewish community institutions turned to me for information and advice. Farmers in the region also contacted me for help. At a 1983 meeting in Iowa of family farmers, I detailed the variety of conspiracy-besotted groups preying on their ranks. In response, farmers came to me with intimate stories from their own communities about events that had long remained below the national media radar. Journalists from Chicago, Minnesota, and points east began calling, and I became a news source. But it was probably my discovery in 1984 of a former Klan leader at the helm of another, more election-oriented group that pushed me out of the ranks of part-time volunteers and into the ranks of full-time professionals.

It was simply a matter of cross-referencing periodicals. In one publication, entitled *White Patriot*, a man named Bob Weems was pictured leading a Klan event in Mississippi. In the second publication, a Washington, D.C., weekly titled *The Spotlight*, the same person was wearing a coat and tie as chairman of a group calling itself the Populist Party. I wrote up my conclusion: the new party chairman was a veteran Kluxer. And I contacted organizations also working in this field, the National Anti-Klan Network in Atlanta and the Klanwatch Project of the Southern Poverty Law Center in Montgomery. Together, they asked me to write a research monograph exposing this new so-called Populist Party, its Klan chairman, as well as its founder, a former salesman named Willis Carto. The two anti-Klan organizations jointly released my report at a press conference in Washington, D.C., in September 1984.[5] What had been an avocation became my vocation.

As the years passed, my research methods became more refined and comprehensive. In addition to cross-referencing a wide variety of printed sources, I watched hundreds of hours of videotapes and listened to audiotapes. I attended trials and collected courtroom documents—criminal indictments, FBI affidavits, bankruptcy filings, and depositions. One year I spent in Atlanta while working at the Center for

Democratic Renewal, attending Klan rallies in small north Georgia communities almost every other weekend. Several men and a couple of women turned to me or my immediate colleagues for help leaving the movement, and they too brought stories of their own. A steady stream of individuals from every corner of the country conveyed information about activities in their communities. Convinced that white supremacists routinely hid the truth from reporters and deliberately misled outsiders, I enlisted several volunteers to quietly attend racist meetings and events. In addition, I did my own straightforward interviews and reporting.

The racists and anti-Semites sometimes wrote about me in their publications. In one I was described as a "bigwig" in the Jewish community; actually I was a "little wig." A second tabloid decided I was "intense and humorless" and generally tried to discredit me. The descriptions veered ever further from the truth after that, and I soon read that my own ideas had supposedly turned me into an ideological descendant of Joseph Stalin. After writing a monograph published in 1986 by the National Council of Churches on the so-called Christian Identity theology, I received a letter from an imprisoned member of The Order, a group of Aryan bandits. For the most part, he thought I had described his beliefs correctly. Nevertheless, he wrote, "you are responsible for the content & accuracy of your report, & you will receive your just rewards for your lies!" Ampersands and exclamation point were included. Others were less charitable in their predictions of my future, and I took the appropriate steps to protect myself.

At each point I carefully regarded nothing and no one at face value. At a 1988 *Kristallnacht* commemoration in Tulsa, for example, I unexpectedly met a retired local college professor active in Holocaust denial circles. We talked together for an hour on the sidelines. He assured me he was interested in scholarly inquiry only. A year later I recognized him parading with skinheads and Klansmen through the streets of a small town in north Georgia. On another occasion I was a guest speaker in Sweden with an English colleague, talking about skinhead neo-Nazis and their white power music bands. In one city, several middle-aged people thanked us for the presentations but politely told us that nothing of that sort had ever happened in their community. After the program's official end, however, a teenager came up to us and quietly said that one such English band, called Skrewdriver, had just been there the week before and played to a large audience of young people.

The transatlantic traffic in white supremacy drew my attention to the way multiple organizations maintained relationships with their ideological counterparts in Europe—particularly the United Kingdom and Germany—further evidence that this was a cosmopolitan, not a parochial, movement.

Over time I developed an emotional armor that has helped me continue studying the movement firsthand. After decades of what my anthropologist friends call "participant observation," its personalities and organizational permutations have became so familiar to me that I sometimes feel as if I know what they are going to do next before they do. This book is the result of those decades of research. Despite my personal engagement, I have taken great care to treat fairly the men and women who populate the following pages. This is their story, not mine.

By dictionary definition, nations are socially constructed groups of people who share a common language, economy, and culture on a common territory. Finding a cohesive notion of national identity is something the United States has struggled with since its beginning. In the present, the dominant view is based on citizenship: if you are a citizen—whatever your race, religion, creed, or place of birth—then you are an American. Political scientists distinguish nations from another type of societal formation: states (often called countries), which are sovereign political entities that establish governments, convene courts, raise armies, and defend their borders. For mainstream Americans, the United States is simply a unitary nation-state, with a federal form of government and a multiracial populace. By contrast, white nationalists turn their skin color into a badge of a distinct national identity, and they exist in a permanent state of self-consciousness about race. They are dedicated to the proposition that those they deem to be "white" own special rights: the right to dominate political institutions, the economy, and culture. They believe that a "whites-only" nation exists in fact, if not in name. And they swear to a duty to create a whites-only nation-state on soil that once was the United States of America.

This white nationalist movement of the twenty-first century grows out of the white supremacist movement of the 1970s and 1980s, a transformation that this book documents. White supremacy is a multisided phenomenon, and a host of scholars have tackled the subject. In a seminal comparison of South Africa and the United States, the historian George M. Frederickson defined it as "the attitudes, ideologies and politics associated with the rise of blatant forms of white or European dominance over 'nonwhite' populations." In colonial America the practices of domination actually came into existence before the ideas that justified them, but as the vignette that opened this preface demonstrates, white supremacy as a political, economic, and ideological structure became so completely ingrained that it was virtually invisible to most white people. It was the way they lived, and they lived it largely without comment— except at those moments when it was most obviously challenged. At times of crisis, such as the Civil War and Reconstruction, or the arrival of large numbers of black people in the North and Midwest and out of the South during World War One, white supremacist movements emerged to oppose any change and recapture the status quo ante. After World War Two, during the 1950s and 1960s, a white supremacist movement tried to stop the civil rights revolution, but that attempt largely failed. It would be a mistake to conclude that the changes wrought in those years completely ended the economic, political, and social privileges that accrue to white people, and a debate remains among people of goodwill over the nature and extent of racial equality. The point here is that the dynamics of the 1960s caused white suprema- cists in the 1970s and 1980s to conclude that their ideological forebears had lost that battle over civil rights. As a consequence, they built a movement around the idea of white dispossession, the notion that the country that they believed had once been the sole property of white people was no longer only theirs. It is important to note that this sense of loss by a segment of white people is not rooted in any particular pol- icy aimed at promoting equal opportunity, such as affirmative action or school busing. This sentiment does not rise and fall in accordance with business cycles and is not contingent on the actual prosperity levels of this particular population. Rather, many different factors contribute to the rise and fall of the white nationalist movement, and these causes will be discussed throughout the following pages.

The ideas underlying the white supremacist movement are mani- festly false. Jews do not run the United States or the world. Black people are not inherently inferior to white people, or anybody else. The economic life and culture of United States have never been exclusively white or European. Nor are the privileges and power accruing to white people God-given or genetically driven. At the same time, political power has rested exclusively in white hands during much of this coun- try's life, and this kernel of truth resides at the heart of the white su- premacist mythology.

While some white nationalists might still wish to rule over people of color in ways reminiscent of Jim Crow segregation, most do not wish to return to the past. Instead, growing parts of the movement want to carve out a new territory free entirely of black people, Jews, and a host of oth- ers they regard as undesirable. If they must burn the entire house down in order to rebuild it from the basement up, they will. If they are able to capture the existing organs of state power and use them for some form of ethnic cleansing, then that will be the path taken. If the current generation has to wait until mid-century for their ideological progeny to plant the flag of an Aryans-only republic, then that will be their choice. Even if they do not reach their final goals, they can push the country into an abyss along the way.

A secondary thread in this discussion reaches over to a related, but distinct, phenomenon sometimes known as the Christian right. It would be impossible to treat both movements comprehensively in one book. But it is necessary here to trace those points at which the two converge, and it is my argument that white nationalists share many of the obsessions that motivate religious and cultural traditionalists. They both believe that feminists, gay men, and lesbians are destroying the (white) nuclear family. And they share the notion (with many outside their immediate ranks) that middle-class white people—men in particular—are actually victims in contemporary society, without adequate political representation. "Christian nationalism," by definition, contends that the United States is or ought to be a Christian nation. As a result, it relegates Jews and other non-Christians to a secondary status. Although a strain of white nationalism has developed without an explicit anti-Semitic conspiracy theory at its root, the focus on Jews is a primary tenet of most forms of white nationalism. And it is the ideology of anti-Semitism—with its belief that Jews act as an alien ruling class that needs to be overthrown—that transforms ordinary racists into would-be revolutionaries.

But this is not a story of paranoids or uneducated backwoodsmen with tobacco juice dripping down their chins, the "extremists" of popular imagination. As a movement white nationalists look like a demographic slice of white America: mostly blue collar and working middle class with a small number of wealthy individuals. Doctors, lawyers, and Ph.D.'s are among the leaders. Almost all the leaders and most of the activists are men, but women play a distinctive part in the movement, not totally unlike the traditional role assigned to them by cultural conservatives in the larger society. The internal dynamics of this movement are much like that of other political movements: some individuals join already fully convinced ideologically; others learn (and accept or reject) the movement's ideas only after becoming active in it. Rank-and-file members read a common set of periodicals and now subscribe to a similar set of cyberspace forums. Organizations and individuals quarrel over money, strategy, and power. But activists and leadership alike have pollinated across organizational lines, creating a single, if not seamless, whole. They employ significant resources in pursuit of their goals. And they look forward with hope and aspirations for the future.

At the dawn of the twenty-first century, thirty thousand men and women form its hard-core populace, and another two hundred thousand plus form a periphery of measurable supporters, giving money and attending meetings.[6] The movement has reached into every geographic corner of the country, although the areas of greatest influence lie outside the more liberal corridors of the Northeast. They have spawned at various times violent criminal gangs, sophisticated election campaigns, churches that worship an Aryan Jesus, and skinheads steeped in Norse mythologies.

Sometimes these different groups act together like the muscles and nerves of a well-coordinated athlete, and at other moments their synapses seem to be in complete collapse. Treating the movement as a comprehensive whole, a viewpoint rarely taken, enables the reader to understand the total dynamic that drives this organism and to draw the connections between its various parts. To appreciate fully the significance of the white power music subculture, for example, it is necessary to see its interaction with other parts of the movement. To grapple with the import of various electioneering efforts, the reader needs to know about the countervailing tendencies pulling at it from *within* the movement. At times activists relate to each other only through their common opposition to outside enemies. But at other times they develop a collective self-consciousness and assess and reassess their own strengths and weaknesses. As a consequence, this book spends some extra time describing the internal life of the movement—its squabbles and strategic differences—in addition to the crimes and campaigns that constitute its more formal life. "The movement" as a single entity, then, is the protagonist of this book. At the same time, it is necessary to understand the main factions that cleave its members.

Within the movement, two political trends, mainstreaming and vanguardism, vie for strategic hegemony. The differences between the two are somewhat akin to the distinctions between reformists and revolutionaries. They both seek the same goal but differ over the manner in which they work toward it. Broadly speaking, mainstreamers believe that a majority (or near majority) of white people can be won over to support their cause, and they try to influence the existing structures of American life. Vanguardists think that they will never find more than a slim minority of white people to support their aims voluntarily, and they build smaller organizations of highly dedicated cadres with the intention of forcefully dragging the rest of society behind them.

As a way of illustrating this, I focus on the two personalities who epit-
omize these trends, Willis Carto and William Pierce.[7] Each man differs
in both temperament and strategy. Carto showed up first. He was an
opportunist by disposition, intent on building a road from his post on
the outer edge of respectability into the political mainstream. Pierce
appeared a decade later, a Lenin-like revolutionary, recruiting an elitist
cadre into a vanguard force aimed at puncturing a degenerate society
and seizing power. Carto and Pierce held each other in mutual personal
contempt. And like elderly godfathers, they helped sire the movement
that followed them. The conflict between Carto and Pierce, as well as
the contention between their respective strategic orientations, shapes
our story from the beginning to the end.

Blood and Politics tells this story in a chronological fashion. Prior
to the 1970s neither Carto nor Pierce was particularly prominent in
the ranks of white resistance to desegregation and the black freedom
movement, though Carto was active in those years, sharpening his
fund-raising skills, oiling up his numerous organizational weapons, and
setting a bifurcated pair of ideological sights. That early part of the story
should be considered a preface to what follows.

When a resurgence of white supremacist activity began in the mid-
1970s, the footprints of both Pierce and Carto were found at almost
every point. At that time, baby boomers such as David Duke imbued
uniforms from the vanquished past, such as Klan robes and Confederate battle flags, with fresh style and vigor. But Klan groups were not the
only ones to grow. An innovative breed of Christian patriots invoked a
pre–Civil War form of constitutionalism lathered with an intense reli-
giosity. And they found new adherents among economically distressed
farmers in the Midwest. Also, a ganglion of would-be academics started
rewriting the Nazi nightmare out of history and reappears at several significant points in this story. During this period paramilitary survivalists
first emerged as well, and they stockpiled weapons and established rural
campgrounds. All these factions shared a set of common beliefs about
the supposedly dispossessed status of those they deemed white. And the
influence of either Willis Carto or William Pierce or the strategic trends
they represented could be found in each permutation.

In the mid-1980s a small band of warriors electrified the movement
with a stunning series of bank robberies and killings. That particular cycle of violence ended with criminal indictments and trials, although the
impulse for murder and mayhem was not permanently stilled. And a
white power music scene added young people to the vanguardist mix.
After an important trial in 1988 of several of the most significant figures,
however, the movement's vanguardist trend felt the squeeze, and main-

streaming became the more dominant strategy. David Duke was elected to the Louisiana legislature.

Despite self-imposed limits, no iron wall separated white supremacists from the larger society. Instead, a semipermeable membrane allowed influences and pressures to flow in both directions. After years of torchlight rallies, preaching, radio broadcasts, and grassroots organizing, the movement has found a distinctive "Middle American" constituency and created a set of counterculture institutions.

A decisive moment occurred in 1990–1991, when the Cold War ended, the Soviet bloc collapsed, and German unification effectively concluded the post–World War Two era. This change of historical epochs has been much commented on by others, particularly as it has affected international alignments and the emergence of ethnic nationalist movements in the Balkans and Caucasus regions. These same events also had an impact on the white supremacist movement at home.

While the Cold War and anticommunism obviously influenced domestic political alignments for more than four decades, they also helped shape Americans' sense of themselves as a people—that is, our national identity. We were defined, in part, by who we were not. We were not communists. Now communists were not communists; thus a new question presented itself: Who are we as Americans? This subliminal change in political atmospherics broke open a long-simmering dispute among American conservatives. Several stalwart Republicans who had supported foreign intervention during the Cold War suddenly jumped over to the anti–Persian Gulf War camp and isolationism. As a result, a new version of America first nationalism appeared. This was not the civic nationalism born of the Enlightenment, defined by state borders and the individual rights of an informed citizenry. Instead, it most resembled ethnic nationalism, marked by race and religion. These nationalist conservatives spun out to the edges of political respectability, where they converged with the mainstreaming wing of the white supremacist movement.

Even as these geopolitical tectonics shifted all around them, the ideological outlooks of Willis Carto and William Pierce did not change. Instead, within the larger political universe, the significance of their movement changed. A transformation occurred, and a white nationalism was born in opposition to the New World Order.

This new form of white nationalism is best exemplified in the (momentary) conjunction of two prominent political figures from dissimilar backgrounds: Republican Pat Buchanan and David Duke. As it would be impossible to fully understand Willis Carto without keeping William Pierce in mind, it is also necessary to see both godfathers at once when looking at David Duke. And without understanding the insurgency David Duke first represented, the meaning of Pat Buchanan's trajectory will remain a mystery. In the 1990s Buchanan captured most of Duke's electoral energy and cemented it to the edge of the Republican Party. Paramilitary survivalism moved from isolated compounds into the militia and a meaner gun lobby, which found support in Congress. And Holocaust deniers wagered that German unification would boost their influence. Overall, mainstreamers were filled with great expectations.

The achievements of Willis Carto's strategic followers, however, did not translate into success for him personally. After a multimillion-dollar bequest was received by one of Carto's corporate fronts, a group of its employees started a dispute with him in the mid-1990s over the fund's ultimate disposition. And what began as the most triumphal moment in his fund-raising history actually turned into his greatest organizational failure.

After the bombing in Oklahoma City in 1995, William Pierce, on the other hand, gained new fame because of a link between a book he had written and the bomber. Vanguardists also experienced some organizational fortune in the wake of this event. But the authorities arrested several squads of would-be revolutionaries and for a moment shut down that wing of the movement. By that time, however, white nationalists had already become a cutting-edge force, cowcatchers at the front of a more respectable conservative right-wing train. Scientific racists enlisted academics and scholars to further their cause. Isolationists influenced the debate about (white) America's role in the globalized world. A definable ideological stratum of white Middle Americans believed that they were threatened by malevolent economic elites from above and a multicultural underclass from below. Nativism and anti-immigrant fever, once banished from the conservative dance card, were back. And a restyled white citizens' council movement found friends inside the Republican Party.

When the millennium ended, white nationalists quietly watched the calendar pages turn, much like everybody else. They were fixated on the demographic changes to come and the birth of a more darkly complexioned United States, rather than any particular anniversary of Jesus. The September 11 terror attacks changed the immediate political environment for white nationalists. But they did not change the character of the movement itself. William Pierce's revolutionary infrastructure grew to include a white power record business, a sophisticated propaganda operation, and a set of seasoned cadres planted from Alaska and Ohio to North Carolina. The whole apparatus relied on the remarkable mystique surrounding his leadership, however, and after he died in 2002, it suffered a set of defections and eventually collapsed. By that time Willis Carto's personal and political fortunes had dimmed to invisibility. The two godfathers did not themselves cross into a white republic, but they left behind a new generation of cadres slapping their boots upon the pavement and preparing for the battles to come.

On my living room wall hangs a framed twenty-four-inch reproduction from the Sarajevo Haggadah, given to me by dear friends. The Haggadah is a book of prayers, stories, and songs used by Jews at ritual meals during the Passover holiday, which remembers the ancient Hebrews' passage from Egyptian slavery to freedom. Jews of every generation and every locale have created and re-created their own editions of this book, the Sarajevo Haggadah being one of the most beautifully illustrated. Written on bleached calfskin around 1314 in Spain, it came to the Yugo peninsula with Sephardic Jews expelled after the beginning of the Inquisition in 1492. At the end of the nineteenth century it entered the Sarajevo Museum and was saved from the grasping hands of German troops only by the clever and brave machinations of the museum's Croatian director. It was then protected by Muslim clerics in a village mosque for the duration of World War Two. Today the Haggadah is kept in the vault of the National Bank of Sarajevo, where Bosnian Serbs, Croatians, and Muslims all regard it as one of their own national treasures.[8]

The Sarajevo Haggadah's existence over the centuries and its survival during the Nazi deluge are a tragic reminder of the former Yugoslavia's multiethnicity, and it remains a sharp contrast with the horrors that ethnic nationalist wars wreaked during the 1990s. It is useful to remember that at one time a hodgepodge of religious and ethnic groups lived together in relative harmony. Places like Sarajevo were cosmopolitan centers of learning and culture for centuries. But in a matter of a few historical seconds the whole place went up in flames, like a refugee hostel attacked by arsonists. People who had lived and worked next to one another for years found themselves with divided loyalties. Families once united by interethnic marriages mourned their dead separately. As they dismembered this multiethnic state in a sea of blood, a generation of combatants cited religious and ethnic grievances hundreds of years past, as well as complaints just weeks and months old, to justify their own nationalist politics. In the end that city's remains stood in stark testimonial to its short steep slide from civilization to barbarism.

The United States, unlike the former Yugoslavia, has well cemented the foundations of its federal order in the 150 years since our own Civil

War, and the election of a black man, Barack Obama, has broken the white monopoly on the presidency. Nevertheless, collective identities based on race and religion have remained just under the skin of American life. As such, we will continue to be vulnerable to the machinations of the generations of white nationalists that follow Willis Carto and William Pierce, particularly as population demographics shift in the next few decades.

For those of us who hope to protect and extend our multiracial democracy, and the cosmopolitanism of the type that preserved the Sarajevo Haggadah, we ignore this white nationalist movement at our own peril. In the book that follows, dear reader, I have sought to make its history available now, so that we may not be destroyed by it in the future.

prequel

1955–1974

The defeat of National Socialism in Europe in World War Two was followed in the United States by a broad-based assault upon legal segregation and the white monopoly on political power. Both were broken by the the moral and political power of the black freedom movement and the judicial edicts and federal legislation that followed. While white supremacists and other segregationists staged a last stand in defense of Jim Crow, they ultimately failed. The two main characters introduced in the following pages, Willis Carto and William Pierce, received little notice during this period. But they prepare to take center stage in the years to come.

The Apprenticeship of Willis Carto

For more than fifty years, Willis Allison Carto marketed racism and anti-Semitism as if they were the solution to all the world's ills. Yet he routinely kept himself out of the public limelight and did business behind a maze of corporate fronts. Most often, what is actually known about Willis Carto's personal life comes largely from the mountains of court documents he created over the decades. At the same time, his role inside the white supremacist movements was well known to his compatriots there. David Duke once told a conference of Aryan believers: "There is probably no individual in this room who has had more impact on the movement today in terms of awareness of the Jewish question than this individual . . . Because he has not only influenced many of you individually . . . but he also has influenced the men and women who influenced you."[1]

Born on July 17, 1926, Carto recalled a Depression-era youth of thrift and enterprise in the Midwest. He mowed lawns in the summer, shoveled snow in the winter, and made deliveries on his bicycle for the local drugstore. From the basement of his parents' house in Fort Wayne, Indiana, he made money operating a small handset printing press. Young Willis attended school in Fort Wayne. After graduating from high school in 1944, he served for two years with the army in the Philippines and Japan. Upon demobilization, he joined the ranks of veterans seeking a college education, attending both Denison University in Granville, Ohio, and the University of Cincinnati.[2]

An aggressive salesman from the start, Carto began his business life in 1950 with Procter & Gamble. He then worked as a Household Finance Corporation loan officer while living in San Francisco. From 1954 to 1959 he sold printing and coffee machines.[3] In November 1958, thirty-two-year-old Willis Carto married twenty-one-year-old Elisabeth Waltraud Oldemeir. A native of Herford, Germany, she eventually took United States citizenship. They never had children. But she was a constant partner in their multiple endeavors.[4]

He also turned friends into enemies and litigated against both.

Carto's first significant enterprise was a monthly bulletin he started in 1955. Entitled *Right: The Journal of Forward-Looking American Nationalism*, it promoted many of the anti-communist, anti-Semitic, and segregationist ideas then circulating on the far right. Editing and publishing under the rubric of a corporation named Liberty and Property, Inc., he developed mailing lists and made appeals for financial support. He became adept at expressing his ideas about race and nationalism in the pages of *Right*—either under his own name or through an oft-used pseudonym, "E. L. Anderson, Ph.D." Like an apprentice entrepreneur, Carto learned during those years many of the organizational skills that later set him apart from other white supremacists.

At that time he also launched a venture called Joint Council for Repatriation. Historically, "repatriation" was the idea that black people living in the United States could best be free if they moved en masse to Africa. Some abolitionists actively supported it during the period of slavery, and after the Civil War some American blacks did settle the territory that became Liberia. In Carto's hands, however, repatriation was another thing entirely. And his correspondence from that period shows that he regarded it as a way to avoid desegregation and the assumption of full citizenship rights by black people. Carto sent out his first letter to a colleague on Joint Council stationery in January 1955—seven months after the decision in *Brown v. Topeka Board of Education*.[5] But the Joint Council died on the vine, and Carto subsequently tried to hide away his advocacy on this point.

Ultimately, Carto became best known as the chief of a multimillion-dollar outfit in D.C. called Liberty Lobby, the origin of which he dated to 1955.[6] At that point, however it existed only in his mind, and it was two more years before he floated this idea with an article in his *Right* bulletin. "Liberty Lobby," he wrote, would ". . . lock horns with the minority special interest pressure groups."[7] Carto imagined a great struggle, with himself at the center. "To the goal of political power all else must be temporarily sacrificed," he wrote.[8]

He shopped the Liberty Lobby idea to both conspiracy-obsessed anti-communists in the North and archsegregationists in the South, promising that it would "complement" their activity rather than supplant it.[9]

Preparing to focus on building Liberty Lobby, Carto closed down his *Right* bulletin in 1960 and spent the summer working at the John Birch

Society offices in Belmont, Massachusetts.[10] A conspiracy-obsessed anti-communist organization with tens of thousands of members, the Birch Society did not share all of Carto's ideological views, and it did not formally endorse his proposal for creating a Liberty Lobby. But a number of observers believe that Carto left Belmont with a copy of the Birch mailing list secretly in hand, ready to use it for his own fund-raising purposes.

Shortly thereafter, Liberty Lobby opened an office in the National Press Building in Washington, D.C. Carto named himself the corporation's secretary-treasurer and hired a staff person, who began courting representatives and senators. A periodic newsletter, *Liberty Letter*, touted the operation's activities. One of its early goals was repeal of reciprocal trade agreements,[11] and Liberty Lobby's nominal chairman, Curtis Dall, testified before the Senate Finance Committee in 1962. An "international cabal" supported free trade, Dall argued, and the "real center and heart" of this cabal was "the political Zionist planners for absolute rule via one world government."[12] Substituting the word "Zionist" when talking about Jews became a hallmark of Liberty Lobby propaganda ever after, as "anti-Zionism" became a convenient cover for anti-Semitism.

One incident from those early years illustrates much about Carto's personality and his relentless attempt to hide his political views. Looking like a mild-mannered model of middle-class probity in coat and tie, Carto walked into the Giant Super Store on Annapolis Road in Glenridge, Maryland, with two accomplices. Once inside the three split up, and each walked to a different section of the store. The thirty-six-year-old Carto grabbed a shopping cart and pushed it through the luggage section, stopping only to open suitcases, insert a fold-over four-inch printed card in each, and snap them shut again before he moved on. Continuing in the book section, Carto sensed that he was being watched. Grabbing his empty basket, he pushed to the front of the store and started to leave. But his path was quickly blocked by first one man and then several others.[13]

A small crowd watched as he was stopped and forcibly detained. Store detectives directed him to a stockroom, where he was handcuffed. The once properly dressed faux shopper now looked madly disheveled. By his own account, Carto "refused to cooperate in any way" and was treated like a "common criminal."[14] From his wallet the detectives took the remaining copies of the four-inch cards.

"Always buy your Communist products from Super Giant" was printed across the front in red ink, beside a hammer and sickle. A quotation from FBI chief J. Edgar Hoover and a list of household products were on the inside. At the time the United States and Soviet Union were locked in geopolitical combat stretching across the globe. The Western bloc and the Eastern bloc glared at each other over the Berlin Wall, which had just been built the year before. The Cuban missile crisis threatened to turn into a nuclear war. American "advisers" were starting to ship out to Vietnam. And Willis Carto was worried about Polish hams, Czech cut glass, and Yugoslav wooden bowls on the shelves at a local market.[15] In the context of the Cold War, Carto's anti-communist card passing seems bizarre, almost cartoonlike. But it was real. He was taken to a local police station, fingerprinted, and booked on a charge of disorderly conduct.[16] Two months later he was convicted before a magistrate judge and fined ten dollars.[17]

Carto subsequently filed a civil suit against Giant Food, charging that he had been called a "communist" and a "Nazi" while being arrested and been "exposed to public hatred, contempt and ridicule." For each of twelve claims, he asked twenty-five thousand dollars, a total of three hundred thousand dollars.[18] While the arrest itself did not expose much about the personality and politics of Willis Carto, his lawsuit ultimately revealed more about his personality and actual politics than he could have possibly wanted.

In civil cases of this sort, one of the first legal steps is known as discovery, a court-sanctioned investigation of the plaintiff by the defendant and vice versa, often taken in the form of oral depositions and written interrogatories. By charging that he had been defamed when called a "Nazi," Carto opened a door to questions about his own political beliefs, and Giant Food responded to each of his claims with a set of interrogatories: Where did the plaintiff go to school? Where did the plaintiff work? Describe all political affiliations. Has the plaintiff made political speeches? Where? Has the plaintiff written political articles? Please identify. Have you ever used any name other than Willis A. Carto? Questions he repeatedly tried to avoid, according to case records, but was eventually required to answer.[19]

Despite his multiple evasions, when the suit came to trial, the jury apparently had enough information to make a decision. Carto lost on all counts. Afterward the judge felt constrained to comment on the speciousness of his claims. "It seems to me, ladies and gentlemen," the Honorable Harrison Winter told the jury, "that only a very benevolent government would make available your services . . . for some four and a half trial days, and the services of the clerk of this court, the services of the court reporter, the services of the deputy marshal . . . my court crier and the services of myself for a case so utterly frivolous and devoid of merit."[20] This would not be the last judge annoyed with Willis Carto, his lawsuits, and his multiple courtroom equivocations. Nor would this be the final time that Carto entrapped himself with a device of his own construction.

Carto faced a dilemma during the early 1960s. He wanted to do more than just talk before congressional committees and surreptitiously distribute propaganda. He sought direct political power within the system of electoral politics. Yet neither the Democrats nor the Republicans fitted his needs. He considered creating a third party but decided against it. A new party would require huge sums of money, he reasoned, and encounter untold difficulties winning ballot status in many states. Worse, it would be ignored by conservative leaders. So he opted for joining the Republicans—but with a twist. Liberty Lobby would try to create its own faction inside the Republican Party, a disciplined "party within a party," as he described it. A short-lived organization calling itself United Republicans of America soon operated under Liberty Lobby's tent.

Carto's group was like a flea on this elephant until the ascent of Senator Barry Goldwater (R-AZ) in 1964. This became Liberty Lobby's first big chance to find new supporters. Although Goldwater lost badly to President Lyndon Johnson that year, he carried five states in the Deep South, states that had previously voted Democrat. The election was a portent of white voting patterns to come. To further its own goals, Liberty Lobby published truckloads of pro-Goldwater literature during the campaign. A *Labor for Goldwater* leaflet argued that white trade unionists should vote for the Republican candidate because he "opposes forcing your local [trade union] to take Negroes as members."[21] The Lobby also produced a tabloid-style biography highly critical of President Johnson. It sold fourteen million copies, and Carto was ecstatic.

"Although many Conservative organizations have expanded their activities since LBJ, none has done so as dramatically as the Liberty Lobby," he crowed. Carto's mailing list grew geometrically. At the start of the 1964 presidential election year, *Liberty Letter* had 17,000 paid subscribers. By November subscriptions had increased almost fivefold to 60,000. Six months after that it doubled again to 125,000.[22]

During this same period a major civil rights bill, with fair employment and public access provisions, was passed in Congress. The Voting Rights Act was passed a year later. Both pieces of legislation represented a significant defeat for segregationists and other conservatives. Liberty Lobby's good fortune in the midst of these setbacks provides an early lesson in a seeming contradiction. A defeat for mainline conservatives can often translate into organizational success for their more radical cousins. Hoping to use these achievements as a platform for the future,

Liberty Lobby published a program after the election titled *The Conservative Victory Plan*. When read five decades later, the *Plan* seems eerily prophetic. It describes how white conservative voters would desert the Democratic Party. "A rising tide of Negro voters will eradicate the Conservatives of one of the two parties in the South, leaving all the Conservatives in one party," it argued in 1965.[23] "A factor pushing the Republican Party into being the natural vehicle for the expression of 'White Rights' is the inevitable movement of the Democratic Party in the South toward becoming an all-Black party."[24]

Although couched in the language of "conservative" politics at the time, the *Plan* promoted many of the themes that Liberty Lobby later gave fuller expression under the banners of "populism" and "America first nationalism." It urged opposition to free trade; it implored conservatives to abandon their hostile attitudes toward trade unions. It also advocated support of "responsible Negro nationalism" and "an end to centuries of racial strife through mutual recognition of the need for racial separation."[25] In essence, it was a call to reverse the *Brown* decision and restore Jim Crow segregation, an idea with murderous proponents in the South at the time.

Despite Liberty Lobby's manifest organizational success, the D.C.-based shop could not fulfill all of Carto's political needs. As a result, he created a separate set of institutions on the West Coast less to pursue immediate practical political tasks than to carry on long-term ideological battles.

Western Destiny and the Fate of Francis Parker Yockey

Despite his expressed support for conservative ideas that aimed at restoring the status quo ante, Carto's heart belonged to the *revolutionary* political philosophy enunciated by Francis Parker Yockey and its advocacy of a new racial order. Yockey was an unusual character by any standard. A figure from the postwar anti-Semitic netherworld, he had graduated cum laude from Notre Dame Law School in 1941. He opposed American military involvement in World War Two, then seemingly reversed himself and enlisted in the army. A year later he went AWOL and was eventually discharged from the service with a medical disability for dementia praecox, an archaic psychiatric diagnosis for schizophrenia. After the war he managed to get a job writing briefs for American prosecutors at war crime trials in Wiesbaden but was dismissed after only eleven months. Yockey then spent the next fifteen years living in Europe, working with the remnants of Hitler's party in

Germany, meeting with Arab nationalists, and fancying the creation of a European-wide "liberation front."[26]

Among American white supremacists, Yockey's reputation rested on a six-hundred-page magnum opus entitled *Imperium*, written in 1948 while he lived in Ireland. Only a thousand copies of the first volume and two hundred of the second volume were initially published in England. Carto had read one of these rare early copies by 1955 and was obviously taken by its ideas.[27]

Borrowing from Oswald Spengler, a turn-of-the-century German philosopher, Yockey treated civilization as a biological organism with a life cycle. Civilizations are born, thrive, stagnate, and die. *Imperium* described in some detail Yockey's version of how Greek civilization, Nordic mythology, and Teutonic traditions provided the original sources of European strength. Yockey argued further that Western Civilization was one unit, undivided by borders based on language, religion, or economic markets. And in his schema the fate of the "West" depended more on developments in Europe than on the United States. Yockey created a specific lingo to tell these tales. "Culture creators," by his account, were the highest stratum of a civilization. "Culture distorters" occupied the lowest rung. He believed mestizo and African populations were a virus infecting the culture of the United States. He also counted the "Church-State-Nation-People-Race of the Jew" as the most destructive of "culture distorters."[28]

Carto claimed that he differed with Yockey on several points. He believed that Yockey downgraded the significance of "race" as a biological structure in the creation of culture. Like Yockey's, Carto's reasoning began with the presumption that a civilization was the product of its culture-bearing stratum. Carto explicitly argued that this stratum was a specific population or racial group. He then extended his syllogism to the conclusion that if nations embodied a specific culture, then nations were composed (only) of a homogeneous racial group.[29]

For Carto the obverse was also true. Western Civilization had entered a period of decline as a result of a polluted gene pool, he contended. And his prescription for renewal called for cultural and economic autarchy: the isolated development of a racially based civilization, unsullied by any other input. Any "influx of alien ideas, ideals, religions and peoples" might ultimately kill the American (white) culture, Carto wrote while using an assumed name. On this count, he specifically faulted the aftereffects of slavery and non-European immigration into North America.[30]

What began as a discussion of culture creation ended up with a call for a blood and soil type of nationalism at odds with the ideas of civic identity that came to the fore after World War Two. Yockey and Carto's argument that the West should be defended through a program of racial purity placed the ideas of both men outside the intellectual conventions of that time. Carto, however, spent his entire political career trying to find an avenue into the political mainstream. By contrast, Yockey lived and died on the edge of society. Despite this difference, when the two men met in person in June 1960, it was apparent that they shared a great affinity for each other. At the time, Carto still lived in San Francisco, the same city where Yockey was arrested on charges stemming from possession of multiple passports and false identification. Carto rushed to visit Yockey at the jail and twice went to his court hearings. And in the years that followed, Carto repeatedly described these events.

At the jail, a heavy screen stayed between them, but it didn't prevent Carto from sensing Yockey's powerful personality. "I knew that I was in the presence of a great force, and I could feel History standing aside me," Carto wrote after the event.[31] At the court prehearings, Carto's fascination bordered on the homoerotic. "His eyes bespoke great secrets and knowledge and such terrible sadness," he wrote as if they were intimates in a lifeboat on an unfriendly sea. "As his gaze swept across and then to me," Carto confessed, "he stopped and for the space of a fractional second, spoke to me with his eyes. In that instant we understood that I would not desert him."[32] Just a few days later Francis Parker Yockey, dressed only in underwear and his knee-high storm trooper–style boots, took a capsule of potassium cyanide that he had somehow obtained and burned his mouth before dying in the jail cell.[33]

After Yockey's suicide, Carto secured the rights to *Imperium* and reprinted it as one volume in 1962, using his own imprint, Noontide Press. He wrote an introduction for the book under his own name.[34] The Yockey faith, he believed, could "reconquer the Soul of the West."[35] Carto also made an unusually unabashed declaration of white supremacist beliefs in the introduction: "Unbiased anthropologists consider the White race to be the highest evolutionary development of life on this planet."[36] Two years later Carto's Noontide Press began publishing a twenty-four-page plain paper periodical, *Western Destiny*. It promoted Yockey's philosophy while discussing topics such as evolutionary biology, classical Rome, and the supposed virtues of the Nordic ideal. Not quite a magazine for theory, neither was it intended for a mass market. Rather, it became a vehicle for ideas then newly percolating among Carto and his ideological peers.

Carto knew that most run-of-the-mill segregationists attracted to Liberty Lobby at that time would find the Yockey faith off-putting, so he kept the two enterprises as separate as possible. Liberty Lobby, after all, was headquartered on the East Coast. *Western Destiny* was published from the West Coast, and Carto often used the name E. L. Anderson when writing in its pages.

"Culture creators," "culture bearers," and "culture destroyers" inhabited the new magazine's pages. One of its first editorials argued, for example, that "tolerance can often be a culture-retarding and culture distorting weakness."[37] Although the magazine's use of Yockeyisms guaranteed it a relatively small audience, Carto modestly considered *Western Destiny* "the most notable publishing venture in the English-speaking world."[38] He was, after all, both its publisher and one of its editors. It attracted an international readership, including Europeans interested in its discussions of art and politics. Its readers included a young David Duke, who cut his first ideological teeth on its pages.[39] And among the Americans associated with the project, several contributing writers became significant personalities on their own terms over the next two decades.[40] One of those, a man calling himself Wilmot Robertson, requires special mention here.

The author who used the nom de plume Wilmot Robertson was actually named Humphrey Ireland. An erudite and well-bred character about ten years older than Carto, he publicly described himself as a native of Pennsylvania with a long American pedigree, dating back before the Civil War. To friends and associates, Robertson claimed to have attended Yale University before World War Two, lived briefly in Germany during the 1930s, and then dodged American wartime repression of Hitler sympathizers.[41] Robertson's *Western Destiny* contributions usually treated cultural issues and the fine arts. Carto's constant huckstering annoyed Robertson, however, and he eventually pursued his own separate path.

In 1972, Robertson self-published a six-hundred-page tome entitled *The Dispossessed Majority*. Part nineteenth-century anthropology, part scientific racism, the text was accessible to anyone with a quality high school education. Unlike the dense Spenglerian lingo of Yockey's *Imperium*, this book could actually be read and understood by activists. Robertson's argument was unabashed in its simplicity: "Minority participation in politics and in every other sector of American life has now increased to where it can be said that the Majority is no longer the racial Establishment of the United States."[42]

Further, he argued, "the idea of innate racial equality had become so firmly established in modern education and in the communications media that no one could question it."[43] The contradictory character of Robertson's claims should not be lost. In his schema, the idea of white supremacy had once provided the rationale for slaveowning, colonialism, and empire. In the context of the 1960s, this same ideological construct described the loss of positions of dominance, in part because of changes wrought by a transformation in accepted ideas about "innate racial equality." Indeed, in the white supremacist mind-set, political power had always been an all-or-nothing contest between the races. And during the last half of the twentieth century, it was a battle they believed they were losing.

Western Destiny devoted itself to questions related to this seeming loss of privilege and position. Carto's editorial partner in this project was Roger Pearson,[44] a British expatriate who had become a devotee of Aryanism while living on the Indian subcontinent. By training an anthropologist, Pearson held several different university positions over the years. From 1956 to 1963 he was best known as the publisher of *Northern World*, a magazine that emphasized eugenics, a set of ideas particularly unpopular in the years immediately following World War Two. It claimed that selective breeding can improve the human gene pool, and thus humanity, and other faux scientific claims. While publishing the newsletter *Right*, Carto had done double duty as a junior editor on Pearson's project. And their partnership extended to the new Yockeyite magazine.[45]

The joint venture fell apart in 1966, and *Western Destiny* ceased publication. It turned out to be the least hostile political divorce among Carto's many such separations. The lack of publicly expressed venom by Carto may have been a result of Pearson's own independent standing and prestige. After his career diverged from Carto's, Pearson too made a mark among a second generation of so-called scientific racists. He stayed in the United States and continued to promote both scientific racism and anti-Semitism.[46] But he left the Yockey cult in favor of a career as a professional anti-communist. In 1978 he became chairman of the World Anti-Communist League, an international conglomeration of South Korean intelligence assets, European far right groups, Latin American death squads, and their North American masters.[47] He was eventually dismissed from that position. During the same period Pearson also served at the Heritage Foundation as editor of *Policy Review*, the conservative think tank's flagship periodical. For these services to the causes of anti-communism and conservative respectability, Pearson later won a letter of support from President Ronald Reagan: "Your substantial contributions to promoting and upholding those ideals and principles that we value at home and abroad are greatly appreciated."

For Carto, the years after *Western Destiny* included his own growth into a major figure among white supremacists. And after Governor George Wallace's presidential bids, Carto emerged as a godfather to the generation of white supremacist activism that followed.

Governor George Wallace, Liberty Lobby, and Youth for Wallace

The story of George Wallace has been told multiple times. He began his political career as a relatively moderate Democrat in the Alabama House of Representatives but soon became famous as a vitriolic defender of the segregated South. His 1963 inaugural address included invocations to Confederates Robert E. Lee and Jefferson Davis, the "Great Anglo-Saxon Southland," and the Christian faith. In words that defined him long after his death, Wallace proclaimed: "In the name of the greatest people that have ever trod the earth, I draw the line in the dust and toss the gauntlet before the feet of tyranny . . . and I say . . . segregation today . . . segregation tomorrow . . . segregation forever."[48] He gained national attention when he stood in a schoolhouse door in a symbolic attempt to block court-ordered integration at the University of Alabama. Acting under Wallace as Alabama's Democratic governor, his state authorities spied on, beat, and jailed civil rights activists. He allowed Klan groups a murderous free rein and paid little attention to their many victims. His closest advisers were hard-core racists and (anti-Semitic) conspiracy theorists, and his chief speechwriter was a former Klansman. When Wallace launched a bid for president during the 1964 Democratic Party primaries, he surprised poll watchers by receiving a third of the primary votes in Wisconsin, Indiana, and Maryland—all states outside his southern base.[49]

Carto and Liberty Lobby supported Wallace instinctively. Liberty Lobby produced a pro-Wallace pamphlet in 1965, *Stand Up for America: The Story of George C. Wallace*, and mailed out 175,000 copies to its own supporters. Another 150,000 copies belonged to Wallace's campaign, which regularly distributed the Liberty Lobby publication on its own.[50] When Wallace's speechwriter convened a meeting of racist and far right leaders in 1966 to jump-start a 1968 bid, Carto was invited and sent a representative.[51]

Wallace decided to run a third party presidential campaign outside both the Republican and Democratic parties in 1968. He named his third party the American Independent Party, but never called a national convention or took other serious steps to build a party apparatus free of his campaign. Instead, his most trusted lieutenants ran a top-down operation from headquarters in Montgomery. Nevertheless, outside the Alabama home base, far right groups provided much of the campaign's muscle. Paramilitary outfits such as the Minutemen in the Midwest and the Klan in the South found themselves Wallace allies. Larger groups such as the John Birch Society worked in tandem with smaller sects. Segregationists rubbed elbows with men from the national socialist world. Within this milieu, Liberty Lobby blipped on the screen much like any other group.[52]

Large areas of congruence existed between Wallace's 1968 campaign and Liberty Lobby's most immediate goals. Yet the matchup was not one-to-one. As Seymour Lipset and Earl Raab point out in *The Politics of Unreason*, Wallace "never developed either a well-constructed conspiracy theory or an ideological racism." Carto had both. Wallace had not started his career and did not end it as a racist. In the 1960s he followed behind the racist sentiment that already existed. Carto hoped instead to lead it. Wallace was a politician *first* who embraced racism *second*. Carto was an anti-Semite and white supremacist first, last, and always.

In order to set himself apart from all the other racists supporting Wallace, Carto created a separate organization called Youth for Wallace. Conceptually, the idea had potential to mine a definable trend among young whites. One poll found that 25 percent of those voters under twenty-nine years old favored Wallace, five points higher than the percentage of support among older voters. Another survey showed a class line among these young whites, with decidedly more support coming from blue-collar families.[53] They saw themselves opposed to both middle-class white antiwar students and the black freedom movement, as well as to the government, which was forcing them to fight a no-win war. Existing conservative student groups, which usually supported the war policy without question, were not positioned to capture this particular sentiment. Youth for Wallace distributed literature during the campaign, organized on campuses, and sent solicitations through the mail. Membership grew to fifteen thousand on the mailing list.

The 1968 campaign year was the most tumultuous since the Civil War and Reconstruction. The Reverend Dr. Martin Luther King, Jr., was assassinated in April by a gunman tied to white supremacists. Robert Kennedy, brother of the late President John Kennedy, ran in the Democratic Party primaries as the peace candidate until he too was assassinated the night of the California primary. Urban rebellions, the Vietnam War, and student unrest further put the country's teeth on edge. That August antiwar demonstrations at the Democratic Party's convention degenerated into a Chicago police riot. On election night in November, Republican Richard Nixon became president. But George C. Wallace and the American Independent Party, in a three-way contest, won ten million votes. He carried the South, winning a majority in Georgia, Alabama, Mississippi, Louisiana, and Arkansas. Although South Carolina, North Carolina, and Tennessee went for Nixon, Wallace received more than 30 percent of the vote in all three states. In Florida, Virginia, and Oklahoma his totals exceeded 20 percent. He also won remarkably high levels of support in the North and Midwest. Altogether, he received 13 percent of the general election total, revealing a stratum in the electorate that white supremacists later sought to capture for themselves.

Wallace's career as a lightning rod for racist sentiment effectively ended after an assassination attempt in 1972 left him partially paralyzed. After the campaigns, groups as varied as the Klan, the Citizens Councils, and the Birch Society drifted without direction. They had invested time and resources into the Wallace movement, but they came out of it with less influence and power than when they had gone in.

But not Carto; he continued to push on, bridging the defeats suffered by old-line segregationists during the 1960s with the resurgence of a new generation of white supremacists in the mid-1970s. Liberty Lobby ended the 1960s larger and stronger than when the decade began. No longer renting office space in the National Press Club, it had its own (three-story) building within blocks of Capitol Hill. Its temporary advisory board had grown into a full-time staff and regular publication of *Liberty Letter*, an all-purpose periodical with 170,000 subscribers. A special mailing list counted 23,000 donors. A third list contained the names of 230,000 former supporters.[54]

Carto sought to transform Youth for Wallace into a new organization, the National Youth Alliance, and he succeeded at first. A founding meeting that November at the Army and Navy Club in D.C. drew many of the old officers from the Wallace support group. Carto started raising funds for the new outfit and selecting a different "advisory board," more radically racist in its orientation. He also hired one of the new organization's members for a position at Liberty Lobby. In the subsequent months the National Youth Alliance sponsored several regional meetings, including a January 1969 event at Conley's Motor Hotel in Monroeville, outside Pittsburgh, Pennsylvania. It was here that the youth organization first began to unravel.

Several officers in the new group objected to the content and tenor of the meeting and an attendant social at a supporter's home. They claimed the affair was awash in Nazi heraldry, including women who wore swastika jewelry and men who sang the "Horst Wessel Lied," a

Nazi Party anthem from the 1930s. The host and emcee promoted a new booklet by Carto's West Coast enterprise, Noontide Press, *Myth of the Six Million*.[55] It argued that the Nazi genocide was a figment of the Jewish imagination. One of the formal presentations was entitled "Plato the Fascist." During his speech, Carto claimed that the United States was disintegrating from moral turpitude and the degenerate influence of democracy, and he reeled out a scenario by which Liberty Lobby could gain state power.[56] But the guts of his talk that night were spent resurrecting the specter of Francis Parker Yockey, detailing their jailhouse meeting and describing the important role that the book *Imperium* possessed.

The dissident officers were more attuned to a Wallace-like conservative racism than to any kind of openly anti-Semitic Yockeyite Hitlerism. They also objected to the direction Carto was taking the organization. A brief seesaw battle for control ensued, but Carto easily vanquished the upstart factionalists.[57] A couple of young Liberty Lobby employees incorporated the National Youth Alliance in D.C. and gave Carto formal control of the name and finances.[58] An office was opened, and a small staff began accrediting the formation of new chapters and reorganizing program priorities. Standard conservative causes went out. Promoting Yockey came in. A special paperback edition of *Imperium* was published.[59] The mathematical sign for inequality, two short parallel lines with a nullifying single crosshatch, became the organization's logo. "Free men are not equal, Equal Men are not free" was the slogan.

The National Youth Alliance was not yet self-supporting, however, and after one of the officers signed a promissory note, Carto pumped fifty thousand dollars into the outfit. By August 1970 the young Yockeyites had run out of funds again; this time the officers refused to sign another IOU.[60] Another fight for control of the corporate identity began. The contest ended differently, however, as William Luther Pierce entered the fray.

William Pierce, National Socialism, and the National Youth Alliance

In contrast with Carto's general silence about his private life, William Luther Pierce wrote an early autobiographical article about his political journey, and he consented to several long interviews about his personal history. He was born in Atlanta on September 11, 1933, and his youth was marked by hardship and instability. His father, named William Luther Pierce II, died in a car accident when Bill was just eight years old. Thereafter his mother, Marguerite, worked hard to support Bill and a younger brother, and her own childhood story may have influenced the future national socialist leader. Marguerite's biological father had run off when she was a child, leaving her fatherless, until Marguerite's mother (Bill's grandmother) remarried. The new stepfather was a Jewish man from New York who had moved south, and Marguerite had a bitter relationship with him. William Pierce's story thus begins with his own absent father and his mother's unhappy tie to a Jewish stepfather.[1]

Marguerite moved about the South with her two young sons in tow. From these travails, William Pierce claimed he learned the virtues of self-discipline and the importance of delaying immediate gratification for a greater goal, values, he said, that became constant themes in his life. He attended a public junior high in Dallas. After Marguerite took a second husband, young Bill was packed off to Allen Military Academy in Bryan, Texas, from 1949 to 1951. At the academy he won a job cleaning the chemistry lab stockroom and prized that opportunity. In contrast with Carto's fond remembrance of childhood commerce, Pierce's best memories were of being alone with his books and studies. He particularly enjoyed science fiction and was an excellent student.[2]

He attended Rice Institute (later Rice University) and was graduated in 1955, the year Willis Carto began publishing *Right* magazine. Pierce spent that summer working at the Los Alamos Scientific Laboratory and started graduate school at the California Institute of Technology in September. During his graduate school career he worked a year at the nearby Jet Propulsion Lab in Pasadena. He also married Patricia Jones, who later earned her own advanced degrees in mathematics. The newlyweds moved to the University of Colorado at Boulder, where Pierce received a doctorate in physics in 1962, the same year the couple had twin sons. His dissertation topic was unintelligible to the nonphysicist: nuclear dipole and electric quadripole resonance in the gallium arsenide crystal. During this period, after the Soviet Union's *Sputnik* entry into space, American interest in physics and science increased exponentially. At that point, the goals of the U.S. government and William Pierce's personal aspirations matched completely.[3]

Pierce became an assistant professor of physics at Oregon State University in Corvallis in 1962, settling down to raise his children and teach. Unlike Carto, who had already spent a decade practicing the art of white supremacist politics, Pierce was then still uninterested in making history. "Until I was 30 years old, I had hardly given a thought to politics, to race, or to social questions," Pierce wrote about himself.[4] But that soon changed.

While at Oregon State, he attended a few meetings of the John Birch Society, the same group for which Carto had once worked before setting up Liberty Lobby's office in D.C. Pierce did not accept the Birchers' beliefs that everyone and everything, from President Eisenhower to the civil rights movement, traced back to communism and alleged communist conspiracies. Explicit theories of racial determinism were off their agenda. "I quickly found out that the two topics on which I wanted an intelligent discussion—race and Jews—were precisely the two topics Birch Society members were forbidden to discuss," Pierce wrote later.[5]

As he studied politics and history on his own, the bookish physics professor step by step exited conventional society and entered the Frankenstein laboratory of white nationalism.

Pierce and Rockwell

Pierce left Oregon State in June 1965 and a month later started working in Connecticut for Pratt & Whitney Aircraft as a senior research associate physicist. He received a salary of $15,400 a year, a solid middle-class income from the defense industry during a period of military buildup in Vietnam. The Defense Department gave him a security clearance, but he never actually worked on classified projects during his year of full-time employment there, according to FBI documents. His colleagues described Pierce as a "real loner," not unusual among research types. But his treatment of subordinates did touch off notice, as he gave only day-to-day instructions and insisted on doing his own machining. His work began to deteriorate during the final months, and when a wildcat strike hit the plant, Pierce tried, but failed, to drive a car through a picket line of a thousand persons.[6]

During this period Pierce periodically visited American Nazi Party headquarters in Arlington, Virginia, and stayed in regular contact with George Lincoln Rockwell, the mini-führer then in charge. Rockwell, who had attended an Ivy League college and had achieved the rank of lieutenant commander in the navy, personally impressed Pierce. And the party's ideology, a version of Hitler's National Socialism, was already at the center of his self-taught belief system. Their brownshirt uniforms and swastika armbands, on the other hand, seemed to Pierce more like Hollywood antics than serious politics.

Pierce took a final vacation from Pratt & Whitney during the last week of May 1966 and came back to work only to formally resign.[7] He moved his family to Virginia. In the next years, Pierce's wife, Patricia, started teaching math at the university level, and for several years she supported her husband's political habits. (Unlike Elisabeth Carto, however, she did not join in Pierce's beliefs and later divorced him.)[8] Over the decades Pierce showed little emotional commitment to his two sons or multiple wives.[9] Only his mother, Marguerite, and his Siamese cats successfully vied with his single-minded devotion to national socialist politics. During these early years, he began a small business selling guns, NS Arms, and registered with the Bureau of Alcohol, Tobacco, and Firearms. His inventory included machine guns. The business folded after passage of gun control legislation in 1968.[10]

In 1966 Pierce reached a deal with Rockwell to edit a new publication entitled *National Socialist World*, which served as a voice for an international grouping known as the World Union of National Socialists. The two men published six issues, but still Pierce would not formally join the brownshirts until January 1, 1967, when Rockwell changed the name of his group to the National Socialist White People's Party (NSWPP). To Pierce, the new name must have represented a switch toward a more sober-minded effort. Eight months later Rockwell was assassinated by a disgruntled member.[11]

After Rockwell's death, the several dozen remaining members began to splinter. Pierce stayed with the largest faction, and by January 1968 he was a top officer and its ideological guide, but not the nominal chief. He produced written propaganda and taped telephone message recordings, then a new way that groups used for spreading their ideas. Occasionally curious university students invited him to speak at their campus. At one such event in April 1970, a speech before 450 students in Scranton, Pennsylvania, Pierce made news after proposing that President Nixon should be "dragged out of his office and shot." His pronouncement caught the eye of the FBI, which already described him as "armed and dangerous" because he carried a handgun while working in the Arlington headquarters.[12]

Pierce became increasingly disenchanted with the NSWPP. He agreed with its philosophical cornerstone—the entirety of the American political and social order needed to be destroyed in order to create a purely Aryan racial state similar to Hitler's Germany. But he wanted an organization with a distinctly American persona to start this revolution, and the party of Rockwell seemed unable to escape the uniforms of its origins.[13] He formally quit in July 1970, subsequently circulating a discussion document he called a "Prospectus for a National Front." "Ideology must never be used to establish tactical criteria," he wrote, and "[we] have to avoid isolating ourselves from the public with programs and images so radical that only a small fraction of one percent will respond."[14] In other words, he understood that wearing swastika armbands was a dead end, and he was finally ready to strike out on his own.

Pierce and the National Youth Alliance

William Pierce set his sights on Carto's National Youth Alliance, which was already embroiled in a multisided factional conflict. The Wallace-era conservatives had abandoned the project, tired of doing battle with both Carto and the young Yockeyites he supported. In the next round of infighting, the Carto loyalists were pushed aside by a band of national socialist types backed by William Pierce. Carto and Pierce each had a different stake in the fight that followed.

For Carto, money occupied the center of this dispute. He charged Pierce's colleagues with stealing Liberty Lobby's mailing lists and selling them. And Carto used those same lists and the National Youth Alliance name to prop up a rival organization. His surrogates attacked Pierce's group and accused it of being agents of some undefined enemy force. Carto presented the Pierce faction with an invoice for forty thousand dollars, claiming the money was owed for rental of Liberty Lobby's mailing lists. When Pierce didn't pay up, Carto had him charged with theft.[15]

For Pierce, ideas mattered most in this conflict, and he and his cohorts hunkered down for a long siege. He reincorporated the National Youth Alliance name in the state of Virginia in October 1970, freeing it from any past encumbrances.[16] The Pierce people filed a civil suit against Carto for libel.[17] They also issued a broadside attack against Carto, a two-page letter with eight pages of "exhibits." They claimed Carto backed a phony National Youth Alliance faction actually controlled by "Zionists." Most of Pierce's other allegations involved Carto's repeated scamming of Liberty Lobby's donors. One document provided evidence that Liberty Lobby routinely rented and sold its mailing lists, all while telling its members that it did nothing of the kind.[18]

Pierce's most significant accusation claimed that Carto had bilked his own followers of fifty-five thousand dollars. The evidence proved so overwhelming that future antagonists of Carto within the movement repeated the complaint over the next three decades, whenever they wanted to prove that the Liberty Lobby mogul was actually a scam artist.

The specifics of this particular charge revealed a portion of the corporate maze Carto had created. Apparently, Carto had first made an emergency appeal to Liberty Lobby's supporters, claiming that the organization could no longer afford to pay rent. Liberty Lobby needed to own its building rather than lease it. As a result, Lobby contributors responded generously. Carto then fooled donors into believing that the office building it already occupied at 300 Independence Avenue SE was indeed purchased by Liberty Lobby and payment made in full. To prove this point, Pierce cited a 1969 issue of Liberty Lobby's newsletter. In it was a photograph of the Lobby's chairman, supposedly giving a $55,235.27 check to a bank holding the building's mortgage. The photo was a fake, according to Pierce, who included exhibits showing that another of Carto's corporate fronts, Government Educational Foundation—not Liberty Lobby—actually owned the building. Liberty Lobby still paid rent.[19]

Carto's scheme worked like a game of three-card monte, and only someone like Pierce, whose colleagues had gotten close to the nerve center, could have figured out which corporate pot held the money. Pierce didn't stop there. One particularly nasty exhibit described Carto as "a short swarthy man of medium build" ("swarthy" being a favorite code for non-Aryan whites). The depiction was meant as a pointed contrast with Pierce, who was six feet four, long-headed, and closer to the Nordic ideal body type at two hundred plus pounds. Pierce went on to reveal five of the pseudonyms Carto employed, including E. L. Anderson, Ph.D.

Obviously, if Carto had actually litigated against Pierce, more secrets would have been spilled in the civil suits than oil from the *Exxon Valdez*. They fought each other to a standstill. Carto dropped the theft charges against Pierce, and Pierce did not pursue the libel complaint. Carto walked away, his Liberty Lobby money machine still intact. Pierce prevailed in controlling the National Youth Alliance corporate name. Despite this victory, Pierce was forced to admit that Carto's battering had taken a toll. "Carto's attacks have been very costly to NYA," he wrote. "By confusing many NYA supporters with his false accusations, Carto has caused NYA's income to drop sharply, seriously hampering its work."[20]

In this round of events, both men had started with the hope that they could recruit young people to their cause. Their immediate goals differed. Carto wanted his version of the National Youth Alliance to form a bridge between Wallace-style conservatives and radical white nationalists. In this vision, the Liberty Lobby building near Capitol Hill would engage in a form of white supremacist realpolitik, while Carto's more ideological enterprises would remain headquartered on the West Coast. Pierce, by contrast, wanted to break completely with all manner of conservatism. He wanted to pull away from mainstream politics and create a separate parallel universe, counterinstitutions uncontaminated by compromise. His concerns were distinctly noncommercial. Pierce aimed at developing talented ideological cadres, not a mailing list of dupes for financial support.

Both men and their respective organizations fell into a lull. After ten years of rapid growth, Liberty Lobby slowed to a standstill. Its influence on Capitol Hill began to wane as the power of hard-core segregationists died out in Congress. And public exposure became one of Carto's biggest problems. A 1971 article in the conservative weekly magazine *National Review* drew a straight line from Yockey and anti-Semitism to Liberty Lobby, uncovering a set of connections that Carto had tried to keep buried from the beginning of his career. The author described many of Carto's assets: "He is the man behind such respectable-sounding organizations as Liberty Lobby, United Congressional Appeal, Save Our Schools, Americans for National Security, the *Washington Observer*, the *American Mercury*." The whole complex, the magazine deduced, had "annual receipts of at least a million dollars." *National Review* had opposed civil rights legislation and supported segregationists in the 1950s, but it had become the flagship publication of the entire conservative movement. The article effectively placed Liberty Lobby outside its fence.[21]

Carto responded with a lawsuit against *National Review*, but he could not erase the damage a small bit of truth telling had done. The magazine's owners countersued, creating a legal imbroglio that lasted for years, until it was decided in the magazine's favor. [22]

During the same time period, Pierce's National Youth Alliance also stalled. Despite its revolutionary rhetoric, it expected to do little more than expand its student membership in and around the District of Columbia. It proposed organizing "Action Units" at six predominantly white universities in the area, and members attempted to sell their tabloid at these campuses and find new recruits. As part of the program, Pierce tried to convince his best student cadres to move to D.C. and work with the national office. But this attempted concentration of forces soon floundered.[23]

An incident at George Washington University caught the essence of the problem. Officially invited to speak by the university's program board on February 3, 1972, Pierce found fewer than two dozen students attending the event. Shortly after arriving at the podium, he was pelted with raw eggs, and orange smoke from a stink bomb filled the room. No one rose to defend the yolk-smeared national socialist, and the session ended quickly. Shortly thereafter the student newspaper received a phone call claiming credit for the protest. The National Youth Alliance had vowed to battle left-wing peaceniks and curb black student associations. But Pierce seemed unable to do as much as safely mount a public podium.

He responded to the incident much like any other aggrieved American. He sued for tort relief, charging the university with negligence, and asked for $10,000 in actual and $40,000 in punitive damages. A year later he agreed to a settlement from the university, whose lawyers allowed that the amount paid was "more than the $2.50 which Pierce had asked for cleaning his suit" and less than $50,000.[24] Not enough to pay for any injured pride.

The raw eggs confirmed the National Youth Alliance leadership's frank assessment of the campuses at the time: antiracists and antiwar sentiment dominated the intellectual climate at most universities.[25] In a certain sense, the racists' analysis on this point rang true. Sentiment mounted against the Vietnam War. Innovative black studies programs gained acceptance. A new growth of feminism took root along with women's studies programs. And a bold gay rights movement was just over the horizon. The National Youth Alliance's arguments for the natural superiority of white men had all the academic salience of Ptolemaic astronomy.

Further complicating Pierce's bid to build an organization of Aryan revolutionaries, the few Wallace-era conservatives left among his membership acted like a hand brake dragging down a car. They were racists and anti-Semites certainly, but conservative nonetheless, more interested in restoring the past than in overthrowing the current regime. "The NYA membership . . . in that early period," he later complained, "showed a definite [nonrevolutionary] reactionary streak."[26]

Pierce tried to keep a small spark going nonetheless. The NYA's tabloid *Attack!* published a set of "Revolutionary Notes" describing various weapons, including which rifles were best for "urban firefights." It also explained the use of explosives. One piece discussed the efficacy of bombing movie theaters. It coldly argued that bombings were just one "short-term" tactic among others less sanguinary, such as picketing and parades.[27] Despite this incendiary rhetoric, the National Youth Alliance at that time was all talk, with few troops and fewer actual bomb throwers.

Pierce traced his immediate organizational misfortunes to larger waves moving through American history: "The United States government has through slow and (until the last 20 years) nearly imperceptible change . . . been transformed from an organic institution embodying the will and aspirations of a free, White [sic] and proud citizenry to a corrupt, unnatural, and degenerate monstrosity."[28] The pejoratives and the language about organicism set aside, this analysis essentially rang true. During most of the hundred years since slavery had ended, black people had remained essentially citizens in name only, as government had rested solely in the hands of white people. This white republic, where the color of your skin determined whether or not you had voting rights and which set of laws protected your person, had been broken, however, by mass movements for civil rights and federal court action, among other factors.

Although the Goldwater and Wallace campaigns had demonstrated the possibility of a mass racist revival in the post–Jim Crow world, the Nixon presidency acted as a brake on its transformation into an autonomous movement independent of the two-party system. After the 1968 election, Nixon effectively absorbed the Wallace vote within Republican Party ranks, thereby diminishing the chances that Wallaceites would create a permanent bastion outside the party. As noted by journalists Thomas Edsall and Mary Edsall in *Chain Reaction: The Impact of Race, Rights, and Taxes on American Politics*, Nixon slowed the pace of federally mandated school integration and nominated ultraconservative southern judges to the Supreme Court. He also championed "law and order," while Vice President Spiro Agnew attacked liberals with the same vitriolic lingo previously used by Governor Wallace. But Nixon also implemented programs such as minority set-asides in construction as well as affirmative action at the same time. Much as in his diplomatic

opening to the People's Republic of China, which angered onetime supporters of a more McCarthyite, anti-communist Nixon, the president
co-opted and then defanged any embryonic movement based on white
racial resentments outside the Republican Party. After the Watergate
scandal forced Nixon to resign in 1974, and the United States effectively lost the Vietnam War, those elements of the far right that had supported both the war and its prosecutor were left (temporarily) adrift.

For white supremacists, the years 1968 to 1974 proved to be an interregnum. After energizing a mass constituency based on racial resentments, they watched Wallace voters move into Republican Party ranks.
Those Klansmen and other hard-core racists who had been at the core
of the American Independent Party, having wasted enormous reserves of
time, energy, and money, found themselves politically homeless. After
losing the contest over civil rights, these activists, much like defeated
armies everywhere, went home to lick their wounds. They became disillusioned, and financial contributions to the remaining troops dried up.

Adding to the situation, the generation that had opposed fighting a
war against Hitlerism and then resisted desegregation following the
Brown decision began to die off. One trenchant obituary, written by a
sixty-two-year-old white supremacist, lamented the times: "The relatively small and closed circle of aging patriots, most of them left from
the 1930's is being constantly diminished by death and despair."[29] The
movement that they had created during the decades immediately after
World War Two ground to a halt.

No amount of huffing and puffing could reinflate white supremacists
during these years. Organizations of all types that had existed on the farthest edge of the conservative movement had the toughest time.[30] Klan
groups declined sharply from fifty thousand plus members in 1964 to
just twelve hundred white sheets in 1972. Segregationist outfits such as
the white Citizens Councils lost members and influence in Congress.
The McCarthyite brand of anticommunism stopped selling, and the
John Birch Society shriveled—even if it did not die. The Minutemen,
which had augmented Birch-style anticommunism with freewheeling
paramilitarism, collapsed also, particularly after its founder went to
prison.[31] Governor George Wallace's American Independent Party splin-
tered into a dozen pieces, each more ineffectual than the other. As
noted earlier, the growth of Willis Carto's Liberty Lobby slowed. And
William Pierce's National Youth Alliance gained no new ground.

Pierce barely took fifty dollars out of the organization's proceeds each
month. He shuttled from the NYA's Arlington offices to his wife Patri-

cia's home in Fredericksburg. With two strapping teenage sons to feed, the family relied heavily on her income. Few calls and little mail came in the door. The recruitment drive on D.C.-area university campuses had sparkled for a brief moment and then faded. Pierce's failure to speak at George Washington University undoubtedly still fresh in his mind, he finally dropped the word "youth" from his organization's name. And on February 26, 1974, he incorporated the National Alliance in the state of Virginia,[32] grandly claiming that the new outfit would provide a "new superstructure for the movement."[33] Otherwise, though, nothing changed. The guiding ideas remained the same. Recruitment practices still aimed at finding a few good men. Even the name of the tabloid, *Attack!*, stayed as before. It continued to augment its usual complaints about Jews and people of color with polemics against conservatives: "Conservatism's belly-crawling fear of the Enemy (real or imagined), its senile retreat into a largely mythical past, its insistence on séances to call back from the dead all that once was—these were some of the symptoms of a species on its way to extinction."[34]

Name-calling could not help his immediate prognosis, however, and with too little money and too much time on his hands, Pierce started to write a novel.

PART one

Emergence, Growth, and Consolidation, 1974–1986

The liberal consensus begins to unravel, and the New Deal alignments of the past break apart under pressure from the Reagan revolution. In this post-civil rights era the ideas of white domination and all things considered "Aryan" are reified by an ideological movement of vanguardists and mainstreamers, including bank bandits, academics, and a coalition of third-party hopefuls intent on overturning the status quo.

The Turner Diaries and Resurgence

January 1975. William Pierce published the first installment of *The Turner Diaries* in *Attack!*. The fictional story line starts with a multiracial government, guarded by the so-called Equality Police and oppressing white people—stealing the virtue of white women and reducing white men to powerless obeisance. Money-hungry conservatives, interested only in the bottom line, sell out the alleged interests of white people. And small bands of Aryan resistance fighters are scattered across the political landscape.

Pierce serialized the novel with each new issue of the tabloid, while other pages were filled with breezy dissertations on "Jews, the USSR, and Communism" and cheerful articles, such as "Does America Deserve to Live?" As the novel took shape over the next couple of years, it became immensely popular with readers. When the protagonist shot Jewish merchants and the black Equality Police, National Alliance members could fantasize a victorious conclusion to their long travail. While the worldview of white supremacists seemed to outsiders like a vision of madmen, it should be remembered that fantasy has a role in any social movement, and this one was not an exception. The prospect of victory, even novelized victory, was so much sweeter than the real-life abyss they had experienced during the early 1970s.[1]

In 1978, under the pseudonym Andrew Macdonald, Pierce published *The Turner Diaries* in its entirety as a two-hundred-page paperback.[2] The book's success ultimately marked a turnaround in the National Alliance's. But in the interim Pierce considered the story akin to an ideological morality play.

Pierce told his adventure story, cast into the near future, through the fictive diaries of Earl Turner, a thirty-year-old electrical engineer turned guerrilla fighter. The imaginary Turner and a few thousand members of an Organization survive a dragnet aimed at violators of a draconian Cohen Act gun control law. They launch an uncoordinated guerrilla war aimed at destabilizing the System. Turner's four-person "unit" murders and robs unsuspecting Jews and blacks, blows up the FBI headquarters building, and kills a *Washington Post* editorial writer—all in the first fifty pages. They live in clandestine safe houses, manufacture new weapons, and survive by their wits. Other units of the Organization aren't as lucky, however, and don't survive. Eventually, guerrilla skirmishes grow into a full-scale war between small enclaves of white people and the disintegrating remains of the multiracial United States government. When the Organization finally gains control of Southern California, it drives the black and Latino population into the desert, kills off all Jews, and terrorizes the remaining white population into submission through the public hanging of white "race traitors." A nuclear war destroys Israel and China, neutralizes the Soviet Union, and leaves radioactive deserts smoldering in patches across the globe. The Organization imposes a dictatorship on the white enclaves it controls, enabling it gradually to gain a military advantage over the remaining multiracial forces. The racists' victory in North America ultimately leads to victory in Europe and finally to complete eradication of all the nonwhite populations on the planet. One hundred years after the revolution, we are told, the white race is on an upward spiral of achievement.[3]

Pierce repeatedly stops his narrative to lard it with political lessons, often combining the explication of revolutionary elitism with an apologia for ruthless terrorism. He describes the mass murder of innocents as regrettable but unavoidable. If only society hadn't been so thoroughly infected, Turner reasons, the cleansing process wouldn't require so much blood. If the masses of white people weren't such sheep, the Organization's method of herding wouldn't be so brutal. In this book's logic, terrorism also has strategic value. Well-placed bombs and assassinations are intended to provoke a police state response by the government and thereby alienate middle-of-the-road Americans from the System. Then they will be pushed into the ranks of the Aryan army.

The white conservative also takes a noticeable beating from the revolutionary ethos in these pages. Like Pierce's Turner, a "conservative" character opposes gun control, racial integration, and the Jews. But his individualistic ethos makes him a poor recruit and an easy traitor to the cause. Unlike true Aryan revolutionaries, who supposedly fight for their race rather than for themselves, the conservatives won't surrender their egotistical search for commercial goods and personal power. The masses of white people are more cowardly and corrupt still, swayed by a false materialism and consumerism. The white race may reign supreme in *The Turner Diaries*, but a dictatorship by a semimystical elite known as the Order makes and enforces the rules.

White women play a subordinate role in this novel, as might be expected. But while Turner describes "women's lib" as a "mass psychosis," Pierce does not simply impose the traditional roles of helpmate and mother on the Aryan women in the book. Instead, some fight side by side with the male warriors, particularly during the period of the guerrilla struggle. Outside the pages of this novel, in magazine articles and elsewhere, Pierce elaborated a unified view of sex and sexuality. And he was unapologetic about linking—nay, chaining—women to racial reproduction. Sex for any other purpose played no role in his worldview.[4]

Immediately after publication, Pierce began a targeted advertising campaign. He purchased ads in *Shotgun News* and other gun publications, as well as *Soldier of Fortune*, a slick monthly magazine for mercenaries.[5] National Alliance cadres and independent vendors sold the novel at local gun shows, where thousands gathered like stamp collectors at a philatelic convention. Other white supremacist groups bought the novel in bulk and sold it from their own mail-order catalogs. Some purchasers turned around and bought other literature off the National Alliance list, which included Hitler-era Nazi reprints, as well as Anglo-Saxon literary classics such as *Beowulf*. A second edition of *The Turner Diaries* followed soon after the first printing sold out.[6]

The book developed a life of its own over the next twenty years. A reported five hundred thousand copies were sold. In 1996 publishing rights were purchased by a small mainstream press.[7] The novel imbued the ideas of white racial nationalism and terrorism with a romanticized sense of adventure. It became the inspiration for a band of white racists building a guerrilla army during the 1980s. And an ex-army gunner turned drifter carried it around in his pocket before being charged with blowing up the Federal Building in Oklahoma City in 1995. Although gun rights were prominent in the story's beginning, this was manifestly not a "militia" book. The militia movement, when it did appear in the mid-1990s, was open and public in its gun carrying. The fighters in this novel belong to secret organizations with tight leadership structures. Clandestinity is the lesson here, even more than the necessity of maintaining your very own .50-caliber machine gun in tip-top shape.

The immediate success of Pierce's novel paralleled an uptick in the National Alliance's prospects. It added a few new highly effective cadres to the hard-core outfit Pierce had been building. "One thing decided during this period was that if we could not be a large organization, we would, at least, be an elite organization," he wrote. "We stuck to the straight and narrow path, and we gradually began to pick up the sort of people we wanted."[8] Pierce looked for people he regarded as intelligent and capable of working for long periods of time without becoming disheartened. And they did more than just sell copies of *The Turner Diaries* through the mail. Members distributed literature at an Oktoberfest celebration in Baltimore, on street corners in Alabama, door to door in Philadelphia, and among high school students in Chicago—all venues that produced new members. A few dedicated cadres purposely joined other organizations on the far right, such as the John Birch Society, and recruited activists attracted by the National Alliance's ideological consistency and relative sophistication. The increased membership resulted in increased revenues, which were quickly converted into more literature, increased staff, a new computer system, and other projects.[9]

Several Carto-related enterprises also grew during these years.[10] Liberty Lobby transformed 25,000 readers of its monthly newsletter into 150,000 paid subscribers for a weekly tabloid entitled *The Spotlight*, known at its beginning as *The National Spotlight*. The first edition appeared on September 17, 1975.[11] Neither Carto's name nor any of his pseudonyms were printed on the masthead, but repeated evidence in court testified to his firm control over the publication. The tabloid became Liberty Lobby's most significant organizational advance since moving to Washington, D.C. It claimed the mantle of muckraking journalism and made money at the same time. Through its pages Liberty Lobby sold everything from vitamin tablets and silver coins to survivalist handbooks and religious tracts. Before the Internet made all things available everywhere, *The Spotlight*'s classifieds and display advertisements became the one place that local propaganda groups found a national market. Carto and Liberty Lobby obviously relished the prospect of using the tabloid to gain hegemony over all the movement's different factions.[12]

It did indeed become the movement's most widely circulated publication. The muckraking claims, however, rested heavily on the only slightly veiled contention that Jews controlled the mainstream media. "Your newspapers, wire services, radio and television networks are controlled by big multinational business organizations and certain 'minority' pressure groups," the first editorial read.[13] Apparently Carto's readers thought much the same. *The Spotlight* rode the right-wing revival to ever larger numbers, and by 1980 paid circulation had reached more than three hundred thousand. Adding to its impact, 410 radio stations broadcast Liberty Lobby's daily program.[14] To keep all the gears turning, Carto now controlled a D.C. staff of forty working in a three-story building near Capitol Hill.

A new breed of self-styled Christian patriots also sprang up in the second half of the 1970s, as did rural gangs of paramilitary survivalists. But none drew the publicity generated by the Ku Klux Klan, which became the symbol of white supremacist resurgence.

David Duke and a New Klan Emerge

October 16, 1977. David Duke stepped out of a rented helicopter and onto the grounds of the San Ysidro port of entry south of San Diego, a federal office used by the Immigration and Naturalization Service (INS) to regulate traffic on the border with Mexico. Dressed in a light blue business suit, Duke was surrounded by an entourage of tough-looking men in street clothes, all members of the Knights of the Ku Klux Klan. They faced a protest group, angry at the Klan's public appearance. An egg splattered on Duke's clothes, and a rock broke the windshield of a Klansman's car. Police arrested the rock thrower while an INS agent in charge welcomed the Klansmen and gave them a guided tour of the port facility. For Duke and company, this visit was the first stop in an effort to stir up opposition to brown-skinned immigrants.[1]

"We believe very strongly white people are becoming second class citizens in this country," Duke told the press. "When I think of America, I think of a white country."[2]

A few days later, in a Sacramento hotel room, he staged a press conference announcing a Klan "border watch." He claimed five hundred to one thousand Klansmen would patrol the back roads and midnight border crossings of "illegal immigrants" coming from Mexico into the United States. At this venue, anti-Klanners tried to force their way into the hotel room, and the protest became part of the news coverage. While in Sacramento, Duke also managed to get a meeting with two aides to the lieutenant governor, and that event became one more headline in the Klan media blitz.[3]

After all the news and hoopla, the actual border watch the following week was virtually anticlimactic. Nevertheless, it generated another round of publicity. Duke and fewer than two hundred Klansmen drove around on the California border, talking to one another on their walkie-talkies. The Knights group in Texas staged a similar border-watch during the same period.[4]

Although the entire affair lasted only a couple of weeks, it was long enough for Duke's Klan to claim a great victory. It published a special border watch issue of its tabloid newspaper, *The Crusader*, and wrote: "No single action in the last decade has done more to bring public attention and awareness on the border problem."[5]

Opposition to immigration later became one of the white nationalist movement's most salient causes, and Duke in effect cut that piece of turf in the 1970s. His own analysis of the events on the border emphasized the media strategy he used then to build the Klan: ". . . when a hundred reporters are gathered around hanging on every word, when they help you accomplish your own objectives by their own misguided sensationalism, if indeed it was a media stunt, it was by their own presence an admission that it was a very brilliant one."[6] By any measure, he had turned California into a sound stage for Klan politics.

Although the Knights of the Ku Klux Klan were the most potent of several white supremacist forces newly resurgent in 1977, ironically, Duke's success owed much to the fact that he was not the stereotypical Klansman of popular imagination. Born in Oklahoma in 1950, he grew up in a middle-class family in New Orleans, attended Louisiana State University, and earned a degree in history. Reporters often emphasized his intelligence. He was handsome, well mannered, and articulate. Unlike the leaders of competing Klan factions, who liked to pose as armed militants for news photographers, Duke never publicly handled a rifle. A psychological portrait might emphasize the fact that his father was largely absent, spending years working overseas, or that his mother was a barely functional alcoholic—or that like generations of other white racists, he was raised and cared for by a black woman, a surrogate parent hired as domestic labor for the family.[7]

The adult Duke's personal relationship with women remained troubled. Although he married Chloe Hardin and had two daughters, he remained an unrepentant womanizer.[8] His own members often complained that they had to worry whether or not Duke would bed their wives when he came to their town. He used the pen name Dorothy Vanderbilt to self-publish a "sex manual" titled *FindersKeepers*. And a long string of young women graced his arm over the years, more a sign of his own self-obsession than any indication that he had found genuine affection. As will become evident, however, whatever insights might be drawn from his family relationships are overshadowed by the importance of Duke's role in transforming the entire white supremacist movement.

While other young people his age joined civil rights organizations and peace groups during the mid-1960s, Duke started his career as a professional racist in high school. When he left home for college, Duke became a student organizer for the National Socialist White People's Party (NSWPP) in 1969, creating first a White Student Alliance and then a White Youth Alliance while at Louisiana State University. He tried selling white supremacy from a soapbox at the school's "Free Speech Alley." In the process of speaking before hostile audiences he honed skills that served him well for years to come. In one incident from those early years, Duke donned a Nazi storm trooper uniform, complete with swastika armband, and strode around for the cameras with a picket sign protesting a campus speech by noted left-wing attorney William Kunstler.[9] The event hounded Duke later, when he tried to become a mainstream Republican.

FBI documents from that early period raise questions on whether or not Duke provided information about members of his own organization to the bureau. According to Tyler Bridges's book *The Rise of David Duke*, Duke was arrested on January 18, 1972, for possession of bottles filled with a flammable liquid and topped with rags.[10] Most people call such items Molotov cocktails, but Duke claimed they were torches for a parade. Notably, FBI documents show that on that same day, January 18, an unidentified source had brought the bureau information *"in person."* That memo indicates that the materials it was provided were *"applications."* These papers were then forwarded to FBI offices in twenty cities, possibly indicating that a membership list with names was dispersed across the country. A week later, January 25, 1972, another memo from the special agent in charge to the FBI director states clearly that Duke had "furnished" information to special agents. The exact nature of the information was not mentioned in the memo, and the agents' names remain unknown, as they were redacted out, a standard practice when the FBI is forced to release documents through the Freedom of Information Act.[11] In any case, the Molotov cocktail charges against Duke were dropped several weeks later. When asked twenty years later about these incidents, Duke denied that he had given the FBI any information or provided his group's membership list in exchange for having the charges against him dropped. He did acknowledge that he had been interviewed by the FBI during that time but claimed the agency must have gotten his membership list through some other counterintelligence program.[12]

Whether or not Duke provided the FBI with information, he soon abandoned both his White Youth Alliance and its successor National Party. Nevertheless, when he created his own Knights of the Ku Klux Klan, described in the beginning of this chapter, it was informed by an underlying national socialist ideology. And Duke easily made the transition to white sheets.

At that moment, in 1973, the white supremacist movement as a whole still lay relatively inert, and Duke's Knights were slow to start. By the time race-based conflicts over school busing broke out in 1975 in Louisville, Kentucky, things had changed. Klan groups sprang "up like wild mushrooms," according to Patsy Sims, who wrote a book about the Klan in that period.[13] Among the many different Klan factions vying for new members, Duke's Klan stood out for the audacity and intelligence of its leadership, and he proved that a postwar baby boomer could successfully reinvent a 110-year-old trademark name.

The history of the Klan began in 1866 with the formation of a social club for six young Confederate veterans in Pulaski, Tennessee. When this Klan turned to night-riding and paramilitary terrorism, it chose Nathan Bedford Forrest as its first Imperial Wizard, or national leader. A former Confederate general, Forrest had been a millionaire slave trader before the Civil War.[14] A statue and Tennessee state park in Benton County, Tennessee, still memorialize his name in the twenty-first century.[15]

Immediately after the Civil War, white people in the South lost many of their special prerogatives. Newly emancipated slaves, once the disposable property of men such as Forrest, gained the right to vote, hold office, and own land—largely because these rights were guaranteed by the Fourteenth and Fifteenth Amendments and the presence of the Union army. Public schools broke the propertied class's monopoly on education, benefiting both black and white. Known as Reconstruction, this period was the most democratic to that point in American history.[16] Forrest's Klan regarded Union soldiers as an occupying army and newly emancipated black men as thieves stealing the privileges he believed should have remained exclusively in white hands. The Klan and similar groups fought to break the Reconstruction governments and push black people back into servitude.

In the first issue of his *Crusader* tabloid, Duke wrote about this earlier history: "A White guerrilla army was formed and it did the job quite well."[17] Although this Klan was quashed by federal force, the canon of white supremacy was reestablished through a combination of racist terror and political power. New laws stripped black people of their civil and political rights, and in 1896 the United States Supreme Court formally recognized the facts on the ground with its *Plessy v. Ferguson* decision, effectively rendering the Fourteenth Amendment moot. Jim Crow segregation became the law of the land.[18]

A second era of Klan growth occurred after World War One, and its enemies list included Catholics, Jews, and others not deemed White Anglo-Saxon Protestants. But Duke disavowed this Klan's anti-Catholicism, arguing that it provoked an unnecessary rift in the ranks of white people. "The original Ku Klux Klan was never anti-Catholic," he wrote, and concluded that white Christians, of whichever denomination or trend, should not "fight against each other." He envied the financial empire that Klan leaders had built during the 1920s, but he was loath to re-create the giant Ponzi recruiting scheme necessary to generate the funds. "If our purpose was fraternal amusement, every possible Province, Dominion and Realm could be filled with corresponding Klan officers," he reminded his members. "But our cause is serious . . . Therefore we will not delude ourselves with high sounding titles, or impressive scrolls of asininity."[19]

Apparently ritualistically burning kerosene-soaked rags wrapped around a forty-foot wooden cross was exempt from said scrolls.

Duke did hope to replicate several other aspects of the 1920s Klan, however, including its size.[20] According to David Chalmers's classic history, *Hooded Americanism*, the Klan had more than three million members in the mid-1920s. Many lived in northern towns and midwestern hamlets, and the Klan was a national force, not a sectional avenger. Dozens of elected officials were members during this period, including U.S. senators and governors.[21] A Hollywood film, *The Birth of a Nation*, extolled the Reconstruction-era Klan's virtues and captured widespread and large, friendly audiences. President Woodrow Wilson and several Supreme Court justices watched it in the White House and concluded that the movie had written "history with lightning."[22] Duke wanted to repeat this political success.

Like its Reconstruction-era forebears, the goals enunciated by this Second Era Klan were reached, even if not by the Klan itself. It campaigned against immigrants from southern and eastern Europe alongside other groups supporting the hegemony of Anglo-Saxon Protestants, and they were rewarded by Congress in 1924 with an immigration law that did just that.[23] In August 1925, Klansmen marched thirty thousand strong down Pennsylvania Avenue in Washington, D.C., a demonstration of nativist and racist sentiment that endured long after that particular Klan collapsed. Segregation remained the law of the land. Anglo-Saxonism was carried on by organizations such as the Reverend Gerald Winrod's

Defenders of the Christian Faith and William Pelley's Silver Shirts during the 1930s. Charles Lindbergh's America First Committee promoted a form of nativist isolationism right up to the entry of the United States into World War Two. And anti-Semitism was a staple feature of Father Charles Coughlin's radio broadcasts.[24] Historian Chalmers concluded that the Klan's decline in the 1920s was due to its own "ineptness," rather than any other "combination of factors."[25]

A third era of Klan resurgence began after the *Brown v. Topeka Board of Education* Supreme Court decision in 1954.[26] In bus stations and public plazas, marauding Klan mobs bloodied Freedom Riders while under the protection and guidance of local police. They bombed churches and homes with impunity. A string of horrific murders shocked the country. Cynthia Wesley, Denise McNair, Carole Robertson, and Addie Mae Collins—four young black girls whose names should never be forgotten—died in the 1963 bombing of the Sixteenth Street Baptist Church in Birmingham. That same year a Klan sniper assassinated Mississippi state NAACP leader Medgar Evers on the doorstep of his home. In 1964, Michael Schwerner, James Chaney, and Andrew Goodman, three activists registering voters, were tortured and then shot to death in Neshoba County, Mississippi. In 1966 another Mississippi NAACP leader, Vernon Dahmer, was murdered. The level of violence cannot be retold in numbers alone. And many of those crimes remained unsolved and unpunished at the time. In several high-profile instances, all-white juries acquitted Klan defendants with little more than a wink and a nod.[27] Only in the 1990s did aggressive reporting and a new generation of prosecutors reopen several of the most egregious cases.[28] With each act of racist violence, the dignity of the civil rights cause grew. Activists broke the edifice of legalized segregation in the public squares of southern cities and pushed the federal government for new legislation. Where so-called states' rights had once held sway, Jim Crow fell. Unlike the Reconstruction-era Klan and the Second Era Klan, this Third Era Klan, despite the casualties it inflicted, lost its war against the black freedom movement.

The invisibility of black people to whites began to change in popular culture, from literature to movies and television. And the attitudes of whites about race, as measured by national opinion surveys, became more enlightened. Having gained the right to vote, black people and other people of color became elected officials and public servants in the South as well as the North. For civil rights activists those years meant tremendous sacrifices and partial victories and ended with an unfinished and unfulfilled agenda. Despite white supremacist claims to the contrary, the dominant position and privileged status of white people remained intact. They remained overrepresented in the halls of political power and more likely to live longer and accumulate greater levels of wealth, which they succeeded largely in passing on to their children. Segregated housing remained the norm, and fully funded, racially integrated public education the exception. Although the United States had not become a multiracial Eden, white supremacists still calculated race relations as a zero-sum equation, in which any advance for civil rights meant a total loss for white people.

The memory of this defeat remained fresh and mean as the Klan grew again in the 1970s. And it presented racists with a paradox. They unabashedly contended that white people were more intelligent and otherwise genetically superior to black and brown people. At the same time, they believed that these so-called inferior people had bested them on the field of civil struggle. To explain this situation, white supremacists invented Jewish control of black people as a way of explaining this supposed white dispossession. David Duke and the Klan borrowed heavily from this argument, particularly William Pierce's writings on the subject.[29] "The blacks in America are not really independent agents and are not fully responsible for their actions, but are primarily the tools of another minority which uses black-White [sic] race conflict for its own ends." It was the Jews "who control the mass media," not black people. And it was the media that conditioned "the White majority to yield without protest to minority demands."[30]

The Pierce imprint, including its demand for total revolutionary change, was plainly visible on Duke, despite the sharp criticism that Pierce leveled at Klan-type groups. "Traditionally, the Ku Klux Klan has been conservative, parochial and Christian," Pierce wrote. "It wanted to keep non-Whites 'in their place,' not separate them geographically."[31]

Duke endorsed Pierce's criticism of other Klan factions. "We of the Ku Klux Klan are not reactionaries longing to return to a previous era of White racial history," the Knights proclaimed in a revolutionary-like credo. "We are not fighting to preserve the systems of weakness and degeneration that have led us to this precipice." And much like Pierce, Duke and others in the new white supremacist movement endorsed the concept of creating a whites-only nation-state. No Jim Crow laws would be needed to keep black people down if the new state just kept them out altogether. Duke also endorsed the notion, shared by both Pierce and Carto, that Jews were the main enemy. All previous Klans had believed that "there is a Jewish problem in the Western world today," as Duke argued. But his Knights of the Ku Klux Klan were the first to regard it as "the most important issue of our time."[32]

Other signs of Pierce's influence abounded. The first issue of the Knights' newsletter carried an ad for Pierce's group. Newsletter editions that followed published cartoons by Dennis Nix, whose drawings also graced Pierce's *Turner Diaries*. Pierce himself came to New Orleans in November 1975 and spoke to more than three hundred people at a Klan rally, according to FBI documents. And he repeatedly sent National Alliance emissaries after that.[33] When Duke switched from a newsletter format to publishing a Klan tabloid, *The Crusader*, he routinely reprinted articles Pierce wrote for the National Alliance. In fact, the Knights' credo, "Why We Fight," reprinted virtually verbatim another article entitled "Why We Fight" from the National Alliance.[34] Duke shortened the text a bit and inserted the word "Klan" to make it appear as if the article had originated with the Knights.

Similarly, the Knights republished Pierce's tract purporting that "the Jews" controlled "the media."[35] For Duke the baby boomer, television loomed larger than newspapers as an instrument of Jewish subversion of the white race. In particular, his *Crusader* tabloid angrily reviewed a January 1977 docudrama miniseries entitled *Roots*. From Boston to Atlanta to Houston to Seattle, white people all watched the same program as black people about the brutal nature of slavery and the innate humanity of black people. The program had a powerful, if short-lived, effect on race relations. And white supremacists complained about it for years.

Nevertheless, Duke successfully manipulated a medium he believed was owned and operated by his racial enemies. From his first appearance on a late-night talk show, Duke impressed TV hosts with his modish appearance, calm demeanor, and articulate presentation. Of course, he had long before honed his forensic skills in the Free Speech Alley. He knew the art of speaking past his antagonists at public venues and talking directly to his own audience. Most of his television hosts, by contrast, had never interviewed anyone quite like Duke. They expected a backwoods bumpkin who gazed unintelligibly into the klieg lights, rather than a sharp verbal interlocutor. Duke often bested them in the sparring. The conflict made perfect television, and the Klansman returned as a frequent guest.

Duke never tired of looking at himself. He added tapes of his television and radio appearances to the list of merchandise he sold out of the back pages of the Klan's periodic tabloid, *The Crusader*. Tom Snyder's *Tomorrow Show*, Phil Donahue, Larry King, and *The Today Show* were listed alongside reprints of the *Protocols of the Elders of Zion*, an anti-Semitic forgery created by the czarist secret police that became a bestseller in the hands of Hitler's Nazis.

At the height of this TV charm campaign, in 1979, a discernible shift occurred in public opinion surveys on attitudes toward the Klan. According to a poll conducted by Gallup, 11 percent of whites held favorable or highly favorable attitudes toward the Klan, while unfavorable and highly unfavorable ratings were held by 88 percent of whites. The biggest shift was in the North—across all educational levels, but most particularly among high school graduates, where unfavorable ratings went down and more closely approximated white views in the South. While still small, these ratings had jumped up from 1965, when Klan violence in the South was well publicized. At that time only 6 percent of whites held favorable or highly favorable views of the group, while 93 percent of whites held an unfavorable or highly unfavorable view.[36]

Duke's ability to find an audience among mainstream white people carried him outside the small circles of vanguard purists and into the ranks around Willis Carto and Liberty Lobby. Early in his career, Duke wrote in his Klan newsletter about the need to engage in electoral politics. In 1975 he announced his first run for public office, this time as a Klansman and a Democrat aiming at a seat in the Louisiana senate. Carto gave Duke's political campaign and the rising fortunes of his Klan a jolt of free publicity in an October 1975 edition of his weekly tabloid, then still called *The National Spotlight*.[37] Carto's tabloid argued the case for Duke: "He sees the Klan, not as a terrorist organization, but as a political movement with ideological leadership." *The National Spotlight* was thrilled. In that race, Duke won 33 percent of the vote, a double-digit portent of the future.

Further, Duke's ideas about movement building and recruiting competent second-rank leaders more closely resembled Carto's than Pierce's. Pierce argued that the first task should be the creation of a dedicated leadership core; a mass organization would follow. By contrast, Duke proposed that the Klan first become a mass organization. A second step would be to identify possible lieutenants and develop them as a group of professional leaders. The Knights' *Handbook* predicted that "our movement, as it attracts millions of adherents, will build its leadership cadre slowly, and carefully—with its eyes trained on the future." Like Carto, finding a mass constituency remained Duke's central concern throughout his career. Practically speaking, however, most of the Knights' initial leaders had long résumés before they joined his outfit, and the internal organization of his Klan actually approximated Pierce's model, which was more appropriately geared toward building a relatively small organization during a period when "millions" were not joining.

.   .   .

In addition to dropping the anti-Catholicism of past Klans, Duke aimed at recruiting women as well as men. History does not recall the involvement of women in the Reconstruction-era Klan and its guerrilla war. Rather, white women were regarded as pure and fragile vessels the Klan needed to protect from a hypothetical ravaging by black men. During the Second Era Klan in the 1920s, by contrast, women participated on their own terms. According to Kathleen Blee's groundbreaking history of that era, *Women of the Klan*, five hundred thousand women joined their own organization, known as Women of the Ku Klux Klan. Ironically, recruits often came from the same organizations that were also wellsprings for the (white) feminist movement, including the Woman's Christian Temperance Union.[38]

Although Duke echoed Pierce's charge that the contemporary feminist movement had been invented by Jews to help destroy the white race, women were able and encouraged to join Duke's Knights itself rather than a second-status women's auxiliary. At one point, Duke claimed that approximately 35 percent of the members nationally were women. Individual women became local leaders in their own right, and an early chief of security was a woman. One of the best-known recruits worked as a horse jockey and enjoyed a reputation for outlandishness. Most women who joined were already married to Klan men. Wives of local leaders became officers themselves, often handling the dues income and other "secretarial" work, much as they did in their local churches. Duke's *Crusader* tabloid did publish one article that argued for including women at all levels of leadership. "Our women must be aware of their unique roles, to be sure. Yet, they must be restored to the even more common roles of our fighting partners, capable of heroism and with a potential for leadership in all areas." And in a remarkably egalitarian statement, the author reasoned that there should be "no chains imposed by kitchen duties not shared by all." That writer's goal was "to free the ones most capable for other tasks."[39]

Otherwise, little of the massive amounts of propaganda the Knights produced aimed directly at recruiting these young wives and girlfriends. When it came to talking specifically about women, the message was directed at men, warning them to protect the sexuality of white women from the supposed rapaciousness of black men, a mythic theme in American life that had emerged after slavery. Most often, by recruiting women, Duke simply managed to get two new members for the price of one. With Duke's Knights as an example, the Klan factions that formed in its wake also admitted women directly to their ranks.

· · ·

The success of Duke's Knights during the 1970s encouraged others to set up their own Klan factions. One of the most prominent was Bill Wilkinson's Invisible Empire, Knights of the Ku Klux Klan. Wilkinson had been a parish-level leader in Duke's operation when he struck out on his own. "I'm the only Klan leader who believes in having guns around," Wilkinson famously said. "These guns aren't for shooting rabbits, they're for wasting people."[40] According to Randall Williams, who interviewed dozens of Alabama Klansmen while serving as the founding director of the Southern Poverty Law Center's Klanwatch Project, Wilkinson's Klan attracted poor and working-class white men in Alabama and Mississippi with a penchant for violence. When the Southern Christian Leadership Conference (SCLC) announced plans to march in Decatur, Alabama, on May 26, 1979, the Invisible Empire planned to stop them. They attacked the SCLC marchers with clubs, starting a three-way melee with a small number of city police in between. Shooting broke out, and two Klansmen and two civil rights demonstrators were wounded. Miraculously, no one was killed.[41]

The following November five anti-Klan protesters were shot to death, and nine wounded, in Greensboro, North Carolina. In this instance, several different neo-Nazi and Klan factions banded together, calling themselves the United Racist Front. Forty white supremacists drove in a caravan of nine cars to the site of a demonstration by a small communist group. The Klansmen and neo-Nazis calmly got out of their cars, took weapons out of their trunks, and began shooting point-blank.[42] According to the most authoritative account of this event, *Codename Greenkil*, by Elizabeth Wheaton, at least one local police informant and one federal agent had infiltrated the Front and driven with the caravan. Apparently, the authorities had not learned to use their informants to prevent violence rather than abet it, and the incident was eerily reminiscent of the murder of Viola Liuzzo by a carload of Klansmen in 1965. At that time FBI informant Gary Thomas Rowe had been in the car but had done nothing to stop the killing.[43] In addition, Bill Wilkinson—Mr. Guns Are Not for Rabbits—served as an FBI informant for seven years, from 1974 to 1981, when a *Tennessean* (Nashville) reporter finally exposed his double-faced role.[44]

Another faction, the Justice Knights in Tennessee, sprayed bullets at five black women walking down the street together in Chattanooga the following April 1980. These incidents were only the most visible acts of violence by members of organized white supremacist groups during these years. From California to Connecticut, crosses were burned and homes were shot at, all in the name of the Ku Klux Klan.[45]

Duke later claimed that this torrent of violence undermined his effort to build a political machine.[46] He had run again for the Louisiana senate and won 26 percent of the vote in 1979 and shortly thereafter began a short-lived presidential campaign. But the final cause of Duke's disillusionment with the Klan may have been money. He had milked the white sheet crowd dry.[47] And competing Klan factions were eating into this base of support. Duke decided it was time to find a new list of contributors. Several weeks after the Greensboro murders, he incorporated a second organization, with the market-friendly name National Association for the Advancement of White People. And he tried to quietly sell his Klan membership list to Bill Wilkinson for thirty-five thousand dollars, only to find that Wilkinson had arranged to expose Duke's plan in the media. To Knights members, the scheme to sell their names was treasonous.[48]

David Duke resigned from the Knights of the Ku Klux Klan in July 1980. In the months and years that followed the once-powerful organization fell into disarray and then split into competing factions.[49] It would be a mistake to conclude that Duke's seven-year stint in the Klan had all come to naught. His innovative use of the media had turned the Klan into the most visible aspect of a broader white supremacist resurgence. He had helped transform the most vital elements of that new movement away from conservative or restorationist ideologies toward a more "revolutionary" emphasis on creating a new Aryans-only nation-state. And he had collected under one roof a set of state and local leaders who became major figures in their own right over the next several decades.

Several important state leaders left the Knights to start their own operations, drawing money and members away from the Knights. One of the most creative tacticians was Tom Metzger, the California Knights leader who had organized the so-called border watch. He had quit Duke early and formed his own California Klan. And then Metzger ran for office in 1980.

The Election of 1980: The Klan and Ronald Reagan

June 3, 1980. Tom Metzger spent less than fifty-four hundred dollars running in the Democratic Party primary for California's Forty-third Congressional District seat. Although he was physically unimposing at five feet eight inches, Metzger loved a good street fight. And as a well-known Klan leader he maintained little separation between looking for votes and knocking heads with clubs and shields. During the campaign Metzger marched his Klan troops into a street brawl in the town of Oceanside, made an appearance at San Diego State University only to be pelted with bottles and fruit, paid for radio advertisements, and shook hands looking for votes. He declared himself the white workingman's candidate and opposed "white collar crime . . . export of U.S. jobs . . . foreign product dumping . . . the unrestricted flow of illegal aliens . . . [and] Asian refugee entrance into the United States." The anti-immigrant message, according to the local press, carried the day. On primary election night, Metzger received 32,344 votes and, with 39 percent of the ballot, defeated the closest Democratic Party contender.[1]

Although the Republican incumbent won the general election, the Klansman's primary victory showed that racially motivated white voters existed in some number. The campaign also dramatized the restless experimentation that characterized Tom Metzger's personal brand of white power politics. His route to the Klan had started in Warsaw, Indiana, where he was born in 1938. After serving in the army, he moved to Southern California and eventually established his own TV repair shop business. He married Kathleen Murphy in a Catholic service in 1963, and their union ultimately produced six children. During the 1964 Goldwater campaign, Tom joined the John Birch Society. He supported George Wallace in 1968 and thereafter became a self-avowed racist and anti-Semite. When David Duke came to California to start a Klan group, Metzger signed on. It was Tom Metzger, by then Grand Dragon, or state leader, who stage-managed Duke's so-called border watch in 1978. When Metzger broke away from Duke's national outfit, he started his own California Klan realm before running in the primary.[2]

Metzger was not the only self-avowed white supremacist running for office in 1980. A National Socialist White People's Party chief, Harold Covington, received fifty-four thousand votes, 40 percent of the total, in the North Carolina Republican Party's primary for state attorney general. And in Michigan, Gerald Carlson, a member of a different national socialist sect, won the Republican Party's nomination in the heavily Democratic Fifteenth Congressional District. Liberty Lobby's *Spotlight* took note of these results and opined simply that "voters [were] ready for a change."[3]

That November, Republican Ronald Reagan won 50.7 percent of the popular vote for president, defeating a sitting Democratic president, Jimmy Carter, and an independent candidate, John Anderson, in a three-way race. Reagan had long been a figure on the far right wing of the Republican Party. He supported Barry Goldwater's candidacy in 1964, won California's governorship in 1966, and campaigned in the 1976 Republican primaries against President Gerald Ford. During the 1980 campaign, Reagan mastered the art of racist innuendo, including talk in his stump speech about the supposed crimes committed by "welfare queens." He aggressively sought the votes of disgruntled white people, including southern Democrats unhappy with their national party's racial liberalism. Just after the Republican Party's convention, Reagan made a campaign stop in Philadelphia, Mississippi, site of the murders of civil rights activists James Chaney, Andrew Goodman, and Michael Schwerner by a gang of Klan killers in 1964. That case had electrified the country at the time, and the acquittals by an all-white jury remained a visible stain on Neshoba County's reputation. Nevertheless, Reagan went to its county fair and, before a sea of thirty thousand white faces, uttered the magic words "I believe in states' rights." The claim to "states' rights" had been used by slavers and segregationists since the founding of the Republic and most recently by Alabama Governor George Wallace. Reagan won the votes of former Wallaceites, along with those of anti-communists, boosters of greater military spending, opponents of federal regulation and antitax budget busters, and growing legions of social and cultural conservatives.[4]

It became common among antiracists and liberals to talk about Reagan's election as if it were the *cause* of conservative and right-wing ascendancy. But his election in 1980 was more the *result* of a right-wing rebirth during the latter half of the 1970s. Organizations, think tanks, and churches known variously as the New Right or religious right had sprouted up after Nixon's resignation. They defeated a drive to pass an equal rights amendment for women. They attacked the Supreme Court, the target of segregationists since its decision in *Brown*, for a 1962 ruling that prayer in public schools violated the First Amendment and for its 1973 ruling in *Roe v. Wade* affirming a right to privacy regarding abortion. They opposed basic civil rights for gay men and lesbians and occasionally remarked that "God does not hear the prayer of a Jew." They watched the Reverend Jerry Falwell on television, believed that the United States was, by rights, a Christian nation, and after 1979 joined Falwell's Moral Majority organization. They also created a broad-based mass movement of angry white people.[5]

Antibusing mobilizations in Louisville and Boston were less about the specifics of educational policy (some black folks also opposed busing) and more about the inclusion of black people in the lives of white people. An antitax referendum in California, Proposition 13, passed in 1978. Support for the measure broke down largely along racial lines, and opposition to taxes became the calling card of white middle-class anger at both the black poor and any government action that seemed to respond to the issues of poverty and racism.[6]

In contrast with the ideology of Carto and Pierce, this new movement simply assumed its whiteness rather than reified it. It identified itself in the political arena according to its faith, not its skin color. It did not respond to calls for racial dominance as such. To this constituency, Reagan articulated "a politics of generalized government restraint . . . [and] mastered the excision of the language of race from conservative public discourse," according to Thomas Edsall and Mary Edsall in *Chain Reaction*, even while attacking policies targeted toward blacks and other minorities.[7] These conservatives regarded Ronald Reagan's election as a shining moment. The period of 1960s-style liberal hegemony had ended.

For white supremacists, Ronald Reagan's election proved more mottled and gray than pure and clear. "There is good news and bad news on Reagan's smashing win over Carter," the remnants of the Knights of the Ku Klux Klan argued.[8] Liberty Lobby also wrestled with its approach to the conservative Republican ascendancy, and it had even more at stake than

Klan groups and national socialist agitators. Four years of opposition to Jimmy Carter's Democratic presidency had been good for Liberty Lobby. It had nabbed new listeners for its radio broadcasts and attracted subscribers to its weekly tabloid, eager to read its latest exposé of the Council on Foreign Relations or the treaty ceding sovereignty over the Panama Canal.

"We were the first to expose to light the drug-soaked Carter regime," *The Spotlight* crowed. "We are proud of the dozens if not hundreds of factual exposures of Jimmy Carter and his gang we exclusively printed."[9]

Just weeks after President Reagan's inauguration, *The Spotlight* celebrated its attainment of "one third of a million paid subscribers." A National Press Club ballroom gala featured congratulations from Congressman George Hansen, a Republican from Idaho who became a recurring figure in Liberty Lobby circles.[10] At the same time, Carto's outfit remained undecided about the new administration taking office. On one hand, it took positive note of Reagan's nationalist rhetoric. On the other hand, it opposed the "Trilateralists, Zionists, and other internationalist stooges he [Reagan] has surrounded himself with."[11]

While Liberty Lobby weighed the new presidency, Reagan's nomination of Warren Richardson to the post of assistant secretary of health and human services became a test of whether or not Liberty Lobby would find a seat in the Reagan administration. Richardson had worked as a professional Washington insider whose employers included the National Right to Work Committee and the National Lumber Manufacturers Association. He had also worked at Liberty Lobby from 1969 to 1973, serving as general counsel and testifying on freedom of the press issues before Congress. For these services, Willis Carto had paid him fifteen thousand dollars a year.[12] After Richardson's formal employment ended, *The Spotlight* still counted him a friend, but when reporters uncovered his past affiliation during the vetting process, Richardson attempted to distance himself from Liberty Lobby and insisted that he was not an anti-Semite. He also wrote a memo denouncing Liberty Lobby's "anti-Jewish and racist actions." Despite these repeated denials, Richardson's connection to Carto's operation doomed his nomination. He withdrew from consideration on April 24, 1981.[13]

At first, *The Spotlight* excoriated news sources that had reported on the matter rather than directly attack the administration. Lobby officials also sent a polite letter to President Reagan contending the organization was not anti-Semitic but simply anti-Zionist. "Opposition to Zionism has nothing to do with opposition to Jews or Judaism," they wrote.[14] When Liberty Lobby did finally criticize the administration for failing to back Richardson's nomination, it used language so obtuse that a casual reader might need a translator to guess that an angry dispute was under way.[15]

By the time the whole affair ended the ambivalence had been squeezed out of Liberty Lobby's analysis. For twenty years Willis Carto had portrayed the Lobby as a "conservative" and "nationalist" institution. Now *The Spotlight* took full aim at conservatism, which "diligently avoids controversy in regard to Zionism, race, money and banking, and Trilateralism."[16]

Reagan Administration Policy on Civil Rights

In its earliest years the Reagan administration had been indifferent to Ku Klux Klan violence. William Bradford Reynolds, who headed the Justice Department's Civil Rights Division, balked at enforcing federal civil rights. When marauding Klansmen shot five black women while they walked down a public street in Chattanooga in 1980, for example, Reynolds refused to indict them, claiming that "there is insufficient evidence on which to prosecute pursuant to the federal criminal civil rights statutes."[17] When a white mob attacked civil rights marchers in Forsyth County, Georgia, in 1987, Reynolds regarded the action as "childish prattle," rather than a significant breach of civil rights requiring federal redress.[18] In fact, for Reynolds, Attorney General Edwin Meese, and President Reagan, the principal civil rights battle was not against racist violence but against affirmative action for black people and women in hiring and education.

According to Drew Days III, who had been the Justice Department's civil rights chief in President Carter's administration, Reynolds sought to repeal policies that had previously guided civil rights enforcement.[19] Instead of addressing discrimination against entire classes of people, Reynolds narrowed Justice Department protection to lone individuals. And instead of aggressive federal intervention, Reynolds and Reagan invoked a post–civil rights era formula based on states' rights and a policy of "benign neglect."[20]

By contrast, where the Reagan administration perceived that the rights of white people were compromised, the Justice Department leaped into action. One of Reynolds's earliest cases before the Supreme Court, for example, was a vain attempt to win charitable status for Bob Jones University.[21] Because of the university's official policies of racial discrimination, the IRS had denied the South Carolina school tax-exempt status. The Reagan administration also cut funding to the Equal

Employment Opportunity Commission, resulting in a sharp reduction in discrimination cases pursued by the agency.[22]

For liberals, divining any significant distinctions between white supremacists and Reaganesque conservatives may seem like an unreal exercise, like counting devils on the head of a pin. For white supremacists, however, these differences were basic to their identity as an autonomous movement. As the year 1981 progressed, *The Spotlight* became increasingly vocal in its criticisms of the Reagan administration.[23] As a result, many of the conservatives who had once subscribed to the tabloid and enjoyed its anti-Carter diatribes now stopped reading. They could not countenance treating Reagan as an enemy. During the ensuing years *The Spotlight*'s circulation fell by half—from 300,000 to 150,000 in 1984.[24] It was still the newspaper of record for white supremacists, but it now operated on a narrower, more ideological, strip of white turf.

To compound the difficulties this created for Liberty Lobby, the *Washington Post* columnist Jack Anderson published an exposé of Willis Carto and Liberty Lobby in a short-lived magazine he produced in 1981, *The Investigator*. Picking up where a similar article in *National Review* had left off a decade before, these articles described Francis Parker Yockey as "America's Hitler." Willis Carto emerged as a secretive racist and anti-Semite pushing his way toward political respectability. Carto sued Anderson for libel, and the exposé became the subject of a long-running legal dispute that wound its way up and down the court system.[25] Other lawsuits plagued Willis Carto during the 1980s, including a libel lawsuit pressed by Watergate burglar E. Howard Hunt. Liberty Lobby won against Hunt. But a lawsuit brought by Mel Mermelstein proved infinitely more troublesome for Carto.[26]

Denying the Holocaust

October 18, 1981. California Superior Court Judge Thomas T. Johnson took judicial notice "that Jews were gassed to death at the Auschwitz concentration camp" and ruled that the Holocaust was an established historical fact. He then ordered a group calling itself the Institute for Historical Review to pay a person named Mel Mermelstein a total of ninety thousand dollars and issue him an apology for any anguish it had caused.[1] In that short courtroom declaration, a whole world of historical events spun around.

The defendant, Institute for Historical Review, had popped up during the crest years of white supremacist revival before President Reagan's election. A marketing operation from the start, it sold a small stock list of books and pamphlets that rewrote the history of World War Two. In these pages Jews were not gassed to death at Auschwitz, and Anne Frank's diary was a hoax. Indeed, the entire Holocaust was deemed a fraud in which the deliberate murder of Jews was invented for "political and economic" purposes. They also argued that President Roosevelt had wrongly pursued a war against Hitler, with tragic results for the West. These ideas, which had circulated on the fringes for two decades without effect, now sought a larger audience.[2]

During the institute's first conference in 1979, its executive director issued a challenge, a fateful fifty-thousand-dollar reward to anyone who could prove that Jews had been gassed at Auschwitz during World War Two.[3] The offer was a bald attempt to garner publicity and mainstream notice, but it failed. Only Carto's *Spotlight* and David Duke's Klan tabloid, *The Crusader*, published articles about the meeting.[4] Otherwise, the general media ignored it. Moreover, no one applied for the reward. At a second conference a year later, the director again made reward offers.[5] When it looked once again as if nobody would take his bait, he sent letters to several Holocaust survivors, soliciting their applications.[6] Mel Mermelstein bit the hook. A seemingly hapless businessman living in southern California, Mermelstein surprised his antagonists and virtually dragged them into the sea.

Mermelstein was born in Hungary and uprooted as a teenager and deported to concentration camps. All of his immediate family perished in this whirlwind of horrors, and he alone survived Auschwitz. Eventually Mermelstein immigrated to the United States, moved to the Los Angeles area, and established a moderately successful business. He also maintained a small museum that memorialized his family and the Holocaust, and he recounted his experiences to schoolchildren in the hopes that such crimes would not be repeated. His personal biography even became the subject of a 1991 television movie.[7]

Angered by the letter from the Institute for Historical Review, he could not leave it unanswered. On December 18, 1980, he formally applied for the fifty-thousand-dollar reward and proffered as preliminary evidence an affidavit to the fact that he had witnessed the disappearances of his family into Auschwitz's gas chambers. In response, the institute juggled Mermelstein's claim while it hoped to draw the famous Austrian Nazi hunter Simon Wiesenthal into the fray. Failing that, the IHR set conditions for evidence from Mermelstein. It became obvious that the institute had no intention of dealing fairly with the application, and Mermelstein sued it and its principals for breach of contract. During the process of legal discovery, his attorney began prying up the layers of secrecy surrounding the IHR's actual workings. All of the institute's correspondence to Mermelstein, for example, had been signed by "Lewis Brandon." The Brandon in this case turned out to be a veteran of Britain's white wing named David McCalden who had answered a help wanted ad in *The Spotlight*, moved to sunny California, and eventually become the institute's founding executive director.[8] Even more significant, the lawsuit also revealed the fact that the Institute for Historical Review was a business name for a corporation known as the Legion for the Survival of Freedom, making the legion's board of directors a party to the case. And the one corporate director that Mermelstein's attorneys zeroed in on was Elisabeth Carto, Willis's German-born wife. During one hearing the attorney argued: "Since Willis Carto bought into and took over [the legion], she has been the one director who has maintained continuity. She was the only corporate officer who was in charge to any extent of the operations . . ."[9]

Both Elisabeth and Willis Carto repeatedly stonewalled and ducked during depositions. In one instance Willis Carto wore sunglasses and an obviously fake nose and mustache while Mermelstein's attorneys asked him questions and the camera recorded his every twitch.[10]

The Superior Court's ruling did not end litigation between Mermelstein and the institute. Over the next dozen years suits and countersuits flew between the parties.[11] Often during these proceedings, the question being asked was whether or not Willis Carto actually controlled the affairs of the Legion for the Survival of Freedom and the IHR. The corporate history of the legion is a story unto itself. It must be told from its first moments in Carto's hands in order to understand how in the end it brought about his fall.

LaVonne Furr and the Legion for the Survival of Freedom

This chronicle of events began, oddly enough, with the ground-up remains of a once mighty magazine of grand letters, H. L. Mencken's *American Mercury*. After Mencken died, the publication and its stock of back issues were sold and resold until they landed with Hoyt Matthews, an aging superpatriot in McAllen, Texas. He published the much-diminished periodical under the auspices of a Texas nonprofit corporation, the Legion for the Survival of Freedom. Sometimes working as a volunteer at his side was a young mother named LaVonne Furr, who lived full-time in Louisiana, where her husband, Lewis Brandon Furr, worked as a parish court clerk.[12]

LaVonne often had the world around her defined by men who requested her assistance. She occasionally helped her husband type up court records, for example, despite having three children to care for. And when she visited her parents in McAllen, her father asked her to help Hoyt Matthews with *American Mercury*. She gladly complied, even accompanying him on a business trip to Washington, D.C. There she briefly met Willis Carto while Carto and Matthews (apparently old acquaintances) chatted in the shadow of the Library of Congress.[13]

When Matthews died in 1964, he left the magazine and the corporation to his daughter. But she had neither the interest nor the capability of keeping any kind of publishing business going. So she turned around and asked LaVonne Furr to take over the enterprise. Needing help herself, Mrs. Furr sought assistance from Willis Carto, beginning with the need to iron out the Legion for the Survival of Freedom's corporate status. Since the original incorporators of the legion were not available, Furr and Carto reincorporated the Legion for the Survival of Freedom in Texas in 1966.[14] For about a year Furr tried to publish *American Mercury* from a Texas address, while Carto helped from his base in southern California. Then Carto offered the Louisiana housewife her first paying job with the proviso that she move the magazine's operations to California. With husband, Lewis, in tow, LaVonne Furr moved to Torrance and filled book orders, kept *Mercury* subscriber lists updated, and copy-edited the magazine—all from her dining room table. Carto set the magazine's direction, made ultimate decisions about prospective articles, and gradually rebuilt it into his own ideological outpost. [15]

With a new corporation and publication in hand, Carto rearranged his publishing miniempire. He stopped producing *Western Destiny* magazine, and made Noontide Press, which had published Yockey's *Imperium*, an imprint of the legion. With both *American Mercury* and Noontide now under one roof, he used the Legion for the Survival of Freedom as the West Coast base for the more overtly ideological activities that his East Coast–based Liberty Lobby eschewed.[16]

The magazine became edgier and nastier. The Holocaust in particular received a drubbing by *Mercury* contributors. In 1966 it published an article entitled "That Elusive Six Million."[17] The following year another article asked, "Was Anne Frank's Diary a Hoax?"[18] Still another claimed to be "The Truth About Dachau Concentration Camp." It recapitulated various anti-Semitic conspiracy theories (the Rothschilds killed Lincoln!), before concluding that three million Jews had smuggled their way from Hong Kong to California and lived happily ever after.[19] And a pearly white profascist thread wound its way through Carto's *American Mercury*, reflected in several articles, including an abridged reprint of a piece by Benito Mussolini entitled "Church, State and Sex." [20]

As remarkable as the articles denying the Nazi genocide was one that affirmed the Hitler regime. Published fifteen years before German unification, it argued that the "Deutsche Reich" was still a legal entity and could therefore be resurrected, complete with its 1945 borders incorporating Austria, the Sudetenland, and a third of Poland. The article also claimed that calling Hitler a dictator was "the greatest distortion of truth." Without the slightest hint of irony it concluded that "the Third Reich under the Fuhrer Adolph Hitler was in the very truest sense a government of the people for the people."[21]

Once the legion was running full steam, Carto resigned his formal seat on its board of directors, preferring instead to direct events from behind the scenes as the corporation's business agent.[22] With more efficient management, *American Mercury*'s paid circulation base grew from six thousand plus in 1966, to about twelve thousand in 1970, reflecting in part the constituency for hard-core racist and anti-Semitic material. By 1975, when white supremacists and Reagan-era conservatives both began to rebound, paid circulation had reached seventeen thousand plus. As articles apologizing for the Hitler regime appeared more frequently, paid circulation started to slide back down, and by 1978 only a core group of eight thousand kept subscribing to the magazine.[23] The circulation's rise and fall during the mid-1970s should not be read as an indicator of the size or prospects of the white supremacist movement as a whole. Consider that David Duke's Klan and William Pierce's National Alliance were considerably stronger and bigger in 1978 than ever before. Support for Liberty Lobby also grew exponentially during this period as well. Rather, *Mercury*'s numbers pointed to a smaller specialty niche for hard-core material exculpating the Nazis' worst crimes. That November, Carto and LaVonne Furr hired David McCalden as an assistant.

McCalden worked side by side with Mrs. Furr. They filled book orders generated by Noontide Press and made the legion an overall success. McCalden saw what was selling off the Noontide list. It was the Holocaust denial materials.[24] And it was his particular genius that sensed this market's existence and Carto's business skills that exploited it.

To capitalize a new project focused on the Holocaust, the legion sold *American Mercury* for twenty-six thousand dollars to one of its contributing editors, who lived in Louisiana.[25] LaVonne and her husband left California and followed *American Mercury* back to Louisiana, helping until that magazine finally ceased publication. Though she retired after this, LaVonne Furr (and her husband, Lewis) remained on the legion's board of directors for years. With Willis Carto legally serving as business agent at the behest of the board, Mrs. Furr had more formal legal power in the corporation. For the time being she simply did as she was told and signed the minutes of board meetings that Carto made up and sent her.[26] As will become more fully manifest, when she finally resigned her seat, control of the Legion-Institute for Historical Review finally slipped from Carto's hands. The IHR's campaign against truth in history, however, stayed the same over time. By its lights the Holocaust remained a hoax.

Carto's Interest in Rewriting World War Two

Willis Carto (and others) needed to rewrite the history of World War Two: it was central, not peripheral, to their white supremacist project. They all believed a civilization-level change had occurred with the defeat of Hitler. "A German victory would have assured that the life-span of the White world would have been extended for many centuries more than now seems likely," Carto wrote in 1973 under his pseudonym E. L. Anderson. "Because of our 'victory,' the Western world is rapidly sinking into a morass of hopelessness and defeat from which there may be neither resurgence nor survival."[27] By placing the word "victory" inside quotation marks in his own text, Carto made it clear that he lamented both the victory itself and its consequences.

Wilmot Robertson also understood the deleterious effect of the Allied victory. Although he tended to trace the supposed dispossession of his white majority to the population loss suffered during the Civil War, he recognized the importance of World War Two's residual effects. "[A]fter the inventory of Hitler's racial excesses was published at the close of World War II, all arguments for racial supremacy were placed beyond the pale of permissive thought by the Western intellectual community,"[28] he wrote.

Mainstream historians, although starting from different premises, reached similar conclusions: the fight against racism and fascism in Europe had discredited these ideologies among America's decision-making elites. "American war propaganda stressed above all else the abhorrence of the West for Hitler's brand of racism and its utter incompatibility with the democratic faith for which we fought," wrote C. Vann Woodward in his book *The Strange Career of Jim Crow*. British historian Eric Hobsbawm noted that World War Two "had eliminated National Socialism, fascism, overt Japanese nationalism and much of the right-wing and nationalist sector of the political spectrum from the acceptable political scene."[29]

While wartime propaganda against Nazi Germany's Nuremberg Laws made it difficult to defend laws that denied voting rights according to race, the defeat of the Axis Powers did not automatically translate into the end of Jim Crow forms of second-class citizenship. That would require the bravery and brilliance of a determined civil rights movement in the 1950s and 1960s. While fascism may have been defeated during World War Two, communism was still very much alive and kicking during the postwar period. And during the Cold War anticommunism gained complete dominance over the heights of American life. As a result, defense of Jim Crow segregation and opposition to civil rights during the 1950s and 1960s often marched under the banner of anticommunism. White supremacy became the ideology that could not speak its name.

William Pierce put it squarely. "A morality which damns the Germans for attempting to rid themselves of a pernicious infestation," he wrote, would also "damn any attempt by White Americans to disinfect the cesspool of mongrelization."[30] The weight of genocide in Europe blocked its repetition in the United States.

Nevertheless, Pierce loathed Holocaust denial as it was practiced by Willis Carto. "There are reckless 'revisionists' who assert that no Jews were killed, solely for being Jews, by the German government," Pierce scolded. "That is certainly not true." He claimed to have talked with Nazi veterans who had assured him that they had shot Jews (solely for being Jews). Furthermore, what purpose was served by denying the existence of gas chambers? Jews could have been gassed, Pierce speculated. The Nazis had killed Jews because they were partisans or communists or commissars or just because they were Jews. What was wrong with that? he asked. The Nazis had done only what needed to be done.[31]

Others were just fooling themselves. "The 'revisionist,' the conservative, the right winger, the anti-Semite who cannot face the Holocaust squarely and judge it on the basis of a higher morality," Pierce wrote, "cannot, for example, cope successfully with the challenges to a White future which are presented by non-White immigration and by a high non-White birthrate."[32] One should not deny the industrialized murder of Jews, Pierce's logic ran, because it may become necessary to repeat it on Jews and "nonwhites" in the future.

Moreover, Pierce lost little time before using the court decision to tweak his archrival about the decision in the *Mermelstein* case. The Institute for Historical Review "has been made to look very foolish," Pierce's *National Vanguard* commented.[33]

Despite Pierce's objections and the financial losses incurred by Willis Carto's extreme litigiousness, the IHR began to prosper and grow. It published a quarterly journal and a monthly newsletter. An editorial board of advisers, many of them with Ph.D.'s after their names, signed up. One of the mainstays was an engineering professor from Northwestern University, Arthur Butz, whose book *The Hoax of the Twentieth Century* set the tone during the early years.[34] The IHR purchased mailing lists of university-affiliated historians and solicited their support. It also began to produce an extensive literature based on a flat earth version of history.

Its conferences remained relatively modest affairs. After the first one in 1979, the meets drew anywhere from 100 to 150 attendees, and the IHR became a coat-and-tie center for the movement's professional intelligentsia. Its ideas took root in every type of white supremacist organization. Klan groups and uniformed Hollywood-style Nazis alike sold its pamphlets. So-called Christian patriots and gun-happy survivalists believed the Holocaust was a hoax. The IHR not only carved a distinctive niche within white supremacist circles, but became part of the interstitial glue that turned disparate organizations into a unitary movement.

As the first years of the 1980s progressed, the movement as a whole slowly continued to gain ground. The Klan groups, which had been the most visible element of the initial resurgence in the 1970s, were joined by a plethora of new organizations taking on differing forms. And some of those completely eschewed the trappings of middle-class mainstream society and opted instead for an alternative lifestyle based on guns and religion.

Survivalism Meets a Subcultural "Christian Identity"

September 25, 1982. Survivalist gear of every kind filled the exhibition room in Kansas City's downtown convention center. Both a display of a model bomb shelter and a booth of dehydrated foods drew curiosity seekers, while serious shoppers thumbed through explosives and gun manuals. Publishers of glossy survival magazines pushed sales next to low-rent newsletter vendors. High-tech biochemical warfare suits hung behind tables displaying the latest in laser-sighted weapons. If you wanted to prepare for impending shortages, you could buy Harvest Pak Low Moisture Survival Foods. If you wanted to remachine your legal semiautomatic into an illegal fully automatic assault rifle, the blueprints were available. If you needed to dress up the weapon with flash suppressors, folding stocks, and thirty-shot banana clips, specialists sold you the parts right there. If you just wanted to dress up, you could pick from the array of camouflage hats, shirts, pants, and jackets.[1]

The Self-Reliance and Survival Expo advertised itself in the daily newspaper and on radio and television as if it were the latest version of a recreational vehicle show. Surviving nuclear war and social chaos appeared as if it might provide the next big entrepreneurial opportunity. The signs proliferated across the popular culture.

"Country folks will survive," sang country and western musician Hank Williams, Jr., in a popular anthem to fishing, hunting, living in the woods, and avoiding the dangers of urban living. Rambo had just made his first big-screen appearance. Pulp novels, magazines, and comic books all exalted a new type of warrior, a working-class man at odds with enemies abroad as well as traitorous elites at home. Most often, the new heroes' values, like Rambo's, were paramilitary and survivalist, rather than official West Point militarist.[2]

The new trend was most marked at gun and knife shows, which had long been cultural bellwethers, particularly in the Midwest and South. At these shows, proud collectors once displayed antique weapons mounted on polished walnut panels and dealers sold bolt-action 30-06s for deer season. Now a new breed seemingly intent on hunting humans traded weapons as if they were preparing for a communist invasion. Large-format illustrations of Civil War rifles appeared in the same exhibit as booklets on revenge killing. Hunter orange was out; brown fatigues were in. Young rootless vendors, living out of their trucks, followed a circuit selling "self-defense" weapons rigged only for murder.[3]

While "survivalism" appeared to have reached the level of the mass market, the market itself was not yet fully developed. Buying a couple of Rambo movie tickets or listening to Hank Jr. on the radio was not the same as plunking down $758 for a seven-month supply of freeze-dried foods. And even paying $200 cash for a blue-steel Mini-14 assault rifle required less time and commitment than actually training with it in the woods. As an epiphenomenon, survivalism, particularly paramilitary-style survivalism, was much like the antibusing movement a few years before. Led by angry white men, the dispossessed majority of Wilmot Robertson's imagination, it provided a pool of potential recruits for the resurgent white supremacist cause.

At the Kansas City Expo, a table for a group calling itself the Covenant, the Sword and the Arm of the Lord demonstrated the case in point. Two men in fatigues stood at an exhibition display with only a couple of books and spare parts for assault rifles on it. A self-published manual gave 175 pages of practical advice on buying and shooting guns, knife fighting, home defense, and nuclear bomb shelters. "A double-edged knife is designed for killing," the text helpfully suggested. "If you believe you will use your knife as a weapon, we suggest you select a double-edged blade."[4]

The books were for sale, but the gear was just for display. The two men were actually marketing a paramilitary training course taught back at their compound deep in the recesses of the Ozark Mountains. They had built an elaborate collection of wooden and stone structures called Silhouette City. For a fee, white (Christian) men could shoot machine guns at pop-up figures, knock down doors, and battle around mock buildings while tires burned to simulate urban riots. Lessons included knife fighting and hand-to-hand combat too. In Kansas City that day the Covenant group, also known as the CSA, tried to ladle some of the commercial gravy into its own small boat, just as it had been doing at gun shows around the Midwest.[5]

The CSA was one of the new breed of organizations that sprang up in the late 1970s and early 1980s. Instead of white robes its members wore camouflage fatigues as their uniform of choice. Unlike Klansmen who paraded down Main Street or national socialists with their spit-in-your-face swastika armbands, at this moment the CSA stayed largely out of the public eye. Electing candidates, effecting public policy, pursuing economic gain, or protecting their enlightened self-interest all were irrelevant to Covenant followers. Living in a tract house, sending their children to public school, and holding down jobs were to be avoided. There was the Beast system on one side, they believed, and the Kingdom of God on the other. They lived in the latter. Here guns and survivalism met race and religion.

Their theology was a nondenominational system known as "Christian Identity." According to this doctrine, northern European whites and their North American offspring are the racial descendants of the tribes of biblical Israel. People of color are sometimes referred to as "pre-Adamic," created by God before Adam and thus without souls, although an even more pejorative term, "mud people," was used as well. Jews are regarded as either the direct embodiment of Satan himself or simply Satanic in nature. And Jesus was an Aryan.[6]

While these ideas might at first sound preposterous, it is helpful to recall that generations of Christians have found in their Bible justifications for racism and anti-Semitism. It was the church that burned Jews at the stake during the Spanish Inquisition. English-speaking slaveholders read Genesis and claimed that Africans were the descendants of Ham, an accursed race bound by God to be "hewers of wood." In the Gideon (King James) edition John 8:44, they read John to claim that Jesus says of the Jews: "Ye are of your father the devil, and the lusts of your father ye will do." The anti-Semitic sap that Identity adherents drew from the Christian tree had risen and fallen for almost two millennia before the CSA set up camp.[7]

So too had beliefs that the end of the world was near, and eschatology—doctrines about the End Times and Final Judgment—remained central to fundamentalist Christianity. In this context, Identity Christians contended that they would live through all manner of evil until the End of Days, when they would be the "Sword of the Lord." By this canon, they were the ultimate survivalists.[8]

In keeping with the notion that they were descended from biblical Israel, the CSA's leaders called their Ozark encampment Zarephath-Horeb. Heavily wooded low mountains and a lake surrounded their 224 acres. Only one road led into the camp from the Missouri village of Pontiac, and on the other side the camp abutted Bull Shoals Lake and the Arkansas state border. At any given time, approximately seventy to ninety people, including thirty to forty children, lived in three small clusters of group homes and single family dwellings. The camp featured freshwater wells, barns and ponds for livestock, a combination school-house and church building, a machine shop, a radio room, and storage sheds. For a time some of the men ran a failed logging business. Others engaged in subsistence agriculture or salvaged scrap. The state govern-ment, hated as it was, provided welfare or food stamps to the indigent. And a select few worked the lathe, milling machine, and drill presses[9] in the machine shop.[10]

The Zarephath-Horeb camp was an odd permutation on an old Amer-ican tradition, utopian communities, with one significant exception: church services were held with a Bible in one hand and an assault rifle in the other.[11] The precision metalworking machinery was used to build silencers and transform semiautomatic rifles into fully automatic ma-chine guns. The CSA also produced homemade hand grenades and claymore-type land mines. A truck frame became the embryo of an armored personnel carrier. Weapons of every description were cached around the camp like sacks of wheat for a future famine. Light antitank weapons, known as LAW rockets, dynamite, and military-style plastic explosives were hidden. So was a thirty-gallon barrel of cyanide and forty thousand dollars' worth of gold coins, or Krugerrands, the currency of the apartheid regime in South Africa. It was the most heavily armed and militarized of the survivalist compounds of that period.[12]

The impressive division of economic labor, tools, and weapons might have made the settlement a haven for superrational *Übermenschen* en-dowed with a supply of white genes for future generations. That was William Pierce's prescription for survivalist communities, and several National Alliance members had taken survivalist training.[13] But the CSA was ultimately a heavily armed and criminal commune for cultists.

Atop this gunpowder dung heap sat James Ellison, like a combination guru and *Gruppenführer*. Originally from Illinois, Ellison attended four years of Christian Church seminary, but he did not graduate.[14] In 1970, at age twenty-nine, he came to the Ozarks and established a supposedly Bible-based, but not yet Christian Identity, church in Elijay, Arkansas. Six years later, with a mortgage from the Campus Crusade for Christ, he moved his congregation of thirty souls to the 224-acre camp. Ellison's top lieutenant was Kerry Noble, also from Texas but twelve years younger. They gathered acolytes from among the region's spiritually dis-solute.[15]

These were not the university-educated souls at the Institute for His-torical Review. One woman joined Ellison's church in Elijay when she was just twenty-three years old, for example, and then later, after a di-

vorce, moved onto the encampment with her three children. She dutifully turned over her possessions and money, as well as welfare checks,
around seven thousand dollars' worth. Another young man, suffering
from heavy drug use and marital problems, thought camp life could
straighten him out. A third joined after a history of drug dealing and alcoholism. And a fourth, who eventually deserted the cause, told the
Arkansas state police: "The problem with half the people out there . . .
when they jump up and threaten to run off," they had no place to go.
Nevertheless, some did leave the camp before it became a destination
with no return.[16]

Like cultic figures elsewhere, Ellison dressed his total control over
other people's lives in biblical language. On one occasion, he instructed
a follower to learn the "mind of a servant" and rub his feet every day for
six months. In another instance, Ellison declared a male camper "spiritually dead," so that he could then "marry" the man's "former" wife. The
woman, the daughter of a Lutheran minister from Minnesota, acceded
to the demand. Already married himself, Ellison lived for a time with
two wives and eleven children, all in the same cabin.[17]

It is useful to compare Ellison's relationship to his followers with that
of other movement leaders. Willis Carto, for example, maintained a financial stranglehold on his organizations but left the personalities of his
employees intact. William Pierce's ideological grip was fierce, but he
wanted strong cadres with intellectual and technical skills, rather than
weak and dependent subordinates. David Duke, whose refracted television appearances were the source of his charisma, thought cults were
tremendous fund-raising opportunities.[18] But he still depended on mailed
appeals, not blind obedience, to raise money. While none of these men
operated an open, democratic organization, neither the Klan nor National Alliance nor Liberty Lobby was a cult. Ellison, by contrast, relied
on the slavishness of his followers and their absolute devotion to him as
a leader. To make the insanity complete, Ellison claimed to be descended from the biblical King David and had himself anointed King
James of the Ozarks.[19]

During the early 1980s the CSA maintained good relations with other
survivalist-type groups in the Midwest. The Christian-Patriots Defense
League, or CPDL, headquartered across the state in southern Illinois,
also adhered to the Christian Identity doctrine. But instead of a cult, it
served as a loosely structured amalgam of paramilitary enthusiasts.[20]
The CPDL promoted an idea called the "Mid-America Survival Zone,"
with the Appalachian Mountains and the Colorado Rockies as imagined
borders. The CPDL argued that the middle of the country had the best

chance to survive a nuclear war or communist invasion. It was an ambiguous quasi-military concept, with its racialism implied rather than
explicit. At private three-day festivals on the estate grounds of its
founder, a thousand people typically camped in trailers or tents, one indication of the movement's drawing power in the Midwest. Vendors sold
white supremacy as if it were the next great consumer gadget. Workshop
attendees learned that Jews sponsored both race mixing and the Antichrist media. Although a few sessions were aimed at women and some
children were present on the grounds, these fests were not actually family affairs. At the fests' end, a small group of men stayed for paramilitary
instruction by a retired army lieutenant colonel, crawling through brush
and shooting at targets.[21]

These events attracted recruiters of various types looking for new followers. William Pierce sent several university students to sell literature
one year, while they took the paramilitary training course. Willis Carto's
Spotlight tabloid reported favorably on these affairs, and Liberty Lobby
sent speakers.[22] For several years, squads of Ellison's CSA soldiers,
dressed in camouflage uniforms with assault rifles slung across their
backs, provided "security." Here they exuded power and prestige, in contrast with the depraved position they occupied at their commander's
feet.

Despite the similarity of the two organizations, the Christian-Patriots
Defense League broke with the CSA after the July 1982 festival and
took the unusual step of explaining its decision in a six-page letter to
supporters. "In the beginning Mr. Ellison's intentions were proper, . . .
but as time progressed they altered and changed to the point where now
he may well be engaged in practices and actions that could endanger his
entire unit, plus set the stage to bring public reproach and damage to
the overall patriotic effort nationwide . . . Some who have lived there
honestly state and believe it could eventually evolve into a Jim Jones
type of tragedy unless numerous changes are made."[23] Apparently, cultlike behaviors were not popular among racists and anti-Semites either.

Despite this particular breach, Ellison kept his ties with other Identity believers in the region, chief among them Robert Millar, who ran a
similar commune-compound dubbed Elohim City. As in Zarephath-
Horeb, Elohim City's residents named their acreage to symbolize their
identification with biblical Israel. Also like Ellison's compound, it was
near a state border, six miles up a dirt road where the eastern edge of
Oklahoma joins northwestern Arkansas in the Ozark Mountains. A collection of self-constructed cabins and trailer homes settled on one corner of four hundred acres, gardens were cultivated, and livestock grazed

on the balance of the land. As self-sufficient as possible, residents also operated their own sawmill and construction company, in addition to a transcontinental trucking fleet. For eight hours each day, Elohim City's full-time residents collectively homeschooled their children. They also attended daily religious services at noon in a white-domed church with polyurethaned walls. Although random visitors were unwanted, the few reporters who gained acceptance were shown the homespun buildings with great pride.[24]

If they considered society around them rotten and doomed for destruction, the campers at Elohim City and the CSA's Zarephath-Horeb all fervently believed they would survive and ultimately see God. By contrast, Willis Carto and William Pierce thought of survivalism in decidedly less ethereal terms. For Carto, it served as another mass-market opportunity, and Liberty Lobby cashed in on the phenomenon early and often. For William Pierce, survivalist events became an opportunity for National Alliance cadres to sell literature and find new recruits.

Pierce wasn't concerned about human existence per se. Rather he worried about "the preservation of [white] genes during a time of racial decay."[25] To ensure this preservation, he needed to influence the larger survivalist movement's direction. As usual, he began with a cold-eyed analysis. "One can recognize three distinguishing traits in the survivalist," Pierce's *National Vanguard* opined. The first was a strong "personal identity"; the second was a "will to survive"; and the third was "alienation from the present society." Despite this positive assessment, Pierce also looked for weak spots. The "largely individualistic approach" bothered him the most.[26] Survivalists were interested in self-preservation (like professionals practicing "lifeboat ethics"), rather than the advancement of the white race. Here Pierce sharply distinguished himself from the survivalists. And his criticism of survivalists turned on the same point as his negative assessment of conservatives: individualism was a curse in both instances, he believed.

Actually, Pierce was no more a survivalist than Lenin was a trade unionist.[27] In his mind, mass movements such as survivalism needed to be transformed by an infusion of white racial consciousness. He argued that the individual home bomb shelter should be abandoned in favor of building entire "survival communities" large enough to defend themselves and create an economic division of labor among those who lived there. He urged these encampments to become self-sufficient with food, fuel, arms, and tools. Pierce could have been describing the Zarephath-

Horeb settlement and the Covenant, the Sword and the Arm of the Lord, but he wasn't. Pierce was most emphatically not a believer in the Christian Identity doctrine or in any Christian doctrine.

William Pierce believed that all of Christianity, including the Christian Identity professed by the Christian-Patriots Defense League, the CSA, Elohim City, and the like, was a useless, and ultimately destructive, myth. Even if Ellison and company believed that Jews were the embodiment of Satan on earth, Pierce argued that Christian Identity was incapable of producing the "ethic" necessary for total victory. According to his take, Christian values provided white people with no protection from the Jews and did little to assert white racial goals. To prove his point, Pierce argued that "the Jewish tribal deity, Yahweh (Jehovah) . . . also became the deity of the Christians."[28]

By Pierce's reasoning, then, Christianity served as an instrument of domination and as an impediment to the liberation of white people. They could buy all the Freeze Pak food they wanted, and they could shoot up Silhouette City from dawn to dusk. But as long as they worshiped "Yahweh," they would never reach their racial destiny. Always Pierce saw a genetic first cause. He argued that there were racial differences between the pre-Christian northern Europeans and the peoples of Asia Minor, where Judaism and Christianity were born. Because of these racial differences, the religions of the Middle East—Judaism and Christianity (and by extension Islam)—did not fill the spiritual requirements of northern Europeans. Christianity was thus incompatible with the true racial instincts of white Europeans.[29]

Pierce's discourse on history, genetics, and religion was, for him, a fight over first principles. Other activists also steeped in the doctrines of classical National Socialism shared this critique of Christianity, including Christian Identity. Some embraced Norse mythology and Odinism as an alternative. A few elevated Adolf Hitler to the status of a prophet or demigod. Pierce created a doctrine he called Cosmotheism, and an entity called the Cosmotheist Community Church, and won tax-exempt status from the Internal Revenue Service.[30] By both personality type and tactical design, Pierce wasn't particularly strident about these kinds of philosophical differences. He was most interested in the prospects for a "resurgent White racial community."[31]

In the early 1980s, intentionally creating all-white communities no longer seemed like an academic question. Unlike the Klan, which still kept one foot in the southern town square, groups such as the CSA lived separately from the rest of society, even mainstream white society. As they grew, these groups created their own system of institutions and allegiances, becoming, in effect, a white nationalist enclave at war with the multiracial state they called the Zionist Occupied Government, or ZOG. If the CSA proved to be the most militarized of these outposts, then Aryan Nations served as its central political address.

Nation and Race: Aryan Nations, Nehemiah Township, and Gordon Kahl

July 11, 1982. Twenty-eight men affixed their names with seals, another thirty signed on, and a notary made it officious, if not official. In a six-page charter, an imagined community, Nehemiah Township, was dedicated to the proposition of "Christian Self-Government" and the "preservation, protection and sustenance of our Aryan Race." Among the signatories were personalities from organizations across the white supremacist spectrum.[1] This township was not a plan for local control. Neither did it imply that just the government in Washington, D.C., was illegitimate.[2] Instead, it was conceived as an alternative to all forms of existing governments—local, state, and federal. Here was a white Christian nation-state, free of all non-Aryans and race traitors.

At the Covenant, the Sword and the Arm of the Lord's commune and inside the Christian-Patriots Defense League's survival zone, the idea of a racial nation was larded with concerns about communist invasions and surviving an eschatological End Times. But at the so-called Nehemiah Township, the ideal of a government—complete with territorial borders, police powers, and taxes—assumed an explicit, even if fanciful, form. Here those calling themselves Aryan Freemen were citizens, governed by what they called common law. Under this common law, contracts were to be signed, courts established, juries picked, and judges selected. And like any state apparatus worthy of the name, Nehemiah Township was to be protected by its own armed forces: a Posse Comitatus and a militia. The charter went so far as to establish the parameters of these militarized bodies. "The Posse Comitatus shall confine its activities to the Shire wherein it is chartered. The Militia shall not be confined to any boundary during its operation." In other words, as in Olde England, this posse operated only at the county level, while the militia could range free.[3]

No roads or highways traveled to this township. No sewer lines were built or water wells dug. And no one lived in any houses there. As an expression of a proposed white Christian nation-state, however, the ideas that animated Nehemiah Township reverberated across several decades. In 1983, after a planning meeting for a North Dakota township ended, two federal marshals were killed. In 1984 a group known as The Order murdered three men and stole from bank cars in the name of an Aryan state. In the mid-1990s, common law juries convened and militias were mustered in the name of white Christian Freemen. And the seed for these events was planted in July 1982, outside the tourist town of Coeur d'Alene, Idaho, at the occasion of the Aryan Nations' annual congress where the Nehemiah Township documents were signed.

Aryan Nations

During most of the 1980s this Aryan World Congress was the movement's premier social event of the summer season. Attendance varied. At its height, three hundred to five hundred men, women, and children spent the night in tents, RVs, or nearby motels for three days.[4] A twenty-acre compound included a church and meeting hall, two trailers for office space, and a bunkhouse with twenty-four beds. A fifty-foot-high guard tower provided a bird's-eye view of the surrounding woods. At the bottom of the property, a gate marked WHITES ONLY stood sentry. Busts of Hitler and swastika flags decorated the halls, and crosses were burned in an open field.[5]

The limited size of the acreage prevented the congress from including paramilitary training on the grounds, like those at Christian-Patriots Defense League fests. Other differences separated Aryan Nations from kindred operations during this period. No cultic leaders took root here, for example. And these meets tended to attract a more exclusive set with national socialist sympathies, hardened cadres at the center of the movement. They withstood years of public opposition and several waves of arrests and prosecutions, as Aryan Nations chief Richard Butler continued holding congresses and attracting new recruits.

Butler lived with his devoted wife, Betty, in a modest cabin on the grounds, which he owned personally. Tall, with tightly combed dirty gray hair, he had worked as an aircraft engineer in Southern California before retiring to northern Idaho in 1973, about the same time Ellison relocated to the Ozarks and Millar established Elohim City. Slightly older than Carto, Butler exhibited few business or entrepreneurial skills. He was a doctrinaire advocate of Christian Identity theology whose belabored speech patterns kept him from artfully articulating his ideas. In fact, he could be either erect or stiff, depending on your point of view. But his devotion to the cause was solid and unmovable, and some followers were obviously attracted to his stern demeanor.

During the early 1980s Butler's compound was the most elaborate administrative movement complex outside Liberty Lobby's offices in Washington, D.C., but none of its arms stretched toward the political mainstream. Here was a vanguardist outfit with a small offset press that churned out a continual supply of booklets, newsletters, and leaflets. A couple of volunteers usually worked in the office, and several stayed on the premises, either in the bunkhouse or in their own trailers. The campground itself did not accommodate more than a half dozen full-time inhabitants, but several dozen others lived in surrounding communities and came over for church services, Bible studies, or meetings. Often, young runaways, men who had left their wives, or wandering activists stopped in the bunkhouse for a couple of days or weeks, worked around the grounds, and either moved on or stayed nearby to be close to "headquarters." Virtually none of the Aryans meddled directly in the community life of the surrounding towns.

Although Butler set the rules by which the compound operated, he was rarely directly involved in its administrative affairs, such as literature sales or correspondence.[6] At any given moment, Aryan Nations' fortunes actually depended on the skills and practices of a revolving door of unpaid personnel, rather than on Butler's personal abilities. He was clever (and militant) enough, however, to give his blessing to whatever new initiatives looked promising.

To the outside world, Butler was a public symbol. His use of the term "Zionist Occupied Government" to describe federal authorities caught the media's attention. Newspaper articles, plays, and movies all focused on his vulgar national socialist beliefs and Hitler worship. Inside the closed world of the movement, Butler served mostly a titular role, brought out for ceremonial events such as cross burnings, marches, and christening of new Aryan warriors. He left the strategic leadership questions to other people.

The Idaho compound remained an open sewer of violence from its first moments of operation until it was finally closed down in 2001. And for most of the 1980s, its significance multiplied as it became a nodal point for Klan factions, small Hitlerite sects, and so-called Christian patriot groups, enabling the creation of a common language across several organizational lines. Some groups would have more sway at one time or the other. And the Nehemiah Township charter signed in 1982 descended from the ideas of the group known as the Posse Comitatus, whose influence was particularly strong in those first years.[7]

Posse Comitatus

Posse Comitatus means "power of the county" in Latin, and the organization has been misunderstood by outsiders almost from the beginning. Commentators described it variously as a tax protest organization, an antigovernment vigilante group, or a ragtag collection of anti–Federal Reserve farmers. In 1982 it was, in fact, all of those things and none of them. Even its founding figure was long in doubt. FBI memorandums listed the founder as Henry Beach, a pre–World War Two Hitler sympathizer from Portland, Oregon, a fiction promulgated by Beach himself. The actual founder, however, was a retired army colonel living in Mariposa, California. Steeped in the anti-Semitic tenets of Christian Identity, William Potter Gale started the group in 1971.[8]

The Posse extended the Christian Identity doctrine into a complex theory of constitutional government based on the notion that the United States is not a democracy but a Christian republic, lawfully governed by so-called Christian common law rather than legislative statutes and court decisions. Posse propagandists argued that the country's governing institutions had been usurped by the "anti-Christ Jewry" and a bloody struggle was needed to set things white.[9]

In the 1970s, during the same years that David Duke re-created the Ku Klux Klan, Posse activists refused to file income tax returns and argued that the Federal Reserve money system was unconstitutional. They disregarded government environmental regulations, convened alternative "lawful" bodies such as grand juries and courts, and formed barter associations to do business.

At one point during the mid-seventies Posse members filed organizational charters at their county courthouses, each listing ten white Christian men who, they believed, constituted the sheriff's posse. The charters staked a claim that the Posse was a lawful party to county government. Most court clerks simply filed the charters away and ignored them. These charters were the first in a long line of pseudolegal court documents, such as liens and common law court judgments, that Posse types used to build their movement and to trouble their opponents.[10]

Although Richard Butler and the others signed the Nehemiah Township documents in Idaho, and a Posse leader from Wisconsin, James Wickstrom, and a group in Shawano County had declared their homestead a "township" and off-limits to government authorities, the center of Posse Comitatus activity had already shifted to the Farm Belt Midwest.[11]

There an acute economic and social crisis gripped agriculture. The farm-based economy and the particular type of rural life that it nurtured had been in chronic decline since the late nineteenth century, leading to a well-documented outpouring of population, white and black, from the countryside into the cities. The multiple causes included the widespread mechanization of agriculture that followed electrification and the market-driven tendency toward economies of scale. The boom-bust of the business cycle usually hit rural economies first, before spreading to industry and finance. The small towns of the Great Plains Midwest, like cotton-producing villages in the Deep South, had been drying up over several generations. And as the twentieth century progressed, the growth of industry occurred in large metropolitan centers. The problems in the farm economy during the early 1980s, however, constituted a unique period of economic, social, and personal crisis.[12]

The difficulties began with the price farmers received for their commodities, which often fell below their cost of production. And since family farmers typically borrowed money every spring for seed, fertilizer, and living expenses during the growing season, add to that the extraordinarily high interest rates of the period. Many farmers were caught in a cost-price squeeze that forced them out of business and off the land they had lived on. Between 1982 and 1985 the market value of farm acreage fell by an astonishing $146 billion, an amount equal to the combined assets of IBM, General Electric, Dow Chemical, and several other major corporations at that time.[13] The drop in land value, which farmers routinely used to secure credit, paralleled a crisis in agricultural banking. As the value of loan collateral fell below the face amounts of the loans to family farmers, government lending agencies and private banks alike foreclosed in an attempt to stanch their losses. In a vicious cycle, one round of foreclosures put even more land on an already glutted market, lowering the land value again, and setting off another round of foreclosures with seemingly no end in sight. Approximately 625,000 family farm operations were lost between 1981 and 1988.[14] These were not the large corporate-style agribusinesses typical of fruit and vegetable production in California and Florida, but smaller farms, producing commodity grains or beef or pork, and with few, if any, hired hands. For every four farms lost in the Midwest, one business on the nearby town square closed down also. The toll on individual families was harder to calculate, but we know community mental health agencies and suicide hotlines were overtaxed. While this problem began in the last years of

President Jimmy Carter's term, the Reagan administration's policies of tight credit and high interest rates exacerbated the situation.[15]

Family farmers searched wildly for answers to their problems. The first signs of revolt showed when the American Agriculture Movement (AAM) brought tens of thousands of farmers to Washington, D.C., in 1979 to protest farm policy. They organized a tractorcade that snarled up traffic around Capitol Hill and became a symbol of farmers' new-found militancy. Born outside the structures of existing organizations, such as the National Farmers Union, the AAM exhibited the freewheel-ing style of militance and ideological diversity of a truly spontaneous mass movement. Among the group that founded the AAM, several em-braced one type of anti-Semitic conspiracy theory or another, and some members adopted ideas promoted by *The Spotlight* tabloid to explain their distress. The Posse-influenced farmers pointed their fingers at the Federal Reserve System. But others did not, trying instead to find a stronger voice for lobbying Congress and state legislatures. Eventually a formal split occurred within the American Agriculture Movement. Daniel Levitas describes this multisided social struggle in *The Terrorist Next Door*, which remains the definitive book on the farm crisis and the Posse Comitatus.[16]

In 1982 the initiative in the rural Midwest still rested with vanguardists such as Wickstrom, who began advertising himself in periodicals widely read by farmers. After several speaking tours through small towns, Wickstrom developed grassroots followers who bought his Christian Identity lecture tapes, read his *Posse Noose Report* newsletter, and started forming Posses of their own. He even published a special pam-phlet for farmers that repeated all the standard anti-Semitic slanders but added an explicit invocation to violence against Jews.

Gale joined Wickstrom in this crusade, and taped "sermons" by the two Posse leaders were regularly broadcast on a Dodge City, Kansas, ra-dio station in 1982.[17] That same year Gale and Wickstrom organized a paramilitary training session on a farm near Weskan, Kansas, just across the border from Colorado. It was advertised as an "Ecological Seminar," and fifty-five participants registered and paid a fee (one hundred dollars for men, fifty for women, and thirty-five for children) to attend. Gale di-vided them into four groups, and for three days they attended sessions on killer teams, knife fighting, usable poisons, and explosives. Several personalities highly visible in farmers' protest organizations trained with weapons; they included activists from the American Agriculture Move-ment, as well as individuals from an ad hoc group calling itself the Farmers Liberation Army.[18] Several Weskan attendees later organized their own bomb-making sessions, without either Wickstrom or Gale, and a couple of them gained prominence in the 1990s as militia and common law court activists.[19]

At the time, one bankrupt farmer told the *Denver Post*, "We're prepared right now for the outcome of the battle that's being waged for this country by the Rockefeller cartel and the international Jew-Bolshevik cartel."[20] Mortal conflict rose on the immediate horizon. Paramilitary training sessions, combined with the drive toward confrontation with the so-called Zionist Occupied Government, ensured that it would begin sooner or later. And it began sooner, off the beaten track in a small town in North Dakota.

Gordon Kahl

Gordon Wendell Kahl, an aircraft gunner during World War Two with two Purple Hearts, never forgot how to handle his weapons. He and his wife, Joan, raised six children, scraping out a living on their Heaton, North Dakota, farm, earning extra money working in Texas during the winter. He also believed the United States had been "conquered and occupied by the Jews" and that taxes were "tithes to the synagogue of Satan."[21] Because of these beliefs, he refused to pay taxes and was wanted for a misdemeanor probation violation related to an original tax conviction. Although he faced a relatively minor charge, he vowed not to be taken alive and always carried a gun.

On February 13, 1983, federal marshals followed Kahl to a meeting in Heaton, where he and other Posse Comitatus members were discussing forming their own township, much like the idea expressed in Idaho the summer before. The marshals lay in wait, hoping to make a surprise arrest on a federal fugitive warrant after the gathering. When Kahl, his twenty-three-year-old son, Yorie, and other family members and friends were stopped at a roadblock, a vicious firefight ensued. Two federal marshals were killed, and three other officers wounded. Yorie was also wounded.[22]

In a letter later sent to Aryan Nations explaining his version of the incident, Kahl argued the shoot-out had been part of a "struggle to the death between the people of the Kingdom of God and the Kingdom of Satan." He also claimed to have killed the two marshals in self-defense. "My bullets appeared to be ricocheting off the windshield and door post" of the marshals' car, he wrote. "I ran around toward the side of the vehicle, firing at the door as I went to keep him down until I got around far enough to get a clear shot at him." When the shooting subsided, he walked up to one of the wounded marshals and shot him twice, point-blank, in the head.[23]

In the aftermath, both Scott Faul, who was in the car at the time of the firefight, and son Yorie were convicted of assault and second-degree murder. But Gordon Kahl escaped into a network of friends and fellow believers who hid him from the authorities until the following June, when an FBI special agent found him living in a concrete-walled cabin outside Smithville, Arkansas, deep in the Ozark Mountains, not far from the Covenant, the Sword and the Arm of the Lord camp on Bull Shoals Lake. Another shoot-out ensued. The local county sheriff was shot dead, and Kahl was killed, first shot in the head by a bullet from the sheriff's gun and later burned up in a fire the FBI started that engulfed the cabin. The entire sequence of events involving Kahl was authoritatively recounted in the 1990 book *Bitter Harvest*, by James Corcoran, who followed Kahl's trail to the end.

During the 1980s, white supremacists contested the circumstances of Kahl's death. Several men in Arkansas launched a semipublic "investigation." They claimed Kahl had been executed and the sheriff shot by one of his own men. (The government later charged two of the "investigators" with conspiracy to murder an FBI agent and a federal judge.) Joining the chorus, Liberty Lobby's *Spotlight* claimed that Kahl, a principled patriot, tax protester, and brave family farmer, was killed while fighting government oppression.

There is a difference, however, between a farmer who is not financially able to make his loan payments and an activist ideologically determined not to pay his taxes. Gordon Kahl was the latter, not the former. His choices were cold-blooded and ideological. Although he was not a wealthy man, he was not a financially and emotionally squeezed bankrupt farmer. It wasn't the local bank or any government agricultural lending agency that foreclosed on his North Dakota farm. It was the Internal Revenue Service, in payment of back taxes. Gordon Wendell Kahl had enjoyed the prerogatives of being a white man in America, and still he chose a struggle to the death.

Eventually, movement mythmaking transformed Kahl from a victim of government wrongdoing into a martyr for a new nationalism, struggling to be free. Like Joan of Arc for the French, he symbolized this white nation's highest virtues. "He was the kind of people that have always built the quality of the nation," lauded son Yorie from a jail cell, "every nation, every culture throughout history; the people that saw further, that cared more."[24]

In the most immediate aftermath, the shoot-out in Arkansas electrified every sector of the movement. The rumor that Kahl had been unnecessarily killed spread from his immediate circle of supporters to the Klan in Georgia and the Aryan Nations in Idaho. When it lapped up on the shores of Cheney Lake in Kansas, a picture formed of Christian patriot constitutionalism at the time and its ability to find a mass type of constituency alongside a cadre of killers.

Christian Patriots After Gordon Kahl

August 20, 1983. The hot wind whipped low across Cheney Lake State Park in south-central Kansas, about thirty-five miles west of Wichita. In the distance, pickup trucks and campers parked half hidden in a tree line. Advertised as the Gordon Kahl Memorial Arts and Crafts Festival, there were no arts or crafts. Fifty middle-aged tax protesters and Identity Christians, some from as far away as Tennessee, Louisiana, and Minnesota, stood in a small clump, surrounded by two thousand unpopulated acres. Several young women on a picnic blanket near a flatbed truck kept their small children occupied. Perched like waterbirds at the edge of a swamp, half a dozen farmers wearing AAM ball caps stood in silent testimony to the continuing influence of Posse Comitatus ideas among a stratum of farmer activists.[1]

The actual memorializing was done by a retired schoolteacher, Len Martin. Martin and Kahl had grown up together in North Dakota, and he described how they had been working together on creating a "township" the previous winter. He had been staying for a while at the Aryan Nations camp in Idaho and had set out from there to talk about Gordon Kahl.[2]

Apparently the enterprise had the blessing of the Aryan chief Richard Butler. "Since the name Gordon Kahl has caught the attention of the nation, it is important that we take this opportunity to awaken our Racial Nation," Butler wrote in a letter to his supporters. "A speaking tour will be a catalyst for awakening the racially uninformed but tax-aware Aryan kinsmen as to the true nature of our Nation's plight."[3]

Len Martin took the Cheney Lake discussion in a different direction. In a nod to the men in ball caps, he argued that the township idea would stop farm foreclosures. As a second to Len Martin's gesture, a bubble-nosed elderly farmer from Halstead, Kansas, Keith Shive, took the stand. Shive billed himself as the chief of the Farmers Liberation Army, the group that had participated in the Weskan paramilitary trainings the previous year. He spit out his complaints: Jews ran the banks, financed the Bolshevik Revolution, and committed an actual genocide against the white Christians of Russia—unlike the Jews' phony Holocaust hoax. Now Christian farmers were losing their land to Jewish usury.[4]

After he was done speaking, Shive stepped into the knot around the platform, handing out leaflets and copies of *The Spotlight*. "Who are the real owners" of the Federal Reserve Banks? The flyers had the answer. "1. Rothschilds of London and Berlin 2. Lazared Brothers of Paris 3. Israel Mossesschif of Italy 4. Kuhn, Loeb & Company of Germany and New York 5. Warburg & Company of Hamburg, Germany 6. Lehman Brothers of New York 7. Goldman, Sachs of New York 8. Rockefeller Brothers of New York."[5]

It was a constant refrain. Many farmers, in the midst of losing their farms and a failed federal farm policy, could recite the same mythic list of "international Jewish bankers" before they could tell you who their congressman was.

Two other speakers testified to their belief in Christian Identity. The first, a mild-mannered twenty-eight-year-old data processor for the Wichita school district in a white cowboy hat, T-shirt, and jeans, stepped onto the truck bed platform and explained that he was an "Identity Catholic" and approached the Lord with prayer through Mary.[6]

The second, a tough-talking army sergeant based at nearby Fort Riley (Timothy McVeigh's base ten years later), added his story. He had been a John Birch Society member, he told the group, because he opposed communism. But the Birchers didn't recognize that communism had been created by the Jews, he complained. So he quit in disgust. Only Christian Identity, he averred, taught the facts about communism, the Jews, and white people—who were the true people of Israel. To top it off, the sergeant offered his own services for anyone interested in paramilitary training.[7]

The combination of appeals to Christian Identity beliefs and opposition to the Federal Reserve System, told with an undertone of sympathy for the plight of distressed farmers and a sheen of anti-Semitic reasoning, typified dozens of Christian patriot meetings in the Midwest during the early 1980s. Plus, every rally had a resident expert on the Constitution. At Cheney Lake Milton Libby filled that role.

A balding middle-aged engineer of medium stature and modest manner, Libby carried the requisite newspaper clippings and dog-eared court documents. A pint-size edition of the Constitution, issued by Liberty Lobby, poked out of the front pocket of his western-style shirt. A wedding band appeared on the pinkie of his right hand. In short order he explained many of the central tenets of Posse Comitatus–style theory regarding the legal system.

While waving a pamphlet entitled *Where You Stand Depends on Where You Sit*, Libby claimed that success in the courts rested on "jurisdiction" and "status." He advised everyone to repudiate his marriage license, driver's license, Social Security card, and all other "contracts" with the state. Instead, Libby prescribed a life under "God's law," where all governed themselves as "natural individual persons." Each individual "sovereign" made a citizenship contract to form a government, as the founders had done with the supposedly "organic" Constitution, the original document and Bill of Rights, but without any of the other amendments. (We the people, in order to form a more perfect union . . .) If such contracts could be made, he reasoned, they could also be broken. This was the principle known as asseveration.[8]

According to this doctrine, a "sovereign" was not just any individual born and residing in the United States. Instead, sovereigns were those originally mentioned in the Preamble to the Constitution in the phrase "We the people." And as any high school student should know, at the time the Constitution was written, "We the people" meant "we the white people." This (white) racial definition of citizenship had then been reaffirmed in the *Dred Scott* decision of 1857, which reads in part: "A free negro of the African race, whose ancestors were brought to this country and sold as slaves, is not a 'citizen' within the meaning of the Constitution."[9] By repeating these arguments, the Posse Comitatus and its Christian patriot look-alikes stood on solid historical, if morally shaky, ground. Before the Civil War the United States had indeed been a "white Republic."

After the Civil War, however, the Fourteenth Amendment had countermanded *Dred Scott* and guaranteed the rights of citizenship to the newly freed slaves and all others born in the United States. The racial definition of citizenship had changed. Like many unreconstructed Confederates and a host of other far-right propagandists, Christian patriots believed the Fourteenth Amendment had not been passed in a constitutional fashion. The southern states had been under military occupation at the time, they argued.[10]

Christian patriot ideologues took their argument a step beyond constitutional validity. The Fourteenth Amendment had created a special class of citizens, they argued. This special class received its rights from the government through an individual's contract with the state. Sovereigns, on the other hand, those descended from the original (white) sovereigns, still received their rights (and responsibilities) from God. By this logic, inconsistent as it might be, sovereigns could either join the compact or asseverate themselves from it.

In order to become a "free man," Libby argued that day, it was necessary to assert your status as a "sovereign" as opposed to a "Fourteenth Amendment federal citizen."[11]

A racial theory is deeply embedded in this concept of citizenship, which postulates rights and responsibilities for sovereign white Christian men different from that of Fourteenth Amendment citizens—that is, everyone else. Although it was expressed in constitutional language as fealty to the Founding Fathers, this was at bottom the same whites-only racial nation as William Pierce's. (On this point, the principal difference between Christian patriots and Pierce: the former found their nationalism in an idealized past; the latter envisioned his state in the future.)

While Libby's talk that day avoided any explicit mention of race when discussing citizenship status, there were others traveling on the Christian patriot circuit who did not pull anything back. One of those was Robert Wangrud, a peripatetic propagandist in the Northwest. He also distinguished between white "sovereigns," whose rights devolved from God, and so-called Fourteenth Amendment citizens, meaning people of color and non-Christians. And he published in detail the constitutional and historical origins of his beliefs.[12]

Wangrud and friends found citations from the infamous *Dred Scott* decision to support the argument that only white people could properly be "citizens"; from Oregon territorial law they plucked sentences stating that only white male inhabitants of that territory could hold political office; and they found old United States statutes stipulating "that no other than a free white person shall be employed in carrying the mail." This juridical hodgepodge was reprinted as evidence that the United States had been founded as a "white nation" and had lawfully remained such in the years following. The Thirteenth, Fourteenth, and Fifteenth Amendments, all imposed by Congress and martial law, were supposedly null and void regarding white people, who were the actual "posterity" of the nation's founding stock.[13]

This form of white nationalism placed itself within the everyday vernacular culture of American life. No gun waving punctuated Wangrud's declarations of sovereignty. He wore no white robes or armbands. And he didn't live on an Ozark campground for cultists. Among those who shared Wangrud's beliefs, however, were some with guns. And they included Richard Wayne Snell.

Snell believed that federal agents had tortured and mutilated Gordon

Kahl's body, and after the shoot-out in Arkansas, Snell became a killer himself. He and his wife, Mary Jo, had moved from their trailer home in Texarkana, Arkansas, to a hilly eighty-acre plot of land near the hamlet of Muse, Oklahoma, just across the state line. Wayne went to auctions, bought government surplus, reworked it, and sold it. He had piles of old machines, motors, and scrap scattered around the property and planned to use them for barter once society collapsed. At least once a week Mary opened a booth at a flea market. They lived in a makeshift house built from Red River Army Depot boxes lined with insulation, without electricity or running water, while Snell was supposedly building them a real home. It was a rough way to live for a couple in their mid-fifties, but after thirty-five years of marriage they were starting over again as survivalists.[14]

Motivated by an all-consuming passion for guns and Identity theology, which he discovered in 1981, Snell had served Gordon Kahl as a courier while the Posse Comitatus farmer was hiding out in Arkansas. He also joined the Christian-Patriots Defense League and became a frequent visitor at Jim Ellison's the Covenant, the Sword and the Arm of the Lord campground in Arkansas.

In October 1982, Snell was charged with knowingly concealing stolen property, in connection with a CSA robbery. Law enforcement officials dug up guns, dynamite, and silver on his Oklahoma homestead. But his troubles with the law did not end there. When a Texas bank attempted to repossess three vehicles that Snell had used as collateral on a four-thousand-dollar loan, Mary Jo Snell chased the repo man off with a carbine. When he returned a short while later, Wayne Snell met him with a "sub-machine gun." Although the Snells kept their cars, three felony warrants were issued in Texas.[15]

That same month, August 1983, CSA members firebombed a gay community church in nearby Springfield, Missouri, and then bombed the Jewish Community Center in Bloomington, Indiana. That November, Snell and another CSA man attempted, but failed, to bomb a natural gas pipeline they believed supplied Chicago.[16]

The crimes continued when CSA members drove over to Texarkana and robbed a pawnshop. During the robbery Snell shot the proprietor, Bill Stumpp, in the head, neck, and back in rapid succession. As the man fell dead, Snell came out of the shop happy. No blood had splattered on him, and his briefcase was full of gold and jewelry. His compatriot carried out a box of guns.[17]

The crime spree continued on a road trip to Texarkana when he was pulled over on a routine stop by a black Arkansas state trooper, Louis Bryant. As Bryant approached his van on the driver's side, Snell rolled out of the front door and shot the trooper twice, then got back into the van and drove off. The reason: Snell claimed he didn't want to go to jail on those "bullshit [repo] warrants" from Texas. But he also said that Bryant, who regularly patrolled that strip of highway and was known to local CB enthusiasts as Blue Flasher, should have known better than to stop him "out in the open." For Snell, it was a clear transgression of God's law: no black person should rule over a white person, especially where others might see. Snell was captured later that day and wounded in another firefight with law enforcement. While he was in the hospital, Elohim City's Robert Millar visited Snell and served as his attending pastor.[18]

Snell later became one of multiple defendants in a seditious conspiracy trial. He was also found guilty of Louis Bryant's murder and sentenced to life in prison without parole, and to death for killing the pawnshop owner, Bill Stumpp. On April 19, 1995, he was executed by the state of Arkansas, just hours after hundreds died in the bombing of the Oklahoma City Federal Building.[19]

Investigators trying to explain Snell's and the CSA's long trail of death and destruction should have looked closely at the contents of Snell's car when he was arrested. Among the tools and paraphernalia police recovered from his van were three hand grenades, a .45-caliber machine gun, and two .22-caliber pistols with silencers. They traced one of the pistols to the pawnshop murder. They also found literature and tapes from the CSA and another Identity church. But the most important title in that collection was a booklet entitled *Essays of a Klansman*, which proved to be a clue to a much-larger development then engulfing the vanguardist wing of the white supremacist movement.[20]

Birth of the First Underground

July 4, 1983

Comrades in Marx and Mongrelism . . .

> *. . . I don't believe in public marches or parades as my own publication and advice to klan leaders has been documented for years . . . You see, I truly believe that Nechayev was correct. The most effective propaganda is that of the deed. My good friend in Marion prison, the Puerto Rican patriot Raphael Miranda and I agreed upon many things and disagreed on many other things but on that point, we both agreed . . . Parades and public meetings are for the guerrilla theatre facets of resistance. I spent six years at Marion because I believe that action recruits far better than posturing.*
>
> *You couldn't have told a Cossack from an SR had you been alive during the real revolution in Russia. You still can't.*
>
> *L'Chaim . . . next life that is!*
> > *(signed)*
> > *Robert E. Miles*
> > *Cohoctah, Mi. 48816*

In this one-page letter to a small circulation antiracist periodical,[1] the venerable Klansman Robert Miles alternately mocked and threatened its recipients, revealed a keen grasp of history and his own operating strategy, and made short shrift of a factual error in reporting. It was classic Miles at his nasty and sarcastic best. Public events such as demonstrations and meetings acted out a "guerrilla theatre," not real drama.

His "propaganda of the deed," on the other hand, translated into a transparent reference to terror and violence. And Robert Miles knew the insides of both political theater and political violence more intimately than most. During the mid-1980s he served as high priest to bands of vanguardist armed robbers and Aryan killers, in the same way that William Pierce stood as their godfather.

In addition, the letter contained revealing references to the author's personal background. Robert Edward Miles was born in Connecticut in 1925, just one year before Willis Carto. He spent several youthful years, however, in New York City, among highly politicized anti-communist Russian émigrés. As a result, Miles knew Russian ideological permutations—from peasant revolutionaries and Bolsheviks to anarchists—better than most history professors. Hence his esoteric mention of Nechayev, an obscure nineteenth-century terrorist. Cossacks may have been well known for their freewheeling and repressive czarist paramilitaries, but who besides assiduous students of twentieth-century Russian history would know that "SRs" stood for Social Revolutionaries, a peasant party at odds with both the czar and the Bolsheviks? Miles's childhood experiences made him a special case.[2]

He had finagled a way into the New York National Guard at age thirteen and trained at Fort Dix. In 1941, at age sixteen, he became a radio operator for the Free French army while stationed in Britain. As soon as age permitted, he joined the U.S. Navy and fought in the Pacific theater, much like Carto. After the war, he later claimed, he worked for British intelligence, monitoring clandestine shipments of arms from New York to Palestine.[3]

With a penchant for poetry and mythmaking, as well as secrecy and information gathering, his character could have jumped off the page of a le Carré novel. Rumors flew among white supremacists that his long career as a public anti-communist covered for a secret life in the British MI6.[4] And he certainly spent years as a solid member of the establishment: as a Michigan executive for an insurance company, the editor of a newsletter for safety engineers, and the finance chairman of the Michigan Republican Party.[5]

Miles left the Republican fold when Alabama Governor George Wallace ran for president on a third party ticket in 1968, and Wallace's inner circle felt glad to have a man of such high caliber aboard.[6] Miles also joined Robert Shelton's old-line segregationist United Klans of America during the same period. Just as his intelligence and talents had lifted him to the top of Wallace's Michigan operation, the following year, 1969, he became state leader of the United Klans and a national officer shortly after that.[7] These were solid credentials in what Miles regarded later as political theater.

As the Wallace campaign apparatus disintegrated in 1970, and Klan numbers declined alongside it, Miles left the open stage for the clandestine world of "action" just below. He was soon arrested for the August 1971 bombing of five school buses used for racial integration in Lansing, Michigan, and for conspiracy to tar and feather a high school principal in a nearby town. Worse, many of his erstwhile Klan comrades quickly deserted him. Both Miles and his wife, Dorothy, turned bitter.[8]

"Robert gave up a $17,000 a year position in the insurance industry," she wrote in 1972, "to fight for people whom [sic]he felt were ignored by, and left out of, the social system as it was operating. He stood up [and] fought at every level." His sacrifices went unrecognized, even spat upon, by his old comrades, some of whom were now running away from their former advocacy of violence.

"To the people inside the old United Klans, who have been so busy trying to destroy everything that my husband built, may the Lord forgive you for none of us ever will," she complained. "The traitors, left within the UKA, have worked unceasingly to destroy what is left of that fraternal group in Michigan."[9]

Miles always remembered that experience, and it helped mold much of his strategic thought during the 1980s. After conviction, Miles served six years in Marion, Illinois, one of the federal system's toughest penitentiaries, and he undoubtedly learned much about clandestine organizational strategies during that time. He never again confused the world of public politics with the underground of racist violence. To those outside his movement, the personality of Robert Miles should be an instant reminder that a successful insurance executive can bomb and burn as easily as any unemployed blue-collar caricature of a racist.

When Miles went to prison, membership in the various Klan factions had sunk to its postwar low of twelve hundred. When he was released in 1979, total membership levels had increased tenfold—thanks in part to Duke's strategy of high-profile publicity, which actually benefited all the Klan groups. Miles became a nonsectarian Klansman for all seasons (although he now stayed away from Shelton's UKA). He naturally assumed a role at the top of the Klan pyramid, commanding by force of personality as well as strategic vision. His intellect made him sure-footed where others faltered. His personal integrity and honor dwarfed the perpetual backstabbing of those around him. He opened his arms to all. Looking past individual weaknesses of his comrades, he extolled what he thought to be their virtues.

He began by analyzing the Klan's various historical incarnations. Miles's rendition was not aimed at creating a political machine like Duke's. Rather, Miles wanted to break with Duke's legacy and turn the cross wheel once again. He planned on creating a different type of organization, more akin to the night-riding counterrevolutionaries of the First Era Klan who had attacked Freedmen and Reconstruction governments after the Civil War. Miles virtually ignored the Klan of the 1920s and scarcely mentioned the Third Era from the 1960s.[10]

"The Fourth Era correctly can be termed the 'Television Era,'" he wrote in a 1983 assessment of Duke's Klan. "It used television to grow and television used it to profit . . . Personal appearances on television, before the press and in the radio forums, became the raison d'etre of the Order and its total program . . . It worked.

"The Fourth Era was an excellent supersalesman," he continued. "Unfortunately, it was not able to deliver the product which it had so competently sold."[11]

In Miles's mind, Duke's Knights had revolutionary *potential* but had been stopped short by a dependence on television and the media. Miles believed a revolutionary consciousness had begun to develop among a stratum of white people, but the Klan that had developed during that period had not been, in fact, a competent *revolutionary* organization.

Ever faithful to the arcana of Ku Kluxery, even when he was reinventing it, Miles decided his new era order should be represented by "33/5" in numerology. The letter *K* was 11, being the eleventh letter of the alphabet; 33 then representing KKK, with the 5 being the Fifth Era. Miles must have recognized the bit of theater attached to his numeric signature. This numeric sign became one way of indicating adherence to a strategy aimed at the so-called Zionist Occupied Government and its supposed lackeys.[12]

As high priest of his own Mountain Church, Miles weaved together Klan factions from the South with small uniformed neo-Nazi groups from the Midwest and the growing Aryan Nations powerhouse in the West. Each spring and fall, nationally known movement personalities along with 100 to 150 rank and filers gathered for a weekend fest at Miles's Michigan farmstead. Second-tier leaders from California to North Carolina shared meals and got to know one another. They listened to an interminable roster of speakers. Some simply bragged of small achievements, such as opening a storefront in southwestern

Chicago. A few presented self-conscious accounts of the movement's weaknesses and proposed remedies for future action. One or two criticized their comrades who still supported President Reagan, particularly mentioning those who supported the anti-communist contra crusade in Central America. But all speakers were politely applauded by the assembly, and each was praised by Miles, who served as master of ceremonies.[13]

Miles's farmstead was not the only locus of factional fellowship. At a less organizationally diverse, more Klan-oriented event in Georgia each Labor Day weekend, a smaller number of speakers pounded a podium before the nighttime cross burning. And the Aryan Nations camp in Idaho became a third regular location for this cross-organizational pollination. There Richard Butler presided over three days of meetings each July. Unlike the Georgia and Michigan gatherings, participants often included wives and children alongside the overwhelmingly male congregants. Hour upon hour was spent sitting in assembly, listening to speeches that varied by place of origin, if not by topic. The real business was often conducted in small groups outside the meetings. Although Miles's Aryan Nations title was only "ambassador-at-large," it was his strategic vision that animated the proceedings. He began referring to a Fifth Era "Order," and his vision of a secret army began to take more complete shape.[14]

Here Louis Beam proved invaluable.

Enter Louis Beam

If William Pierce served as the vanguardists' godfather and Robert Miles as their high priest, then Louis Beam was their commander in chief.[15] Picture Napoleon with a soft Texas drawl: five feet seven inches, a small build, mottled skin, black hair, and brown eyes with "Born to Lose" tattooed across his upper left forearm.[16] Born in 1946 and raised in the east Texas town of Lufkin, Louis Beam joined the army at age nineteen and served as a helicopter gunner in Vietnam. He claimed "1,000 hours combat flying time: 12 confirmed, 39 probable kills."[17]

Like tens of thousands of young American volunteers, he hated losing the war and remained a proud anti-communist. "A bloody joke it was although we American G.I.'s didn't realize that fact until May 1, 1975, when communist troops rolled into Saigon . . . After all the blood, the sweat, the heat, the death and dying—nothing."[18] Like millions of others, he quickly concluded that the heroism of frontline soldiers in Southeast Asia had been undermined at home. Beam took his analysis one step further. He decided that it was not just failed policies (or the determination of the Vietnamese opposition) that had lost the war. A secret conspiracy had been at work.[19]

Returning home to Texas in 1969, before the war's end, he enlisted in the old-style United Klans of America, the same Klan organization that Miles was then leading in Michigan. The two first met in 1971.[20] Beam later claimed he had joined the Klan because of the "current political and social conditions and a desire to taste the blood of my enemy."[21] This mix of faux rationalism and savage emotion became Beam's characteristic calling card.

Beam boasted that he was suspected of, but never convicted in connection with, several high-profile offenses, including blowing up a left-wing radio station's transmitting tower, shooting up a communist organization's offices in Texas, and attacking Chinese leader Deng Xiaoping during a state visit to Houston.[22] The incidents all were related in some fashion to the Vietnam War or the fight against communism.

Attracted by David Duke's revolutionary ideas, Beam left the old-style Klan and joined the Knights of the Ku Klux Klan at its height in the 1970s. He eventually became its Texas state leader. While Duke primped for the television cameras and primed himself for electioneering, Beam trained a local paramilitary calling itself the Texas Emergency Reserve. It started harassing immigrant Vietnamese fishermen in Galveston Bay and was stopped only after a lawsuit was brought by the Southern Poverty Law Center. Beam resigned from the Knights but continued to refer to himself as a Klansman.[23]

In 1982, after his second wife filed for divorce and won custody of their two-year-old daughter, Beam grabbed the child and fled north to Richard Butler's Aryan Nations camp in Idaho. (He subsequently worked out a more favorable custody arrangement.)[24] From Idaho he published a collection of short essays analyzing the Klan's history, strengths, and weaknesses. Beam's line of argument was cogent and bloodcurdling at the same time. Unlike much movement writing, which employs liberal doses of euphemism and code language, Beam was brutal and direct. *Essays of a Klansman*, the booklet found in Richard Snell's car, became a classic statement of the emerging underground. In contrast with Miles, whose call for a new-era Order in the 1980s was based on a critique of the "television" Klan prominent in the 1970s, Beam took his analysis back a step farther, to the 1960s.

"Had the so-called 'civil rights' movement of the 1960's been a movement propagated, controlled and led by blacks," Beam was certain, "there can be no doubt that this . . . would have been stopped by the Ku

Klux Klan."[25] His white supremacist assumptions, after all, axiomatically precluded black people from winning the battle by way of their own courage, intelligence, and political savvy.

It had been whites, he argued, not blacks, who had defeated his Klan brethren on the fields of southern segregation. These traitorous whites, Beam believed, had been either cynical careerists or misguided followers of the obviously false doctrine of equality and brotherhood. In both instances they had been directed by the real manipulators of events, the Jews. His rationale for the defeat on civil rights was identical to the reasons he believed Americans had lost in Vietnam. And it shared the same outlines of the argument that David Duke and others had made about the lost battle to defend Jim Crow in the 1960s. But instead of a political machine, Beam wanted war.[26]

Like Miles, he believed the terms of engagement needed to be changed. Violence needed to be redirected away from everyday black people on the street. At one point, after praising the bloody bombing of black churches in Mississippi, he implicitly conceded it had been a strategic mistake: "Victory is not won by removing the enemy's pawns." If instead "the culture distorters and destroyers [had] suffered [they] might have considered it too expensive . . . to have continued."[27]

(An interesting side note here: The term "culture distorters" was not a euphemism common in Klan or Aryan Nations circles at the time. It was, by contrast, common coinage among Yockey admirers, including Willis Carto. Carto would never openly advocate the bloodbath Beam was seeking to encourage, but both obviously went to the same reservoir for ideas.)

To further his argument about switching targets, Beam published a "point system" in his *Essays* that awarded "Aryan warriors" only one one-thousandth of a point for killing an ordinary black person, but a full point for the murder of policy makers. Government officials and Jews were his preferred targets, not because he "hated" them more than black people but because he considered them ultimately more powerful.[28]

Compared with David Duke, who expressed the same ideas in a less bloodthirsty form and wrapped his program in a facetious concern for "majority" rights, Beam had a simple, straightforward goal: "a Racial Nation of and by ourselves."[29]

In this way, Beam broke with the strategy of white supremacists in the 1950s and 1960s. "We do not advocate . . . segregation," he wrote. "That was a temporary political measure that's time is long past." Nor did he want to carve out a small whites-only island on a multiracial continent. "Our Order intends to take part in the Physical and Racial Purification of ALL [emphasis in original] those countries which have traditionally been considered White Lands in Modern Times," Beam's compatriot John C. Calhoun wrote, meaning North America, Europe, South Africa, and Australia. "We intend to purge this entire land area of EVERY [emphasis in original] non-White person, gene, idea and influence."[30] A more forthright call for ethnic cleansing and genocide would be hard to find in any of the white supremacist tracts published after World War Two.

The partnership then emerging between Robert Miles and Louis Beam did not require them to agree on the exact location of any future whites-only landmass. It was based first on a common vanguardism. While Miles counseled his kinsmen to "pull away" from mainstream institutions and create their own alternative counterculture, Beam directly addressed the weakness behind the vanguardist strength. "The vast majority of the White Race will," he wrote, "oppose the Klan and any other racial movement."[31] This one statement undergirded the entire vanguardist project and most differentiated Miles, Beam, and godfather Pierce on one side from Carto's competing mainstreaming mission on the other.

In addition, Miles and Beam shared a common assessment of parade politics and a candid agreement on the necessity of creating a clandestine apparatus. "There should be no doubt that all means short of armed conflict have been exhausted," Beam wrote in his *Essays*. Even his critique of the Duke era echoed with the same insights motivating Miles: "Political involvement—either openly or sub rosa—is an excellent means for exposing our view to the public and recruitment of new members." But he reminded those about to run for office that electioneering was only a supplement to the main objective: utterly destroying their enemies.[32]

In 1983 Louis Beam and Robert Miles started jointly publishing the *Inter-Klan Newsletter & Survival Alert*, a small circulation bulletin initially produced at Butler's Idaho campground. At that point, both men also bore the title of Aryan Nations ambassador-at-large in addition to whatever other memberships they claimed. Distinct affiliations with particular organizations meant less than their common association with other vanguardists. In these pages, the term "Klan" was often substituted for the word "Order," and both words came to mean any clandestine organization of white supremacists. Here they promoted strategies they believed would protect a developing underground from penetration from without and perfidy from within.

Miles remembered being betrayed from within and had watched his Michigan Klan go down the drain after his conviction. That Michigan

Klan had been organized much like a traditional business, with lines of authority running from the top down. A small number of officers knew and controlled the entire operation below them. When a few leaders decided to cooperate with the authorities, they effectively could and did turn over the entire enterprise to the police. Miles wanted a structure that would continue to stand, even if one or another of its supports did collapse. He proposed a web.

While this web would not prevent individuals or even small groups from betraying those around them, Miles and Beam argued that it could minimize damage to the movement as a whole. No one person or organization would be indispensable. "We conceive of the Order to be a WEB, instead of a chain," Miles wrote. "In any web, each intersecting point is tied to many other points. In a chain type organization, one link is suspended by only the one above it. Let one link fail, and the function of the entire chain fails. Let one strand, on the contrary with a Web, break and the function of the web is unimpaired."[33]

Here was a new theory of organization. In this web the sins of fractiousness and egoism turned into virtues. Instead of trying to get all the members of the Klan; Aryan Nations; National Alliance; and the Covenant, the Sword and the Arm of the Lord to amalgamate and follow one führer only, each organization itself formed a strand in the web. Further, as individuals drifted from one faction to another, the web as a whole stayed strong. A decline in Klan membership in the early 1980s, for example, was complemented by the growth of the new hybrid paramilitaries.

In the first issue of the *Inter-Klan Newsletter*, Beam published a short essay to expand the point. Traditional forms of organization inevitably lead to failure, he wrote. Instead of choosing a chain as his metaphor, as Miles did, Beam invoked the pyramid. It was as simple as a chart in a corporate boardroom. "The orthodox scheme of organization is diagrammatically represented by the pyramid, with the mass at the bottom and the leader at the top." It was a schema for disaster: "an infiltrator can destroy anything which is beneath him in the pyramid of organization."

Such concerns are not urgent if all you are doing is burning crosses in cow pastures on Saturday night, but if you plan to assassinate your enemies, rob armored cars, and bomb synagogues, then the stakes are much higher. "This [traditional] structure [is] . . . extremely dangerous for the participants when it is utilized as a resistance movement," Beam instructed.[34]

Beam then analyzed cell-type organizations used by communist undergrounds. In these, small groups of people worked together but were known only to one another. Other small groups worked independently, and the participants of one cell remained unknown to the personnel of another. Thus an enemy infiltrator could possibly betray one cell but couldn't break up the entire underground. While this cell structure was an improvement over the traditional pyramid, Beam decided it also had weaknesses. The problem was it required a central command to give direction to all the cells, and their new vision of vanguardism did not support one single leadership.

Beam proposed, instead, a structure composed of cells (like the communists), each operating independently of the others, but without a headquarters. The thorny problem of command remained. Beam promised to elaborate in future issues of the *Inter-Klan Newsletter & Survival Alert* as he continued to wrestle with the problem of creating a leadership for a movement that defied leadership.[35]

At one point he briefly flirted with the idea that a single computer bulletin board could dispense the leadership's "accumulated knowledge" to any patriot. (He was occupied with setting up Aryan bulletin boards at the time.) In another article, the newsletter reprinted a complex text on the "science of rebellion." It proposed a quasi-centralized series of "bands" with "sleepers," "couriers," and auxiliaries. Although he described the functions necessary to create an underground, that essay did not solve the problem of command and control.

Finally, Louis Beam stood by an essay he had first published in the *Inter-Klan Newsletter* in 1983 entitled "Leaderless Resistance." The strategic task at hand had already been established: utterly destroy the movement's enemies. The underground would be composed of cells that already understood their mission, safely separated from one another and without a central tactical leadership.[36] Beam's ideas were not without critics from within vanguardist circles. One Aryan Nations state leader disputed the concept as a matter of national socialist principle. "There can be only one army," he wrote. "There can be only one leader of the army."[37]

William Pierce also disagreed and cogently argued for a centralized leadership. In his fictional *Turner Diaries* saga, the Organization is a complex multilayered apparatus, a "legal" political front operated on one hand and an illegal armed front operated on the other, both under a single military-style structure. Further, inside the larger Organization, a small mystical secret society known as the Order made all the commanding decisions. Pierce's idealized Order was composed of only the most self-sacrificing and race-conscious cadres under a single authoritarian leadership.

.   .   .

Regardless of the actual strategy and organizational model promoted by Miles, Beam, or Pierce, the vanguardist wing of the movement had been gathering steam since before Duke quit the Knights. In 1981 the first attempt at actually overthrowing an existing government had failed miserably. In this case it was the government of Dominica, a tiny nation-state in the West Indies closer to Venezuela than to the United States. A small band of North American Klansmen and neo-Nazis, financed by Canadian mob sources, had planned to join a putsch and install a malleable former prime minister as a puppet dictator. They hoped to use the island as a criminal, financial, and paramilitary base camp for operations in the United States. But the Afro-Caribbean coconspirators on the island were arrested, and the entire plot collapsed even before it began. FBI agents arrested ten men in New Orleans as they prepared to set to the sea. Their rented boat contained several dozen weapons, dynamite, and thousands of rounds of ammunition, as well as Confederate and Nazi flags. The most notable of those arrested was Don Black.[38]

Black had started his movement career as an Alabama teenager enlisting in several organizations, notably a youth group of the National Socialist White People's Party, then under the influence of William Pierce. An obviously intelligent and well-spoken youth, he briefly attended the University of Alabama and then joined David Duke's Knights of the Ku Klux Klan in 1975. Black became the Alabama state leader, known in Klan parlance as the Grand Dragon. When Duke resigned after the mailing list fiasco in 1980, Black was installed as Grand Wizard, or national director.[39] After Black went to jail in the Dominica affair, a factional fight in the Knights broke out, and when he returned from the federal penitentiary, he lost his leadership post.[40]

Despite this setback, developments leading to the creation of a violent underground continued apace. Gordon Kahl had already started a one-man battle against ZOG, killing two federal marshals before being reduced to a burned corpse by the FBI. Richard Wayne Snell and the CSA had started their murderous crime spree. And at an Aryan Nations meeting in Idaho during July 1983, Robert Miles and Louis Beam turned up the rhetorical heat. Miles called for robbing armored bank cars, and Beam wanted blood spilled for a new nation.[41]

Among the three hundred Aryans listening that day sat a well-muscled, strong-willed thirty-year-old named Robert Mathews, who joined Beam that summer in a propaganda effort called the National Organization of Farmers and Independent Truckers, or N.O.F.I.T.

Actually, that entire enterprise consisted of a couple of issues of a newsletter with an eye-catching slogan: "Don't throw a fit, throw a bureaucrat." The articles explicitly rejected any attempt at mainstream politics and exhibited a shrillness that seemed more like screaming than just bad agitprop.[42] This "organization's" big moments were two pages of favorable coverage in *The Spotlight*.[43]

Although N.O.F.I.T. did little else of substance, Robert Mathews was impressed by the experience. At that point, Mathews lived near the remote settlement of Metaline Falls, Washington, just south of the Canadian border but within driving distance of the Aryan Nations camp. He worked forty hours at a local cement plant, was clearing his small plot of land, and lived with his wife, Debbie, and their adopted boy, Clint. His résumé included youthful stints with the Birch Society and tax protesters. In 1980 he had joined the National Alliance. And in the recent past he had started frequenting Aryan Nations events. At a rally in a Spokane public park shortly after the congress, he easily warded off a handful of antiracist protesters and was accepted as one of Butler's own. Despite the excitement of working with Louis Beam and attending Aryan Nations, Mathews's primary political identification remained with William Pierce and the National Alliance—at least for the time being.[44]

Enclave Nationalism and The Order

September 4, 1983. For the sixth time since founding the National Alliance, William Pierce gathered its members to a convention in Arlington, Virginia. They came from across the country for a chance to rub shoulders with Dr. Pierce, as he was always deferentially called, and to make new friends. Pierce used the occasions to cull the ranks for individuals he thought had leadership potential and to continue a process of instilling a new method of recruitment, personal solicitation. In years previously, most new members had joined through contact with the national office in Arlington. Now Pierce wanted his geographically dispersed cadres to advertise the organization, find qualified membership prospects, and sign them up.[1] To help inspire others along this path, Pierce selected Bob Mathews to speak about his work with Louis Beam in the Northwest distributing N.O.F.I.T. newsletters.

Mathews's speech blended the general approach taken by white supremacists toward (white) family farmers with the specific analysis the National Alliance made of its own vanguard role. Farmers were faced with losing their livelihood and their "whole life," he reasoned, "mostly from the Jew usury system." Since farmers were prime racial stock, "living monument[s] to masculinity," he said, National Alliance members had special responsibilities. As "members of the vanguard of an Aryan resurgence," he argued, they must "radicalize American yeomanry and bring them into our vanguard for victory." And Mathews described a specific example of such a farmer he had met while distributing newsletters.

Notice the specific wording here. He did not argue for a plan of building the farmers' own autonomous organizations. Neither did he call for a broad propaganda campaign against "Jews" and "usury." Instead, he urged the "radicalization" of farmers, which meant spotting those who already exhibited anti-Semitism and imparting to them a sharply defined ideology, then recruiting them into the National Alliance "vanguard." Mathews's formulation was akin to Lenin's when he organized the Bolsheviks: those workers who were the most militant and angry at the czar and the bosses should be given an education about the capitalist system and recruited into the Communist Party.

Mathews's convention speech revealed dual loyalties. On one hand, he leaned heavily on Pierce's ideological underpinnings when discussing propaganda and recruitment to the "vanguard." And he believed that only the National Alliance could lead their white revolution.[2] His belief was almost religious in nature. "Through the Alliance lies the salvation of our entire race," he said.

On the other hand, Mathews's talk also reflected the months he had spent with Beam. The erstwhile Klansman had "shown us the way,"[3] he claimed. He emulated Beam's hot rhetorical style as well, including an invocation to "stand up like men and drive the enemy into the sea." For Pierce, violent destruction of the enemy was a necessary, but future, task. Beam's call to arms, by contrast, was immediate.

Mathews also exhibited two minds when thinking about white people. In his right brain, he had bitter contempt. "I was thoroughly disgusted with the American people," he wrote; "our people have devolved into some of the most cowardly, sheepish, degenerates that have ever littered the face of the planet."[4] In his left brain, he was willing, even eager to give his life for a semimystical future for white children.[5] Just a few weeks after the convention, Mathews made up his mind. He decisively chose one direction only, from which there was no escape.

William Pierce called it the Aryan Resistance Movement. Robert Miles called it the *Bruder Schweigen*, German for Silent Brotherhood.[6] The press called it The Order. Most outsiders identified this band as an Aryan Nations splinter group, while others emphasized its connection to Pierce's *Turner Diaries*. If Mathews's Order resembled Pierce's fictional Order, it also followed from the dicta in Miles and Beam's *Inter-Klan Newsletter & Survival Alert*, which had prescribed the immediate creation of a Fifth Era–style underground. Mathews did not initially follow the precepts of "leaderless resistance," but Beam's influence during the months prior to The Order's formation was unmistakable.

Although Mathews did draw recruits from Butler's Idaho campground, The Order was much more than an Aryan Nations splinter group. Of the original nine, Mathews and two others came directly from the National Alliance. A fourth was simply Mathews's closest neighbor and friend, and a fifth had joined a Colorado Klan faction before trekking to Butler's Idaho camp. Only four came directly and exclusively from the ranks of Aryan Nations. As the band of bandits and their immediate accomplices grew to include dozens more, they came from virtually every vanguardist corner: the Covenant, the Sword and the Arm of the Lord; Posse Comitatus; Knights of the Ku Klux Klan; and Invisible Empire Knights of the Ku Klux Klan. The factional heterogeneity of Bob Mathews's Order made it the product of the *entire* vanguardist wing of the movement. And its remarkable success endowed it with a prominence far exceeding its size.

The action began when Mathews and eight other men pledged their sacred honor and declared war against the Zionist Occupied Government in a makeshift ceremony at Mathews's Metaline Falls homestead. The first nervous stickup occurred on October 28, 1983, at an adult bookstore in Spokane, Washington, with a total take of $300. Two months later a shifting cast of characters robbed $25,000 from a Seattle bank and $3,600 from a Spokane bank. In between they took $8,000 from a Shoney's restaurant courier and started counterfeiting $50 bills. In March 1984 they hit their first armored car and came away with $43,000. A month later they targeted the same Seattle car, this time clearing $230,000 in cash. On April 29, a synagogue in Boise was bombed.[7]

On June 1 they murdered one of their own. Two gang members took Walter West out in the woods, hit him on the head with a hammer, shot him, and buried him. They were afraid he would talk. His body was never recovered.

On June 17 Mathews and three others gunned down a Denver Jewish radio talk show host, Alan Berg, who was known for his on-air quarrels with anti-Semites.[8] The murder was the basis for Eric Bogosian's play *Talk Radio*. Just one month later, on July 19, 1984, they staged their most successful heist, $3.6 million from a Brinks truck on the highway outside Ukiah, California.

In just nine months Mathews and company went from an anxious crew of wannabes to a self-confident and vicious band of Aryan guerrillas. A few intrepid women joined the overwhelmingly male battle group. They gave themselves salaries; bought weapons, camping gear, vehicles, and electronic equipment; and treated themselves to steaks and beer while hiding out in safe-houses from Idaho to Georgia. They paid cash for a 300-acre tract of land in southern Missouri and a 110-acre plot in Idaho. An electronic stress test specialist ran a buzz box, looking for informants. Code names, false identification, and elaborate communication systems became de rigueur. Each soldier was given a special silver medallion. Robbery proceeds were distributed across the movement, from a couple of thousand for individual comrades in need to alleged hundred-thousand-dollar allotments given to a few key leaders. They hoped the money would help their cause.

At first, law enforcement officials knew little about this gang. That ended when Mathews inadvertently left a handgun behind in the armored car at Ukiah, however, and it became the FBI's first real clue linking the robberies to white supremacists. Once the feds stumbled over the robberies and counterfeiting, an ever-widening dragnet enveloped the group.

A second mistake proved even more fatal. Mathews had recruited a former National Alliance comrade in Philadelphia, Tom Martinez, to help pass counterfeit money. Martinez used the phony bills near his home, was quickly arrested, and just as quickly turned informant. He then led the FBI to Portland, Oregon, where they picked up Mathews's trail. After a brief firefight that left him wounded, Mathews escaped to Whidbey Island in Washington State. There he hid with several others until their safe house was surrounded. Everyone but Mathews surrendered. He preferred to shoot it out. On December 8, 1984, after a forty-hour gun battle with a helicopter and FBI ground troops, Robert Mathews died as the house burned to the ground around him.[9] Like Gordon Kahl, he was incinerated.[10]

Over the next five months, most of the rest of The Order were captured in groups of twos and threes in a massive roundup from Georgia and North Carolina through Missouri to Montana. With each new arrest, the FBI turned Aryan warriors into abject informants. The underground apparatus unraveled as half the soldiers squealed on the other half.

Unusual in this instance was nineteen-year-old Order soldier David Tate. His father had been Butler's number two man at the Idaho camp, and his mother acted as church secretary to the group. His two sisters subsequently married noteworthy movement personages. Tate hoped to escape down the back roads of Missouri and hide at the Covenant, the Sword and the Arm of the Lord camp. On April 15, 1985, during a traffic stop, Tate rolled out of his van—much as Richard Snell had the year before—and killed a Missouri highway patrolman, Jimmie Linegar. Authorities arrested a tired and hungry Tate several days later without further bloodshed.

The incident highlighted the connection between the Aryan bandits and the CSA compound in the Ozarks. On the fateful day of April 19, more than four hundred law enforcement officials surrounded the remote camp. They knew its inhabitants were heavily armed, and they sought help negotiating the CSA's surrender. The FBI called upon

Robert Millar from Elohim City in Oklahoma, and he talked his old friend James Ellison into vacating the encampment without a firefight. Ellison, his lieutenants, and several Order members were quietly arrested on weapons and conspiracy charges. The last days of Mathews's Order also effectively became the last days of Ellison's paramilitary CSA.

April 1985 also marked the eighth and last issue of the *Inter-Klan Newsletter & Survival Alert*. This edition was markedly different from the previous seven. The names of Louis Beam and Robert Miles, which had graced the masthead of all previous issues, were gone. Instead of a return address and mailing permit from Idaho, this issue was posted from Camden, Arkansas. Rather than neatly typed essay-style articles discussing strategy and organization, a few newspaper reprints detailed Robert Mathews's fiery death. It was unknown who published this last newsletter, but it gave pointed instructions: "The Second American Revolution will be a revolution of individuals, a revolution without exact precedent in recorded history. Because individuals can accomplish complex acts of resistance without peril of betrayal or even detection by the most advanced snooping devices, missions FORMERLY ASSIGNED TO GROUPS MAY BE UNDERTAKEN BY INDIVIDUALS EQUIPPED TO FIGHT ALONE [emphasis in original]."

The Seattle Order Trial

James Ellison and a few others at the top of the Covenant ammo dump quickly pleaded guilty to weapons charges and were convicted of racketeering in a federal court at Fort Smith, Arkansas. With Ellison in jail, the remaining campers returned to their cabins. But the entire 224-acre Ozark business went bankrupt, and the action shifted to Seattle.

The U.S. attorney for western Washington needed six assistant attorneys to bring a ninety-three-page indictment against twenty-three of the approximately four dozen people involved in The Order.[11] The martyred Robert Mathews, of course, was not indicted. Individuals who had simply aided or abetted the bandits while they hid from the law were left off the Seattle list and tried elsewhere. A couple of unknown Canadians rumored to have been members escaped into the ether. Robert Miles, Louis Beam, and William Pierce—the three men who had most motivated Robert Mathews—were not indicted.

In federal court, the case turned on charges of conspiracy and racketeering. Originally designed as an anti-Mafia statute, the Racketeering Influenced and Corrupt Organizations (RICO) Act prohibited running a criminal enterprise, such as a prostitution ring or drug dealership. Bank robbery, for example, is not simply grand larceny under RICO if, and only if, it is an element of a larger business operation. Evidence that the indicted had paid themselves salaries and bought properties became more legally salient than their "Declaration of War." No state murder charges were ever filed for the deaths of Alan Berg and Walter West, but those murders were among the overt acts listed in Seattle as furthering the racketeering and conspiracy. Another twenty charges were based on specific federal violations, such as disrupting interstate commerce.

Of those indicted, only ten went to trial in September 1985. At that time Order member Richard Scutari had not yet been captured. Young David Tate remained in the custody of the state of Missouri, awaiting trial for the murder of Patrolman Linegar. Eleven others pleaded guilty prior to trial. Several testified against their (former) comrades. Those numbers meant that 50 percent of these indicted revolutionaries "turned over" for the prosecution, an unusually high rate for people supposedly motivated by ideology rather than greed.

Prosecutors were careful not to let First Amendment concerns become a factor. The defendants' ideas, a special assistant U.S. attorney argued, were "significant only because those feelings, those hatreds, those animosities are what motivated them to commit the crimes." And there were dozens of crimes for him to present as evidence. The prosecutor also argued that "there will be evidence, not completely, but there will be evidence that to a certain extent Bob Mathews and this group followed the principles, if you will, of the *Turner Diaries*." Referring to the novel apparently riled the defendants, who objected. The judge overruled their objection, however, a sign that the defendants' politics would, in fact, be germane to the proceedings.

One particular moment vibrated with the rhythms of battles to come. In an opening statement, a defense attorney acknowledged that his client was a Klan member and an avowed white separatist. "Now I say white separatist," he continued, "because there is a significant difference in an individual who professes to be a white supremacist as opposed to a white separatist." What was that difference? "The white separatist is nothing different than a black nationalist who advocates a separation of races, wants to live only with those members of his race. He advocates the fact that races when mixed together cannot survive because of their division in their cultural backgrounds, their upbringing and their history."[12]

The Seattle jury did not buy this spurious distinction between white supremacy and "white separatism" in 1985, any more than the U.S. Supreme Court was willing to endorse the "separate but equal" doctrine in 1954. Neither did the jury believe defense efforts to impugn the credibility of Aryans who became prosecution witnesses. Nor did jurors accept contentions that the defendants' beliefs were unrelated to the enumerated crimes. After four months at trial, all were found guilty.

Judges and juries, however, can change with the tides of public opinion. And the Seattle racketeering trial was not the last of its kind.

The Legacy of The Order: The Search for a White Christian Enclave-Nation Continues

The Order changed everything. Years after its last soldier was sent to jail, it remained a nodal point in the development of the movement. In the aftermath of the police crackdown, a debate pitted the violence-prone wing of the movement against proponents of mainstream politicking. And the mainstreamers' fortunes plumped up like the fat end of a toothpaste tube while the vanguardists' enterprise was squeezed by the authorities. Long prison terms highlighted tactical differences between those who supported the "one army, one leader" thesis and Louis Beam's leaderless resistance strategy. A more concentrated discussion began about carving a white nation-state out of the multiracial North American landmass. But first and foremost, Robert Mathews and his band of bandits inspired admiration.

In the Southeast, hundreds of camouflage-clad white supremacists marched in rank under Confederate battle flags in downtown Raleigh, North Carolina, WE LOVE THE ORDER on the banner at the front. In Idaho, a small group called Order II detonated a string of bombs in Coeur d'Alene. Among several West Coast groups, the day Robert Mathews died, December 8, became "Martyr's Day." Several memorial events included camping overnight on Whidbey Island, as close as possible to the shrine of death.

On multiple occasions, William Pierce embraced Mathews's courage wholeheartedly, even while asserting a difference in tactics between The Order and the National Alliance. "He took up arms against the enemies of his race, knowing that he had virtually no chance of defeating them, or even of surviving more than a few skirmishes," he wrote in 1985.[13]

But their ultimate goals were the same. The Order, Pierce noted, "set its sights on a full-scale, armed revolution, ending with the purification of the U.S. population and the institution of a race-based authoritarian government." It was aimed at the future.

Here it was again: no status quo ante, no black cities and white suburbs, no genteel bourbon and branch water racism. That segregated past was part of the problem. The solution was an all-white nation.

"Men have died for the concept of nationalism. Men and women both. Both have died to be free of strangers. Robert Mathews died for that belief. Gordon Kahl died for that belief," Bob Miles wrote shortly after Mathews's death.

Even while the FBI was still rounding up the vestiges of The Order, Miles projected a new nation in the Northwest. He later fleshed out the idea of five states—Montana, Wyoming, Idaho, Oregon, and Washington—seceding from the United States. He called it the "10 percent solution." "The history books are full of people of all races and all nationalities, who died to be free. God willing we shall live to be free! Ourselves alone willing, we shall begin to form the new nation even while in the suffocating embrace of ZOG."

Four months after the racketeering convictions in Seattle, in April 1986, Miles convened two hundred souls in a large shed he called the Hall of the Giants on his northern Michigan farmstead. They licked their wounds. Robert Mathews's young widow, Debbie, stood to receive a round of applause. So did other wives and even parents of imprisoned Order soldiers. There was the usual round of speeches, but it was Miles's proposal to create a white nation-state in the Northwest that dominated the conversation. Miles had an Ohio comrade explain again the benefits of moving to the Northwest, this time with statistics about population density and the number of nonwhites currently living in the territory. Miles made his case for the "10 percent solution." It was still possible to wring victory from defeat, he argued. "Can we gain such a nation? Yes. [But] it will take time and patience."

One by one he criticized the alternatives. Plans for a mid-America survival zone were "illusionary," Miles argued in a direct hit on the idea once promoted by the Christian-Patriots Defense League. A survival zone was not a new nation created through population transfers or guerrilla warfare. Its racial character was the subtext, not the main theme, he explained.

The Northwest could be a refuge. "Consider," he said, "it has all we want. Space that is not jammed already with hostiles, indifferents or aliens. It has a sea coast. It has mountains. It has water. It has land areas yet to be developed. It has a border which is definable. It has the warmth of the temperate zones but the cold which our Folk require in order to thrive."[14]

Miles's lesson in geography had a larger point. He proposed an outtrek by white nationalists, from inside a multinational empire they once controlled, but no longer did, to a territory where they could reinvent themselves. "We are not the majority in the USA," he had written the year before. "We are a distinct minority. We are outsiders living in our own lands."[15]

This "minority" was not a historically constituted community with a distinct language on a specific territory. It had no internal market of goods and services it was trying to protect by establishing borders and tariffs. And it had no common religion; although many already believed the Christian Identity doctrine, some did not. Nor was Miles proposing a common theory of government; some believed in a strong authoritarian central state, but others were almost anarchists. Neither did they descend from a common ethnicity, as that term is conventionally understood. They were Scots-Irish from the Carolina piedmont, German and Scandinavian from the Midwest, and even of Italian and Slavic descent.

Political scientist Benedict Anderson refers to nations as "imagined communities." As Miles conceived it, white nationalism was mostly a product of imagination.[16] "Let us be considered a Racial Nation of Aryans, living within the man-made boundaries of a political state," he wrote in a declaration of independence. "Let us be recognized as a Folk who have different beliefs, values, and different life-styles than those which comprise your 'loyal' citizenry."[17] His nation was founded on a mythical common culture and racial self-identity. It should be remembered, however, that nation-states had been created in the past out of little more.

Ultimately, the idea of creating an Aryan republic on a *piece* of North American territory served as a bridge between the white supremacist discourse of the past and the new white nationalism that would emerge after the end of the Cold War. But this particular proposal, in the mid-1980s, was due in large measure to the explosion of ideas following The Order, and its exponents had to take account of other ideas competing for adherents.

Recall that during the 1960s, Willis Carto's white nationalism centered itself in Europe, with American civilization an extension of European civilization. By these lights, the Founding Fathers were unique only insofar as they continued a European lineage on North American soil. Carto attempted to re-create Eurocentrism and reestablish it as racial nationalism via the American political system, not to carve out a small enclave in the mountains or anywhere else. He claimed to speak in the name of white Americans as a whole (or the antielite popular

strata) against multiracialism, alien, and inferior cultures, internationalism, and the small elite clique that represented these trends.

By contrast, Pierce, Miles, Beam, and Mathews all saw themselves as
a small band at odds with the majority of whites.

Miles's schema also differed from southern nationalism and southern
independence movements, and not just because of geographic location.
These southern movements projected themselves back in U.S. history
to the Confederacy, maintained an unbroken lineage to the past, and
regarded the South as a conquered territory. The neo-Confederates
claimed the South's cultural heritage and national and regional distinc-
tiveness. Southern nationalism represents itself as the vehicle for the
popular masses in the region (sometimes including blacks, although as
second-class citizens), not just a small vanguard called to leave their
brethren behind. In this regard, southern nationalism is more like ethnic nationalisms of the former Soviet bloc, with their combinations of
historical grievances, martyrdoms, and unrealized (or only briefly realized) national ambitions.

The proposal for a Northwest Republic was not readily accepted by
everyone. Several National Socialists from Chicago, for example, opposed "abandoning the industrial heartland to the Jews." On the other
hand, a couple of California National Socialists quickly heeded Miles's
call and moved to The Dalles, Oregon.[18] An Illinois state Klan leader followed to Washington State. Others moved into the region as well.[19]
Miles won wider support after Aryan Nations met in Idaho that summer
under the banner of the "Northwest Territorial Imperative."[20]

Miles aside, the most trenchant ideas were those of William Pierce. He
shared many of Miles's vanguardist assumptions about ordinary white
people, but he took that critique two steps further. "The ills that we see
today are not the result of a Jewish conspiracy, they are the culmination
of processes that have been at work within our society, within our race
for centuries," he argued. "And I think we can no more cure western civilization by passing new laws or getting new leadership than a 100 year
old man can cure his old age by recommending a new diet." The momentary failure of Mathews's Order had long-term causes. "The degen-
erative processes have gone too far and they've affected every part of our
society."

If the purpose of Miles's pure republic was separation from the polyglot United States of America, Pierce was proposing a total separation
from everything contemporaneous. "We think in terms of making a new
beginning. We think in terms of building a seed that can germinate and

grow and become something new while western civilization" continues to deteriorate. Pierce wanted to plant his seedbed far from the teeming metropoles. He had moved the National Alliance headquarters from Alexandria, Virginia, to remote mountainside acreage in Pocahontas County, West Virginia. He was of course less separated from people of color than he claimed. Brown-skinned people had manufactured his clothes, picked whatever fruit he ate, and helped build his car. He relied on the post office, including its black employees, to transport packages for his National Alliance book business. In 1985 he distributed seventy thousand dollars' worth of books and pamphlets published by others, not including his own *Turner Diaries*, which itself was selling well. Distributing books was just one part of Pierce's plan for building an infrastructure in the period after The Order.[21]

The other was to turn the West Virginia land into a "new living and working environment more conducive to moral and spiritual health than the one we left."[22] Pierce and several families dug wells, constructed homes, laid underground electric utility cables, and built a six-thousand-square-foot two-story combination school and administrative building.

If Pierce's West Virginia headquarters camp sounds suspiciously like a step back to Jim Ellison's survivalist CSA commune in the Arkansas Ozarks, to Pierce they were as different as the quality of people who lived on the land. Pierce wanted only an elite breed for his seedbed. They were there to prepare "the way for Higher Man." Jim Ellison may have sat atop his brood of downtrodden misfits for the greater glory of an Aryan Jesus, but William Pierce was clearing the brush and digging pipeline ditches for the Übermensch.

Whatever philosophical face Pierce painted on his retreat up the misty West Virginia mountainsides, his post-Order plan was for himself only. He was not trying to create an Appalachian substitute for the Pacific Northwest.

The most complete alternative to the Northwest Republic and all its vanguardist permutations came from the mainstreamers. David Duke was directly critical. "Is this the way American civilization will topple, as more and more whites flip off their TV sets, quit their jobs, trash their word processors and desert the suburbs in favor of weapons and revolution?" his tabloid asked of Mathews's example.[23] Duke's answer was negative. "The best way we can fight," he wrote, "is through nonviolent political action."[24]

Willis Carto and Liberty Lobby virtually pretended The Order and its crimes had not happened. At the same moment Bob Mathews was plundering bank cars, Willis Carto was busy starting a "third" political party.

Origin of the Populist Party and the Break with Reaganism

April 21, 1984. At Mount Nebo State Park in northwestern Arkansas, the casual tourist can camp or rent a lodge, fish or go swimming, hike through the Ozark Mountains, or drive to Russellville and shop for antiques.[1] The beauty of the environment belied the violence that had taken place in the surroundings. Not far from here Gordon Kahl had died, Richard Wayne Snell had killed a black highway patrolman, and James Ellison plotted mayhem atop his gunpowder Dogpatch. Robert Mathews's war against ZOG was still raging half a continent away.

Here three hundred gray-haired Christian patriots gathered quietly in the main lodge and listened to a small roster of speakers on this Easter weekend. They tacked a twelve-foot-tall American flag to the wall and sang an off-key, but vigorous, version of "America the Beautiful."[2] The emcee, a former American Nazi Party captain turned Ku Klux Klansman turned Christian Identity minister in a dark business suit and red power tie, brought three preliminary speakers to the platform.[3] The first offered a prayer. The second, a woman dressed in a pioneer period costume, talked about old-fashioned values such as self-reliance and patriotism. The third, one of the shooters from the murders in Greensboro back in 1979, blasted communism and communists.[4] Finally, the emcee introduced the principal speaker for the day, Robert Weems, who turned the audience to the business at hand, testing the waters for a new organization calling itself the Populist Party.

A thickset six-footer speaking with a southern accent and gas station grammar, Weems bounced back and forth across the room and waved his arms windmill style. He sweated his way through a sixty-minute soliloquy on the slings and arrows white people had endured since being dethroned in post–World War Two America. Weems had given up his post as Mississippi state chaplain for the Invisible Empire (but not his penchant for wearing white robes)[5] and signed up with Willis Carto and Liberty Lobby. In contrast with Klan members who had joined The Order, he was a mainstreamer, an accomplished propagandist, and a dedicated organizer.

At Mount Nebo, Weems echoed the same theme around which David Duke had rallied his Klan in the 1970s: the supposed racial and cultural dispossession of white Christians. But Weems added economic-based complaints to his talk. In fact, he married the issues that had marked the Klan's growth to those matters on which Posse Comitatus types had focused: the Federal Reserve money system, taxes, and the Constitution. This grand theory he called populism, using the same vocabulary Willis Carto minted soon after President Reagan had taken office.[6] The actual underlying ideology bore little resemblance to the populism of William Jennings Bryan. Indeed, the ideas expressed that day were virtually identical to those once expounded by Carto under the banner of "conservatism."

Many of the elderly people in the audience undoubtedly regarded themselves as conservatives. Their past reference points were Senator Barry Goldwater's 1964 campaign and Governor George Wallace's 1968 and 1972 ventures. Weems needed all his considerable rhetorical skills to convince this crowd of graying patriots to identify themselves as "populists" rather than as "conservatives." To help facilitate the process, he cleverly identified himself as a disillusioned conservative (rather than as a former Klan chaplain). And he spent most of his speech focused on the relationship between conservatives and populists.[7]

First, he created a grand schema of (white) American history and divided the Founding Fathers into two distinct groups: populists and conservatives. They had taken turns governing the country, he told the assembly. Weems spent little time explaining the supposed differences between these two historical camps because his main point was that they all had been patriotic, loyal men. That was important. Something terrible had happened to change that dynamic of white racial loyalty, he explained.

It had occurred in 1913, Weems told the crowd, when "the international bankers took over the country" and established the Federal Reserve System. That was it. Then followed a list of ill effects marking decline: Jewish immigration from eastern Europe, World War One, and American involvement in the League of Nations. Weems claimed there was a brief respite when the Klan reemerged in the 1920s and during Calvin Coolidge's conservative administration. Franklin Delano Roosevelt had been a disaster.

Weems's history lesson had a moral. By his clock, the dispossession of white people hadn't taken place all at once, but one step at a time. It was the same way "the Chosen took over Hollywood," he said, using a snide euphemism for Jews. At first they made a lot of patriotic films. Then they started "bobbing noses, changing names, and joining churches," he roared as the audience came alive with laughter. "Then in the 1960s," he emphasized, "they let it all hang out."

Once Weems got his audience to agree that the white world had been turned upside down, it remained for him to convince these Christian patriots that the only way they could be redeemed was through a movement of "populists" rather than "conservatives." So after establishing the consanguinity of conservatism and populism, he drew the sharpest possible criticism of the contemporary conservative movement. The latter had been taken over by "kosher conservatives," he argued, who were guilty of supporting the state of Israel and acceding to Jewish domination in general. One problem with conservatives was that they "assume the government is loyal." But the government was not loyal, Weems argued; it was treasonous. Although he never used the words "Zionist Occupied" that day, Weems's argument differed little from Bob Mathews's conclusion that the government was in the hands of his racial enemies. "They've put us on the subversives list," Weems exclaimed in utter amazement.[8]

After telling the crowd that he had voted for Ronald Reagan in 1980, he asked, "We spent fifty years trying to elect a conservative, and what have we got?" Weems's disappointments with the Reagan administration fell into three categories that day.

First, they "don't take on the international bankers and the Federal Reserve; they think that's part of our glorious capitalist heritage," he argued. Second, "they don't take on the Zionists at all because they are The Chosen and our Number One ally in the Middle East." And finally, they don't "take any stand for the white race and its preservation either."

The assembly needed a new political party to represent true Americans, he said. "Since the George Wallace movement," Weems reminded the Mount Nebo audience, "there hasn't been a viable patriotic right-wing third party in the United States." Now that Willis Carto was gearing up the Populist Party, he argued, there was a chance for success. The "Populist Party has potential right now because it's backed up by the Liberty Lobby and the *Spotlight* newspaper, which has a paid mail circulation of 150,000," he told the crowd. And over most of the next decade the Populist Party served as an extension of Liberty Lobby, much as Youth for Wallace once had, complete with fights over money and political control.[9]

. . .

In 1984, talk about "populism" was much in the air. Democrats such as Congressman Vin Weber from Minnesota used the term to describe a program of rehashed New Deal liberalism. The right-wing fund-raiser Richard Viguerie wrote a book on "conservative populism" that equated populism with a strong uncompromising opposition to communism.[10] Carto used the same label, originally manifested as a movement of farmers who opposed the gold standard and pressed for a policy of easy money for debtors, to call for a return to the gold standard (which would tighten the money supply). Populist movements of the past had sometimes fought to protect and extend the system of white supremacy, and the icon of southern populism in the 1890s Tom Watson had ended his career as a raving anti-Semite and racist.[11] Populism, it turned out, was an elastic term devoid of any actual ideological or defined content. Instead, it was more of a political style than anything else, an antielite style, according to Michael Kazin in his book on the topic, *The Populist Persuasion: An American History.*[12]

Consider then the actual character of the antielitism projected by Weems. Like others of his ilk, he considered the government of white elites to be on the same side as the black poor, and he opposed them both. His so-called populism was just as surely arrayed against the black poor as it was against the white elites. He didn't call for measures such as stronger trade unions, an increased minimum wage, or even parity prices in agriculture. Further, specifically agrarian or rural concerns were not even mentioned that day in Arkansas. As a matter of style, Carto's Populist Party was a picture of white-sheeted racism in a Grant Wood frame of pitchfork Americana.

Four months after Weems's prayer day in Arkansas, on August 17–19, 1984, the Populist Party held its founding convention in Nashville. A facade of unity stretched over the six hundred "delegates" from forty-two states and dozens of organizations. Anyone who registered at the door and paid thirty-five dollars to be a party member could be a delegate and vote. It was a plaid shirt and polyester suit group, much like at Mount Nebo. Approximately two-thirds were aged fifty or older, and almost 50 percent were women. A noticeable minority of farmers was present. Almost half the delegates came from Tennessee, although Florida, California, and Illinois had sizable contingents.[13]

If the party was to succeed at all, it depended on various small groups working smoothly together. But they all had come to Nashville with different agendas. One wanted to repeal the income tax; another opposed the separation of church and state; still another wanted an investigation of Israel's mistaken attack on the USS *Liberty* spy ship in the Mediterranean in 1967. Mini parties such as the Conservative Party in Kansas and the Constitution Party in Wisconsin had to agree to subordinate their own egos to the larger superego.[14]

The most important organization affiliated with Carto's newest enterprise was the American Independent Party in California, led by William Shearer. His party had something Liberty Lobby didn't: ballot status in California and the largest reservoir of potential candidates for local office—a prerequisite for any party hoping to win votes.[15] Carto and Shearer agreed to work together. "The ideological merger is a major step," Weems concluded in a *Spotlight* article publicizing the party. To effect this "merger," a deal was cut. Shearer became the "dean" of the party's so-called school of politics, and his wife, Eileen, was given the post of national campaign coordinator. Carto became the school's "assistant dean," not its top spot. But he remained in control of those things that really mattered, like the money. Liberty Lobby also controlled the party's propaganda, through *The Spotlight*.[16]

The conventioneers nominated for president Bob Richards, an Olympic decathlon champion featured on the Wheaties breakfast cereal box. Maureen Salaman, a bright-eyed, quick-witted mother of two grown children from California, was nominated for vice president. Richards ultimately felt pinched and uncomfortable in his role, like a man wearing someone else's shoes. Salaman seemed to fit right in, on the other hand, although she was one of the few women in leadership.[17]

"We're up against the most evil and powerful conspiracy the world has ever known," Salaman said during her acceptance speech. She was the president of the National Health Federation, a foe of the American Medical Association and government regulation of cancer treatment. Her book *Nutrition: The Cancer Answer* and five years as a radio personality seemed to make her an attractive candidate.[18] Salaman's nomination may have been inspired by the fact that she represented alternative health activists. A significant percentage of *The Spotlight*'s paid advertising promoted unusual medical treatments, vitamins, and whole foods. The same merchandise, usually available at shops in upscale urban neighborhoods, also sold well at survivalist expos and Christian patriot meets.

Despite Salaman's credentials, some of the delegates grumbled about nominating a woman for vice president. Keith Shive, the farmer at the Gordon Kahl rally in Kansas, received some unexpected votes for the vice presidential nomination.[19] Carto and Shearer both backed the health foodist rather than the farmer. Although *The Spotlight* had covered farm-related events since the first tractorcade protests, the party leadership at Nashville missed the initial indication that a program of opposition to farm foreclosures might win votes. Nevertheless, during a resolutions session farmers sponsored an unanticipated motion for an immediate moratorium on farm foreclosures. It passed unanimously.[20]

From the Nashville Station

The Populist Party's election campaign failed before it got started. Recruiting a personality with unproven bona fides, such as Olympic champion Bob Richards, might have given the party more visibility and new adherents. But that inexperience also made him politically unreliable. Almost from the first, Richards talked positively about Jews in Israel and how he had personally witnessed the furnaces of the Holocaust. Both points put him at odds with Carto and Liberty Lobby, which controlled the party's money as well as its major vehicles for publicity. Richards tried to compensate by opening a campaign bank account that he alone controlled. But he raised little money, and after the convention *The Spotlight* dropped Bob Richards's name from its pages faster than an Old Bolshevik purged from the history books by Stalin.[21]

The candidate or the party or one of its state affiliates managed to get on the ballot in only fourteen states and win 66,168 votes in November 1984. The party's treasurer reported that the campaign spent "just under one million dollars" and left a $280,000 debt, according to William Shearer, Carto's ostensible partner in this enterprise.[22] The paltry showing at the polls was only exceeded by constant bickering by party officials over the debt and other factional differences, including charges made by anti-Klan groups that the party was a vehicle for promoting racism and anti-Semitism.[23]

William Shearer used his California newsletter to defend the party: "The Populist stands . . . include no attacks on any ethnic group, nor could such an attack properly be made. Both Jews and non-Jews can be found in the ranks of international bankers, pornographers and usurious lenders, just as both Jews and non-Jews may be found among victimized borrowers, farmers and crusaders for decency."[24] Carto reprinted Shearer's defense in *The Spotlight*, but the issue never went away. Fallenaway Klansmen and defrocked national socialists remained firmly ensconced among the national and local leadership. Later Shearer felt compelled to add that "there are always those who will try to misuse a political party as a vehicle for some prejudice or passion."[25] The internal bickering continued, and before the 1988 election season Shearer pulled his American Independent Party apparatus back out of the Populist Party.[26]

Despite the presence of Carto, Weems, and other well-known white supremacists at the center of this effort, most of the movement's hardcore cadres could not be convinced to join. A man like Aryan Nations führer Richard Butler would not climb down off his compound and vote. "A political party, even though called 'Populist,' will never remove our bondage, nor prevent our race's slaughter to gratify the blood lust of the eternal, destroying Jew," Butler wrote. "Politics as we know it today is nothing more than Jewish duplicity and deception, bemusing the befuddled goy 'sheep' while they are being sheared."[27]

Similarly, common law activists, like those at Cheney Lake who memorialized Gordon Kahl, were unlikely even to register to vote after rescinding their driver's licenses and other "contracts" with the state. The new party's inability to unify the existing pool of white supremacists was compounded by its failure to develop new voters in the one place it could have possibly won a following, among the debt-ridden farmers of the Midwest.

The Populist Party and Family Farmers

Dozens of small-time anti-Semites like Keith Shive had joined the Populist Party and pushed it to include farm foreclosures in the platform. By 1986 a Nebraska farmer had become the party's "national vice-chairman for agriculture," a post with little pomp and even less circumstance.[28] The Iowa state party filed a lawsuit against the Federal Reserve, and for only thirty-five dollars farmers could add their names as plaintiffs.[29] Like the common law liens, this lawsuit went nowhere. But it did recruit a few genuine farmers to the party's ranks. One of them, Johnny Vogel, ran unsuccessfully for Iowa's state senate.[30]

The Populist Party's efforts to fish in the sea of farmers' discontent suffered from competition that came from every corner. In addition to the Posse Comitatus mentioned earlier, William Pierce's National Alliance had sent out a team of pamphleteers to entice any true Aryans parading in the American Agriculture Movement's first tractorcades in D.C. Even Louis Beam and Robert Mathews had put a line in this stream. Numbers of scam artists sold phony loan schemes, bogus common law lien kits, and land patents along with anti-Semitic and racist propaganda tracts. One particularly popular pamphlet, authored by a Christian Identity preacher, argued that Hitler had solved the problems of debt and economic crisis by removing the "international bankers" from Germany.[31] Each of these snake oil salesmen developed a following just large enough to take energy and money away from campaigns for the ballot.

While the Populist Party's electioneering could not capture all of this activity, Liberty Lobby's *Spotlight* did speak in broad enough terms to win a significant subscriber base in the Midwest. One East Coast reporter even suggested that the tabloid was read by farm revolt leaders in the same fashion that investment bankers read *The Wall Street Journal*.[32] And the years of propaganda about Jewish banking conspiracies had a cumulative effect on community attitudes that showed up in carefully constructed public opinion surveys.

A 1986 Louis Harris poll of rural Iowa and Nebraska residents found 42 percent of respondents agreeing with the statement "Jews should stop complaining about what happened to them in Nazi Germany." Forty-three percent agreed that "when it comes to choosing between people and money, Jews will choose money." Most significant, 27 percent agreed that "farmers have always been exploited by international Jewish bankers." Harris's conclusion: this was a mass phenomenon, even if it wasn't massive.[33]

Despite these numbers, farmers were not inherently anti-Semitic or immune to alternatives to both the Populist Party and its Posse-type competitors. Progressive-minded farmers ultimately drove the white supremacists and anti-Semites out of their movement. During the mid-1980s, liberal nonprofit agencies and state farm-church coalitions entered the fray. They remembered fondly the Roosevelt-era farm programs that protected the commodity prices that farmers received at the grain elevators. A new foundation, Farm Aid, took center stage in 1985, as Willie Nelson and other musicians raised funds through high-profile benefit concerts, funneling money to progressive and mainstream grassroots organizations, many of them springing up as an alternative to the dead-end politics of the Posse. Farmers joined with union members and civil rights activists to protest foreclosure sales on the steps of county courthouses. They lobbied state legislatures as well as Congress. In Missouri, progressive farmers held a 145-day protest at the doors of a county office of the Farmers Home Administration (FmHA) and succeeded in having a particularly onerous supervisor removed.

In the end, organizations with liberal policy agendas like Farm Aid prevailed. Significant blocs of (white) farmers supported the Reverend Jesse Jackson during his run in the Democratic primaries. Farmers won an important policy change with the Farm Credit Act of 1987. A multistate class action lawsuit against the Farmers Home Administration resulted in a stay in government foreclosures that same year.[34] Many of the remaining farm families were able to restructure their debts, and the crisis receded a bit. In its place chronic decline returned to much of the rural Midwest, and a new wave of corporatization threatened to overturn what remained of family-size agriculture. Invoking "Christian common law" and charging after mythical Jewish conspiracies had not saved a single family farm. After 1988 the followers of these theories dissipated as a force in family farm politics. And the Populist Party had missed its main chance to win a mass constituency.

Nevertheless, both the Populist Party and its Posse Comitatus competition did leave a lasting imprint on the white supremacist movement. In the mid-1990s, Posse types—although no longer attached to a genuine mass farm movement—became the seedbed for a revival of Christian patriot militias. And the Populist Party carved out its own distinctive niche, serving as a point of intersection for second-tier leaders and local activists. The party helped restart David Duke's career. And it identified issues that were later picked up by Pat Buchanan. While the Populists sometimes suffered from their association with Willis Carto's Liberty Lobby and *The Spotlight*, the party managed to add a distinct Americanist counterbalance to the European focus then dominant at the Institute for Historical Review.

Europeans and Southerners
at the Institute for Historical Review

February 15, 1986. At a sunny venue in Southern California, the tone of the Institute for Historical Review's seventh conference fluctutated between that of a dank European *Bierstube* and a mint and magnolias southern plantation. An ethnic Croatian lectured on the link between "B'nai B'rith and Yugoslavia's Tito." A German national blamed World War Two on Churchill and Roosevelt. A Romanian-born medical doctor living in Chicago, Alexander Ronnett, extolled the virtues of the fascist legionary movement in prewar Romania while distinguishing it from Hitler's National Socialism. The institute's George Orwell Free Speech Award went to a Canadian attorney whose moment of glory rested on defending Ernst Zündel, a German Canadian propagandist indicted for "falsifying history."[1]

Several Americans added to the East of the Rhine atmosphere. A one-man operation called the World Service Film League, for example, distributed a catalog of films including Leni Riefenstahl's classic on the 1936 Nuremberg Party rally *Triumph of the Will* and Goebbels's crude agitprop piece *The Eternal Jew*.[2] One Californian had to be told to remove his swastika stickpin before entering the room.[3] During a strategy session, a participant from Cleveland ventured the comment that if accused of being anti-Semitic, "we should just say yes and not be afraid to say it." That prompted the IHR personality Bradley Smith, who was moderating the discussion, to assert that for the record he was not an anti-Semite.[4]

To the uninitiated, getting to the conference seemed a bit like entering a pornographic peep show. Six weeks before the event, potential participants had to sign loyalty oaths and submit them along with their two-hundred-dollar registration fees. They swore not to "advocate or practice . . . repression" of revisionists. "Revisionists" were described as "those who question or deny establishment notions about gas chambers, Hitler, National Socialism and related issues."[5] After passing that test, prepaid registrants then were given a phone number to call when they arrived in the Los Angeles area. Finally, they were directed to the Pacifica Hotel in Culver City. Once attendees surmounted all these hurdles, however, Willis Carto's friendly German-born wife, Elisabeth, let down her guard and welcomed out-of-town participants as if they were traveling salesmen checking into the home office.[6]

The secretive conferences and national socialist undertow combined with accents from Central Europe tended to limit the appeal of IHR events on American soil. At one conference during this period the featured speaker was Otto Ernst Remer, an aging former *Wehrmacht* officer who had brutally suppressed an incipient German military revolt in 1944 after an unsuccessful assassination attempt on Hitler.[7] Another speaker had been August Klapprott, a German American Bund officer who had been charged with sedition by the Justice Department during World War Two.[8]

At this meeting, a formal presentation about Abraham Lincoln by a Georgia attorney, Sam Dickson, offered a strong counterpoint to the European obsessions. By Dickson's account, Lincoln was a dishonest demagogue, cut from the same "leftist" material as Presidents Wilson and Franklin Roosevelt. Lincoln, he said, pursued only sectional interests, rather than national interests. As proof Dickson proffered the fact that Lincoln, while still a freshman congressman, had opposed President Polk's war against Mexico. Among his other purported crimes, Lincoln had also opposed slavery and supported racial equality from his first days in the Illinois legislature but had mischievously crafted his views according to the political opportunities of the moment.[9]

In discussing Lincoln, Dickson revealed much about his own beliefs, including his views on slavery. "The Union had existed half slave and half free from its inception," he argued. "There appears to be no logical reason why it could not have existed in that fashion, given responsible leadership and good will on both sides, until slavery was eliminated by the progress of technology."[10] Apparently Dickson did not consider opposition to one human's holding another as property to be a "logical" reason.

While Dickson's speech was unremarkable in its content—merely repeating the commonsense white supremacist understanding of the past—Samuel Glasgow Dickson the person was an important figure on his own terms. A dark-haired son of a Presbyterian minister born in Georgia in 1947, he came of age just as the racial customs of his beloved

South were being wrenched out of the nineteenth century. He was polite and clever, and you could hear sweet tea pouring in his long vowels
and taste the corn pone in his droll humor. He practiced law from a
small office in the Atlanta suburbs and cultivated the company of other
white middle-class professionals. He extolled tradition and traditional
authority, and he considered white supremacy a natural, biological
thing. He didn't hate anybody, he said, and took occasion to remark on
his own Jewish cousins.[11] He believed the Ku Klux Klan gave white
people a bad name. Underneath his soft charms, however, Dickson had
a hard, even nasty edge. And on questions of race or the Holocaust, he
unsheathed a rapier wit.[12]

He had run for lieutenant governor in Georgia's 1978 Democratic
primaries, at a time when most white supremacists in the South still registered as Democrats. He raised few contributions and received only
72,621 votes, or 11 percent of the primary total.[13] Afterward he traded
vote chasing for small private meetings of like-minded souls.

Just a few months before this conference in California, Dickson had
sponsored an event in Atlanta designed to "promote a feeling of fraternity and solidarity throughout the English-speaking world." Guest speakers from Canada, Australia, and South Africa discussed such topics as
"International Finance and the Assault on Individual Freedom and National Sovereignty."

When asked if he had convened this international fete in Georgia,
Dickson replied that he was just the local contact for it. "I didn't personally convene it," he said. Yet his signature was at the bottom of a letter
that began, "You are invited to attend a unique and extraordinary gathering," and then listed the meeting's time, place, speakers, and topics.[14]
"Inviting" but not "convening" the meeting? It is a revisionist thing. The
average reader wouldn't necessarily understand.

As for revisionism and the Holocaust, Dickson averred that Hitler
"was a disaster for European history and for the European white man."[15]
He was equally assured Jews had been persecuted during World War
Two. But "to the extent to which six million of them were killed, is something I do not know." It was obvious to Dickson why certain people kept
talking about it, however: "to intimidate, psychologically bully people of
European extraction, to create in us a sense that we are an especially
guilty people."[16] On this point, Dickson's own ideas matched perfectly
with those undergirding the Institute for Historical Review.

A contingent of southerners joined Dickson and the Europeans at
this conference. The most veteran of this group was Ed Fields, or more
precisely Dr. Ed Fields, as he preferred to be called. Fields had started
his career after World War Two as a member of a Naziesque group in the

Southeast known as the Columbians. He had also managed to get a degree in chiropractics from a college in Iowa. Fields claimed to have been one of the founders of the National States Rights Party in 1958 and served as editor of its publication, the *Thunderbolt*.[17] By the time of the conference in Los Angeles, Fields was living in the Atlanta suburb of Marietta, and his publication was a low-circulation *Der Stürmer*–like tabloid with lurid headlines. Although he made repeated stabs at creating his own groups—a Klan faction here, a "third party" there—Fields never mastered the art of winning a mass following. Permanently consigned to the middle ranks of movement leaders, he maintained a fiefdom of followers in north Georgia, and his red head and flushed face were oft seen bobbing in Klan street parades.[18]

Other attending southerners included David Duke, who was looking for new opportunities to reenter the limelight after his six-year absence from the Klan. Alongside Duke came James K. Warner, a onetime American Nazi Party national secretary who had joined Duke's Klan in the 1970s but was now running an international book distribution enterprise from a New Orleans suburb.[19] Another Georgian, Martin O'Toole, set up a conference display for *Instauration*, the high-toned monthly magazine edited by the *Dispossessed Majority* author Wilmot Robertson. An activist for all seasons, O'Toole at that time ran a business service that included *Instauration* among its customers.[20]

The southerners babbled like mockingbirds on a telephone wire. They debated among themselves about the role religious cultism might play in the building of mass movements. They differed on the tactical efficacy of excoriating Jews versus attacking black people, all while drinking and talking too long. During one such session, James K. Warner proclaimed that Sam Dickson's real name was Humphrey Ireland. (Ireland, as noted earlier, used the pseudonym Wilmot Robertson.)[21]

Although Dickson, the middle-aged attorney, and Ireland, the elderly reclusive author, were two different people, their views were similar on a number of key points. Germany after World War Two and the South after the Civil War each was a "victim of inflammatory lies about atrocities," Dickson proffered in his speech.[22] By Ireland-Robertson's understanding, the beginning of "white dispossession" should be traced back to the Civil War. Remembering that Holocaust denial had the goal of removing from white supremacists the moral burden of the Holocaust, linking the fate of the Confederacy with that of Nazi Germany seemed natural to men like Dickson and Robertson.

Robertson underscored the fact that in Hitler's Germany "theories of race superiority" had been "state doctrine." At the same time, he also questioned the claim that the Third Reich had been the first government of this kind in history. As evidence, he pointed to the Confederate States of America and a speech by its vice president, Alexander Hamilton Stephens, in 1861. Stephens averred that "the negro [*sic*] is not equal to the white man, that slavery—subordination to the superior race—is his natural condition. This, our new government [the Confederacy] is the first in the history of the world based upon this great physical, philosophical, and moral truth."[23]

"The decline of the Majority began with the political and military struggle between the North and South," Robertson wrote.[24] He constructed an elaborate sequence of events to demonstrate this idea. Prior to the Civil War, he argued, almost all whites were of "Northern European descent" (the kind he valued most). During the war, however, 610,000 were killed, and the Anglo-Saxon population fell sharply as a result. The remaining white population was unable to reproduce itself in adequate number. Further, he claimed, "the war's dysgenic effect fell more heavily on the South."[25] As a result, when the railroads plowed west and industrialization intensified in the decades after the Civil War, the number of Anglo-Saxons available to fuel this economic development was insufficient.

Thus began, he wrote, "the importation of vast numbers of white immigrants of disparate races and cultures."[26] Among the white immigrants that Robertson lamented were Catholics who refused to adopt his Protestant norm. These southern Italians, Slavs, and even some Irish he designated as "white minorities." They could assimilate and become completely white in his mind, but there were other immigrants from Europe who could not. The most unabsorbable of white minorities, in his taxonomy, were the Jews. They had a special place in his schema, in part because he believed they dominated the country.[27]

In Robertson's view, the decline of Anglo-Saxon hegemony after the Civil War had been followed by a pre–World War Two attack by scholars who argued that race was a socially created category rather than a scientific or biological fact, and he cited the work before the war of anthropologists such as Franz Boas in this regard. Hitler's defeat then added to this change in intellectual climate.[28]

By tying the fate of Nazi Germany to the Confederacy and then to a grand theory of majority dispossession, Robertson helped anchor Holocaust denial to the entire white supremacist enterprise. By 1986 that relationship had become relatively fixed. It no longer simply served a niche market for books and materials, as it had at its founding. While the Institute for Historical Research never approximated its grand vision of itself as a center for historical research, it nevertheless could be considered the closest thing to a think tank that white supremacists had at that time. Here a small number of ideologues sought mass influence without the annoyances of mass participation. And in the absence of a natural constituency, the institute provided a place for movement intellectuals and middle-class professionals to meet and exchange ideas in a secure environment. At the same time, many of its publications and ideas trickled down the movement's ranks, so that by the mid-1980s Klansmen, Aryan warriors, Posse Comitatus sovereigns, and Populist Party members knew that the Holocaust was a hoax invented by the Jews to trick white society.

Regardless of its relatively insular character, Carto had long hoped that the institute would help change history's verdict on World War Two, as well as find new customers and supporters for his ideas. To pursue those goals, he endorsed a shift in the IHR's tactics, which emphasized first and foremost a libertarian and free speech approach. Rather than simply proclaim that the Holocaust was a hoax, institute staff now argued that all points of view on the subject should be heard, including the view that Hitler didn't do it. This new strategy was extended into a "radio project," whereby the IHR attempted to get on talk radio shows. The watchwords became "First Amendment" and "freedom of speech." The *IHR Newsletter* eagerly reported on the number of programs the institute had managed to get on and recounted in glorious detail if it suckered a rabbi or other Jewish representative to debate it on the airwaves.[29] The IHR also tried promoting itself to Louis Farrakhan's Nation of Islam, and Arthur Butz, the engineering professor and author of *The Hoax of the Twentieth Century*, who had presented at the institute's first conference, was consequently invited to speak at a 1985 Nation of Islam convocation in Chicago.[30]

Despite the added buzz that such efforts created, Holocaust denial remained under the sole proprietorship of a relatively marginal movement. Only very small groups of people want to sit in a hotel room for two days and listen to long perorations on Romanian fascism. On the surface it seemed as if the white supremacist movement had hit a moment of stasis. Although the warrior set still posed a murderous threat, it had already reached its peak. Subscriptions to Liberty Lobby's *Spotlight* tabloid had started to taper off. As a whole, the number of movement cadres had grown only slowly. At times stasis seemed to be the principle most at work in a movement dedicated to change.

You learned it in high school. Bodies at rest tend to stay at rest—until an outside force exerts itself. And then bodies in motion tend to stay in motion. This isn't rocket science. It is the physics of throwing rocks and bottles.

PART two

Mainstreamers and Ballots Take the Lead, 1987–1989

Even as federal prosecutors take another crack at Aryan leaders, a second strand of movement activists finds an enlarged following among a stratum of regular white folks. A whites-only ideology takes form as a family-friendly theology, and bands of young subculturalists declare themselves through music and style.

White Riot in Forsyth County on King Day

January 17, 1987. Chicken plants and textile mills had supported the tradition-bound towns and isolated villages of the north Georgia piedmont for generations. But life changed after 1980, when the twisting curves of Highway 19 out of Atlanta became a four-lane turnpike, speeding a torturous two-hour drive into a thirty-minute commute from the metroplex. The low-rent rural reaches of Forsyth County were invaded by upper-middle-class professionals. The green hills and browned-out factories were transformed into an exurban bedroom community. Well-read bourgeois children pushed their blue-collar cousins to the back of area classrooms. Luxury sedans crowded pickup trucks on the local roads. With all these changes, Forsyth County still remained essentially all white, as it had been since the early 1900s. And then, as if to compound further the culture clash, a new multiracial challenge emerged at a crossroads outside the county seat on this Saturday, just days before the Dr. Martin Luther King, Jr., national holiday.

The King holiday weekend had become a flashpoint for white supremacists in the 1980s. Several groups distributed pamphlets attacking King personally and the holiday. One of the most popular was a reprint of a speech by Republican Senator Jesse Helms of North Carolina, who had led the opposition. In fact, only after a long campaign and great pressure did President Ronald Reagan finally sign the bill in 1983 authorizing a national day memorializing Dr. King in the same manner as George Washington and Abraham Lincoln. Almost all the states had done likewise, the notable exceptions being New Hampshire and Arizona, but even these states recognized King Day before the century ended.[1] Dr. King took his place as a founder of the post–Jim Crow American nation.[2]

In Forsyth County an assemblage of white working-class locals and black civil rights veterans from Atlanta planned to commemorate Dr. King's birthday with a solemn "brotherhood march" through the county.[3] During the weeks prior to the march, Klan groups in north Georgia plotted to stop it. One Klan flyer argued in hyperbolic type that "OUTSIDE AGITATORS AND COMMUNIST RACEMIXERS want to defile our community." Racist rhetoric often carries sexual undertones, a connection that has been repeatedly explored by scholars.[4] These Klan groups weren't organizing a journal of literary criticism, however. They called for a "White Power Rally" and made plans to be at the same place at the same time that the brotherhooders would march. "LOOK FOR REBEL FLAGS," the Klansmen instructed. They signed their leaflet "The Committee to Keep Forsyth and Dawson Counties White," a fake front for the awful events to come. A confrontation was inevitable.[5]

On that frosty Saturday morning in 1987, a bus of mostly black Atlantans met two dozen local whites at a convenient crossroads, and together the multiracial group rode to a spot on Bethelview Road, just three miles away from the Forsyth County courthouse.[6] Seventy-five brave souls disembarked from the bus and were immediately confronted by an angry mob of four hundred white people screaming racist epithets. The Klan's choice of a bogus "committee" to rally their followers had proved effective. Nine out of every ten in the mob were not Klan members, but run-of-the-mill working people intent on protecting their white enclave.[7]

Among those commanding the mob, however, were cadres from two different Klan factions, the Southern White Knights and the Invisible Empire Knights of the Ku Klux Klan. Some Klansmen wore white robes or camouflage fatigues, but most wore regular street clothes. They brought professional-looking banners proclaiming ABOLISH THE KING HOLIDAY and FORSYTH'S SECURITY IS RACIAL PURITY.[8] Klan and non-Klan, they all waved large Confederate battle flags, displayed ropes tied into nooses, and surrounded the marchers and their bus on both sides of the rural road. Roving bands threw rocks and bottles and flitted through the nearby woods, evading the small contingent of state law enforcement officers and the even smaller sheriff's squad. Soon the barrage became so thick the brotherhood marchers were forced back onto the bus in defeat.[9]

That afternoon the Klan groups quickly claimed victory with a rally outside the Forsyth County courthouse that had all the earmarks of a 1960s-style Jim Crow celebration, including appearances by J. B. Stoner, who had been released from imprisonment for bombing a black church in 1958,[10] and Lester Maddox, who had become infamous for wielding an ax handle to ward off integration of his Atlanta chicken restaurant and was subsequently elected governor.[11] The next day one Georgia Klan leader traveled to an anti–King Day rally in North Carolina and advised his comrades: "If those blue-gummed, gorilla-smelling niggers come sticking their nose in your business, you ought to send them home like we did, with bottles and rocks upside the head."[12]

Certainly some, like the Klansman above, understood the Forsyth violence only in terms of the crudest racist invective. Others romanticized it as if the great glories of the Civil War were being relived. "Now comes the Confederate counterattack. Shot and shell crack through the air," Ed Fields boasted in his *Thunderbolt* tabloid. Fields's description of events had the ring of a first-person account. "Next the Confederate forces charge down the line on both sides of the Brotherhood Bus. Battle flags flying the troops swing in front of the bus [which has] been outflanked and cut off from the rear," he continued. Fields's account of the attack was a surprisingly candid statement of how the brotherhood marchers had been denied use of a public highway.[13]

The mass attack, draped in the Old South's symbols and sympathies, had all the hallmarks of the past. Adding to the Faulknerian scent hanging over the drama was Forsyth County's particular history.[14] In 1912, an eighteen-year-old white girl had been raped and murdered there. Three black men were immediately arrested for the crime. A mob formed quickly and took one of the prisoners from the county jail, beat him to death, and hanged his mutilated body from a telephone pole. The other two were placed in jails outside the county, tried, and hanged six weeks later before a crowd of ten thousand.

When a black minister protested the illegal lynchings, he too received a beating (which he managed to survive). Shortly thereafter all one thousand of the county's black residents were forced from their homes and farmsteads and lost their properties without compensation. In a fashion not untypical for the times, a nearby newspaper blamed the victims for the violence: "The conduct of those Negroes in Forsyth County has caused the organization of White Caps, who have notified the blacks to move out and where they acted slow about it their homes were destroyed."[15]

Lynchings were common during that period. The NAACP has counted the lynching of 3,436 people between 1889 and 1922, including 28 who were publicly burned to death in the four years immediately after World War One.[16] And more people were lynched in Georgia than in any other state.[17] Significantly, many of these lynchings were ostensibly the result of alleged violations at the intersection of race and gender, such as rape. Just six years prior to the 1912 Forsyth County debacle, white mobs in Atlanta had dragged black people from their homes and stores, beaten them, and burned their buildings in a pogromlike riot supported by the city's business and political elite. Again, race met sex as the city's newspaper published inflammatory accounts of supposed "assaults by black men upon white women."[18] While the overwhelming majority of Georgia lynch victims were black, a young Jewish man, Leo Frank, was lynched by an Atlanta mob in 1915, just three years after the Forsyth expulsions. Again the crime supposedly involved the rape and murder of a white woman. White riots drove black people from their homes in Rosewood, Florida, in 1923. Similarly, black residents were murdered and their homes burned by mobs in East St. Louis in 1917, Chicago in 1919, and Tulsa in 1921. In each of these instances the riots were mass events involving hundreds of white people without direct affiliation to a group like the Klan.[19] (Forcing black people from their homes had precedents, of course, in slavery and Indian "removal.")

During those decades, mass violence and spectacular public lynchings enforced the customs of everyday Jim Crow and reified the distinction between black people's secondary status and the first-class citizenship of those with pale skin.[20] As a result, the campaign against lynching became a central part of the fight against legal segregation.

The ghosts of lynching victims past may have hung over the brotherhood marchers, but this was 1987, not 1912. De jure segregation had been constitutionally ended, even if de facto segregation, as in Forsyth County, remained. Hundreds of rock-throwing, screaming white people no longer enforced the social order; they destabilized it. The ideology of biological white supremacy no longer enthralled society's commanding heights. Rather, these ideas were embodied in a relatively distinct social movement. Area newspapers heaped contempt and rebuke upon this mob, instead of understanding and respect as they had when black people were first driven from the county.

Almost as soon as news of the violence in Forsyth County reached Atlanta, civil rights organizations began planning a response. They too invoked the past, not of lynchings and victimization, however, but of bravery and transcendence. During the official King holiday commemoration that Monday, Coretta Scott King announced that she and others would go to Forsyth the following Saturday to "complete the march," using tones reminiscent of her late husband after a 1965 voting rights march from Selma to Montgomery had been stopped by police violence.

Mass rallies in Atlanta that week attracted thousands. An ad hoc Coalition Against Fear and Intimidation in Forsyth County formed. Union officials, politicians, and activists from across the country announced plans to attend the second march.[21] The mob violence in north Georgia had hit a national nerve.[22]

Just seven days after the Klan-led mob had stopped the busload of brotherhood marchers, more than 25,000 civil rights advocates marched into the Forsyth County seat of Cumming. Instead of a small ineffective sheriff's squad, an army of law enforcement personnel protected the demonstration. They included 1,700 national guardsmen, 600 police from jurisdictions all over the state, and 185 Georgia Bureau of Investigation (GBI) agents. The mayor, the governor, and even Senator Sam Nunn welcomed the march, as did a relatively unnoticed delegation of local (white) clergy.[23] For that day at least, official opinion was mustered on the speakers' platform in the town square. It was the largest civil rights demonstration in the South since the 1960s. The alignment of civil rights leaders and Georgia's political leadership seemed like the triumph of enlightenment and racial progress over violence and the past.

However, there was another side to the events that second weekend, less visible to the international media, which focused its cameras on the multiracial multitudes and the celebrities onstage. Along the roadside and in the town square, several thousand white people gathered, periodically chanting, "Nigger go home," or throwing rocks and bottles. Once again they flew Confederate battle flags, a reminder that a supposed symbol of southern heritage had been irretrievably marked as a banner for contemporary racism. In this crowd of white rebels, a colloquy of nasty signs held forth: PRAISE GOD FOR AIDS and KEEP FORSYTH WHITE, along with one of the Klan's favorites, SICKLE CELL ANEMIA, THE GREAT WHITE HOPE. Dozens of Kluxers, as well as neo-Nazis representing every faction from Florida to North Carolina, showed their faces, some wearing robes and uniforms, others not. J. B. Stoner, the aging church bomber, walked like a Hollywood celebrity, autographing business cards for well-wishers and shaking hands.[24]

Among the most notable movement personages present that day was David Duke. This was his first public appearance in five years, and he took advantage of the situation to lead an impromptu parade on the edge of town. Using a bullhorn, he told the crowd that Forsyth County was theirs to protect. He claimed that the civil rights march that day was similar to the putative crimes that occurred during the Reconstruction era. Sounding a theme from his Klan days, he said another revolution was needed.[25] At his side was Don Black, the onetime Alabama state leader who had gone to federal prison in 1982 for violating the Neutrality Act in the Dominica affair.[26] Now that he had served his sentence, he attended this event without any formal organizational identification. Before the end of the day, fifty-five people were arrested, many on charges of public drunkenness or throwing rocks. Among them was Duke, who later pleaded no contest to a misdemeanor charge of obstructing a roadway.[27]

At the beginning of the day, while civil rights paraders were still approaching the downtown square, these three thousand white counterprotesters waited, playing a seesaw game of push and shove with the National Guard and a tough squad of GBI agents. Rocks were thrown from the back of the crowd, and the agents charged in to make arrests. The crowd would then surge, taunting the troops and protecting the offenders, their spirits buoyed by the conflict. But the raucous tenor of the white protest quickly changed as the first group of brotherhood marchers began to arrive. "Well, there they are boys. There's your future communist party," somebody said clearly as the crowd began to quiet. As row after multiracial row filled the town, the white mob began to lose its bounce. They hadn't expected so large a civil rights demonstration, and the number of white participants began to shake them up. They had expected a much smaller, virtually all-black march. "Goddam boys, we've lost this country," one white-robed man said. "That's it. We've lost this country."[28]

As will become evident, David Duke drew an opposite conclusion from the same set of events.

Other events in the Southeast pointed at the complexity of white supremacist activities during this period. An amalgamation of groups paraded on January 17 through Pulaski, Tennessee, the town in which the post–Civil War Klan had first formed. Ceremonially lead by the Aryan Nations chief Robert Miles, the Pulaski parade was organized by the Knights of the Ku Klux Klan, now led by Thom Robb. From the same postwar boomer generation as David Duke, Robb had been born in Michigan and in the mid-1970s settled down near Harrison, Arkansas, just a few miles down the road from where James Ellison had established a church. While a member of the Knights of the Ku Klux Klan, Robb still published his own periodical, *The Torch*, which ostensibly purveyed a version of Christian Identity theology. The tabloid combined national socialist ideas with Klan-crafted Americana. In one edition Robb wrote: "we endorse and seek the execution of all homosexuals."[29] In another he reiterated the common theme of white dispossession: "It is not our government that is working to promote homosexuality, race-mixing, abortion and the destruction of our Christian faith—it is their government."[30] He had become the Knights' national chaplain in 1980, the year David Duke resigned from the Klan. When Duke's successor, Don Black, finally went to prison in 1982, Robb pledged undying fealty to his incarcerated leader.[31] Shortly thereafter, however, Robb proceeded Brutus style to undermine Black's leadership and win effective control (if not the highest title) of the Knights of the Ku Klux Klan. Following the language used by Robert Miles, Robb had maintained that his Knights group was a Fifth Era Klan. Like much else said by Robb, it was a hollow claim. Instead of creating a secretive night-riding paramilitary, as Miles had envisioned the Fifth Era, Robb had only adopted its symbols, such as emblazoning his propaganda with the numeric code designating clandestinity. Nevertheless, Robb's Knights became a visible force in white supremacist circles, and it continued public rallies, paraded through town squares, and burned wooden crosses. This event in Tennessee showcased his Klan's strength in the Southeast in the same way as a July congress in Idaho displayed Aryan Nations' strength in the Northwest. One hundred Kluxers walked two or three abreast before retiring to a nighttime cross burning at a nearby farm on the Saturday before the King holiday, the same day as the first brotherhood march had been stopped with rocks and bottles in Georgia.

A completely different Klan faction marched in a similar fashion that same weekend in Summerville, South Carolina.

A fourth rally also occurred on Sunday, January 18, in Raleigh, North Carolina. In previous years North Carolina events had been organized by a group called the Confederate Knights of the Ku Klux Klan that had then changed its name to the White Patriot Party.[32] The hybrid organization grafted uniformed paramilitarism and Naziesque ideology onto its roots as a white-robed Klan group. This troop had grown geometrically during the mid-1980s, and its annual mid-January parade through the state capital routinely drew several hundred men and several dozen women. They carried Confederate flags, wore camouflage fatigues, and marched in tight military-style columns behind a banner declaring their "love" for Robert Mathews's Order or hatred of the "Zionist" government. The White Patriot Party considered itself the militia of an emerging Carolina Republic for Aryans, one of the many mininationalisms dancing around in movement heads at the time.[33] At its height this organization had more than one thousand members, most of them in North Carolina. Party leaders recruited active-duty marines, obtained heavy weapons, including LAW rockets (light antitank weapons), and concocted a detailed military plot for seizing power.[34] The Raleigh event in 1987 was smaller than past anti-King rallies in North Carolina, as an ideologically focused troop of eighty-five political soldiers carried on the tradition under the name Southern National Front.[35] But it was no less significant.

Nevertheless, the Raleigh march was dwarfed by events the night of January 17 in Shelby, North Carolina, where five men were shot in the back of the head as they lay facedown in an adult bookstore. Three died immediately, as the perpetrators set the shop on fire. Two managed to survive. The complete story of the Shelby bookstore murders remains unknown, forever shrouded by fear and bigotry. The bookstore, which was known for catering to gay men, had been a local target in a statewide "antiporn" drive by the U.S. attorney, and few would leap to the defense of its habitués. Local police and press speculated at first that the assassination-style murders were drug- or organized crime–related, ignoring evidence to the contrary. The father of one of the victims claimed his son was only at the bookstore as a Christian witness against pornography.[36]

Months after the killings, a reporter for *The Fayetteville Observer* developed a source that claimed that known white supremacists believed the bookstore victims were gay and shot them to "avenge Yahweh on homosexuals."[37]

Eventually two men associated with the White Patriot Party were indicted for the murders and arson, and one of them went to trial more than two years after the crimes. The prosecutor relied heavily on testimony by White Patriot defectors and turncoats to make his case. He missed real opportunities to turn defense testimony to the prosecution's advantage. And the criminal case collapsed completely as the defense team accused one of the turncoat witnesses of being the crime's actual perpetrator. Essentially one faction of the White Patriot Party accused the other of murder, leading to a situation in which the jury could not determine who was actually guilty. The prosecution's ineptness was compounded by deep social conflicts about homosexuality, which were an unstated influence upon the all-white jury, according to Mab Segrest, who monitored the trial daily for a civil rights group and later wrote about the case in her book *Memoir of a Race Traitor*.[38] In the end, one former White Patriot Party warrior was found not guilty. The other never went to trial. Nobody was ever convicted for these heinous crimes in North Carolina.[39]

The bookstore murders were one moment in a seeming eternity of violence aimed at gay men and lesbians. The National Gay and Lesbian Task Force documented 2,042 incidents of antigay violence in 1985. Reports doubled in 1986, and the task force documented 4,946 incidents, including 80 homicides.[40] Of course, homophobia is not the sole province of white supremacists, and only a small percentage of crimes motivated by antigay bigotry were perpetrated by members of organized groups. During that period, laws against "sodomy" remained on the books in many states, and the basic civil rights of gays and lesbians often remain unprotected. Society stayed at odds with itself over everything gay and lesbian, from military service to officially sanctioned marriages. For many religious fundamentalists, homosexuality is a biblical abomination, and they say so regularly from their pulpits and on their television ministries. The repetition of noxious remarks about gays and lesbians often goes without public censure. Discrimination and violence have naturally followed, including constant campaigning against the so-called Homosexual Agenda by the Christian conservative wing of the Republican Party.

For members of the White Patriot Party, such as those indicted but not convicted in the Shelby murders, homophobia was a salient part of their total ideology.[41] Like the cultists at the Covenant, the Sword and the Arm of the Lord compound and the warriors at Aryan Nations, the White Patriot Party adhered to the tenets of Christian Identity. For these Identity believers, homosexuality is a sin, much like interracial marriage.[42] Within this framework, an individual committing murder to prevent interracial sex or stop homosexuality is regarded as morally upright. Similarly, a mob like that in Forsyth County is believed to be justified when throwing rocks and bottles to preserve white enclaves from racial integration. (By racist reasoning, integration leads to mixed matings in any case.)

These similarities between the Forsyth riot and the Shelby bookstore murders should not obscure the differences. Even if both events occurred on the same day in the same region of the country and the perpetrators shared a common set of ideological preconceptions, they were separated by more than just the differing targets (multiracial marchers versus gay men) or the level of violence employed (felonious assault versus homicide). Shelby was presumably the work of a small band of hardened ideologues, much like those Order members who murdered talk radio host Alan Berg. (Remember no one was ever convicted under state law for murder in the Berg case because no murder charges had been brought.) Forsyth County, on the other hand, was a mass action by hundreds of ordinary white people.

Klan groups had spent the last ten years cultivating the small towns and villages of north Georgia. Almost every resident had driven by a Klan "roadblock" at one street intersection or another, where white-robed crusaders distributed propaganda while collecting money in buckets. Saturday afternoon parades through small town squares and nighttime cross burnings were also commonplace, particularly during the summer months. Dropping a dollar bill in a bucket or picking up a piece of racist propaganda did not mean that you had joined the Klan. But the constant presence of public activity tended to normalize these groups. In this fashion, Klan groups influenced social standards without ever being elected to office or lobbying public policy makers. Turning ordinary non-affiliated white youths into a racist, violence-prone mob thus took little more than a presumptive threat and a fake front leaflet from the Klan.

The differences between vanguardists, like those who had presumably pulled the trigger at the Shelby bookstore, and mainstreamers were most stark at this moment. Robert Mathews had started his small guerrilla army because he reasoned that most white people were "cowardly, sheepish, degenerates." Now David Duke argued the opposite: that white people actually agreed with the movement on gut issues. Even if most whites didn't have a "scientific" understanding of race, Duke surmised, they were against affirmative action, integrated neighborhoods, school busing, and immigration. They simply needed a "voice" to say in public what they really thought in private.[43] He wanted to be that voice but had difficulty over the next year finding an organizational platform tall enough to enable him to be heard. His first stop was a Populist Party meeting.

David Duke, the Democratic Party Candidate

March 7, 1987. "I've been active for fifteen years," David Duke told a hotel room of Populist Party activists meeting outside Pittsburgh. "This was the largest pro-white demonstration I've ever seen," he said of the three thousand white counterprotesters the day he had been arrested. Duke thought more than just a large demonstration had occurred. "I believe that Forsyth County was the genesis of an entirely new movement." Duke had long exhibited a sixth sense for fresh chances to stir the white protest pot, and he regarded the Forsyth events as an omen of greater events to come. "There are going to be tremendous opportunities to take this country back . . . for the founding majority," he said. "Forsyth County was a tremendous victory."[1]

On these points, Duke proved correct. An insurgency was definitely in the offing. But he had picked an odd venue to announce this latest bit of tea leaf reading. While the Populist Party's founders presumed it would become the vehicle to build a voting bloc, at that moment it was obviously ill prepared to capitalize on any kind of spontaneous mass development. Similarly, Liberty Lobby and *The Spotlight* did not even recognize that something out of the ordinary had occurred in Forsyth County. The tabloid waited until the week of the March meeting to mention it. When *The Spotlight* did finally report on the white counterprotest, it was only to excoriate the supposed "communist" presence at the civil rights march and the arrest of Duke.[2] Not a word about an "entirely new movement." While David Duke was geared up to lead, the Populist Party was not yet ready for him.

After the 1984 election year, the party had been troubled by financial and organizational wrangling. A rapid succession of national chairmen had followed Mississippian Bob Weems's short tenure, adding instability to the money troubles. The alliance between Willis Carto and William Shearer had disintegrated into a faction fight over party funds. Carto claimed that the Populist Party owed Liberty Lobby $289,326.19 for expenses incurred during the party's formation and abortive presidential campaign.[3] Shearer, who controlled the party's nominal national office, didn't want to pay Carto's bill. He claimed that Liberty Lobby's expenses were not the Populist Party's concern.

The Shearer faction brought several significant assets into this fight. With its roots in the American Independent Party, it had demonstrated a stronger record of running candidates for office. For a time, Shearer's faction also controlled most (but not all) party activists in California and the upper Midwest as well as the putative national officers. Shearer did not control a publication as widely circulated as *The Spotlight*, however, and could not sustain a national organization without Carto's support.

One leader then loyal to Carto demonstrated a remarkable self-consciousness about the party's prospects: "The '84 effort had no follow-up, as ineffective chairmen and then a nasty public feud between the original founders of the Party and the unpopular but shrewd Bill Shearer sapped much of the remaining energy that had been created," he wrote in the party's newsletter.[4]

After a break occurred, Carto followed a three-track strategy to rebuild a party without Shearer's faction. First, Carto loyalists started seceding from Shearer's outfit state by state. Where that wasn't possible, as in California and Wisconsin, Carto established parallel state operations. Next, he convened a meeting of loyalists to sign documents formally acknowledging the party's financial debt to Liberty Lobby.[5] Carto's third track led him, once again, to search for a mainstream public figure to front for less reputable but more ideologically dependable activists.

All three tracks converged at this March 1987 meeting outside Pittsburgh.[6] While most of the 150 attendees came from Pennsylvania, a smattering of others "represented" twenty-six states, giving the event a national veneer.[7] From the podium Carto pushed through his agenda. He moved adoption of the original Populist Party platform, which he had written with Bob Weems. It passed unanimously. Gathering steam, Carto read the new bylaws to the crowd. They cheered when the office of "parliamentarian" (Shearer's old post) was abolished. Then they passed the bylaws unanimously by voice vote—despite complaints from the back of the room that what was being read (no printed copies were available) couldn't be heard. Brooking no opposition, Carto then nominated Tom McIntyre for chairman. McIntyre's credentials consisted of a 1986 run for Congress in which he won 5 to 9 percent of the vote "in some precincts."[8] There were no other nominations, and the forty-seven-year-old electrician from the Pittsburgh area was elected unanimously. Still standing impatiently at the front, Carto then nominated the vice chair and the secretary. They also were elected unanimously. His control complete, Carto stepped aside and let the new secretary nominate a new treasurer.[9]

Carto's loyal assistant, *Spotlight* reporter Michael Piper, gave a state-by-state assessment of the party. Pennsylvania had the strongest state organization. The South, Piper noted, wasn't the stronghold that had been expected. Sturdy organizations existed only in North Carolina and Georgia. The state of Florida required 150,000 petition signatures to get ballot status, so the Populists didn't even try to run as a third party there. When Piper asked the crowd how many had ever worked on an electoral campaign, only one-third of the conventioneers raised their hands. Even fewer, about thirty, had ever directed a campaign, and only twenty had ever been candidates.[10]

For want of any other obvious avenue toward renewal, the party's hopes rested heavily with its banquet speaker, the former congressman George Hansen, a hard-core conservative Republican from southern Idaho. Hansen had won a seat in the House of Representatives in 1964, the year Senator Goldwater lost the presidential election. Hansen prevailed in six subsequent congressional elections but lost two bids for the Senate.[11] While in Congress he became known for opposing taxes and the Internal Revenue Service. In 1984 he was convicted of violating recently passed congressional ethics laws. He was initially sentenced to five to fifteen months in jail.[12] Hansen was so popular, however, that while his case was on appeal, he won the Republican nomination for Congress and lost the general election by only 170 votes out of 200,000 cast. He went to jail for six months in 1986 but was later exonerated.[13]

George Hansen had a long-standing connection with Willis Carto and the Liberty Lobby. As noted earlier, he had spoken in 1981 at the event celebrating *The Spotlight*, which published numerous articles supporting him while he was in prison. His wife, Connie, had returned the favor, signing a fund-raising letter for Liberty Lobby.[14] After he was paroled, *The Spotlight* published a laudatory interview with him as a three-part series.[15] At the same time, Liberty Lobby's tabloid and the Populist Party's newsletter began promoting him as a potential candidate for president in 1988. It reasoned that Hansen would fill its most pressing need, a magnetic leader with broad appeal.[16]

Hansen's speech at the Populist meeting in Pennsylvania that March was remarkable mainly for his open display of friendship with Willis Carto. He turned to Carto several times, referring to him with a familiar

"Willis" and seemed to be pleased with the crowd. He blasted the predictable targets: the IRS, the Justice Department, and other federal agencies. At the end a planned demonstration took the floor, complete with HANSEN FOR PRESIDENT placards.[17]

While finding, courting, and using mainstream figures typified Carto's approach to party building, Hansen had no intention of becoming the Populist Party's candidate for president in 1988. But he didn't want to seem like an ingrate either. So he told the cheering convention that he would allow himself to be its stand-in candidate until someone else more suitable was found. Hansen eventually turned down the Populist Party's entreaties altogether and developed his own Christian patriot road show, focusing on tax protest and the IRS instead.

With the Populist Party still fixated on making Hansen its candidate, David Duke went to an Atlanta suburb (rather than his hometown in Louisiana) and announced a campaign for the Democratic Party primaries still seven months away. For the occasion, on June 8, he secured a meeting hall at the Marriott Hotel. Before the event actually started, attorney Sam Dickson strolled by in earnest conversation with Don Black, both dressed handsomely in dark suits.[18] Outside the room's double-doors two thickset biker Klan goons stood guard under the direction of Frank Shirley, a less physically imposing member of Duke's National Association for the Advancement of White People. Shirley buzzed with energy. He had helped instigate the white riot in Forsyth and strutted like a north Georgia rooster that night—full of authority and command. Not quite mainstream material. Shirley and the bodyguards were joined by assorted grand dragons and their less augustly titled brethren from Florida, Alabama, the Carolinas, and Georgia. A crowd of a hundred took their seats.[19]

After the doors closed, Jim Yarborough arrived. Tall, balding, and bland, Yarborough was from the same generation as Willis Carto and lived in Gainesville, Georgia, just a fifteen-minute jump down the roadway from Forsyth County. Yarborough was then national vice chairman of the Populist Party, the latest in a series of posts he held whenever Carto controlled the party's apparatus. That night he was Carto's eyes and ears in Georgia, assessing Duke's future prospects. Forsyth County was still on everyone's mind, and Duke had not yet plea-bargained his charges from the second march. The new energy (and money) created by these battles, it was presumed, could launch Duke's presidential campaign. Yarborough said he would give Carto a good report, although Duke announced a run in the Democratic primaries and not (yet) as a

Populist.[20] Inside the room Duke gave an updated and sanitized version of his old standard Klan stemwinder. The crowd loved it.

But if Duke's campaign was to be any different from his bids as a Klansman for the Louisiana state senate in 1975 and 1979, he needed more than the attention of a few grand dragons in an Atlanta hotel. His first task was to be noticed outside the movement's immediate circles. Carto and Liberty Lobby obviously thought Duke's notoriety would get him the necessary publicity. Then money and votes would follow. "The establishment media won't be able to resist talking about Duke's former Klan connections," *The Spotlight* gloated. "It will guarantee automatic publicity for his campaign."[21] That estimate might have been right, but it wasn't.

Duke had long practiced the art of racist ambulance chasing. Like a shyster attorney soliciting for clients at fires and traffic accidents, he sought out every racial conflict from busing in Boston to immigration on California's southern border. He would show up with just a few troops but often capture local media interest nonetheless. And he would walk away with new recruits and their money. His recent foray into Forsyth County, for example, had projected him to the front of a large racist demonstration and flushed his pockets with dollars for a defense fund. Not bad for a couple of days' work.

He decided to follow the same path with the Democratic Party. That meant chasing after the Reverend Jesse Jackson, who was running a genuine campaign through the primaries. Duke figured he could seek out an altercation, and a war of words would make him a contender among anti-Jackson Democrats. Two decades before, Jackson had emerged as a Southern Christian Leadership Conference lieutenant, followed by years as a Chicago-based civil rights figure. Jackson had transformed presidential politics in 1984, however, with a credible run in the Democratic Party's primaries. Although that first campaign had been marred by Jackson's alliance with Louis Farrakhan's Nation of Islam as well as his infamous reference to New York City as "Hymietown," Jackson had mobilized some of the party's most liberal constituencies. By the time Duke announced, Jackson was the most visible black leader in the country.

Duke thought he smelled money and votes in a confrontation with Jackson. Running in the Democratic Party as Wallace did in 1972 offers tremendous advantages for "us," Duke explained. The candidacy of Jesse Jackson gives "us" an opportunity unparalleled in recent American politics, he told followers.[22]

He conjured up the specter of Jesse Jackson at every available opportunity, whether it was a speech to a small group in Georgia or to tens of thousands of direct-mail recipients. When Jackson announced his own candidacy in North Carolina, for example, Duke rushed to the spot. He and a small band of protesters raised picket signs in hopes of finding a cooperating television camera. "I have news for Jesse Jackson," Duke proclaimed, "the people who founded this country are no longer going to stand idly by while we lose our rights and heritage."[23] Only Duke's followers heard the pitch. The general media, for once, did not tune into his megaphone.

Duke also tried to gain entry to the Democratic Party's public debates. But the national committee chair, Paul Kirk, instructed state party chairmen to freeze him out of public forums.[24] And when Democrats debated publicly in Houston, Duke was forced to sue to try to gain a place at the table. The suit failed, and so did the anti-Jackson gambit. Boxed out of regular Democratic Party functions, Duke took a step back and leaned heavily on his existing networks, in the process preparing himself for the explosion of support that would come later.

If David Duke's plans to turn the Democratic Party into a racist launch pad fizzled, Willis Carto's Populist Party could not even find a fuse. A Labor Day weekend event in St. Louis was supposed to be a national convention. Only one hundred Populist diehards dragged into a hotel near the airport, however, fewer than had gone to the meeting in Pittsburgh six months before.[25] Far less attended than the Nashville convention in 1984, when six hundred enthusiastic souls had cheered the ill-fated candidacy of Bob Richards. Three years of party building had produced a net loss of five hundred conventioneers—not an auspicious start for the 1988 elections. If this rate of decline continued, the party would disappear completely in less than a decade.

In contrast with the anemic showing in St. Louis, 275 Klan types marched vigorously through Stone Mountain, Georgia, that same September weekend. They staged a nighttime cross burning, attended by another hundred souls. Two of the speakers that night were Frank Shirley and Ed Fields, both of whom had listened favorably to Duke's announcement speech the previous June. The two missed the Populist meet in St. Louis, however. Cross burnings apparently excited them in ways that stuffing envelopes and walking precincts never could.[26]

At the so-called convention, the new chairman, Tom McIntyre, tried to pep up the crowd, but he succeeded only in reminding everyone how much it depended on *The Spotlight* and Liberty Lobby. "There would be no patriotic movement in America today without him," McIntyre said while introducing Carto to the platform. Carto, in turn, gave a long-winded introduction to Bob Weems, the former Klansman with the windmill delivery. Weems understood populism better than anyone else,

Carto averred. At the very instant Carto finished a relatively august introduction, Weems jumped up, mumbled something about going to the "little boys' room" and ran off to the restroom. Instead of Tom Watson and William Jennings Bryan, Carto and Weems seemed more like Laurel and Hardy.[27]

Weems returned to the convention only slightly embarrassed and rehashed the basic themes of his 1984 speech in Arkansas: populism was the unique philosophy of white American nationalism, different from all variants of conservatism, libertarianism, and liberalism and opposed to internationalism and Zionism. Another Mount Nebo figure, the former American Nazi Party captain Ralph Forbes, also spoke. Forbes's campaigns for a county board in 1985 and the Republican Party primary for Arkansas lieutenant governor in 1986 practically made him a veteran candidate. Keith Shive was also back. The Farmers Liberation Army chief cum Kansas state party chairman also had a turn at the platform, reminding everyone about the "Jew families" that owned the Federal Reserve. Any of the attendees caught napping in their seats could have recited the litany in their sleep.[28]

The party's finances were equally squalid. Through the end of July, it had raised $41,749.82 and spent around $31,700. There were local Rotary Clubs with bigger budgets than this so-called national third party. The "convention" officially nominated George Hansen, contingent on his final acceptance. (Hansen was not present.) Carto prepared the body for a rejection by Hansen and passed a resolution that empowered the executive committee to choose another presidential and vice presidential nominee if Hansen ultimately turned down the party's overtures, as he did.[29]

While this charade was acted out in the hotel's forum room, the one candidate who would have accepted the Populist endorsement, David Duke, sat in the bar, making small talk with flight attendants. He was waiting his turn to address the meeting, but it never came. Duke may have been the buzz among the delegates, but Carto wasn't quite ready to put him back on the program.[30] Duke would have done better to campaign that weekend at the Stone Mountain cross burning.

Nevertheless, a string of events reinforced Duke's conclusion that a new mass insurgency was in the offing. Throughout 1987 whites continued to mobilize after Forsyth County. Klan activity and related violence occurred in twenty-six Georgia counties, and in several of those counties cross burning and rallies occurred on multiple occasions.[31] Georgia aside, the first features of this embryonic insurgency were its seemingly spontaneous development, its relative autonomy from established hard-core cadre formations, and the involvement of a new generation of youths born in the years after desegregation became law. And it was national in scope.

Just weeks before the first Forsyth riot, young whites had chased three black men through the streets of Howard Beach in New York City. One of the three, Michael Griffith, was hit by a passing car and killed. Most noticeably, when civil rights advocates marched in protest through the Howard Beach neighborhood, they were met by more than one hundred jeering whites. That June in Chicago's Marquette Park neighborhood, more than a thousand curious young (white) people listened politely at a Klan rally, then turned into a violent mob of five hundred to attack a small anti-Klan picket across the street. But the young and the racist were not simply blue collar or on the streets in that period. University campuses were hit by one incident after another: racist graffiti at Smith College; assaults on Mexican-American students at a California community college; two masked white students' attack on a black student at the University of Texas; formation of the Great White Brotherhood of the Iron Fist at the University of Chicago; and more.[32] In addition, racist squads known as skinheads began to spontaneously emerge, often with violent consequences. (They became increasingly important in the years following.) Despite the Populist Party's poor showing that weekend, David Duke was correct: something was happening.

Not everyone agreed with Duke's diagnosis. The *National Review* columnist Joe Sobran, for example, commenting on the Howard Beach violence, concluded that racism "has no definition" and was "liberal billingsgate."[33] The Reagan administration also took a dim view of claims that Forsyth County signaled a turn for the worse. A spokesman for the Justice Department's Community Relations Service told the House of Representatives that "enclaves such as Howard Beach . . . or Forsyth County" are not "a reflection of a rising tide of racism."[34] This view was reinforced by the Civil Rights Division head William Bradford Reynolds, who claimed that the Forsyth riot was merely "a small band of bystanders whose childish prattle" should have gone unnoticed.[35]

Future events proved Duke right. Even if the Populist Party demonstrated little ability to take immediate advantage of the new opportunities, the steam coming out of white Middle Americans would find (or create) organizational vessels for itself. During the years to come white supremacist groups were to influence a growing sphere of the populace. And the events of 1987 marked a nodal point in the development of their movement. As the mainstreamers' wing was poised to plump up with growth, federal prosecutors were squeezing the vanguardists. Indeed, at the very moment the Reagan administration was pooh-poohing events in Georgia, it was pursuing the most significant government action against the white supremacist movement since World War Two.

16

Crackdown and Indictment at Fort Smith

November 6, 1987. Louis Beam lay flat on the ground in the American tourist district of Lake Chapala, Mexico, a large-caliber pistol pointed into his left ear. The groceries and his seven-year-old daughter were still in the car. While he stayed inert, Beam's twenty-year-old wife, Sheila, scurried around indoors, looking for safety in the two-story house. A second unidentified man in a T-shirt toting a shotgun was inside, coming up the stairs after her.

"Come here," he demanded, threatening her with his raised shotgun.

Half hidden by the wall, Sheila pulled her own heavy Beretta pistol from behind her skirt. She fired three times down the staircase, hitting the intruder each time. Then she turned to run but was grazed on the leg by a bullet. Bleeding, she dashed from one room to the next, firing shots out the upstairs windows. In response, a five-minute fusillade peppered her house.

In the heavy night air outside, car lights shone on men dashing around, setting up a siege. Watching the men, Sheila finally figured her assailants were law enforcement officers, not criminals. She surrendered to a joint task force of Mexican *federales* and American FBI agents.[1]

That was only the beginning of the ordeal. Sheila was taken to Guadalajara, where she was interrogated before being sent to the women's prison in Puerto Agrande.[2] "On the eighth day," Sheila swore later, "officials suddenly came to me and told me that the charges of intentionally wounding a Federal Police Officer and possession of a weapon" had been dropped. She was processed and returned to her family in Santa Fe, Texas.

Louis Ray Beam had been on the FBI's most wanted list for six months. A poster described him as "armed and extremely dangerous."[3]

After months of searching, the FBI had finally traced him through friends in Texas to a Mexican mail drop.[4] To win the cooperation of Mexican authorities, Beam claimed later, the FBI had told the federales he was a drug pusher. In any case, the arrest didn't meet American legal standards, subsequently complicating the juridical use of evidence the agents had seized.

Years later Beam told and retold the tale of his arrest in Mexico, reveling in his fourth wife Sheila's brave shoot-out. There were several ways he might have told the story. He could have described her as an Aryan warrioress, something like the female guerrillas who populated William Pierce's futuristic fantasy novel *The Turner Diaries*. Those tough women equaled men in every capacity except decision making. Beam instead chose a more accessible nationalist myth, that of a brave white woman facing native savages on the frontier. "My wife did nothing that no American pioneer woman did not do for her husband when the Indians came," he said. "[She is] a true, red-blooded American lass."[5] Her release from the Puerto Agrande jail had been "a miracle" by Yahweh, he said.

Beam himself was not released. From Chapala, he was taken in shackles to the Guadalajara airport, flown to Nuevo Laredo and then on to an Arkansas county jail.[6] His days as the underground resistance's commander in chief appeared to be over. Louis Beam had gone into hiding knowing that he would be indicted for plotting to overthrow the United States government. Now he would go to trial with other named coconspirators. With his capture the Justice Department closed the penultimate chapter of its multiyear crackdown on white supremacist bank robbers, killers, and bomb plotters. The finale would be an epic trial of multiple defendants charged with seditious conspiracy.

The attempt to squelch these violent vanguardists began just months after government officials realized the full import of the accomplishments of Robert Mathews's Order gang, and the path to this point had passed through a number of federal and state prosecutions. It needs to be noted that the Reagan administration's Justice Department was unprepared for the task. It had previously demonstrated little interest in federal prosecutions of attacks by white supremacists on black people and other ordinary civilians, preferring to leave such cases to state courts and county attorneys. Where these local channels were unresponsive, lawsuits pursued by nongovernmental organizations became the primary avenue for legal redress.[7]

However, once white supremacists started killing law enforcement officials and robbing banks in 1983 and 1984, Attorney General Meese and the FBI took a more aggressive federal posture. The FBI planted more confidential informants inside white supremacist groups, started tapping phones, and made arrests in a number of incipient criminal conspiracies. The Justice Department coordinated several prosecutions over a multiyear period, in a program dubbed Operation Clean Sweep. After the FBI broke the back of The Order and arrested James Ellison's CSA crew, the Justice Department succeeded in securing racketeering (RICO) convictions in Seattle and Arkansas courtrooms by the end of 1985. Also that year, the FBI stopped a plot to kill a government informant, sending the Aryan Nations' security chief off to prison. Another Aryan Nations grouplet was apprehended after bombing the rectory of a local Coeur d'Alene priest, and then bombing the Coeur d'Alene federal building and two local businesses in September 1986.

In Nevada, federal agents arrested Posse Comitatus founder William Potter Gale and his coconspirators from the Committee of the States in 1986. They were convicted of plotting to attack the Internal Revenue Service, which continued the antitax and promilitia bent of his previous Posse activity. Gale was convicted a year later and then died quietly from emphysema while awaiting an appeal. In a similar case in December 1986, the FBI arrested eight members of the Arizona Patriots on gun and conspiracy charges, including plans to rob banks to finance their activities. And in the troubled state of North Carolina, the U.S. attorney issued an arrest warrant for Glenn Miller, after the former leader of the White Patriot Party jumped bail on other charges. Miller made a half-suicidal "Declaration of War" before being captured on April 30, 1987, at a hideout near Springfield, Missouri. He then quickly decided to turn state's evidence.

The next to the last event in the federal campaign took place in Denver, just weeks after Louis Beam's capture in Mexico. Federal prosecutors charged four Order members with violating the civil rights of radio talker Alan Berg by murdering him. The defendants were already serving long sentences for Seattle racketeering convictions when they went to trial before Judge Richard Matsch, a law and order Republican appointed by President Richard Nixon.[8] The mixed verdict did not bode well for the seditious conspiracy trial pending in Arkansas: two convicted, two acquitted.

This coordinated multistate crackdown ended in Fort Smith, a sleepy federal court district in the northwestern corner of Arkansas, just across the state line from eastern Oklahoma. After a yearlong grand jury investigation, the Justice Department announced on April 21, 1987, a sweeping set of charges: interstate transport of stolen money, conspiracy to manufacture illegal weapons, conspiracy to murder federal officials, and seditious conspiracy—that is, conspiracy to "overthrow, put down and to destroy by force the government of the United States and form a new Aryan nation," according to the federal documents. Ten men were indicted on charges of seditious conspiracy. Four others were named for conspiracy to murder a federal judge. (One was indicted on both sets of charges.) A total of fourteen men were accused.

In court documents, the federals asserted that a plan to overthrow the government had been agreed upon at a meeting in July 1983 and then put into action. It listed 119 overt acts, including the robberies, bombing, counterfeiting, and murders committed by The Order as "furtherance of the [seditious] conspiracy" headed by Robert Miles, Richard Butler, Louis Beam, and an unindicted coconspirator, James Ellison.[9] The heart of the case was directed against Miles, Butler, and Beam. The others charged were secondary players whose alleged crimes simply lent credence to the charges against these three principals.

If the federals intended to close down the vanguardist wing of the movement with this case, several escape holes existed from the very beginning. While Robert Miles and Louis Beam played a direct role in creating a clandestine submovement, as discussed earlier, other men had had a hand in the process as well. Most significantly, William Pierce, the ideological godfather of this trend, was left untouched by any prosecution—state or federal. And Tom Metzger, who had emerged as the spokesman for the street warrior set, remained free from any charges. As the repression of those most closely associated with The Order, the CSA, and Aryan Nations continued, the large reservoir of remaining activists began moving over into other organizations.

There is evidence that the Justice Department understood this weakness in its larger effort to stifle the vanguardists. An early FBI affidavit contended: "Despite the convictions of . . . members of the racketeering enterprise known as THE ORDER [it] continues to exist and is being led by [Robert] MILES, [Richard] Butler, [Tom] Metzger, [William] Pierce, [and Glenn] Miller."[10] Although they correctly named Glenn Miller, William Pierce, and Tom Metzger, the statement betrayed the prosecutors' failure to understand how the underground groups operated. The pending seditious conspiracy case rested on the notion that the various violent white supremacist gangs simply continued The Order, once led by Robert Mathews.

But in fact the group known as The Order had stopped operating after the arrest and imprisonment of its original members. Only its mythos lived on in movement minds.

.   .   .

Go back to 1982 and 1983, when Robert Miles and Louis Beam first articulated a strategy for creating a secretive underground. They argued for two complementary organizational forms: leaderless resistance and a weblike structure of clandestine cells. Beam had signed his name to the leaderless resistance manifesto in 1983. Clandestine groups should be small, he wrote, without any direct organizational contact with any other cells. These unconnected cells would follow common leadership with a common ideology, rather than a specific group of individual commanders. In a slightly different mode, Miles had argued that clandestine warriors should be completely separated from public activities, which he labeled "theater." As discussed earlier, Miles prescribed an underground without a single leadership but "horizontally" constructed through a series of interconnected cells operating like a web.

FBI documents, by contrast, conceptualized the Aryan underground as a pyramid, a more traditional vertical organizational model for clandestine structures. In this construct, a person or persons at the top commanded the troops at the bottom through a series of vertically connected links. The FBI theory was understandable, given that Robert Mathews tended to operate The Order like a pyramid in which he gave all the instructions.[11] But the violent underground as a whole functioned more like the web prescribed by Miles and Beam. Because of this difference between the FBI's concept and the way events actually transpired, the prosecution failed to understand the essential roles played by each of its central defendants—Richard Butler, Louis Beam, and Robert Miles—and thus could not satisfactorily explain them to a jury.

Several problems also existed with the legal case itself. Many of the overt acts cited were the same crimes for which twenty-two of The Order's warriors had already been convicted in 1985. At that trial in Seattle, the Justice Department had contended that these robberies, etc., were part of a racketeering enterprise—that is, a business that engaged in organized crime. Now at Fort Smith the same crimes were considered instead part of a plan to overthrow the government. And five of those charged with seditious conspiracy were already serving long sentences for racketeering. Several of the defendants believed the government charged them twice for the same set of crimes. Technically, no double jeopardy existed, since the charges in Fort Smith were different from those prosecuted in Seattle. But to potential jury members, it might look as if government prosecutors were overreaching. The most vulnerable spot in the prosecutorial edifice, however, was the charge of seditious conspiracy itself.

. . .

According to the United States criminal code, a seditious conspiracy occurs when two or more people plan or "conspire" to overthrow or destroy the government by force. Other clauses prohibit levying war against the government or hindering the execution of its laws.[12] A key element is "force." To violate this anticonspiracy law, however, no overt acts, such as killing a judge and robbing a bank, need actually be taken. It is necessary only to make an agreement or cook up a plot specific enough from which an overt act can ensue. Although the statute claims to distinguish between seditious conspiracy violations on one side and activities protected by the First Amendment on the other, the thin line has tended to disappear during the course of American history.

During World War One about two thousand cases were filed under a complex of laws designed to limit wartime dissent.[13] A Sedition Act passed in 1918 criminalized virtually any criticism of the government, according to the respected legal encyclopedia *American Jurisprudence*.[14] These laws were aimed specifically at those who opposed the war and were enforced against labor radicals and socialists of various stripes. Today it would seem natural that these same activities would be protected by the First Amendment, even if the Sedition Law had not been repealed in 1921.[15] And the attorney general acknowledged the unjust character of these prosecutions in 1924.[16]

World War Two engendered questionable prosecutions based on the antiseditious conspiracy law passed in 1940 and known as the Smith Act.[17] As originally written and enforced, the Smith Act was as broadly constructed as its 1918 antecedent. It criminalized "teaching" or "advocating" the overthrow of the U.S. government and didn't require even the intimation of an overt act for a conviction. In 1942 its first victims were leaders of a communist splinter group opposed to the official Communist Party.[18] That same year the Justice Department charged a group of Nazi sympathizers and isolationists.

The latter indictment generated intense opposition from isolationists, racists, and anti-Semites in Congress and was dismissed by the court. John Rankin, a segregationist congressman from Mississippi who later opposed the GI Bill of Rights because it would assist black veterans returning from World War Two,[19] was a typical opponent. Rankin read the indictment into the *Congressional Record* and concluded:

> Mr. Speaker, I hesitate to use the word Jew in any speech in this House for whenever I do a little group of Communistic Jews howl to high heaven. They seem to think it is all right for them to abuse gentiles and

to stir up race trouble but when you refer to one of them they cry "anti-Semitism," or accuse you of being pro-Nazi.

Read this indictment and then read it again and ask yourself if the white gentiles of this country have any rights left that the Department of Justice is bound to respect.[20]

This indictment was dropped, and a second set of charges was thrown out by the courts in 1943. Finally, in January 1944, thirty people were charged under the Smith Act; twenty-eight went to trial in *United States v. McWilliams*. Those indicted included most (but not all) of the leadership of the prewar far right. Among them were the leader of a uniformed group known as the Silver Shirts, William Dudley Pelley; a fundamentalist minister from Kansas, Reverend Gerald Winrod; a Harvard-educated former Diplomatic Service employee, Lawrence Dennis; and a German American Bund minif%uhrer, August Klapprott (a somewhat dignified bunch, none apparently attracted to the far right because of economic distress).

The trial itself was a drawn-out ferocious affair, beginning with a monthlong fight over jury selection. The prosecution introduced volumes of evidence confirming the defendants' Naziesque sympathies and beliefs, but little evidence of direct collaboration with Germany or Italy once the war started. The defendants challenged the prosecution at every turn, sometimes transforming the courtroom into a circus of contempt and calumny. But the evidence was never fully adjudicated. The trial ended abruptly after eight months, in November 1944, when the judge suddenly died.[21]

The Roosevelt and then the Truman administrations let the case drop, and there were no other sedition-related charges brought against the far right until Fort Smith. Nevertheless, the aborted trial effectively sprayed the Silver Shirts and Bund with the smell of treason. It also blunted the effective menace of America first–style isolationism for almost forty-five years.

After World War Two, the Cold War and McCarthyite fevers sent federal prosecutors after the far left. Twelve leaders of the Communist Party were indicted under the Smith Act in 1948. Remember that the Smith Act outlawed teaching and advocacy but did not require even the beginnings of a plot to overthrow the government. Little evidence was needed of any overt acts. Most of the prosecutor's case rested on a recitation of communist doctrine. Eleven were convicted.

In 1951 a majority of the Supreme Court declared these convictions constitutional, although Justice William O. Douglas's dissent remains instructive: "The vice of treating speech as the equivalent of overt acts of a treasonable or seditious character is emphasized by a concurring opinion . . . The doctrine of conspiracy has served divers and oppressive purposes and in its broad reaches can be made to do great evil. But never until today has anyone seriously thought that the ancient law of conspiracy could constitutionally be used to turn speech into seditious conduct. Yet that is precisely what is suggested."[22]

Despite Douglas's warning, 160 communists were indicted under the Smith Act, and most were convicted. The Supreme Court voided several of these convictions on technical grounds after McCarthyite temperatures cooled. Eventually the Smith Act went into judicial mothballs.[23]

Instead of the Smith Act, federal prosecutors began using a statute against seditious conspiracy descended from the Civil War era, Title 18 Section 2384. After Puerto Rican nationalist and *independista* Lolita Lebrón and three of her comrades fired pistols into a 1954 session of Congress, Lebrón and seventeen other Puerto Ricans were indicted under Section 2384.[24] They were quickly convicted. That case, *United States v. Lebrón*, became the legal model used by Reagan administration officials in several cases during the 1980s.

Two of those cases were against Puerto Rican independistas deemed soldiers in the Fuerzas Armadas de Liberación National (FALN). They were charged with 120 bombings between 1973 and 1983 and seditious conspiracy, and sixteen of the seventeen defendants were found guilty.[25] A third case was prosecuted against a mostly white group of anti-imperialists calling themselves the United Freedom Front. They were charged with ten bank robberies and fifteen bombings of targets they believed supported the apartheid regime in South Africa. One black member of the group pleaded guilty. One white woman was convicted in a separate trial. The remaining six whites were either acquitted or had their sedition charges dismissed, although most all were sentenced to long terms on racketeering and other more distinctly criminal charges.[26]

At Fort Smith the requisite memorandum filed by prosecutors prior to trial cited the statutes used against Lolita Lebrón in 1955 as the legal basis for their current case. "In this instance we anticipate that the government's case will precisely parallel these prior prosecutions," the U.S. attorney wrote. They argued that they would need to introduce evidence of the defendants' beliefs because "these cases recognize that there is a strong ideological element to any seditious conspiracy. Typically, the defendants in a sedition prosecution are driven to desperate, violent acts by violently held political convictions."[27]

At the broadest nonideological level, Robert Miles, Richard Butler, and Louis Beam had expressed no more loyalty to the U.S. government than had Lolita Lebrón. By the Aryans' account, the government administered a multiracial state and that multiracial state was anathema to their white nation. Miles and the others had long called it a Zionist Occupied Government. Butler's most overused phrase was that his "race was his nation." Beam had many times declared his intention to spill blood in a new war against the state. But Lebrón's loyalty had been to the independent island nation of Puerto Rico, which had been seized by the United States military in its war with Spain in 1898. The white nation of Aryan imagination, on the other hand, was dredged out of a past filled with slavery and genocide.[28] Distinctions such as these did not have the power of law in federal court, however. When the U.S. attorney began his case in Fort Smith, American courts had a history of convicting dozens of Puerto Ricans and communists for seditious conspiracy, but not one white supremacist or Nazi.

Before the Trial Begins

February 16, 1988. On Saturday, two days before the seditious conspiracy trial began, two hundred men and a few women paraded through downtown Fort Smith. They carried homemade signs. FREE AMERICA, FREE SPEECH, FREE MILES BUTLER & BEAM, typified the placards. CITIZENS AGAINST SEDITION LAWS and SEDITION LAWS ARE UNCONSTITUTIONAL made the same point. The usual Klan robes, swastika armbands and Hitler paraphernalia had been left at home. A half dozen Klansmen wore white power T-shirts under their jackets, however, and a skinhead crew from Dallas didn't completely conform to the Middle American dress code. At the front, five men marched with a twenty-five-foot banner reading REPEAL THE ANTI—FREE SPEECH SEDITION LAW. A hammer and sickle logo was pictured on one side of the slogan, and a Star of David on the other side, a set of symbols designed to show that Jews and communists were behind the charges against the Aryans. Thom Robb in suit and tie dominated the speakers' platform. After taking over the leadership of the Knights of the Ku Klux Klan, Robb had adopted Aryan Nations' call for creating a Northwest Aryan Republic. However, while one of his lieutenants, Kim Badynski, moved from Illinois to Washington State, Robb and the rest of his klaverns stayed safely tucked away in the South and Midwest. As the trial neared, Robb had made it appear as if he would be Richard Butler's successor. Robb focused his remarks that day on the First Amendment rights of the three principal defendants. Betty Butler and Dorothy Miles, the defendants' wives, stood stoically nearby while six stern men with plywood shields guarded them. Only Badynski didn't understand the theater being staged. He made his speech while wearing a white construction hard hat with a clear plastic drop-down visor.[1]

Curious local residents watched silently from the sidelines, but none stood up to denounce the white supremacist display. That had not been the case during fifteen rallies Robb's Knights of the Ku Klux Klan held in the squares of towns within the orbit of Fort Smith's potential jury pool during January 1988, the month before the trial began.[2]

The judicial district of this federal court encompassed most of northwestern Arkansas. Within these counties, Gordon Kahl's final firefight had taken place, and the Covenant, the Sword and the Arm of the Lord had launched its final battles. Bob Weems had made that Populist Party speech in a state park. Except for an artists' colony in Eureka Springs and the university at Fayetteville, the region's towns and villages were culturally conservative and fervently fundamentalist Christian. An unreconstructed passion play was still being produced on an outdoor stage each summer.[3] While 10 percent of the city of Fort Smith's seventy thousand inhabitants were black, the surrounding counties in the district were virtually all white. Robb's traveling Klan show had been ill received, however.

At Ozark, a town of twenty-five hundred, white Arkansans had visibly opposed the Klan. "At rally time . . . the pickup trucks rolled in fully loaded with rowdy Ozarkians ready to stomp," complained one Klansman.[4] The local anti-Klanners shouted down Robb's attempt to give a speech and forced his outfit to pack up and leave. In nearby Alma a different crowd also gave the Klan a hard time. Here local white Christian ministers led the opposition. "A large group of Judeo-Christians equipped with crude placards and led by wild eyed ministers," the same Klansman moaned, "again tried to shout down the sound system."[5]

At that point, it had been decades since white supremacists mounted a public defense campaign prior to trial. Nothing had been done to influence the potential jury pool before the Seattle racketeering trial. And during all the crackdown cases afterward, nobody had lifted a finger to win sympathy for the defendants prior to trial. Although his tactics were limited by his organizational imagination, Robb pioneered a trail used again later when a man named Randy Weaver faced charges.

Nine months prior to the demonstrations, when the indictments were first issued, Robb had tried to make himself the voice of free speech. "The government is attempting to silence those individuals who disagree with the government-supported policies of homosexuality, race-mixing, secular humanism, abortion and Zionism," he said. "Surely you can see that Pastor Miles and Butler were not indicted for an illegal act or a violent crime, but were indicted because the government wanted to silence" them.[6]

He had also published a Klan tabloid devoted to a defense of Butler, Beam, and Miles. "There have been some people who have committed illegal acts or violent crimes that were also associated with the Christian Identity Movement, Aryan Nations or Ku Klux Klan," he wrote. "Is it really fair to condemn all the members of the above because of the actions of a few?" he asked.[7]

Throughout this campaign, Robb distinguished between the three Aryan generals and their codefendants, the blood-splattered soldiers, who were already serving long jail terms. On this point, as well as many others, Tom Metzger from California emerged as a counterpoint to Thom Robb's narrowly constructed free speech defense. Metzger had traveled beyond Duke's Klan and electioneering to ever more provocative forms of activism. He had used the technological know-how he had garnered in his occupation as a television repairman to pioneer the movement's use of community access cable television in the mid-1980s, and one of his first guests was a soon-to-be member of The Order, Frank Silva.[8] Along with Louis Beam, Metzger had been one of the first to use computer bulletin boards—several years before the Internet became a mass phenomenon.[9] And he published a tabloid five or six times a year, amplifying his voice across the country. During that last pretrial rally in Fort Smith, Metzger marched with a white armband reading REMEMBER WHIDBEY ISLAND over his dark suit. By invoking the site of Order founder Robert Mathews's fiery death, Metzger asked that the protesters support all the defendants at the trial—even those Robb considered bad apples. "I went not just for the three, but for all prisoners who are loyal to their race," Metzger explained. "I was taken aside by conservative right wing Thom Robb and told I could speak, but not for the other prisoners." Metzger concluded that Robb and others were "trojan horses" and unprincipled "mailing list milkers," eager only to raise funds. He decided not to speak from the platform at all rather than muzzle his support for the other defendants.[10]

The conflict between Robb and Metzger spilled over into a meeting. The featured speaker was Ed Fields, the Atlanta-area publisher who had reveled in the chaos in Forsyth County the year before. If these men could be convicted for speaking out against the admittedly powerful influence organized Jewry held over the government, he claimed, well, then just about any free man could be charged with sedition.[11]

In the dispute over how many of the defendants to support, Fields had already aligned himself with Robb and against Metzger. Fields claimed The Order "had no official connection with any legitimate Right Wing organization" and drew a line between Mathews's bandits and the

movement as a whole. "No legitimate Patriotic Christian group con-
dones any of the action taken by The Order. The conspiracy here is on
the part of the Justice Dept. to overtly FRAME three innocent men by
putting them on trial with the 'bad apples,'" Fields had written in his
tabloid.[12]

During the trial Fields even testified for the defense that he initially
thought that Robert Mathews was a government agent sent to disrupt
his movement.[13]

Fields was simply rewriting his own history. Just three years before,
he had issued a special tabloid edition memorializing Bob Mathews with
bold headlines: "His Legend Had Just Begun." At that time Fields lion-
ized Mathews. He published a favorable summary of Mathews's movement career, reprinted his last testament in full, interviewed his widow,
Debbie, and declared the "public idolized Bob Mathews." Now Fields
acted as if he had never written any of that.[14]

Like Fields, Robb tried to have it both ways. "Some thought that by
my limiting myself to defense of Pastor Butler, Pastor Miles, and Louis
Beam I was condemning the men of The Order," Robb wrote. "We had
long disagreed with the methods of The Order, but have never condemned the spirit, the zeal or will of those men and the courage they
displayed." If he wanted to inherit Butler's spot at the top of Aryan Nations, Robb had to reconcile his short-term trial strategy with the avant-
garde's larger objectives. He tried: "I have always defended The Order
members even though I have been equally critical of their method."[15]

In contrast to Fields and Robb's double-talk, Tom Metzger's single-
minded militance that day attracted skinhead marchers from Texas,
Oklahoma, and Minnesota as well as several of Robb's own top state
dragons. In addition to a shared contempt for Robb's market-driven
opportunism, they all despised the market itself. Metzger was the vanguardists' vanguardist, ensconced in his own sectarian principles, which
he treated with religious-like devotion. He was certain that the conservative white Arkansans who would form the jury pool would similarly
follow their religious convictions—into the government's arms.

"Why did the vermin feds hide this trial in Ft. Smith where the jury
will undoubtedly be made up of Bible-beating Falwell types who tend to
believe every statement that comes from the mouth of ZOG," Metzger
asked, "why not L.A., San Francisco or other cities where people are
more prone to be suspicious?"[16]

In this rift over pretrial public strategy, Robert Miles and Richard
Butler took a slightly different tack, directed more to their own followers than the broader public. They weren't the only ones going to trial,
they argued. The entire movement was. A "concerted, orchestrated pro-

gram of intentional criminal harassment of the white racial movements" was afoot, Butler warned. If the prosecution succeeded, he worried, "it will leave us barren and naked before the enemy. The rebuilding process will be long and painful."[17]

Robert Miles extended the impact of impending events beyond his own movement to the entire right wing: from conservatives such as the Reverend Pat Robertson, who supported Israel, to dissidents opposed to immigration and gun control. "If we lose, the so-called rightwing will be lost as far as its effectiveness is concerned . . . Let the kosher rightwing understand that all of its rhetoric about the Constitution and the laws, will avail them nothing once we who are their spearhead are broken."[18] More than Butler or Pierce, Miles consciously projected his own sub-cult as the narrow vanguard of a much broader right wing.

Miles's wife, Dorothy, reached even further. If the government succeeded in convicting her husband at Fort Smith, then all government opposition of every kind would be lost. "If the right wing loses this fight, then all Americans will have lost too," she wrote in a fund-raising letter. It seemed a hyperbolic claim, but she'd seen the force imperiling her movement at work before. "The left has already been stilled, either by incarceration, financially breaking them or even by adopting some of their stands."[19] She feared white nationalists would be silenced through a similar combination of incarceration and co-optation.

At the same time, Butler and Miles mixed bravado in with their fears about the future. "Does ZOG realize how truly honorable it is in times like these to be charged with sedition," the Aryans asked. They talked as if each were a Nathan Hale on the way to the British gallows, rather than two retired engineers whose blueprints for racial chaos had finally been taken seriously by the cops. "The pleasure of making the trial scene, giving opening and closing arguments to a jury that we have helped to choose . . . cross-examining ZOG's perjured witnesses," they wrote, ". . . all of this appeals to us."[20]

They did not know then what they learned later: how much would turn in fact on those alleged "perjured witnesses."

Seditious Conspiracy Goes to Trial

February 16, 1988. The courtroom was medium size, better suited for prosecuting interstate car theft rings than far-reaching conspiracies to overthrow the federal government. The narrow elevator to the third floor chamber seemed to reinforce feelings of routine inconsequence. Across the street from the federal courthouse, a statue commemorating Confederate Civil War veterans stood on the Sebastian County courthouse grounds as an icon of a remembered past. An American flag flew nearby. Erected during the early years of the twentieth century by the Daughters of the Confederacy, similar statues grace the landscape at county courthouses across the Old South. In 1861, after state troops had seized Fort Smith's armory, Arkansas had seceded from the United States.[1]

Presiding U.S. District Judge Morris Arnold seemed intent on keeping dramatic flourishes to a minimum and the judicial calendar unclogged. Thirty reporters from across the country recorded the trial's opening moments, but after the first week it became simply a local story with a wire service feed. The judge picked the jury with less care than he might have chosen apples at a grocery. Dispensing with any meaningful voir dire, he questioned the ninety-eight jury prospects himself. The defense's preemptory challenges removed the half dozen black people in the pool. In less than one day an all-white jury was chosen to decide the first seditious conspiracy case against self-avowed racists since World War Two. Ten men and two women, representing a thin slice of blue-collar life, sat in rows on the judge's right-hand side.[2]

The prosecution's table was commanded by veteran adversaries of the movement's violent vanguard. Assistant U.S. Attorney Steven Snyder had managed this case from the first grand jury witnesses. Snyder was backed by Jack Knox, the FBI agent who had investigated white supremacists since the Gordon Kahl shoot-out in 1983. An additional special consulting attorney was shipped in from Washington, D.C. And when the occasion demanded it, U.S. Attorney Mike Fitzhugh made a guest appearance. Prosecutors planned to call two hundred witnesses, introduce twelve hundred pieces of evidence, and overwhelm the defense during a trial they expected to take three months. The judge soon cut those numbers in half.[3]

The defense team sat in U-shapes around their tables; fourteen defendants crowded in with their attorneys. Fourteen federal marshals stood nearby. One by one the accused faced their judge and jury.

Robert Miles was their natural leader. He managed to maintain an august presence despite the obvious wear endured by his sixty-two-year-old body since being indicted. The government's case placed him at the center of the conspiracy as a whole. His loyal wife, Dorothy, who had survived his six-year imprisonment in the 1970s with the fortitude of a soldier's wife, sat behind the gate with other visitors each day. N. C. Deday LaRene, Miles's quick-witted attorney from Detroit, dominated the courtroom floor and quickly became the defense team's commanding figure.

Richard Butler, at age seventy and with a history of heart trouble, looked even more worn than Miles. Like Miles, Butler stayed with his prim wife, Betty, in rented rooms not far from the courthouse. After escaping prosecution in every other Order-related criminal proceeding, he now faced the most serious charges of his racist career. His main street Idaho attorney, Everett Hoffmeister, focused on proving that the aging Aryan was more a spiritual leader to his congregants than a warrior himself. Would a Catholic priest be indicted if one of his parishioners had bombed an abortion clinic? Hoffmeister asked.[4]

Unlike Miles and Butler, who were free on bail, Louis Beam was brought from the jail to the courthouse in chains each day. Of the three most prominent figures charged with leading the seditious conspiracy, he was the only one to speak on his own behalf and question witnesses. Dressed in a dapper business suit, Beam seemed most conscious of the drama in progress: homeboy with the jury, deferential to the judge, and suspicious of prosecution witnesses. He acted at times like William Wallace of Scotland defying the king of England. At other points he adopted the chivalrous pose of Robert E. Lee surrendering his sword. Beam was flanked by his two attorneys, one court-appointed and the other his friend from Texas Kirk Lyons.

Lyons was just over thirty years old at the time, and his still-boyish face was incongruous with the gravity of the proceedings. Before the Fort Smith trial, Lyons was a small-time lawyer in a Houston personal injury firm. But Beam's stamp of approval and his role at Fort Smith enabled him to quickly enter the movement's most inner circles.

Lyons's exact relationship to Beam remains a mystery. He gave reporters two different stories about how he first met the Texas Klansman. In 1988 Lyons told the *Southwest Times Record* (Fort Smith) that he had met Beam in December 1985, when two men in fedoras and trench coats unexpectedly knocked on his apartment door in Houston and took him outside to meet Louis Beam in the backseat of a car. In this *Godfather*-like scene, Beam reportedly told Lyons that he expected to be arrested shortly and asked Lyons to arrange bail. Lyons told the *Record* he only recognized Beam that night from a chance meeting the two had had at a Houston gun show in 1980.[5]

Lyons told a different story to *The News & Observer* (Raleigh) in 1992, claiming their first encounter had been in the Hofbrau Restaurant in Houston. Lyons and his buddies were drinking and singing German songs. Beam and his party began singing "The Star-Spangled Banner" in response.[6]

Whatever the actual circumstances of that initial meeting, Lyons had leaped into action after Beam was arrested in Mexico. He quit his Houston job, and despite making little contribution on the courtroom floor, he sat at the defense table every day. At night he often drove across the state line to Oklahoma and slept at Robert Millar's Elohim City encampment, beginning a long and fateful friendship there. And as we shall discover, Lyons popped up during several key events in the future.[7]

Alongside "Generals" Beam, Butler, and Miles, a second group of defendants included those who were supposedly "soldiers" in this seditious army. These defendants were being tried a second time (and in some cases a third time) for the same Order-related crimes on which they had already been convicted in the racketeering trial. Although not technically considered double jeopardy, because the Fort Smith charges were different from those in Seattle, their complaints of double-dipping obviously resonated with the jury.

At the Seattle racketeering trial in 1985 Bruce Carroll Pierce appeared at first to have spent his life helping customers at the local hardware store and taking the kids camping on the weekend instead of soldiering for The Order. Twenty-eight months later in Fort Smith, he seemed weary and defeated, an ordinary man turned killer, then turned again into a permanent prisoner.[8]

Three years of prison had visibly aged David Lane. His sandy hair had turned gray, his sidearm had been traded for a pair of reading glasses, his six-and-a-half-foot frame was drawn and thinned. Once a Klansman, he had been central to The Order and he was already serving long prison sentences.[9] Richard Scutari was testament to the ever-changing definition of "whiteness" in the late twentieth century. His dark features, medium build, and elaborate tattoos were more suggestive of a Mediterranean pirate than a Teutonic knight. (The Scutari district of Istanbul is not in Europe but in Asia.) The Klan in the 1920s had marched down Pennsylvania Avenue to keep his kind of visage offshore. Of all those indicted for racketeering, Scutari avoided arrest the longest. He wasn't captured until March 1986, long after the Seattle trial had ended. The federals didn't want to go to the expense and trouble of putting him on trial alone, so they convinced him to plead guilty to racketeering by promising not to indict his wife, Michelle, and put his children in foster homes. His gallantry came to naught, however, and his wife filed for divorce and testified against him at Fort Smith.[10] Andrew Barnhill, like Scutari, had come into the movement through the guns and survivalism circuit. He was recruited into The Order at the age of twenty-six and was already serving a forty-year sentence when marched to the Fort Smith courthouse in chains.[11]

Ardie McBrearty was the last of The Order soldiers added to the indictment. McBrearty had been in court against the IRS since the 1970s. Clever and amiable, he could have been a successful town square attorney, eating breakfast in a diner every morning and chatting with the same crowd of farmers, office clerks, and shopkeepers for forty years. Instead, he had joined the Posse Comitatus and wound up giving stress analyzer tests for The Order and setting up its phone communications system. Now, at age sixty, he was already serving a forty-year sentence and facing another jury.[12]

The most tenuously connected to any conspiracy was Robert Smalley, a small-time Fort Smith gun dealer who had been convicted in Seattle of racketeering and sentenced to five years. Adding Smalley, a local firearms dealer, to this sedition case only troubled the prosecution and added to the perception that small-fry "soldiers" like him were unfairly facing double jeopardy.[13]

A third set of defendants had little direct dealings with Bob Mathews's Order but had been party to the acts swirling around the Covenant, the Sword and the Arm of the Lord. They were charged with conspiracy to kill federal officials and various related weapons violations. Presumably, prosecutors reasoned that lumping together the seditious conspiracy case with the conspiracy to murder case would save money and time, since the major witnesses were the same for both sets of charges. As events turned out, however, combining these two prosecutions turned these supposed crimes into an unwieldy hybrid of charges. Economy of scale doesn't always increase the profit margin.

Prosecutors contended the murder conspiracy was hatched in December 1983 to avenge the death of Gordon Kahl. Bill Wade and his thirty-year-old son, Ray Wade, were native Arkansans, farmers like Kahl who believed the government was in Satanic hands. Bill Wade had owned the concrete-walled cabin in which another couple, the Ginters, had harbored Kahl. The Wades believed the cops had set fire to their cabin to cover up this badly bungled operation. They had asked for a grand jury investigation of the whole affair. When that failed, they filed a pro se lawsuit, seeking compensation for damages to their property. That too died on the vine. Meanwhile, the Ginters, who had rented the cabin from the Wades and harbored Kahl, were brought to trial before H. Franklin Waters, a federal judge in Fort Smith. The Ginters were convicted on harboring charges. And it was this Judge Waters who was the supposed object of the murder plot. In this conspiracy charge, Bill Wade and Ray Wade were joined by Lambert Miller, a former member of the CSA; David McGuire, who had once been married to the CSA chief Ellison's daughter; and Richard Wayne Snell.[14]

Snell stood out from the other defendants on several counts. He was the only one indicted for both conspiracy to murder and seditious conspiracy. And he was already on death row for the 1983 murder of a Texarkana, Arkansas, pawnshop owner. He was also serving a life sentence for the 1984 murder of a black state trooper. At Fort Smith, the fifty-seven-year-old looked like a walking stack of ashes. His wife, Mary, stayed with Bob and Dorothy Miles in a rented duplex and attended the trial every day, just as she dutifully published his prison newsletter, *The Last Call Bulletin*. The events in this Fort Smith courtroom were an empty formality for Snell. For federal prosecutors the trial was to go from bad to worse.[15]

Assistant U.S. Attorney Steven Snyder opened the prosecution's case with a dizzying ninety-minute recitation. He detailed the founding of the Covenant, the Sword and the Arm of the Lord on the Arkansas border in 1981, the formation of The Order in 1983, the fall of both in 1985, and every crime in between. Weapons were collected, bombs set off, banks robbed, murders committed, and moneys distributed. But Snyder talked little about the connection between this crime spree and an actual seditious conspiracy. Instead, he practically pinned his entire case on a late-night gathering in July 1983 at the Aryan Nations camp. It was at that moment, he argued, the conspiracy was hatched. At this meeting Robert Miles, Louis Beam, and Richard Butler, among others, had made plans for the violent overthrow of the government. The logical conclusion of Snyder's opening remarks placed the prosecution in a precarious position. If the evidence didn't support his argument about the July 1983 meeting, then there was no conspiracy.[16]

The defendants' opening statements varied with their current status before the courts. Those already convicted of crimes in other courts assailed the credibility of government witnesses. Those not already so convicted added a defense of free speech to the argument. The most stunning opening was Louis Beam's, delivered as if he were once more on the stump before a crowd of potential Klan sympathizers.

"The only reason I'm here is because I said what I think," Louis Beam said as he rose from the crowded defense table. "If the Constitution is still alive, I'm innocent."

He discussed the evidence that would be presented against him and told the jury which witnesses he would call in his own defense. He talked about his early Klan membership and his relationships with the other defendants and painted himself as an idealist who had disappointed his mother. (And who in the jury box hadn't disappointed their mothers at one time or another?) "Junior, quit this and get a good job," Beam said his mother told him repeatedly. Beam claimed he sacrificed financial success as a computer consultant for his political and religious beliefs. He admitted setting up movement computer bulletin boards in Idaho, Houston, Dallas, North Carolina, Chicago, and Little Rock but denied they were used for secret communications.

If the conspiracy was supposedly set at Butler's home, as the government alleged, Beam told the jury, then he missed it. He must have been changing his daughter's diaper, and he called the government's case the "baby diaper conspiracy." In fact, the discussion around Butler's kitchen table was "just a coffee break," he told the jury, and the 1983 Aryan Nations meeting "just like a hundred others I've been to."[17]

Beam ended with a speech he had given to dozens of audiences: how he had come home from Vietnam to find antiwar demonstrators burning an American flag. In fact, it was taken almost verbatim from his booklet *Essays of a Klansman*:

> As I sat there watching the flag disintegrate, rage and bitterness began to engulf me—the flames consuming the flag changed to flames enveloping an armored personnel carrier in the Hobo Woods north of Saigon. The cheers of the demonstrators became screams of a nineteen year old soldier over his radio as he burned to death, trapped inside what was fast becoming his coffin. The clapping of hands as the flag fell to the ground,

became the deafening roar of my M-60 machine gun as I literally melted the barrel in an attempt to pin down the enemy long enough for the dying soldier's friends to reach him. Finally, at last, came the laughter of those demonstrators as they spit on the ashes at their feet, blending in my mind with the sobs of grown men as I remembered the armored personnel carrier disappearing in a ball of orange flame.[18]

The courtroom was spellbound by Beam's soft Texas accent and Vietnam stories. The wave of empathy from the jury was palpable. They were teary-eyed and visibly exhausted.[19] How could they convict this genuine American war hero of sedition? He was no dark-skinned, curly-haired Puerto Rican bomber.

The prosecution's case disintegrated from there. Of the forty-eight pieces of evidence seized when Beam had been arrested in Mexico, for example, the judge allowed only two, citing the gross disregard by the arresting officers for American constitutional protections. One piece he did allow was Beam's *Bruder Schweigen* medallion, the one worn by Order members. To win this seditious conspiracy trial, however, Assistant U.S. Attorney Snyder needed to do more than simply reprosecute The Order.[20]

Snyder paraded a string of broken white supremacists before the jury to present evidence, just as prosecutors had done at the Seattle RICO trial. This witness had procured illegal weapons; another described bank robberies and counterfeiting; a third told of taking secret oaths and making plans to divvy up the country between "civil administrators." A defendant's former wife testified she had helped edit a "declaration of war," written by Bob Mathews.

One of the weakest government witnesses was Glenn Miller. The formerly ferocious chief of the White Patriot Party claimed to have given up his hatreds and become a born-again Christian. He whimpered and crawled before the jury, displaying malice toward none but cynicism toward all. Miller's testimony was a particularly bitter moment for Robert Miles, who had touted the retired army sergeant as the next best thing after Hitler's storm trooper boss Ernst Röhm. During a brighter, whiter moment Miles had written of Miller: "Good-looking straight Aryan men, rank on rank, file on file, legion on legion, stand behind him because they trust him, because they have faith in him, and because he has never betrayed either their trust or their faith."[21]

If Miller disappointed his former Aryan comrades, he didn't do the government's case any good either. According to another prosecution witness, for example, Miller had been assigned control of the Southeast region of the United States by the conspiracy's supposed "civil administrators." But instead of confirming the testimony of that other witness, Miller contradicted it. When a defense attorney asked Miller about being an "administrator," he denied any knowledge of it.[22] Rather than risk a lengthy redirect, prosecutors pulled Miller off the witness stand before he had warmed up the seat.[23]

Glenn Miller was simply unconvincing. James Ellison, the paramilitary preacher with two wives and a cultful of followers at the Covenant, the Sword and the Arm, drowned the government's case in a sea of absurdity. The prosecution needed Ellison to testify that the numerous criminal acts were tied together in a single conspiracy. Otherwise its case consisted mainly of "speech" (protected by the First Amendment). Because of his past role at the center of events, he was the one government witness who might have proved its case. Assistant U.S. Attorney Snyder spent two days with Ellison, plodding through evidence in each of the indictment's four counts. On the plot to kill federal officials in Arkansas, Ellison said he had the names, dates, and places because he was there, conspiring along with the rest at every step. On the government's most important count, seditious conspiracy, he claimed the plot to overthrow the government had been launched at private leadership meetings held during the Aryan Nations congress in the summer of 1983.

From the very beginning defense attorneys destabilized the prosecution's presentation. Deday LaRene objected to Snyder's opening questions five times in the first ten minutes, throwing both the assistant U.S. attorney and his witness off-balance. To the evident dissatisfaction of the judge, an hour into his testimony Ellison was still talking about events in 1982, long before the conspiracies at issue were supposedly hatched. Snyder also incurred the judge's reproach by attempting to use Ellison's testimony as a vehicle to reintroduce emotion-laden Nazi lingo and swastikas, a tactic the judge had deemed prejudicial and proscribed during the trial's first witnesses. "I am not going to allow any more evidence in about Nazi flags and swastikas," the judge declared. "You have run that into the ground."[24]

Further, Snyder often elicited testimony from Ellison on specific events without establishing to which count or defendant the evidence was pertinent. If Snyder had succeeded in bundling all the incidents together into one undifferentiated incriminating mass, then stronger pieces of evidence could have helped carry the prosecution's weakest claims. But this attempted bundling failed after it was challenged by the entire defense team, from the least literate pro se defendant to the most masterful, Deday LaRene.

In a moment that exemplified the prosecution's ineptness, Snyder attempted to introduce an unflattering videotape of Louis Beam by having Ellison testify that the tape was a complete reproduction of Beam's speech at the 1983 Aryan Nations congress. After approximately a half hour of courtroom viewing, however, it was clear that the tape was not complete. It was a double whammy: not only did the judge disallow it as evidence, but Ellison's prior testimony that the tape was complete proved to be one more instance in which he clearly did not tell the truth.[25]

Only when Ellison rattled on effortlessly about weapons—the differences between bolt-action rifles and fully automatic assault weapons or how his troops standardized their ammunition caliber—was he convincing and transparently truthful.[26]

Snyder presented the heart of the government's case in a series of questions about the seditious conspiracy itself, agreements at private meetings to form a coordinated national leadership and launch military operations. Ellison mapped out the plot's parameters: The four central figures were supposed to be Robert Miles, Richard Butler, Louis Beam, and himself. The commander in chief was Robert Miles, who Ellison said oversaw the "general operation" and was constantly urging others to rob banks in order to accumulate necessary funds. Richard Butler was in charge of the Northwest (a demotion, it should be noted, from Butler's media-mythic role as Aryan Nations' national leader). Louis Beam, in this scenario, was to run the Southwest territory and oversee the national conspiracy's computer operations. And by his own account, Ellison's job was to train the soldiers, raise funds, and oversee Arkansas.[27]

As proof of the seditious agreement, Ellison offered the flimsiest of evidence. At one evening side caucus, he said, he had passed a sheet of paper around the room for everyone to sign. "When the paper came back to me, after making the complete circuit, I took the paper and I read off each name. And I looked at each man and I said, I hope you realize that by being present in this meeting and by signing this paper that you are guilty of conspiracy and treason against this government. And I said your presence here and your willingness to participate in this meeting makes you guilty, so therefore, you better be serious about what you are doing."[28]

Defense cross-examination quickly homed in on Ellison's recollections of these agreements and meetings. How many meetings were there, Mr. Ellison? In your grand jury testimony you said there were two meetings. Now you are telling the jury about three meetings. Which one is it? Eager to catch him in this obvious discrepancy, each defendant and his attorney tried to trip up Ellison on this issue. Finally the judge tired of the questions and said he had heard enough about the number of meetings.

Then the defense challenged Ellison's characterization of the meetings. In direct testimony Ellison described one private meeting as a "young leadership" gathering. But on cross-examination he was forced to admit there was nothing youthful about several of the participants. Was John Ross Taylor at this meeting? defendant David Lane asked. Yes, Ellison answered. And how old was Taylor? In his seventies, Ellison replied.[29]

The jury could not help noticing that Ellison's testimony eroded piece by self-contradictory piece. He was forced to confess that he had decided to become a government witness after being denied parole. He also admitted that he wanted favorable treatment for himself and his family. "The jury's tax money is going to go to provide for the support of your two wives as part of this deal?" one defense attorney asked rhetorically.[30]

After two days of cross-examination the defense had whittled Ellison's expansive claims down to the self-interested nub of a lying, thieving sociopath. The sharpest cuts were delivered by Louis Beam in one quick set of questions.

Beam asked Ellison to describe his coronation as King of the Ozarks.

"I didn't know that it happened," Ellison answered.

"There was no ceremony where oil was poured over your head and you were declared James of the Ozarks?" Beam asked again.

"I believe that you're confusing an anointing with oil with a coronation."

"Okay. Well, then describe to the jury the anointing."

"On one occasion at CSA when Robert Millar and a number of his people were present and a number of people, some of the defendants, were present, Robert Millar did anoint me as James of the Ozarks, or King of the Ozarks," Ellison replied.[31]

After Louis Beam's questions finished revealing James Ellison's obviously fanciful pretensions, it was hard to believe anything he said about seditious agreements or anything else.

The defense's weakest spot was Bruce Carroll Pierce. When he was first arrested, Pierce had told FBI officials that The Order had distributed hundreds of thousands of dollars in robbery proceeds. Among the recipients he named, some were now his codefendants. His statement could have potentially linked Miles, Butler, and Beam directly to The Order and made the idea of a conspiracy much more plausible.[32]

When the U.S. attorney tried to introduce the statement as evidence, Pierce naturally wanted it suppressed. He claimed it was given under duress. The FBI, he said, had threatened to arrest his wife, Julie, and send their children to foster homes unless he cooperated. Pierce's spirits sank when Judge Arnold said he would probably accept the statement as evidence.

Ashamed at his own collaboration with the government, Pierce then attempted to plead guilty. Admission of guilt by any one defendant would have harmed the case of all, however, and the judge wouldn't immediately accept his plea. It was at that moment that Robert Miles's sage leadership made a difference. Miles forgave Pierce whatever statements he had previously made and helped dissuade him from giving up. Miles had no ill will toward Pierce for his momentary weakness. "What Bruce did in order to save his own wife and children was understandable," Miles wrote later. "None blamed him for trying . . . He does not deserve any criticism. He deserves our support and comradeship."[33]

Pierce then withdrew his guilty plea. Judge Arnold ultimately decided the statement was inadmissible because it was not a spontaneous confession. The judge's decision severely hurt the prosecution, one of several blows the government's case received during the proceedings. Before the defense even called their first witness, the judge dismissed the charges against the former Fort Smith gun dealer Robert Smalley. At that point, every observer knew the prosecution could sink.[34]

The defense case was short. It was summed up by Louis Beam, whose closing statement argued that he and the others were protected by First Amendment freedoms. Once again he invoked history, albeit badly: "In McCarthy's case, they called it communism and said they were trained to infiltrate the government. They're calling us Nazis and saying we attempted to overthrow the government."[35]

After seven weeks of trial and more than seven hundred thousand dollars in expenses the case went to the jury.[36] In three days the verdict came back: not guilty, all defendants on all counts.

After the trial Robert Miles and Richard Butler held an impromptu press conference on the courthouse steps. The trial had been about freedom of speech, they argued. The verdict had proved that the First Amendment was still alive.

Then they walked across the street to the Sebastian County courthouse grounds and celebrated at the foot of the Confederate war memorial. Kirk Lyons raised a Confederate battle flag on the courthouse pole as the Aryans mixed with the assembled television cameras and print reporters. "This flag, this statue, represent the ideals that I believe in," Beam told a Fort Smith reporter.[37] The irony went unremarked. The last of the prosecutions in the feds' extended multiyear crackdown lay in dust.

It is a basic law of Newton: for every climax there is an anticlimax. James Ellison served the balance of a much-reduced sentence for racketeering and eventually resettled at the Elohim City compound in Oklahoma. Wayne Snell went back to death row in Texarkana. Andrew Barnhill, Ardie McBrearty, Richard Scutari, and David Lane were taken back into the bowels of the federal penitentiary system for long terms. Lane may have walked out of the courtroom in chains, but he still regarded himself as a modern-day Viking warrior. During the next ten years his fourteen-word motto, "We must secure the existence of our people and a future for White children," was adopted by skinheads in Europe and North America. He became more important to the movement as an imprisoned martyr than he ever was as a Klansman on the street in Denver. He died in prison at age sixty-nine in 2007.[38]

Ray Wade, Bill Wade, and Lambert Miller left the trial and tried to put their lives back together. Juror Carolyn Slater returned to her job as an inspector at the local Whirlpool factory. But she couldn't forget defendant David McGuire. Almost as soon as she had slipped through Judge Arnold's voir dire, Slater had fallen in love with the youngest defendant. During the proceedings, they had exchanged furtive glances and laughed with each other. When he was found innocent, he mouthed the words "thank you" to her. So after the trial Carolyn wrote David a friendly letter and mailed it to his attorney, who forwarded it to him in Indiana. David followed up quickly with a telephone call. Three months later the former defendant and the former juror were living together. They married and settled down, not far from the courthouse.[39]

A second juror expressed, after the trial ended, agreement with some of The Order's actions, and a third said that he admired Louis Beam.[40]

Richard Butler returned to northern Idaho, but he never reestablished the supremacy of his twenty-acre camp in the Aryan constellation. Louis Beam began the next stage of his career.

Of all the former defendants, the sage and venerated Robert Miles's fate came to symbolize the meaning of the white supremacist victory in Fort Smith. Miles should have been excited and happy after the verdict, and he did perfunctorily denounce the government and the movement's enemies at the time. But he and his wife, Dorothy, soon began to despair. Why had the movement failed to win more support, Miles wondered, when white people should naturally recognize their racial destiny? The vast majority of white people were still lost in a cesspool of racial mongrelism and Jewish commercialism, he sadly concluded. "America . . . is a land of sheep. They are content to graze, to romp in the grass and to procreate."[41]

He was tired of the vanguardist dilemma. "Can we endure and survive by simply shaking our heads, reading more of our own literature about our foes, and then go on about our lives in the midst of the sewerage?" he asked.

Miles grew increasingly bitter about what appeared to be a hollow victory at Fort Smith. He began to receive letters that recycled old rumors that he had worked for one of the secret services. Few sent any financial support, and he faced paying his attorney's fees alone. Each letter was a bitter pill. He had gone to Fort Smith to fight for the movement, but the movement had disappointed him. "After the trial ended we knew there would be some jealousies and nose out of joint reactions," he wrote. But he wasn't "prepared for the Alice-In-Wonderland reasoning" of his comrades.

Miles retreated into a shell of cynicism. "We fight ofttimes despite the ones on our side, rather than because of them," he decided. Instead of looking forward, he started to spend his time reminiscing about past Klan comrades.[42]

Then, in May 1991, his life was further complicated when he and his daughter, Marian, were subpoenaed for their fingerprints in a North Dakota bomb case. By then he was spending all his time caring for his seriously ill wife, Dorothy. They had always been close and had occasionally signed their newsletters "Fafnir and the Dragon Lady," the only couple in the movement to present themselves to others as such. When Dorothy died of heart failure in May 1992, Bob was at her side. Without her he was completely adrift. "She was my raison d'être," he wrote. "Now no reason, no purpose."[43]

About six weeks later Miles awakened in the middle of the night to investigate a noise outside his house, which was on a remote farmstead. He was hit on the head from behind and hospitalized for two days. Some thought he was the victim of ZOG or its lackeys. Others thought he was silenced before he could spill any secrets. His daughter, Marian, never called the police. "It was not my father's wish at the time, nor is it mine now, to invite the police on our property."[44]

He died on August 16. The rumor circulated that he had been killed, but the actual cause of death was never announced. Instead, daughter Marian asserted that "he loved and missed my mother so much that he didn't wish to remain here without her."[45]

He had already written his own obituary in the form of a birth announcement: "The Movement is dead . . . long live the movement! The movement which we built and saw pass, will live on in other movements yet to be born . . . The old is dead. It has passed with time. It is now for a new wave, a new age, to be born. For those of us who were the leaders from a generation now dying, the hour is late. We can aid in the birth but we must not delay such new birth from happening."[46]

Miles's prediction carried a germ of truth. Although the defendants had won their case in court, the extended crackdown had taken its toll on the vanguardists' wing of the movement. And it would be several years before the squads of bombers regained their footing. Nevertheless, a new surge of white supremacist activism did occur after the trial, and the mass energy evident in Forsyth County flowed into the multiple engines powering the mainstreamers. One of the consequences: a new family-oriented trend became more prevalent among Christian Identity believers, leaving the gun-toting cultists to their jail cells.

Pete Peters's Family-Style Bible Camp for Identity Believers

July 24, 1988. At this summer Bible camp, hundreds of families spent a week taking meals together, studying scripture, listening to live music presentations, and vying good-naturedly in contests of strength and spirit. Teenagers played volleyball, and adult men ran an obstacle course race. Families stayed in cabins or camped in RVs and tents. A special event catered to singles, and several couples were married during one of the nighttime assemblies. More than fifty adults were baptized in a nearby mountain river. A children's choir of sixty performed a special camp song entitled "We Are Israel." This could have been any other Christian gathering at beautiful Camp Cedaredge in the Colorado Rockies, except that the doctrine taught here was the so-called Christian Identity theology favored by a segment of the white supremacist movement that grew after the Fort Smith trial.

Much like the Aryan warriors who had been tried for seditious conspiracy, these campers believed the federal government was occupied by a Satanic force. But this was not a vanguardist gathering. No machine shop manufactured automatic weapons as at the Covenant, the Sword and the Arm of the Lord compound in Arkansas. Paramilitary training most manifestly did *not* cap the week of summertime activities, as it had at Christian-Patriots Defense League survival fests. Camp Cedaredge was not a compound, but a rental facility where like-minded souls enjoyed the company of one another. On the Janus-faced Christian Identity countenance, this was what the mainstreamers looked like. They wore plain street clothes, not white-sheeted uniforms. They had marriages like any others, enrolled in higher education at the same rates as any other group of white people, and enjoyed commensurate income levels. If you didn't grasp the underlying meaning of their heavily coded lingo, the special nature of their cause might escape the nonbeliever.[1]

Peter John Peters presided over this camp. A dark-haired and mustachioed six-footer with close-set eyes, Peters spoke with an angry Middle American accent and cultivated the stern demeanor of a cowboy preacher in western-style suits and boots. Born in 1947 and raised on a ranch in the underpopulated stretches of western Nebraska, Peters harkened back to a time before hippies and civil rights activism. Like many graduates of small high schools on the Great Plains, he was startled to find the state university he attended in Colorado larger than his hometown. He had hoped to become a veterinarian but left the program, he said, because of conflicts with zoology teachers who taught evolution. He finally earned a Bachelor of Science degree from Colorado State University in Fort Collins and worked as a loan administrator for the Farmers Home Administration.[2]

He also graduated from the fundamentalist Church of Christ Bible Training School in Gering, Nebraska, became a pastor in that denomination, and established his LaPorte Church of Christ. Peters's flock was more than just a Sunday morning fellowship in someone's living room. They maintained a modern church building and all the usual trappings of a small but devoted congregation. And when he embraced the Christian Identity doctrine during the early 1980s, Peters brought most of his congregation along with him on the trail from fundamentalism to Identity.

Much of Pete Peters's pastoral success was due to the energetic contributions of his bright-eyed wife, Cheri, a Donna Reed 1950s mom type on the surface with a harder Carrie Nation–style zealotry burning underneath. Like many non-Identity fundamentalists, she insisted that men were endowed with God-given abilities and biblical rights that placed them "at the head" of women.[3] She left most matters outside her family to her husband and devoted herself to raising their two children. At the same time, she participated fully in the life of the church, including the summertime Bible retreat, where she led workshops and acted as husband Pete's camp cohost.

At one of these summer camps Cheri Peters scripted a corny practical joke for a contest to crown a "Woman of Grace" from among the campers. More than sixty-five women answered an extensive questionnaire about their faith and practices. Three finalists then were selected to serve meals to three male judges, apparently to test their skills as homemakers and servants before a nighttime assembly. Just as it appeared the women were all dutifully bound to servant status, they poured water in the men's laps and slopped spaghetti on their clothes.

As the audience roared with laughter, the three women slapped cream pies in the judges' faces in a slapstick routine worthy of any Catskills summer resort.

Despite the comedy of that moment, the nature of a "godly" relationship between husbands and wives was a much-discussed topic at these camps. Several workshops focused on teaching women how to be non-assertive "helpmates," smiling sweetly in Christian obeisance to their husbands. Cheri Peters presented one workshop only for married women on the subject of "intimacies in marriage." It was a subject she often visited. At another summer camp she called a similar workshop "God's Perfect Triangle." It covered "sensitive issues of submission and wisdom in a godly marriage."

Like other fundamentalists who strictly defined gender roles in a patriarchal fashion, Christian Identity believers tried to reinforce a pattern of submission and servitude for women while often relying on the same women for the most important social tasks that bound together the family, clan, or tribe.[4] The result was a contradiction: powerful women with no independently recognized power. No one at the Peterses' Bible camp personified this internal conflict better than Peggy Christiansen, a Montana woman well-known among tax protesters.

She titled her workshop "The Wife Secret Behind Husband's Courage." A large, ruddy-faced woman with a bob, she had the ability to command a crowd that seemed at variance with the demure flower print dress she wore and the Bible she cradled while talking to several dozen women sitting in chairs under a tree. Christiansen told stories about her own audacious adventures, laced with homilies about how she didn't do *one thing* without her husband's permission. Although she spent weeks traveling from one tax protest hot spot to another, she assured the other women that she did not neglect her children. It was her husband, she claimed, who had sent her out into the world because she had a special gift to give. That was the "wife secret." Her husband told her it was okay, so she engaged in everything from making mischief at the United Nations' Year of the Woman meeting in the Houston Astrodome[5] to counseling men to stop paying their taxes to the IRS.

By the reckoning of those around her at Camp Cedaredge, Peggy Christiansen had boldly stood up against a Beast system imposed upon Bible-believing Christians. The Beast would have women standing "at the head" of men, in direct disobedience to God's Law. It wasn't Peggy's husband who demanded submission but God who commanded her to obey his leadership. In this fashion, she added to the guidance that the summer camp provided on how to live.

This was the third Scriptures for America summer camp. The Peters couple provided the motivating force behind these Bible camps, which served as movement-wide gatherings for Identity believers. More than periodic weekend conferences or even regular Sunday morning church services, these weeklong affairs enabled believers to socialize with their brethren and create the interstitial tissue of a social movement. Occasionally personalities such as Kirk Lyons and Louis Beam attended. Even the reclusive Willis Carto showed up one year.[6]

A select group of men, designated as Elders, deliberated over theological issues and conducted ceremonies during the week. They led congregations and churches of their own at home and traveled long distances—from North Carolina, California, Wisconsin, and Arizona—to participate. The end purpose of these summer camps, after all, was to guarantee the spread of a specific variant of their doctrine.

At the 1988 session, Peters presented a "special recognition" plaque to Liberty Lobby's aging secretary, Lois Petersen, who led three workshops during the week. Kirk Lyons lectured on the recent acquittals in the sedition trial. Gordon Kahl's widow, Joan, told her side of the story, five years after the Posse farmer's death in Arkansas. Other workshops covered subjects such as tax protests, gun rights, and the supposed wrongs of the hated Fourteenth Amendment, which had guaranteed citizenship rights to freedmen after the Civil War. The speaker who gave a history lesson on the Reconstruction-era Klan that year requires some additional note, for his biography tells much about the trajectory of the white supremacist movement and the attraction of Christian Identity.

Richard Kelly Hoskins was a mild-mannered and well-educated stockbroker, with a stiff military bearing, punctilious manner, and patrician Olde Virginia accent. He traced ancestors back to 1615 in Virginia and a plantation near the Rappahannock River in the 1780s.[7] Born in 1928, he joined the air force during the Korean War and afterward remained a reservist. He married in 1957 and had six children and multiple grandchildren. He went to New York to learn the investment business and returned home to work for Francis I. du Pont and Co.[8] He later joined the local office of Anderson & Strudwick, Inc., and became a vice president.

His activities spanned more than four decades, all while he "vehemently" denied that he was a white supremacist.[9] In the 1950s he joined a group called The Defenders of State Sovereignty and Individual Liberties and fought under the banner of states' rights against the dismantling of Jim Crow segregation. In a 1959 pamphlet entitled *Our Nordic Race*, he wrote that the entire world was seething with a "line of conflict . . . wherever the protective ring of outposts of our western civilization comes in contact with the now belligerent and aggressive nations of the colored world."[10]

His segregationist activities got him in trouble with the air force reserves, but sympathetic politicians, including Senator Harry Byrd and Senator Willis Robertson, bailed him out.[11] (Willis Robertson was the father of the Reverend Pat Robertson, who became a leader of the Christian Coalition.) Hoskins also joined Wilmot Robertson, Roger Pearson, and other acolytes of Francis Parker Yockey, writing for Willis Carto's *Western Destiny* magazine.[12]

The secular Yockeyite suffered from a bout of alcoholism in the early 1960s.[13] Then, Richard Kelly Hoskins says, "on April 28, 1965, at 4:00 in the afternoon, in the green rocking chair on the front porch," he got religion.[14] "When He saved me all He got was a drunk with a nervous breakdown who couldn't work and who had no money," he recounted. The Jesus who saved Richard Kelly Hoskins wasn't the Jew from Galilee. He was an Aryan, or, to use Hoskins's term from the 1950s, a Nordic. Hoskins became a devotee of Christian Identity.

Hoskins self-published a history of the world entitled *War Cycles, Peace Cycles* in 1985 and developed a readership among Christian patriots of all types. He presented himself like a mainstreamer, while promoting a form of vigilante vanguardism. He had stood up in a Posse Comitatus–style rally in a business suit and fedora and sounded completely rational, while other speakers in overalls and blue jeans advocated a farm strike with guns. And his history of the post–Civil War Klan doubled as a critique of the contemporary Klan and an endorsement of Christian Identity Bible camps.

These multiple lessons struck home. One camper from Texas expressed a typical reaction in a letter: "I honestly can't find the words to express adequately how edifying, educational, how emotionally and spiritually uplifting and how revitalizing and refreshing your camp was."[15] Another from Connecticut wrote, "What I find particularly satisfying is that each camp retreat is unique and not a facsimile of [the] previous year's retreat."[16] Each year more believers attended the camp, and Peters grew increasingly important within his end of the white supremacist movement.

As Peters's following spread beyond the walls of his LaPorte Church of Christ, he held meetings across the country: this month in Virginia, that month in Wisconsin, another visit to southern Illinois, and still another regular stop in either Georgia or Florida. He issued bimonthly newsletters, published tracts on every topic, and distributed Bible lessons and weekly sermons on cassette tapes. Prior to the wonders of the

Internet, his materials were widely and easily available. He bought a regular time slot on almost twenty AM and FM radio stations to broadcast his sermons everywhere from Washington State to Georgia. The cost of the radio time was covered by the free will donations of his listeners in those locales. (Later he developed a satellite television program.) At the core of this nationwide ministry, Peters's Colorado church was growing. During 1988 he acquired new high-end video production equipment and made other technological improvements in his operations. All this was done with the goal of spreading his message.

Like other ideological white supremacists, Peters self-conciously conflated race with nation, believing that those who were not white (and Christian) were "aliens" rather than first-class citizens. Unlike others, however, who drew their reasoning from National Socialist or Dred Scott Americanism sources, Peters justified his beliefs almost entirely by his reading of scripture, and his source of authority was available to anyone in the pews with his or her hands on a Bible. Identity believers contend that understanding the racial identity of the ancient "people Israel" is the key to understanding everything else. In their hands, the Bible is both a history of the Twelve Tribes of Israel and a prophecy for the future of their genetic offspring. As such, Identity theology is rooted in a nineteenth-century phenomenon known as British Israelism.

British Israelism was a creature of the British Empire, a period of unparalleled power for the Anglo-Saxon island. This "ism" retold the story of ancient Israel's division into two kingdoms after King Solomon's reign. In the northern kingdom, then known as Israel, ten of the twelve tribes lost themselves in the customs of the surrounding non-Hebrew peoples. Approximately 150 years before the first Temple fell in 585 BC the northern kingdom was completely conquered by the Assyrians, and the newly subject people were exiled. These ten tribes, the Lost Tribes of lore, then supposedly migrated north and west into Europe, according to this doctrine. The southern kingdom, composed of the tribes of Benjamin and Judah, which had been conquered and carried off to Babylon, returned to the land between the Jordan River and the Mediterranean Sea only to be dispersed also into northern Europe.

This supposed migration was described in one British Israelist publication in a quick paragraph: "When the people of the Northern Kingdom went into Assyrian captivity, they did not remain there. During the subsequent dissolution of the Assyrian power through its involvement in foreign wars, the people of Israel escaped in successive independent waves, leaving the land of their captors when the opportunity came to do so. Under different names (Scutai, Sak-Geloths, Massagetae, Khumri, Cimmerians, Goths, Ostrogoths, Visigoths, etc.) they moved westward into the wilderness, across Asia Minor, then into Europe and eventually into the Scandinavian countries and the British Isles."[17]

From the British Isles and northern Europe it was a quick hop over the Atlantic to North America, and the United States and Great Britain are linked, according to this dogma, by a common biblical prophecy. The blessings of Joseph, the favorite of Jacob's sons, are supposedly national destinies passed through his two sons. Manasseh, a "company of nations," is supposedly the United States. Ephraim is Great Britain. It is their birthright to be the wealthiest, most powerful nations, dominating and colonizing the world by divine right. The white man's burden, it turns out, had been mandated three thousand years before Rudyard Kipling.

"This included territorial expansion and a multitudinous seed," one magazine tract argued. ". . . Now that's the worth of our identity with Israel. It establishes our claim to the great things God said should be Israel's in the latter days . . . It explains why the Anglo-Saxon-Celtic nations have been the only successful colonizers; why they possess the gates of their enemies . . . why the United States occupies the position it does."[18]

In this fashion, British Israelism explained why Britain developed an empire and the United States became a superpower. In short, it was a set of ideas that rationalized power and privilege. The Identity doctrine, by contrast, developed after World War Two, during the period of decolonization and the political emergence of the Third World and the United Nations. Great Britain lost its colonies in Asia and Africa and no longer possessed the gates of its enemies. In the postwar period, white supremacy in the United States was hammered by Supreme Court decisions, a vibrant black freedom movement, and a change in the civic attitude toward civil rights. Wilmot Robertson described this same transformation as the "dispossession" of the white majority. Identity thus became a theology that explained this dispossession (while promising a grand redemption in the future). In this reading of scripture, Aryan Israel's enemies now possess *their* gates. And looming large in this construct is Satan, a metaphysical rival to the Lord and an all-powerful force or personage able to directly sway events on earth.

Who Is Satan?

Satan. Beelzebub. Diablo. In John Milton's *Paradise Lost* he is one of God's angels, who rises in rebellion with one-third of the hosts and loses a great battle on the plains of heaven. Alas, poor Lucifer once vanquished is thrown into hell's grasping pit. Goethe's Mephistopheles must first ask the Lord's permission before tempting Faust with promises beyond comprehension. In the end, Mephisto's realm is not a glowing celestial orb, but the rotting proverbial dungheap of yore. In the Hebrew reading of the Bible it is the people of Israel's own loss of faith—the worship of false gods—that undoes them. Jews do not blame Satan for the ten tribes' adopting Assyrian ways and becoming lost. When Satan appears in the Hebrew Bible, he is a provocateur, making his argument to God but with no direct power on earth. He is a tease, but he is not equal to the Lord and cannot remake God's creation. The devil in the Book of Job, for example, only confirms God's power in the end. If the devil is a second-rate, subordinate character in the Hebrew reading of scripture, he is just the opposite in the hands of Christian Identity. And Peters's Satan is "the Jew."

Where did Peters's Satanic Jew come from? Such a question never entered the deliberations of those, like William Pierce, who did not adhere to any of Identity's concepts. For them, Jews were simply a distinct species, a biological genus forever at war with Aryandom. That was that. For Carto, Jews were (alternatively) an alien virus infecting Western Civilization or engineers of a grand "Zionist conspiracy." It mattered little to Carto where Jews came from, only that they should go back there. Identity believers, on the other hand, had to find the Jew as Satan in the same place they found themselves as Aryan Israelites, the Bible. Without Adolf Hitler's *Mein Kampf* or Francis Parker Yockey's *Imperium* as guides, Identity discovered everything and everyone in its Bible.

Actually, while Identity believers all share the same view of themselves as the progeny of Israel, they remain divided over the exact nature of Satan and the Jews. Within the movement, the different points of view are often referred to as "Two Seed" and "One Seed." Both camps of course seek to explain the modern status of Satan through an explication of his origins in the Bible. Two seeders believe Satan and the Jews are consanguine, whereas one seeders believe that Jews are a "mongrel race" that resulted from interbreeding with other peoples. Both tendencies teach that a supposed enmity between Jews and white people (Christians) started with antagonisms between biblical brothers. Nevertheless, the disagreement within the movement about the nature of a Jewish Satan is real. Two seeders believe that Jews are the descendants of Cain, who murdered Abel; one seeders believe that Jews are descendants of Esau, whose birthright was given to his brother Jacob. For those outside the white supremacist movement, trying to comprehend this part of Christian Identity theology may seem like an unnecessary distraction filled with biblical arcana. Yet Christian Identity as a whole cannot be fully grasped without understanding the difference between naming Cain or Esau as the first embodiment of the Jewish Satan.[19]

This distinction is a central difference among Identity followers. According to one leading preacher, "the doctrine of seedlines enables the believer in Yahweh to build a conceptual vision of all Scripture."[20] Since scripture is the foundation of their worldview, this difference takes on added significance, including practical and tactical consequences. The one seeders are mostly mainstreamers like Peters. The two seed camp is composed primarily (but not exclusively) of vanguardists.

For two seeders, Satan makes his first biblical appearance as the snake in the Garden of Eden. By most non-Identity interpretations, the snake convinces Eve (and, through her, Adam) to disobey God's command and eat from the Tree of Knowledge. For many Christians, this is the moment of original sin. But Identity followers believe the Satan snake encounters Eve and impregnates her. At the same time, Eve is pregnant by Adam. Eve is thus carrying two seeds: Satan's and Adam's. Remember Cain and Abel were considered twins. In this story, Satan's seed produces Cain. And Adam's seed produces Abel. Cain is evil incarnate, the personification of Satan himself. And it is Cain himself whom two seeders regard as the father of the Jews. Satan thus now walks upon the earth in the personhood of the Jews, and it is through their evil deeds that Satan manifests his wickedness. Again, remember the Book of John, where Jesus is talking about the Jews in Chapter 8 Verse 44: "Ye are of your father the devil, and the lusts of your father ye will do. He was a murderer from the beginning, and abode not in truth, because there is no truth in him."[21]

According to this doctrine, Jews are thus genetically predetermined to be the embodiment of Satan on earth, just as white people are to be the children of God. By stressing the story in the Garden, two seeders push the determining moments of racial history back to the beginning of time and the origin of life.

One seeders, on the other hand, believe that both Cain and Abel are sired only by Adam. Peters, for example, contends that although Cain is obviously evil for murdering Abel, the two brothers aren't racial antagonists.[22] Instead, enmity between Jews and (Anglo-Saxon) Christian Israel purportedly derives from the conflict between Jacob and Esau.

According to the Hebrew reading of the Bible, Esau was the oldest son of Isaac and by tradition was to be his father's heir. While Esau is a hunter, his younger brother, Jacob, tends the fields at home. Upon returning home exhausted and hungry from a hunt, Esau implores his brother to feed him. Jacob gives him a bowl of pottage, but only after Esau trades his birthright inheritance for it. Jacob then receives the blessings that were to go to Esau. Jacob later takes the name Israel, or "wrestler with God."[23]

Christian Identity's one seed believers pick up the story at this point and contend that Jacob-Israel became the genetic father of the "Anglo-Saxon-Celtic and kindred peoples." By this same telling, Esau's descendants, also known as Edomites, are supposedly the first incarnation of the Jews. These Edomite-Jews intermarried with non-Aryan tribes, which violated God's Law. And they became a Satanic *force*, even if the *personhood* of Satan didn't reside within them.[24]

According to this one seed story, the Satanic nature of Jews is not derived from the personhood of their supposed father. But it is no less immutable for that. Jews cannot shed their Satanic character by becoming Christians, as the Catholic Inquisition in Spain forced many Jews to do. The one seed doctrine does not include a nonracist version.[25]

Among one seed Identity adherents, the Satanic nature of the Jews is regarded as unchanging and unchangeable and considered biologically derived and racial. One of Pete Peters's acolytes, Charles Weisman, from Minnesota, explicated this problem in great detail, leaving no room for a nonracial view of the Jews to emerge within any Identity camp. He frequently spoke at Peters's Bible camps and wrote the booklet *Who Is Esau-Edom?* to explain his views. According to Weisman, the descendants of Esau and Jacob "were regarded by God as two different nations or racial groups."[26] They acted differently in public, had dissimilar worldviews, and obeyed different moral codes. These differences, he argued, were based not on differing cultures or environment but on genetics. "This contrasting and conflicting ways and thinking between Jews and the white European is not artificial or a result of their environment," Weisman wrote, "but is based on the nature of their physical constitutions."[27]

According to this biological determinist argument, these differences, symbolized in the Bible, are genetic and unchangeable, a sign of God's hatred of the Jews.[28] "God's hatred of Edom is not a temporary thing but is perpetual," Weisman says of the Jews.[29] Accordingly, Christian Identity believers conclude that Jews have a "hereditary hatred" for Christians and white people.[30]

Although Pete Peters and Charles Weisman reject being identified with Hitlerism, Identity theology rings with many of the same themes as Hitler's secular anti-Semitism. In *Mein Kampf*, Jews were painted as the source of both capitalism and communism; they allegedly provoked international war to destroy Aryans and parasitically sucked the life from others' culture. Weisman located the same nonsense in his Bible.[31]

Man Before Adam and White Weakness

Despite the seeming omnipotence of Satan in Christian Identity doctrine, Pete Peters did not cede to the Jews total power over the white race's sorry condition. Rather, he believed Jews prevailed because white people had failed to obey God's Law. "God has told His people they must obey that Law or suffer the curses that come from disobeying it," Peters wrote. Once again mixing biological determinism with religious mythology, he concluded: "This is a genetic reality, i.e. the curses of disobeying God's Law follow His people wherever they go, from generation to generation. One of those curses involves alien people, that is, people of races other than the Israel people (today we use the term minorities rather than aliens) rising above and oppressing God's people."[32]

In Identity parlance, strangers and aliens are scriptural terms for people who aren't considered white Israelites. Peters and others use biblical language to transform religious differences between the ancient Hebrews and other tribes into racial-national differences between peoples today. These racial-national differences are then supposedly codified by God into mandates to maintain strict racial segregation.

If failing to obey God's Laws was the sin for Identity believers, according to this doctrine, then *Brown v. Topeka Board of Education* desegregation was the punishment. Peters argued that black mayors and elected officials were just one example of "aliens rising above and oppressing" whites. Interracial marriage was another, considered one of the most heinous of crimes.[33]

In this construct, people of color are not simply members of a racial nation distinct from the white Israelites. Interracial marriage is not regarded as something akin to an Italian's marrying a Swede, deciding to have children, and live in Switzerland. Interracial sex is thought to be more like a form of bestiality, because black people are not considered human in the same way white people are. They are regarded as descendants of man before Adam, the pre-Adamites. Again, the Book of Genesis is marshaled to establish the origins of different peoples and their supposed genetic traits. Unlike the Jews, who represent the agency of Satan, in this construct nonwhite peoples are considered part of God's creation. But they are formed *before* God makes the first white man, Adam, on the sixth day.

Having determined the origin of black people in God's creation among the beasts before Adam, Peters still fixes the blame for white people's condition on their own misdeeds. It should be noted that this assertion that white people are responsible for their own racial misery challenges the liberal assumption that scapegoating and prejudice, rather than a cosmology or worldview, motivate individuals in the white supremacist movement. In this instance, Identity believers cite their own failure to live up to God's Law as the cause for their "dispossessed" status.

"Illegal aliens, reverse discrimination, economic hardships, devastating taxes and rejection of Bible Law in America is a precise repeat of the Bible history," Peters wrote. He claimed that "a historical cycle" had repeated itself since biblical times. Whites supposedly enjoyed peace and prosperity until they forgot their God, turned from his Laws, and were punished. To end their supposed suffering and dispossession and be redeemed, these Aryan Israelites must simply obey God's Law, as Pete Peters understood it. First they must establish their own white Christian nation-state free of "aliens" and "strangers." (Repealing the Fourteenth Amendment would be a start.)

They also needed to end sinful practices, such as abortion. As noted earlier, women must return to their position two steps behind men. And women and men must no longer tolerate homosexuality. Peters cited scriptural verses from Leviticus, Corinthians, and Romans and declared: "Intolerance of, discrimination against and the death penalty for homosexuals is prescribed in the Bible!" Much like enforcing male "headship" in the family or prohibiting interracial marriage, antigay discrimination fulfilled Peters's version of God's Law. The United States of America either enforced this law, according to Peters, or was a Baal-worshiping Sodom on the quick slope to hell. Either the death penalty for homosexuals or death and destruction would envelop the country, he reasoned. "If we as a society refuse to repent and acquire righteous government to punish this crime with the death penalty, then even more will die," Peters wrote.[34]

Peters and other advocates of Christian Identity were not alone in their opposition to acceptance of homosexuality. Tens of millions of Americans cite aversion to gay men and lesbians as part of their core beliefs.[35] And the politicians most identified with the issue of discriminating against gays are those influenced by the so-called Christian right, theologically driven cultural conservatives such as the Reverend Jerry Falwell and the Reverend Pat Robertson.

Elections 1988: David Duke and Pat Robertson Out on the Hustings

February 9, 1988. During the period when prosecutors and defendants in Fort Smith were still preparing for trial, the rest of the country was giving its attention to the presidential primaries. In Iowa, George H. W. Bush, President Reagan's sitting vice president, was heavily favored in the Republican caucuses. Journalists expected votes for Senator Bob Dole, from the neighboring state of Kansas, and Dole did actually win. But no one predicted that the Reverend Pat Robertson would come out of right field, gather 25 percent of the GOP's caucus vote, and place second in the pack of candidates. Before the primaries ended, Robertson had won the Washington state caucus and finished second in the Minnesota and North Dakota caucuses. He polled almost six hundred thousand votes on Super Tuesday alone and raised more money than any Republican contender other than George Bush. His candidacy collapsed in the southern primaries, but it was not a fluke showing. Rather, Robertson's campaign proved to be a bellwether of Christian conservative electioneering to come.[1]

Marion G. "Pat" Robertson was then arguably the most successful entrepreneur among the preachers on the Christian right. He founded the Christian Broadcasting Network in the 1960s, and by 1988 its Family Channel was the eighth-largest cable network in the country.[2] He started Regents University for undergraduates and the American Center for Law and Justice as a legal advocacy institute. He wrote several substantial books enumerating his views and for a time became the preeminent religious voice for ultraconservative views outside the Republican mainstream.[3] Even as others on the Christian right foundered financially in President Reagan's wake during the mid-1980s, Robertson prospered.[4] While white nationalists pressed their noses against the glass, looking into the dining rooms of American politics, Robertson sat in the public's living room via television and the Christian Broadcast Network.

Robertson, born in 1930, is from the same generation as Willis Carto and William Pierce. He is the patrician son of Senator A. Willis Robertson, a segregationist Virginia Democrat whose House and Senate career spanned thirty-four years. The Reverend Robertson's father had been one of the architects of the South's strategy of "massive resistance" to court-ordered desegregation.[5] But the reverend lived in a different era from his senator father. Jim Crow had been replaced by an amiable black cohost on the reverend's daily *700 Club* television program. Although Robertson the younger supported the apartheid regime in South Africa because it was fighting godless "Communists," he forsook the open advocacy of white supremacy in favor of ideas that were popular among Christian conservatives.[6]

The Reverend Robertson's Bible taught him that God had put man as the head of women; thus he opposed the Equal Rights Amendment and other measures aimed at creating gender equality. He fought anything that smacked of civil rights protection for gays and lesbians. Jeremiah Chapter 1 Verse 5 reads: "Before I formed thee in the belly, I knew thee," which Robertson interpreted as reason for overturning abortion rights.

At his core, Robertson believed that the United States was founded as a Christian nation and should live under God's Law, as understood and interpreted by men like him. This supposedly Christian nation had come undone after being placed under the despotic thumb of secular humanists. And he adapted classic conspiracy theories dating back to the French Revolution to explain how.[7]

Robertson's nationalism was of the Christian kind, a first cousin of the white variety. Both were similarly rooted in a mythology based on the Founding Fathers and the first moments of the Republic. The Christian right dated the moment of its dispossession to 1962, when the Supreme Court outlawed prayer in public schools, while its white nationalist cousins believed the 1954 *Brown v. Topeka Board of Education* decision had stolen their national birthright. Both Christian nationalists and white nationalists regarded the United States of America as a country that was no longer theirs to control.

Despite this shared political kinship, in 1988 white supremacists such as Willis Carto could not abide Pat Robertson's Republican candidacy, primarily because of his pro-Israel policies. On this point, Robertson's eschatology—his version of God's plan for the End Times—determined his politics. According to Robertson, the regathering of Jews in Israel and the reclamation of Jerusalem, after almost two thousand years of dispersal, were a sign of events to come. It meant a Satanic one world government would arise, persecute Christians, and crush Israel. In the End, Jesus Christ would return and a remnant of Jews would convert to Christianity and be saved, along with all true believers. Everyone else would be thrown into the pit of hell. The Kingdom of God would be established. In this scenario, Christ's Second Coming can't occur without Jewish control of Jerusalem. As a consequence, Robertson supports the state of Israel, notwithstanding his conspiracy theories about how the Rothschilds and "international bankers" run the world.[8]

During the early 1980s, when Robertson first became prominent, Carto's *Spotlight* enlisted Cornelius Vanderhaggen for a series of articles on Israel and the End Times. According to the Liberty Lobby tabloid, Vanderhaggen had met Robertson in 1956 and catalyzed the latter's born-again experience. Thus Vanderhaggen was the perfect authority to assure readers that Robertson's view on Israel and the End Times "is totally contradicted by the Bible." In this way, Carto first drew a line between his own camp and Robertson's.[9]

After Robertson made it known that he would run in the 1988 primaries, Carto faced a quandary. *The Spotlight* opined that Robertson came "closest to the populist views of most" of its readers, excepting, of course, on Israel and the Middle East.[10] So Liberty Lobby soft-pedaled its differences with Robertson during the primary season. Instead, *The Spotlight* directed most of its criticism at Senator Bob Dole (Vice President George Bush was already known to be beyond acceptance). That left Robertson untouched.

"We believe Pat Robertson does a great deal of good in his work. We saw no reason to get into a bitter shouting match with a television minister with whom we agree on almost every other issue but the Middle East," Liberty Lobby's secretary, Lois Peterson, reasoned.[11]

Robertson did not return the favor. *The Spotlight* reported that Robertson had once held the tabloid aloft on his nationally broadcast *700 Club* program and "urged his followers to stop reading" it. Robertson apparently described Carto's crown jewel as "one of the most rabid, vicious publications and unfortunately a number of well-meaning Christians think that it is the truth and buy it."[12]

Shortly before the Iowa caucuses *The Spotlight* found a platform from which it could air its problems with Robertson. It published an interview with the Populist Party chair Tom McIntyre. The Populists couldn't support any of the Republican contenders, McIntyre declared. "Pat Robertson comes close, but on the foreign policy question, he has declared himself as an all-out supporter of the state of Israel." After all, supporting Robertson "would be contrary to the Populist Party platform which cautions nationalism and non-intervention in U.S. foreign policy." Robertson was dangerous, *The Spotlight* decided.[13]

Robertson's campaign in the Republican primaries that year paralleled a similar effort by David Duke in the Democratic camp. Robertson's advantages over Duke included more spendable money, an only slightly off-key conservatism, and the celebrity that comes from having your own television network. His constituents flooded into the Republican Party, worked their precincts, and set up voter mobilization phone trees. They were practiced at the art of lobbying elected officials on such issues as opposition to abortion rights. And in the years to come Robertson's supporters ensconced themselves in the heart of the Republican Party. They were ready to run for, and be elected to, everything from school board and county commission to Congress. Duke's erstwhile supporters, by contrast, sometimes preferred to attend weekend cross burnings rather than labor dully over the little things that make a campaign go.

If the Reverend Robertson roiled the Republican waters, David Duke barely created a ripple among Democrats. His campaign relied on existing white supremacist networks for money and human matériel. He rented mailing lists of potential donors from Liberty Lobby and *The Spotlight*, paying thousands trying to prime his financial pumps. To those who contributed relatively large sums early, the David Duke for President Committee gave copies of Wilmot Robertson's book *The Dispossessed Majority*, the same title he had sold ten years earlier from his Klan offices.[14]

With these contributions, Duke paid himself office rent through a business front he called B C & E. (Duke rarely missed an opportunity to line his own pockets.) He also hired some part-time staff: Matt Anger, a college-age Virginian who fancied himself a "political soldier"; Allen Baylough, once a sharp Pennsylvania organizer for William Pierce's National Alliance; and William Rhodes, a future Aryan Nations associate and videographer. To this crew, he added Ralph Forbes, the Arkansas state Populist Party chair, who became his campaign manager but failed to ensure that Duke met the requirements for receiving Federal Election Commission matching funds.[15] These all were relatively capable men drawn from several organizations. But Duke could have more easily hired these same people to run a Klan organization, as they all lacked significant election experience.

His major stops included a Pittsburgh Populist Party fund-raiser and an Identity gathering in Cape Canaveral, Florida. At a motel stop outside Philadelphia, Duke handled pointed questions about his attitude toward the former California state Klan dragon Tom Metzger, who had made a noticeable mark at Fort Smith. Duke was circumspect in his response, not directly criticizing Metzger—despite the Californian's widely broadcast and vehement denunciations of Duke as an unprincipled opportunist.[16] Such were not the kinds of questions that decided votes at the ballot box.

Duke had originally hoped to leverage up a Democratic Party bid by picking a high-visibility fight with the Reverend Jesse Jackson. But Jackson emerged as a serious contender, an alternative to the Democratic front-runner, Massachusetts Governor Michael Dukakis. And the civil rights activist refused to get in a mud wrestling match with the former Klansman. And in none of the primary states did Duke outpoll Jackson. In Texas, Duke's second-best primary state, Duke received 8,808 votes. By any count, that was 8,000 more than had ever joined his Texas Klan operation, but Jackson received 433,335 votes—about fifty times more than Duke. The embarrassment was worse elsewhere. Duke had once announced of his prospects in Georgia: "I don't know if I can win, but I know in this state I can beat Jesse Jackson."[17] In the end, however, Duke could not qualify for the state ballot, while Jackson received 247,831 votes.[18]

Despite these constraining factors, Duke purchased a thirty-minute bloc of television advertising time in Louisiana and found himself a base of support, pulling 23,390 votes in that state, more than Arizona Governor Bruce Babbitt or Illinois Senator Paul Simon. Although David Duke's run in the Democratic Party ended with the March 1988 primaries, his vote totals in Louisiana augured a possibly more successful future on a different ticket.[19]

Meanwhile, in Carto's reassembled Populist Party, few members showed any interest in running for local office. When they did run, they received little financial support and even fewer votes. Instead of focusing on building the party from the bottom up, they fantasized about a mainstream presidential candidate who could build it for them from the top down. Carto still lamented former Congressman Hansen's rejection of the Populists' nomination: "No candidate of national stature will abandon either of the two old parties until we have proven that we have something to offer."[20] So at a national committee meeting in Cincinnati, they asked David Duke to be their candidate. And he said yes.

The party newsletter ecstatically hailed Duke as the "charismatic, ar-

ticulate champion of America's dispossessed majority."[21] When Lieutenant Colonel James "Bo" Gritz (ret.), a POW-MIA champion who had
spoken at Liberty Lobby's convention the previous October, came to
Cincinnati and agreed to take the vice presidential nomination, the
Populists were thrilled. Alas, Gritz went home, thought about it, and
withdrew several weeks later.[22] Duke, on the other hand, switched
seamlessly from a Democrat label to the Populist one.

His rhetoric still used Jesse Jackson as a symbol of white dispossession. But he was no longer running against the civil rights advocate.
"Unless we change the immigration rates into America, unless we slow
down the welfare birth rate," he told the Cincinnati meeting, "Jesse
Jackson is the future of America." It was his standard "the United States
is becoming a Third World country" speech. "The only all-White country is Iceland and Iceland's not enough," he said.[23]

Although issues such as welfare, affirmative action, school integration, and crime had been targets of white racial resentments since before Duke's days as a Klansman, Duke was less concerned with the
economic costs of "welfare dependency" and more concerned with the
"welfare birthrate." When this was paired with "immigration," he conjured an explicit worry about the threat to the majority status of white
people. Duke and other white supremacists predicted a milk chocolate
future with low living standards and a declining civilization. They had
the milk chocolate part correct.

Immigration had been a movement issue since Duke's first trip as a
Klansman to the California border with Mexico. One of the most widely
circulated pieces of propaganda was a map of North America with broad
colorful arrows from the South demonstrating the danger of brown and
black immigration from Central America and the Caribbean. By railing
against immigration during his 1988 campaign, Duke hoped to catalyze
a phenomenon already visible in Europe, where France's Front National
campaigned for the immediate expulsion of North African immigrants.
The Front National drew four million plus votes in the first round of
French elections that March.[24] Its success goaded David Duke and the
Populist Party into open imitation. The number one issue on David
Duke's ten-point Populist Party platform was: "Restrict immigration to
protect employment for American workers, and to preserve the spirit,
the heritage and traditional values of our nation."[25]

Duke also tried blending immigration and welfare with a menu of
economic grievances, such as job loss and low wages. This was a slight
change of course for Duke. He had long understood race, but the technique of transforming economic grievances into racial resentments was
new for him. At first, Duke borrowed heavily from Carto and *The Spot-*

light, which had mastered this art during the farm crisis in the mid-1980s.

Duke's initial propaganda was clumsy. One of his early newsletters featured a cartoon drawing of farmers singing: "We are the farmers. We built America. We fed the World. But now, for our rights and heritage, there is only one. So, we hope and pray that David Duke will run!"[26] Actually, farmers were praying for higher commodity prices and debt relief, not "heritage and rights."

In an earlier instance, Duke reacted to a sharp drop in stock market prices with a Carto-like belief that lower prices for IBM shares signaled a reawakening of white people. "Don't look upon the stock market crash or a currency collapse as being a misfortune for this country," his newsletter read. "It may be that a disaster of this kind will bring with it the very opportunity white people need to have Majority views examined and permit the education and re-education of our people."[27]

Revolutionaries of every stripe have awaited cataclysms of all kinds to usher in their new orders. Communists, for example, saw the final collapse of capitalism in a declining rate of profit. Aryans had predicted a race war whenever different physiognomies appeared on the same continent. Duke could have been merely restating a piece of revolutionary dogma, but he wasn't. As the movement matured in the late 1980s, the economic concerns of ordinary white people were increasingly addressed in a new fashion. Duke added calls for tariffs, preserving the family farm, and cleaning up Wall Street to his list of ways to right racial wrongs such as immigration and the "welfare birthrate."

We must not be afraid to say that we are protectionists, he said. We seek the protection of American industry and jobs, the safeguarding and keeping of American land and property.[28]

There is of course a racial edge to this brand of economic nationalism. Willis Carto had drawn the link between racial nationalism and economic nationalism long before. "If the U.S. imports automobiles, steel or any other commodity, it can import labor just as well," Carto argued. "The movement of entire populations of North Africans to Europe, Caribbean 'refugees' to the U.S.; hordes of Mexican and Latin American mestizos to America [is] likely to accelerate in coming years."[29] Simply put, Carto, Duke, and the Populists opposed the free movement of capital goods because they opposed the free movement of labor.[30]

At a Washington State Populist Party convention in July 1988, Duke added international bankers to his enemies list. But he focused on "Zionist" control of the media rather than the banks. He qualified his call to abolish the income tax, which many Christian patriots believed was unconstitutional, with a more Republican-sounding advocacy of a flat tax. In the end, money issues, such as the Federal Reserve, didn't matter to Duke if the racial "heritage" of the country was swamped by an uncontrolled black population, nonwhite immigration, and Zionist mind control. In one moment of truth, he told the Washington State Populists that the problem wasn't just Zionism, but the Jewish religion itself.[31]

All the rhetorical blather aside, however, the Populists needed to build their party infrastructure and get on the ballot. And on this point Duke was untiring on their behalf. He traveled from one meeting to another in the hopes of creating a real third party. Duke crisscrossed Florida, went to southern New Jersey to speak on the second floor of a grocery store, and stimulated a record number of Populist candidates to run for local offices. Because of Duke's multiple efforts, the Populist Party did make some organizational gains that year. Yet it still did not cross over the line that separates an ideological sparring partner from a viable third party contender. The party managed to secure ballot status in only twelve states. Even the party's chairman acknowledged the failure. He had hoped that Populists would go further into the mainstream, "just as the student radicals of the '60's went straight into the System."[32] But Duke's campaign had underscored weaknesses that no one person could have fixed. "I truly believe that the major obstacle the Populist Party faces is to overcome the fear so many of us have of immersing ourselves in the political process," the chairman had predicted. "Until we become involved in electoral politics with regularity, we will remain a non-entity."[33]

While Duke finished the election year as a Populist Party candidate, a conflict embroiled Pete Peters in a different kind of campaign. Soon after his summer Bible camp ended, city council members in Fort Collins, near the town where Peters's home church was located, considered a simple question: Would the country's civil rights laws be extended to cover housing and employment discrimination against gay men and lesbians? Spurred on by the black freedom movement in the 1960s and the wave of feminist organizing that followed, a nascent gay liberation movement had emerged in the 1970s. As the AIDS crisis became an epidemic in the mid-1980s, gay men and lesbians became more public and prominent. Hollywood film stars wore red ribbons to show a sense of solidarity with the AIDS-stricken. Political action committees in Washington, D.C., pressed for federal legislation. Radical local groups staged dramatic protests, including acts of civil disobedience. And annual gay pride parades ranged from outrageous exhibitionism to quiet determination in the pursuit of change. Pressure built up to add protection based on "sexual orientation" to local ordinances, state statutes, and federal laws. Following the national trend, activists in Fort Collins documented dozens of instances of local discrimination because of sexual orientation. They took their concerns to the city council and asked for statutory protection.

After expert testimony supporting a change in the law, the city attorney drafted the requisite legislation outlawing such discrimination, and the city council appeared ready to pass it. At that point, Pete Peters and his LaPorte Church of Christ mobilized to oppose the measure. Peters and two hundred others attended two different council meetings that summer. They used the scriptures to justify discrimination against homosexuals much the way Mississippi planters had once employed the biblical story of Ham to deny black people their rights. After a hotly contested August meeting, the Fort Collins City Council decided to put the issue on the November ballot for a referendum-style vote rather than pass the legislation themselves.[34]

Peters led the opposition to the measure, which included other non-Identity Christians. His church spent more than twelve hundred dollars for radio advertising on a local AM station. He purchased the time like a pro: a ten-second spot that ran ten times a week for forty weeks and one two-hour slot on Monday night for four weeks. He also bought newspaper advertising, and his coalition distributed leaflets door to door. One leaflet threatened an increase in AIDS cases and "boy prostitution" if "pro-homosexual legislation" was passed. Another argued that "gay rights laws" were only the first step to "full social acceptance." A third leaflet pressed the main opposition point: "Homosexuals' civil rights are identical to yours. They can vote, seek office, get an education, own property, assemble, worship . . . Do they deserve *special* treatment [emphasis in original]?"[35]

These campaign expenditures eventually ran afoul of the Colorado secretary of state, who required that those spending money in an election register as political action committees. Legal proceedings concerning such registration dragged on for years. Peters lost the political money issue in the courts.[36] But he proved successful in the electoral arena, nevertheless. In a high-turnout election the antigay coalition won more than fifteen thousand votes, while the civil rights advocates received only eleven thousand.[37] The "no special rights" argument against protecting gay men and lesbians eventually was redeployed in several higher-profile statewide contests, including a 1992 election in Colorado.

On November 8, 1988, while George Bush soundly defeated Michael Dukakis, Populist Party candidate David Duke eked out a mere forty-five thousand votes in his run for president. Duke's time had not yet arrived.[38] His long months as a Democratic candidate and then as a Populist candidate had, nevertheless, turned him into an adept campaigner. He now also possessed a list of willing financial supporters from all over the country. Further, the fight against gay civil rights, like that pursued by Peters, contained a lesson for all white supremacists. If they could find the right propaganda package and an acceptable vehicle for their core ideas, white supremacists too could find mass constituencies, even voting majorities. In the months that followed, David Duke did precisely that.

Populist Party Meets in Chicago After David Duke Wins a Legislator's Seat

8 February 1989

Dear Friend,

We are making history in Louisiana.

As an open defender of the rights of White people, I have stunned the media and political establishment by finishing a strong first in the recent election here for representative. In a field of seven candidates, I received 33% of the vote! That was almost twice as many as my nearest opponent, John Treen.

. . .

Our enemies know, perhaps more than anyone else, the potential represented by this campaign for our people's basic civil rights.

I have addressed the real issues that no other candidate will dare to discuss. I am the only candidate in recent America who has made a major issue out of the anti-white racial discrimination called affirmative action. I am the only one who points out that poverty can never be cured without curbing the welfare illegitimate birthrate. I am the only candidate addressing the true causes of violent crime and the deterioration of our schools and neighborhoods.

There are millions of Americans who talk about these issues every day among their friends and families, but no serious candidate seeking political office has dared to discuss them openly and fearlessly. Until now!

. . .

With your help, February 18th will mark the beginning of a new political era.

Sincerely,
David Duke.[1]

David Duke's fund-raising letter, sent to activists living in Forsyth County, Georgia, among others, promised the political breakthrough he had been touting for almost two years. His exuberance over the white riot in Georgia had stretched seamlessly into a run for president and then extended again into a run at the Louisiana statehouse. The once and future candidate now aimed at a representative's seat from the Eighty-first District. In the months after the November election, Duke had switched his registration to the Republican Party as easily as he had once made the transition from a brown-shirted national socialist to a white-sheeted Klansman. He tried on party labels as if he were shopping for a new suit, Democrat, Populist, and Republican all in a short eighteen months.[2]

According to Duke, the largest factor affecting his decision to run for the legislature was his potential for success.[3] He had sized up the Metairie district, just across the causeway from New Orleans. Of the 21,600 registered voters, only 60 were black. The seat had been vacated after its occupant had been named to a judgeship and there was no incumbent. Issues such as crime and drugs had already taken on a racially tinged cast. In 1979, when he ran as a Klansman for the state senate, he had placed second among voters from this district. And in the 1988 Democratic primary, he had received more district votes than most of the other candidates.[4] While Duke saw his own name in future headlines, all the other candidates ignored him as a miscreant.

During the weeks before the primary, Duke campaigned the old-fashioned way—by knocking on doors. When voters answered, there stood a pleasant-looking, earnest gentleman wearing a sportscoat and tie while talking their talk. No scowling bigot in a white sheet or swastika armband. Duke told voters he was for "equal rights" for whites. Could he have their support? Once they said yes, they rarely changed their minds. Could he put a DAVID DUKE FOR REPRESENTATIVE sign in their yard? Enough people said yes that his campaign gave the appearance of momentum. Politics is, after all, the grandfather of all performance arts. The *appearance* of momentum produced momentum itself. His signs popped up on front lawns and busy intersections like mosquitoes swarming in a hot Louisiana swamp. Soon he wasn't a miscreant pest at all, but a contender.

Instead of picking a former American Nazi Party captain as his campaign manager, as he had done in the presidential race, Duke enlisted two tough ex-cops whose street skills translated easily into the mechanics of political trench warfare. Soon they were supervising a raft of volunteers and defending Duke from spurious charges of anti-Catholicism. The two men became the campaign's unsung workhorses.

Duke startled the political establishment by winning the first-round primary just two weeks before the above letter was mailed. Out of a field of seven, Duke had received 33 percent of the total—13,995 votes. His nearest competitor, Republican John Treen, whose brother had once been governor, received 2,277.

Candidate Treen marshaled all the resources he could command for the runoff. The president's son (and future president himself) George W. Bush came to town and campaigned for the Republican regular. President Ronald Reagan, just months into his retirement, endorsed Treen in radio advertisements. President Bush publicly called Duke a racist. Lee Atwater, the strategic mastermind behind Bush's victory that November, offered to come to Louisiana to help, but Treen's campaign demurred.[5] And as might be expected, Treen sent voters pictures of Duke parading around with a swastika armband, and reminded them that voting for a Klansman was no longer fashionable behavior.[6]

Those who had already decided to vote for Duke dismissed the big-time advertisements. They had their own opinions. Duke was for keeping the homestead exemption on taxes; Treen wasn't. Duke was really against crime and the "welfare underclass." His Klan credentials proved it. Treen was just another pretender. As one young white kid told his (white) playmate, "My Daddy says David Duke is gonna get rid of all the niggers."[7]

On February 18, 1989, David Duke slipped past John Treen with 224 more votes out of the approximately 16,500 cast. For the next three years, debates raged among campaign professionals, academics, journalists, and civil rights activists over the "real" nature of voters' support for Duke. Were they poor, uneducated bumpkins, down on their luck and looking for scapegoats? Was voting for Duke an act of "symbolic racism," or did they really mean it? Weren't they just angry and sending a message to the elites they loved to hate? Or was this the Republican Party's southern strategy come home to roost; after twenty years of race-baiting, wasn't it to be expected that a genuine white supremacist would win office? Or was it the other way around: Was David Duke leading where Republicans would soon follow? Polls would be taken. Studies were conducted. And books were written, but no conclusions were immediately in sight.

At that moment, however, David Duke had his own answer. He had beaten the president of the United States and the entire political establishment because he had vocalized what white people had privately thought, but could not say. Also, during the campaign, he had avoided talking about those parts of his belief system that he knew were still out of bounds.

Almost every corner of the movement hailed Duke's victory as its own. One small-circulation newsletter from California claimed it was a "morale-booster" that "legitimize[d]" the desires of whites to "live racially-separate."[8] Ed Fields's *Truth at Last* tabloid claimed "a new dawn for white people."[9] Willis Carto's *Spotlight* was more circumspect, relegating the story to page sixteen and describing Duke as a "populist maverick," not a consensus-shattering pioneer. Nevertheless, the tabloid did announce plans for Duke to speak at an upcoming Populist Party meeting. For their part, the Populists treated Duke's victory as if a new earth had entered a new heaven. Despite the fact that Duke had jumped registrations, their newsletter gave him a full-page cover photo under a banner headline. Of Duke's victory as a Republican, the party concluded: "The idea of using the political process for change has been conclusively proven. Aware Americans must stop giving money and time to every conservative organization and unite behind the Populist Party."

The party's leadership thought Duke's election would redirect money and personnel from the movement generally toward its particular niche, electioneering. "The most obvious and undeniable lesson of all this is that David Duke has proven that it is through the electoral process we must work," the newsletter opined. In a low-key criticism of other formations, it also claimed that "hundreds of patriotic educational organizations and debating societies have striven mightily . . . with precious little success." On the other hand, "David Duke has achieved the long-sought goals of those groups overnight through one legislative race."[10]

On March 4 the Populist Party national committee met at the Bismarck Hotel in Chicago and celebrated Duke's success. Otherwise, the Populists wrestled once again with their long-standing liabilities. Obligatory reports on the party's finances revealed that small amounts had been raised and spent on election year activities during 1988.[11] Fewer than half of the party's state affiliates sent voting delegations. Attendance was confined to the usual group of whiners and moaners, with the exception of a few new skinheads and Klan types from the Chicago area. While the party's customary villains were discussed ad nauseam, campaign management and ballot access were remaindered to a few exhortations from the speakers' platform.[12]

The election of officers revealed a new split in the Populist ranks, this time between Willis Carto and Don Wassall, who served as the party's executive director from an office outside Pittsburgh. Articulate and a generation younger than Carto, Wassall had been the Populist Party state chairman in Pennsylvania. He regularly published a newsletter,

The Populist Observer. Under his leadership, the Pennsylvanians fielded local candidates and looked almost like a small third party. When Carto reorganized the party's apparatus in 1987, he had relied heavily on this infrastructure in Pennsylvania. Wassall began drawing a small salary, $19,500 a year,[13] to run the headquarters, and his *Populist Observer* became the national party's newsletter. As Wassall's stature inside the party grew, *The Spotlight* reporter Mike Piper regularly promoted Wassall in Carto's tabloid, adding to his prominence.

Because of his differences with Wassall, Carto did not attend this meeting in Chicago and was not elected to its executive committee, the first time since the party's formation. Their dispute boiled down to a naked fight over control of the Populist Party's decision-making apparatus. Any differences they exhibited over political strategy were secondary in nature. The problems started while making plans for the meeting. Carto wanted the program to pair conservative tax cutter Paul Gann with iconoclast Eugene McCarthy, known for his liberalism. It was a combination, Carto was sure, that would make "the media's eyes . . . bug out."[14] Wassall rejected McCarthy, however, opting instead to feature the recently impeached former Arizona governor, Evan Mecham, a stalwart of ultraconservatives. Apparently, Mecham initially agreed to attend but pulled out at the last minute.

Wassall accused Carto of sabotaging the ex-governor's appearance, presumably in a fit of spite following their differences over Gene McCarthy. Carto responded coyly to Wassall's charge. He admitted calling Mecham's office prior to the March meeting but claimed that the former governor had pulled out solely because of local pressures. Carto claimed that news had leaked back to Arizona Republicans that their former governor would be on the same platform as David Duke, and the former Kluxer was still considered out of bounds.[15]

What began as a genuine dispute over the meeting's program soon degenerated into a petty spitting contest over the timing of the opening session. At one point Carto claimed, "I resent having to twiddle my thumbs for five hours," while waiting for the event to start. Carto's petulance at his underling's impertinence would have worn better if the Populist Party had ever done anything more than eat, greet, and meet under his guidance. Wassall's brash junior partner revolt, on the other hand, ventured little because there was nothing to lose. In the end, Carto's tabloid spent the next several years describing Wassall as a drug-using, money-hungry "office manager," like a bad secretary run amok.[16]

For the moment, Wassall held the upper hand inside the party. Tom McIntyre, the party chairman, was reelected. A. J. Barker, the North Carolina state chair, was elevated to national vice chairman. And three former Klansmen—Don Black, now living in Florida; Van Loman, from Ohio; and John Warnock, from Arkansas—were among those elected to the executive committee.

The reshuffling of the leadership aside, the Chicago meeting's grandest moment was the appearance of David Duke, who strode to the speakers' podium as if he were the president of the United States about to address a joint session of Congress. He gloriously recounted how he had surmounted great obstacles and beaten the elites just three weeks before. He had countered the national Republican establishment and "New York" media with an aggressive grassroots campaign, he said.[17] "It was a small enough district that we had a real chance to reach the public without a great expenditure of money," he continued.[18] Unstated was the importance of contributors Duke had developed during his national campaigns. He had raised thirty-five thousand dollars during January 1989, at the height of the race. Of that total, Louisiana supporters provided only fifty-eight hundred dollars, or 17 percent. California, Florida, Illinois, and New York, on the other hand, contributed the largest amounts of the balance. Duke knew that much of the money was raised from Liberty Lobby and Populist supporters in those states but didn't say it out loud that day.[19]

He did tell the Populists, however, how he had mixed local and national issues. The homestead property tax exemption may have been a more important issue than his constant carping about the cost of maintaining the "welfare underclass." He had campaigned against minority set-asides in state contracts and claimed they meant fewer jobs for white people. Affirmative action was similarly on his list of issues. But he had dropped other issues, such as immigration and the Federal Reserve "banksters" that he had promoted during his Populist campaign. Unlike any other self-avowed white supremacist at the time, Duke sensed his constituents' concerns and was able to render "majority dispossession" into a palpable sentiment among a sector of white voters.

Duke also understood that his base of support had a class character. People "that have the high fences . . . guard dogs, the security systems, the people who can afford to send their kids to private schools," didn't support him, Duke reminded his Chicago audience. Those people voted for the mainstream Republican opponent.[20]

In fact, the base of Duke's District 81 support came from Reagan Democrats, who had voted for Republicans in national elections but registered (and voted) Democratic in local elections.[21] Louisiana Republican

Party officials were cognizant of the sea change represented by Duke. He was the first registered Republican to pick up these votes in a local election. Unlike the national party, state Republican officials feared that criticizing Duke would alienate his working-class voters.[22]

Duke too was aware of the repercussions. "We're having a tremendous shift going on right now in this country," he told the Chicago Populists. "We have started something; we have really started something from a small little race in Louisiana."[23] Much as he had felt after the 1987 mob violence in Forsyth County, Georgia, Duke saw in his District 81 election the nodal point of a transformed white movement. While Duke's analysis was prescient, it also reflected his own solipsism. Whatever *he* happened to be doing at the moment, Duke usually considered it the most important historical development at that time. Like narcissists who worship their own reflections, when Duke saw his own image on the television, he believed it was reality.

Despite Duke's mediagenic presence, the Populist Party was itself not ready for prime time. Immediately following his closed-door speech to the party faithful, Duke planned an open-door press conference for local media. Before the press conference started, however, one of Duke's bodyguards, Art Jones, started pushing a television reporter around and calling him names. Jones was well known in Chicago as an American Nazi Party activist and sometime candidate for local office, and his thuggish behavior that day was recorded for local and then national news.[24] Thus, as the Populist meeting ended, the party projected a public image of neo-Nazi gangsters and dissembling pretty-boy racists trying to deny the obvious. Gone was the picture it had hoped to project: an elected official concerned about affirmative action and minority set-asides.

Duke's imbroglio in Chicago followed him home to Louisiana in the person of Beth Rickey. Then a pert Republican Party state central committee member from New Orleans in her early thirties, she had been a Republican long before being a Republican in Louisiana was cool. Her father, whom she revered, had been a Republican businessman in the era of Huey Long, when being a Democrat would have been more profitable. He had come home from World War Two with a firm line in his own mind between fascism and his own anti-communist conservatism. Beth considered her own politics a continuation of her father's, and she had been an eager Ronald Reagan delegate to the Republican Party's 1976 convention, which nominated Gerald Ford. With Reagan's ascension to the presidency, Beth found herself at the top of the state party apparatus. During the race for the District 81 seat, she had worked on her friend John Treen's campaign, only to have David Duke come across her radar screen like a Stuka bomber. Appalled that someone who had worn a Nazi Party uniform, the uniform her father had fought, would win office, Rickey put Duke in her political sights.[25]

After the election, Rickey followed Duke up to Chicago, where she attended the Populist Party meeting and taped his speech. After witnessing Art Jones's thuggery and sitting in a room with tattooed skinheads, she brought home the news that Duke's days with neo-Nazis and Ku Kluxers were not over.

During the campaign, Duke's past in the Ku Klux Klan had cut both ways. Remember that Carto's *Spotlight* had predicted that Duke's notorious past virtually guaranteed press coverage of his presidential bid. (It had been a bad estimate.) During the state race, Duke used his Klan past to remind white voters that he was a serious racist and not a one-time dilettante. At the same time, Duke repeatedly argued that his Klan membership had been a youthful indiscretion, replaced by a more mature advocacy of "equal rights for all and special privileges for none." He was a different person now, he said. And he sounded this theme at every available opportunity.

Duke's argument that he had changed was inadvertently aided by his opponents. While candidate Treen and *The Times-Picayune* (New Orleans) constantly replayed images from Duke's past, they did little to expose his contemporary connection to the white supremacist movement.[26]

The attitude of District 81 voters toward Duke's Klan past became a salient indicator of how they would pull the lever. Of those who voted for Duke, 83 percent believed he had changed from his days as a Kluxer, but 98 percent of those who voted for Duke's opponent believed he had not changed.[27] And as Duke constantly reminded his constituents, American public life was littered with respectable political figures who had once been Klan members. Robert Byrd had been a Klan minichief before he became a senator from West Virginia. Hugo Black had joined the Klan in 1923, and his resignation two years later had been a mere question of electioneering tactics, not ideological principle. Only later did Senator Black become a liberal and win nomination to the U.S. Supreme Court.[28] Could ex-Klansmen become only liberals? Duke asked. Was his conversion less legitimate because he had become a Republican conservative rather than a Democratic liberal like Byrd and Black?

Republican Rickey's complaint was more pointed. Duke had been first a national socialist, before becoming a Klansman. And polling data showed that white voters disapproved of Duke's days as a neo-Nazi in greater numbers than they disapproved of his past as a Klansman.[29] (Apparently Duke had understood this distinction between the perception of a German-tinged neo-Nazi and a native Klansman when he first decided to become a Kluxer.) Rickey and a newly formed political action committee, Louisiana Coalition Against Racism and Nazism, argued that Duke had never forsaken the biological determinism or anti-Semitic conspiracy theories common to both the Klan and national socialists. After the Chicago meeting, her message was simply that Duke's past and present were essentially the same.

One of New Orleans's local television newsmagazines picked up the question in the weeks after Duke was caught with Art Jones and crowd in Chicago. When a reporter asked him about his Populist Party candidacy (an issue that had rarely come up during the campaign), Duke danced around the question. When you are at the "bottom of the political bucket," he told the reporter, you take help where you can get it. When asked about Art Jones, Duke replied that Jones was just a "Nazi kook running for office." No hint of irony showed on his televised face. Asked about denying the Holocaust, Duke was equally evasive. Sure, there had been atrocities, but "it was possible that some of the atrocities were exaggerated." And asked about anti-Semitism, he said, "What am I saying against Jewish people? Tell me one thing."[30]

In response to Duke's claims that his views had changed, Rickey's colleague at the aforementioned Louisiana coalition, Lance Hill, analyzed Duke's current ideology and political behavior and compared it with Adolf Hitler's prior to the Nazi seizure of power in 1933. Hill's conclusion, in a monograph that became the basis of the coalition's work: despite changes in costume and coloring, Duke's ideas had remained essentially unchanged since his days as a national socialist youth.[31] It took the coalition two more years of campaigning, but eventually a significant minority of white people in Louisiana drew the same conclusion.

Meanwhile, convinced that the newly elected legislator represented an evil and corrupting influence on her party, Elizabeth Rickey began a lonely battle to save it. She met with national Republican leaders in D.C., who had already roundly condemned Duke. The Louisiana state Republicans, by contrast, had stayed quiet and tacitly accepted Duke. Rickey knew that one of the party's best strategists was even helping Duke learn the backroom ropes. So Rickey tried to take a half step. She decided to ask the state central committee for only an investigation, rather than immediate censure.[32] Three months after the election, she submitted a resolution that read in part:

> Whereas, while Representative David Duke maintains publicly that he has abandoned his former Ku Klux Klan perspective, he continues to disseminate virulent anti-Semitic, white supremacist, and violent literature through the auspices of his legislative office in Metarie, Louisiana, and
>
> Whereas, these actions undermine the principles of the Republican Party and call into question Representative Duke's fidelity to the party and respect for the legislature.
>
> Therefore, be it resolved that the Republican State Central Committee appoint a sub-committee charged with investigating the above evidence and submitting a report within sixty days.

Rickey could have compiled a list of whereases and therefores longer than the snake in Pete Peters's Garden of Eden, however, and her Republican colleagues would neither censure nor investigate the newest addition to their caucus. In addition to bringing the party new votes from Democratic precincts, Duke quickly established himself as the point man opposed to a tax reform plan offered by Governor Buddy Roemer. When voters rejected Roemer's proposals in April 1989, it became immediately apparent that Duke owned a statewide constituency, extending far beyond blue-collar voters in District 81. Although none of his legislative proposals was made law that summer, Duke's Republican colleagues decided not to challenge him directly. It wouldn't have mattered if he'd shown up in Baton Rouge in black leather jackboots; some would have decided his suit was haute fashion and worn boots themselves if it meant winning votes. On Saturday, September 23, four months after she had first offered it, Beth Rickey's resolution was officially tabled in committee. The inability of Republican state officials to withstand David Duke's blandishments was a sign of the full-scale political battles ahead.

Duke's relatively rapid transformation exemplified the contradictions within and around the white supremacist enterprise in the late 1980s: the movement's vanguardists had beaten the government's prosecution at Fort Smith but lay weak and shattered in the trial's aftermath. Pete Peters's Bible camp had supplanted the CSA's paramilitary training, and he had successfully led the opposition to civil rights for gay men and lesbians. Nevertheless, Christian fundamentalist leaders such as Falwell and Robertson still considered his Identity theology off-limits. Willis Carto's Populist Party, after four years of nurturance, had finally produced a winning candidate—who was a Republican. It seemed as if white supremacists could find a niche inside the mainstream as long as they did not name their true politics.

Skinhead International in Tennessee

October 7, 1989. It was a warm, sunny fall day in Pulaski, Tennessee, the 1866 birthplace of the Ku Klux Klan. Klan robes that day, however, were out of vogue. The fashion statement du jour was T-shirts, ball caps, and the skinhead uniform: red suspenders snapped to blue jeans over black Dr. Martens boots. T-shirts were emblazoned with the names of bands—Skrewdriver and Bound for Glory—or slogans such as "Just Say No to ZOG" in white letters on black. "David Duke for State Representative" across the chest with a camouflage-colored ball cap was also popular. The Aryan Nations had called this rally ostensibly to honor Confederate war hero Sam Davis, but the youthful attendees showed a variety of affiliations and allegiances.

A tall, finely featured, bleached blond skingirl, barely out of her teens, adorned her black bomber jacket with multiple patches: Confederate flag, Aryan Nations, and Church of the Creator. One youthful contingent held black shields painted with white SS lightning bolts; another carried a large red flag with a black swastika in the middle. Others kept a more southern fried theme: battle flags on long poles, gray War of Northern Aggression costumes, or shields painted with Confederate bars and crossed hammers, fasces style.

A small group of slightly older Kluxers up from Georgia wore modest blue jeans and Southern White Knights T-shirts. A forty-year-old Oklahoman mixed and matched with a black-and-white swastika pin on his hunter orange ball cap plus a traditional white Klan cross with a red teardrop patch on his jacket. A few other men didn't mix at all, sticking with brownshirts and swastika armbands.

Half a dozen young men played Praetorian guard, swaggering around the town square with walkie-talkie headsets and "Sam Davis Security" shirts.[1] A statue of Sam Davis stood on the town square, much as other memorials remembered rebel soldiers in every county seat of the Old Confederacy. Like the statue in Fort Smith, this one had been erected by the Daughters of the Confederacy. Davis had been from the local area, Giles County, a war hero hanged at age twenty-one by Union troops certain he was a spy.

A flyer promoting the rally directly linked Confederate war heroes of the distant past with the new generation of skinhead racists then emerging. "In Sam Davis' veins ran the blood of sacred honor," the flyers read, "the same sacred honor that ran in the veins of the signers of the Declaration of Independence, Col. Travis, Crockett, Bowie of the Alamo, Forrest of the Confederate Calvary [sic]—the sacred honor of which our Aryan youth have heard little today."

Aryan Nations leaders in their forties and fifties, who had organized the rally, were hoping for a bit more than an outdoor history lesson, however. They wanted to recruit skinheads into their shrinking ranks or at least exert some influence over a movement that was growing spontaneously and proving difficult for the established groups to control.

The leadership promised a nighttime party of white power rock bands and a short daytime march around the town square with Louis Beam. Beam, the Vietnam helicopter gunner turned Klansman turned Aryan strategist, had become a movement demigod after the victory at the Fort Smith sedition trial. His reputation and rhetoric endeared him to skinheads, despite the generational gap between them.[2]

For this occasion, Beam was the image of a plantation aristocrat, wearing an all-white suit with a red rose boutonniere. With three hundred skinheads gathered at his feet on the town square, the short, unimposing Beam swelled into a fire-breathing *Sturmführer*. He claimed a blood right to the soil of the South:

> My ancestors lived over here in Franklin, Tennessee. There were ten Beams enlisted in the first Tennessee Confederate Infantry. So I come here not as an outsider . . . to tell you poor dumb southern people how to think about us. You let these carpetbaggers and scalawags come in and run your town . . . You don't need damn Yankees to tell you what to do . . . My ancestors lived in this state five generations. Four of them died fighting for the Confederacy in the Tennessee army.

At points Beam also sounded like an overexuberant cornpone politician, reveling in the glories of Confederate nationalism.

Sam Davis means so much, so much to me. And I know to you. Sam Davis was brought over here into this courthouse, surrounded by three thousand Yankee soldiers who occupied these streets in 1863 . . . Sam Davis was brought here by these tyrants and despots, and he was brought forward in there and said, if you'll just tell us, tell us, who gave you the information about the movement of the Yankee army, you can go home Sam. You can go home to your mother, to your sisters, and to your brother. Right here, you stand on holy hollow ground. Sam Davis looked those Yankee tyrants in the face and said if I had a thousand lives I'd give them all right here before I would betray a friend or a confidant.

Despite this invocation of history and heroism, Pulaski's town fathers drew a line between their own reverence for the Confederate past and the unreconstructed white nationalism Beam represented in the future. Civic leaders took several steps to disassociate themselves from Klansmen and Aryan Nations types who had been gathering periodically in the town's center. They had recently remortared facedown on a brick building a bronze plaque that commemorated the Klan's founding there in 1866. Faced with the prospect of the rally at hand, the city's merchants had decided to shutter their businesses on that day and deck the town with orange ribbons as a show of protest.[3]

This sentiment was expressed in the local press, *The Giles Free Press*. Sam Davis was its hero and could not be legitimately claimed by Aryan types. "Sam remains a revered fellow here-abouts," the paper said. "He is not equated with hate groups, instead honored as a bonafide hero of the Confederacy who gave his life to protect his friends."[4] Pulaski's semiofficial mythology distinguished between honoring martyrs who had died defending white supremacy in the past and present-day proponents of the doctrine. For Beam and company, however, the South, the white South, and an Aryan Republic were all one and the same.

"The message from us," Beam continued, "and the message from Sam to us is, if we had a thousand lives, we would give them all for our people, our heritage, and our culture."

Beam was a powerful orator. Just as he had captured the Fort Smith jury's sympathy with his emotional opening remarks about Vietnam, he reached into the guts of the skinheads standing around him. "Will you give those lives for those things that mean something, or will you spend your life in front of a Jewish worship machine called a television?" he screamed. "Will you spend your life there while your children are being molested, while your wives are raped, or will you fight for America? I say, we will fight.

"We will fight," Beam barked.

"We will fight," the crowd barked back, their fever growing.

Beam again: "We will fight."

Again the crowd responded, and again until the fever broke in a final catharsis.

The obligatory march around the town square was anticlimactic, almost a formality. An overinflated Kirk Lyons, who had been Beam's sedition trial attorney, acted as a legal adviser. Lyons stood next to the parade marshal, dressed in a three-piece brown suit, red power tie, and tan hat; he looked "imperious in a Walter Mittyish sort of way," according to one observer.[5] His appearance that Saturday afternoon in Pulaski was another stop on Lyons's long trek from survivalist camps to Waco firestorms to National Rifle Association meets back to Confederate flag rallies.

Soon after Beam's speech, three hundred skinheads and their middle-aged suitors motored over to a remote pasture for a rally. At that point, the public demonstration became part cultural carnival, part political convention, complete with interminable speeches and sideline propaganda booths. As at all skinhead events, there was an aura of impending violence. Guns were prohibited, but many carried knives. Nevertheless, the beer flowed peacefully, an impromptu tattoo parlor operated, and two young couples made wedding vows. While they waited for the bands to start, half the crowd partied and half watched the speakers.

About 7:00 p.m., Pete Peters, the Identity preacher from Colorado, came onto the stage. Peters had more in common with Willis Carto's mainstreamers than with the movement's vanguardists. His radio ministry was aimed at new movement recruits, the Joe Six-Packs so disdained by William Pierce. That night outside Pulaski, Peters dressed in cowboy boots, ten-gallon hat, and western-style suit. He warmed up for what should have been his usual forty-five-minute harangue by ridiculing his potential audience and immediately clashed with the crowd.

"I thought in the South you had manners down here," he complained. "I always heard that the southerner was very mannerly. I tell you something, out in the West, when you've got a man speaking, and he spent a lot of money to come out, you don't have a bunch of loudmouths along the sidelines trying to outdo him talking." That brought a few jeers and catcalls from the crowd, many of whom clearly weren't listening anyway.

Then Peters insulted the skinheads: "Now I understand that, tell me if I'm wrong here, skinheads are the SS troops of the right. Is that right? What's that stand for? Stupid sissies. Does it stand for stupid sissies, or does it stand for strong soldiers?"

At that point a young skinhead rushed the stage, ripped open his shirt, pointed to his knife scars, and started screaming about "niggers."

Peters was rattled by the less than deferential response and left the stage after a short thirteen minutes. His first sermon to skinheads had been drowned in a sea of beer.

On reflection, however, Peters expressed sympathy for the skins. He saw in their revolt an echo of the youth culture from a generation before. It was a remarkable observation, but colored, as always, through his Identity prism. The skins were a "natural outgrowth of a sick, dying, decaying society, of a race that's going extinct," he said. "I met their counterpart, their dialectical counterpart about twenty years ago, those that were on the left. They were the longhairs called the hippies."

Peters also recognized a concordance between his own white nationalism and theirs. "The skins know that you can't have a nation of people without a race," Peters later told his congregation back home in Colorado. "And most people don't seem to understand that. And the skins are smart enough, are willing to fight for their race and their territory."[6]

While that core agreement was enough to initially draw him to Pulaski, Peters's cowboy Americanism was repulsed by the skins' Naziesque internationalism. "You know, as you point to these young people out there and say this is our heritage and our people and our culture," Peters complained, "and yet you see them going 'Sieg Heil, Sieg Heil.'" The Hitler salute was not part of American culture, Peters argued.[7]

Actually, Peters decided that both swastikas and Confederate flags symbolized a form of nationalism he didn't share. His Colorado congregation didn't imagine a southern white republic. His midwestern and western constituency may have included ethnic Germans, but America, not Europe, was the Promised Land. Besides, Peters's theology promised eventual victory, not defeat. "When you march around with a Nazi swastika, you carry the flag of a loser. It is stupid to only venerate and exalt losers as heroes," he reminded his followers. "How can you deny the fact that the South lost . . . You can respect that flag, but when you carry it understand you carry the flag of the side that lost. Robert E. Lee, great general that he was, lost the war."

It wasn't solely that the South and Hitler's Germany had lost their respective wars. Peters believed that secular ideologies could not redeem white people from their national sins: "When you have a society that has the problems of our land today, you've got to understand that it goes back to a spiritual problem. You've got to read more than the Constitution . . . You've got to hear more than *Race and Reason* TV programs. You've got to read more than *Mein Kampf.* You've got to go to the word of God. You've got to go to the spiritual cause of the whole problem."[8]

The Pulaski rally and Pete Peters's unceremonious rejection caught the currents then swirling through survivalist camps and at cow pasture cross burnings. Skins were tough new additions to the violent wing of the movement, which had been battered by arrests and the Fort Smith conspiracy trail. But they were not simply street fodder for existing *Gruppenführers*. While they certainly respected William Pierce, for example, skins were not yet ready to be disciplined cadres in anybody's organization. Perhaps Pierce understood that skins would not bend easily to his will at that time. Only later did he intervene in the white power skin scene, make a little money, and recruit a few top cadres.

The conflict at Pulaski was repeated dozens of times. On one occasion a Klan chief planning a protest in Dallas tried to keep the skinheads away from his event. "The day before our rally about twenty of those garish looking suckers showed up at our hotel," he told a daily newspaper. "My advance man knew I didn't want anything to do with them and told them not to show up. They didn't know what we're all about. They're just scary."[9] A few skins showed up nonetheless.

Earlier more than one hundred skinheads prepared to join a march in Georgia. This time the same Klan chief tried to coax them into cooperation.[10] Shortly before the parade began, he walked over to the parking lot where the skins were gathering. He told the skins that personally he agreed with them. But this was a Klan rally, he said. Chants of "white power" were appropriate; the skins' more usual "Sieg Heil" shouts were not. Moments later a local Klanswoman in charge of mothering the parade to birth repeated the plea, urging the out-of-town skins to "act white." With those words the skinheads spontaneously broke into a rhythmic "Sieg Heil" with their stiff right arms popping up in the air in unison. Clearly chagrined, the Klanswoman walked away.

Skinheads were not always at odds with the movement's existing leaderships, however. Remember that skins had participated harmoniously in the movement's free speech protest march before the trial in Fort Smith. In 1989 the difficulties stemmed from the skins' origin in an autonomous youth subculture with its own organizations, leaderships, and ideas.

The skinhead phenomenon arrived in Pulaski from Britain virtually unnoticed, through a self-invented musical subculture of small affinity groups grafted onto a borrowed ideology. After years of incubation it finally burst into public view on daytime television talk shows. On both sides of the Atlantic, the skinhead movement was shaped by the interaction of global electronic communications—records, television, and computers—with local tribes of alienated white youths. In America, these skinheads were from the first generation born after the civil rights movement.

On the other side of the Atlantic, British skinheads first emerged in the late 1960s, one of several post–World War Two youth cultures to define themselves through fashion and music. These young people were a self-contradictory mix.[11] They listened to Afro-Caribbean music, but attacked Pakistani and East Indian ethnic immigrants as well as homosexuals. They rejected their parents' social conformism at the same time that they exalted their working-class roots. In fact, the skinhead uniform represented an idealized industrial worker: shaved heads or brush-cut hair, Dr. Martens work boots, short-hemmed blue jeans, and broad suspenders. Their coda emphasized personal toughness and intense group loyalties, manifested in an eagerness to battle both other youths and the authorities.

After that first generation, British skinheads returned in the mid-1970s as two ideological movements, both of which claimed the same subculture origins. One wing associated itself with antifascism and the left. The others identified themselves with a growing movement against nonwhite immigrants. This second group organized themselves through white power music and shops selling Nazi paraphernalia, such as stylized swastika badges. Initially, both antifascists and white power skins listened to the same music, and they often battled each other for control of the dance halls.

Skinhead concerts lacked Leni Riefenstahl's cinematic finesse but had the emotive force of a Nuremberg rally nonetheless. Center stage a thuggish, sweating lead singer with close-cropped hair and large tattoos snarled lyrics into a microphone, while several dozen men crashed into one another in a rhythmic dance known as slamming. Between songs the slam dancers would often chant, "Sieg Heil, Sieg Heil," their right arms jerking up in salute, one of the few rhythmic and coordinated movements of an entire concert. The lyrics amounted to cheerless national socialist agitprop: "Hail the New Dawn," "Boots and Braces," "Europe Awake," "Smash the IRA," "Blood and Honour." But the crowd often clapped and sang along: "We will fight and die to keep our land." Hundreds of young men, and a few women, pumped full of rage while drinking beer to the thudding beat, transformed themselves into soldiers of a great white army. Violence was inevitable.[12]

In the United States, skinheads first appeared out of a schism within the punk rock scene, itself another subculture initially expressed through style and music.[13] British punk bands developed an audience in the United States, and homegrown bands, such as the Ramones, began playing clubs in the mid-1970s. Aspects of punk rock later made it to the edges of the mass market, and some of its particular style was adapted by Hollywood and the fashion industry. In the beginning punks sported wild multicolored hairstyles and nose rings and pierced their skin with safety pins. To stand middle-class values on their head, they often threw beer cans at bands to show appreciation.[14] Clapping was too bourgeois. Their core values were nihilism, antiauthoritarianism, and extreme individualism—not patriotism or racial nationalism. Nevertheless, punks sometimes wore Iron Crosses or Naziesque paraphernalia for its shock value, further marginalizing themselves.

Despite the antiestablishment flirtation with Nazi symbols, William Pierce's National Alliance quickly rejected punk style and music in the 1970s. "Punk rock and 'Nazi' rock have a similar appeal to a jaded, Judaized, deracinated youth," said one National Vanguard commentary at that time. "The quasi-military uniforms, the chains, the safety pins . . . have nothing whatever to do with the inherently healthy worldview of National Socialism."[15]

Pierce's quick rejection of punk was in part an accurate assessment of punk's expressed politics. In part it also reflected his cultural tastes. At the time National Alliance publications regularly promoted classical German music and national socialist romanticism as art. The sculptor Arno Breker, for example, was a favorite. Most significantly, however, Pierce tended to reject alternative youth subcultures of any type. His experience of 1960s left-wing social movements was certainly still uppermost in his mind during the 1980s. Pierce's sledgehammer aversion to alternative subcultures led him to miss completely the nuances within the punk scene, as well as the opening moments of the white power skinhead phenomenon itself.

At first the identities of punks, white power skins, and antiracist skins were mixed together. They attended the same music shows and often read the same zines (cut-and-paste, do-it-yourself periodicals usually produced at the local copy shop). One early skinhead conflated all three identities in a letter to a music tabloid. "I feel it's about time we skins/Nazi skins stood up and told it like it is," he wrote. "I agree with sporting swastikas as a symbol of Blitzkrieg style revolution. That's why I joined the punk movement . . . it presented me with an aggressive, angry, stomping, fighting mad type of movement." This elemental rage and confusion was oft-repeated.[16]

Gradually, differences in music, dress style, and attitudes toward violence separated the nationalistic skins from the nihilistic punks. Each developed its own zines. American white power skins listened to tapes and records of British bands, but they had not yet birthed their own homegrown American bands. So for a while in the mid-1980s, punks and both types of skins shared music events. In Denver, for example, one notorious skinhead fought repeatedly in the mosh pit of area punk clubs until he left the city. When he returned, he started a small-time business distributing British neo-Nazi skinhead music and paraphernalia. (He eventually became a regional organizer for a Klan group.)[17]

A crew in San Francisco, one of the very first, followed a similar trajectory into the white phantasm. They began as punks in the same city that had once produced beatniks and flower children. Gradually this crew rejected the mores, values, and style of their punk brethren. At the same time, they began adopting dress styles and tattoos from British white power skinheads and listening to British bands. They also started battling punks for control of the music scene. Sometimes the punks struck back, and one punk band, Dead Kennedys, had a national following with its song "Nazi Punks Fuck Off."[18]

Unlike the British skins they imitated, however, most American skinheads invented their "working-class" character. One early study found that most were "high school dropouts from middle-class, politically conservative, suburban backgrounds."[19] One prominent young woman in a San Francisco group was from a wealthy family. She adopted punk styles while attending elite art schools before dropping out and joining the skinhead scene.[20] Hardly the story of angry unemployed working-class youth so often told to explain the skinhead phenomenon in the United States.

What skinheads did provide one another was intense comradeship and a set of family-like relationships. They often lived communally, eagerly defended one another, and physically attacked outside groups. By the late 1980s the line between punks and skinheads had been firmly demarcated. One white power skinhead group in Cincinnati, obviously annoyed at the confused identities, distributed a crude handwritten leaflet: "We are *not* idiotic punk rockers and do not wish to be associated with such left-wing scum . . . We are the exact opposite in ideals . . . We are part of a world-wide white nationalist movement of youth."[21]

This internationalist version of white nationalism was bred into the subculture by its origins as an imitation of British styles, music, and political sensibilities. At Pulaski the appeal to neo-Confederate nationalism or Pete Peters's theology was less powerful than the thudding magnetism of electric guitars and growling calls for blood and soil. Although a small segment of skins did embrace Christian Identity doctrine, most found their religious icons in Norse mythology, Viking history, and runic symbols. While Peters and his Identity kinsmen regarded America as a special promised land, for skinheads it was just one more landmass, like Europe, on which the white gene pool reproduced.

Even if William Pierce was paying scant attention to skinheads at that time, his own dogma closely paralleled theirs, particularly regarding Christian Identity's claims to historical accuracy. In *Hunter*, his second novel after *The Turner Diaries*, published in 1989, Pierce has one of his mouthpiece characters remark on Christian Identity's claim that the biblical people Israel were Aryans: "They have this completely nutty version of history, which no one who's paid attention in his high school history class can believe."[22] If Pierce had been out in the cow pasture that night, he might have whooped and hollered Pete Peters off the stage along with the rest.

But Pierce was not at Pulaski in 1989 or any other venue where he might rub shoulders with the undisciplined minions that made up the vanguardists' new rank and file. He spent the year ensconced in his West Virginia camp, installing a new computer system and preparing the text of *Hunter* for publication. He noticed that "more and more people [had] become receptive to the message" and were buying his magazines and books. But more sales did not translate easily into new recruits. "It's still very difficult to find more good people for our team," he complained. "The fact is that we need more people involved in our work, and we need more money to support those people."[23] Apparently, Pierce did not draw the simple conclusion that sitting on the side of a mountain and writing a novel would not build the kind of cadre organization he wanted.

Pierce and National Alliance made one attempt in those years to reach out to mainstream white people, a stockholders' initiative like that used by consumer groups.[24] In 1986, the same year he had moved his headquarters from a Washington, D.C., suburb to West Virginia, National Alliance bought one hundred shares of AT&T stock. A year later it submitted a proposal against affirmative action for a vote by stockholders. AT&T's management responded by not submitting the proposal to a vote, but a Securities and Exchange Commission ruling placed it on the agenda for an April 1988 vote. Amid great controversy and protests, the resolution was voted down. National Alliance resubmitted a similar resolution for the 1989 meeting, but that too was voted down. As skinheads were marching around Pulaski's town square, Pierce's cadres were preparing still another resolution for the 1990 AT&T stockholders' meeting. Whatever stockholders actually thought of affirmative action, it was unlikely they would vote for a resolution sponsored by an outfit advocating a white revolution.

Why would Pierce and National Alliance bother with such a misguided scheme? A *National Vanguard* magazine article describing the resolution process reminded readers that they believed "equality is a despicable goal." Not much news in that statement. So an additional rationale was invoked: "The aim is to take the offensive against the enemies of White America, to show what can be done with the weapons at hand, and to inspire others to take them up and join the fight."[25]

Pierce soon abandoned this experiment with stockholders' resolutions. At that point, mass organizing—even among the rough-and-tumble skinheads, much less ordinary white stockholders—was still beyond the National Alliance's ken. A few years later, however, that changed.

If William Pierce dressed once or twice in Willis Carto's more mainstream costume, then Carto did the reverse, putting on Pierce's vanguardist clothes for an occasion or two. Carto made a stab at promoting the skin scene in the 1980s, when his *Spotlight* tabloid published a three-page photo and text spread glorifying skinheads. "They live by a macho creed of two-fisted values such as personal courage and fighting skills," it gushed.

"[They] represent a total rejection of the system by a still small, but possibly pace-setting, element of today's youth . . . In increasing numbers they are turning to the struggle to replace this order with one that will truly care about their race and their nation . . . given the toughness, determination and fearlessness of the skinheads, they are certainly prepared to do their part to bring a new social order to America," *The Spotlight* marveled. The spread had been written and photographed by Robert Hoy, a middle-aged American who had published a magazine spread of photographs on British skinheads.[26] (In a most ironic twist, Hoy later was on the receiving end of that macho creed, much to his regret.)

At that time Carto did not follow Hoy's heroic photo display with any initiatives aimed specifically at recruiting the young subculturalists to his enterprises. The established British far right racist parties had already tried and failed to turn violence-prone dance hall drunkards into semirespectable electioneering Tory look-alikes. Americans like Carto were to have had even less success than their British counterparts.

There was one established leader, however, who had a loyal following among skinheads as the decade ended: Tom Metzger. More than anyone else, Metzger churned the skinheads' raw power into usable ideological steam. Metzger had long ago forsaken the electioneering model he had adopted immediately after leaving Duke's Knights of the Ku Klux Klan. He now sneered at both Duke and Carto. Like Pierce, he had little more than contempt for ordinary white people, chained as they were to their television sets and conservative values. Unlike Pierce, however, Metzger exalted spontaneity over discipline, small "wolf packs" over large organizations, and street action in metropolitan centers over mountainside retreats. And his prescient reading of white youth subcultures and freewheeling approach transformed him into the skinheads' godfather. "White revolutionaries have no dogmas," he proclaimed.[27]

Compared with Carto's weekly *Spotlight* or Pierce's glossy *National Vanguard* magazine, the tabloid Metzger published looked like an amateur effort. But the cartoons, polemics, and sloganeering were the envy of comrades such as Louis Beam. "You are producing the kind of publication others have only dreamed about," Beam wrote to Metzger.[28]

During the early 1980s Metzger's closest associates had pushed him toward the skinheads. Perhaps most important among them was Wyatt Kaldenberg, a former New Leftist who claimed to have campaigned for Tom Hayden and had once joined a Marxist sect.[29] The physically imposing Kaldenberg was particularly attuned to marginal subcultures. He worried that veteran white nationalists would not recognize new opportunities in unexpected places. He lamented what he regarded as a lost chance for the Aryan cause, when the early punk movement in Southern California, he claimed, had been dominated by "Nazis." Punk clubs, Kaldenberg wrote, had been a "great recruiting ground for the young White Racists." But the opportunity was missed because "Jews dominate the music industry and now they control the punk scene." The emergence of skinheads, Kaldenberg argued, was "a present given to us from the English [*sic*] National Front." It was a subculture "sweeping the nation and . . . is our greatest in road into Aryan Youth."[30] He proposed providing white power bands with places to play and other support.

Metzger took the hint. In 1983, six years before Aryan Nations held its Pulaski event, Metzger promoted British skinhead music.[31] He sponsored skinheads on his community access cable television program and defended the young racists on national news programs. His tabloid became a forum for skins, publishing their letters and articles, advertising their organizations, and promoting their events. Odinist graphics and skin-style cartoons dominated the tabloid's design. The middle-aged former Klansman who had once won a congressional primary election disappeared under a blanket of white power rock music and Viking tattoos. "Ancient barbaric qualities are just what our effete, overcivilized and self-abasing society needs," his *WAR* tabloid cheered.[32]

In 1988, Metzger sponsored the first "Aryan Fest" with homegrown American bands in northeastern Oklahoma. More than a hundred skinheads from Minnesota to Texas turned up for a day of music and speeches. It was the first in a string of outdoor "Reich 'n Roll" concerts.

Stealing a page from the 1960s, Metzger even advertised one California gathering as an "Aryan Woodstock."[33]

Tabloids of cartoons, daylong rock fests, and computer bulletin boards may have helped bring skins under Metzger's wing, but taken altogether, these elements still could not change a small subculture into the most visible national symbol of white youth rebellion. Mainstream television talk shows did that. From the well-regarded *The Oprah Winfrey Show* to a dozen other lesser lights, white power skinheads took advantage of the electronic soapbox provided them. Their TV hosts were unprepared for the skins' willingness to flout the rules of television etiquette, and the shows usually turned into verbal race riots.

Finally, on November 4, 1988, skinhead TV turned violent on *The Geraldo Rivera Show*. Rivera opened his program with the proclamation that "sunlight was the best disinfectant" for hatred. On the television stage he arrayed Tom Metzger's son John and two skinheads against a rabbi and a black man. When a melee ensued, chairs were thrown and Wyatt Kaldenberg charged from the audience and broke Rivera's nose.

The fight was replayed on the nightly news, and the following morning daily newspapers across the country printed pictures and long stories. One of the syndicated comics ran a strip on Rivera's nose. Overnight, for millions of young white people, defiance of convention and authority became visually intertwined with white power skinheads. It was as if Geraldo Rivera had paid for and distributed forty million copies of an *Aryan Youth Movement* tabloid.[34] Contrary to Rivera's initial claims, nothing was disinfected.

The Metzgers went home and claimed victory. "Thousands of inquiries and millions of viewers now recognize a White separatist movement exists," they crowed.[35]

Even William Pierce sent word of his approval. "I just saw someone who looks a lot like your son John punch out Roy Innis on the Geraldo Show on the NBC Evening News," Pierce wrote in a letter to the elder Metzger. "Tom Brokaw identified him only as a 'hatemonger,' but I thought I recognized the face. If I was right, please give my warmest congratulations to your son."[36]

By the time of the Pulaski event the number of hard-core white power skinheads had grown from 350 in a few major metropolitan areas to 3,500 from every corner of the country. Thousands more young white people dressed the part, emulating their brave contemporaries. Still, the numbers were small. The total number of white nationalist cadres had drifted up from about 15,000 in 1980 to slightly more than 20,000, with about 150,000 sympathizers who bought publications or attended meetings. It was still a relatively insular ideological epiphenomenon, however, and not yet a mass-style movement.

Mass and weight are different physical properties, however. The movement's mass may have been small, but its weight was increasing, primarily because of gravitational forces outside its control. Principal among these forces was the centrifugal breakup of the communist bloc in Eastern Europe and the end of the Cold War.

PART three

The End of Anticommunism, 1990–1991

German reunification, the collapse of the Soviet Union, and the First Persian Gulf War change the geopolitical alignments upon which anticommunism and American national identity were hung during the post-World War Two era. New forms of nationalism—racial, ethnic, and religious—assert themselves. In the United States a new white nationalism is born.

German Unification and the Reemergence of Nationalism

February 12, 1990. Leipzig, Deutsche Demokratische Republik. A strange quiet bounced across the tracks of the *Hauptbahnhof*. Everyone politely waited his turn to step down off the train and into the long concrete corridors out of the station. Not a soul pushed or shoved. No graffiti covered the gray walls. No dozed-out druggies or homeless women wrapped in rags and newspapers sat in the corners. One young entrepreneur, stationed at the end of a long, empty shadow, illegally traded currency: ten *Ostmark* for one *Westmark*, more than three times the official rate. He knew that the Ostmark and East Germany were already dead, even if the official burial was months away. Once the site of the Soviet bloc's premier manufacturing exposition, Leipzig now sat at the center of a political maelstrom that belied the tranquillity of its train station.[1]

During the previous summer and fall, mass rallies of nonconformist intellectuals, artists, and clergy had protested the regime's tyrannical powers with candlelight vigils in the streets. Long before ultranationalists or anyone else dared defy the secret police, these dissidents spearheaded a prodemocracy movement that had spread across East Germany. During the same months a parallel drive by tens of thousands of East Germans had pushed into the brightly neon-lit streets of West Germany. Eventually the combination of open protest and mass defection forced the East German authorities to open the Berlin Wall on November 9. Like almost every date and place in German history, November 9 has at least two meanings. In 1938 it was *Kristallnacht*, the pogrom that marked in blood and glass the beginning of German Jewry's physical destruction. In 1989 it marked the end of the Berlin Wall as a dividing point between Germans, East and West. The Brandenburg Gate changed from a nearly forgotten Prussian military monument hidden behind miles of concrete wall to the scene of a freedom festival broadcast live across the globe.[2]

This Monday night in February, a noisy crowd of thirty thousand elbowed its way into the plaza by Leipzig's Opera House. Clumps of people made a mad grab at carloads of brightly colored posters and literature from West German political parties. One stack of Christian Democratic Union newspapers was yanked from the hands of a young woman. When it fell to the ground, the crowd pushed her out of the way and snatched the papers. Just as quickly, many of these same papers were discarded and trampled underfoot, as the crowd surged toward the next new bundle. Banners that had previously read WIR SIND DER VOLK, meaning "We are the people" (and should be able to rule ourselves), became WIR SIND EIN VOLK, "We are one people," and DEUTSCHLAND EINIG VATERLAND, "Germany United Fatherland." The movement for basic civil liberties and human rights in East Germany had morphed into a nationalist demand for unification of the two German states.[3]

Standing uneasily at the edge of this crowd, a small band of the early dissident intellectuals circulated typewritten half sheet leaflets. Where were all these people during the summer of 1989? one asked. Democracy was more difficult than shopping for new shoes, another said glumly. But the crowd paid them scant attention now. These intellectuals wanted free expression, but they didn't relish paying for it in the capitalist marketplace. And they didn't fully endorse unification. As the black, red, and gold West German flags replaced the pale glow of candlelight vigils, the protest leadership had shifted out of their hands.

Across the plaza, stern young men circulated, distributing flyers from an anti-immigrant party, *Die Republikaners*: "*Sozialismus ist Beschissmus*," a play on words that translates roughly as "Socialism is Shitism." At that point, the Republikaners were still illegal in the East. Amazingly, not one of these circulars was discarded that night. Several older women handed out booklets proclaiming that the "six million" were a "legend," as well as flyers advertising a speech the following night in Dresden by a well-known Holocaust denier, David Irving.

On the steps of the Opera House, lit against the nighttime darkness by television cameras from around the world, speaker followed speaker as the crowd waited uneasily to begin its march through the streets. Representatives from the main West German political parties were followed by a speaker from the marginal National Democratic Party. "There are too many Turks in Germany," he complained. The German Democratic Republic (East Germany), he said, actually occupied *Mitteldeutschland*, or Middle Germany. In this revanchist description, the provinces under Russian and Polish sovereignty since 1945 were in fact the real eastern part of Germany. Obviously, if a new Germany had tried to reclaim these territories as part of its unification process, a conflict with Poland in particular would have been inevitable. But the crowd greeted his claims in the same manner as they greeted all others.

Approximately two hundred skinheads roamed the plaza, distributing leaflets from far right parties and bullying foreign reporters and television camera crews. With their black bomber jackets and shaved heads they matched their American counterparts in both style and ideology. Only the jacket patches differed. *"Ich bin stolz ein Deutscher zu sein"* (I am proud to be German), they read. Several dozen clambered to the top of the Opera House with a banner declaring FOREIGN TROOPS OUT, a radical demand at that time but later part of the unification pact. When the march finally started out of the plaza into the streets, the skinheads started chanting, *"Deutschland erwache, Jude verrecke"* (Germany awake, Jews perish). A small group of marchers responded to the chants by blowing stadium air horns in protest, but otherwise the skinheads went uncontested.[4]

As the march reached its conclusion, the crowd dispersed into the dark streets and the night became quiet. A few *Polizei* reappeared in the plaza, and others took posts inside the train station. Foreign journalists earned a quick glance at their passports as they boarded the midnight express to the West, but otherwise the once-feared East German police state now seemed curiously inert as a revolution swept it aside.[5]

East and West Germany had been the quintessential symbols of the geopolitical order. At the end of World War Two, Allied victors had dismembered the Twelve Year *Reich* and redrawn the borders of Europe in the process. Those provinces of the German Reich not reallocated to the surrounding countries were divided into four zones of occupation: French, British, American, and Soviet. As tension mounted between the Soviets on the one side and the Western powers on the other, two different states were created in 1949: the Federal Republic of Germany in the West and the German Democratic Republic in the East. Berlin, situated in the provinces under Soviet control, was divided and at the center of Cold War contention. The Wall, built in 1961, had become a sign of the division of Europe between communism in the East and capitalist democracies in the West.

After the Berlin Wall fell, the East German state followed, a first step in the unraveling of the Soviet bloc in Eastern Europe. West German parties such as the Christian Democratic Union and the Social Democrats developed large branches in the East. Stores in Leipzig, Dresden, Halle, and East Berlin became stocked with products from the West, everything from Sony sound systems to soft toilet paper. The West German deutsche mark became the official currency in the East. And then on October 3, 1990, the lands formerly known as the German Democratic Republic became part of an expanded Federal Republic.[6]

The skinheads, Holocaust deniers, and anti-immigrant racists in the streets of Leipzig that night became a prominent feature of the new Germany. For *Ossis* (East Germans), they seemed little different from the sudden presence of superior consumer goods. They (wrongly) assumed skinheads were manufactured only in the West and imported into the East. The *Wessis*, on the other hand, assumed skinheads were products only of unemployment and hard times in the East. Both were wrong. Skinheads in Germany did emerge first in the West during the 1980s, just as they had in the United States and other countries after they had spread from the United Kingdom, and they reached the East long before unification. These white power skinheads shared a common revolutionary zeitgeist. Like their American counterparts, they embraced Hitlerian symbols, such as the swastika and the stiff-armed salute. And far right and ultranationalist parliamentary parties in Germany eagerly sought them as recruits.[7]

Anti-immigrant fevers had also existed in West Germany prior to unification. The foremost parliamentary party on the far right had been the Republikaners, which polled ninety-four thousand votes and won eleven seats to West Berlin's city parliament in the January 1989 elections. Franz Schönhuber, the Republikaners' most visible spokesman, personally linked present-tense racism to that of the forbidden past by writing a book that favorably recounted his stint as an SS officer during World War Two. Undeterred by this association with Hitlerism, his party won two million West German votes in the June 1989 elections for the European Parliament.[8]

The path from the Republikaners to the ruling party, the Christian Democratic Union (CDU), was traversed quickly. The CDU adopted much of the Republikaners' anti-immigrant program, deporting refugees and changing the post-Hitler constitution that granted liberal asylum rights. In addition, militant ideological youth gangs known as *Kameradenschaften* prowled the cities—East and West—in search of the homes of *Ausländers*, or foreigners. (Third-generation ethnic Turks, born in Germany like their parents, were still considered "foreigners," and the government had not yet allowed them an immediate constitutional right to citizenship.) The youthful arsonists stood only a flaming petrol bomb outside the mainstream, and for several moments it seemed as if all Germany would be engulfed in the flames of burning refugee hostels.[9]

Old-fashioned racial nationalism swept across Germany like a whirlwind from hell. When the graves of playwright Bertolt Brecht and his wife, Helen Weigel, were defaced with the epithet *Jude Sau* (Jew pig), Brecht's family left the graffiti up as a warning. For a brief moment, a wave of candlelight protests marched against murder and mayhem. Otherwise, the barrier between polite society and barbarism collapsed more quickly than the Berlin Wall itself. Here, at this time, the reconsideration of German national identity took center stage. If a reevaluation of values was to take place, then a reexamination of the Holocaust did not trail far behind. [10]

German Unification and Auschwitz

By constitutional law the Federal Republic officially annexed the German Democratic Republic on October 3, 1990, marking for history the end of the post–World War Two period. During this postwar period, East Germans had been told that their state was the legacy of antifascist resistance, and they felt unburdened by the past. West Germans, on the other hand, had felt as though they were being punished for crimes committed during the years they euphemistically referred to as the "Hitler time." After occupation by Allied armies, NATO troops had been deployed, and the American military and intelligence established command centers. The loss of territories to Russia and Poland had been compounded by the separation of families on either side of the East-West line. Children felt burdened with the acts of their fathers and grandfathers, who, they were told, had fought for a criminal regime. It was their homeland that had plunged the world into a war that had cost fifty million lives, including those of six million Jews. Holocaust Memorial Day became a national holiday set on the day Soviet troops liberated the Auschwitz concentration camp, officially intertwining national identity with "Auschwitz," which became the idiomatic term for the persecutions, concentration camps, and industrial murder that constituted the Holocaust. Could any expression of German nationalism ever be untarnished by these crimes once done in its name? [11]

The desire to escape the onus of the past extended from machinists laboring in the Ruhr Valley to politicians at the summit of international prestige. The Bavarian prime minister had vowed, "We must once again become a people that does not walk with the stoop of a convict of world history."[12]

When the stain of postwar division was erased by unification and annexation, many believed the period of punishment had ended. German nationalism could now be separated from "Auschwitz," they reasoned. It was a notion similar to that held by many in the United States who felt that Confederate nationalism should be considered separately from the horrors of chattel slavery. In the first moments after formal unity, a commentator for one of the Federal Republic's premier liberal newspapers hoped that "Auschwitz will not remain a standard of condemnation at which Germans reflexively lapse into intense self-analysis."[13]

The logic may be circular, but it was compelling. If Germany had been divided as punishment for "Auschwitz," then "Auschwitz" was directly linked to German national identity in the postwar period. And if unification ended the punishment, then it should also lead to a reconsideration of German nationalism. To complete the circle: a reconsideration of German nationalism then would mean a reconsideration of Auschwitz. By this reasoning, unification and the attendant freshly assertive nationalism—rather than the outrageous insults of skinheads in the plaza or small groups of deniers meeting in a hotel room—altered the German debate on the Holocaust.

Unification did in fact transform much of Germany's thinking about its own history. And not just in the East, where the history of Soviet occupation and Communist rule was rewritten. One study conducted during this period found that 58 percent of Germans agreed with the statement "It is time to put the memory of the Holocaust behind us." A separate question found that 39 percent agreed that "Jews are exploiting the Holocaust for their own purposes."[14] The debate over the link between the Holocaust and German national identity, however, had actually emerged first among scholars in West Germany prior to unification. Known as the *Historikerstreit*, or historians' debate, in the mid-1980s, it prefigured a wider reconsideration in 1990.

The central figure in this debate was the historian Ernst Nolte. To Americans, Nolte is probably best known as the author of *Three Faces of Fascism*, a 1963 overview of German National Socialism, Italian Fascism, and the Action Française. To Germans, Nolte was a commanding personality among postwar intellectuals who taught modern European history at the Free University in West Berlin prior to unification.[15]

Nolte's camp of historians expressed the victimization felt by West Germans and their quest for relief from the burden of "Auschwitz." (In 1986 one German newspaper commissioned a polling study that concluded that the German people were subject to "humiliation" and that

Germany was an "injured nation" because of the national identification of its history with Hitler's crimes and anti-Semitism.[16]) To that end, Nolte sought to disassociate the uniqueness of the Holocaust from Germany.

In 1986 Nolte unofficially opened the debate by decoupling the annihilation of European Jewry from anti-Semitism. Instead, he argued, Hitler's crimes were consequences arising from Lenin's ghost and Stalin's crimes. "Auschwitz is not primarily the result of traditional anti-Semitism and was not just one more case of 'genocide,'" he argued. (The quotation marks are Nolte's.) Rather it was "the fear-borne reaction to the acts of annihilation that took place during the Russian Revolution."

More than just an argument that Russian Communists forced Hitler to murder the Jews, Nolte claimed that the Nazis did only what the Bolsheviks had done first: "the so-called annihilation of the Jews by the Third Reich was a reaction or a distorted copy and not a first act or an original," the once-respected historian wrote.[17]

Prior to unification, Nolte's denial of the centrality of anti-Semitism did not extend to denying the genocide itself—despite his use of qualifying quotation marks when using the word "genocide." He also conceded that the Nazis were more efficient murderers than the Communists. While he recognized the irrationality and horror of Germany's "quasi-industrial" murder machine, his argument provided solace for the guilt-stricken. The machine patent belonged to the Soviet Union, after all, not to German engineers.[18]

After unification (and the Cold War's end), however, the terms of the Historikerstreit debate changed. Nolte was explicit. "With German unification, of course, everything has changed, because one of the main points made by [my opponents] was that if you do not accept their way of interpreting German history, then you endanger peaceful coexistence [between the West and the USSR]. You also show yourself to be a German nationalist who wanted to reunite the nation by annexing the communist 'German Democratic Republic.'" Since East Germany had already been annexed and war had not broken out, Nolte believed his opponents' entire position was "no longer valid."[19]

While Nolte's brand of nationalism had been a marginal set of ideas prior to unification, now these same concepts were Chancellor Helmut Kohl's government policy. The change in discussion was reflected in a thousand venues large and small. Even the museum of Nazi atrocities at the site of the Sachsenhausen concentration camp outside East Berlin added a small exhibit on the Soviets' postwar use of the camp. The force of the *Wende* (turn-around) was so strong that one of Nolte's preunification opponents switched sides. "Nolte's approach, the center of the so-called Battle of the Historians, was actually philosophically correct," the former antagonist conceded.[20]

In essence, Nolte stepped forward first to argue for a new method of historical inquiry. If unification legitimized German nationalism, then the normalization of German nationalism meant that the murder of European Jews should be reexamined. Although he did not deny the "genocide," he did demand that Germany's national claims be considered free from the burdens imposed by Hitler and Holocaust. Willis Carto and the Institute for Historical Review aimed at the same target, even if they were shooting at it from a different ideological spot. Nolte's success in the Historikerstreit encouraged the hopes of white supremacists and Holocaust "revisionists" in the United States, who believed a larger attempt to rewrite history was afoot.

Germany long occupied pride of place for the American movement. For so-called Christian Identity adherents, Germans were regarded as descendants of the biblical tribe of Judah, and Germany by right was the Lion of Europe. Mainstreamers and vanguardists alike saw in Germans a reflection of themselves: embattled Aryans with fingers in the dike protecting Western Civilization from flooding. Tom Metzger's White Aryan Resistance, among others, gloried at the similarities. "Right now the Skinheads in Germany are very strong and united," he argued. "They are extremely White Power and they don't tolerate anything from anyone. They basically have the same problem we do with immigrants."[21] William Pierce also considered Germany Aryandom's once and future fatherland, although prior to 1990 he had few followers. And in Nebraska a character named Gary Lauck turned himself into a middle-aged bag carrier for hard-core National Socialists in the Federal Republic, producing German-language literature in the United States and then smuggling it into Germany, where it was ruled illegal.

The broadest, most effective ties with German anti-Semites, however, were held by Willis Carto. His wife was a German national, and *The Spotlight* carried occasional articles written in Bonn. And his Institute for Historical Review published German-language literature for distribution in Europe. As a result, it was natural for the institute to examine many of the same questions posed by Nolte when it met for its tenth conference just thirteen days after German unification.

A cautious optimism animated the meeting in a D.C. hotel ballroom. The IHR was being heard on talk radio, a perfect medium for angry white men and unverifiable rumormongering. A deliberately controversial advertising program in campus newspapers had turned into a clever two-for-one publicity bonanza. One of the IHR's offshoots contacted student newspapers with a basic it-didn't-happen-let's-talk-about-it display ad. Whether or not the newspapers accepted the paid advertisements, a debate on "free speech" and "free inquiry" followed. The IHR then got free coverage in local radio, television, and newspaper markets, something that had eluded it since the days of the so-called fifty-thousand-dollar reward. In addition, the market stayed solid for the IHR's books and insiders' journal. With the changes in Germany, a breakthrough appeared possible for the first time in decades.[22]

Nolte's advocacy of an explicitly nationalist German historiography registered high on the list of positive portents. That weekend Robert Countess, one of the IHR's prized scholars, brought news of his own discussions with Nolte. Countess, who held a master's degree from Georgetown University and a doctorate in religion from Bob Jones University, taught history at the University of Alabama in Huntsville until his death in 2005. While in Berlin during the summer of 1990, Countess said, he had met with Nolte.[23] He was respectfully received by the German historian, but his efforts to convert Nolte to IHR-style revisionism had failed. Nevertheless, Countess invited Nolte to address a future IHR conference.

According to Countess's conference remarks, Nolte had said he would agree to a future invitation, with a proviso. An eminent Holocaust historian, such as Yehuda Bauer, must also speak at the meeting. Countess concluded that Nolte might never become a "full-fledged" revisionist, but he could serve as a "bridge" between the IHR and the wider public since he held ideas common to both mainstream historians and the institute.

Like the IHR, for example, Nolte contended that Jews had attained an unwarranted permanent, privileged status because of the Holocaust.[24] In addition, during the Historikerstreit he had smeared William Shirer's classic account of Hitler's Germany, *The Rise and Fall of the Third Reich*, as "clearly anti-German."[25] Further, Nolte contended that a statement by Zionist leader Chaim Weizmann in September 1939 claiming that in the event of war Jews would fight on the side of England could have justified "treating the German Jews as prisoners of war."[26] Most important, Nolte ratified the heart of the IHR's claims that its "revisionism" was unfairly vilified. "All attempts to make the National-Socialist past knowable like any other past and to strive for 'objectivity,'" he wrote during the Historiker debate, "are stigmatized with the word 'apologist.'"[27]

Nolte never fully embraced those he called radical revisionists, and he never stooped low enough to attend any of the IHR's conferences.

His reference points remained in Germany, where rewriting the history of the twentieth century occupied everyone, from skinheads distributing swastika stickers to government officials charged with creating a national consensus encompassing territories East and West. The question facing IHR regulars that weekend was straightforward: Could they translate the changes in Europe into an American vernacular?

Mark Weber shouldered the task that weekend in Washington, D.C. Uniquely suited to the task, Weber had studied history in Munich and remained fluent in German. As a young editor for Pierce's National Alliance, he had tackled international issues. And now, about to be in the employ of Willis Carto, Weber had started "debating" the Holocaust on network television.[28] In an hourlong keynote speech, Weber connected the dots between the transformation of Europe and the IHR. "While revisionism is going full scale ahead in Eastern Europe," he told attendees, "it is needed now here in America."[29] By Weber's telling, the IHR was about to vanquish its foes. The fall of the Berlin Wall meant an accelerated retreat by the "Holocaust lobby" at home. And American victory in the Cold War would soon mean the end of foreign aid to Israel. All would combine to stimulate public support for the IHR.[30]

At its banquet dinner, the IHR presented evidence that greater public acceptance awaited it with the appearance of John Toland. The author of several bestselling military histories, his 1971 book about Japan, *The Rising Sun*, had won a Pulitzer Prize. Toland's prominence far exceeded that of anyone previously associated with the IHR. None of his books, including his biography of Hitler, questioned the facts of the Holocaust. Nevertheless, the IHR considered Toland's Pearl Harbor tale *Infamy* "strongly Revisionist." Its newsletter could justifiably claim that the "participation of so prestigious and courageous a writer" was a milestone.[31]

Toland's banquet speech, although considered the "catch of the conference," added nothing to the historical record. Instead, it was a self-absorbed recounting of his meetings with Nazi war heroes and stories about research and writing. Still, the IHR was thrilled by Toland's presence because it meant that "we Revisionists are no longer talking to ourselves."[32]

Despite these changes, a bunker mentality informed this conference, just as it had dominated meetings past. Precautionary steps again kept the conference's actual location secret until the last moment. After preregistering by mail, attendees were given a phone number to call upon arrival in D.C. At that point they were diverted to a hotel on Dupont Circle in Northwest Washington. There, in a rented room, Elisabeth Carto checked credentials, issued ID tags, and directed traffic to the conference site itself, a ballroom in another hotel.[33] The circuitous route reinforced the participants' belief that the IHR was victimized by the "enemies of free speech."

At that moment the IHR, however, remained a political enterprise atop a borderline movement, not an academically accepted organization of historians.[34] The same number attended that weekend as had in the past: about 125. Half were returnees. Half the speakers' list repeated performances as well. The usual excuses for small attendance fooled only the IHR themselves: the group didn't want large numbers, the staff contended; big crowds were too hard to control. And most of the speeches emphasized the idea that they all were victims, a certain sign of their marginality.[35]

Along the meeting's sidelines, nasty Jew baiting remained customary, augmented by speakers who told thin routine jokes about such Jewish personalities as Elie Wiesel. Mark Weber exemplified the contradiction between the IHR's thoroughly anti-Semitic roots and its attempts to grow more acceptable. He told the conference that of course "we all express our sympathy" for the Jews' wartime suffering. The next moment he angrily promised to deride the United States Holocaust Museum, then under construction amid other Washington monuments, as soon as it opened to the public. It was a "monument to foreigners," he scoffed. He promised to make it an object of public scorn. "We're going to love pointing out the mistakes," he crowed, ". . . we're going to have great fun."[36] Weber's sneering aside, when the Holocaust Museum did open, exhibits drew more Americans in one week than the deniers could distribute pamphlets to in fifty-two.

While the Historikerstreit and the collapse of the Berlin Wall changed the conditions under which the Institute for Historical Review tried to rewrite the Holocaust, German unification did not change this small band of anti-Semites into genuine historians. Other world changes, however, eventually did transform the entire American white supremacist movement. The disintegration of the German Democratic Republic in the East was soon followed by the collapse of the entire Soviet bloc in Eastern Europe. Like a string of dominoes falling from Berlin to Moscow to Washington, D.C., the communist collapse ended anticommunism as a glue unifying American conservatives and the far right. A split opened in the conservative establishment over war in the Persian Gulf. And in a completely counterintuitive development, the white supremacist movement was saved from its own internal weaknesses and marched back onto the stage of History, that fickle judge.

The First Persian Gulf War and the Realignment of the Far Right

September 1, 1990. Liberty Lobby held its convention at the very respectable Stouffer's Concourse Hotel in Arlington, Virginia, outside Washington, D.C. Approximately 250 supporters gathered, much like any other politically concerned middle-class Americans in their fifties and sixties. A dinner ship cruised down the Potomac with conventioneers on board. Longtime financial contributors received wristwatches in a ceremony designed to honor them. Willis Carto eulogized the Lobby's recently deceased secretary, Lois Peterson. *The Spotlight*'s distribution was discussed, and policy statements were voted upon.

Plenary speakers hit Liberty Lobby's usual targets: the Federal Reserve banking system, the American Medical Association, secret drug trafficking by the CIA, and the perfidy of American support for Israel. Robert Weems popped up again, and the Mississippi Klansman turned Populist Party chair gave an abridged edition of his standard stump speech. The events in Germany were not on the agenda. The coming war with Saddam Hussein and Iraq, by contrast, was the number one topic of discussion.[1]

One month before, Iraqi leader Saddam Hussein's military had occupied neighboring Kuwait. The invasion destabilized the world's most important oil-producing region and provoked an immediate international response. As the United States posted hundreds of thousands of troops to the Persian Gulf, President George H. W. Bush constructed an unprecedented diplomatic and military coalition. In addition to longtime Western European allies, Arab countries such as Saudi Arabia, Egypt, and even Syria signed on to United Nations resolutions opposing Iraq's invasion. A United Nations resolution established January 15, 1991, as the deadline for Hussein to withdraw. For the first time since the outbreak of the Cold War, an American-led international military expedition was not conducted under the banner of anticommunism. And it went unopposed by the Soviet Union and its surrogates. "This is an historic moment," Bush said when the battle against Iraqi troops in Kuwait began. "We have in this past year made great progress in ending the long era of conflict and cold war. We have before us the opportunity to forge for ourselves and for future generations a new world order—a world where the rule of law, not the law of the jungle, governs the conduct of nations. When we are successful—and we will be—we have a real chance at this new world order, an order in which a credible United Nations can use its peacekeeping role to fulfill the promise and vision of the U.N.'s founders."[2] Bush drew a line between the past era, dominated by conflict with the Soviet Union, and an (illusionary) future of international peace and cooperation.

Meanwhile, at Liberty Lobby's convention, opposition to the impending war stood as a matter of principle. At a luncheon, the former Mississippi congressman David Bowen, then the director of the Council for the National Interest, a pro-Arab lobby, praised Liberty Lobby for "standing up for America for 35 years."[3] Comedian Dick Gregory told the same crowd that he was fasting in protest of the growing American military buildup aimed at Iraq. Mark Lane, an old friend of Gregory's then serving as Liberty Lobby's house attorney, introduced the black comedian. In a previous incarnation, Lane had been a liberal Democratic state representative in New York. And Gregory was known for his civil rights activism in the 1960s, just as Liberty Lobby was known for its segregationist platform. Nevertheless, Gregory told the assembled patriots, "[y]our group has the power to help change our foolish policy in the Persian Gulf," and the crowd gave him a standing ovation.

Across the months of the crisis, *The Spotlight* railed against Israel and blamed "international bankers" for the dire consequences of war. One early tabloid "exclusive" claimed that Israel would go to war against Iraq the week after the November 1990 election, thereby preempting any United States "offensive."[4] When military hostilities actually began, Israel stayed out of the conflict, despite Iraqi missile attacks on its cities. Liberty Lobby republished articles from the 1970s and 1980s that criticized American military policy. Each article reiterated Liberty Lobby's nationalism and its opposition to internationalism, and all aimed at proving the deleterious effects of foreign intervention.[5] One article, reprinted under Willis Carto's byline, had been first published in 1981 as President Reagan prepared to invade Grenada. It argued that imperial adventures actually weakened the United States. "Involvement in all foreign wars beginning with the Spanish-American," Carto had written, "have resulted in varieties of disaster, culture distortion, economic over expansion resulting in depression or inflation, growth of government and a weakening of American nationality."

By conflating "international intervention" with "culture distortion," Carto reiterated ideas redolent of his old infatuation with Yockeyism. Remember that for Carto, culture had always been determined by the race of the people who created it. And culture distortion was caused by racial integration or "amalgamation."[6] Thus *The Spotlight*, by reprinting the 1981 piece, warned that U.S. involvement in a Persian Gulf War would negatively influence (white) American culture because of its future impact on race relations.

In addition to Liberty Lobby, every other white skin sect saw its own archenemies reflected in the developing conflict. Sometimes their language was crude and inflammatory. "WAR IN THE MIDDLE EAST? Another Blood Sacrifice on the Alter of International Jewry," ran a banner headline on one Klan's bimonthly tabloid.[7] The "sacrifice" lingo conjured up a specific type of false charge dating from medieval Europe, the blood libel. A second group had a more contemporary slant. It complained that parity for women and racial integration had crippled the military. "The American army is demographically unsound," the group declaimed. "It is 10% female and 35% non-White. The non-Whites are over-represented in the combat forces, and they have little commitment to their country beyond their pay."[8] While some groups, like the Klan above, used the occasion to heap calumny upon Jews, and others insulted blacks and women in the military, the Populist Party did both and neither at the same time.

In West Palm Beach, Florida, a small band of Populists joined a local left-wing "peace and justice" antiwar protest. A few wore "Duke for Governor" buttons while distributing flyers and mingling with the crowd.[9] "It is the children of the conservative, white, working class who will bear the bulk of the casualties," the Populists claimed. In contrast with previous practices, these Populists lauded the left—without the usual insults directed against white liberals or black people. "The most conspicuous foes of war have been on the left and we in the Populist Party support their efforts," the leaflet read.[10]

In Pittsburgh, twenty-five pickets circled the sidewalk in front of the downtown federal building. The placards read NO WAR FOR BIG OIL PROFITS and BRING THE TROOPS HOME. Most of the pickets were middle- and working-class men and women in plaid flannel shirts, stocking caps, and pink-collar office wear; one well-dressed exception carried a sign that said JUST SAY NO TO NO-WIN FOREIGN WARS. A young boy, about ten years old, held his own sign declaring KUWAIT SHEIKS ARE GEAKS as he walked in line.

Picketing was an unusual form of street action for this party. Its members had sat through innumerable meetings, nominated themselves for public office, and even filed suit against the Federal Reserve Board. But they had rarely marched with bullhorns and placards. Such immodest behavior was best reserved for Klansmen, skinheads, or uniformed neo-Nazis. Nevertheless, the pending war with Iraq forced a small attempt at changed tactics. Despite the earnestness of their signs and slogans, the whole affair had a katzenjammer atmosphere about it. The protesters tired easily, and the group never grew larger than the original twenty-five pickets—even with a half dozen area high schoolers and Populists imported from Ohio. Don Wassall, who made himself chief of the national party, had called all the area news bureaus. Yet only one local television camera showed. "The higher-ups want to stifle us" became the explanation for lack of media interest. At one point Wassall tried to rouse the others to a round of chanting, but nothing happened. One high school student started shouting, "Death to Israel," but stopped after his girlfriend punched him in the arm.[11]

Another woman stood on the corner, handing out party leaflets. "If the Populist Party were in power," the leaflets read, "we would have hundreds of thousands of troops on the Mexican border, not in desert sand dunes ten thousand miles away . . . There would be no 'affirmative action,' quotas and other anti-white racist schemes." She soon gave up because only black people were walking past, and she was too embarrassed to hand them obviously offensive leaflets. Two young men left the demonstration briefly, bought a Confederate flag, and then returned, waving it for the duration. For these two, the battle banner was probably less a standard for America first nationalism than a simple symbol of rebellion.

The group left after an hour on the sidewalk and reconvened at a VFW hall for a "victory party."[12] Van Loman, a Cincinnati Klansman turned party officer, avowed that the afternoon's protest was bigger than anything he could organize in Ohio. Even though the event had been dispirited and poorly attended, Wassall also declared it a success.

At that point the Populist Party grabbed at the smallest shreds of good news. When a Populist candidate running for the Rhode Island state legislature received 700 votes, or 34 percent of those cast in that race, the party virtually declared victory. When another candidate, in New Jersey, received 19,957 votes (about 1 percent) in a statewide race, that too was considered a step up because their person had outpolled the miserable showings of the other third parties. The party's electioneering was "following a long-term strategy, and is right on track," its newsletter assured any doubters.[13]

Long march or short hike, this third party of known racists and anti-Semites would never muster the hundreds of thousands of votes necessary to win an election. Nevertheless, the Populist Party played a unique role. As the one white supremacist grouping closest to the conservative movement, it paid attention to developments on the Republican far right. A few key members commented favorably on an increasingly radical nationalist tendency within the broader conservative movement. The personification of that trend was Pat Buchanan. This small but significant group of conservatives broke ranks with President George H. W. Bush over his plans for a New World Order and his war in the Persian Gulf.

Enter Pat Buchanan

A brawl had started on television soon after Iraq's invasion of Kuwait. At that moment President Bush was still out on the international hustings, drumming up support for his anti-Saddam coalition. Pat Buchanan sat with four other commentators around a horseshoe-shaped broadcast studio engaged in one of America's best-known political pundit food fights, the *McLaughlin Report*. While arguing that little domestic or international support existed for a new war, Pat blurted out: "There are only two groups that are beating the drums for war in the Middle East— the Israeli Defense Ministry and its amen corner in the United States."[14]

Later in the same program he repeated the charge, implying that Israel was pulling the United States' foreign policy strings, urging Americans to spill blood in a proxy war Israelis were unwilling to fight. "The Israelis want this war desperately because they want the United States to destroy the Iraqi war machine. They want us to finish them off. They don't care about our relations with the Arab world."[15]

Substitute "amen corner in the United States" for "Zionist Occupied Government," and the verbal flourishes of Buchanan and white supremacists start to sound remarkably alike. On these points and others, differences between white supremacist rhetoric and Pat Buchanan talk disappear before the naked eye. Buchanan's stature as a former Nixon and Reagan White House aide and his nationally syndicated column and television celebrity, however, gave him a bigger megaphone than any Aryan Nations believer screaming at the top of his lungs. Here was a biography moving from a hard-edged but nevertheless establishment conservatism, out to the unrespectable reaches of white nationalism.

Pat Buchanan was born in 1938 (eleven years after Willis Carto). His early heroes included Senator Joseph McCarthy and the Spanish dictator Francisco Franco, both ultra-authoritarian and anti-communist. Buchanan's Catholicism was pre–Vatican II and traditional. While an aide in the Nixon White House, he opposed efforts at racial integration, often in the most caustic terms. As a columnist he flirted with an anti-egalitarian critique of democracy. He claimed homosexuality lead to the "decay of society." By the mid-1980s he had started waving the banner that became white nationalism's clarion call in the twenty-first century. "The central objection to the present flood of illegals," he wrote in 1984, "is they are not English-speaking white people from Western Europe; they are Spanish-speaking brown and black people from Mexico, Latin America and the Caribbean."[16]

Buchanan even explicitly posed the question of whether the United States would "remain a white nation."[17] (Apparently the descendants of Africans brought in chains, the mestizo population of the Southwest, and the Chinese laborers who built the railroads were either invisible to Buchanan's historical eye or not to be counted as natural citizens of his nation.)

He also exhibited a nervous disbelief in the charges leveled against those believed to be war criminals. At different times he rose to defend Arthur Rudolph, Karl Linnas, Kurt Waldheim, John Demjanjuk, and others. In the Demjanjuk case Buchanan's skepticism of Justice Department actions ultimately proved justified on several key points of evidence. Buchanan challenged more than just the rules of evidence used in cases against war criminals, however. As an aide to President Reagan he helped formulate a 1982 trip to the military graves at Bitburg, Germany. At Buchanan's behest, Reagan memorialized the Waffen SS along with ordinary Wehrmacht soldiers, setting off international protests at the honoring of Hitler's henchmen. Buchanan added to the outrage when he claimed that Jews could not have been gassed by diesel engines at the Nazi concentration camp at Treblinka. He was soon publicly and widely accused of giving "aid and comfort" to those, like the Institute for Historical Review, that maintained the Holocaust hadn't happened.[18]

Shortly after his Persian Gulf "amen corner" remarks, charges and countercharges about Buchanan's personal prejudices flew among media elites. One highly regarded *New York Times* columnist, A. M. Rosenthal, accused Buchanan of repeated anti-Semitism. Buchanan replied in turn that Rosenthal was accusing him of anti-Semitism in order to silence all political opposition on foreign policy matters. Other commentators, both liberal and conservative, defended Buchanan on these same grounds. They knew Pat Buchanan, they said. They had been to dinner with Pat Buchanan, and the refined Pat Buchanan was not a bigot. Buchanan's opponents, on the other hand, rehearsed a string of his offending remarks and actions, including his defense of Nazi war criminals.[19]

The debate over going to war in the Persian Gulf so roiled Buchanan's ideological peers that months later *National Review*, the conservative movement's publication of record, published a long William F. Buckley, Jr., essay devoted to anti-Semitism. "Buchanan could not be defended from the charge of anti-Semitism," even if some of his best friends were Jews, Buckley royally concluded.[20]

Something more was afoot than Pat Buchanan's personal tastes in friends. He had been a reliable, traditional conservative, an anti-communist who had backed the Vietnam War while working in President Nixon's White House and during President Reagan's invasion of the tiny island nation of Grenada in 1983. Buchanan had been formed in the mold of anti-communist interventionism that dominated the conservative movement during the Cold War. Although he quieted his dissent after the shooting started in Iraq, during the months prior he was the most visible Republican opponent of President Bush's war plans. He broke the pattern of past conservative thought in favor of a new form of isolationism.

"In shaping a post–Cold War foreign policy," Buchanan wrote, "the contest will be between acolytes of globalism and advocates of a new nationalism, America First."[21]

The Populist Party, always on the lookout for any potential rift within conservative ranks, noticed the change almost immediately. By its lights, Buchanan was fighting the same battle it was, while using virtually identical terms of debate. He had become transformed from a "fearless conservative to [a] fearless nationalist," the party's newsletter averred.[22] It declared him the "personification of Populism." The party's enthusiastic display of support for Buchanan's new politics equaled its encouragement of David Duke. "There are others who can be considered Populists, because of their stand on several issues, but Buchanan is 100% Populist in his outlook," one party officer concluded.[23] Some even fantasized about Buchanan's leaving the Republicans and becoming the presidential candidate of their "third" party.[24]

Since the Populist Party's founding in 1984, its leadership had searched for an avenue into the conservative movement, hoping to recruit a standard-bearer from outside the ranks of known white supremacists. Each effort had failed. Olympic gold medalist Bob Richards smelled the party's anti-Semitism. Former Republican Congressman

George Hansen turned down the nomination. Arizona Governor Evan Mecham decided against attending a meeting with David Duke. For Richards, Hansen, and Mecham, going from the mainstream to the margins was a losing strategy. Now Pat Buchanan was doing exactly that, abandoning a position within the borders of accepted conservative opinion and heading straight to the outside. The Populists argued that a realignment of the right was taking place via a "melding of Populism and nationalist conservativism into a powerful new force."[25]

On this point the Populists proved to be essentially correct in their analysis. Among conservatives, Buchanan's opposition to Bush's war plans and the "New World Order" was not unique. A split among conservatives over issues such as immigration, free trade, and national identity had been brewing since the mid-1980s. Now, at the occasion of the Persian Gulf War, the differences in approach became unbridgeable. George Bush's wing was still globalist and interventionist. The other tendency, following Buchanan, became nationalist and isolationist. At the same time, a different political force, consisting of David Duke and the mainstreaming breed of white supremacists, was self-consciously moving toward the edge of the Republican Party. It would only be a matter of time before these two different vectors ended up at the same white nationalist nexus.

The significance of Buchanan's transformation should not be lost in the minutiae of petty party politics. He still did not fully embrace a biological determinist view of society. But without any evident intervention by white supremacists, Pat Buchanan was talking and walking much as they did. Contrary to natural intuition, however, Buchanan himself had not changed much. Unlike Kafka's Gregor Samsa, Buchanan had simply stood still while the world changed around him. His metamorphosis from establishment conservative into an anti–New World Order propagandist was a function of the change in the geopolitical gestalt and not an existential crisis. The Cold War ended. The New World Order was just beginning.

The Collapse of the Soviet Union and the Transformation of White Supremacy

December 31, 1991. Fifteen months after the unification of Germany, and nine months after the Iraqi army had been pushed out of Kuwait, the Union of Soviet Socialist Republics formally dissolved. It had encompassed fifteen republics and numerous autonomous regions populated by more than one hundred recognized nationalities. It had stretched from a border with Poland in Europe to China and the Sea of Japan in Asia, from the Arctic Circle in the north to the Black Sea in the south. With a population approximating three hundred million, a literacy rate of 99 percent, and a strong military possessing its own nuclear weapons arsenal and space program, the Soviet Union had been the second strongest superpower, after the United States. Buffered on its western borders by a string of sycophantic socialist regimes, it had projected itself across the globe as the communist alternative to capitalism.[1]

Despite this empirelike power, the Soviet Union had cracked apart like a three-minute egg. After a small clique of Stalinist military officers staged an abortive coup, Russian President Boris Yeltsin had seized the moment, put down the plotters, and supplanted the reform-minded Communist Party chief Mikhail Gorbachev with a promise to bring democracy and a market economy. During this period, republics and nationalities linked to the Great Russians since the czars broke away in quick succession. The republic of Georgia declared its independence, as did the Baltic republics of Lithuania, Latvia, and Estonia. Ukraine, long considered an appendage of Russia, also announced its independence. So did the Caucasian republics of Kyrgyzstan, Uzbekistan, and Tajikistan. Inside Russia itself Leningrad became St. Petersburg again. Several of these republics reconstituted themselves as a loose federation known as the Commonwealth of Independent States, and a segment of the Russian leadership never lost its designs to remain a world power. Communism as a geopolitical power, however, was dead. The Cold War was over.[2]

Hungary and Poland quickly sold off their state-owned industries and adopted free market economies as they moved out of the Soviet orbit. The bonds of "communist internationalism" dissolved, and long-suppressed sentiments of ethnic and religious nationalism came to the fore in several of these new "democracies." In Czechoslovakia, an amalgamation put together by the entente powers after World War One, the Czech and Slovak republics separated peacefully, leaving two nation-states where there had previously been one country. But in other places, declarations of independence precipitated ethnic wars. Two former republics of the Soviet Union—Christian Armenia and Muslim Azerbaijan—engaged in a bitter military contest over the territory of Nagorno-Karabakh until a cease-fire was imposed in 1994. Similar conflicts broke out in the Caucasus region and Eastern Europe. A conflict between Romanians and Russians for control of the newly independent republic of Moldova and an ethnic independence war inside Russia by Chechens continued into the 1990s. In Yugoslavia, an ethnic civil war became the most widely recognized symbol of ultranationalist fratricide in the years immediately following the Cold War.[3]

Before the Soviet bloc's last gasp and final collapse, Willis Carto had already recognized the epoch-changing character of the events in Germany and Eastern Europe. "Now that the distraction of communism has been removed," *The Spotlight* opined, *"we are entering a new era where the battle lines are clearer than ever. The new struggle (actually an old one)—the struggle of the 21st century—will pit nationalism vs. internationalism"* (author's emphasis).[4] In this view, little distinction was drawn between the growth of ethnic nationalism across the ruined borders of Eastern Europe, the anti-immigrant racism of political parties in Western Europe, and the emergence of Buchanan-style America first nationalism in the United States. While Carto's notions of "nationalism" and "internationalism" were not widely shared outside his movement, he had in fact struck at a much larger truth: as the Cold War receded from view, ethnic and religious wars began to take its place.

William Pierce's views on the shift in world events mixed prescience with ideological illusion. He correctly predicted that once the Soviets failed to use military force to stem the moves toward independence in Eastern Europe, the collapse of communism was a "foregone conclusion."[5] As will become evident, Pierce's anti-Semitism (temporarily) blinded him to the opportunities—domestic and foreign—emerging for racial nationalists like himself. The National Alliance did happily report that every nationalist organization in Russia, including the highly visible Pamyat, was anti-Semitic. It also noted that nationalists in Hungary, Romania, Lithuania, and Poland had similar beliefs. Pierce's analysis suffered, however, from fears that the various reform movements were infected with Jews. One by one, Pierce ticked off the list: in Poland, where the Solidarity movement had first shaken loose Communist Party control, he believed Jews had actually increased their power. Romania had always been too friendly to the Jews after World War Two. Hungary had too many Jews, and one of the top two reformers there was, well, a Jew. In the lands of the former East Germany, reformed communists had elected a Jew, Gregor Gysi, as their chief. "And that in a country which officially numbers only a few thousand Jews among its population of 17 million," *National Vanguard* noted with evident exasperation.[6]

From the day Pierce had first formed the National Alliance and started publishing *National Vanguard*, he had argued that communism was a Jewish creation. Now, fifteen years later, as communism in Eastern Europe collapsed, he believed the Jews were still in control. Such views also led him to misunderstand the changes within his own organization, which had benefited from a spike in membership applications as the decade turned. He believed this growth reflected a "palpable sense of unease" among white people, caused in part by "signs of a major setback" in the economy.[7] He did not count German unification or the Persian Gulf War or the Soviet Union's collapse—or any combination of these three world-shattering events—among the causes of his good fortune.

For the most ideologically internationalist of America's white tribalists, Pierce's blindness was an ironic twist in his twenty-year rivalry with Carto. For Pierce, the initial moments of the Soviet collapse simply signaled a change in the face of Jewish-run regimes. Carto, on the other hand, sensed a set of new opportunities in the changes ahead. With or without their self-conscious understanding, however, the end of the Cold War meant a significant realignment.

Outside of white supremacist circles, scholars, politicians, and journalists all attempted to make sense of the geopolitical earthquake under their feet. British historian Eric Hobsbawm put it best in his magisterial history of the twentieth century *The Age of Extremes*. "There are historic moments which may be recognized, even by contemporaries, as marking the end of an age," Hobsbawm wrote. "The years around 1990 clearly were such a secular turning-point. But, while everyone could see that the old had ended, there was utter uncertainty about the nature and prospects of the new."[8] Several commentators noted the emergence of new nationalist movements in Eastern Europe, and one carried that same analysis over to France and Quebec.[9] As Hobsbawm noted, the sudden disintegration of alignments between nation-states would create unknown future changes in the "structures of the world's domestic political systems."[10] And the United States was not exempt.

Scholarly opinions about these changes ranged from blind triumphalism at the end of Soviet communism to the bleakest pessimism at the flesh-eating horrors unleashed in places such as Yugoslavia. Francis Fukuyama, a former State Department policy director and well-regarded scholar, contended that after Soviet communism collapsed, only the ideology of "liberal democracy" remained on the stage of History (with a capital H). Conflict itself had not ended, he argued. But other major ideological alternatives, such as monarchism, fascism, and now communism, were no longer viable. Theocratic regimes, such as those in Afghanistan and Iran, may continue to linger on, he wrote, but theocracy itself had no future. The Communist Party may still rule in China, but one-party dictatorships and state-run economies were now universally proven failures. Nationalism need now serve only the liberal democratic ideal in this schema.[11]

An opposing, less exultant set of ideas was articulated by Samuel Huntington, a former National Security Council policy director. Like Fukuyama, Huntington argued that the eclipse of communism had ushered in a new era in international relations. But Huntington posited a future world of conflict between "civilizations," rather than an end to ideology and History. By his argument, "Western Civilization" in Europe and North America was at loggerheads with an "Islamic Civilization," headquartered in the Middle East. In addition to conflicts between regions, fault lines ran through areas such as the Balkans, where an Orthodox Civilization (Serbs) clashed with a Western Civilization (Croatians) and a Muslim Civilization (Albanians, for example). By this account, another mode of conflict also occurred within civilizations, such as that in Europe between immigrant children of the Saracens and the resident grandchildren of the Crusaders.

Huntington extended his argument to the United States and Hispanics. "If assimilation fails in this case, the United States will become a cleft country, with all the potentials for internal strife and disunion that entails."[12] He warned against both multiculturalism at home and globalism abroad. Instead of the universal liberal democracy that Fukuyama had envisioned, Huntington saw a world at war along religious and ethnic lines.[13]

Other views of the post–Cold War world stressed a transition to a "global" economy, organized horizontally across countries. Accordingly, they emphasized the formation of a transnational juridical structure of free trade compacts, environmental treaties, and world courts. By this account, the nation-state no longer controlled its own economic borders. A free market in capital was matched by the increasing transience of labor. The European Union became the example par excellence of this view of the future: increasingly integrated economies, unchecked transportation across borders, and the development of an overarching set of political institutions.[14]

While each of these theories differed with the others, they held one element in common: a new era had been born. Like the transition from Ptolemaic to Copernican astronomy, many of the same planets and stars were still in the sky, only they meant something new and different. A paradigm shift had occurred. Categories associated with the old order changed. And just as the defeat of the Axis powers in World War Two had given birth to new political alignments and the post–World War Two period, the collapse of communism brought new political forces into the fray and, among other things, transformed the character of the white supremacist movement.

Two decades before, at the height of the Cold War, Aryan Nations had declared that its race was its nation. The Covenant, the Sword and the Arm of the Lord camp in Missouri and the Nehemiah Township charter had tried to create an enclave for this nation on a small swatch of land and with a set of rules to guide its conduct. Pete Peters had made his race the basis of his religious beliefs and attached a notion of white (national) redemption to his salvation. David Duke had gone to the border and told reporters that he thought of America as a white nation. A gang of Order bandits had tried to finance a revolution, not a return to Jim Crow segregation; they wanted a territory established free of everything they regarded as "nonwhite." And Willis Carto and William Pierce had helped birth these various strands and had articulated a complete worldview in the process. Theirs was a zero-sum equation, in which white people had it all or they had nothing. And in the post–Cold War era, this white nationalism fitted neatly into the ethnic and religious nationalism that was breaking out in fits of barbarism across the globe.

.   .   .

One of the most important new developments was the end of anticommunism as a politically unifying theme. Anticommunism had been the one agreed-upon tenet of the entire right wing. Now no such agreement existed, noted Louis Beam. His hot-blooded rhetoric had inspired skinheads and brought the Fort Smith jury to tears. Now he coolly parsed the meaning of the Soviet bloc's collapse. "Anti-communism as a political tenet and bedrock of faith has been second only to belief in freedom by those in America to the political right of Karl Marx," he wrote. "It has been the *one single issue* [italics in original] that all who love liberty have agreed upon. Now that the threat of a communist take-over in the United States is non-existent, who will be the enemy we all agree to hate?"[15]

Beam's analysis twisted to a conclusion. Like the anticommunism of all white supremacists in the postwar period, Beam's had been a derivative concern, following his primordial fear of racial equality (and the Jews he believed promoted it). Nevertheless, when Beam and his comrades looked up, they saw the anti-communist umbrella covering their heads also. Remember, he had been proud of his "12 kills" as a helicopter gunner in Vietnam and included them in his Klan biography.

As Hobsbawm had noted, anticommunism was at the core of the American national biography as well. As an ideology it enshrined values, such as free enterprise and individualism, which were older and more deeply embedded than the principle of individual liberty without regard to race.[16] In addition, anticommunism was broadly popular as a glue binding the American people together. As such, anticommunism during the Cold War period both dictated foreign policy and constituted the cornerstone of national identity.[17]

With the end of communism, and thus of anticommunism, the question was asked: What would become of the American national identity? Beam and other Aryans had a ready answer. "People occupying the North American continent today now define themselves more by race than by any other criterion," Beam wrote. "Where one lives, works and plays in America is all a product of race . . . There are in fact, no more 'Americans,' only competing racial groups."[18]

"What will be the issue of main concern for conservatives, right-wingers and nationalists in the United States?" he asked in his small-circulation newsletter *The Seditionist*. For Beam, the answer was self-evident. The enemy would become the federal government in Washington, D.C., headquarters of the New World Order. "The evil empire in Moscow is no more. The evil empire in Washington D.C. must meet the same fate."[19] Beam saw in the ashes of Yugoslavia a renaissance for his Aryan-only state.

. . .

Like the Soviet Union, Yugoslavia had once been a multinational state. For hundreds of years the Balkans had been the point at which empires and civilizations had clashed. "Roman popes, Byzantine emperors, Hungarian and Hapsburg kings, and Ottoman sultans" each had taken a turn ruling over all or a part of the southern Slavs, according to Jasminka Udovicki, a Belgrade-born sociologist. Each regime left behind its own religious following: Catholics, Orthodox Christians, and Muslims. In addition, a small Jewish population lived scattered across the region.

In the nineteenth century these religious differences became the badges of ethnic nationalism, and the crazy quilt of population concentrations alternated between peaceful amalgamation and separatist warfare. Then, in 1912 and 1913, two Balkan wars pitted Serbs and other Eastern Orthodox Christians against both one another and the Muslims of Ottoman Turkey. In 1914, World War One began in Sarajevo, after a Serbian nationalist assassinated an Austrian archduke. After that war, a kingdom of Serbs, Croats, and Slovenes was governed by a Serbian monarch. World War Two again cleaved the region's peoples by religion and ethnicity. The most Catholic territory, Croatia, became a nominally independent modern state for the first time, ruled by a fascist puppet party known as the Ustache. A Catholic Croat and Bosnian Muslim federation was also established under the Axis powers. Ustache Croatians aligned with Hitler and Mussolini forced hundreds of thousands of Serbs into concentration camps. The dispute over whether forty thousand or four hundred thousand or more Serbs died in the process remains a point of ethnic contention.[20]

After World War Two, communists under the direction of the partisan leader Josip Broz Tito attempted to knit together a federation of six republics—Slovenia, Croatia, Bosnia-Herzegovina, Serbia, Montenegro, and Macedonia. Instead of perpetuating centuries of ethnic conflict, Titoists tried to establish a common Yugo culture. To promote homogenization, Serbs and Croats spoke a single language known as Serbo-Croatian. Ethnic populations were dispersed rather than concentrated, to encourage integration. At the same time, Tito's police dealt harshly with any dissent, jailing opponents much like any other authoritarian regime. Nevertheless, the postwar period was largely a time of ethnic peace, as a cosmopolitan and secular civil society developed outside the strictures of the socialist state. "Before May 1991," the author Misha Glenny noted in *The Fall of Yugoslavia*, "Croats and Serbs lived together in relative contentment throughout the region."[21]

As the Soviet Union whirled apart, nationalist and ethnic pressures grew inside all the Yugo republics. Serbian nationalists, led by a strong set of leaders, held sway in a republic that had been at the core of the federation. Slovenia and Croatia declared their independence. Slovene sovereignty established itself easily. But tens of thousands of ethnic Serbs living inside Croatia, egged on by the regime in Belgrade, feared the newly established independent government, and fighting began. Croatia's leaders only exacerbated the problem. They raised the same flag that Ustache fascists had flown over their puppet regime during World War Two. They adopted the Ustache monetary unit. And to compound the crisis, Croatian president Franjo Tudjman continued to circulate a book he authored in 1988, *Wastelands—Historical Truth*. "The declared estimated loss of up to six million dead is based too much on emotionally biased testimonies as well as one-sided and exaggerated data,"[22] Tudjman had written as if he were auditioning for a spot next to Mark Weber at a "historical revisionism" conference. During this stage of the civil war, neo-Nazis from across Europe (and a few from the United States) joined a kind of international brigade fighting on behalf of the Croatians, whom they regarded as the second coming of the Ustache regime. Although their impact on the actual battlefields was minimal, much was made of the military unit by Aryan propagandists in the United States.[23]

As the battles between Serbs and Croatians quieted, a second round of fighting began in the republic of Bosnia and Herzegovina. In these territories, the Serb, Croat, and Bosnian populations were more tightly interlaced than in Croatia, and the bloodshed more horrible. The fate of two cities—Mostar and Sarajevo—was emblematic of this stage of the civil war. In Mostar, Bosnian and Croatian paramilitaries combined forces to drive out the Serb-dominated Yugoslavian Army. After they succeeded, however, Croatian (Catholic) militias opened fire on the Bosnian (Muslim) part of the city and destroyed the historic bridge that had once linked the two communities. In Sarajevo, perhaps the most cosmopolitan place in southern Europe, ethnic Serbs concentrated in the suburbs around the city laid siege to the populace, indiscriminately firing mortar rounds into breadlines and schoolyards. This stage of the civil war ended only after the Serb territorial enclaves were recognized as their own autonomous republic inside an independent country smaller than the state of West Virginia.[24]

A third round of fighting pitched Albanian-supported Kosovar militias against the Serbian republic itself, and these battles quieted only after President Clinton's bombing campaign against the Serbs. In the end, the former Yugoslavia completely dissolved, as the last remaining republics—Macedonia and Montenegro—became independent.[25]

The Yugoslav civil war became an object lesson in the dangers inherent in the new ethnic nationalism. When President Clinton went to Paris in 1994 to participate in the commemoration of D-day, he delivered a statement on this new threat: "Militant nationalism is on the rise, transforming the healthy pride of nations, tribes, religious and ethnic groups into cancerous prejudice, eating away at states and leaving their people addicted to the political painkillers of violence and demagoguery."[26]

During the Cold War, nationalist sentiment was discouraged inside the Soviet bloc, while communist internationalism was favored. After the Cold War, within the countries once dominated by the Soviet Union, nationalism came to the fore. As often as not, this new nationalism possessed an ethnic or a religious character, rather than the liberal civic type of nationalism dominant in Western Europe and North America. Within Western Europe and Canada, civic nationalism based on a system of shared rights and responsibilities had held sway during the Cold War. Movements imbued with sentiments of racial and national chauvinism, such as Jean-Marie Le Pen's Front National in France, existed, but both the movements themselves and the ideas they supported were regarded as threats to the mainstream consensus. During the post–Cold War era, however, resurgent nationalist sentiment emerged on two fronts: one, as an opposition to economic and political global integration and two, as an opposition to the language, religion, and culture (and skin color) of non-European immigrants. Immigrants were also regarded as an economic threat to wage rates and social welfare costs. While still minority movements, on the whole, white nationalists affected both government policy and the political discourse.[27]

Within the United States during most of the Cold War, the situation was only slightly different. Both liberals and conservatives had supported a foreign policy based on containment of any communist advance. Although a noninterventionist form of anticommunist liberalism developed during the Vietnam War, conservatives remained united around the belief that opposition to communism entailed both direct foreign military intervention and support for anticommunist insurgencies. At that point, the dominant form of nationalist sentiment had expressed itself as a form of opposition to communism and the Soviet Union. Americans saw themselves as freedom-loving non-communists, democrats (with a small *d*).

After the Cold War, a vacuum developed where the definition of

American national identity had once firmly existed. White nationalists rushed in to fill the void. It took about ten years for a new form of white nationalism to take shape in the United States. But its outlines had been prefigured in the Yugoslavian civil war, as multicultural communities were torn apart by the demands of ethnic nationalism.

Transatlantic Traffic

March 23, 1991. Munich, Germany. The Kuwaiti oil fields still burned, and the Soviet Union had not yet teetered off its last leg, but white nationalists from the United States were already traveling across the newly unified Germany, helping plant the flag of historical revisionism and Holocaust denial in the land of Ernst Nolte and marauding skinheads. The Institute for Historical Review editor Mark Weber joined a bevy of propagandists from Canada, France, and the United Kingdom.

The Germans had planned for an elaborate public *Kongress* in a palatial hall at one of the city's most prestigious museums. They claimed that two thousand nationalists would attend, enabling their Holocaust theories to "break through" into the realm of relevant public debate. They intended to make an august presentation of "scientific evidence," (illegally) collected at an Auschwitz concentration camp memorial, which supposedly proved that no mass gassings had occurred there. But any hint of respectability eluded the participants. The museum canceled its rental contract and the Kongress ended up on the street outside. Instead of two thousand inquiring minds, only three hundred fanatics rallied, and eight of them managed to get themselves carted off to jail. Despite the setting, speaker after speaker droned on for hours from the back of a truck.[1]

In addition to Weber, there was a widow of a World War Two–era Nazi, a movement attorney from Hamburg, the IHR's German advisory board members, and the British historical writer David Irving. All attacked the Federal Republic's suppression of their views. At that point Irving served as the dean of the so-called revisionist movement. His early books on World War Two had received a few good reviews. But after he claimed in a two-volume tome entitled *Hitler's War* that the

Führer had not known about the deliberate genocide of European Jews, it became evident that the British writer was also a propagandist. He had became a regular at Holocaust denial events in North America and Europe, including a Munich beer hall meet the year before on the anniversary of Hitler's birthday. By the time of this Kongress, Irving had little prestige left to lend and contributed only his flawless German. Mark Weber also gave his speech in perfect German and translated Robert Faurisson's French talk into German as well. Despite the Munich event's obvious failings, Weber gave it good grades. "It was the most public challenge in Germany to the crumbling Holocaust edifice," he wrote in a newsletter account of the event.[2] And because it was on European soil, a greater number of activists from across Europe and the United States quietly got to know one another.[3]

Also on the platform that day in Munich, Kirk Lyons introduced himself to the German scene, which he described in terms very similar to those he had used in the United States. In the three years since the Fort Smith seditious conspiracy trial, Lyons's biography had changed considerably. He had married Brenna Tate, the sister of convicted Order killer David Tate and the daughter of Richard Butler's second-in-command, Charles Tate. Butler performed the nuptials at his camp in northern Idaho. Lyons wore a Scottish kilt, and an Arizona Aryan played the bagpipes for the occasion.[4] Louis Beam was the best man and got so drunk that he tried to climb a ladder while it lay horizontally on the ground. The guest list read like a page from the movement's *Who's Who*. Among the luminaries was Robert Millar, the guru atop the Elohim City camp in Oklahoma.

Lyons also spoke regularly at Populist Party events and participated in Aryan Nations events, including the skinhead march in Tennessee. He quietly joined William Pierce's National Alliance and after Lyons opened an office in Houston and incorporated a nonprofit organization, Patriots Defense Foundation, the National Alliance's members-only bulletin applauded the effort.[5] He publicized the foundation with a newsletter, compiled lists of potential donors, and solicited contributions so the foundation could underwrite the defense of major criminal cases. To the newspapers he billed it as a "conservative American Civil Liberties Union" that defended constitutional rights.[6] To his comrades, however, he stressed the foundation's origin in discussions at Aryan Nations camps.[7] His first big case was in North Carolina, where he successfully defended a white patriot accused of killing three men because they were gay.

While he was in Germany to speak at the Munich event, Lyons used the opportunity to express his solidarity with the German racists and anti-Semites. "Europe is the land of my forefathers," he told a German skinhead zine, *Volkstreue*. "White Americans are nothing else than Europeans planted somewhere else . . . We share common origins, Volkstum [nationality] and culture." His was more than a statement of Eurocentricity, however. "We are in a common fight against a common enemy," Lyons added.

Here Lyons expressed a view shared by William Pierce, Tom Metzger, and other vanguardist leaders. Who or what was this enemy? he was asked. Was it liberals and the left? No, he told the skinhead magazine. "The Left is no problem in the USA." Instead, "the police are the big problem." What about democracy? "Democracy is a farce and a failure. I don't believe in democracy," he told his interviewer in German. And what was his wish for the future? Short term, he answered, "to smash internationalism." For Lyons and other speakers that day in Munich, the future burned bright for a resurgence of nationalism, including American white nationalism.

Despite this oft-repeated opposition to "internationalism," an active transatlantic traffic in racism and anti-Semitism reached virtually every corner of the American movement, particularly during this period. That May the scene shifted to Atlanta, where John Tyndall landed for a two-week, six-state speaking tour. Playing the role of a proper fifty-six-year-old British gentleman, Tyndall stepped off the long plane ride from London into the Atlanta airport wearing a white shirt and sports coat. A plaid tie several inches short of the belt buckle and a long, wary horse-face seemed to give him away. A photographer snapped his picture, and it appeared the following month on the cover of *Searchlight* magazine, a British investigative monthly that had been dogging his steps for years. *Searchlight* periodically republished photos of a younger Tyndall in a brownshirt uniform, stiff with respect before a swastika flag and a portrait of Hitler. With Tyndall that day in Atlanta was Sam Dickson, the sharp-tongued attorney who had been with the southern contingent to the Institute for Historical Review conference in 1986.[8]

Among British white supremacists, Tyndall combined both the mainstreaming role of Willis Carto and the vanguardist strategy of William Pierce. He had started his career in the 1950s and graduated in the 1960s to the National Socialist Movement, a group much like the National Socialist White People's Party to which Pierce had once belonged. (It was during that time Tyndall wore homemade uniforms and saluted a swastika flag.) During these early years he was convicted of threatening Jews, controlling a paramilitary outfit, and a gun offense. By the mid-1970s he had switched tacks, left the uniforms in the closet, and attempted to find a broader following. He helped organize the British National Front, a more successful coat-and-tie group similar to Willis Carto's own Liberty Lobby and Populist Party confections.

For a brief moment in the mid-1970s the National Front became Britain's "fourth party" by campaigning against Afro-Caribbean and Asian immigrants. It also brokered the marriage of white supremacy to a subset of the skinhead scene. Tyndall's front ran into problems, however, after the national socialist undergarments beneath its electioneering cloak became public information. And when Tory candidate Margaret Thatcher opposed immigrants in the 1979 election, she stole that issue away from Tyndall's front. In the aftermath of that election, internal factionalism gripped the National Front, virtually destroying it as an electoral force. Tyndall later formed a new group called the British National Party. The new party enshrined his leadership as a matter of principle, the so-called *Führerprinzip*, and started to grow.[9] By the time Tyndall got to Atlanta, however, his party had stagnated at around fourteen hundred members.[10]

Despite, or perhaps because of this history, the relationship between Tyndall and Dickson ran deep. Soon after Tyndall had gotten out of jail in 1987 for violating the Race Relations Act, Dickson rushed to England to videotape an interview with him for distribution in the United States. And in 1988, when Tyndall published a six-hundred-page tome entitled *The Eleventh Hour*, Dickson arranged to distribute it from his Georgia post office box.[11] Now Dickson and leaders from a half dozen outfits welcomed Tyndall to the United States as if he were an angel sent to redeem a poor melanin-deprived race from suffering at the hands of Jewish demons and black witchery.[12]

For this effort he traveled over six states in two weeks and spent thousands of dollars in expenses. This tour turned into one of the movement's largest cross-organization collaborative efforts. It demonstrated the similarities in ideological outlook among white nationalists in the United Kingdom and the United States. The trip also encapsulated the paradox underlying the movement at that time. The mainstreaming wing had become the dominant trend at the moment. Its leaders included an educated set of middle-class professionals who now eschewed survivalist boot camps and cow pasture cross burnings. They campaigned for public office instead, rewrote history from computer workstations, waged war from hotel lecterns, and searched for personalities to bridge the gap between them and Middle Americans. While they hoped to hold court in the palaces of public opinion, these mainstreamers were more often left on the street outside. They were also repeatedly undercut by the vanguardist urge to smash and kill. Riven by a split personality, the movement, driven to change society from within, was at odds with itself. With a self-contradictory ideology and competing strategies, organizational factionalism was sure to follow as John Tyndall trekked across the United States.

His first stop was a relatively sober and respectful visit with the reclusive Wilmot Robertson, the author of *The Dispossessed Majority*. The two had established a friendship back in 1979, during an earlier tour by Tyndall across the South. Now tucked away in North Carolina's Nantahala Mountains, less than four hours north of Atlanta, Robertson had remained a reclusive figure during the two decades since he published his magnum opus. In fact, his actual identity, Humphrey Ireland, had been a closely kept secret.[13] However, his publishing house, Howard Allen Enterprises, was a matter of record with the state of Florida, where it was registered. Humphrey Ireland and his wife, Mary, were the only two officers of the corporation, which was named after their sons, Howard and Allen. During the last productive years of their lives, the couple settled in a substantial middle-class log house with a two-bedroom guesthouse deep in the southern Appalachian Mountains near Whittier, North Carolina. Mary conducted the couple's affairs with the outside world, and their political identities remained unknown to their neighbors, several of whom were Jewish. Gray-haired, blue-eyed, wrinkled, and slightly stooped on a six-foot plus frame in old age, Robertson occasionally held court for visiting white nationalist dignitaries, and Tyndall enjoyed several days of pleasant hospitality during this visit.[14]

Dickson played a loyal Sancho Panza to Tyndall's delusional Don Quixote. In addition to organizing the national speaking tour, Dickson issued the invitations to the event in Atlanta.[15] "Mr. Tyndall deserves a hearty American welcome by virtue of his life long devotion to our cause," Dickson wrote in an invitation letter.[16] Using the name Anglo-American Forum, Dickson booked an area Marriott Hotel.[17] (The previous year he had used the name of his Atlanta Committee for Historical Review for invitations to an event that was canceled after Tyndall was denied entry to the United States.)[18] At the hotel, a few area Klan chiefs mixed with clumps of skinhead youths. But the majority of attendees appeared to be educated and domesticated middle-class citizens. About two hundred paid a five-dollar fee at the door. Dickson, clever as always, opened the meeting. He complained about coverage in the local press, denied the charge that he personally was an "extremist," and then gave a glowing introduction to Tyndall. Although Tyndall had been convicted of crimes at home, Dickson argued, American courts would have treated the same matters differently. In any case, Tyndall's record proved his leadership mettle.

After Atlanta, Dickson handed Tyndall off to Ed Fields, who had changed the name of his tabloid to *The Truth at Last*. Fields chaperoned the Brit across the country. The two men shared a penchant for bullhorn-in-the-street parades, and like Tyndall, Fields flitted back and forth between uniformed sectarianism and coat-and-tie opportunism. (When Tyndall last visited the States, he had stayed with Fields and his wife, Jayne.) The two were old friends and a perfect fit. As they snaked their way across the country, Tyndall and Fields encountered a dizzying number of individuals and organizations, each alternately collaborating and combating the other for pride of place.

At the stop in North Carolina, A. J. Barker served as host and used the meeting to promote his own goals within the Populist Party. Since the Chicago meeting two years earlier, when the fight between Willis Carto and Don Wassall first started, Barker and other party activists in the South had stepped away from both factions. At this meeting he drew together a group of party units from across the Southeast. Don Black, now living in West Palm Beach and married to David Duke's ex-wife Chloe, represented the Florida Populist Party at this event. He argued that the prospects for a pure third party option seemed dim when compared with the success Duke was then enjoying as a Republican. Attorney Kirk Lyons, freshly returned from his speech in Munich, also attended and spoke from the lectern. Here Tyndall was virtually an afterthought.

A similar situation surrounded Tyndall several days later at his speech in Maryland, where the event was ostensibly sponsored by the Maryland Populist Party. This state party was completely controlled by Carto's Liberty Lobby. While visiting its offices in D.C., Tyndall taped an interview for future broadcast over Liberty Lobby's radio network. And when he spoke at the nighttime event in the suburb of Lanham, Maryland, Carto used the event as window dressing in his fight with Don Wassall. Bob Weems was rolled out to speak once again, establishing Liberty Lobby's credentials as the founding agency of the Populist Party. Carto made a rare public appearance to announce the creation of a Populist Action Committee. He said the new "committee" would support "populist" candidates, whichever party they ran from—Democrat, Republican, or Populist. It would raise funds to do this work, but the money would stay inside the Liberty Lobby complex rather than be contributed to specific candidates. The formation of this "committee" was a shrewd recognition that David Duke's Louisiana victory had shifted much of the far right's electoral action back inside the Republican Party. It also established a virtual competitor to Wassall for precious movement funds. About one hundred people heard the pitch.

If Tyndall understood that one of his tour's sponsors, Liberty Lobby, was using his visit to help eviscerate another of the tour's supporters, Wassall's Populist Party, he did not publicly acknowledge it. After Maryland, Tyndall and Fields were hosted in the area around Clifton, New Jersey, by Populist Party activists tightly aligned with Wassall. At that meeting the most imposing figure on the platform was not John Tyndall or Ed Fields but Chester Grabowski. A silver-haired publisher of a community weekly tabloid, *The Polish Post Eagle*, Grabowski had been a Populist Party candidate the previous November. His fervent émigré-style Polish nationalism seemed out of place next to the Hitlerite Tyndall. But Grabowski proudly printed accounts of the meeting, which drew a few Klansmen down from Canada, in addition to about 150 anti-Semites from the New York–New Jersey area.[19] For his part, Tyndall glowed. "We should salute our Slavonic fellow-Whites for standing up," he wrote in his account of the trip.[20]

Next Tyndall flew to Los Angeles, where he spoke at another forum for Wassall loyalists. While in Southern California, he also met at the Institute for Historical Review offices with staff there. The final speaking event was in Chicago, organized by a longtime Klan state leader, and drew about a hundred people, many from the harder national socialist edges of the movement.

At each stop, Tyndall sold crates of his *Eleventh Hour* tome. He gave roughly the same stump speech, regardless of the factional intrigue around him. Over and over again he told his audiences that the twentieth century, and World War Two in particular, had virtually sunk the white race's prospects. "The retreat of the white man is universal," he claimed, obviously ignoring (white) Europe's most recent military adventure among darker-hued Arab peoples. "We have seen in one place after another the blacks taking control." There was a small grain of truth in Tyndall's assessment. Black people in the American South, for example, could now vote and elect people to office. Britain had lost most of its empire. Black people in South Africa were about to elect their first majority rule government. Nevertheless, Tyndall's reasoning was a bit over the top. Listening to him, you might have thought it had been African nations that had convened the 1888 Berlin Conference to carve up Europe and that Eastern European Jews had started World War Two. "The greatest lunacy of all," he added, had been "the lunacy of World War II in which the best of American, British, and German manhood died on the battlefields of Europe." Once again the background music was familiar.

If each speech rehashed bleary old complaints, Tyndall usually concluded his remarks with a clear perception of the prospects for change. The post–World War Two era was dying, and a new period was being born. The twenty-first century, he believed, would mark a new beginning. "We are coming to an era in the century to come when the great white race, with all its genius and glory, is going to get off its knees and stand up straight," he said. "We are living in a time of great historical change," he repeated. "The system has collapsed in the East," Tyndall thundered. "Let us work to make it collapse in the West."[21]

John Tyndall's visit to the United States revealed many of the cross-organizational bonds that created a movement out of what looked like a series of uncoordinated single enterprises. It was also an early manifestation of the increased level of transatlantic interchange by white supremacists in the years that followed the collapse of the Soviet bloc. In addition to visits by American Holocaust deniers to Germany, white power skinheads were to find their counterparts across Western Europe and Scandinavia. Eventually, the traffic was to flow farther east into Russia and Ukraine, where anti-Semites of all countries could unite in a common cause.

Within the United States, sectors of the white electorate, defined less by its economic fortunes and more by its ideological concerns—i.e., race—began to see themselves as a group, much like a traditional "ethnic group." Some believed that their group had already lost its dominant place in American life, a view that is usually imbued with some variant of anti-Semitism. (Jews run the government, media, etc., and act in other ways like a ruling class.) Others believed that their group would soon lose their dominant place in American life, usually through what they described as racial "swamping"—i.e., multiculturalism, immigration, special rights for black people, etc. Over time these sectors of the white populace became increasingly self-conscious of themselves as a distinct group. Many adopted ideological characteristics similar to those of oppressed racial minority groups. And like Croatians and Serbians who could not countenance each other while under the same Yugo roof, the most "advanced" elements saw themselves as white nationalists, no longer willing to live in a multinational state—even if they were still objectively the dominant racial and ethnic group. They needed only a strong leader to break open the political terrain. And that happened first in Louisiana with David Duke.

PART

The Movement Matures, 1992–1993

With a newly energized race-conscious constituency, white nationalists enter the fray of presidential politics and seek a marriage of convenience with Christian nationalists opposed to abortion, homosexuals, and Bill Clinton. Debacles at Waco, Texas, and Ruby Ridge, Idaho, tip the tactical advantage to the white-ists.

The Duke Campaign(s) and the Louisiana Electorate

November 16, 1991. Louisiana is not the former Yugoslavia. When medieval Serbs were still fighting Ottoman Turks at the gates of Europe, Choctaw and Caddo civilizations lived peacefully on opposite sides of Lake Pontchartrain. But the state does suffer its own history of split personality disorders. Prior to purchase in 1803 and statehood in 1812, the territory flew both Spanish and French flags. A civil law system rooted in French conventions thus remains underneath the Anglo-American juridical system. The Spanish division into parishes, rather than counties, remains also as a reminder of an era when no wall separated church from state. And the flags of the Confederacy may have ceased flying from government buildings, but the residue of white supremacy still hangs in the air like moss in a cypress swamp.

For a brief moment after the Civil War, democracy swept across the plantations, and black people joined white people at the polls and in government. Under the protection of Union troops, three black lieutenant governors sat in Baton Rouge during the Reconstruction era. But white marauders overturned this first attempt at black enfranchisement and restored white supremacy. In 1874 the Klan-like White League defeated police and black militiamen in an armed battle on the streets of New Orleans.[1] Reconstruction nationally ended with the presidential election of 1876, when Louisiana's electoral delegates were traded to Republican Rutherford B. Hayes as part of a compromise that effectively withdrew the protection of federal troops from freedmen in the South.[2] Twenty years later the U.S. Supreme Court formally institutionalized its "separate but equal" doctrine in *Plessy v. Ferguson*, a case originating in Louisiana when Homer Plessy, a thirty-year-old light-skinned shoemaker, attempted to buy a first-class (white) train ticket. The Four-teenth Amendment, ratified in 1868, had supposedly rendered uncon-stitutional laws that enforced badges of inferiority. But the *Plessy* case proved that constitutional guarantees established in one era could be disestablished in the next.[3]

A system of legal apartheid formed atop one of North America's most heterogeneous populations. Creoles mixed their French and Spanish heritage with the bloodlines of Africa. Cajuns spoke a French patois generations after their ancestors had fled Canada. Africans brought voodoo from the West Indies and gave New Orleans its own distinct music. And of course, it was the ill-paid labor of African-descended cane cutters and cotton pickers upon which the fantastically wealthy non-African plantation elite lived. This racial schizophrenia was passed down like a hereditary disease, until it reached Louisiana's 4 million plus inhabitants in contemporary times. Black people numbered 1.3 million, or 31 percent of the populace. And those counting them-selves white were split between Protestants (Baptists) in the north and Catholics in the South.[4]

After Democrats in D.C. passed the Civil Rights Act in 1964, the white majority started voting Republican in presidential elections, yet remained Democratic in its local registration. In 1968 Louisiana's whites voted overwhelmingly for Governor George Wallace's segrega-tionist campaign. The trend was interrupted in 1976, when the (new) black vote pushed the state into Georgia Governor Jimmy Carter's col-umn. Fourteen years later the black vote once again proved decisive, this time in the 1991 race for governor. David Duke carried a sharp ma-jority of votes by whites, 55 percent, yet lost the election to former Gov-ernor Edwin Edwards, 701,024 to 1,086,820. Without the black vote, a dedicated national socialist would have lived in the governor's mansion.[5]

David Duke mounted the platform at the Hilton Inn ballroom in Baton Rouge and claimed that his defeat in the governor's race was actually victory. "The candidate may have lost," he told the assembly of volun-teers and reporters, "but the message goes out across Louisiana and across this whole country." Dispirited by the loss, the crowd chanted, "Duke, Duke, Duke," with less than obvious enthusiasm. "The time has come to help people become more responsible for their lives and to teach them responsibility and all the things that go with it," he contin-ued. "This is an issue which goes forth across the country. The time has come to realize that government is not going to solve the problems of the individuals of this nation. Only we as free and independent individuals can solve these problems."[6]

His speech that night sounded as if it had been copied straight from President Ronald Reagan's conservative issues playbook, not from *The Spotlight*'s back pages. But mainstream respectability carried a high price. Three years after making himself the eye of Louisiana's political hurricane and establishing himself as a viable candidate, Duke was now the victim of his own success. This election was his second loss in as many years. Although he was to run again and again, he had reached the end of his career as a credible candidate.

When we look back at the start of his career as a professional full-time candidate, Duke's emergence seems inexplicable. How could someone who had screamed "white power" in front of a burning cross be elected to office or win a majority of whites' votes? One knee-jerk explanation looked in the rearview mirror at the 1950s, seeing in Duke a reflection of the Jim Crow politicians of that era.[7] A more apt response, however, would have been to look through the windshield at the twenty-first century to come. A thousand threads knotted the past to the future, and the most significant tie-in was Duke himself.

Over decades he had developed a set of skills only the most veteran politicians possessed. As a nineteen-year-old national socialist in Louisiana State University's Free Speech Alley, he had learned how to debate his opponents under the most difficult of circumstances. As a young Klan leader he had given hundreds of impromptu stump speeches, jumped into fawning crowds to shake hands, and learned to motivate volunteers and generate contributions. Most significantly, he had learned how to harness the power of television. He could speak over the head of any talk show host or news personality and reach directly into the living rooms of his potential constituents. His talent for smelling opportunity where others saw only chaos was uncanny. Witness his ability to turn mob violence in Forsyth County, Georgia, into a launching pad for his own comeback. And before finally winning an election, he had campaigned regularly over a period of a dozen years. He had run first as a Klansman for state office in 1976 and 1979, before his short stint in the Democratic Party's 1988 presidential primaries. As a Populist Party candidate he learned to build the components of a viable (non-Klan) campaign machine and constructed a nationwide list of contributors. And in the state legislative race, as a Republican, he had knocked on doors and talked to voters one-on-one in a shoe leather campaign his opponent did not replicate.

All the lights were on and all the buttons pushed when he seamlessly switched from freshman state legislator to candidate for the United States Senate in 1990 and then for governor in 1991. Like the White League more than a hundred years before, David Duke's conjoined campaigns almost pushed Louisiana to the breaking point.

In the Senate race the seat was held by Bennett Johnston, a wily oil business Democrat first elected to the Senate during the Nixon landslide of 1972. To oppose Johnston, the Republican Party officially nominated a mainstream conservative state senator at a convention in January 1990. Party leaders hoped to push Duke out of the race, and he had received only 52 of the 792 delegate votes.[8] Duke decided, however, not to accede to the leadership and seemed to understand intuitively that his Republican opponent was a weak candidate. While anyone could imitate Duke's rhetorical attacks on affirmative action and minority set-asides, it soon became apparent that a majority of white voters liked the real thing.

Duke's Senate campaign began with rallies in the northern end of the state, far from his legislative district in Metairie. He drew 1,000 people in Bossier City, outside Shreveport, and 750 people in Monroe. Just days later in Lafayette 500 attended. The same number showed in Baton Rouge.[9] At each rally Duke's charismatic presence and rhetorical skills swept away any doubts that he was a statewide contender.

In the first three months of 1990, Duke the candidate registered $575,305 in contributions with the Federal Election Commission, and the totals grew significantly through the summer months. By July he had eclipsed his principal Republican opponent in the opinion polls, despite repeated declarations by national Republican leaders that Duke was an unwelcome intruder. As the October primary neared, the party leadership began to panic. Louisiana's nonpartisan primary system, first created to ensure the supremacy of a whites-only Democratic Party, now worked to Duke's advantage. Democrats, Republicans, and candidates of any other nominal stripe all competed against one another in one primary election. Duke could pull from blue-collar Democrats and Republicans at the same time. If one candidate did not win an absolute majority in this first election, a runoff was held four weeks later. A runoff could turn into a short but fevered event. Having lost all hope of defeating the sitting senator, Democrat Bennett Johnston, Republicans nationally hoped to spare themselves the embarrassment of Duke's representing their party in a high-profile postprimary runoff. Eight Republican senators endorsed Johnston.[10]

On October 6, 1990, Senator Bennett Johnston received 752,902 votes, 54 percent of the total, to Duke's 607,391, or 44 percent. There was no need for a runoff. In conventional terms, Duke had been routed.

At the same time, he received almost 59 percent of the white vote and carried twenty-five of the state's sixty-four parishes, including Jefferson Parish, one of the wealthiest and best educated. He won every parish in the Fifth Congressional District save two. His support ran from the white Protestant piney woods north of Baton Rouge to the ethnically diverse and Catholic southern half of the state, making him Louisiana's most successful Republican statewide candidate.[11] Moreover, he had raised and spent approximately two million dollars that year, a respectable sum by any standard; but a particularly large amount compared with the budgets of his white supremacist colleagues. Only Willis Carto raised and spent more each year.[12] Duke could justifiably claim to have emerged from the election as the spokesman for a majority of Louisiana's white people.

Nevertheless, Carto's *Spotlight* tabloid ignored Duke's success, drowning a one-line comment on the Louisiana election in an ocean of ink otherwise devoted to the crisis then looming in the Persian Gulf. Even the small-time eat-and-greet Liberty Lobby conference in D.C. received more coverage. It was an odd twist in a relationship that dated back to the first editions of Carto's tabloid in 1975, when it had favorably covered Duke as an up-and-coming Klan leader. Perhaps Carto sensed that Duke had already outgrown *The Spotlight* constituency and no longer needed a boost. William Pierce's *National Vanguard* magazine, for its part, never did get around to mentioning the Senate race. Running for office carried little immediate import for him. Otherwise, while Louisiana wrestled with itself like an alligator chasing its own tail, the rest of the country focused on the coming war with Saddam Hussein.

The Governor's Race

During the last week of January 1991, Duke virtually ignored American tanks crashing into Iraq. He shaped his own battle plans instead, as he switched from the Senate race to a campaign for governor without so much as a change of suits. On the first floor of 550 North Arnoult in Metairie, volunteers stuffed seventeen thousand letters to non-Republican supporters, urging them to register with the party.[13] Only as Republicans would they be able to vote for Duke delegates to the state convention.

For their part, state Republican officials once again tried to outmaneuver Duke, rather than confront him directly. The sitting governor, Charles "Buddy" Roemer III, a Democrat about to switch registrations at the behest of President George H. W. Bush, ignored Duke completely. Roemer considered himself the odds-on favorite in the coming election, but his relationship with the state party leaders remained sour, at best. They decided to back a conservative evangelical Christian, Congressman Clyde Holloway, and planned a convention to name him rather than Roemer or Duke. They pinned their hopes on the convention as a way of avoiding the havoc Duke had caused in the party the year before. (Meanwhile, Edwin Edwards, a former Democratic governor, twice indicted for corruption but not yet ever convicted, aimed at confounding the odds and winning back the spot in the Baton Rouge mansion.)[14]

Against the party's official machine, Duke assembled his own engineers and skilled craftsmen. They set schedules, turned raw materials into workable tools, and maintained the power grid. A circle of shop floor veterans established departments, enforced labor discipline, and instructed the rank and file. The machinery wheezed and groaned, but it sputtered on for six months with one goal in mind: winning delegates to the Republican state convention that June. Volunteers worked the phones from computerized lists to mobilize known activists for areawide meetings. Slates of Duke delegates were drawn up district by district, and a leader, who functioned much like a legislative whip, was selected for each district. Then, in the days before the actual party caucuses, volunteers again made calls, this time urging supporters to attend the caucuses and vote for a slate of delegates committed to Duke. A half hour before the caucuses started, Duke's supporters met, and the whips received the list of delegates designated by central command.[15]

Despite months of aggressive computer list phone calling, at the end of caucus day Duke received only 160-plus designated votes. By contrast, Congressman Holloway won 3,170 delegates in the caucuses, plus the promise of an additional 150 state party officials with automatic voting rights.[16] Because Holloway and the leadership secured a larger number of delegates, they mistakenly believed their political machine had beaten the former Kluxer's. But they didn't understand Duke's campaign operation any better than they fathomed the depth of popular support for Duke himself. When the party convened on June 14 in the Lafayette convention center, Duke decided to make a splash big enough to ensure that his campaign could not be ignored.

Convention rules required that anyone whose name was officially placed in nomination had to pledge in advance his or her unconditional support for the official nominee. The rules worked against Duke, who did not have enough delegates to win the nomination and was loath to give his support to anyone else. The same was true for Buddy Roemer, the sitting governor and recent Republican convert. Neither man planned to drop out of the race or take the pledge. Therefore, they each decided not to officially enter themselves into nomination. Instead, Duke and Roemer both instructed their delegates to vote no endorsement, as a way of forestalling Holloway's formal selection.[17]

At the same time, Duke thought that he had a deal with party officials that would allow him ten minutes at the convention podium. That was all he really wanted: a chance to get a minute on the local news broadcasts around the state. At the last minute he discovered that in fact there was no deal. As word came back that he would not be allowed to speak, tension built inside the Duke camp.

At a side caucus, Duke assembled his delegates. At the appropriate moment, he told them, launch a loud and noisy convention floor demonstration that would force officials to allow him to speak. All 180 brimmed with excitement. They were going to get a little chance to fight after all. The moment finally came when Duke's campaign manager was formally recognized to make a short speech supporting no endorsement. Instead of making a speech, the manager quickly tried to cede his time to David Duke. When Duke was ruled out of order, his delegates broke into prolonged pandemonium, chanting, clapping, and disrupting the proceedings for a half hour. Duke egged them on by dashing past the sergeant at arms and onto the stage, although not to the podium. Ultimately, the demonstration failed to force Duke to the platform at that moment.[18]

After he had been officially elected the party's nominee, however, Congressman Holloway asked Duke to make a few remarks. It was the first in a long line of Chamberlain-like appeasements that ultimately doomed Holloway's candidacy. The demonstration was instant proof that Duke was willing to break the rules and that the party lacked the will to stop him. He got the publicity he wanted from the convention. And his machine was fierce, loyal, and capable. Duke had founded fierce and even loyal organizations before, but this was the first to be genuinely capable. Contrasted with the gaggle of warring Klan factions or the schismatic Populist Party, Duke's campaign machinery purred like a twentieth-century assembly line compared with a seventeenth-century blacksmith's shop. Finally, the "white political machine" he had envisioned in his first Klan newsletter almost twenty years before was up and running.

If his Republican operation ran qualitatively better than his Populist campaign, it was not due to any change in Duke himself. He was still an organizational oaf, charismatic and charming for the public, but little concerned with the volunteers and activists who made the calls and stamped the envelopes. Duke had neither the temperament nor the skills to actually manage a complex mechanism.[19] The difference was the paid staff and volunteers he had gathered to run it. At headquarters in Metairie, top campaign jobs remained in the hands of the tough ex-cops who had run his legislative election unburdened by a direct connection to the Klan. A few veteran national socialists worked quietly behind the scenes. Longtime movement personalities served as regional coordinators in Shreveport, Bogalusa, and Baton Rouge. At the same time, a new generation of activists functioned as both paid staff and volunteers. They kept the New Orleans headquarters on track, managing volunteers, tending databases, and handling media calls. One campaign staffer even contributed articles to Duke's noncampaign tabloid, the *NAAWP News*.[20]

The line separating Duke's campaign committees from the National Association for the Advancement of White People (NAAWP), not always sharp at the start, blurred further through each successive election cycle. The NAAWP was a nonprofit corporation, not a political action committee, but its solicitations sometimes asked for support for Duke as a candidate. At headquarters it wasn't always clear to volunteers whether they were working in space belonging to NAAWP or the election committee. And as the campaigns grew to crusadelike proportions, the NAAWP grew as well—at least initially.[21]

The campaign structure—with its mix of hard-core cadres and first-time volunteers—proved that Duke was developing a new mid-level rank of activists with skills beyond the ability to wrap a wooden cross in burlap and set it on fire. This was most true among Generation Xers. Young Republicans at Northwestern State University sponsored Duke's first Senate campaign speech at a college. The campus chapter also voted to endorse him, despite the state party's official nomination of someone else.[22] Similarly, at Southeastern Louisiana University in Hammond, the Kappa Delta Theta fraternity made Duke an honorary member, and a campus rally attracted five hundred. If Duke had run with a Populist tag, these kinds of endorsements would have eluded him. It was slightly different at the University of Southwestern Louisiana in Lafayette, where a White Student Union formed to support Duke. In that case, the Republican label would have mattered less. But with just a few exceptions, the young people signing up for Duke's Senate campaign would have been unlikely candidates for either the Klan or the skinhead scene. Walking into a semipublic office and stuffing envelopes or making phone calls on behalf of a charismatic state representative whom you had just seen on the television news the night before was a fundamentally different experience from secreting yourself away in a subcultural hangout. Nevertheless, both skinheads and young Duke volunteers shared a common generational experience. They had been born in the years after legal segregation, and their experience of "whiteness" was inherently more problematic than it had been for their parents and grandparents at a similar age. Not everyone in the society around them assumed that being "American" meant being "white." Instead, the United States of America had started to take on the aspect of a multiracial democracy, as black people voted, ran for public office and served in Congress. Not everyone assumed that white males should be the only ones talking or running the place. There was also something testosteronic in this young constituency. A poll commissioned that summer by Duke's opponents showed his support to be higher among young white males than among white women.[23]

After the convention the campaign pushed hard toward the primary in October. Duke's speeches at rallies and political advertisements remained focused almost exclusively on the same theme that had informed his public politics since his years in the Klan: white majority dispossession. His rhetoric was more cleverly embroidered than ever before, but it was no less pointed. Typically, Duke began his stump speeches by attacking the media. It was a predictable shtick built on the decades he had recirculated William Pierce's propaganda pamphlet with a cartoon of Uncle Sam chained by a Star of David to a television. From his first moments in a swastika through to his candidacy as a so-called Populist, Duke had claimed explicitly that it was "the Jews" who owned the nation's media. Pointing at the Jews was the line around which his worldview rotated. During the state legislative race, he had coded the point by emphasizing that *The Times-Picayune* (New Orleans) was "New York owned" ("New York" often serving as a stand-in for "Jews"). But in the conjoined candidacies that followed, Duke needed a campaign package more than an ideological device. He emphasized the New York angle less and focused on the media simply as an oppressive elite. By constantly referring to his years as a Klan leader, he argued, the media unfairly attacked him—and by extension all those around him. Even if his past was "controversial," he would claim that he was a victim of calumny, just as whites as a people were also victims. By the same reasoning, minorities pressing for affirmative action were the "real racists." And he would assert, with some justification, that he was simply saying out loud and in public the same things that his audience said quietly and at home. This supposedly shared victimization and vocalization established a connection between Duke and his constituents. At the same time, the constant reference to his "controversial" past was offered as proof that he was a strong leader whose views were honestly held.[24]

His preaching against the corrupting influence of "special interest" political contributions added cross stitches to his central message but did not change it. Duke was concerned less with "good government" re-form than with the need to generate campaign contributions and volun-teers. He pledged never to accept any PAC funds (but of course he was never offered any). So his talk about big-money funds was usually a prel-ude to passing the bucket. Significantly, when he talked about jobs and the economy, Duke was unusually inarticulate. (During one televised debate a reporter asked him to name Louisiana's largest employers. He could not do it.[25]) Although the state was then suffering from a decline in the oil industry, he rarely mentioned the multinationals. When he tried to explain his position on jobs and deindustrialization, the audience would fall politely quiet and remain virtually still while he sputtered on about "smaller government" and "taxes." (His direct mail to voters often hit at taxes as well.) If Duke's vote totals had depended just on eco-nomic resentments, he would never have threatened any of the main-stream candidates. Only after he had started attacking the use of taxes for school busing and for welfare did he generate a visible response. And that was when David Duke hit his stride. He could talk for hours about race issues, and the growing crowds would respond viscerally.

The number one problem facing the country, in every media ad and every speech, was the "growing welfare underclass." It was this "under-class" that cost so much in taxes and was responsible for crime and drugs (drug addiction was "worse than slavery"). In a quick rhetorical phrase, the same underclass was responsible for the decline in academic performance in public schools because of busing "for integration." The underclass also lowered standards in the economy and universities through the "massive" program of racial discrimination against whites known as affirmative action. In sum, it was this underclass that most threatened the "Christian" and "European" majority. There was almost nothing they couldn't be blamed for (except maybe controlling the me-dia). And if the time permitted in Duke's Fidel Castro–length speeches, he would get to the bottom line: it wasn't the economic cost of the un-derclass that most worried the once-and-future biological determinist. It was the class's reproductive potential. Simply put, the population growth of black people threatened the majority status of white people. During the Senate and governor's race he left explicit mention of the Jews off the platform. Otherwise the message remained essentially the same as when Duke had chanted "white power" at Klan rallies ten years before.

From virtually the beginning of the dual campaigns, however, it had mattered less to voters what package Duke used to dress his message.

His core ideas were a known item. The battle was over whether or not Duke the person was considered a socially acceptable candidate. As the Tulane political scientist Douglas Rose noted about the Senate race, the crucial contest "may have been the one for acceptability, not the one for support."[26]

To gain further acceptance, Duke attempted a gambit in the final months of the governor's race that ultimately did him more harm than good. After two decades as a secularist, Duke decided it would be advantageous to portray himself as a born-again evangelical Christian. Although he had often risen to defend the "Christian" nature of Western Civilization, and his rallies often opened with some kind of prayerful invocation, he was not a religious man. (Christian Identity had never caught his fancy.) As a result of this patently transparent ploy, hard-core national socialists who had been supporting his campaign pilloried Duke for opportunism. And several important evangelicals publicly doubted this professed faith.[27] Further, as reporters stopped treating him as a three-headed monster (to be looked at but not touched), they asked questions that easily pierced his born-again veil.

Nevertheless, on October 19, 1991—just one year after the Senate race—Duke upset all expectations and forced himself into a runoff with Democrat Edwin Edwards. In a field of twelve, the Republicans' official nominee, Congressman Clyde Holloway, pulled just over 5 percent of the vote. The sitting governor, Buddy Roemer, once so smug and confident, polled 27 percent. David Duke easily topped both with 32 percent. Only the disgraced Democrat from Acadiana, Edwin Edwards, beat Duke on primary night—but by a scant two points. As the entire country looked on, the final weeks turned into a contest between Duke's thinly disguised brownshirt racism and Edwards's corruption-soaked patronage politics. Signs sprouted in New Orleans's French Quarter and on the back bayous, VOTE FOR THE CROOK, IT'S IMPORTANT. Split by race, ideology, and ethnic personality, Louisianans voted in record numbers. With a remarkable 80 percent turnout, Edwards walked away in the final election, 61 percent of the vote to Duke's 39 percent. Buried inside those seemingly lopsided numbers were questions that needed to be asked. The answers would have meanings long after David Duke stepped down from his election night platform in Baton Rouge.

Who were the six hundred thousand voters Duke had attracted in the 1990 Senate race and the seven hundred thousand plus he won over in the 1991 governor's contest? Why did they punch the button for a man widely reviled for his days as a Klansman, proved to still hold the tenets of his faith in scientific racism, and denounced by local business interests worried that his election would engender a tourist boycott? Who voted for Duke, and why? Duke, the white supremacist, was a known item. The core staff, volunteers, and contributors who made up his campaign machinery were also relatively identifiable. But the most enigmatic questions remained.

Some observers chose not even to ask about this white majority Duke had won, perhaps (mistakenly) believing that ignoring these voters would make them go away. Typical in that regard, William F. Buckley, Jr., declaimed in *National Review*: "What happened, we now know, was not a close race but a total repudiation of a reptilian creature."[28] If Duke had in fact been repudiated in the governor's race, it had not been by a majority of whites, and Buckley was not known for setting his compass by black voters. Another *National Review* column claimed that Duke was for the most part a symbol of the electorate's dissatisfaction. "The less viable Duke is as a nominee, the more attractive he will be as a protest vehicle."[29] When such a view was ventured as an explanation for voter behavior, it was only undermined by the facts. In the future, as Duke became "less viable" as a candidate and thereby potentially a greater "protest" candidate, he received qualitatively much smaller vote totals. A similar view had been advanced by Vice President Dan Quayle after the Senate race. Duke voters were angry at the federal government and wasteful bureaucracy, he said. But *National Review* and conservative politicians were not alone in the attempt to omit race and racism from explicit consideration.

Those at the center of the established terrain did the same. One consensus view held that Duke's vote was an anomaly peculiar to the state's "hot and spicy" political tradition. "Duke's message is more economic than Southern," a national television news broadcast explained during the Senate race. "It feeds on resentment in a state where the oil business is still slumping and unemployment is over six percent." By this typical account, the Bayou State was virtually a banana republic. "America's Third World: that's what Louisiana almost is," *National Journal*'s 1992 edition of *The Almanac of American Politics* averred.[30] A standard reference work akin to the *Encyclopaedia Britannica* in status, the *Almanac* did ask the most important question: "Why did such an anomaly [the anomaly being Duke] get so many votes?" But its answer was most telling by what was missing. "Duke seems to have been the right person in the right place, a tax opponent in a time of economic distress, a plausible speaker in the state with a great weakness for demagogues and a carelessness about civil liberties, the only prominent opponent in an anti-incumbent year of an incumbent who had not been working the state intensively for years."[31] Unless racism comes under the umbrella of "a carelessness about civil liberties," and it doesn't, the *Almanac* did not mention race as a factor.

The notion that the Duke vote rested, in the final analysis, on financial distress, the downturn in Louisiana's oil industry, or some other proximate economic cause echoed across the political center and re-echoed on the left. One West Coast sociologist, an astute critic of conservative movements such as the Christian right, ventured the idea that Duke's supporters "were downwardly mobile not so much as a status group but as an economic class. Duke's electoral success is better explained as the result of voters' declining economic conditions."[32] It was a sentiment repeated in left-wing forums from Cambridge to Berkeley.

Such a conclusion was certainly reasonable. As we have seen, it had been depression-like conditions in the Farm Belt just a few years before that had opened the way to a steady stream of far right racists and anti-Semites in the rural Midwest. They had plied farmers with forests of propaganda that blamed Jews directly for high interest costs and low commodity prices. The constant refrain that eight Jewish families "owned" the Federal Reserve Bank had spoken directly, even if falsely, to the concerns of bankrupt farmers. And the solutions offered by the radical right, although ultimately specious, at least offered a glimmer of a chance that a family's way of life could remain intact. But Duke didn't offer any plans to create new jobs. He didn't speak out in favor of raising the minimum wage or supporting trade unions. And when discussion turned to the oil industry during the governor's race, Duke claimed to be an "ecologist," a term usually understood to mean he was an opponent of an expanded oil industry.[33] As the votes were tallied in the governor's race, few signs showed that "economic distress" had mattered.

In fact, overnight surveys showed that David Duke's voters came from a broad swath of the white working and middle classes, regardless of whether or not they actually experienced declining economic conditions. A quick look at the numbers reveals a visible class line in the Duke vote, but no real correspondence to an experience of distress. While he took 55 percent of the total white vote, Duke's pull rate was slightly higher at 60 percent among those with middle-class family incomes ranging from thirty thousand to fifty thousand dollars a year. Among the working poor, those with family incomes between fifteen and thirty thousand, it was higher still at 63 percent.[34]

The surveys also asked Duke's voters about their economic condition. Those who reported that their economic condition had "stayed the same" voted for Duke at marginally higher rates than those who reported that they were "worse off": 60 percent for the "sames," 58 percent for the "worses." Only those who reported that they were "better off" voted at levels below the white norm, but at 47 percent it was not much below that norm. In fact, that last number is a stinger. Almost half the white people who said their economic situation had improved voted for the former Kluxer.[35]

If economic distress did not predict much about Duke's voters, what did? Education told a bit. Among whites with a high school diploma or less, he took 68 percent of the vote; of those with at least some college, he won 48 percent. A gender gap showed also. Among all voters (white and black), he took 41 percent of men and 37 percent of women. The measurable gap in gender would have been greater if just white voters had been counted. The religious identification of white voters revealed a bit more, as he took 69 percent of those calling themselves Christian born-again fundamentalists. A composite of the most likely Duke voter thus emerged: a financially stable, middle-class white male, with a high school education and a born-again Christianity. Conversely, black people from all classes and whites with college educations earning above seventy-five thousand dollars a year were most likely to vote against Duke.[36]

While economic status, education level, religion, and gender helped draw a partial picture of who Duke voters were, these factors did not explain why the white electorate voted as it did. The Democratic Party, of course, had an immediate interest in finding out more about the "Duke-Democrats" who had been deserting their party in favor of an identifiable racist. Here a poll conducted by Garin-Hart Strategic Research in the midst of the Senate race offered some preliminary advice. Duke voters were noticeably not economically distressed. "Indeed, voters' feelings of *political* alienation were a far better predictor of support for Duke than their feelings of *economic* hardship [emphasis in original]." They advised Democrats to champion middle-class interests against "the wealthy special interests" on issues such as tax fairness.[37] In a pair of elections in which race and racism became the defining issues, telling Democrats to focus on taxes was as useless as telling Republicans to nominate Holloway.

After the elections passed into history, a dozen academics jumped into the fray, analyzing opinion poll surveys and parsing precinct-level voting and demographic data. They ran statistical programs of every sort and wrote up their conclusions for scholarly publication. This was the first clearly identified vote for an undisguised racist since Alabama's Governor George Wallace had run for president in 1968 and 1972. Studies of the Wallace vote had been the benchmark for understanding the angry white vote in the late 1960s. The Duke vote in Louisiana could have played the same role for understanding the early 1990s. Perhaps the most thorough analysis of opinion poll surveys was conducted by Tulane's Douglas D. Rose. After considering six different kinds of motivations, Rose concluded that each told only a partial truth: "As we have seen, all these explanations account for some of Duke's support. The least powerful are those picturing Duke primarily as a populist candidate who draws on distrust of government among marginal and disappointed citizens." Race and racism, he argued, rather than any kind of right-wing populism predicted whether or not white people would vote for Duke.[38]

Although virtually every scholar concluded that the central factor motivating Duke's voters was "racial prejudice," several controversies emerged around the edges of this debate. Some questions, such as whether or not it was possible for pollsters to gather accurate data over the phone from Duke's voters, had limited significance. Other points of contention did have significant implications for the decades to come: Was the Duke phenomenon specific to the open primary process, or could someone like Duke replicate his success outside Louisiana? Outside the South? Was the racism exhibited by Duke's voters a new development or simply a reincarnation of an older white supremacy dating from the Wallace years and farther back? Two different edited collections of studies, *The Emergence of David Duke and the Politics of Race* and *David Duke and the Politics of Race in the South*, starting from opposing points of view, actually ended up pointing in the same disturbing direction, although neither expressed its conclusion in terms used by the other or even the terms used here.[39]

Simply put: David Duke had been right when he claimed victory. One, he had emerged personally as a strong leader. On this point, Duke's willingness to break the rules was considered an asset. Two, his leadership had further polarized the people of Louisiana.[40] Although he was not as powerful as Serbia's Slobodan Milošević or Croatia's Franjo Tudjman, the lack of open conflict in Louisiana was due to the comparative stability of American institutions and the sizable white minority that had opposed racism rather than to Duke's own actions. Three, his leadership had imbued a definable sector with a distinct sense of itself as a "victim" group, a dispossessed white majority. "Supporters in part saw Duke as a voice for whites, in the same sense that minorities have spokespersons," Douglas Rose's study concluded.[41] All three points are related.

For a significant number of white people qua white people to desire or want a unique voice such as Duke's, an important change in self-consciousness needed to have occurred. They needed to identify themselves as white people first, rather than as Americans. As one former neoconservative analyst, Michael Lind, noted in his book *The Next American Nation*, white (Christian) people had thought of themselves as the quintessential real Americans since before the country's founding.[42] They drew no distinction between their identities as white people and their identities as Americans; and for two centuries that congruence was cemented in laws relegating black people to second-class status. Even after the laws were changed, most white people still saw themselves as first-class citizens. David Duke, on the other hand, had spent three consecutive years telling white voters that no!, white people no longer ride in first class. Instead, he said, black people have special rights that you don't. (In smaller circles he argued that white people no longer ran the government, but that Jews did.) A statistically measurable segment of Duke's voters now believed they were not just Americans or the American majority, but a distinct white (minority) facing a black threat perceived as real (not symbolic) and dangerous. In this white mind, they were not consciously trying to preserve Jim Crow or the material prerogatives of pale skin. However wrong the notion, they believed political power was a zero-sum game: the more power for black people, the less power for white people. It didn't matter that they all were Americans.

This odd transformation was implicitly measured in one statistical study that asked if the perception that black people constituted a "racial threat" to white political dominance might influence white voting behavior.[43] From the period of legal segregation through the Wallace campaign in 1968, whites in the South had tended to vote for explicitly racist candidates at higher levels in counties with correspondingly higher percentages of black populations. Prior to the civil rights movement, one study after another had concluded that this trend resulted from white fears of losing "their" dominant political position. (It was actually a behavior that only further disempowered and impoverished the white poor, however, as it left them at the mercies of the region's [white] economic elites.) After 1968 an increase in the number of black voters pushed the study of "racial threats" off the map of analytical inquiry. But in the Duke campaigns, "racial threat" re-emerged as a factor motivating white people to vote for Duke. That is, with other variables being accounted for, the higher the percentage of black voters in a county or metropolitan area, the higher the percentage of white voters who pulled the lever for Duke. (Conversely, in those areas with lower percentages of proximate black voters, whites tended to vote for Duke's [more racially tolerant] opponents.)

It is virtually a truism among human relations professionals that one way to smooth over America's racial fault lines is for black people and white people—indeed people of every hue and description—to live together in the same neighborhoods, eat together in the same restaurants, attend the same houses of worship, go to the same schools, and vote in the same precinct houses. Here was at least some evidence of the contrary. White people tend to be "tolerant"—a mealymouthed term—up to a certain point. At that time, when the percentages change and white people approach minority status, they tend to run. The sociological literature on housing segregation makes that point over and over. The question that emerges from Louisiana in 1990 and 1991: What is (at least one) electoral equivalent of "white flight"? The answer appears to have been: David Duke.

What does this mean for future generations? The U.S. Census predicts that in the years between 2035 and 2050 white people will become an actual demographic minority in a nation of minorities. If unchecked, the trend mid-century will produce larger numbers of David Duke types, each pushing the perception of a racial threat upon an even more statistically receptive white constituency. Deprived of the monopoly of voting rights they enjoyed during the Jim Crow era and thus unable to enforce their political will through the ballot box, will white people seek other means?

Within days of losing the runoff for governor, Duke announced his candidacy again, this time in the 1992 Republican primaries for president. He promised to run hard at President George H. W. Bush in the South, and his threat now seemed considerably more potent than his fanciful stab at the Democratic primaries had been four years before.[44] But after two years and more than two million dollars, Duke was no longer a credible candidate. He had proved that he could not win an election statewide with any significant minority of black voters, and he no longer had the seat for District 81. Duke was hoisted by the petard of his own mainstreaming success. Commanding hundreds of thousands of votes had turned him into a conventional candidate. And as a conventional candidate he looked less like an insurgent racial rebel and more like a perennial loser. Key personnel abandoned the Metairie headquarters. Some hard-core movement cadres went home, disgusted at his pandering to Christian fundamentalists and evangelicals in the last moments of the governor's race. Others, more pragmatic in their racial politics, prepared to join seemingly less quixotic campaigns. And when Duke did finally stretch his campaign apparatus outside Louisiana, Republican regulars became unavailable as staff. He was forced to rely on movement personnel with embarrassing track records.[45]

Nevertheless, the constituency Duke had awakened and the hot buttons he had pushed still existed, not just in Louisiana and other southern states but from New Hampshire to California as well. In the next election cycle, the threat of white majority dispossession helped elect Governor Kirk Fordice in Mississippi and pushed Senator Jesse Helms past the popular black mayor from Charlotte, Harvey Gantt. In addition, new issues animated a new (white) nationalist campaign. Absent a communist threat, foreign intervention would be opposed by an America first isolationism. As multilateral agreements, such as the North American Free Trade Agreement, became policy, protective tariffs became the cry of economic nationalists as well as nationalist charlatans. As the free trade in capital mobilized an increasingly global workforce, a renewed nativism would target immigrant rights in the name of opposition to "multiculturalism." And once again, the refuge of states' rights would emerge as the last redoubt against the federal Leviathan. Each of these issues (and others) would mobilize constituencies nationally similar to Duke's Louisiana voters. The intrepid former Klan wizard had opened the door. But it was Pat Buchanan who walked through.

Pat Buchanan Runs Through
the Republican Presidential Primaries

December 10, 1991. As the presidential primaries came into view on the near horizon, a number of would-be challengers appeared, each hoping to replace President George H. W. Bush. The post-Duke Populist Party presidential candidate blustered his way along a route of superpatriot stops and survivalist fest flops. Ross Perot, a blunt-talking Texan, railed against establishment politics while readying his own millions for a third party independent run for president. On the Democratic side, seven contenders vied for the public's attention. In Republican ranks, Pat Buchanan formally announced his candidacy for president, reclaiming the party's right flank for his own anti–New World Order politics.

Just weeks before, Buchanan had urged Republicans to adopt Duke's issues: "The way to do battle with David Duke is not to go ballistic because Duke, as a teenager, paraded around in a Nazi costume to protest William Kunstler during Vietnam, or to shout to the heavens that Duke had the same phone number last year as the Ku Klux Klan. Everybody in Metairie knew that. The way to deal with Mr. Duke is the way the GOP dealt with the far more formidable challenge of George Wallace. Take a hard look at Duke's portfolio of winning issues; and expropriate those not in conflict with GOP principles."[1] Buchanan believed Duke's message was "Middle Class, meritocratic, populist and nationalist."[2]

Buchanan quickly assembled a competitive campaign apparatus, with his sister, Angela "Bay" Buchanan, as manager. While her brother worked as President Richard Nixon's speechwriter, she had kept the books for Nixon's reelection campaign in 1972. Four years later she enlisted in Governor Ronald Reagan's first (failed) presidential primary bid. After that campaign Bay was the comptroller for a nonprofit organization known as Citizens for the Republic, which continued stoking

Reagan's presidential ambitions while working his contributor lists. When Reagan launched a renewed bid for the presidency in 1980, Bay served as the campaign's treasurer. She was subsequently appointed treasurer of the United States in the new Reagan administration.[3] A few blocks away her brother sat ensconced in the president's communications offices. When brother Pat began thinking about running in the 1992 Republican primaries, according to the book *Mad as Hell*, Bay secured the endorsement of New Hampshire's conservative newspaper, *The Union Leader* (Manchester), and walked him into the race.[4]

Buchanan gained ballot status and began battling through the primaries. Only in delegate-rich New York State did the sitting president's functionaries manage to deny the challenger a primary ballot line. Duke faded. Buchanan surged. At the level of pure campaign strategy, Buchanan attempted in 1992 to replicate the kind of insurgency staged by Democratic Senator Eugene McCarthy in 1968, which had forced President Lyndon Johnson to withdraw from the race. In the months prior to New Hampshire's primary, Buchanan visited factory gates and small-town diners, talking one-on-one with voters. Direct contact with the state's electorate enabled him to hone his message more sharply than any poll or focus group would have. President Bush, on the other hand, virtually ignored Buchanan's efforts.[5] On February 18, Buchanan won a respectable 37 percent of the total—65,087 votes. Although he didn't quite reach the 42 percent McCarthy had received in 1968, the total was large enough to justify his continuing the campaign past New Hampshire. Per McCarthy and Johnson in 1968, Buchanan subsequently asked Bush to step out of the race, a request the president declined even to acknowledge.[6]

To Buchanan's civic opponents the election results felt much like David Duke's initial win in District 81. Once again a significant percentage of (white) people had voted for a candidate whose most salient credentials were as an unabashed bigot. The former Reagan White House insider succeeded so well at co-opting Duke, that Wilmot Robertson's *Instauration* magazine declared the intrepid columnist a "clean" version of the erstwhile cow pasture cross burner.[7]

Duke's own run through the Republican primaries was short. In Georgia he managed to meet the qualifications, but party officials removed him from the ballot anyway. He made one quick foray into South Florida at the invitation of some Cuban right-wingers, but party officials there also denied him ballot status.[8] In the process, his campaign machinery broke down. By February 1992, Duke's campaign had only fifty-eight thousand dollars in the bank, and fifty thousand of that was a carryover from the governor's race. His top managers dropped out, apparently fatigued after three years of constant campaigning. And Duke never established any strong state organizations outside Louisiana, with the exception of South Carolina. There William Carter, a chiropractor and former Populist Party state chair, raised money and brought Duke in to speak and shake hands. Despite spending more time in the Palmetto State than either George Bush or Pat Buchanan, Duke received only 7 percent of the vote—10,553 ballots on primary day. His totals were equally squalid elsewhere. In both Texas and Tennessee he got 3 percent. Mississippi was his best state, at 11 percent, and 16,426 votes. Even at home in Louisiana he polled only 9 percent—11,955 votes— and did not carry his home parish. By April David Duke had officially quit the race.[9]

Carto's *Spotlight* quickly analyzed Duke's failed primary bid. His core supporters were weary, it said, "afraid he was becoming a professional office-seeker." Most important, however, *The Spotlight* pointed to the real nerve center of white nationalism in 1992, Pat Buchanan. "Any hope Duke had of mounting an effective challenge to George Bush ended with the entrance of Buchanan into the Republican race."[10] When Duke finally withdrew from the race, he endorsed Pat Buchanan; an endorsement Buchanan formally ignored.

Buchanan proved a formidable insurgent in the Old Confederacy on Super Tuesday, March 10. In Georgia he virtually repeated his New Hampshire performance with 36 percent of the vote, and in Florida he tapped a nerve at 32 percent. In both states party officials had kept David Duke off the ballot. Still, in Louisiana and Mississippi, Duke was listed, and Buchanan was forced to split their joined constituency. In Louisiana many of Duke's key supporters, including his former campaign lieutenant Kenny Knight, voted for Buchanan.[11] Buchanan won 27 percent of the Republican vote there. Duke pulled only 9 percent. In Mississippi, Buchanan received 17 percent to Duke's 11 percent. In both states their combined totals approximated Buchanan's New Hampshire percentage. Nevertheless, as the weeks turned into months, it became obvious that the president was winning majorities in every contest. Buchanan's national support slipped into the low twenty percentages and then the teens. At the time Alabama voted on June 2, Buchanan won a miserable 8 percent in the state that once boasted the Confederacy's capital.

In the Pacific Northwest, where the idea of a white republic had drawn many militants to live, Buchanan did poorly on primary day. Christian patriots of varying strands were noticeably active in the region, particularly in Oregon, certainly more so than in New Hampshire. Survivalists had settled in the three states around the Aryan Nations camp in the Idaho Panhandle. Their inability to influence the Republican vote in the region evidenced the tactical gulf between mainstreamers, such as those in Louisiana, and the subculturalists billeted away in the mountains. The adjutant then answering the phone at Richard Butler's camp, for example, declared Buchanan "basically anti-Christ."[12] In Oregon, Buchanan garnered 19 percent of the Republican vote, in Washington State only 10 percent, and in Idaho 13 percent. Even if all the Christian patriots had been concentrated in one state, it is unlikely that they would have much influenced the totals. For many Aryans, registering to vote was akin to endorsing the Beast system.

By the end of the primaries Buchanan had collected 2,988,380 votes in thirty-four states and Washington, D.C. And during the campaign year he had raised a total of $14,521,899. More than $7 million of the total was from individual contributions, most of that in relatively small amounts. The other half came from Federal Election Commission matching funds. Both the vote totals and contribution amounts dwarfed anything David Duke could have hoped to muster. The financial numbers unequivocally demonstrated that Buchanan had established an independent fund-raising base within the Republican Party. But numbers alone can't convey the complexity of his run through the primaries.

In addition to his more widely reported opposition to abortion rights, Buchanan had courted Duke's constituency, touted issues such as white majority dispossession, and received endorsements from throughout the movement. "Buchanan is saying—practically to a word—what *The Spotlight* has been saying on the big issues for many years," Carto's tabloid opined.[13]

At points Buchanan's relationship to explicit movement operations such as Liberty Lobby seemed a bit like the Reverend Jimmy Swaggart's flirtations with virtue. Sometimes his association with potentially embarrassing personalities remained undetected. Such was the case with Boyd Cathey, who floated in the Holocaust denial etherworld, but was more firmly planted among a small band of neo-Confederate intellectuals.[14] Cathey volunteered as Buchanan's official North Carolina state campaign chairman, but his vote-mobilizing skills were unremarkable. In that state's primary, Buchanan received 55,420 votes, or about 20 percent of the Republican total. At the time, Cathey also served on the Institute for Historical Review's editorial advisory board and as a senior editor at *Southern Partisan*, a glossy quarterly magazine dedicated to Confederate honor in the history of the War Between the States. The magazine declared the television commentator cum presidential aspirant "the current leader of the conservative movement in America."[15]

Cathey and *Southern Partisan* were not exactly rewriting the history of the Civil War; they were simply keeping alive the Confederate historical view that had dominated (white) historiography for decades, until the civil rights movement forced a reconsideration of its claims. And Cathey apparently preferred to obscure his exact relationship with the Institute for Historical Review. When interviewed, he claimed to have resigned from the advisory board in 1992. The way Cathey told it, a reporter might have reasonably concluded that his name was listed on the IHR's board by accident.[16] Despite Cathey's claims, a July 1989 *IHR Newsletter* squib described him with familiarity and pride in his educational achievements. Cathey had received a master's degree in history at the University of Virginia in 1971 and a doctorate from the Pontifical University of Navarra in Spain. He had also studied at the International Seminary of St. Pius X in Switzerland and taught at the St. Pius X Institute in Argentina. At home in his native North Carolina, Cathey worked in the archives of the state's department of cultural resources. And he was still listed on the IHR's advisory board during the years Buchanan ran for president.

If the connection between Buchanan's North Carolina chairman and the Institute for Historical Review went unnoticed in the press, some of Buchanan's other supporters did create minicontroversies. Consider the campaign's New Jersey state volunteer coordinator, Joe D'Alessio, who also served as the New Jersey chairman of the Populist Party and temporarily embarrassed the candidate. An Associated Press reporter had heard D'Alessio publicly compare interracial marriages to mongrel animals. "If you have two purebred dogs and you mate them, what do you get? You get a mutt," he had said.[17] As a result, D'Alessio was forced to resign.[18]

Despite the snub of D'Alessio, the Populist Party's enchantment with Buchanan overshadowed any parochial organizational concerns. And the party's monthly newspaper didn't mention its state chair's slip from grace. In fact, one of the Populist Party's eleven national committee members, John Justice, gave Buchanan a thousand dollars just five months after the incident.

John Justice was just one among four thousand donors who gave in excess of $250 to the campaign and fewer than a handful who were even remotely associated with the movement. John Toland, the Pulitzer Prize–winning author who had spoken at an IHR meet but was not otherwise active in movement circles, gave Buchanan $400. A reverend from Virginia who often carried water for Liberty Lobby gave $900. From Nebraska, a regular donor to Holocaust denial efforts gave $250. Samuel G. Dickson, the attorney from Georgia, gave $500.[19]

Dickson had supported Duke's first bid for the presidency in 1987, but his contribution to Buchanan's campaign, unlike D'Alessio's, had no visible deleterious effect. And Ed Fields, who along with Dickson had sponsored the British führer John Tyndall's 1991 American tour, lent his own dirtied hands to Buchanan. With the same energy that he had once used to laud Bob Mathews's Order gang, Fields mailed Buchanan's campaign materials to hundreds on the *Truth at Last* subscriber list. Bearing a February 24 postmark and containing a "Dear Friend" letter signed in blue ink by Pat Buchanan, Fields's envelope was filled with brochures obviously intended to help in the primary.

Not all white supremacists supported the Republican insider. In one confrontation prior to the California primary, Pat Buchanan fared poorly at the hands of Tom Metzger, then still prominent among skinheads and other subculturalists. As part of Buchanan's campaign against darkly hued, Spanish-speaking immigrants, he planned a photo opportunity on the Mexican border—not far from where Duke had created his own media story more than a dozen years before. Near a hole in the fence oft used as a crossing point, a small group of Buchanan's advance men and supporters waited—along with the requisite television news cameras— for the candidate to appear and take appropriate verbal umbrage at those dashing across the border. The only problem was Metzger, who waited with great fanfare for Buchanan to appear. Where was the "great white hope"?, he sneered like a perfect villain in a street theater, "I want to talk with him." When Buchanan did finally appear, he was forced to huddle in a small circle of supporters to avoid contact with Metzger. But the ornery Aryan worked his way into camera range nevertheless. "Pat," he yelled as all the cameras swung away from the candidate and toward him, "what are we going to do about all those rich Republicans making millions off the wetbacks in the Imperial Valley?" As the cameras swung back and forth, Buchanan beat a hasty retreat after less than fifteen minutes of photoless opportunity. With the cameras all to himself, Metzger then staged his own press conference. If he were president, he argued volubly, he would station National Guard troops like a picket fence along the border with orders to "shoot to kill." The immigration problem would be over in one night, he declared.[20] Tom Metzger played footage from the border incident on his community access cable program, *Race and Reason*.[21]

In the middle of the primary season riots broke out in Los Angeles, affecting the campaigns of every Democrat and Republican, and Buchanan was not immune. Touched off by the verdict in a highly charged trial of four white police officers, the riots had their roots in a case that had originated the year before. Police had kicked and clubbed an unarmed black motorist, Rodney King, fracturing his skull, breaking his leg, and smashing his teeth in an orgy of ganglike violence. Unbeknownst to the officers, an inadvertent witness videotaped the incident. In the days and months that followed, footage of the beating was played and replayed on television, further enraging a local population already angry over years of police misconduct and brutality.

As a result of the outrage, local authorities appointed an independent commission headed by Warren Christopher, President Jimmy Carter's former deputy secretary of state, to investigate the Los Angeles Police Department. The commission's official report found a "significant number of officers in the L.A.P.D. who routinely use excessive force." It also examined digital messages transmitted prior to King's beating, and it found a complete repertoire of racist, sexist, and homophobic banter across the police airwaves. "Batten down the hatches," read one, "several thousand Zulus approaching from the North." Another message was even more pointed: "I'm not happy until I've violated somebody's civil rights and then put them in jail." Additional insults were recorded in seven hundred different messages over a period of less than two hundred days.[22]

As the commission's conclusions were debated in Los Angeles, a national discussion of police racism and brutality ensued. Local police departments found themselves under increased scrutiny, and President Bush's Justice Department re-reviewed fifteen thousand complaints of misconduct.[23] Although the department could have brought federal charges against the four officers under a 120-year-old civil rights statute first passed to curb Klan-style violence, it ceded prosecution to the state. The defendants were granted a change of venue to Simi Valley, California, a predominantly white suburban enclave of homeowners, quite unlike the multiracial neighborhoods of Los Angeles. Their attorneys succeeded at shifting the blame from the police to the victim. Prosecutors failed to pursue vigorously any racial animus underlying the incident. The Simi Valley jury found the officers innocent.

"From Boston to Berkeley," *The New York Times* reported, "people searched for ways to vent their anger and astonishment" after the jury announced its decision.[24] Even President George H. W. Bush felt compelled to say, "Yesterday's verdict in the Los Angeles police case left us all with a deep sense of personal frustration and anguish," and the Democratic Party presidential nominee-to-be, Governor Bill Clinton, took a half step further. There is a feeling, he said, that "the system is broke and unresponsive and unfair."[25] A dozen major cities soon experienced violence or the threat of violence. But the epicenter was Los Angeles's South Central district. Businesses were looted and burned, unwitting passersby attacked, and gunfire rang out in every direction. When police finally restored order after three intense days of conflict, businesses and homes were ruined, at least eight thousand people were arrested, and at least fifty deaths counted.

Into the ensuing political maelstrom stepped the intrepid Pat Buchanan, blustering across California and shooting from his lip. In Northern California he argued that the riots were caused by "the politics of appeasement."[26] At a stop in Whittier he blamed illegal immigrants.[27] And at still another stop, he blamed Los Angeles's Democratic mayor, Tom Bradley, for "giving moral sanction to the mob."[28] In addition to the sound bites in California, he gave a fuller exposition to the Reverend Jerry Falwell's graduating class at Liberty University in Lynchburg, Virginia. "While we conservatives and traditionalists were fighting the Cold War against communism," he said, "we were losing the cultural war for the soul of America. And we can see our defeat in the smoking ruins of Los Angeles."[29]

To this budding generation of religious fundamentalists, Buchanan reduced the economic, political, and social problems of Los Angeles to a simple moral equation: on one side stood "Christian truths" and "Western Civilization"; on the other side were the "barbarians" of an "adversary culture." He posed George Washington against Robert Mapplethorpe, Easter against Earth Day, and Custer National Battlefield against the descendants of Crazy Horse. Of all the things he lamented just days after the riots had ended, the Republican candidate did not include Rodney King's fractured skull or the failure of justice in Simi Valley. Instead, he rued the removal of Confederate statues "because Dixie's cause was not [considered] moral." According to the presidential candidate, the true legacy of the Confederacy—"family, faith, friends and country"—had fallen victim to the vicissitudes of this culture war. Buchanan's constant harkening to the past rendered his white nationalism fundamentally backward-looking. He wasn't a revolutionary like William Pierce, who sought an Aryan superman in the future. Nor did Buchanan then explicitly find Western Civilization in the genetic code of those Europeans who created it, as did Willis Carto's pseudonymous E. L. Anderson, Ph.D.

In fact, when Buchanan first announced his run, the issues that had most animated his candidacy were those particular to disappointed conservatives: President Bush had reneged on his "read my lips" no new taxes pledge and signed civil rights legislation that he had earlier promised to veto. In addition, Buchanan sought conservative votes as the most uncompromising opponent of abortion rights and as a staunch defender of the so-called Christian right. When he projected a renewed isolationism, he couched it in terms that would have pleased Robert Taft prior to World War Two. With the Cold War's conclusion, he reasoned, the imperative to contain the Soviet Union had ended. He called for pulling back from multilateral institutions such as NATO and the International Monetary Fund, ending all foreign aid, and withdrawing American troops stationed in Europe and Japan.[30] And from New Hampshire to California, Buchanan had complemented this America first–style foreign policy with a correlate economic nationalism and nativism. He promoted tariff protections as a way to stem transnational capital flows and endorsed immigration barriers to restrict the movement of labor.

After a consideration of his ideological predispositions, one must still question why voters pulled Buchanan's lever: Was it because he promised to keep factory jobs in the United States and stop Mexicans at the Rio Grande, or because he would outlaw abortions at safe hospitals, or because he invoked a culture war to explain the Los Angeles riots? As will become evident, white nationalists believed the Buchanan candidacy had helped birth a new moment for their politics. At the same time, exit polling in Colorado, Georgia, and Maryland showed that more than three-quarters of Buchanan's voters supported him mainly to "send a message" of opposition to the sitting president, George H. W. Bush, rather than to affirm votes for Buchanan's nationalism. As further proof of this anybody but Bush thesis, commentators offered as evidence the South Dakota primary, where Buchanan was not on the ballot. There 31 percent voted for "uncommitted," rather than Bush, just a few points less than Buchanan received in his best states.[31] As Ross Perot was to demonstrate, dissatisfaction with both the Republican and Democratic parties was running high in 1992, and Pat Buchanan obviously tapped the votes of Republicans unhappy with their party.

If Buchanan's three million votes were, in fact, little more than a protest vote, they would have been remarkable nevertheless. Consider that just as the primaries had begun, William Buckley had argued in *National Review*—the conservative periodical of record—that Pat Buchanan "could not be defended from the charge of anti-Semitism." Nevertheless, just two months later, *National Review* urged a "tactical vote for the challenger in New Hampshire."[32] While the association with anti-Semitism hung around Buchanan's neck throughout the primaries, it did not seem to matter to the three million Americans who voted for him. Instead, commentators were rankled more by the candidate's support for protective tariffs than by any supposed animosity toward Jews.

Differences over the meaning of the Buchanan vote continued rattling around inside the Republican Party for another eight years. Adversaries from within the conservative movement argued that his campaign was less about winning the presidency of the United States than about gaining the upper hand among movement intellectuals.[33] But Buchanan's innermost circles did not believe that his candidacy was simply a bid for ideological hegemony or protest votes. Instead, they believed something totally new was in process.

"What has happened in the Buchanan revolution," wrote Sam Francis, "is the emergence of a new political identity."[34]

Enter Sam Francis

Samuel Todd Francis was in a unique position to gauge the campaign's import. He and Buchanan were fellow columnists, and Francis had long urged his friend to jump into the electoral fray. When Buchanan finally did announce his candidacy, he handed off his nationally syndicated column to his colleague. Both men had once been part of the conservative establishment, privy to the elite at either end of Pennsylvania Avenue. Now they were part of the opposition, the white nationalist opposition. Comrades called Francis the Clausewitz of the Right. But he was an intellectual rather than a strategist. A more apt sobriquet might have been philosopher-general. His influence did not end or begin with Pat Buchanan's presidential campaigns, and he was able to explain the intellectual underpinnings of his ideas in a common sense fashion.

Francis's pen was as sharp as his body was round. A postwar boomer native of Chattanooga, Tennessee, the large, flush-faced Francis graduated from two first-rank institutions, earning a bachelor's degree at Johns Hopkins University in 1969 and a doctorate in history at the University of North Carolina at Chapel Hill in 1979. His dissertation may have focused on the first earl of Clarendon in 1660, but Francis's interests were very contemporary.

At the Heritage Foundation, the ascendant think tank on the conservative right in the late 1970s and early 1980s, Francis churned out background briefing papers on international terrorism, southern Africa, and issues related to American intelligence agencies. (He recommended that intelligence agencies be exempt from the Freedom of Information Act.)[35] During that period he also wrote for *Southern Partisan* (the same magazine that Boyd Cathey later edited), as well as for journals managed by Roger Pearson. Pearson, who had left Willis Carto and *Western Destiny* fifteen years before, was then making a splash in D.C. Pearson edited his own journal, for which Francis wrote, as well as briefly serving on the Heritage Foundation's *Policy Review* board.[36]

Francis's intellectual products were genuine, not crackpot propaganda paperbacks promoting race war. His book *The Soviet Strategy of Terror* was published in 1981. Three years later the University Press of America published his study of James Burnham, who predicted the dominance of a new managerial class over the owner-operators of pre-monopoly capitalism. Francis showed residues of his ideological debt to Burnham, a Marxist turned conservative, for years to come. And as the 1992 election cycle concluded, Francis finished collecting his essays into a book published by the University of Missouri Press, *Beautiful Losers: Essays on the Failure of American Conservatism.* Published at the end of twelve years of Republican presidential rule, the title conveyed Francis's assessment of the Reagan Revolution.

Francis had also served as a senior aide to North Carolina Senator John East, who sat on the Senate's subcommittee on terrorism, from 1981 to 1986. (East's office was then a nesting place for a bevy of future Buchananite intellectuals.) After the wheelchair-bound East committed suicide in 1986, the impeccably credentialed Francis went to work alongside Pat Buchanan, writing editorials and columns for *The Washington Times*, a daily newspaper that had marked itself during the Reagan years as the conservative alternative to *The Washington Post*. (He eventually won two awards from the American Society of Newspaper Editors.) It was Francis's prodigious intellect that propelled the Buchanan brain trust. And at the vortex of this intellect swirled his conception of Middle American Radicals.

When Francis had written that Buchanan's Middle American Radicals represented new social forces, he didn't mean "new" as in "born yesterday." In fact, he had said much the same thing in 1981. By his account, Middle American Radicals (or MARs) were the social constituency of what was then known as the New Right. At that time, Francis argued that Middle American Radicals had expressed themselves in a string of movements throughout the 1970s: against school busing for racial integration, against the Equal Rights Amendment, against the ceding of the Panama Canal, and finally in electing Ronald Reagan president. MARs were both a social movement and a class: "not simply a middle class and not simply an economic category . . . [but] in the broadest sense a political class."[37] Arguing in much the same way as Marx did about the proletariat, Francis contended that MARs' will to power, while it was self-motivated, would actually benefit all society. That early essay was two-sided. It burned with personal anger at the Middle American's "threatened future and . . . insulted past." And it borrowed extensively from the dispassionate analysis of the Michigan sociologist Donald Warren, who had first discovered and named this ideologically complex class while studying Governor George Wallace's presidential campaigns.[38]

According to Warren, MARsians were radically alienated from institutions that reproduced social consensus, such as the government, trade unions, and churches. But they were neither unambiguously of the traditionally plebeian left nor the aristocratic right. He found this generation at the center of society, rather than at its so-called extremes. Unlike the inhabitants of the conservative right, MARsians were antielite. At the same time, they were vehemently opposed to the aspirations of black people, quite unlike the left. According to Warren, MARsians saw themselves "caught in the middle between those whose wealth gives them access to power and those whose militant organization . . . gains special treatment from the government."

MARsians were not antigovernment per se (as libertarians are); rather, they were hostile to government because they claimed it didn't represent their interests as a group or as individuals. MARsians considered themselves dispossessed opponents of the status quo. Dissecting a constituency that opposes itself to those it considers beneath it in social status, while also opposing those it regards as elites, may seem commonplace thirty plus years after Wallace. But at the time Warren's findings stood many conventional analyses on their head.

One of the most remarkable findings in Warren's study was buried in the middle of his 1976 book *The Radical Center: Middle Americans and the Politics of Alienation*. After dissecting his population samples by income, education, and opinion, he asked: "As a social group are MARs more similar to the white majority of society or to more conventional minorities?" That is, did MARsians tend to think of themselves as members of a racially defined subgroup? The answer was yes, and at levels much higher than other whites, with percentages approximating those of black respondents. Thus MARs were not just angry antigovernment militants; they regarded themselves as an oppressed and exploited white subgroup, with a distinct racial consciousness. And if the Wallace vote in 1968 and Duke's votes in 1990 and 1991 were indicators, there were millions of white people who saw themselves in this mirror.

At the end of the opinion polling, survey questions, number crunching, and peer review by other sociologists, it seemed as if Donald Warren had discovered the "dispossessed majority" at about the same time as Wilmot Robertson. When unburdened by the baggage of anti-Semitism, these MARsians appeared to Francis to be the class basis for a (white) social revolution.

Picking up the analysis at the beginning of the Reagan ascendancy,

Francis had demurred that MARsian "values were anti-business, even anti-capitalist."[39] He even engaged in a bit of Burnham-like class analysis to make his point. The reason the pre–World War Two Old Right could not be resurrected, Francis argued, was that its social base was gone. Main Street businessmen, who had kept precious Anglo-American traditions alive, had been replaced with corporate managers seeking world markets and low-cost brown-skinned labor. At the same time, Francis believed postwar conservatives were also doomed. The business conservative's obsession with "low taxes and small budgets, anticommunism and law and order" had ignored the real concerns of their once and future constituents, such as the maintenance of Anglo-European culture.

Two decades later Francis imagined his MARsians engaged in a process of self-transformation that would distinguish them as the agents of change throughout society. He argued that Buchanan's primary campaign provided "an organized mode of expression" that would foster the development of Middle American "consciousness and power."[40] Francis also believed Middle American Radicals had been changed by the end of the Cold War. Where Middle Americans had once advocated foreign intervention, now their new nationalism was isolationist. The change was visible in Francis himself. In a 1981 essay he had argued for "the military and economic preeminence of the United States" and "international activism." After the Berlin Wall fell, however, he argued the reverse. Nationalism should "emphasize less expansionism and activism abroad and more opposition to a globalist foreign policy that jeopardizes Middle American economic and cultural interests." Middle American Radicals were transformed into Middle American Nationalists.

If Buchanan failed to represent Middle American interests after the primaries, Francis remained certain the heart of his new social force would continue beating on, either inside the Republican Party or outside it. As Republican regulars prepared for their national convention in August 1992, Francis's assessment of Middle American prospects brought him full circle. "Mr. Buchanan was by no means the first to give political expression to this force, and he may not be the one who brings it to revolutionary fulfillment. Perhaps it was David Duke who actually initiated it in recent times, and perhaps it will be H. Ross Perot who brings it to fruition," he wrote in a style more suggestive of Karl Marx than of William Buckley. "Yet regardless of who began it and who will finish it, the Middle American Revolution is not going to go away."[41]

At the same time, Francis deplored what he called paramilitary infantilism and conspiracy mongering on the political right. Sympathy with issues associated with white survivalists and Christian patriots— whether of the Pat Robertson or the Posse Comitatus variety—did not extend to their strategies or even their worldview. Like Lenin excoriating errant trends in the Communist International, Francis's critique of his erstwhile comrades reeked of hard-eyed realpolitik. Paramilitarism as a response to the power of the police was infantile. Conspiracies were the hobgoblins of demon-obsessed minds. Nevertheless, Francis brimmed with the same anger that motivated David Duke's and Pat Buchanan's candidacies.

Like few others inside the beltway, Francis understood the feelings of white victimization. "There was a subtext to what Mr. Duke explicitly and formally said in his speeches and campaign literature," Francis wrote. "The historic core of American civilization is under attack. Quotas, affirmative action, race norming, civil rights legislation, multiculturalism in schools and universities, welfare, busing, and unrestricted immigration from Third World countries are all symbols of that attack and of the racial, cultural, and political dispossession they promise to inflict upon the white post-bourgeois middle classes."[42]

At the Republican Party convention Buchanan gave a speech some liberals credited with handing the 1992 elections to the Democratic Party and Bill Clinton. President Bush obviously believed that Buchanan's three million primary votes represented more than just a protest against a sitting president, because he gave the former presidential speechwriter a prime-time speaking slot, right before the Gipper himself. Buchanan's claim that a culture war *between* Americans had replaced the Cold War with the Soviet Union reverberated across millions of television screens like a hand grenade tossed into a crowded theater. "My friends," Buchanan said, "this election is about much more than who gets what. It is about who we are. It is about what we believe. It is about what we stand for as Americans. There is a religious war going on in our country for the soul of America. It is a cultural war as critical to the kind of nation we will one day be as was the Cold War itself."[43]

Compared with his culture war commencement address at Falwell's Liberty University the previous June, Buchanan's convention speech on August 17, which had been vetted beforehand by Bush aides, was actually fairly mild.[44] He called for the party's dissident right wing to come "home" and vote for President Bush. He didn't mention any opposition to the president on matters of trade, tariffs, taxes, or immigration, although issues of economic nationalism had been his most distinctive campaign calling card in the primaries. On issues dear to the Christian right—abortion, gay rights, and state aid for religious schools—Buchanan rallied the convention and excoriated the Clinton-Gore ticket. In so doing, he highlighted the grip on much of the party's grass roots held by the antiabortion movement and the Reverend Pat Robertson's Christian

Coalition. According to a *USA Today* survey, 47 percent of the delegates to the Republican convention considered themselves born-again Christians.[45] In their book on the 1992 election, *Mad as Hell*, Jack Germond and Jules Witcover concluded that something new in national party politics had emerged: "the delegates of the religious right were a different breed of activists who believed those who disagreed with them were not just wrong but evil."[46]

Pat Buchanan presented himself to the convention as a defender of the faith. But at heart he understood that the battle was about power. Here Sam Francis's footprint showed itself repeatedly in Pat Buchanan's walk and talk. In a later speech re-rehearsing what he called the "savagery of the reaction" to his convention talk, Buchanan invoked his friend by name. What is the cultural war about? he asked. "As columnist Sam Francis writes, it is about power; it is about who determines the norms by which we live, and by which we define and govern ourselves.

". . . Who decides what is right and wrong, moral and immoral, beautiful and ugly, healthy and sick? Whose beliefs shall form the basis of law?"

There it was, completely undisguised. The question at issue for Buchanan was not *what* the common beliefs of the Republic should be, but *whose* beliefs. Not which ideas should hold hegemony, but which people should rule. Whose nation is it anyway? Buchanan and Francis often asked. Their answer was always the same: the United States was and should be a white nation, a Christian nation. If others happened to be citizens, they should submit to the will of the real Americans.

By the third week of August 1992, all the drama had been drained from the Republican Party convention. Pat Buchanan's culture warriors went home. And President George Bush and Governor Bill Clinton prepared for their respective post–Labor Day campaign sprints. Out of the range of television cameras and most print reporters, however, a political volcano boiled with paramilitary infantilism and conspiracy mongering on the remote edge of Ruby Ridge, Idaho. Before we watch that part of the story explode into gunfire, however, it is necessary to retrace the first months of 1992 and the Populist Party candidate's campaign travails.

The Populist Party Goes with Bo Gritz

February 8, 1992. The presidential campaign played like a late-night police television soap opera. Bill Clinton sagged down in the pack, stung by the first charges of impropriety. President George Bush paced in the wings, unsure about how to tell voters how much he really cared. Ross Perot took potshots at all the candidates, like a sniper on the edge of town. Pat Buchanan danced in close enough to land a few heavy blows on the otherwise distant president. David Duke tangled with state party bureaucrats, trying unsuccessfully to unravel access to their primary ballots. And at the Holiday Inn in Clemmons, North Carolina, a small group of young Klansmen patrolled the parking lot while about eighty people from a dozen states attended a meeting ostensibly under the rubric of the Populist Party. The party's state chairman, A. J. Barker, presided like a precinct house captain directing a crew of squabbling detectives. Ed Fields announced his support for Pat Buchanan's anti-immigrant policies. Otherwise the room was divided over whom to support in the race for president.[1]

Only Kirk Lyons, recently moved from Texas to North Carolina, seemed to have a grasp of the fundamental tasks at hand. "Don't worry about field marshalling and building long lines of tactics. You've got to get to the grass roots," he told the assembly. Later he asked, "Well, folks, how are we going to take power? You've got to get somebody out there. This is your moment of opportunity. Get into the Duke campaign. Get into the Buchanan campaign. Get into the Gritz campaign."[2]

The "Gritz campaign" Lyons mentioned was that of retired Lieutenant Colonel James "Bo" Gritz, the same person who four years before had accepted and then declined a spot as David Duke's running mate for the Populist Party. Now he was its presidential candidate. A charismatic figure with a natural knack for telling his audience what it wanted to hear, Gritz could have been a successful politician in any mainstream party. But his penchant for things paramilitary made him a better stump speaker than a legislator. Gritz remained an enigmatic figure, full of personal and political contradictions. In a movement dominated by purists and subculturalists on one side and mass-market opportunists on the other, Bo Gritz was none of the above. He was a military man and a brother to all those Americans under arms. Although graying and increasingly thickset and paunchy, he still carried himself like a drill sergeant. And his path to the Populist Party passed from trusted Pentagon insider to conspiracy-mongering outsider.[3]

Born James Gordon Gritz in 1939, he enlisted in the army in 1957, served faithfully for twenty-two years in hot spots from Southeast Asia to Central America, and retired as a lieutenant colonel with sixty-two medals and citations, including ten Bronze Stars and two Purple Hearts. The military was his home. While in the service he graduated from college and then earned a master's degree from American University in Washington, D.C. He forever considered himself a Special Forces commander and referred to "SF" as his "mistress." During the Vietnam War, Gritz led a force of South Vietnamese in off-the-grid special operations, including recovery in Cambodia of a spy plane's electronic record (black) box. He claimed to have personally killed "400 Communists." Gritz's military service record was sufficiently glorious to merit five laudatory pages in General William Westmoreland's own memoirs of Vietnam. Gritz left the military as an underwater demolitions expert, a sixth-degree black belt in karate, a skilled aviator, and with a commander's love for his fellow soldiers.[4] The experience defined him for life thereafter.

After formally retiring from a Pentagon desk job, Gritz led several (officially) unauthorized forays into Southeast Asia, searching for American POWs still held by the Vietnamese. Among Gritz's early backers was H. Ross Perot, who had famously arranged the rescue of his own employees from Ayatollah Khomeini's new regime in Iran. Arrested inside Laos in 1983 with a small group of others, Gritz became an icon in the minimovement to recover POWs and MIAs. (He often asserted that he, Bo Gritz, was the real-life inspiration for Sylvester Stallone's movie hero John Rambo. But Rambo's artistic creator denied any connection to Gritz.) Over the next few years this certifiable war hero turned into a Cassandra of disappointment, conspiracy, and imminent doom. From his home in Sandy Valley, Nevada, Gritz traveled widely, sometimes as pilot of his own plane, speaking to meetings of true patriots and conspiracy buffs. Picked off the POW-MIA circuit by Willis Carto, Gritz had been a popular speaker at Liberty Lobby's convention in 1987.[5]

While digging into the far right's bunkers, Gritz also flitted around the edges of the conspiracy-sotted sections of the left, joining with a few other disgruntled military and intelligence personalities working with the Christic Institute. A small outfit headquartered in D.C., Christic was then raising fistfuls of money from liberals to pursue a fatally flawed lawsuit aimed at a so-called Secret Team operating deep in the bowels of government. For his part, Gritz rolled up U.S. covert operations, intelligence agency subterfuge, and drug smuggling into one big plot to establish a "one-world government." He knew about it, he said, because he had been there and seen it with his own eyes. And his war record and chestful of medals bestowed him with credibility as well as honor. When Gritz self-published his six-hundred-page memoir cum exposé, *Called to Serve*, he subtitled it *Profiles in Conspiracy from John F. Kennedy to George Bush*.[6]

Gritz sold his memoir at every available stop and inscribed it to one and all: "Forever your Brother." He also acted as if he meant it. Gritz's memoir was devoid of the biological determinism that often permeated David Duke's talks. And the Vietnam vet countered charges that he was a racist by pointing at pictures of his two obviously Amer-Asian children, often alongside his Anglo wife, Claudia, in the book. At the same time, *Called to Serve* repeated the usual anti-Semitic canard about the Federal Reserve's being controlled by "Eight Jewish families." Gritz included on his list of American Jewish banking families the venerable (American Baptist) Rockefellers, presumably because all the other anti-Semites did the same.[7]

By the time Populist leaders selected Gritz as their presidential candidate, he was already a known personality at Christian patriot meets and Identity retreats. He was a favorite of Pete Peters's, and the Colorado preacher expedited publication of the memoir with a much-needed check. Gritz thanked Peters at a summer Bible camp in 1991. "I am telling you that He [God] has given us all that we need," Gritz told a crowd of five hundred. "He's given us the likes of Pete Peters. He's given us the likes of the Christian Identity movement." Although Gritz had not yet fully embraced the Identity theology, he had little problem adopting its rhetoric about Jews. At that same Bible camp he told an assembly: "The enemy you face today is a satanic overthrow of the United States of America, a nation under God, into USA Incorporated, with King George [Bush] as chairman of the board. And a Zionist group that would rule over us as long as Satan might be upon this earth. That is your enemy."[8]

Despite these unambiguous, undeluded assertions of loyalty to white supremacist institutions and ideas, Gritz continued to walk and talk as if he did not comprehend the racist world around him. He claimed a genuine support for Pete Peters on the one hand, while complaining about David Duke on the other. In a letter to Willis Carto, written in the middle of the factional dispute between Carto and Wassall over control of the Populist Party, Gritz complained that *The Spotlight* had ignored his looming presidential campaign, while still covering David Duke in a positive fashion.

> You have yet to do a single article favorable to my campaign. David Duke is a loser. He has done more harm to the Populist Party and third party movement than Hitler would have. Why do you continue to ride a dead horse? Why support a young man who has never worn the uniform of the United States, but chosen to sport a nazi emblem that brave Americans (including my Dad) fighting [sic] against? Either you are an American in this fight against Bush's new world order, or you are part of the problem. Decide which it is.[9]

Gritz's campaign for president more often resembled a circus act on a circuit for paramilitary advocates than a genuine bid for the attention of ordinary white people. In fact, he seemed oblivious of the tension within the movement between mainstreamers and vanguardists, acting at times like both and neither.

During these earliest years of the 1990s, several factors had combined to shift the movement's center of gravity. After the Fort Smith sedition verdicts in 1988, Richard Butler's role inside the movement had declined. And Robert Miles's withdrawal and subsequent death had left Aryan Nations bereft of its best strategist and long-term thinker. A law enforcement crackdown in Tulsa nabbed a band of skinheads, who were convicted on federal civil rights charges. Three Aryans were convicted for conspiring to blow up a gay nightclub in Seattle. Another was convicted of killing a black sailor in Jacksonville, Florida. Tom Metzger was sued in a Portland, Oregon, civil court by the Southern Poverty Law Center and judged to have incited his followers to kill an Ethiopian immigrant. The day before the trial started, three thousand local residents marched to protest bigoted violence; it was the largest outpouring of such public sentiment since the civil rights march in Forsyth County in 1987. Metzger's trial and conviction, described in Elinor Langer's book *A Hundred Little Hitlers,* only added weight to the shift toward the mainstreaming tendency.[10]

David Duke's four-campaign transformation—from a marginal run as a Populist to Louisiana's best-known Republican—added weight to the notion that Middle American money and votes waited for white supremacists willing to work for them. Pat Buchanan's conversion from a White House speechwriter into a white nationalist rabble-rouser demonstrated the promise of the growing split in conservative ranks. And Buchanan's run through the Republican primaries, along with the insurgency represented by Ross Perot, revealed a great unhappiness with the two-party alternatives. Among this evidence of a change was the temporary growth of Thom Robb's Knights of the Ku Klux Klan into the largest national Klan faction, precisely because it now eschewed association with revolutionary violence. Robb had removed the "33/5" signature from his organizational propaganda after it had been attacked for years as a ubiquitous symbol advertising adherence to an "underground" Klan strategy. He also published a disclaimer in the *White Patriot* tabloid: the Knights were "not engaged in: 1) Seeking to overthrow the UNITED STATES [caps in original] government, 2) Harassing Negroes or other 'Minorities,' 3) Paramilitary camps, or 4) Paramilitary training."[11] He presented his Klan as a reasonable proponent of "white Christian revival" instead.

Robb also promoted David Duke imitators, particularly those who presented themselves well on afternoon television talk shows, which were then pumping their ratings with appearances by racists and anti-Semites of various persuasions. In one instance in Colorado, Robb managed to convince a seasoned skinhead leader to put a dress shirt on over his swastika tattoo. The erstwhile skinhead talked rationally about running for office, whereas his immediate past practice had been to growl racist epithets and bash heads in mosh pits.[12] The television appearances brought in a string of new recruits and money, which Robb turned to good effect by underwriting organizing drives in such new territories as Wisconsin and Iowa. He even claimed that the Knights were "beginning to meet with success in our effort of putting *sleepers* [italics in original] within the Republican and Democratic Party." These were supposedly secret Klansmen who were also "prestigious" members of a community, such as businessmen or doctors, who would quietly join a party and work their way up to "positions of power and influence."[13] The "sleeper strategy" sounded good in spy novels, but it was an unproven claim in Robb's case.[14]

The one place where one of Robb's top lieutenants did make a difference was in the Washington State Populist Party. There Kim Badynski and his wife, Debbi, transplants from Illinois to the Northwest Aryan Republic in 1987, openly organized meetings, made telephone calls, and otherwise did the day-to-day work of trying to build a viable third party apparatus. The Badynskis were not the only bed sheet and brown-shirt types leading the Washington State Populist Party. The state chair kept the Bo Gritz campaign moving with one hand, while distributing

Holocaust denial material and attending Aryan Nations camps with the other.[15]

Into this mélange of activity, Gritz tried to root his presidential campaign. He established his own America First Coalition, headquartered in Florida, to try to bridge some of the gap between Wassall's Populist Party apparatus and other factions. It worked for a while. A. J. Barker, for example, was not then associated with Wassall but was named as Gritz's campaign chair in North Carolina. Similarly, state chairs in Oregon, Maryland, and a half dozen other states were not Populists.[16] And to further create an illusion of movement unity behind his campaign, Gritz announced that appointments to his future cabinet would draw from a wide range of movement personalities.[17]

Gritz never won *The Spotlight's* endorsement, however, and his vote totals were only marginally better than those won by Populist Party candidates in 1984 and 1988. With ballot status in eighteen states, he received 107,002 votes, at a total cost of $371,648.[18] The Populist Party chief Don Wassall averred that Gritz "did a great job of getting his message out."[19] In fact, most of the credit for the Populist Party's showing in 1992 adhered to Gritz personally, as he did best in states, such as Utah, where Wassall's party had little actual organization.

Gritz also fared better than Howard Phillips of the U.S. Taxpayers Party, another marginal third party candidate. Phillips's résumé included long service at the centers of power. He had attended Harvard College and served as president of its student council. He had worked his way up Republican Party ranks until he became President Nixon's director at the Office of Economic Opportunity in 1973. In 1974 he founded the Conservative Caucus, one of the most important addresses in the creation of the so-called New Right. And he hailed President Reagan's election in 1980 as a victory for conservatives. As the Reagan administration and then the first Bush administration failed to fulfill Phillips's political hopes, however, he turned farther to the right.[20]

The Taxpayers Party campaign rested heavily on its no-compromise opposition to all abortion rights, although the platform embraced the entire panoply of Christian nationalist issues. It could have attracted votes from Christian Coalition activists unhappy with the Reverend Pat Robertson's support for President Bush, and it should have garnered some noticeable percentage of the 3 million voters who voted for Buchanan in the primaries. But it didn't. Phillips received 43,398 votes—less than half that received by Gritz—and at a greater cost.[21]

All the evidence pointed to the Republican Party as a lasting, if unhappy and dysfunctional, home for the panoply of forces that groups such as the Taxpayers Party and Populist Party were trying to capture.[22]

One feature of Gritz's presidential campaign endured, however, long after the vote counting was completed: an appeal for patriotism wrapped in a blanket of distrust for such established institutions as government and the media and guarded by a zealous paramilitary (white) nationalism.

During his campaign stops Gritz typically unfurled a small black POW-MIA flag on the podium. He told war stories about searching for MIAs and urged the establishment of militias. Gun control was hitting the target on your first shot, he would say in repetition of a standard gun lobby one-liner. And after asking for members of the "unorganized militia" to raise their hands, he would say: "U.S. Code 10 and U.S. Code 32 designates who is in the unorganized militia . . . Now how many of you are between 18 and 64 here. Oh a lot more people just joined the unorganized militia. Good."[23] It was nonsense wrapped up in the Constitution.

The gun talk and militia mongering could have just been the usual movement braggadocio. Telling audiences that they were members of the militia did not turn them into camouflage artists carrying heavy assault weapons. That is, until the Randy Weaver incident on Ruby Ridge.

The FBI Aims for Randy Weaver on Ruby Ridge

August 21, 1992. There are moments when modest men and women—of goodwill and ill—change the course of events simply by obeying their most intensely held beliefs. So it was with Randall Claude Weaver, a forty-three-year-old unemployed outsider living high on a ridge in northern Idaho, who started a rockslide of events with an act of defiance based on an unambiguous fear. His name became an icon for the convergence of guns and religion on Pat Buchanan's cultural battlefields. Congressional hearings and a television movie were to make this private man a public figure.[1]

Born January 3, 1948, into a stable, devoutly Presbyterian, small-town Iowa family, Randy Weaver graduated from high school in 1966, joined the army and Special Forces (but never saw Vietnam), married his wife, Vicki, in 1971, and returned home to work and raise a family. During the same period that James Ellison was attracting spiritually dissolute baby boomers to the Covenant, the Sword and the Arm of the Lord compound on the Missouri-Arkansas border, the more resolute Randy and Vicki Weaver found the same Christian Identity theology in their Fort Dodge hometown. Iowa, just starting to slide into the farm crisis of the early 1980s, was then being honeycombed by a host of Identity pamphleteers and Christian patriot salesmen. At the John Deere plant in Waterloo, where Randy worked, a representative of Aryan Nations declaimed loudly about the virtue of Butler's Idaho enterprise and the vice of the Zionist Occupied Government (ZOG). Although there is no available evidence that this man directly influenced Randy Weaver, it is unlikely that the two did not know of each other. Whatever the case, after a period of Bible study and preparation, Randy and Vicki Weaver decided to move to the mountains and there await the final battle of Armageddon and the ultimate triumph of white Christian believers.[2]

In 1983, just as Bob Mathews was gathering his Order troops to create a white bastion in the Northwest, the Weaver family settled in Boundary County, in the narrow neck of northern Idaho, just sixty miles north of Butler's campground, forty miles from the Canadian border, twenty miles from Washington State, and thirty miles from Montana. On a remote mountainous perch known as Ruby Ridge, Randy and Vicki constructed a roughshod cabin and outhouse, chopped firewood, raised chickens, and grew vegetables. Infant Elishiba was cradled like any other baby. Daughter Sara and son Sam played like other children, except that they also carried loaded weapons like sentries. Always short of cash, Randy worked periodically for local employers. The family both squabbled with neighbors and befriended a circle of settlers who believed as they did. As in many families in which the woman keeps the religious flame alive, it was Vicki more than Randy who imbued the family's life with the Identity message. But Randy did his part for white supremacy. In 1986 he drove down to Aryan Nations and attended its annual conference; he did so again in 1989, this time with the whole family. He never signed an Aryan Nations membership card on the dotted line, but he often wore the organization's belt buckle and sported a T-shirt emblazoned with "Just Say No to ZOG." The exact nature of his beliefs later became subject to public dispute. But any reasonable account of the facts would have to conclude he considered himself a member of a theologically based movement defined by its belief in the Satanic nature of Jews and the secondary status of people of color—that is, white supremacy. He was neither a leader nor even a mid-rank activist, yet he would become an unlikely movement-wide symbol of government evil, an oversize role for an unassuming third-rank believer.[3]

That story began with a fishing expedition into the Aryan Nations by Bureau of Alcohol, Tobacco, and Firearms (ATF) agents. The agents concocted a plan to catch Weaver breaking the law, threaten him with arrest and jail, then turn him into an informant, using him to gather evidence on those higher up the organizational ladder. It didn't work. They did trap him selling illegally sawed-off shotguns in October 1989, a misdemeanor. He was indicted the following month. But he would not agree to become an informant. It wasn't his unwillingness to snitch on others that changed the course of events, however, but his refusal to turn himself over to authorities. Rather than have Randy face arrest, the Weaver family decided to stay up on their mountain ridge. Vicki wrote a letter to Aryan Nations explaining their situation: "We cannot make deals with the enemy. This is war against white sons of Issac [sic]. We have decided to stay on this mountain. You could not drag our children away from us with chains."[4] It was their belief that Satan personally walked the earth in the guise of (Jew-controlled) federal agents who turned Randy Weaver's mountainside misdemeanor into a spark in the tinderbox of history.

Finally, on January 17, 1991, ATF agents managed to arrest Randy Weaver on the outstanding firearms charges. According to *Every Knee Shall Bow*, a book on the Weavers by the reporter Jess Walter, the local authorities had mishandled the original notification of trial. In any case, the Aryan Nations security chief vouched for Randy Weaver's good character in a bond hearing, and he was released. Once again it was wife Vicki who wrote a letter explaining the family's beliefs to the authorities: "Whether we live or die, we will not bow to your evil commandments." Randy Weaver subsequently failed to show for trial, and a fugitive warrant was issued. Meanwhile, the family members fortified themselves at their ridgetop cabin and refused to come down. To complicate matters, friendly neighbors and Aryan comrades trekked up the mountainside's dirt trail and kept them in fresh supplies.[5]

Federal marshals charged with arresting Weaver faced several difficulties. The marshals actually knew very little about Randy Weaver or his family, even after targeting him for an arrest on gun charges. The ridgetop was inaccessible to casual entrance, and the entire family was known to be armed. In addition, a twenty-four-year-old friend who had been living with the family, Kevin Harris, was believed to be similarly armed and willing to use his weapons, adding to the family's potential firepower. Marshals began establishing posts in the woods that summer, surrounding the Weaver home, listening, watching, and presumably waiting for an opportune moment to nab the fugitive. The presence of the marshals, who were armed as if for war, was subsequently discovered by the Weavers, who were themselves heavily armed whenever they left their cabin.

On August 21, 1991, the unavoidable happened. A brief firefight erupted out on the ridge after a federal marshal shot the family dog, which had barked at the marshals in the trees. Federal Marshal William Degan was killed. Samuel Weaver, fourteen, was shot in the back and died. Overnight the reconnaissance and capture mission turned into a siege. Hundreds of law enforcement personnel ferried into the region and established a military-style barricade and command post. Road-building equipment moved up the mountain to construct a path to the cabin. Armed personnel carriers, helicopters, and a robot were deployed. The next day gunfire again erupted, this time near the house. Kevin Harris was shot in the arm and chest. Randy Weaver was wounded. An FBI sharpshooter, Lon Horiuchi, shot Vicki Weaver through the head while she stood in the doorway, holding her ten-month-old baby, Elishiba.[6]

Violent conflicts between movement activists and law enforcement were not new. After killing two federal marshals in North Dakota, Gordon Kahl was shot and his Arkansas hideout burned down by the FBI. After a fifteen-month spree of robberies and murders, Order founder Robert Mathews was killed when he refused to surrender, and FBI agents burned down his safe house. And Arthur Kirk, a hopeless Nebraska farmer, was shot and killed by an area SWAT team after a short exchange of gunfire. A similar pattern had marked other violent standoffs. When law enforcement cornered members of a leftist California group calling itself the Symbionese Liberation Army in 1974, a short gunfight ended after the safe house burned to the ground, killing several men and women in the fire. And in 1985 six people were burned to death and an entire city block in Philadelphia destroyed when local police tried to dislodge a radical black group known as MOVE.[7] As the Weaver siege began in earnest, it appeared that there could be only one horrible end to the story. Something unprecedented developed at the foot of the mountain, however, changing once again the course of events.

A twenty-four-hour vigil of movement activists and neighbors began, quickly growing to a permanent presence of almost two hundred men, women, and children standing nose to nose with the FBI at the barricades. Aryan Nations members gathered from Canada, Montana, and, of course, Idaho. Skinheads traveled from Las Vegas, Utah, and Oregon. Identity believers from throughout the Northwest joined with unbelievers to bear witness against federal agents. A camplike cook kitchen fed the protesters, who formed bonds across ideological lines. They cried with grief at the news of the deaths and screamed with rage at each newly arrived federal agent. They held aloft a bevy of homemade signs: DEATH TO ZOG, of course. F.B.I. BURN IN HELL. But also more temperate pleas: KIDS KILLED TOO. TELL THE TRUTH. STOP. COME WALK WITH US. THE WEAVERS TODAY! OUR FAMILIES TOMORROW. And an even more remarkable sign that read REMEMBER KENT STATE. RED SQUARE. TIANANMEN SQ. MY LAI. RUBY RIDGE.[8]

As the vigil grew in size and self-consciousness, participants invoked the names of Gordon Kahl and Bob Mathews. Some understood that their presence at the foot of what they now called Weaver Mountain was acting as a brake on further bloodshed. Others wanted to join the battle, and five skinheads were arrested in a vehicle stuffed with weapons when they attempted to sneak up a back road to the cabin.[9] Violent or nonviolent, enraged or prayerful, the protest represented a break with the movement's past practices. It brought together mainstreamers and vanguardists alongside nonmovement people who were concerned about the immediate situation, but not sympathetic to the movement's final goals. All were engaged in an action with direct consequences.

At the same time, a similarly remarkable sequence of events ensued off-site. Before the siege ended, *The Spotlight* published the first in what became a long line of articles on the Weaver incident. Under the headline "Confrontation in Idaho Harbinger for America," Liberty Lobby's tabloid declared: "George Bush and the U.S. military may not be able to dislodge Saddam Hussein from power in Baghdad, but it looks like one man and his family in Idaho are goners." Similarly, Tom Metzger began broadcasting messages in the midst of the siege. He claimed Weaver was "a subscriber associate" of White Aryan Resistance, meaning Weaver probably subscribed to the *WAR* tabloid. Metzger encouraged "white separatists and anti-Iron Heel citizens . . . to move into the area to protest a planned murder" but did not get directly involved otherwise.[10] These first indirect reports occurred about the same time that Bo Gritz decided to make a direct intervention.

Five days into the siege, Gritz arrived with a sidekick, Jack McLamb. Before Bo appeared on the scene, however, Pete Peters had contacted him. Peters was at that moment convening his annual summer Bible camp in Colorado. After a year of planning, the camp started on August 22, the second day of the siege. Everyone already knew that Weaver's son Sam and the federal marshal were dead, although they did not yet know that Vicki Weaver was also dead. Peters convened a late-night three-hour session of "Elders" to decide what to do. They issued a press release signed by someone not known by the media as an anti-Semite. That small decision indicated that Peters intended to speak out beyond the confines of the white supremacist movement. The Elders also asked campers to phone the Bush administration's U.S. attorney general's office in protest.[11]

Knowing that Bo Gritz was then en route to Idaho, Peters also wrote a letter to Randy Weaver and sent it to Gritz, asking that it be delivered to the family. "Dear Randy," it began, "Please know that the murder of your son has not gone unnoticed. Five hundred Christian Israelites from 40 states gathered at my 1992 camp in Colorado are right now praying for you and the Gideon situation you face."[12] There is no evidence that Gritz delivered the letter or that it had any impact on the final outcome. (As we shall see, one late-night camp decision by Peters's crew did have broad repercussions later, after he had convened a meeting of "Christian men" specifically to discuss the Weaver episode.)

Meanwhile, Gritz arrived at Weaver Mountain and began a complex dance that ultimately ended with Randy Weaver's safe surrender to federal authorities. At first, Gritz read with great fanfare a multipage "Citizen's Warrant for Citizen's Arrest," at the behest of the protesters, then placed it under a rock at the FBI's barricades. The next day Gritz handwrote a personal note to the special agent in charge of the siege: "We aren't trying to make your task more difficult. We want to help. We believe that we can convince Randy to come out . . ."[13] The FBI, stuck at an impasse, agreed to let Gritz try to negotiate directly with Weaver. On the second day of negotiations, Gritz talked the severely wounded Kevin Harris into surrendering. The next day, August 31, Randy and his daughters came down the mountain. The immediate crisis ended quietly.[14]

Despite Gritz's success at diffusing the situation, an anticlimactic moment at the bottom of the hill proved more revealing about his character. While explaining the last stages of his negotiations to a group of protesters (and the press), Gritz stopped, raised his right arm in the typical Nazi salute, and said: "By the way, [Weaver] told me to tell you guys to give you a salute. He said you know what that is." Certainly, a skinhead in the back of the crowd understood, even if Gritz then pretended that he didn't. The skinhead returned the Sieg Heil white power salute and then turned his thumb up. Gritz continued explaining the surrender. When a local television station, KXLY-TV, aired tape of the incident, it appeared as if Gritz, who had started the year chastising David Duke for his Hitlerian sympathies, was about to end the year subject to the same criticism. That day he told the press that he gave the Nazi salute at Weaver's request. But two nights later he told the audience of Chuck Harder's right-wing *For the People* nationwide radio broadcast that the Nazi salute was not a salute at all; he was merely waving to supporters. When questioned about the incident again, he continued to deny what was manifestly evident to the naked eye.[15]

The whole affair was pure Gritz. In his speeches, "intelligence briefings," burning of United Nations symbols, and other histrionics, Gritz continually flirted with the imagery, code words, and stock phrases of the movement, all the while acting as if he weren't sending signals to his audience. At that point in his life, Gritz did not want to be known as anything other than a true American patriot, a fighter against evil conspiracies, and a brave candidate for president. And the successful negotiation of Weaver's surrender certainly gave his Populist Party candidacy a moment of fame.

Gritz went back to electioneering, and he drew larger crowds during the presidential campaign's last months than during the first months. But the venues hadn't changed. He still rode the Christian patriot and survivalist circuit, primarily in the West. He told five hundred people in Nampa, Idaho, "We'll either take it with ballots in 1992, or we may be required to defend our rights with bullets in 1996."[16] In Spokane he drew eight hundred one night and five hundred two nights later. He repeated the performance in Seattle, stumping a bit (just a bit) for president and selling his book. In Montana he drew enthusiastic crowds, which watched him shred a United Nations flag and declare himself a steadfast defender of American sovereignty. To the outside world he may have still been a crank third party candidate, but to these crowds his negotiation skills had made him a celebrity.[17] Nevertheless, for Bo Gritz the events on Ruby Ridge became just one more talking point. For other activists, by contrast, the battle over Randy Weaver was just beginning.

After the Shoot-out, the Militia

September 19, 1992. Another preparedness expo, another town; this time Spokane, Washington, an hour's drive from the Aryan Nations camp, two hours from Ruby Ridge. Crowds of herbalists and food hoarders mixed with defenders of the Second Amendment and opponents of the New World Order. Vendors stood at their exhibit tables, hawking their wares like salesmen with the latest in home show gadgets. From the main stage, Bo Gritz and a few celebrity marketeers pitched their latest theories of dismay and disarray. Despite these and other distractions, the Weaver debacle was most on everyone's mind. Off to the side, Louis Beam sat in a natty brown suit and casually discussed plans to buy land in the Northwest. Four years after the Fort Smith seditious conspiracy trial, he still hunted out conflagration like a coon dog searching for prey. (And there was plenty of conflict to come.)

In the evening Beam met with a dozen men and women from the area and began making plans. First on his list was the relatively mundane task of distributing a flyer that looked like a wanted poster, much like the bulletin the FBI had issued in 1987, when Beam was hiding out in Mexico. Across the top in bold type it read, "Wanted by Citizen Committee for Justice" a "U.S. Marshal, FBI or ATF Agent." Two rows of fingerprints were pasted underneath the headline, a faceless photo to the left, and a description on the right. "The U.S. Marshall, FBI or ATF agent is usually accompanied by others whose specialty is persecution, the suppression of religious beliefs and/or the assassination of Christian Patriots and their family members." Beam told the group he had printed an initial ten thousand flyers and wanted to distribute one million ultimately. If anyone needed more copies, Beam said, he had an 800 number to call. Ask for "Rudolf Hess"[1] (as in, the aide to Hitler who had flown to Britain in 1941 and was imprisoned ever after). Distributing the flyer was only a small first step in a long propaganda campaign. In fact, at Beam's side that night was Chris Temple, then one of the most adept and analytical organizers in the movement. Over the next few years Temple's strategic acumen blended with Beam's thirst for militia-style madness and shaped the post-shoot-out Weaver campaign.

Unlike Beam, Temple had not served in Vietnam, never been a Klansman, and shied away from violent revolutionary rhetoric. Born in 1961 and raised in upstate New York, Temple claimed he had worked for Jerry Falwell's Moral Majority before learning in 1986 "who my Heavenly Father was and who I am and who our race is."[2] He became a dedicated Identity adherent and an open admirer of Hitler's National Socialist Germany.[3] While living in Cortland, New York, during this period, he wrote more than three thousand dollars in bad checks, as a protest, he said, against the banking system, and he was subsequently convicted of a felony. Despite this incident, Temple never lost the taste for working within larger constituencies. He moved to Montana and with his wife, Sue, established a large family and became a small-town Main Street businessman.[4] He also wrote regularly for a monthly tabloid, *The Jubilee*, which promoted Christian Identity, and coordinated the Gritz presidential campaign in western Montana. He was a busy man who had stood with the others protesting the FBI at the foot of Weaver Mountain.

Three days after the Spokane expo, Temple and Beam helped launch the post-Weaver campaign in Naples, Idaho, the village nearest Ruby Ridge. Forty people met in a local resort lodge, established committees, and picked officers and a name, United Citizens for Justice. They decided their initial goal was to ensure that a local grand jury convene and indict federal agents for murder. This United Citizens meeting was quite unlike the congress held by Aryan Nations at its compound in the weeks after Gordon Kahl's death in 1983. Plans there to elevate Kahl to martyrdom had never reached beyond readers of *The Spotlight* and a handful of activists. And it was Bob Mathews and his Order bandits who had followed Kahl, virtually assuring that he remained known more as a perpetrator than as a victim.

At Naples, by contrast, longtime movement activists joined with unaffiliated local residents angry at the injustice done the Weaver family. Here Temple pulled the train of events into the mainstream, not into the underground. When Louis Beam arose in this assembly, he used his best rhetorical skills to argue for a class-action lawsuit against the federal government, a course of action that his friend Kirk Lyons was considering. "Randy Weaver and his family had a grip on the rope of liberty," Beam intoned. "As their bloody hands slipped off, we must be ready to take it up."[5]

Two weeks later, October 6, Beam was the featured speaker at another United Citizens for Justice meeting, this one in Sandpoint, Idaho, twenty-two miles down the highway from Naples. More than two hundred attended. Beam told the crowd he was living "in a small East Texas community raising black-eyed peas and blond-haired children until I heard about the events in North Idaho," a down-home aw-shucks line he repeated on multiple occasions. Chris Temple also spoke, explaining that "we" had opposed the Soviet Union for the past fifty years but "should have been worrying about people who have been minding the store here."[6] Thus the post-Weaver campaign started in the spot where the hearts of local people ached the most. But Chris Temple and Louis Beam, among others, were hard-eyed strategists, intent on creating a new nationwide movement, beyond the border of Weaver's home state. The next step was Colorado.

Estes Park Meeting

To fulfill the late-night promise made at his summer Bible camp, Pete Peters convened a meeting of 160 "Christian men" on October 22 in Estes Park, a quiet resort town at the entrance to Rocky Mountain National Park. For two and a half days they met in committee, deliberated in plenary sessions, and engaged in the kind of one-on-one conversations known, in the parlance of business professionals, as networking. They made decisions in the name of Jesus Christ and Yahweh, sang "Onward, Christian Soldiers," and otherwise conducted themselves in a manner of quiet resolve appropriate for their surroundings, a YMCA facility abutting the park. No guns were waved, and even the most heated rhetoric seemed to have the blood drained out of it. (A brief second of excitement bubbled when a police surveillance team was discovered taking pictures.) Otherwise, not much indicated that this meeting would become the foundational moment for a new militia movement in the 1990s.[7]

Peters made no secret of the meeting. He mailed out notification and registration forms to everyone on his Scriptures for America list. He sent a pro forma invite to William Barr, President Bush's attorney general, who didn't bother to respond. The roster of those who either declined the invitation or did not answer it at all is as instructive as the list of those who did attend. James Dobson of Focus on the Family did not even answer Peters's invitation, despite their mutual opposition to civil rights for gay men and lesbians. Similarly, the Rutherford Institute, a legal advocacy group, said no. "The Rutherford Institute will not send a representative . . . and will not participate in the Randy Weaver matters.

These matters are not within the guidelines of cases in which the Institute becomes involved." Christian Identity pastors were still officially off the grid for these two mainstays of Christian nationalism.

David Duke did not respond either, despite Peters's entreaties. Having made the transition from Klan wizard to Republican politician, Duke was apparently not quite ready to revert.[8] Bo Gritz's buddy Jack McLamb, after hemming and hawing, decided not to attend, a decision that might have been influenced by Gritz, one of the few not to receive an invitation. Although Peters had tried to use Gritz as a courier to Weaver, both men remained at odds after Gritz refused to endorse Peters's call for the "death penalty for homosexuals."

Willis Carto and William Pierce did not attend this gathering either or send emissaries. Pierce in particular had no taste for any meeting of "Christian men." Once the postmeeting action started, however, they both would participate in the Weaver aftermath, each after his own strategic fashion.

Who was there at this foundational moment? As might be expected, Peters's fellowship of Identity pastors, who usually functioned as a council of elders at other camp gatherings, acted in a similar fashion over this weekend. Most of the male members of Peters's LaPorte congregation also attended. So did a small tribe of Aryans, headed by the aging Richard Butler. (Butler was given the platform to confess publicly that he was a "bigot.") Add to this plaid shirt affair a very few faithful gray-suited souls more typically found lobbying Congress than mixing it up with the mountainside Aryans. The total number of "Christian men": 160.

Louis Beam starred at the podium. He used the occasion to retell the story of his own persecution at federal hands, his arrest in Mexico prior to the Fort Smith trial, and the bravery of wife Sheila during the shoot-out with the federales. (The marriage with Sheila broke up five years later with the young wife claiming she wanted nothing to do with her husband's Hitlerite racism.) Beam called for a new unity among militants, but he did not publicly discuss his longtime strategic goal, to create a decentralized and clandestine arm of the movement. Nevertheless, in his semiofficial report of the meeting, alongside the committee decisions and audiotape advertisements, Peters republished Beam's three-page 1983 essay "Leaderless Resistance."

Almost ten years after their first articulation alongside Robert Miles's notes for an underground in the *Inter-Klan Newsletter*, the essay and strategy obviously were being revived, and not just by Beam. A group calling itself the Divine Ways and Means Committee put itself on record as supporting "vigilante action" and other acts it described as "carrying out directives from God." A second group, calling itself the Sacred Warfare

Action Tactics (SWAT) Committee, specifically endorsed leaderless re-sistance: "Whatever resistance is done should be done without an earthly leader. Because we have been INFILTRATED as a nation [em-phasis in original]." Among the examples of resistance the committee cited was an incident in the Book of Judges when "Ehud put a sword in the fat belly of King Eglon."[9] (Biblical violence always seemed more jus-tified than the contemporary kind.)

Kirk Lyons, Beam's attorney from the Fort Smith trial, addressed the meeting with the stature of a veteran movement man for all seasons. Lyons was trying to elbow his way into the Weaver case and told the crowd that he would represent the family in a civil suit against federal agents—despite the fact that Randy Weaver had already signed with an-other criminal defense attorney. "We've got to be part of this, gentle-men," he told the assembly. "We have got to make sure that we as Christian Israelites are represented."[10] Despite his perpetual pleas for fi-nancial support, Lyons also understood the significance of the develop-ing situation. His movement was changing direction, and the Weaver incident was a pivot point. "This is the fight of the decade," he argued. "This is the crucible. This is the turning point."

Chris Temple, Beam's pal from United Citizens for Justice, amplified that point. The movement had arrived at a strategic moment. As horri-ble as the murders of Sam and Vicki Weaver had been, Temple said, the killings provided a great opportunity. "All of us in our groups," Temple told the assembly, ". . . could not have done in the next twenty years what the federal government did for our cause in eleven days in Naples, Idaho . . . what we need to do is to not let this die and go away."

Temple and Lyons both argued the same point: mobilize all available resources around the Weaver case. Accomplishing just this would mark a change. The movement had a tendency to leave its dead and wounded untended and undefended, a sore spot for those who believed *all* the de-fendants at Fort Smith should have been supported.[11] They often com-plained that the left had a better record helping unpopular defendants in the courtroom, as well as remembering those who went to prison. But Lyons and Temple thought the Weaver case could be different. Weaver's son and wife had been killed in a bald case of abuse by federal authori-ties. Randy himself was criminally guilty of only a misdemeanor gun charge. And his up-on-the-ridge version of Christian Identity looked relatively harmless to the naked eye, like a leave-me-alone variant of Armageddon theology. By movement lights, the Weaver case equaled religion and guns, a good combination of organizing issues. To take ad-vantage of this opportunity, Temple argued for a new kind of unity, not just among white supremacists but between white supremacists and

others—particularly their cousins on the Christian right who were neither biological (racial) determinists nor explicitly anti-Semitic.

"We need to remember the Muslim's saying that my enemy's enemy
is my friend. You know, we've got a common goal . . . to restore Christian
government in this land so that our people, the descendants of Abraham, Isaac and Jacob—and any strangers that live among us, until we
take care of that problem—so that everyone can live their lives free of
fear."[12]

Despite the grammatically challenged phrasing, everyone in the room
understood its meaning, *"any strangers that live among us, until we take
care of that problem."* In Identity parlance, "strangers" are nonwhites.[13]
Temple argued for a strategic shift, a two-stage revolution. First, build
unity to establish a "Christian government." In other words, deempha-
size rhetoric and direct action on race, perhaps even build alliances with
some willing black or brown people, during the revolution's first stage.
Attack the federal ZOG. Later "take care" of the problem of the non-
whites. Of all the overwrought verbiage at Estes Park, the most important was this enunciation of a shift in strategy by Chris Temple and Kirk
Lyons.

For Temple's two-stage strategy to actually work, a few patriots, not
known as white supremacists but intent on establishing a Christian government over a Christian nation, had to be available for building an alliance. Thus add Steve Graber and Larry Pratt to the expanding list of
characters at Estes Park. Under most circumstances, Steve Graber
would have been an unlikely attendee for a meeting dominated by such
men as Peters, Beam, and Lyons. But as noted, this was not an ordinary,
everyday meeting. Graber was a devout Mennonite from central Kansas,
an attorney, and a former regional organizer for the aforementioned
Rutherford Institute. Graber made sure everyone else understood that
he was "not here as part of the Rutherford Institute." He understood
that Peters's Christian Identity was not his. "I'm not here to embrace
your theology and I know you're not here to embrace my theology."
Graber also told the assembly that he understood that associating with
the likes of Louis Beam and Richard Butler would not enhance his career as an attorney or a community leader. "I'm associated with the Lord
Jesus Christ, plus or minus nothing," he told the Christian men. Nevertheless, "unprecedented attacks" on God's people required a response.
"We are in a spiritual battle," Graber averred. At another point he hinted
at his own End Times theology. "We are in a time when God is wrapping
things up." Despite his manifest differences with so many of the atten-

dees, Graber had advice for all: be confident, stay in God's way, and make an unemotional presentation of your facts. God's people, assuming the assembly was of God's people, would prevail.

The presence of a person like Graber, who followed a more widely accepted fundamentalist theology, embodied the type of alliance that Chris Temple's strategy required. But the perfect partner was Larry Pratt, who resided at the axis of religion and guns . . . and the militia.

Larry Pratt did not look like a militiaman. He presented himself as something akin to a mild-mannered accountant: glasses, gray suit, and grandfatherly. He exuded faithfulness and loyalty. And although he didn't mention these facts publicly, he had been married to his wife, Priscilla, for three decades, had four children, and was a devout member of Harvesters Presbyterian Church of America. He spoke softly, almost sotto voce, and understated his ideas for emphasis, rather than turn bellicose. Yet as he stood before Pete Peters and the assembly of Christian men, he was already a self-confessed veteran of what he called spiritual warfare. He had served two years in the Virginia legislature as an antiabortion, antitax representative. He had directed a constellation of conservative organizations in the Washington, D.C., area, much like other figures on the Christian right. Unlike most others, however, he had also traveled extensively in Central America and the Philippines, witnessing to the gospel of armed citizen militias. As the executive director of Gun Owners of America, a public-interest lobby headquartered in Springfield, Virginia, with a hundred thousand members nationwide, he arrived at Estes Park with the largest constituency of any of the speakers. For Pratt, detailing the intricacies of antigun legislation and advocating for a militia was all in a day's work, and he did both that weekend.

This was an unusual audience for Pratt, though he shared many of its obsessions. One and all were fervently anti-communist, opposed any form of gun control, and believed the establishment of the United States as a Christian republic was in God's plan. Yet Pratt was neither a Christian Identity adherent nor a biological (racial) determinist. Chris Temple's two-stage strategy may have opened the door to men such as Pratt, but it remained for Pratt to figure out a way to walk in without overtly compromising his own beliefs.

Pratt began his speech by dissecting the Brady Bill, then under consideration in Congress as a way of curbing weapons. He believed the Second Amendment guaranteed unrestricted individual ownership of guns—machine guns, LAW rockets, and assault rifles . . . whatever.

"The Second Amendment is not about duck hunting," he told the crowd. By Pratt's interpretation, the Constitution and the Founding Fathers had intended for the Second Amendment to provide personal protection from individual criminals as well as criminal governments. Although all the relevant Supreme Court decisions had declared the Second Amendment a collective right accruing to state governments, Pratt argued that a contemporary rationale for guns (and more guns) resided in the failure of government. "We need to keep reminding people, because people won't hear it from anybody else, that the police can't protect the individual citizen. The policeman can't provide personal security. I suspect everyone in this room understands that. But a lot of the American people didn't understand that, never had thought about it, until the riots in Los Angeles, literally, [brought it] home to them, by means of their television."[14]

Pratt also advocated lobbying. "When we have a chance to testify," he instructed the assembly, "what we do is to go and confront the legislators directly with the illegality of unconstitutional action."

With just a few exceptions, the Estes Park Christian men were unlikely lobbyists. On the other hand, starting up paramilitaries would be almost as natural as not shaving on the weekend. Pratt provided the rationale. He told them he believed it was perfectly reasonable to walk into the office of a state secretary of state and declare: "My name's Larry Pratt, and I'm the commandant of the Nathan Hale unorganized militia." What would happen next? "That would be that. Then you've got a recognized, but unorganized, militia, one that's not being provided for or commanded by the governor of the state, or the legislature."

Pratt's militia mind had been born in the battle against communism, particularly in Third World countries, as a way of defending dictators and mobilizing armed opposition to revolutionary insurgencies. He had gone to Guatemala three times during the 1980s and once to the Philippines. There, while the Soviet Union still existed and the United States was still fighting the Cold War, Pratt promoted a militia that turned ordinary civilians into death squads. "We find that the value of the Second Amendment," he had written, "guaranteeing the right to keep and bear arms as the way to insure that there be a militia made up of armed people, has been discovered in foreign settings."

In 1990, as the Soviet bloc collapsed, Pratt published a book recapping his experiences and pointing toward militia formation in the post–Cold War world. At that time, the war on drugs had replaced the war against communism as his rationale. "America has been losing the War on Drugs, and it is probably safe to predict that the United States will continue to lose this war until the . . . professional monopoly in civil defense are replaced," he wrote. His answer was a return to "an armed people with functioning militias involved in civil defense (or police work, if you will)," an explicit call for vigilante action in the war on drugs. (It was an argument that would make even Clint Eastwood's Dirty Harry blush.) Pratt had also previously developed a line of reasoning that was more applicable that day in Estes Park: form a militia to oppose the government. "When a government no longer fears the people, atrocities become possible," he had written as if he were one of the insurgents in Guatemala instead of one of the regime's defenders. "Long live the militia! Long live freedom! Long live a government that fears the people!"[15]

Pratt also argued: "We have to take every thought captive to the obedience of Jesus Christ and then all disobedience will be punished . . ." In his theology, "punishment" loomed larger than guns.

Pratt's corporate complex rivaled Willis Carto's in its intricacy. The largest entity, Gun Owners Foundation, is a nonprofit educational corporation, contributions to which are tax deductible. The second company is Gun Owners of America, Inc., a nonprofit corporation. Attached to GOA Inc. is a third group, a federal political action committee, Gun Owners of America Political Victory Fund, which contributes money to sympathetic congressional candidates. Together, GOF, the GOA, and the Victory Fund all operated in tandem as a more militant alternative to the National Rifle Association.

In addition to directing the gun groups, Pratt formed the Committee to Protect the Family Foundation, a Virginia nonprofit corporation he used for various Christian right causes, including a bit of gay bashing for money. In one fund-raising letter, Pratt called for the quarantine of anyone with AIDS: "Our judges coddle criminals instead of caring for the victims of crime. They've chased God out of our schools, defended abortions . . . and now they are trying to infect us and kill us with strange and horrible diseases."

Among its other jaunts along the edges of respectability, Pratt's Family Foundation raised funds for an antiabortion group, Operation Rescue, run by Randall Terry, at a time when Terry's group was under a court order restricting its activities. Operation Rescue's modus was staging large-scale sit-in–style blockades of women's health clinics. Beginning in Atlanta during the Democratic Party's 1988 convention, Terry called for hundreds of activists from around the country to descend on a city, mobilized local sympathizers, and then blockaded the clinics and clogged the city's jails with arrests. When Terry came to New York City in 1989, the National Organization for Women (NOW) got a court injunction ordering Operation Rescue not to interfere with the clinics. Terry flouted the court order, attempted a blockade, and was arrested. Operation Rescue was fined fifty thousand dollars. After Terry refused to pay the fine, the U.S. attorney's office seized two Operation Rescue bank accounts, and the group was essentially closed down.

At that point Larry Pratt entered, wearing his hat as president of the Committee to Protect the Family Foundation. During the first six months of 1990, Pratt sent potential contributors three letters from the Committee to Protect asking contributors for money to pay the debts and operating costs of Operation Rescue. Pratt's first letter stated his sympathies: "Many of us are grateful for the work of Randall Terry and Operation Rescue over the past two years . . . As you well know, the federal government has seized Operation Rescue's operating and payroll accounts . . . We have set up a separate account to pay off . . . [its] debt."[16]

A July 16 letter was slightly more hysterical: "THE GOVERNMENT IS DOING THE FEMINISTS' DIRTY WORK WITH YOUR TAX DOLLARS [emphasis in original]."[17]

The Committee to Protect spent more than $146,000 on Operation Rescue's debts that year. When a U.S. district judge ruled that it could also be liable for Operation Rescue's fines—since it was raising money and paying bills—Pratt stopped sending letters, and Terry shuttered his Operation Rescue office.

Pratt's Christian nationalist résumé at the Committee to Protect the Family Foundation and his gun rights profile at Gun Owners of America were a remarkable combination. While he did not personally accept the obvious racism of men such as Richard Butler and Louis Beam, Pratt did not raise any public objections during the course of the meeting. He made it abundantly clear he was ready to work with the group at Estes Park if it was ready to work with him. (In his speech Pratt charitably described his audience as Bill of Rights–style constitutionalists. No Fourteenth Amendment in that Founding Fathers document. Pratt told the assembly he had a problem with it anyway.)

Gun rights and (white) Christian nationalism: upon those two rocks the contemporary militia movement was founded in the 1990s. Perhaps Beam summed up the anger and danger present at Estes Park in a leaflet he was circulating: "The federals have made a terrible error in the Weaver case that they will long regret. Their cruelty and callous disregard for the rules of civilized warfare will have the effect of solidifying opposition to them. Long after Weaver has been tried and has been freed by the courts as an innocent man wrongfully accused, there will be 10,000 White men in this country who harbor in their hearts a terrible hatred for the federals and all they stand for . . ."[18]

Historical Weight of Estes Park Meeting

In the first years after the formation of the militia movement, the importance of the Estes Park gathering was much debated. Ken Stern wrote of the meeting in his book on the militia movement, *A Force upon the Plain*: "The Estes Park meeting . . . may have laid the groundwork for the militia's formation . . . Yet, its importance should not be overrated. Meetings happen every day."[19] Conversely, Morris Dees and James Corcoran in their book on the militia, *Gathering Storm*, assigned a singular importance to the meeting.

Certainly, common sense argues that there are limitations to the ultimate importance of any particular meeting, except those where specific overt acts are planned. But the participants at Estes Park did not behave as if they were bank robbers plotting a heist. Louis Beam was not the gunman with a watch, ensuring that his cohorts escaped before the cops arrived. Neither was Pete Peters the getaway driver or Larry Pratt the man with the alibi for all. The militia movement was not the result of any conspiracy, although as a movement it eventually engendered dozens of actual criminal conspiracies.

History is always ambiguous about the meaning of specific events. Consider, for example, the January 1942 conference of Nazi leaders at Wannsee. Did they plan the "final solution" to the Jewish question at that place and only at that place? The Holocaust would have probably occurred without Wannsee. An ideology that regarded Jews as a subhuman menace guided Nazi policy long before 1942, and the mass murder of Jews had already started before that particular meeting.

Similarly, both the view that the federal government was a menace to white people and the actual formation of militias predated Estes Park. In fact, the "unorganized militia" had been a basic tenet of Posse Comitatus practice since the early 1980s. The ideology and social forces that manifested themselves in new and explosive ways after Estes Park had been in the process of (re)developing since Willis Carto and William Pierce had rescued the white supremacist movement from complete eclipse in the very early 1970s.

Nevertheless, Estes Park was unique and of significant historical weight on several counts. This was a relatively calm and deliberative meeting, absent the usual bombast and conspiracy mongering—not an everyday occurrence among racists and anti-Semites. This band of

Christian Identity leaders and Aryan types planned to organize around an issue that resonated widely and had immediate consequences. While their southern kinsmen had already campaigned à la David Duke, and those in the Midwest had created a minimovement out of dispossessed farmers in the 1980s, most of those in the Northwest tended to withdraw into the mountains. A few robbed bank trucks. But Estes Park was a new departure, in part because the urgency of Randy Weaver's and Kevin Harris's coming trial loomed over virtually every point.

Another unique aspect of this gathering was its truly collaborative leadership. Despite Pete Peters's role in convening the meeting, there was little planned agenda or preapproved list of speakers. By contrast, at Peters's summer Bible camps he was the unchallenged chief, and each speaker in each time slot had been arranged in advance. At Estes Park a group of men made decisions ad hoc, during the proceedings.

Although the militia movement in the 1990s eventually traced directly back to the Estes Park meeting, the most singularly significant aspect of the meeting was less the initiation of the militia than the participation of such men as Larry Pratt. Temple and others like him had nosed their way into groups such as Moral Majority or lobbied legislatures on gun issues in the past. But in those instances, others outside the movement had set the political agenda. On this occasion, however, it was Pete Peters's tent, it was Louis Beam welcoming the guests, and it was Chris Temple setting the strategy. And it was the likes of Larry Pratt walking in on an expanded white nationalist turf. The shift that had manifested itself with the collapse of the Soviet Union continued. Much like Pat Buchanan's adopting the rhetoric of David Duke and Willis Carto's *Spotlight*, a number of activists and organizations associated with Christian conservative causes adopted a more militant opposition to the status quo. A new Christian nationalism emerged, distinct yet entwined with the post–Cold War white nationalism. And a mixture of guns with religion burst like the muzzle flash of a .38 revolver. No metaphor intended.

Clinton's First Year and the Culture War

March 10, 1993. At 9:40 a.m. Dr. David Gunn drove his 1992 Buick up to the Pensacola Women's Medical Services Clinic on Bayou Boulevard. The detritus of commuting hundreds of miles from his home in Eufaula, Alabama, to clinics in Florida, Georgia, and Alabama was scattered around him: a McDonald's bag of fast-food trash, a carton of empty beer cans, a jar of peanuts, empty coffee cups, several changes of clothes, and various legal and bank documents. A slight, unimposing forty-seven-year-old gynecologist, Dr. Gunn provided abortion services in a region where they were legal but not widely available. So he traveled, a moving target for antichoice activists aiming at what they considered the weakest link in abortion services, the doctor. In front of the clinic, a crowd of protesters had gathered. Some stood in a knot off to the side, apparently in deep contemplation. A band bunched in the middle of the drive, making it difficult for women to pass into the clinic. Gunn parked in the west lot, away from the front and closest to the employee entrance, and got out of the car.

At that moment a well-dressed man in a brown sportscoat stepped up from behind and shot him three times in the back. One bullet entered his body in the back of the right shoulder, puncturing his lung. Another bullet entered between the left shoulder and the spinal column and lodged itself in the muscles on the left side of his neck. A third bullet also entered on the left side and left a gaping bloody exit wound on the right side of his chest.[1]

As the doctor crumpled to the ground in a pool of blood, the shooter dropped his chrome-plated .38 revolver to the ground, walked to the front of the clinic, and said, "I just shot a man in the back of the clinic." A police officer observing the pickets immediately took the shooter into custody.[2] Three hours later Dr. David Gunn died at Sacred Heart Hospital, assassinated in cold blood and in broad daylight for the crime of providing safe and legal medical services to women.

Up until just a couple of months prior, the shooter, Michael Griffin, was a Joe Regular Guy. His father was a dentist, and Griffin passed through Pensacola's best public high school without comment.[3] He wed young, had children, and by mid-marriage had enlisted in the navy. In the military, Griffin repeatedly earned high marks from his superiors and was regarded as an excellent electrician.[4] Upon return to civilian employment, Griffin scored well with supervisors at a chemical plant and at his annual work evaluation rated "excellent" on "cooperation with others."[5] His cooperation apparently did not extend to his family, and his wife won a restraining order after he had (repeatedly) physically abused her and their two daughters.[6] After a reconciliation, the couple started volunteering at a local home for "troubled" women, and it was there, under the tutelage of John Burt, the home's founder, that Griffin became a soldier in the pro-life crusade.

Unlike Griffin, Burt had a long association with racially and religiously motivated violence. After a stint in the Marine Corps, Burt enlisted in the Klan and spent two years during the early sixties as a Kluxer in St. Augustine and Jacksonville. When questioned, Burt admitted that he was "very active" as a Klansman. "I thought that the race problem was a communist conspiracy to disrupt America," he said. "I was in St. Augustine when they had race riots there. We moved to Jacksonville and we continued our work."[7] In fact, a drive to integrate St. Augustine in 1964 was met by significant Klan violence.[8] When asked if he had broken the law during those years, Burt replied, "Oh, yeah, sure."

Burt claimed that after he left the Klan and became a born-again Christian, he dropped any animosities based on skin color. "You can't be a bigot and be a Christian," he claimed. Nevertheless, in the years following, Burt replaced his battle against civil rights for black people with an attack on the constitutional rights of women. He began regular pickets at a Pensacola health clinic that performed abortions, and on Christmas Day 1984 that clinic and two associated doctors' offices were firebombed. No one was arrested for that first arson, but Burt reportedly told followers that he had "no qualms" about such attacks.[9] (Four people, none of them Burt, were arrested after the same clinic was bombed a second time several months later.) In February 1985, Burt barged into one of the doctors' offices, and was convicted of trespass. In another incident thirteen months later, Burt along with three others again broke into a Pensacola clinic, while it was operating. He was arrested and placed on probation. Then, still on probation, Burt was arrested once more for allegedly showing a would-be bomber the location of the clinic in Pensacola. He was sentenced to two years of house arrest, ending until 1991 his crusade to intimidate medical professionals and their patients.[10]

After Burt's house arrest ended, he rejoined the irregular armies attacking clinics and doctors as if they were infidels at the gates of holy cities. In 1991 and 1992 he twice blocked the entrance to a clinic in nearby Fort Walton Beach and twice was convicted of criminal trespass. Apparently unrestrained by these multiple arrests and convictions, he zeroed back in on Pensacola, the women's center clinic, and Dr. Gunn. Burt led repeated pickets at the clinic. He hung a bloodstained effigy of Dr. Gunn in the home for women, replete with a rope around its neck and a biblical verse attached. He also issued a wanted poster with Dr. Gunn's photograph, address, and telephone numbers. He harassed, threatened, and intimidated the doctor and ensured that Michael Griffin was personally able to identify him. And when Burt took his troops to the front of the clinic on that fateful March 10, Griffin's assassination of Dr. Gunn fell like the last step in a long march from mayhem to murder.

Despite Burt's past Klan membership, he never couched his opposition to abortion in specifically racist or anti-Semitic terms. Most contemporary white nationalists, by contrast, regarded abortion as a secondary question, deriving its importance only because of its presumed connection to the demographic fate of white people. When William Pierce offered an opinion on the topic, it was only to lament the role of abortion in the declining birthrate of whites. He certainly preferred measures such as abortion and sterilization if aimed at nonwhites. Tom Metzger took a slightly different tack. "Almost all abortion doctors are Jews. Abortion makes money for Jews. Almost all abortion nurses are lesbians. Abortion gives thrills to lesbians," Metzger reasoned. His concern on this issue was only for abortions among white people. It was a sentiment shared by mainstreamers and vanguardists alike, despite any other disagreements they might have. Ed Fields, who had opposed Metzger's strategy at Fort Smith, for example, said much the same thing: "We favor abortion on demand [paid by the taxpayers] for any and all colored people . . . Abortion for White people should be totally banned."[11] If that day should ever come, Metzger proposed a sanguinary conclusion to the whole phenomenon: "When abortion is declared to be murder they [Jewish doctors and lesbian nurses should] be hung by piano wires for the holocaust of twenty million white babies."[12]

While Metzger's call for killing doctors and nurses in the future might seem farfetched, the level of actually existing violence was disturbingly high nonetheless. The National Abortion Federation recorded 155 instances of vandalism directed at clinics during the two-year period of 1993–1994, as well as 29 arsons, another 20 attempted arsons, and a total of 5 murders and 9 attempted murders.[13]

The campaign of intimidation and harassment of women's clinics had initially grown out of a movement to change public policy on abortion. In the 1970s broad coalitions sponsored by the Catholic Church and Protestant fundamentalists sought to elect politicians who would stop abortion through state or federal legislation, or a constitutional amendment, or even a change in the Supreme Court's composition. This so-called right-to-life movement helped elect President Reagan in 1980. But Reagan was unable to end reproductive freedom of choice, and a more militant wing of the movement began a clandestine crusade, bombing clinics and committing other acts of violence. Another wing of anti-choicers began mass civil disobedience campaigns to shut down clinics by blockading their doors. These were the so-called rescue operations that the Gun Owners of America executive Larry Pratt had supported.

The turn to murderous violence began in earnest after all these other avenues for changing policy had been exhausted, according to a persuasive argument by James Risen and Judy L. Thomas in their comprehensive book on antichoice killers, *Wrath of Angels*. Both mass militance and political lobbying reached their limit when the Supreme Court decided in 1992 in *Planned Parenthood of Southeastern Pennsylvania v. Casey* to uphold the core of the *Roe* decision endorsing abortion rights. "With Clinton's election, anti-abortion militants now felt disenfranchised and increasingly were willing to follow extremists . . . into radical fringe groups," Risen and Thomas wrote.[14]

The election of President Clinton and Democratic Party majorities in both the House and Senate precluded any immediate ban on freedom of choice. And the Christian right fought the Clinton presidency from day one, turning the president into the preeminent symbol of the dope-smoking, antiwar, sexual revolution of the 1960s, everything that conservatives of all types abjured. After Clinton proposed normalizing the presence of gay men and lesbians serving in the military, religious and cultural conservatives used the opportunity to ratchet up their profile as an opposition force. Organizations whose financial fortunes had sagged during the Reagan-Bush presidency now experienced a rapid surge of growth and money. The Reverend Jerry Falwell, who had been operating at a deficit since the midyears of President Reagan's administrations, installed a 900 phone line, which charged callers to express their views on the issue. According to *The Washington Post*, more than twenty-four thousand people paid the cost of calling within the line's first hours, and the antigay crescendo grew from there.

Broadcasters on both radio and television urged their audiences to let their representatives know they opposed gay men and lesbians in uniform. Headlines on the Reverend Pat Robertson's Christian Coalition monthly tabloid screamed about "Homosexual Soldiers." And Falwell's and Robertson's weren't the only operations to benefit by opposing the new president. Other sectors of the conservative movement also gained from the growing opposition to the new Democratic administration. William Buckley's mainline *National Review* magazine, for example, enjoyed a jump in paid circulation figures. In the end, Clinton was forced to abandon his initial proposal and adopt a much-ridiculed "don't ask, don't tell" policy in the military.

The forces unleashed by Pat Buchanan's run through the 1992 primaries had not abated. Buchanan's fierce invocation of a culture war during the Republican convention had struck a chord among a distinct stratum of voters. On that November's ballot in Oregon a proposed amendment to the state constitution had lumped in homosexuality with "pedophilia, sadism and masochism" as behaviors that were "wrong, unnatural and perverse." Known as Measure 9, it forbade state funding for educational programs regarding homosexuality and denied civil rights protection to gay men and lesbians. Proponents of the referendum produced clever propaganda, including a videotape of gay pride marches featuring provocative public displays of sexualized behavior.[15] By conventional standards the measure lost badly, 44 percent to 56 percent; nevertheless, it took one point more than Clinton, who won the state.[16]

A similar initiative in Colorado that year, known as Amendment 2, proposed changing the state constitution to ban any local or statewide civil rights legislation: "No protected status based on homosexual, lesbian or bisexual orientation" was to be legal. Municipal statutes protecting gay men and lesbians from discrimination in housing and employment would become unconstitutional.[17] This measure passed with 53 percent of the vote—thirteen points more than Clinton took while winning the state. Amendment 2's foes brought suit after it passed, and the United States Supreme Court ruled it unconstitutional on the ground that it violated the equal protection clause of the Fourteenth Amendment:[18] "We cannot accept the view that Amendment 2's prohibition on specific legal protections does no more than deprive homosexuals of special rights. To the contrary, the amendment imposes a special disability upon those persons alone."[19]

Although ultimately unsuccessful, these campaigns shifted away from purely a theological opposition to gay rights toward propaganda that claimed that homosexuals wanted "special rights" not available to others. It was an argument similar to the one David Duke had popularized in Louisiana regarding racial equality for black people. And focus group studies showed that the antigay sentiment expressed by ordinary nonideological white people was similar to their objection to policies such as affirmative action.[20] The high levels of opposition to abortion and civil rights for gay people demonstrated that the proponents of culture warfare did not lie down after the 1992 election; rather, the prospect of a Democratic presidency turned them into a highly energetic mass base for the new forms of white Christian nationalism being born in the early 1990s.

While men such as Pat Buchanan aimed to turn these warriors into a vigorous, more broadly defined force for America first nationalism, the Christian Coalition executive Ralph Reed tried to tie this growing constituency firmly to the Republican Party establishment during Clinton's first year. Convinced that so-called family issues were too narrowly defined a platform for electoral success, Reed hoped to graduate from abortion, gay rights, and prayer in public school to issues such as free trade and health insurance.

In the Heritage Foundation's monthly journal, *Policy Review*, Reed wrote: "The most urgent challenge for pro-family conservatives is to develop a broader issues agenda. The pro-family movement has limited its effectiveness by concentrating disproportionately on issues such as abortion and homosexuality . . . To win at the ballot box and in the court of public opinion, however, the pro-family movement must speak to the concerns of average voters in the areas of taxes, crime, government waste, health care and financial security."[21] The Heritage Foundation had been the preeminent think tank supporting President Reagan's administration, and it was a logical place for Reed to discuss strategy. Much of the Republican leadership, following former President George Bush and Senator Bob Dole, was then pressing Congress for the NAFTA treaty's passage, despite the fact that President Clinton was leading the effort to sign it into law. It was therefore natural for Reed to announce his support for NAFTA at a Heritage Foundation luncheon, and he planned to have the assembly at the September Christian Coalition conference officially endorse the free trade agreement.

Two thousand activists gathered at a Washington hotel under the banner THE TIDE IS TURNING, but the Christian Coalition conference itself was swirling with conflicting currents. On one hand, Ralph Reed loaded the platform with Republican Party regulars, including Kansas Senator Bob Dole and Texas Senator Phil Gramm, who talked about such economic issues as taxes and health care. They received polite Republican applause. On the other side were the cultural warriors, best represented that day by Pat Buchanan, who urged no compromise with the Republican Party establishment. He thumped the issue of "multiculturalism" and argued that "our culture is superior because our religion is Christianity." He also pounded free trade and NAFTA with all the pent-up ferocity that his primary campaign had produced. Opposition to NAFTA too was a cultural issue. "The battle over NAFTA is also a struggle about what it means to be a conservative in 1993," he wrote later. "Who defines the term?" he asked. "America first" or "New World Order" were the choices Buchanan posed.

White supremacists had opposed free trade since before Willis Carto's Liberty Lobby had testified before Congress on the issue in the early 1960s. And Buchanan had made it one of his signature issues during the 1992 primaries. As *The New York Times* reported, this conference crowd endorsed Buchanan's America first thumping over Ralph Reed's free trade conservatism. Reed's resolution endorsing NAFTA never came to the floor after Buchanan spoke. For those who believed the Christian right represented a homogeneous movement of biblically motivated evangelicals, Buchanan's dashing of Reed's plans showed that a rift on fundamental issues existed within the ranks. At that moment, at that convention, Buchanan-style nationalist forces held the highest hand.

The debate over free trade at the Christian Coalition contained, in miniature, differences within the right wing over the meaning of fighting a culture war as well as the nature of the so-called religious right itself. In this discourse the most forceful and clear-eyed account was not put forward by Pat Buchanan but by his friend and colleague Sam Francis. In speeches and in columns for the monthly magazine *Chronicles*, Francis argued that the religious right's constituency was motivated primarily not by theological concerns, but by the attempt to defend its traditional white civilization. In his account, conflicts over issues such as abortion and gay rights were really clashes over the "traditional middle-class social and economic dominance . . ."[22] The promotion of religion was only one moment in a "social convulsion for the preservation of class, ethnic and cultural dominance."[23]

Rather than a movement to implement a particular vision of God's Law, he argued, "the religious right . . . is merely the current incarnation of the on-going Middle American Revolution."[24] Accordingly, the Reverend Pat Robertson's Christian Coalition and like groups were not the most effective instruments "because the Christianity of the right simply doesn't encompass very many Middle American interests."[25] Francis prescribed a formula that called for adding support for gun rights, opposition to immigration, and opposition to free trade to the cultural warfare agenda.[26] He wanted this war, fought under the banner of tradition, essentially to reconquer the American state and reinstall the pre–civil rights regime. It was a fight for power and control. Francis put it bluntly: the "white middle-class core of American society and culture was being evicted from its historic position of cultural and political dominance."[27] And he wanted it back.

The concept of dominance loomed large in Sam Francis's analysis. He sometimes spoke of "preserving" dominance, an implicit acknowledgment that society's commanding heights were still held by his brand of white people. And his movement, whether marching under the banner of the religious right or Middle American Radicals, was seeking to conserve and protect the privileges which that dominance accrued. At other times Francis argued that "dominance" had already been lost and needed to be regained.

"The first thing we have to learn about fighting and winning a culture war is that we are not fighting to 'conserve' something; we are fighting to overthrow something," Francis contended. "If our culture is going to be conserved, then we need to dethrone the dominant authorities that threaten it." At a conference convened by Pat Buchanan, Francis did not mince his words about the total upheaval he sought: "When I call for the overthrow of the dominant authorities that threaten our culture . . . it involves the almost total redistribution of power in American society— the displacement of the incumbent governing and cultural elites, the dismantlement of their apparatus of domination, the delegitimization of their political formulas and ideologies . . ."[28]

He did not advocate anything illegal or violent, nor did he propose the immediate seizing of political power. The governing elites, he believed, did not rule through a monopoly of violence or the naked exercise of raw state power. Rather, they exercised ideological hegemony first, thus guaranteeing their stranglehold on the minds of the white majority. For this analysis Sam Francis, the ultraconservative anti-communist, explicitly invoked the name and the theories of the Italian Marxist Antonio Gramsci, who had died in 1937, a victim of Mussolini's prisons.

Francis demonstrated a keen grasp of Gramsci's intellectual contributions. Gramsci had used the concept of ideological hegemony to explain how exploited workers borrowed parts of their worldview from the same capitalist class that oppressed them. From his prison cell, Gramsci posited a war of position—that is, a war for the ideologically commanding heights—prior to launching a war of maneuver, the fast-paced battle for state power. When applying these ideas to the culture war,

Francis believed that the dispossession of the white majority was legitimized by the widespread acceptance of concepts such as egalitarianism. This was the meaning of ideological hegemony in this context. As a result, a war of ideas had to be fought and the notion of egalitarianism itself had to be attacked.

Framing his disquisition on winning the culture war, Francis had started with a critique of the religious right and ended up on territory already occupied by white nationalists. Wilmot Robertson had made much the same argument two decades before: white men were a dispossessed majority in their own homeland and were ruled over through control of the political culture by a government and a class of elites hostile to their interests.

During the next years, events seemed to confirm Francis's views. Angry white men took center stage in the electoral arena. The Republican Party led the battle against immigrant rights. Scientific racism once again entered public discourse and presented a theory contrary to the concept of natural equality. At the same time, however, the Republican Party leadership and the probusiness wing of the Democratic Party managed to pass NAFTA in both houses, and President Clinton signed it into law. After Congress combined several gun control measures into one piece of legislation, Clinton also signed the Brady Bill. Named after James Brady, an aide who was shot and severely wounded during an assassination attempt on President Reagan, the bill had previously languished in congressional committees for years.

An extraparliamentary common law and militia movement flourished during and after 1994, motivated by ideas rooted in the old Posse Comitatus. It challenged these existing institutions of authority and control and fed off the opposition to NAFTA and free trade as well as a mass resistance to gun control. The election of President Clinton and an administration of cultural and racial liberals seemed to accelerate these developments, particularly in places geographically or culturally farthest away from the centers of ideological hegemony. To understand these future events, however, it is first necessary to take one step back in time to Waco, Texas, and the trial of Randy Weaver.

Inferno at Waco and Randy Weaver Wins at Trial

April 19, 1993. A helicopter and tanks and armored personnel carriers driven by FBI agents began a military-style assault on a seventy-seven-acre compound populated by a religious sect known as the Branch Davidians. After hours of gunfire and tear gas, a fire started and swept from one building to the next. The origins of the fire remained in dispute, as did the exact number of deaths from the fire. But at least seventy-six Davidians died altogether, including twenty-one children. For hundreds of thousands of Americans they became symbols of the federal assault on gun rights and religious beliefs.

The Branch Davidians started as an obscure splinter of the Seventh-Day Adventists, itself one of the hundreds of smaller Christian sects that abound in a land that prides itself on religious liberty. They established a religious commune called Mount Carmel outside Waco, Texas, and garnered little interest from government authorities until 1987, when a fight for control of the sect ended in a gun battle. Eight Davidians were charged with attempted murder; they included a young man who later changed his name to David Koresh. A deadlocked jury ended in acquittals, and Koresh emerged as the unquestioned guru of the Mount Carmel cult.

Davidian theology focused on an arcane set of revelations and End Times prophecies. Except to the most trained eschatological eye, it was an unfamiliar and inaccessible set of beliefs. But as Koresh transformed the commune into a heavily armed walled fortress, it began to recognizably resemble camps like the Covenant, the Sword and the Arm of the Lord compound James Ellison once controlled on the Arkansas border. The Davidians shared none of Identity's theological preoccupation with Zionist Occupied Government or the belief that spiritual grace was attained via biological race. In fact, a mix of approximately one hundred varied multiracial souls from Australia, the United Kingdom, Jamaica, and the United States inhabited the commune in mutual and complete obeisance to Koresh's supposedly God-inspired will.

Early in 1992 a Texas state welfare department investigated charges of child abuse at Mount Carmel. (Like James Ellison and other cult leaders, Koresh took multiple wives, including in this case a fourteen-year-old girl.) At the same time, a local reporter began inquiring about possible plans by communards to commit mass suicide at Koresh's instruction. Bureau of Alcohol, Tobacco, and Firearms (ATF) agents also opened an investigation and learned that Koresh and associates were buying large numbers of guns and manufacturing illegal weapons. The ATF described the religious commune in terms usually reserved for paramilitaries, and undercover agents reported that Bible lessons and shooting assault rifles on a firing range were part of communal routine.

According to a report by the Treasury Department, on February 23, 1993, the Davidians showed an ATF informant a video, produced by Larry Pratt's Gun Owners of America, that portrayed the ATF as a threat to liberty. Five days later ATF agents raided the compound on a warrant for illegal weapons. From the first minute this raid bled disaster. Four ATF agents were killed, and another twenty wounded, by an incredible barrage of gunfire from civilians. ATF bullets killed three cult members, and three others were killed either by other cultists (in mercy killings) or by suicide. Four were wounded, including David Koresh.[1] Only a nego-tiated cease-fire allowed the ATF to disengage and carry off all its dead and wounded. With President Clinton's administration less than six weeks old, a siege by the FBI began in the wake of the failed ATF raid.

A semipermanent camp of observers soon grew up outside the barri-cades. Relatives and friends of those inside the compound, their attor-neys, media professionals, the merely curious, and a smattering of activists of all stripes converged. Unlike Randy Weaver's cabin on Ruby Ridge, the Branch Davidian compound on the plains of Texas was visible to both television cameras and the gathering crowd. Virtually every FBI misstep became the subject of international news broadcasts, as did the Davidians' theological invocations of the End Times. A month into the standoff, Louis Beam and Kirk Lyons joined this apocalyptic spectacle.

Beam's appearance at Waco was short-lived and of little consequence to either the Davidians inside the compound or to the FBI outside it. While presenting himself as a journalist representing a California-based Christian Identity monthly tabloid, he created a small ruckus at an FBI press briefing, got himself arrested, was represented briefly by attorney Lyons, and the charges were dropped. Nevertheless, the apparent sup-port for a multiracial (and race-mixing) sect by a former Klan dragon who had once pledged to rid North America of every nonwhite gene signaled a significant shift in strategy. Waco became a test of the ideas enunciated at Estes Park: first establish a common front for a Christian nation and against the Beast government. Worry about the ultimate fate of people more darkly hued later.

Kirk Lyons injected himself into the legal imbroglio growing around the standoff. Before it was all over, he pressed four different lawsuits against the federal government and sought financial support for those cases from the multimillion-dollar budget of the National Rifle Association. Although he received an initial pledge of funds, the country's biggest gun lobby ultimately decided not to support him. Despite this setback, the events at Waco enlarged the political space Lyons, Beam, and other white nationalists opened after Ruby Ridge.[2]

Randy Weaver Trial

On April 13, six days before the final fiery conflagration at Waco, the trial of Randy Weaver and codefendant Kevin Harris started in Boise, Idaho. Both were indicted for conspiracy to murder as well as for the murder itself of Federal Marshal William Degan during the siege at Ruby Ridge. In addition, Weaver faced the charges that had initially provoked the conflict, selling a sawed-off shotgun and failing to appear for trial. While federal prosecutors might have believed these were sound criminal charges, untainted by public sentiment or political concerns, the defense proved otherwise. By the trial's end the government case against Weaver was a more wretched failure than the prosecution at Fort Smith, where charges of seditious conspiracy had evoked libertarian concerns for "free speech."

Comparisons between these two most important cases demonstrate that white nationalists had learned from their own past, a sure sign of the reflexive self-consciousness that separates living social movements from stick figure data. At the same time, the federal government seemed to have remembered little from its loss in Fort Smith and acted as if it were determined to repeat itself in the Weaver case.

Weaver's supporters rallied for the defense at the trial's opening, for example, just as protesters had in Fort Smith. In contrast with the marchers in Arkansas, however, Weaver's supporters in Boise displayed no anti-Semitic imagery on their placards. The new tone evinced at Estes Park held sway instead. One quiet woman held a picket sign reading WHO STANDS TRIAL FOR MURDERS OF VICKI AND SAM WEAVER? The poster board of another gentleman in a sportscoat and tie read, THE MOST DESPICABLE CRIMINALS ARE THOSE WHO WEAR A BADGE. FREE WEAVER AND HARRIS.

While the rallies for the defense at Fort Smith had largely been organized by one Klansman, Thom Robb, supporting Weaver became an imperative across almost the entire movement. In addition to the Boise picket, others rallied at federal courthouses in Philadelphia and in Van Nuys, California. Further, Carto's *Spotlight*, which had published little about the sedition defendants, ran Weaver coverage front to back, issue after issue. Skinheads from Utah joined Christian patriots from Oregon in the courtroom seats behind Weaver's defense table. White nationalists had not shown such internal cohesion since the movement's reemergence in the mid-1970s.

In Boise the defense successfully turned the deaths of Vicki and Sam Weaver into a prima facie case of government wrongdoing. Weaver's attorney showed jurors bloody photos of Sam and Vicki, had them handle the FBI sharpshooter's rifle, then asked them to imagine the screaming coming from the cabin. The prosecution's evidence might have been able to address the initial shootings on Ruby Ridge: of the dog, Federal Marshal William Degan, and even young Sam Weaver. But the image of mother Vicki's head blown off while she was holding her ten-month-old baby could not be erased by any mountain of testimony about her belief in a final battle between good Aryans and evil race mixers.

Additional self-inflicted blunders undermined the case against Weaver. The government tried to introduce photos of "reconstructed" evidence, in an almost unbelievable display of prosecutorial arrogance. After the FBI had taken apart and removed certain materials from Ruby Ridge, it realized that it would need them for trial. So the feds brought them all back to Ruby Ridge and reassembled them for picture taking, a clear violation of the rules of procedure. Further aggravating their case, the FBI failed to provide other (discoverable) evidence to the defense in a timely fashion. The judge angrily levied an initial fine of $3,240 against the government.

Finally, the disaster on April 19 at Waco burned the prosecution's case completely to the ground. Televised images of government tanks attacking civilians, flames, smoke, and death compounded the growing unease that law enforcement officials had turned from defenders of the public order into unrestrained thugs. Weaver's judge instructed jurors not to watch or read the coverage. But at least twice during the proceedings, Weaver's defense attorney deftly introduced a comparison of FBI conduct on Ruby Ridge and the horror at Waco, binding the two events into a single mental picture.[3]

White Supremacy and "White Separatism"

Parallel to the battle in the courtroom, a subtle contest for the moral high ground had implications far beyond Randy Weaver's immediate fate. Weaver's attorney, as well as a number of white nationalist cadres, attempted to change the words the public used to identify Randy Weaver. They argued that this hapless ridge sitter was a harmless "white separatist," not a dangerous "white supremacist." Weaver's attorney of course had an immediate interest in portraying his client as an innocent victim. And if Weaver was just a "separatist" who wanted to be left alone, then the movement of which he was a part became a white separatist movement by extension. He was thus just one more dispossessed white male victim of affirmative action and multiculturalism. David Duke's Kluxers, after all, did not hate anyone. They just loved white people. Willis Carto's Liberty Lobby claimed it was populist and nationalist and oft asserted that white nationalism was a beneficent twin to black nationalism. William Pierce's National Alliance cadre, skinheads, and a host of others also claimed that they were white separatists rather than white supremacists.[4] What was wrong with wanting to be *white* anyway and just living, working, eating, and going to the water fountain with just *white* people?

Weaver's supporters started this exchange over nomenclature during the first days of the siege in Idaho, and these efforts were reflected in the regional media at the time. In one early article in the Boise-based daily newspaper *The Idaho Statesman*, ran the headline "Friends Say Weaver a Separatist, Not a White Supremacist." The text quoted one of Weaver's friends on the topic. "A supremacist believes the only race to have rights to life is the white race," the friend decided. A separatist, on the other hand, believes in "staying separate with his faith and his race."[5] As a counterpoint to these claims, the *Statesman* simply closed the article with the self-evident observation that "members of the Aryan Nation white supremacist group" were supporting Weaver.

Later, when reporting on Weaver's first postsiege court appearance, the *Statesman* continued to describe Weaver as "a devotee of the Christian Identity Movement which combines Old Testament and white supremacist beliefs," a statement of uncontestable veracity. But Weaver's attorney used the occasion to claim that when the case finally went to trial, the issue would be government misconduct, "not whether this man believes in separatism, or his religious views."[6]

The attorney's statement turned out to be true enough, as far as it went. But the government indictment contended that Weaver's beliefs had lead to his actions. According to prosecutors, Weaver and Harris intended to advance "their views of 'white' or 'Aryan' supremacy or separatism and the political, social, and economic ascendancy of persons of a 'white' or 'Aryan' background."[7] By arguing that Weaver's actions had been motivated by his white supremacist ideas, the government placed the exact nature of his beliefs at the center of the government's case. It then simply became a matter of the defense attorneys' countering the prosecutors' description of Weaver's motivations. Thus the defense team was pushed by the logic of the case to claim that Weaver was not a "supremacist" at all. At one point they even asked the judge to stop government prosecutors from publicly referring to it as a "white supremacist case."[8] Weaver was simply a "separatist," the defense told reporters.

As the case finally came to trial, and the prosecution's case collapsed under the weight of its own mistakes, the ambiguity dropped out of media coverage. Weaver became an unadulterated "separatist." If the indictment alleged that Weaver's "white supremacist" beliefs were the premise motivating a conspiracy, then the government's failure to prove the existence of a conspiracy undermined the premise. "The government's image of Mr. Weaver as a political extremist bent on armed conflict has been eclipsed by courtroom revelations," one reporter concluded even before the verdict was reached.[9]

After eight weeks of prosecutorial misfires and a sharpshooter defense, the judge dismissed two of the multiple charges against Weaver and Harris and sent the rest of the case to the jury. Twenty days of deliberation later, on July 8, came the verdicts: not guilty of murder and conspiracy. Harris walked away completely free. Weaver was convicted only on the original gun charge and of failing to appear for trial the first time around. By anyone's account, Weaver had won and the government had lost.

The not guilty verdict sealed Weaver's claims in cement. If he had been convicted of murder, subsequent efforts to paint him as a benign white separatist might have failed. But the jury had decided that there were no plans for Aryan domination. In effect its decision made it official: Weaver was a separatist who had truly just wanted to be left alone. And media coverage of the trial and the verdict sealed the less loathsome description in the public mind.[10]

This change in nomenclature became an enduring legacy of the Ruby Ridge tragedy, part of a larger posttrial shift best understood in comparison to the period following the verdict at Fort Smith. After the seditious conspiracy trial, David Duke–style mainstreaming rose to the fore, pushing guns and gunmen into the background. By contrast, following the Weaver case, government agents, rather than Aryan bandits, were regarded as heartless killers.[11] A renewed drive for mainstream acceptance was paralleled by a rise in mass gun-toting militia militancy. A sector of Christian nationalists began intersecting with white nationalists. A new cohort of militants again robbed banks and killed for their cause.

While these actions took place and were recorded in newspaper head-lines, a second sequence of events occurred outside the public's view. A new generation of Aryanists took the stage and shaped their own cul-tural institutions while the older generation quietly lost control of the movement and began to die out.

A Suicide in North Carolina and the Birth of Resistance Records

August 8, 1993. In the numerology of Hitler worshipers, the number 8 stands as a symbol for the letter *H*, the eighth letter of the alphabet. Thus the salutation "Heil Hitler," or "HH," is represented by the number 88, and like the number 33 for Ku Kluxers, National Socialists are fond of using the symbol like a secret handshake. Following suit, in past years at the Church of the Creator camp in North Carolina, the eighth day of the eighth month, August 8, was a day for special celebration.[1] But on this day in 1993, the camp's seventy-five-year-old founder, Ben Klassen, swallowed multiple bottles of sleeping pills and committed suicide. It was a quiet end to a long career, first at the center of resistance to desegregation and then at the furthest edges of the white supremacist movement. During his last years, Klassen helped empower Generation X skinheads, those born between 1965 and 1980, setting the stage for the emergence of a white power music business in the United States. At the same time, Klassen's suicide revealed a weakness inherent in the movement as a whole, which was built around individual personalities (like Klassen), rather than formalized through institutions. The strategic wisdom gained by years of activism as well as the organizational power and accumulated assets was difficult to transfer from one generation to the next.

Benjamin Klassen was born in 1918 into a Mennonite colony in the Ukraine, then a region ravaged by war and revolution. His family immigrated first to Mexico in 1924 and then to a German-speaking Mennonite community in Saskatchewan, Canada. He taught school for a brief period and later studied electrical engineering at the University of Saskatchewan. Klassen claimed he first read Adolf Hitler's *Mein Kampf* in the original German at the age of twenty and became, in his words, "political." After World War Two he moved to South Florida and made money in the real estate market. Like other white-ists of his generation, including William Pierce, he joined the John Birch Society in 1963. Klassen won a seat in the Florida legislature in 1966 from Broward County and subsequently became the state chairman of Governor George Wallace's American Independent Party, then at the center of de jure segregation's last defense.[2] In 1968 Wallace received 624,000 votes in Florida (part of his 10 million votes nationwide), an indication that Klassen was not alone in his public sympathies.

Despite Wallace's relative success, Klassen felt "a key ingredient" was missing from the right wing at that time. He resigned from both the Wallace party and the Birch organization the following year.[3] During the same period that Klassen enlarged the fortune he had made in Florida's booming real estate market, he also searched for a philosophy that matched his own. Finding none, he decided to invent a "religion." He named it Creativity.

As a theology Creativity was uncomplicated. Whatever "benefited" the white race, Creativity deemed good because it regarded the white race as "Nature's finest creation of all time." (The N in "Nature" was always capitalized in Klassen's alphabet, as were the W in "White" and the R in "Race.") Jews were "the most sinister and dangerous parasites in all history." Neither precept particularly distinguished Klassen's Creativity from the other ideologies floating around his end of the spectrum. What made Klassen's Creativity unique was its explicit and rabid opposition to Christianity of all types—from mainline Protestantism and Catholicism to the Reverend Pat Robertson–style fundamentalism to the Identity variety. Despite agreement on much else, in Klassen's eyes Identity Christians—with their claims to be the actual (racial) descendants of the biblical tribes of Israel—were just wannabe Jews. Over time it was this anti-Christian mania that gave Klassen's "church" its own legs and walked the former Bircher out to the white rim of the universe.

In the early 1980s Klassen moved to Otto, North Carolina, a village nestled into the Appalachian Mountains five miles north of the Georgia state line on Highway 23. That tristate area of Appalachia—western North Carolina, northern Georgia, and eastern Tennessee—remains a beautiful and remote region, hidden away from large metropolitan areas. It is also home to significant pockets of white supremacists. Klassen and his wife, Henrie, turned their twenty-plus-acre tract into a headquarters complex, with an additional "church" cum office and apartment building. From this base, Klassen announced that Latin would become the language of the new white religion and anointed himself its Pontifex Maximus (supreme leader). He self-published books and produced a periodical, but his writings tended toward the scurrilous and vulgar, and he found few converts at first. At this point his Church of the Creator remained without structural form and was devoid of any motivating idea other than an Aryanist opposition to Christianity. By Klassen's reckoning, Christianity was a "Jewish creation . . . an unholy teaching designed to unhinge and derange the White Gentile intellect and cause him to abandon his real responsibilities." Klassen concocted his "religion" as a substitute doctrine, in which salvation rested with Nature (with a capital N) and the doctrines of Adolf Hitler.[4]

Initial "church" activities consisted mostly of distributing a tabloid titled *Racial Loyalty*. The first edition was dated June 1983 and set the pattern for the next decade: twelve pages of fourteen-point type, almost all of it written by Klassen, punctuated by a few cartoons and a page of book advertisements. Over time the letters to the editor section grew, a sign that somebody somewhere was reading it, and a couple of contact addresses came and went. He bequeathed the title of Reverend on a few white souls. The tabloids and books were long on ideology and exhortations to violence, but short on reporting actual church-type activity. No summer Bible camps here. Business stayed slow.

During the early and mid-1980s most of the action at the Hitlerite end of the movement gravitated around the Aryan Nations–Klan–Posse Comitatus axis. All three organizations considered themselves Christian Identity. And their leadership failed to appreciate Klassen's repeated gibes at worshiping "spooks in the sky." Nevertheless, after Klassen hired a competent organizational secretary in 1988, the Church of the Creator's footprint began to be seen with more frequency. Overseas branches developed in England, Sweden, and South Africa. And as the decade turned, a new generation of skinheads looking for an ideological home began to populate its ranks.

Klassen exhibited little taste for the youthful subculturalism of white power skinheads. Nevertheless, the interaction between Klassen and the skins worked to the temporary advantage of both. A segment of skins were drawn to Creativity's explicit worship of Hitler, its open abhorrence of everything Christian, and its glorification of random violence. As Tom Metzger's star dropped in the skinhead sky, and Kluxers such as Thom Robb turned toward Duke's mainstreaming, overzealous and violence-prone young men joined the Church of the Creator. "RAHOWA," short for "racial holy war," became their battle cry. From Klassen, the skinheads inherited an organizational structure, a codified set of ideas, and a literature. From the skinheads, Klassen gained his first real constituents since the George Wallace campaign era. His tabloid's contact list grew quickly to thirty addresses and chapters in the United States and three in Canada.

Soon Klassen was the victim of his own success. In May 1991, one of his so-called reverends, George Loeb, shot and killed a black sailor, Harold Mansfield, in the parking lot of a Jacksonville, Florida, convenience store. After the Reverend Loeb was convicted in criminal court, rumblings that a civil suit might be filed against Klassen's church threw a chill over the heated organizational growth. If the church was found liable for its reverend's actions, the sailor's family could possibly win possession of the twenty-acre campground. Compounding Klassen's anxiety, his wife, Henrie, died the following January from cancer, sinking the surviving spouse into a prolonged period of mourning. Klassen began searching for a replacement Pontifex Maximus and started talking openly of suicide, which his own Creativity doctrine had long held to be a positive virtue. Of the two end-game tasks, finding an organizational heir proved more difficult than killing oneself.

The problem of organizational succession has remained unsolved for white nationalists. Most organizations are basically sole entrepreneurships, small family-owned businesses dependent on the energy and vision of their founders. Those that avoid repression by law enforcement agencies or survive the vagaries of insurgency rarely turn into self-sustaining institutions. A trade name, such as the Ku Klux Klan, may pass from generation to generation, but each Klan organization has reinvented itself at the turn of the historical wheel. Klassen was one of only a few with any organizational assets to pass on: a plot of land and an inventory of books worth thousands in a very specialized market.

Klassen alone had the authority to choose his successor. His first choice was a failed businessman, a Nebraska meatpacker then in jail for selling tainted meat to school lunch programs. In one article after another, the *Racial Loyalty* tabloid extolled the meatpacker's racist virtues, as Klassen prepared his followers for their new führer. After the meatpacker's release from prison, however, he turned the job down. As a brief alternative, Klassen enticed one of his loyal reverends from Maryland to move to North Carolina in expectation of taking over the remote camp. But just as quickly, Klassen changed his mind and sent the man home again. A letter from William Pierce to Klassen discussed this dilemma: "The failure of your plans . . . [for the meatpacker] must have been very disappointing," Pierce wrote. "I hope that you do not act too hastily now and put your faith in people unable or unwilling to carry on in the right direction."[5] Pierce and Klassen were not particularly close. They had corresponded off and on since the mid-1970s and had visited with each other only a couple of times. They shared an ideological aversion to Christianity and a mutual admiration for Hitler, but as Pierce said, they had different styles of work. Nevertheless, in a series of quick decisions, Klassen sold his plot to Pierce at a price below market value, while turning over the remaining church assets—money and books—to a much-younger generation.

The future of Creativity resided with Generation X skinheads in large metropolitan centers rather than with middle-aged has-beens seeking refuge in the remote regions of Appalachia, Klassen decided. He was particularly impressed with a crew in Wisconsin, and he chose one of them, Mark Wilson, to take over as Pontifex Maximus. Wilson had solid entrepreneurial skills and was linked to skinheads across the upper Midwest and into Canada. For a brief moment, it looked as if Klassen would be the first leader from the World War Two generation to understand the potential brewing on the edge of the twenty-first century. But this anointment was not to be.

Soon after Mark Wilson had finished unloading three truckloads of COTC books brought from North Carolina to the new headquarters in Wisconsin, Klassen inexplicably backed down from his choice. He decided instead to go with a middle-aged chiropractor named Rick McCarty, who had recently endeared himself to Klassen and was appointed the new Pontifex. McCarty showed up in Wisconsin with his own truck and carried the books back to his home in Niceville, Florida, which he then named the new "international headquarters" of the Church of the Creator.[6]

McCarty turned out to be the worst of both generations, just the type of person Pierce had warned about. Unlike Klassen, McCarty had no writing skills. The tabloid, once dense with type, now looked like every other low-rent racist publication: big headlines, small blurbs for articles, and many reprints from the daily press. And unlike Wilson, McCarty had no natural constituency and few established ties in the movement. It was almost as if McCarty had been dropped into the Church of the Creator in a clever counterintelligence operation aimed at wrecking the organization from the inside. Except that role belonged to a man called Joe Allen.

Mr. Allen announced in May 1992 that he had "been converted to the one and only true White racial religion structured toward the survival, expansion, and advancement of the White Race."[7] Allen moved to Southern California, converted a warehouse space into a gym and office area, and started working with a group of Creator-allied skins calling themselves Fourth Reich Skinheads. "Rev. Allen has always been there for us," McCarty wrote in a spring–summer 1993 edition of the new lightweight *Racial Loyalty*, "call him." No sooner was the ink dry on the tabloid than several of the Fourth Reichers were arrested, charged in a plot to murder Rodney King, the black motorist whose beating precipitated the Los Angeles riots. The skinheads also were charged with planning a machine-gun attack on a black church and a plot to send a letter bomb to an area rabbi. The conspiracy was uncovered by Reverend Joe, who was in fact an undercover FBI agent. In the end, McCarty's lack of journalism skills and middle-aged distance from the young recruits was compounded by a shortage of basic street smarts—an inability to smell a cop when he met one. The two events—the conspiracy in California and the murder in Florida—added to Klassen's declining morale. Within just a few weeks of the California indictments, he committed suicide.

A few months later, on February 22, 1994, McCarty tried to officially close down Klassen's church. But two weeks after, the Southern Poverty Law Center, acting on behalf of the sailor's family, sued the Church of the Creator as a corporation. McCarty failed to respond, and a default judgment of one million dollars was entered against the church by a Florida court the following April. A year after that, the Southern Poverty Law Center sued William Pierce for the profit he had made by selling the Klassen property originally purchased at below market value. Ultimately a judgment against Pierce was sustained in that case as well. And only a portion of the original Creativity book stock remained extant. Klassen had spent years as a sole proprietor. But he had failed to secure an organizational heir or safely pass his assets to the next generation of activists.[8] The Church of the Creator smoldered in ruins, its führer dead by his own hand.

Birth of Resistance Records

While the tangible assets in Klassen's estate went up in smoke, the young people who had joined his enterprise made their own marks on the walls of history. Chief among them were Mark Wilson, the twenty-something from Wisconsin whom Klassen once designated as his successor, and George Burdi. A self-obsessed product of Toronto's tolerant upper-middle-class suburbs, Burdi liked to tell reporters that he tested at the "genius-level IQ" in the fifth grade and was an avid reader.[9] While still attending a private Catholic high school, he started learning his national socialist alphabet. In his mind, youthful vigor, music, and politics were bound up in a quasi-Nietzschean philosophy and a romantic idealization of Viking history. He assumed the pseudonym Eric Hawthorne, worked a stint at Klassen's North Carolina headquarters, and served as the Church of the Creator's chief Canadian representative. In 1989, at the age of nineteen, he started a band known as RAHOWA (for Racial Holy War, one of Klassen's slogans), and it was this persona that became the force driving the creation of the premier homegrown skinhead music company on North American soil.

Using contacts established through the Church of the Creator and a network called Northern Hammerskins, Burdi started Resistance Records with a combination of ideological zeal and basic business sense. He signed bands one by one to the label, arranged recording studio time and then a manufacturer for CDs and tapes. They sold and publicized their product through a combination of concerts, niche media, and hype.

The first Resistance Records Report, produced during the summer of 1993, was a black-and-white zine-style copy sheet entitled *Under the Hammer*.[10] It whispered a bit of in-house gossip, loudly announced new releases, and asked fans not to make bootleg copies of the recordings. "If you care about the future of White Power music," it warned, "be fair and do the White thing—don't dub your albums!" The profits were needed to pay the musicians. That summer, while Klassen was committing suicide in North Carolina, a Victory of Valhalla concert tour in Canada featured bands from Canada, three American groups, and a band from England. In addition, periodic gigs began at a clubhouse on Detroit's west side. At a show called "Two Nights of Terror," on December 31, 1993, and January 1, 1994, seven bands thudded through the evening, hailing the new dawn.

Before the Two Nights ended, Burdi and two other former Church of the Creator members from Canada, Jason Snow and Joseph Talic, officially affixed their names and registered Resistance Records Incorporated with Michigan's secretary of state. Ten thousand shares of common stock, valued, they hoped, at one dollar each, were issued. Rumors circulated that the start-up capital had been siphoned off the Church of the Creator by Mark Wilson during his brief tenure as the Pontifex. But George Burdi always claimed that the initial money for his band RA-HOWA to make a record had come from France and that low production costs and high profits had allowed the enterprise to grow rapidly after that.

Much like movement elders who had turned living room political hobbies into lucrative stand-alone businesses, the corporate principals created an institution out of producing and selling music to their Generation X cohorts. And as the white power music scene grew over the next years, those one-dollar shares increased in value. Resistance Records went from a young do-it-yourself operation to a full-line company. Wilson moved from Wisconsin to the Detroit area and served as Resistance's corporate agent. From a house in the suburbs he ran the business on a day-to-day basis. That spring it launched a twenty-eight-page promotional magazine, complete with high-quality graphics and a glossy cover with *Resistance: The Music Magazine of the True Alternative* across it. George Burdi, the Canadian, was editor.

Over the next three years *Resistance* became the most graphically innovative and stunning publication across the entire white nationalist movement. In these pages, Pat Buchanan was a virtual nonentity, and his Republican campaign went unmentioned. Neither Weaver nor Waco was mourned. The militia of the mid-1990s, with its invocation of an iconic red, white, and blue American patriotism, was out of place in this swastika-bedecked publication. Instead, articles puffed up bodybuilders and muscle tone. Bands playing "neo-pagan fascist hate metal" were celebrated. Thor and the Norse gods reigned supreme. Vikings strode like mighty men. And page after page featured pale male torsos dressed in dark tattoos.

The names of the bands told much of the story: Berserkr, Brutal Attack, Aryan, No Remorse, Vit Agression, and Bound for Glory. Rock and roll was retrofitted with a history of whiteness that excluded Elvis Presley's debt to the original music of the Delta blues. One bandleader even claimed that the chords in his songs were derived from the music of Richard Wagner, the anti-Semitic German composer. A lone folk singer, an anomalous figure in this crowd of hard rockers, was advertised as a misspelled "Bob Dillon for Ubermenschen." The magazine's fascination with the will to power was exceeded only by its smart sales technique, marketing and mayhem wrapped in a package that looked much like the hard-core metal magazines on the racks of downtown bookstores.

This was a males-only world. In just a handful of the many scene photos were women present. A few advertisements did picture romanticized graphics of long-haired, Valkyrian blond women, noticeably unmarred by tattoos and the paraphernalia of skindom. Outside the fantasies of the magazine, however, few of these idealized women associated themselves with the "black metal mafia" men glorified on the pages inside. In one article, a writer lamented the interracial dating habits of high-status blond beauties. "It is my belief that interracial matings are the result of a desire for self-annihilation," he argued. And with an almost Spenglerian flourish, the writer lamented the decay of "white" civilization and values. It was unlikely that the tattooed, shaved head readership seriously regarded such metaphysical musings. But its inclusion signified the publication's strategy of combining music madness within a broader cultural enterprise.

Small forays were made into the universe of liberal concerns. One magazine article critiqued the "Politics of Meaning," a set of ideas generated by liberal Jewish writers for the magazine *Tikkun*. Another writer revisited the author Jack London and the white racial socialism he had advocated a century before.[11] These pieces showed that the *Resistance* team was listening to the cultural babble around them, but they did not signify any genuine intervention into those larger discussions. Similarly, one article described the demographic changes due in the next fifty years and repeated the white nationalist mantra about becoming a new racial minority in a "third world" country. But *Resistance* did not plot any new strategy in that regard, and it did not revisit the topic for any further serious discussion.

By Burdi's account, Resistance Records tapped into the essence of white generational revolt. Skinheads felt betrayed by their elders, he wrote in *The Spotlight*. In an attempt to explain his followers to Carto's readers, he described young people scarred by a "society in decline" and guilty of being born White (with a capital *W*). They had spontaneously rebelled against black rap music and the white "effeminates" on MTV. Like the Vikings of old, he wrote, skins were "semi-nomadic tribes who lived to plunder and wage war." They might not be able to raise up a civilization, he argued, but their "violence-laced brand of music" was "born from souls of a generation preparing for Ragnarok [a world-destroying battle between the Norse gods and the forces of evil] once again."[12]

Statistics showed that these would-be Nordic warriors did in fact engage in an uncommonly large number of violent incidents. Although there were fewer than four thousand white power skinheads in the core of the subculture at the time Burdi launched the magazine, they committed thirty-two politically or racially motivated killings between 1987 and the end of 1994, according to documentation provided by the Center for New Community, a small civil rights organization in Chicago. These murders were brutal and personal, even if many of the victims were randomly chosen. Ten were the result of beatings, and ten were stabbings, crimes in which the perpetrators often found themselves covered with blood. Even shootings were up close, rather than instances of faraway sniping. By the end of 2001 the number of murders had reached fifty-one. These killings were only the smallest part of the violence committed by white power skins, and untold numbers of assaults, arsons, and other crimes went unreported to the police.

It became a commonplace for reporters, human rights activists, and cops all to refer to skinheads as the "street warriors" of the "hate" movement, a designation that reduced the subculture down to its violent expression. Some law enforcement professionals tended to treat these shaved head youths as if they were gangs, white versions of the Crips or

Bloods, and gang intelligence units in some cities were used to monitor the activity of all young people, sometimes hopelessly confusing racist and antiracist skinheads and both subcults with punks. A corollary view considered them of note only as the obedient street soldiers of older, established organizational bosses—disciples, not leaders; followers, not innovators. One criminologist declared that skinheads had developed only through the direct intervention of adults, not through the medium of subcultural self-discovery.[13]

The ganglike rituals practiced by a number of the crews, however, were secondary to the culture and style modes from which the skinhead phenomenon had sprung. Hairstyles, dress, and tattoos had initially defined skinheads. As the subculture matured, a more generalized system of beliefs and icons came to sustain it. Music and myth bound together these pockets of alienated white youths. As an autonomous social rather than criminal phenomenon, skinheads existed in their own social milieu with a distinct leadership and organizational impetus. These Gen Xers developed their own political style and counterinstitutions. And at the heart of this subculture beat the bands and their music. In this regard, Burdi's magazine played an outsize role.

Prior to the formation of Resistance Records, skinheads in the United States and Canada depended largely on their European counterparts to provide recorded music. In Britain enterprising skinheads had already seized control of their own music business. American white power bands, by contrast, had languished in their suburban garages. The would-be stage performers practiced, drank beer, and waited. One or two groups toured the skin music scene in Europe. Others played an occasional outdoor fest or rally. A few ran small distribution outfits with catalogs of European imports: music tapes, T-shirts and Naziesque paraphernalia. The one standby, Scene Zines, proliferated as fast as copyshops could turn cut-and-paste graphics into low-cost black-and-white newsletters. Before Internet use became commonplace, any white boy with an electric guitar and a post office box could reinvent himself into a newsletter warrior. Although several businesses catered to this set, none produced any homegrown music. *Blood and Honor* magazine published band news from Southern California. Skrewdriver Services in Colorado and Thunor Services in Georgia sold music from the U.K. and skinhead paraphernalia. Bound for Glory, a Minnesota band that had played at the Aryan Nations' 1989 rally in Tennessee, recorded its own LPs in Germany, and the band sold them from a St. Paul post office box under the rubric of Wolfpack Services. Once Resistance Records formed, however, it drew energy and resources from across this spectrum and began taking in tens of thousands of dollars in revenue.

. . .

Resistance Records' business success indicated the existence of a niche market in a political subculture ignored only at the larger society's peril. Here twenty-something skinheads registered heavily. Nevertheless, it was still a small boutique taste, not a musical department store. In the realm of mainstreamers and electioneers, however, this demographic showed not at all.

As the skinheads aged, they came to more closely resemble other white nationalists. Some grew their hair out or dressed professionally for regular jobs in the economic mainstream. A select few learned the intricacies of national socialism and became competent propagandists. Like members of the movement as a whole, skinheads came from family roots across the class spectrum, and those like Burdi with upper-middle-class roots tended toward positions of visible leadership.[14]

Nevertheless, the contrast between these Generation Xers and older parts of the movement remained sharp. Skinheads never became simply clay pots fired by their elders. Tom Metzger may have wanted to recruit skins to his banner, but he did not invent them. And as the conflict with a Bible-thumping Pete Peters in Tennessee had demonstrated, young activists pushed and pulled the older set in a generational contest of wills. If the young subculturalists (briefly) borrowed ideas or an occasional propaganda outlet, they also learned not to depend on their elders for organizational resources. Generational revolt within the white nationalist movement was not confined to the skin scene, however. Soon after Klassen's suicide, a long-simmering dispute within the Institute for Historical Review broke out into the open. In this instance, it was the boomer-age cadres that staged a coup against the older Willis Carto.

Willis Carto Loses Control of the Institute for Historical Review

October 15, 1993. At a battle at the Institute for Historical Review's offices in Costa Mesa, California, Willis Carto tenaciously ceded nothing without a determined fight. The pushing and shoving started just before noon. Mark Weber, the IHR's journal editor and ambassador to Germany's Holocaust deniers, was gone from the premises, along with three other (male) staffers. They were waiting for a prearranged meeting at their attorney's office, supposedly with Carto. Meanwhile, at the warehouse the secretary was left in the offices and talking on the phone when she was accosted by an outsider. "I was sitting at my computer with my back to the warehouse door," she later told police. "A strange man came up behind me and yanked the telephone out of my hand and pulled the chair I was sitting on back away from my desk. I asked who he was and he responded, 'We're taking over control.' I said, 'Do you mind if I finish this phone call, I have a customer on the line.' He said, 'No one is on the phone. That was us.'"[1]

Willis Carto, Elisabeth Carto, a locksmith, and a couple of thugs had entered the IHR's offices surreptitiously while Mark Weber and his staff were out of the building. In short, the Cartos and their hired-hands were quickly trying to regain control of the premises. They started changing locks and copying computer data, grabbed the phone lines, and briefly detained the remaining staff. After Weber and the others discovered they had been tricked, they left the lawyer's and rushed over to the institute offices, just in time to push their way through a door whose lock had not yet been changed. A battle began: the elderly Cartos and their thugs on one side, Weber's would-be historians on the other. The scrappy Willis came at his opponents with a makeshift wooden club. The elderly Elisabeth waved a concrete doorstop. One of Carto's hired hands knocked Weber to the floor and began pummeling him. In response, one of the other IHR staffers pulled a gun. At that point the muscle started backing off. Willis and Elisabeth, however, would not stop charging at their former comrades. So one of Weber's cohorts forced the elderly publisher to the door but did not succeed in pushing him completely out of the building. With one foot inside, Carto clung to the door while Elisabeth waved her doorstop like a character out of a Hitchcock thriller. Finally the police arrived, hauled off the Cartos, Weber, and his gun-wielding colleague. Weber's two remaining associates resecured the offices. And the Cartos were officially shut out.[2]

This failed attempt to take over the warehouse offices turned into one of the most humiliating defeats for Willis Carto in his decades of merchandising and mongering. The staff that he had once effectively directed had figured out how to seize control of the Legion for the Survival of Freedom, the parent corporation behind the Institute for Historical Review. Carto had controlled that corporation for almost thirty years. Now he was being unceremoniously pushed out the door—literally. All these combatants had until recently been on the same team, not using clubs or a gun against one another. They all had braved the disdain of historians and other keepers of the past in their self-described noble search for the truth. Now, by their own actions, they had reduced themselves to the status of back alley muggers. And the results had more far-reaching consequences—particularly on the fortunes of Willis Carto and his ability to eventually pass a legacy of his own making on to the next generation.

The dispute began at an editorial meeting between Carto and the senior staff on April 6, 1993. This session was "punctuated by loud and abusive" outbursts by Carto, according to a staff account of the meeting. He threatened and hammered on the table while trying to declare his intention to change the editorial direction of the *Journal of Historical Review*. He was tired of the sole focus on the Holocaust and wanted to join the parade of publications attacking "multiculturalism."[3] By changing the political direction of the journal, Carto also aimed to shift the entire IHR enterprise. He planned to replace Mark Weber as journal editor with a writer described by the staff as a past "Nazi propagandist."

Staff members began accumulating other complaints. They accused Carto of dragging the IHR into a swamp of fiduciary and legal trouble. Among other grievances, they cited Carto's reckless disregard for copyrights. On several occasions he had reprinted protected book titles after a cursory copyright search. As a result, the institute had been sued and forced to pay damages. The staff also claimed that Carto pursued worth-less publishing projects, including a book aimed at Mel Mermelstein, the Holocaust survivor who had already been through two rounds of lawsuits with Carto and the IHR. The staffers were tired of fighting with Mermel-stein. He had already cost them the ninety-thousand-dollar settlement, thirty thousand dollars in legal fees, and countless hours away from their main pursuit. During a second round of legal bouts in 1991, Carto had transferred the legion's hard assets—inventory, furniture, etc.—to an-other corporation. The staff believed these transfers amounted to "fraudulent conveyances."[4] Another lawsuit could possibly undo the en-tire corporate structure.

The staff also took umbrage at Carto's plan to publish a "10-volume flagrantly pro-Hitler" biography by Leon Degrelle, a Belgian general in the Waffen SS who had lived in Spain since World War Two.[5] Carto planned to pay Degrelle twenty-two thousand dollars in advance royal-ties for each volume. In addition, the IHR would incur translation, printing, and advertising costs—a large expenditure that would cost money it did not seem to have.

Any objective observer would have to conclude that the staff's sense of institutional responsibility certainly exceeded Carto's, whose imperi-ous decision making brought the legion ever closer to danger. Yet a cer-tain irony underlay the staff's description of these events: the same editors who had claimed that Nazi gassings had not happened com-plained about their journal's becoming unscholarly. The man to replace Weber was a "past Nazi propagandist." Degrelle was flagrantly pro-Hitler. These adjectives and adverbs were used by a crew anchored by former top cadres in William Pierce's National Alliance, who had gloried in the bloody shadow of the Hitler henchman Otto Ernst Remer and whose journal routinely stepped onto the white side of scholarship. Nevertheless, the staff's delineation of the fiduciary issues dividing the two camps was closer to the mark than the fulminations by Carto, who soon began describing Weber and crew as agents of the Israeli secret service and the Anti-Defamation League of B'nai B'rith. Faced with Carto's implacable opposition, the staff began researching its options.

Two facts quickly became apparent. First, although Willis Carto exer-cised complete control over the Legion for the Survival of Freedom, he had not been an actual member of its board of directors since 1969, when he had resigned. Legally, Carto's corporate power rested solely on his role as the designated "agent" of the board of directors. Second, the staff could find only three board directors formally registered with the state of Texas, where the legion was officially domiciled; and only two of them were listed as officers: LaVonne Furr and her husband, Lewis.[6] It had been fourteen years since LaVonne had handled the legion's affairs from a desk in her apartment. When she left California in 1979, the legion's niche market in Holocaust-related publications had not yet been created. Mel Mermelstein had not yet sued for the fifty-thousand-dollar reward, and Mark Weber was still working for William Pierce. The Institute for Historical Review did not exist in name or fancy. Once she left California, she never returned—either to attend a conference or visit the legion-IHR offices.[7] At this point in 1993, LaVonne and Lewis lived in Arkansas and were increasingly infirm and troubled financially. They had conducted such legion business as they did with Carto while talking over the phone. The staff reached a simple conclusion: the Furrs were the legal linchpin to Carto's decision-making powers.

Carto had managed to obfuscate the precise nature of his relationship to the legion and its board of directors for more than two decades. The mystery he had created had allowed him to survive, even prosper, while involved in one tortuous lawsuit or another during virtually his entire career. Only those inside the palace were in a position to topple the king. The mechanics of the coup in 1993 would determine whether or not the turnover could withstand Carto's legal counterattack in the years to come.

Two months after the April meeting at which Carto had screamed and banged, the staff began contacting the Furrs directly. The first letters and phone calls established a friendly relationship between the two parties. The staff began telling the Furrs about legal liabilities that the legion had incurred because of Carto, particularly those involving violations of copyright protections. These liabilities worried the Furrs, who felt burdened by their own distressed circumstances. But their continued presence on the board did not begin to reach a crisis point until a critical phone call on August 21, 1993. At that point the staff informed the Furrs that Carto had transferred one hundred thousand dollars of legion-IHR funds to Liberty Lobby. He had also distributed funds, by his own account, to other "good causes" as he saw fit. LaVonne Furr told the staff that she objected to these transfers. "He can't do that," she said. "It's not his money." The staff sent the Furrs a package documenting its claims and in a phone call a week later, on August 28, suggested that the elderly couple seek legal advice. LaVonne agreed.

Three weeks later Weber and crew learned that the Furrs had formally resigned from the legion's board on September 16. "The press of current family responsibilities, our ill health, and age urge us to be relieved of any outside obligations," the short and sad six-line letter read.

The staff was prepared. It immediately contacted Tom Kerr, the third name legally registered as a director. Until that moment Kerr had been even less involved than the Furrs in the legion's corporate affairs. But on September 24 he was the sole individual empowered to convene a board meeting, and at the staff's insistence he added three new board members to the legion: Andrew Allen, Friedrich Berg, and John Curry, according to court documents. This new board then appointed new officers from the staff, including Mark Weber as secretary. And in short order they terminated Willis Carto's corporate "agency," the fig leaf behind which he had ruled the legion's affairs.[8]

Carto's first response was to try to undo the Furrs' resignations. But his ham-handedness quickly undid him. Carto asked LaVonne to sign a set of minutes for a meeting (which never took place) on September 16. According to these phony minutes, a meeting was attended by four supposed board members: LaVonne Furr, Lewis Furr, Tom Kerr, and Sam Dickson, the Atlanta attorney who had hosted (alongside Ed Fields) the British National Party führer John Tyndall and otherwise contributed to various racist and anti-Semitic causes. In this piece of Carto's revisionist history, the Furrs resigned only to be replaced by Elisabeth Carto and Henri Fischer, an Australian residing in California who worked closely with the Cartos. For some reason Carto also created a second set of minutes, these for a meeting (which also never took place) on October 25. In these minutes, the September 16 minutes were described as "prepared only for strategic reasons," an admission that the first meeting was a fiction. At this supposed second meeting, LaVonne and Lewis Furr, Tom Kerr, and Sam Dickson were once again in attendance, but this time they were alongside three other names. Once again, the Furrs resigned, only this time they were replaced by Elisabeth and Willis Carto, as well as one other loyalist. In this Alice in Wonderland world, Carto obviously believed the second meeting placing him on the board of directors would forestall the legal ascension of his former underlings and protect his corporate control. But in the real world these fictions had no agency.

Why would Sam Dickson, an attorney with a full understanding of the way boards of directors legally function, even temporarily allow his name to be used for such shenanigans? At least part of the answer may be that Dickson believed that the staff "acted deceitfully and duplicitously." Nevertheless, in a statement to a California court, Dickson later acknowledged that he had not been present at any board meetings—on either September 16 or October 25.[9] And early in the dispute he offered to mediate between the warring parties. The staff, by its own account, accepted his offer. Willis Carto, however, immediately went into court, attempting to void the board of directors constructed by his usurpers and install his own board instead.

After two days of hearings in the Orange County Superior Court, on December 31, 1993, Judge Robert J. Polis ruled decisively for Mark Weber and the staff. The staff-friendly board, appointed on September 24, legitimately governed the organization and was now fully empowered. Carto's board was out, but one simple adverse court decision could not convince him to surrender.

Unlike Ben Klassen, who had once hoped that young skinheads would inherit his legacy and who then committed suicide, Carto would not go quietly into the political night. Among other assets at stake was a bequest to the legion of $7.5 million. He had battled in courts on two continents for more than five years to secure these funds, and Willis Allison Carto was not going to let go of them now.

Jean Farrel and $7.5 Million

Seven and a half million dollars is a lot of money on anybody's books. To a marginal sales operation like the IHR, it might have ensured long-term viability. To Jean Farrel, an American with Colombian citizenship living in Switzerland, the $7.5 million was less than half her estate, which totaled more than $16 million at the time of her death. An enigmatic figure, Farrel, born in 1920, kept her financial affairs and personal life as private as possible. Farrel, whose mother's maiden name was Edison, remained single throughout her life and often used Edison as her surname. In fact, she signed her will Jean Farrel Edison. (The Edison name often led to her being described—by IHR associates and others—as a scion of the inventor, Thomas Alva Edison, either his grandniece or granddaughter.) Despite her expatriation, Farrel apparently maintained an active interest in the American far right, including the IHR. In 1983 she had started corresponding with Willis Carto over the best method to protect her huge financial holdings from unnamed "sharks in the background who would destroy me."[10]

As a result, she decided, in an extraordinarily complex maneuver, to place her assets in a corporation registered in Liberia, NECA. Ownership of NECA was controlled by twenty stock certificates scattered in safety-deposit boxes around the globe: eight shares at Crédit Suisse Lausanne near her home in Lutry, Switzerland; three shares at a bank in Henderson County, North Carolina; three more in London; three in Singapore; and three shares at Volksbank in Herford, Germany, the birthplace of Elisabeth Waltraud Carto. Her other assets, which included gold, coins, diamonds, and precious stones, were similarly distributed. Willis Carto claimed to have keys to the safety-deposit boxes and obviously expected one day to control NECA's assets.[11]

Farrel periodically sent six-thousand-dollar donations to the IHR during the early 1980s.[12] The staff also gave her a grand tour when she visited the California offices in 1984. Carto believed a large bequest was eventually on its way. Seventeen months later, on August 11, 1985, the sixty-five-year-old Farrel died suddenly at her home in Switzerland. The same distrust that had led her to form NECA in the first place and to scatter proof of its ownership across the globe was written into her will. She asked that someone watch over her body for five days before burial, to ensure that she was in fact deceased. It also stipulated a "simple and raw" wooden coffin and a short funeral without any Christian rites. Despite Carto's expectations to the contrary, only one "universal heir" was named: a Swiss woman named Joan Althaus. Only if Althaus was incapable of fulfilling her duty as executor did the will designate the Legion for the Survival of Freedom as secondary heir.[13]

Farrel was gone, but the fight over her legacy was just beginning. Upon learning of her death, Carto rushed to take control of the safety-deposit boxes. Banks have rules, however, and attorneys for Joan Althaus were making the same claim on the same assets. Carto needed to do more than just show up with a key. He tried several avenues of approach. His first correspondence to the North Carolina bank was done in the name of "NECA Corporation," for example, with an address in California and Carto on the letterhead as "president." He claimed that the contents of the safety boxes were not part of Farrel's estate (and therefore subject to probate) but were owned exclusively by NECA. A month later, after the bank's vice president turned aside Carto's claims, he shamelessly changed tack. In a letter to the same bank officer written on the same NECA letterhead, Carto argued that "the box in your bank is the sole property of the Legion."[14]

Over the next five years, Carto, representing himself as the agent of the Legion for the Survival of Freedom's board of directors, fought tenaciously in the corporation's name. He went to courts in North Carolina, London, and Switzerland to void the will. He mustered affidavits, sought control of the safety boxes, and countered every one of Joan Althaus's legal maneuvers with his own. Finally, on July 17, 1990, the battle ended. Althaus could war no more, while Carto's ability to fight in the courts seemed endless. She settled the dispute. The distribution agreement, filed in Switzerland, was a compromise. Althaus received 55 percent of the estate. The Legion for the Survival of Freedom received 45 percent, or $7,585,189, which was delivered to a Swiss public notary to be held in trust.

At that point, Carto alone knew that a deal had been finally completed. By 1993, however, the IHR staff had learned that Carto had secured the money. They launched the coup with full knowledge that the generational battle for corporate control of the Legion for the Survival of Freedom was a fight for these funds. And with Judge Polis's initial decision in the case, the courts seemed to be lodged completely against Carto's claim. Ultimately, the entire affair brought down his Liberty Lobby empire and marched him off the movement's main stage. He did not immediately relinquish the money, however, or anything else. He still believed that History was standing with him.

PART

Against the
New World Order,
1994–1996

Opposition to the New World Order invigorates the civic debate about national identity. The issue of immigration directly poses the question of who "we" are. A set of counterinstitutions, including militias, pose a challenge to the authority of government. But the Oklahoma City bombing starts a chain of events that reverses gains made by vanguardists, while the mainstreamers thrive.

The Common Law Courts, Partners to the Militia

January 27, 1994. On this day in the former Yugoslavia, Serbian military forces prepared to crush their Bosnian opposition in the Drina river valley. In South Africa's first free election the apartheid regime's last white president, F. W. de Klerk, campaigned in the Eastern Transvaal. In Mexico, Zapatista guerrillas consolidated control over villages seized in a rebellion that had started on New Year's Day, when NAFTA treaty provisions went into effect. In Virginia, Oliver North opened his bid for the U.S. Senate, notwithstanding a conviction for obstructing Congress during the Reagan-era contragate hearings. In Texas federal court a Treasury Department agent testified about his undercover assignment inside the Branch Davidian compound at Waco.[1] And in the empty stretches of Montana, three dozen desperate white men began a revolt that helped trigger a mass-style insurgency. They called themselves Freemen, and eventually landed in jail. But not before a prolonged siege by the FBI rekindled memories of both Randy Weaver and Waco.

Jordan, Montana, is a double-wide spot in the road, the government seat of Garfield County. Across this county, fourteen hundred residents are spread in an area four times larger than the state of Rhode Island (with its population of almost one million). Here the armed Freemen pushed their way past the county's court clerk and into the main hearing room. They convened a so-called common law court with all the pomp and ceremony available.[2] One Freeman acted as presiding judge, while another served as a prosecutor. The offending party was absent, of course. Nevertheless, this group conducted itself like a duly constituted jury. It produced paper documents that it claimed were lawfully binding writs, liens against property, and warrants, even notarizing them with its own seal.

The cause of the invasion was petty, a family dispute. A local judge had ruled against one of the Freemen's kin in a divorce proceeding. Nothing the Freemen could do that day could change anything related to the divorce. Even so, the Freemen walked away satisfied that a true, lawful de jure court had met. "We have the law back in the county now," the so-called presiding judge declared at the end of the pseudoceremony.[3] "Supreme Court of Garfield County comitatus," they called it.

The county's actual law enforcement officers—a sheriff and two deputies—did not try to bar the intruders. Instead, they videotaped the event. The county attorney, a part-time employee working in his office a half block down the street, came rushing over to watch the common law court from the sidelines. After the event the courthouse clerk knew enough to ignore the bogus liens or writs the Freemen produced that day. Nevertheless, for that moment, in that place, the Freemen challenged local officials with their own authority. In time, such actions would constitute a virtual dual power.

The appearance of Freemen in Montana in 1994 testified to the persistence of ideologies with their roots in the Posse Comitatus and the mixture of Christian Identity theology and Dred Scott constitutionalism upon which the Posse had rested. It had been eleven years since Gordon Kahl shot two federal marshals in North Dakota and turned the Posse Comitatus from a tax protest and farm gate battle cry into a newspaper headline. One Freeman explicitly asserted this connection between common law courts in the 1990s and the Posse Comitatus of previous decades. "Our law of posse comitatus," he wrote, "is derived from 'Holy Scriptures.'"[4] Here they distinguished between the rights of white Christian citizens and those of nonwhite, non-Christian residents. Accordingly, the former received their rights from God, while the latter supposedly derived citizenship from the Fourteenth Amendment. Thus the Freemen vowed allegiance to a white republic, much like those who had signed the Nehemiah Township charter in 1982.

The Freemen did not invent Christian Identity. Long before they crashed the door at the Garfield County courthouse, this theology had sanctified everything from family-style Bible camps to clandestine killing. While casting the heavens in a presumed racial order, it named a particular Satan who conspired against its Lord. And at every common law seminar, the Freemen studied Identity, spreading its message like worthless bank drafts. This crew adhered to the hard-edged so-called two seed version. In this fiction Jews personally incarnated Satan on earth. For white people to stay true to their Lord, they had to choose between making covenants with the devil and establishing a common law "pursuant to the Word of Almighty God." The Freemen wrote this Identity doctrine into their documents again and again, as if they were bar association attorneys citing case law in a pleading. One twenty-page paper on "Israel/Appointing Power" rambled on with a punctuation and capitalization style that only the initiated understood. Yet within a paragraph it restated the fundamentals of the Posse Comitatus doctrine:

> How many of the People of Israel [Adam/white race] have rejected the words of Almighty God and rejected their "**faith**" [surety] **in Almighty God**, to worship man made laws; "**color or law**", such as applying for a 'social security card/number'; marriage licenses, drivers' licenses, insurance, vehicle registration, welfare from the corporations, electrical inspections, permits to build your private home, income taxes, property taxes, inheritance taxes, etc., etc., etc.,

In essence, they argued much like the Posse Comitatus–influenced engineer at Cheney Lake in 1983 who claimed that a white person with a Social Security number could not attain the "status" of a (white) free man.[5] Accordingly, inalienable rights belong only to "we the people," the population mentioned in the Constitution's Preamble. In this view, all others were like the slaves who gained their citizenship from the Fourteenth Amendment. Those people had lesser rights, devolved only from the government. By contrast, most legal scholars and historians trace an ever-expanding tradition of individual liberties from the Magna Carta to the U.S. Constitution and amendments, leading from the divine right of kings to representative democracy in a republican form of government. For the Freemen, however, this trajectory was about racial lineage, not developing institutions. The biblical tribes of Israel, the Anglo-Saxons of medieval England, and American white people all were hung from the same single genetic strain. By this account, the Book of Deuteronomy, the Magna Carta, and the Constitution are all God's Law written only for God's People.

As odd as it sounded in 1994, this particular reading of the Constitution was rooted in the United States' founding moments. From the beginning of European settlement in North America, two different visions of citizenship, the political state and national identity, have contended for hegemony. One view sought a country without inherited privileges, envisioned a citizenry with unalienable rights and a government of all the people. According to a competing view, African slaves had no rights that a white man needed to respect. Neither did the Native Americans.

And while the political state granted citizenship rights to non-Christians and eventually to former slaves and their progeny, according to this second view, the real American nation and its cultural expressions remained Anglo-European (and Christian). The adherents of this second view are, in effect, if not always self-consciously, white nationalists. They may have tolerated a multiracial federal state, like Serbs in multinational Yugoslavia during the Tito era, but they never fully accepted it. Like ethnic nationalists seeking separation from a multiethnic Bosnia, the Freemen sought to establish themselves as an entity distinct from the multiracial United States.

This was the nasty white thread running through barrels of Freemen ink. It connected the phony court documents they filed on everything from family civil matters to computer-generated larcenous bank drafts. The United States is peopled by two nations, they argued, not one: "American nationals" (or organic sovereigns) versus "U.S. citizens." The latter, they said, were unfortunate denizens of a corporation headquartered in Washington, D.C. This attack on the Fourteenth Amendment is the core of the Freemen ideology and the basis of their specious reasoning about the other issues on their minds, such as the Uniform Commercial Code. If the original white republic no longer existed according to congressional statute, then the Freemen denied the "lawfulness" of that legislation and the supporting constitutional amendments.

Over a several-year period, the Freemen established themselves inside Montana community life. In one instance a town's mayor became a member. In another, authorities shied away from arresting Freemen for fear of provoking an armed conflict. And at moments they came dangerously close to their goal of establishing themselves as a dual power, with authority rivaling that of local and federal governments. Their Montana garrisons became the most important transfer points in a network whose strongest links stretched from the Northwest to the Midwest and south to Oklahoma and Texas. An estimated eight hundred camp followers attended their classes on convening common law courts and then used fake court writs to write fraudulent bank documents. Six men from Columbus, Ohio, for example, spent four days in Garfield County and then established a common law court back home. In another instance, a former state prison guard returned from a Freemen "school of learning" and set up courts in Kansas. One organizational descendant of the Freemen called itself the Republic of Texas and claimed to reestablish the original white republic there. A band from Oklahoma called itself United Sovereigns of America and joined in 1995 with the Colorado veterinarian Gene Schroder to convene, in Wichita, Kansas, a common law convention of five hundred activists from across the country, further boosting the Freemen's ideas and the common law court phenomenon.[6]

Model Militia in Montana

Another early admirer of the Freemen was a group with a similar ideological lineage, the Militia of Montana. According to this militia, the Freemen had discovered the essence of "our fore-fathers plan for self-government." The militia newsletter repeated the Freemen's core argument: a fundamental constitutional distinction existed between white Christians and others. "If you are a Fourteenth Amendment citizen then you have inalienable rights which can be liened. If you are a sovereign 'Freemen' then you have unalienable rights which cannot be liened."[7] Upon this mutually asserted citizenship, the common law court and militia movements combined to assert a white nationalism at odds with the federal government. Like the double helix at the heart of a DNA molecule, militias and common law courts would spin and thread through each other from Montana to Texas and from Oregon to Florida, with a single white chromosome at the root of a diversified complex of movement organs and tissues.

The Militia of Montana's chief figure, John Trochmann, filed his own declaration of common law citizenship in 1992. Like the Freemen, he claimed a local court had no jurisdiction over him because he was an organic "sovereign"—that is, a free white Christian male whose rights trumped the Fourteenth Amendment.[8] And in 1992 he declared himself to hold a Freemen-like "sovereign" status.

With a bushy beard and wild eyes, Trochmann looked like the apparition of a nineteenth-century mountain man. In fact, he was a former Minnesota snowmobile salesman, a shrewd operator looking for his next main chance. Trochmann's extended family had settled during the mid-1980s in Sanders County, Montana, a remote 2,749-square-mile mountainous expanse populated by fewer than nine thousand souls, 98.5 percent of whom were classified as white in the 1980 census. Only 45 percent were native Montanans.[9] The mix of settlers included 1960s-style countercultural leftovers, as well as white supremacists gathering for a future Northwest Republic. The Trochmanns gained a small measure of local notoriety by distributing Christian Identity and so-called constitutionalist pamphlets.[10] John Trochmann also attended several Aryan Nations conclaves at the Idaho campground, speaking at the 1990 session. There he met a fellow resettled midwesterner, Randy Weaver, and the two families became friends.[11]

When the FBI siege started on Weaver's mountain, the Trochmanns joined the protest at the police barricades. After the siege, John attended Pete Peters's stage-setting conference of "Christian men" in Estes Park, Colorado, though he did not speak from the dais or otherwise make a name for himself.[12] After the meeting, however, Trochmann transformed himself from a pamphleteer in his own home region into a creative and energetic national leader. When Louis Beam and Chris Temple kick-started the United Citizens for Justice to press Weaver's case with the public, Trochmann became a cochair alongside Temple. Despite the self-evident fact that Weaver was a white supremacist of the Christian Identity persuasion, the United Citizens had (successfully) pressed the case that the hapless ridge sitter was simply a harmless white "separatist."

After Weaver's exoneration at trial in July 1993, Trochmann might have returned to local obscurity. It had been Temple and Beam, after all, not Trochmann, who most clearly articulated a new post–Ruby Ridge two-stage strategy. Trochmann, however, became the new strategy's more accomplished practitioner. Almost as if he were following instructions from Chris Temple's Estes Park speech, Trochmann aimed at the federal government first. The racial "strangers" targeted by Aryan Nations could wait for a second stage. Trochmann's bushy-bearded face became synonymous with the militia at small-town meetings, gun shows, and preparedness expos. At a Senate subcommittee hearing, he claimed his militia was simply the Montana version of a neighborhood watch. To reporters, he sold himself as an average American, angry with the federal government.

The Trochmann clan certainly handled its share of weapons and ammunition, but John Trochmann did his best podium pounding in public. In this sphere only a few others rivaled his notoriety and his gift for making nonsense sound as if it were God's truth. During the first months of 1994, he crisscrossed Montana's small towns and villages, holding open meetings in local schools and halls as if he were selling memberships in the Grange. These were not suit-and-tie affairs, with stuffy European atmospheres like those held behind closed doors by the Institute for Historical Review. Neither did they require long nights of travel out of state, like Liberty Lobby or Populist Party events. These were blue-collar and plaid shirt meets held in a familiar venue with speakers in the most American of tongues. Trochmann drew hundreds to long descriptions of various perceived threats: gun control and the federal government, of course, but also the United Nations and World Bank. Almost always, a foreign invasion was imminent. He could make long lists of individual facts, but his whole speech was always less than the sum of the parts, a classic sign of what Richard Hofstadter called a "paranoid style" of politics. (As Hofstadter used it, the label was neither a clinical diagnosis nor an ideological statement, but a description of a certain type of political fashion.) The underlying message was defense of hearth and homeland from menacing forces emanating from a cabal of New World Order globalists. No true (white) American would want to surrender to the United Nations.

Trochmann's Militia of Montana was the "mother of all militias," as one reporter trenchantly wrote.[13] The actual relationship of this founder of this militia to white supremacy and the Aryan Nations became a question of moment. Like others seeking more mainstream acceptance, including Randy Weaver, Sam Dickson, and David Duke, Trochmann always denied that he was a white supremacist. Asked about his Christian Identity beliefs, he claimed not to hold them. Asked about his speeches at Aryan Nations meetings, he would say he was just warning the campers of the dangers of race hatred. As militiamen spread across the media and gained a public hearing, the nature of Trochmann's core beliefs—and by extension the militia's founding ideology—became a point of public interest.

One commentator argued that although Trochmann had attended three or four Aryan Nations meetings, this was "hardly a fair criterion for membership." Further, he wrote that "racist ideas were conspicuously absent" from Trochmann's public presentations. The point being, this person wrote, the role of racism in the militia should not be overemphasized.[14]

The Aryan Nations staff at the Idaho compound took a completely different point of view and issued its own press release about Trochmann's denials. "Why lie about the number of times here, especially when you came over several times for Bible Studies?" Aryan Nations asked of Trochmann. "John, you even helped us write out a set of rules for our code of conduct on the church grounds. For all the problems you claim you found at the Church . . . why did you immediately move skinheads to your place and then whine about the conduct? Maybe you're just a first class whiner when things don't suit you."[15] To this charge from Aryan Nations, Trochmann was left, essentially, without a reply.

With or without Trochmann, the roots of this phenomenon lay in the white supremacist movement. Taking a look back, Daniel Levitas's book *The Terrorist Next Door* described in minute detail the Posse-like ideological spine at the center of both the militia and its Siamese twin, the common law courts. Though the militias of the Clinton era were direct descendants of the Gordon Kahl–era Posse Comitatus, these two movements were not identical, according to Levitas. Tax protest in the 1970s and the farm crisis of the 1980s had fueled the Posse. By the 1990s the farm movement had been recaptured by progressive farm organizations, and the few Posse farmers still active had no influence. Gun rights and national sovereignty, not grain prices and farm policy, filled the air like fertilizer and fuel oil waiting to explode.

Three events precipitated the rebirth of the militia movement: the FBI siege at Ruby Ridge in September 1992, the Waco inferno eight months later, and President Clinton's 1993 signing of the gun control Brady Bill, which sent National Rifle Association members and the like into apoplexy.[16]

Militiamen told themselves that their Second Amendment right to keep and bear arms was being unconstitutionally abridged and that the Weaver family and Branch Davidians had been made targets by virtue of their religion. Militias were never simply a bunch of conspiracy mongers with guns, however. Rather, they asserted a particularized (white) nationalism, couched as opposition to the New World Order. It was upon this basis that the militia spread quickly across the country.

First in Idaho and Montana, next in Michigan and the Midwest, and then into the Confederate South and every other region, militiamen popped up like cardboard targets on a rapid-fire shooting range. The gunners outstripped the paper hangers from the common law courts. Dozens of local and regional militia leaders emerged and then faded, only to be replaced by new paramilitary enthusiasts. Bo Gritz's presidential campaign promoted militias for the purposes of "preparedness" and "survival." He talked constantly about "ballots in 1992 or bullets in 1996." And he turned himself into one of the militia's biggest megaphones.[17] In this environment, newsletters flourished like antiwar rags on college campuses in the 1960s. A half dozen periodical magazines and tabloids gained a national readership, although none rivaled *The Spotlight* for paid circulation. Militia groups built websites, used shortwave radio programming, and distributed videotapes. The militia became the most significant mass-style phenomenon of its kind since the 1960s, when white supremacist gunners had shot, burned, and bombed in defense of Jim Crow.

The word "militia" became an eponym, a proper noun changed into a common reference for so-called antigovernment radicals, much the way the term "Klan" had once referred only to a specific organizational subspecies but that with widespread use had become an uncapitalized reference to white racists in general. The actual militia membership became conflated with the much-larger numbers of preparedness buffs, gun enthusiasts, and active sympathizers. The militia face became so familiar that even those who could not describe the difference between a .38-caliber revolver and a 9-millimeter pistol understood that guns had become once again a symbol of resistance, this time to a specter known as the New World Order. Thousands of articles by hundreds of journalists created a public record of militia activity. Unlike Aryan bandits such as The Order, which protected itself with a veil of clandestinity, these gun toters flashed themselves into the public's eye as symbols of mass resistance. For the first time in ten years, white men carrying assault rifles allowed themselves to be photographed and videotaped. Television news programs found militias irresistible. Weekly and monthly magazines covered militias on one page and news about FBI wrongdoing at Waco and Weaver's mountain on the next. Militia spokesmen often sounded as if they were indicting the government for hate crimes, and much of the public's discourse accepted the militia's self-description at face value. United States senators called militiamen to testify and accorded them the graciousness of a national platform.

They emblazoned themselves with icons of colonial-era minutemen, dressed in camouflage fatigues, carried assault rifles, and often gave themselves military-style titles—Colonel This, Major That. Many militia groups were actually private armies of the type proscribed by laws in most states. If these cammie-coated ivories had been black-jacketed ebonies marching through the woods and firing armor-piercing cop-killing ammunition, the entire movement would not have lasted five minutes, much less five years. Yet not one state militia was ever prosecuted as a private army. Only after Timothy McVeigh and others known and unknown killed 168 men, women, and children with one bomb in Oklahoma City did the militia and the weapons-trafficking subculture surrounding it receive any special attention from law enforcement officials.

On the continuum between mainstream electioneering at one end and subcultural vanguardism at the other, the militia and common law court phenomena existed somewhere in between, at a point that might be called mass resistance. Unlike vote-seeking campaigners such as David Duke, the militia and the Freemen took up arms and repeatedly expressed their willingness to use them. But rather than dive deep into national socialist ideology and iconography, they expressed themselves in the most American of terms and used symbols such as the minutemen at Concord to identify their nationalist heritage. Much like civil disobedience activists of other movements past, they urged defiance of existing laws—regulations of gun ownership and private armies and use of judicial proceedings and banking practices. They defined themselves as counterinstitutions to those that demarcated the political state: law enforcement agencies and the military as well as legal and financial authorities. And in places where they held some measure of communal power, either through sheer force of numbers or through intimidation of their foes, both the common law courts and militias existed as an embryonic (and revolutionary) dual power.

Whether or not militiamen and common law court activists believed the Holocaust happened, whether or not they used slur words to describe black people, whether or not they wanted to send nonwhite people and race traitors into the proverbial desert, the militia in the 1990s marched to the same drumbeat that other bands of white paramilitarists had heard before them.

Those who actually formed militias rested their rationale on a notion of state citizenship that fundamentally "predated" and opposed itself to the federal citizenship of the Fourteenth Amendment. Many militia groups consciously adopted the organic sovereign status, whereby only white Christians had natural inalienable citizenship rights. A few militia groups did not explicitly justify themselves by such Dred Scott reasoning. However, they did alternatively predicate themselves on a notion of states' rights and state citizenship at odds with the Fourteenth Amendment, enforcement of which is the single most important *constitutional* roadblock to the restoration of a Jim Crow–style white republic. And citizenship status of course is a central element when delineating one nation or nation-state from another.

Birth of *American Renaissance*

May 28, 1994. At first glance it appears to be another quiet suit-and-tie meeting at the Atlanta airport Hilton Hotel. University professors, journalists, and religious leaders deliver academic-styled lectures in the most convivial of fashions. Instead of the fervid secrecy and thick European atmospherics attending gatherings on topics such as "Race and Civilization," this conference, held under the auspices of a newsletter entitled *American Renaissance*, exhibits a relative openness. No loud white power rockers chant in locked arm unison. No skinhead tattoos. No swastika armbands or white robes. No Populist Party faction works the room, although a savvy, newly emergent group known as the Council of Conservative Citizens unmistakably holds the franchise on the sidelines. Neither Willis Carto nor William Pierce attends. Neither the Federal Reserve System nor the Holocaust is on this agenda. Nevertheless, Mark Weber and a small gaggle of Institute for Historical Review regulars dot the room. Ed Fields sits quietly. No one needs his flush-faced oratory here, but he is not the only cow pasture cross burner in the hotel. David Duke mills about the restaurant, a candidate without a campaign, telling whoever will listen of his plans to write a book. As the proceedings begin, however, the conveners close the door on Duke. He is not welcome. Instead, a small band of obviously Orthodox Jews, identifiably dressed in black suits, hats, and beards, enter the room alongside 150 others committed to white supremacy.[1]

A few speakers set the event's tone. Among them was Sam Dickson. Despite the presence of Jews at this particular event, the Atlanta area attorney was no stranger to the world of the politically *Judenfrei*. In the past he had operated a small Historical Review outfit in Georgia and had attended at least one Institute for Historical Review conference in California. He had danced British führer John Tyndall across the Atlantic in 1991 and supported Pat Buchanan in 1992. Nevertheless, Dickson was as gracious as any southern gentleman could be and treated the Jewish speakers with deference and respect. Not even a euphemistic mention about "our traditional enemies" passed his lips. Instead, Dickson simply affirmed the theme of the meeting. "To me the whole idea of racial equality was preposterous from childhood," he averred.[2] Over the course of the weekend it was stated and restated by others, with nuance and without: black people were mentally inferior, genetically prone to violent crime, and biologically unfit to live as social and political equals among whites.

Dickson's unique contribution was a droll sarcastic wit. His target: white liberals. He turned the verbal tables by using psychologically loaded language to lampoon left-wing activism, the same lingo that liberals often used to describe the "paranoid" right wing. Ever since the *Brown v. Topeka Board of Education* decision, he said, the consensus view had been that racists were emotionally disturbed, perhaps best institutionalized for the benefit of society. The truth was the reverse. "Liberalism is a form of mental disorder," he drawled. "It is a neurosis or a psychosis that has swept the world." Among other emotional problems, liberals exhibited an unreasonable mania. They protested this cause and that, nonstop. "And they're meeting constantly, and writing and printing and picketing. I mean these people have an abnormally elevated energy level," Dickson chuckled. Worse, liberals were undaunted by failure. Look at public education, he said. Is there any evidence that "race mixing" has improved the lot of anyone? Of course not![3]

Sam Francis, the former Senate aide turned conservative think tank analyst cum *Washington Times* columnist, also stood at this podium. Francis displayed little of Dickson's dramatic delivery, but he packed twice the analytical punch. Unlike Dickson, the Middle American philosopher-general had always eschewed dalliances with crass *anti-Semitica*, like that at the Institute for Historical Review. As Pat Buchanan marched through the primaries two years before, however, Francis had tried honing the inchoate revolt against Republican conservatism into an ever more tightly defined white nationalism. For the purposes of this meeting, he made two points.

First, American civilization was a white (biologically determined) racial civilization. "The civilization that we as whites created in Europe and America could not have developed apart from the genetic endowments of the creating people," he told the *Renaissance* audience. "Nor is there any reason to believe that the civilization can be successfully transmitted to a different people." In Francis's mind, those descended from African slaves, Chinese railroad workers, Mexican peasants, and Native Americans had few claims on American nationality. He added a caveat to the point: race alone could not explain "historical and social affairs," but without "racial, biological and genetic explanations" nations could not exist. Second, Francis contended that while white people existed objectively, "whites do not exist subjectively because they do not think of themselves as whites."[4] Ergo his task at hand was the development of white consciousness in explicitly racial terms.

During the entire post–World War Two, post-*Brown* era, similar ideas had animated white supremacists of every stripe, usually coupled with an explicitly anti-Semitic set of corollaries. Willis Carto had argued a link between race and civilization in his early pseudonymous article on Evotism. William Pierce had predicated a Leninist-style vanguard on Francis's second point: white people's lack of race consciousness rendered them incapable of saving themselves without National Alliance's leadership. Unlike Pierce, however, Francis counted European Jews among the ranks of white people, and unlike Carto, Francis found anti-Semitic conspiracy theories an annoying distraction from real politics. As a consequence, Francis believed the presence of a few Jews did not necessarily detract from his white nationalist cause.

Rabbi Mayer Schiller proved the point. A forty-three-year-old native of Brooklyn and long-time educator, he taught Talmud and coached the hockey team at Yeshiva University High School in Manhattan. At the same time, Schiller pursued a virtual second career as a self-proclaimed "white separatist," speaking alongside black nationalists and "third way" revolutionaries in England and meeting with Afrikaner neo-Nazis in South Africa. As a featured speaker at a conference of conservative Jews and Christians set by Rabbi Daniel Lapin's Toward Tradition, Schiller later decried "egalitarianism" and the supposed destruction of the white race, unusual claims at a meeting featuring Ralph Reed and other Republican luminaries. However, at the Atlanta meet Schiller's speech added little to the mix. If anything, he simply restated an assemblage of racist propositions already familiar to all. He assailed Vatican II Catholicism and lamented William Buckley and *National Review*'s retreat from the segregationist cause. The black-hatted rabbi from New York urged this congregation of unreconstructed southerners to read books about Confederate generals to their children. (Perhaps that is the true definition of "chutzpah.") His one unique contribution to the weekend was a theory of Western Civilization's five sources—"Sinai, Bethlehem, Greece, Rome and the Northland"—thus writing Jews, and himself, into this version of whiteness.[5]

.   .   .

The presence of Schiller and the half dozen other Jews testified to the originality and genius of the conference's motivating personality, Samuel Jared Taylor, and the particular brand of white nationalism he pursued.[6] A handsome, even elegant son of the South, he was born to missionaries and raised in Japan, where he attended public school, rendering American English a virtual second language to him. He graduated from Yale University in 1973 and then continued his education outside the United States, receiving his master's degree from the Institute for Political Studies in Paris. Later he worked as an international loan officer and then as a consultant for American businesses with interests in Japan.[7] A respectable New York publisher, Quill—William Morrow, issued his first book, *Shadows of the Rising Sun: A Critical View of the Japanese Miracle*, in 1983. Taylor worked as *PC* magazine's West Coast editor in the mid-1980s, at just the moment when Silicon Valley technologies were entering middle-class markets.[8] He obviously did not go over to the white side out of a sense of economic disenchantment, and he exhibited nothing of the paranoid style or apocalyptic fever so often attributed to white nationalists. But his beliefs were no less firmly held because he did not conform to the common stereotype of a "hater."

Taylor began his public foray into the white nationalist arena with a newsletter he edited called *American Renaissance*. The first issue was dated November 1990, one month after Germany's formal unification and just at the cusp of epochal change. Although the newsletter was about the size of a skinhead zine, ten pages, and was similarly obsessed with race, any resemblance between the two publication types stopped there. *Renaissance* advertised itself to readers as a "literate, undeceived, journal of race, immigration, and the decline of civility." In tone, topic, and style it most closely resembled *Instauration* magazine, minus Wilmot Robertson's fixation on Jews. *Renaissance*'s first front page owed a direct debt to Robertson's concept of white dispossession. "In another half century, if whites continue to cooperate in their own dispossession, this nation will have no core and no identity," the newsletter opined, as if a transformation from majority to minority status also meant white people would lose their passports.[9]

Thus Taylor began reasserting a pale-skinned Americanism at precisely the moment that changes in geopolitical alignments had precipitated a transformation of the role nationalism played on the global stage. A nation, Taylor's newsletter noted, was not simply an undifferentiated "crowd" of people. It must have a common "culture, language, history and aspirations."[10] Race was not mentioned directly. That would come later. But as *American Renaissance* began to appear every month without fail, it began to attract readers. And it was under the rubric of the newsletter project that the Atlanta meeting was being held.

While editing the newsletter, Taylor also finished writing a second book, *Paved with Good Intentions: The Failure of Race Relations in Contemporary America.* Like his book on Japan, *Paved* was published by a well-regarded house, Carroll & Graf, and received mainstream attention. *The Wall Street Journal* published a gushing review that concluded: "Mr. Taylor's book is easily the most comprehensive indictment of the race-conscious civil rights policies of the past three decades."[11] Peter Brimelow, a senior editor at *Forbes* magazine, was even more forcefully favorable in *National Review*. Racism against black people had disappeared, Brimelow argued, only to be replaced by racism against whites.[12] Brimelow later lamented that the fact that "this book did not transform public debate on this topic is a signal condemnation of American intellectual life."[13] Other reviews were less sympathetic, and a few were scathing. Taylor appeared on Pat Buchanan's *Crossfire* television program during the book's initial promotion cycle. The attention focused on Taylor turned him into a figure on the edge of conservative discourse, with a place in American literary life that the positive review he received in Willis Carto's *Spotlight* could not alone have engendered.

Paved was written as if from the vantage point of a disappointed liberal. It began with a feint toward Gunnar Myrdal's classic formulation of race as an American dilemma and acknowledged the centuries of oppression of Native Americans and exploitation of African slaves. "No one would argue that America is free of racism. A nation that enslaved blacks, freed them only after a terrible war, disenfranchised them, segregated them, lynched them—such a nation cannot entirely free itself from its past." But sixteen pages into the text he declared the problem essentially solved, at least as far as the prejudices and practices of white people were concerned: "Though America is by no means perfect, racism is no longer central to its national character." Three hundred and fifty pages of anecdotes and analysis later, it was overwhelmingly evident that Taylor believed that centuries of white supremacy had been replaced in a single generation by "white guilt" and "reverse racism." After passage of the Voting Rights Act and other civil rights laws in the 1960s, he decided, any remaining problems of race lay with the inadequacies of black people.

Taylor eventually coupled up with Evelyn Rich, who came to the partnership with her own understanding of white supremacy.[14] Born in Scotland, Rich began her university education in England and received her bachelor's degree from Lafayette College in Pennsylvania. She

earned a doctorate in history from Boston College in 1988. Her dissertation topic: "Ku Klux Klan Ideology: 1954–1988."[15] While doing research, Rich had formally interviewed many of the white supremacist
movement's leading figures, attended semipublic events such as Institute for Historical Review conferences and Bob Miles's fests, and been
privy to a number of meetings, including a one-to-one visit between
David Duke and William Pierce.[16] Rich seemed to have a particularly
intense interest in Duke, whose Knights of the Ku Klux Klan loomed
large in her dissertation.

On each of these occasions, she would tape her interviews and take
extensive notes and then share notes and transcripts, along with her observations and analyses, with several civic organizations that monitored
racist and anti-Semitic activities.[17] To the anti-Klan groups, she reported with a scholar's precision on the ideological arcana of each organization she encountered. With the scalding sarcasm of late-night
television comics, she recounted several bouts of movement infighting.
And with an apparently anti-racist perspective, she detailed the failures
of the individuals she met. Of one activist she wrote: "[He] seems to be
on the fringe of just about everything, but at the center of nothing. He
is a 3rd degree Mason, a former communist party member and presently
a member of NAAWP." This particular individual, she noted, was "very
impatient and keen to get in on some 'action.'"[18]

Rich grasped the subject of her inquiry like few others, including the
national socialist character of Duke's ideas in the 1970s and the role
anti-Semitism played in transforming a backward-looking Klan movement into a revolutionary vanguard. When her dissertation was completed in 1988, Rich understood that after conservative racists publicly
tarred themselves with the brush of anti-Semitism, their claims to mainstream respectability were compromised.

Eventually Rich's interview transcripts became part of the library
archives at Tulane University in Louisiana, and when David Duke ran
for governor in 1991, Rich lent her name to the anti-Duke opposition.
Particularly revealing segments of her audiotapes were broadcast as part
of anti-Duke radio commercials. Nevertheless, Rich continued to keep
her reports to the anti-Klanners quiet.[19]

At some point Evelyn Rich must have dropped any scholarly distance
she had from white nationalists. She attended the Atlanta meeting that
May in 1994 alongside Jared Taylor, quietly tending to their first child
while he carried on the conference. Rumors swirled around the room
about "Taylor's wife." One held that the couple had met at an Institute
for Historical Review conference in California; if true, that meant Taylor, despite keeping Holocaust revisionism off the agenda, had more

than a passing acquaintance with its claims.[20] True or not, Rich's antipathy to David Duke was well known; it was also rumored that she had suggested the once and future candidate be excluded. None of the rumors suggested that just a few years earlier she had been making notes on meetings such as these and sharing her observations with the movement's opposition. Soon, however, Mark Weber used quotes from Evelyn in the IHR's promotional material, although the spelling of her name varied from time to time. On one brochure, "Dr. Evelyn *Fitch*" described revisionists as "Intelligent, rational, objective people."[21] On another, the author of that same quote was "Dr. Evelyn *Rich*."[22] Despite this declaration of support for IHR personalities, Rich's actual sympathies remained a subject of some speculation.[23]

American Renaissance's debut conference marked the beginnings of a more mature, less adolescent white nationalist movement: open, not furtive, self-assured rather than boastful, and smart rather than sophomoric. Its proceedings were semipublic, followed by a press conference and the sale of audio- and videotapes of the presentations, a stark contrast when compared to the secretive cadres-only sessions William Pierce's National Alliance convened. This forum also differed from other events that were relatively accessible, such as Willis Carto's Liberty Lobby conventions. There speakers were less scholarly, and self-conscious debate was eschewed in favor of celebratory hoopla. In addition, the *American Renaissance* conference differed from other supposedly academic-styled outfits, such as the Institute for Historical Review, which focused on events two generations past, whereas Renaissancers talked about present conditions and the future. Nevertheless, whether the conference was open or closed, rewriting the past or predicting the future, the unique aspect of Jared Taylor's project was his deliberate inclusion of Jews among those to be considered dispossessed and white. Jews were not on everybody's list of favorite conference invitees.

Are Jews White?

As previously noted, whiteness is an arbitrary, socially constructed category, invented at the dawn of colonization. White skin had been codified into custom and law, and it marked a set of prerogatives that need not be earned or merited. It was, as has been frequently observed, the first form of affirmative action.[24] While skin color appears to have a biological or zoological significance akin to the difference between blue jays and cardinals, it is actually more like the divine right of kings, a social construct the definition of which is subject to human action and constant change. Initially the property of only Anglo-Saxons, whiteness was denied to the first Irish immigrants and then granted in the nineteenth century. Italian, Polish, and Jewish immigrants went through a similar transformation.[25] Early in the twentieth century, racists and anti-Semites of all stripes worried about the supposedly dysgenic effect of Jews entering the country. Scientists had, after all, tested the dark-haired, Yiddish-speaking newcomers and proved that they had low IQs and carried rare, incurable diseases. It was thought to be in their Jewish genes. In time, as whiteness was transformed yet again, Jews too became white, even as their non-Christian status continued to set them apart in the larger American society.[26]

Despite changes in the postwar universe, Jews existed as not quite white aliens in the smaller world of white supremacists. For national socialists and Aryanists, Jews were wholly of another race, a biological breed apart. And a Christian Identity tenet asserted that Jews were inherently Satanic—either through their descent from the mating of Eve with Satan or through a slightly less penetrating inheritance of racial mongrelization. Wilmot Robertson's influential *Dispossessed Majority* had cast Jews as a particularly pernicious "unassimilable" white minority, a classification mixing Aryan-style anthropology and genetics. A less caustic but still anti-Semitic mythology contended that Jews were not eligible for the rights of natural sovereign citizenship, as the United States was constitutionally a "Christian republic." In each of these instances, and in all the permutations in between, a Jewish conspiracy ran either the media, the Federal Reserve banks, the federal government, communism, capitalism, or all of the above. The Jews' best trick was supposedly inventing the Holocaust, which burdened Europeans with guilt and won support for Israel. As discussed previously, these Jewish conspiracy theories provided a grand explanation for world events as well as for the particulars of white dispossession. And as Evelyn Rich correctly noted in her doctoral dissertation, it was this explicit anti-Semitism that gave white supremacists their revolutionary ideology.[27]

Rabbi Mayer Schiller's convivial presence in a room with men such as Ed Fields, Mark Weber, and Sam Dickson casts doubt on his common sense, but it signaled no change in the liberal mainstream of the Jewish community. Neither did it suggest any swing among conservative or neoconservative Jews, who might have truckloads of grievances with black people but would have little truck with either Holocaust deniers or so-called scientific racists. That said, Schiller's behavior is not without precedent. In every age and in every land there have been a few Jews who sought a separate peace with anti-Semites. If Mayer Schiller's common platform with the Renaissancers created not a ripple of interest among Jews, Jared Taylor's invitation to the rabbi provoked a continuing wave of controversy among white supremacists. The common refrain: What was Taylor thinking?

Several possibilities were proffered. The first came in the form of a brief review of the conference published in Wilmot Robertson's *Instauration*. It noted the presence of Schiller and several other men of Jewish descent on the platform. But the monthly's usually strident anti-Semitism remained remarkably restrained. A bit of nuance was needed by white activists, the reviewer suggested: "The time-honored strategy of fighting two enemies is to pretend to be the friend of one while zapping the other." And for this meeting, attacking just the so-called Negroes, while leaving the Jews off the hook, worked quite well. "Maybe after the Negroes are put in their place," the reviewer speculated, "another conference in a few decades will take on those who purists contend are the real enemy."[28] By this favorable account, Taylor's overture toward Schiller was little more than a clever chess move, a tactical decision of little long-term consequence.

Other views were less friendly toward the inclusion of any Jews on the platform, and a debate over Taylor's motivations and the prospect of ultimate success for the *American Renaissance* project rankled during the years following the first conference. Some activists accepted at face value Taylor's inclusion of Jews but objected nonetheless, using terms familiar on the vanguardist side of the movement. There were no "good Jews" and "bad Jews," they argued, just Jews—who were poison, one and all. Another faction thought Taylor's tactics were wrong, but they weren't sure of his motivation. *American Renaissance* was "more or less racial," but it avoided the "Jewish Question like the plague," wrote another activist. "I often wonder where their minds are really at, and whether they just think they are clever by putting up the PC front."[29]

These questions continued to roil *American Renaissance* supporters well into the future. It would be wrong to conclude that Taylor was by any means philo-Semitic. Shortly after September 11, he issued a statement blaming the attacks on American support for Israel and claiming that "if we go to war, it will not be because we are the land of freedom and opportunity, but because we are the best friend and benefactor of Israel."[30] Nevertheless, a couple of Jews continued attending conferences. And a contingent of young National Alliance cadres in 2002 kept a subterranean murmur of dissent going during the course of the weekend.[31] The anti-Semites chafed at the Jews, and the Aryans-only whisper occasionally broke out into the open during question and answer sessions. One observant young Aryan woman, writing on the Internet under the sobriquet the Cat Lady, may have ventured the most insightful parallel. She compared developments within *American Renaissance* to recent changes of focus by the British National Party. The British Nationalists' approach was "very appealing," she wrote. It was a racial nationalist, a socialist party but not "explicitly anti-Semitic." She also noted that at a side meeting a British representative who had spoken at an *American Renaissance* meeting had "pointed out that when Hitler was pursuing power, he hardly ever spoke publicly about the Jews either."[32] While the Cat Lady and the Brit may get failing grades as students of history, his remarks and her assessment—whether true or false—of Taylor's full intentions are useful when considering *American Renaissance*'s import and strategy.

For its part, Liberty Lobby and *The Spotlight* ignored *American Renaissance*'s weekend meeting during 1994. In the three months that followed, *The Spotlight* gave a full page to promoting a conference on "states' rights" sponsored by a Christian Identity tabloid. It spent pages attacking the Holocaust Museum in Washington, D.C. And almost every week it exposed the United Nations and other supposed threats to American sovereignty. When *The Spotlight* did cover Taylor, it folded a critique into its ongoing faction fight with Mark Weber's Institute for Historical Review. Taylor and Weber, *The Spotlight* argued, were "enigmatic" figures. It claimed to have heard accounts of Taylor's wife receiving a friendly phone call from the Anti-Defamation League, one of the largest of bogeys in Liberty Lobby's pantheon of enemies. (Given that Evelyn Rich had a history of working with such groups, such a call was not impossible.) *The Spotlight* also claimed that Jared Taylor and Mark Weber were longtime friends, and in one tabloid edition it wrote about their first meeting in Ghana in the 1970s, as if the event were somehow a cover story for more undefined but nevertheless nefarious doings.[33]

Minus an implication that their meeting was connected to any secret company, the friendship between Taylor and Weber was hardly news. Taylor served, for example, as Weber's best man at his wedding eight weeks after the conference.[34] Weber's betrothed, Priscilla Gray, had once worked for Phyllis Schlafly, an iconic figure on the far right who had led the opposition to the Equal Rights Amendment in the 1970s. Gray had also served on staff for Buchanan's presidential campaign in the previous election cycle.[35] A priest who had spoken at the *American Renaissance* conference, Father Tacelli, officiated at the St. James Roman Catholic Church in Falls Church, Virginia.[36] The wedding of a former Schlafly staffer with a former National Alliance cadre should have received notice on somebody's society page. Taylor's relationship with

Weber extended back to the days when he was still a leading cadre of Pierce's organization. Weber had received a special mention in Taylor's acknowledgments for his 1983 book on Japan. Ten years later Taylor continued to think highly of Weber. "Any man of whom Mark Weber speaks highly is a men [*sic*] worth knowing," Taylor wrote in a 1993 letter to a new *American Renaissance* subscriber. Then in a remark that might have pleased Taylor's detractors in white nationalism's traditionally anti-Semitic ranks, he made an oblique reference to the "frolic" surrounding the Holocaust Museum in Washington, D.C. "The march of folly never rests," he wrote.[37]

Perhaps Taylor's abstinence on the "Jewish question" was not about Jews at all. Just as anti-Semitism is often more about explaining world events than about a personal fear or phobia, so perhaps Taylor's thoughts about Rabbi Schiller or Jews in general were not germane to the *American Renaissance* project. Taylor's lack of overt anti-Semitism may have been about constructing a white nationalist movement freed from the conspiracy mongering that often accompanies belief that an international Jewish cabal runs the world. If he was quietly sympathetic to the claims of Holocaust revisionism but kept it off the agenda at the Atlanta conference nonetheless, perhaps he was not alone in that regard.

Consider the case of Wayne Charles Lutton, then a rising figure among the anti-immigrant intelligentsia. By almost every account that weekend, immigration from countries such as Mexico was threatening white majority hegemony. One speaker argued that "our immigration policy . . . is in fact turning America into a non-white country, dispossessing white America and its culture."[38] Lutton's talk was of similar measure, but with a focus on legal and legislative changes since the end of World War Two.[39]

The author of dozens of reviews and essays as well as coauthor of several small books, Lutton lacked natural gravitas. Nevertheless, his balding, bespectacled presence, framed by a salt-and-pepper beard, projected a scholarly mien. At home in Michigan, he enjoyed classical music concerts, read widely, and carried on an active correspondence with other intellectuals.[40]

Like most of the other conference speakers, Lutton, born in 1949 in Illinois, was part of the postwar boomer generation. While others of his age gravitated toward cultural rebellion and antiwar protest, Lutton's youth was taken with Christian fundamentalism and fervid anticommunism. Well educated, he received a bachelor's degree from Bradley University in Peoria and a doctorate in history from Southern Illinois University in Carbondale. His dissertation topic: Allied and Axis military strategy during World War Two.[41]

While still in graduate school, he found a megaphone for his views on the far right. *Christian Crusade Weekly* published a two-part article by Lutton on Soviet naval power. And in July 1975, Representative Larry McDonald, a Democrat from Georgia and then chairman of the John Birch Society, read the essay into the *Congressional Record*.[42] During the same period, Lutton also published in *American Mercury*, by then firmly within Carto's institutional empire. Both *Mercury* articles touched on Jewish-related topics. A review of Arthur Koestler's *The Thirteenth Tribe* noted that Koestler's claim that European Jews were descendants of a tenth-century kingdom in the Caucasus was a "devastating blow to international Zionism." An article in 1978 on the "Arab boycott" was similarly pointed.[43]

Although *American Mercury* under Carto was marred by the same politics that later informed the Institute for Historical Review, it was not solely identified with Holocaust denial, and Lutton used his own name when writing for it. As he became directly involved with the Institute for Historical Review, however, his political life came to resemble binary stars. One named Charles Lutton quietly associated itself with Holocaust revisionism. The other, Wayne Lutton, assumed increasingly important roles in the fight against immigration. While his anti-immigrant persona was well known and highly visible, for reasons unknown he kept the other personality secret.[44]

Wayne Lutton eventually landed at the Social Contract Press in Petoskey, Michigan, publisher of a small-circulation journal. During the Reagan years, he regularly wrote book reviews for William Buckley's *National Review*, did articles on AIDS for Christian right publications, and won recognition as an expert on population and immigration. He coauthored *The Immigration Time Bomb* for the American Immigration Control Foundation in 1985 and *The Immigration Invasion* for the Social Contract Press in 1994. The onetime Democratic presidential aspirant Senator Eugene McCarthy thought enough of the second book to write a two-page foreword. "I recommend study of the immigration issue and of this thoughtful book to all Americans."[45]

During the same period that Wayne Lutton was gaining a solid reputation at the center of the conservative movement and respect from Capitol Hill insiders, his alter ego, Charles Lutton, careened out to the edges of the universe at the Institute for Historical Review. This persona first wrote for the IHR's *Journal* in 1980 and continued writing book reviews and small essays for the institute into the 1990s. His usual beat was Axis military strategy, much like his dissertation topic. And he did not challenge directly the facts of the Holocaust itself. Nevertheless, he personally gave a presentation at the IHR's 1981 conference, joined its editorial advisory board in 1985, and, when one of its perennial personnel disputes emerged, interceded on the staff's behalf with Willis Carto (to no avail).[46]

In each instance, he used the name Charles Lutton, in an apparent effort to hold up a veil between the identity of the mainstream conservative and the Holocaust-obsessed activist. Sometimes, however, that veil slipped. A tape of his talk at the 1981 conference on "Axis Involvement with Arab Nationalists" was advertised in a catalog as the work of Charles Lutton, but the tape itself is imprinted with a label bearing the name Charles Sutton. (The voice on the tape of this IHR "Charles Lutton-Sutton" is exactly the same as that of Wayne Lutton on tapes sold by *American Renaissance*.)[47] Sometimes the veil fell to the ground altogether. For example, a 1991 letter written by the Institute for Historical Review's staff editor on its letterhead ends with a paragraph describing Lutton: *"One last thing: today I talked with Dr. Wayne Lutton, who received his Ph.D. in 20th-century European History from Southern Illinois. Wayne is an old friend, an ardent Revisionist, and a great guy"* (author's emphasis).[48]

The fictional split in personas disappeared entirely, however, in a pair of letters Wayne Lutton wrote to a colleague. In one, dated March 7, 1992, he chatted about a book manuscript deadline, and his plans to attend a concert by the Dresden State Orchestra and gave instructions to call only after 9:30 p.m. Over the signature of Wayne Lutton he also wrote, *"If you have the Winter JHR, you will have seen the long review essay on the literature of Pearl Harbor written by Charles Lutton . . ."* The ellipses in the original obviously meant to convey a wink and a nod. In a second letter, dated October 1, 1992, over the same signature, he was more explicit: *"Wish I were going to the IHR Confab this year (I gave a paper at one ten years ago, tho not as 'Wayne' Lutton)."*[49]

Lutton's list of accomplishments as an anti-immigrant activist alone merit notice, as does his work with *American Renaissance*, which eventually included multiple conference presentations and a seat on the board of directors of its parent corporation, New Century Foundation.[50] But Lutton's attempt to cloud his association with the Institute for Historical Review may reveal more about his ultimate aims than he wanted to show. Perhaps this version of white nationalism hoped to include anti-Semites, while occluding anti-Semitic ideology as a motivating force. Unlike William Pierce's wing of Aryan vanguardists, and different even from Willis Carto's attempts to find a mainstream constituency, Jared Taylor, Wayne Lutton, and the *American Renaissance* crew already had a seat on the (far) edge of conservative respectability, and they were apparently loath to lose their perch in a controversy over Jews and Hitler.

Over the next several years, *American Renaissance* became the premier gathering place for intellectuals in the white nationalist movement, firmly supplanting the Institute for Historical Review and all other venues. The IHR still maintained a unique status in the movement, however, particularly in its role as an international transfer station.

Holocaust Denial: To the Moscow Station

September 3, 1994. Now under Mark Weber's control while continuing the battle with Willis Carto, the Institute for Historical Review gathered its congregation once again in a California hotel.[1] Factional contention had come to dominate the internal life of Holocaust denial circles. Various pivotal figures chose the staff's side, including those whose only interest was a long and abiding dislike of Carto. Carto mustered his own loyalists, of course. One major personality unexpectedly maintained a facade of disinterest in the feud: William Pierce. At least three of the central anti-Carto actors, including Weber, had once been inside National Alliance's most trusted circles.[2] Yet Pierce refrained from publicly positioning himself, despite his own twenty-five-year feud with Carto.

Most of the IHR domestic regulars, as well as its European stable of writers and speakers, aligned themselves against Carto. And the staff proudly recounted a string of sturdy accomplishments over the previous twelve months: five issues of the *Journal* released; a bookstall sold seventy titles. In addition, the institute had received repeated mention in mainstream periodicals and made several appearances on network television. All were causes for self-congratulation. Carto's hectoring, nevertheless, had a noticeable effect.[3]

In a stern keynote address, Weber warned that "our financial situation is not good."[4] At the conference's end the staff held a special session on the dispute. Its report bordered on grim. Institute funds were being channeled into a never-ending series of lawsuits. The assistant editor had suffered an emotional breakdown and left town.[5] The remaining senior staffers all had worked without paychecks for several weeks. The Farrel estate funds were still under Carto's lock and key. A lawsuit seeking recovery of the funds, staffers explained, was still winding its way through the court system. Those knowledgeable about the IHR's problems but not in attendance, such as Wayne Lutton, worried from a distance that Weber might not survive the battle with Willis Carto.[6]

For his part, Carto used *The Spotlight* to regularly besmirch individual IHR staff members. He also launched a monthly magazine to compete directly with Weber's *Journal*. Entitled *The Barnes Review*, the first issue was dated October 1994. The August 29 edition of the *The Spotlight*, published just prior to the IHR's Labor Day meeting, carried a three-page spread announcing the magazine, including its first editorial. And Carto demonstrated that he had learned a lesson from this dispute. Rather than hide his control, he prominently posted his own name on the magazine's title page. The first issue published twenty plus congratulatory "letters to the editor." LaVonne Furr and Tom Kerr, the two Legion for the Survival of Freedom board members whose (temporary) perfidy had enabled Weber's crew to seize control, re-signed up with Carto. Not surprisingly, five people closely associated with Liberty Lobby, including its counsel, Mark Lane, formally added their names. Two additional attorneys, Kirk Lyons and Sam Dickson, sent letters of support as well. Finally, Jeanne Degrelle, widow of Waffen SS General Leon Degrelle, wrote her special regards.[7] Each name provided a clue to Carto's standing among his peers.

Although the IHR's 1994 conference counted as a significant marker in the staff's nine-year battle with its former boss, the most remarkable event that weekend was a speech by Ernst Zundel. Born in southeastern Germany in 1939, Ernst Christof Friedrich Zundel grew up under the occupying Allied forces before immigrating to Canada in 1958. By the mid-1970s he had become a fully fledged apologist for Hitler while eschewing the uniforms and buffoonery of Hollywood-style neo-Nazism, according to Stanley Barrett, a scholar whose 1987 book on Canada's right wing, *Is God a Racist?*, chronicled much of Zundel's early career.[8] Under a barely disguised pseudonym, Zundel authored a book entitled *The Hitler We Loved and Why* and contributed regularly to an unabashed national socialist monthly bulletin produced by another German émigré then living in West Virginia.[9] Despite this history, Zundel exhibited an almost endless capacity for self-promotion. From a house in Toronto, he did business using the name Samisdat Publications, evoking the image of an underground dissident press battling a totalitarian state. It was only one of Zundel's many clever marketing gambits. One of the booklets on his distribution list was *Did Six Million Really Die?*, and it was this piece of propaganda that turned Zundel's name into a Canadian newspaper headline.[10]

In 1983, following a criminal complaint by a private citizen, Canadian prosecutors charged him with willfully publishing false news that "is likely to cause mischief to a public interest." They cited the *Six Million* pamphlet and one other publication. When the case finally went to court in 1985, Zundel was convicted. But not before he had wrung "one million dollars" of publicity out of the six-week trial. Dressed each day in a bulletproof vest and a hard hat inscribed with the slogan "Freedom of Speech," he walked into the courthouse surrounded by a gaggle of supporters, also wearing hard hats. Television cameras could not resist the action.[11]

Zundel appealed the conviction, and an Ontario court overturned the verdict on technicalities in 1987. A few months later a second trial on the same charges began. During this second trial, defending Zundel became the business of the entire revisionist industry. Widespread financial support enabled him to mount a vigorous legal defense. David Irving traveled from England and testified on his behalf, as did Mark Weber and several other lesser-known figures. Zundel supporters even underwrote a thirty-five-thousand-dollar expense to send a team of "experts" to take rock brick samples from Auschwitz in an attempt to prove that gas chambers never existed. Despite the elaborate defense, Zundel was once again convicted on the facts and sentenced this time to nine months. On this occasion he showed up for prison in a concentration camp costume with television cameras in tow, once more squeezing every possible ounce of publicity from his legal travails. He served only one week before being bailed out while his case was appealed to the Canadian Supreme Court.[12]

When Canadian justices rendered their final decision in 1992, they noted that the statute under which Zundel had been charged dated from the year 1275 in England, "a society dominated by extremely powerful landowners." The justices noted that England had already abolished this old law and that the United States had never adopted it. They decided that the statute prohibiting "false news" abridged the freedom of expression guaranteed in the Canadian Charter of Rights and Freedoms, and the charges against Zundel were dismissed.[13]

Fifteen years after attending the IHR's first convention as a German émigré with a small personal footprint, Zundel returned to the 1994 conference after these battles as a veritable yeti. At the Saturday night banquet address he was formally introduced as the "leading distributor of revisionist" materials. The staff added an unusual disclaimer: the IHR's goals were "fundamentally different" from Zundel's, an apparent reference to his open advocacy of national socialism. Nevertheless, he was described to great applause as the "ring master" who had tamed the "huge media circus" attendant at his two trials.[14]

The heart of Zundel's talk that night was about his recent trip to Russia, not his victory in the Canadian courts. Still a German national traveling on a German passport, Zundel had made arrangements to visit Russia through contacts in Germany, who acted as an advance team and made the appropriate arrangements. With a group of five and a formal invitation from a member of the Duma, Vladimir Zhironovsky, Zundel had spent two weeks in Russia. At that point, ultranationalists of every stripe multiplied across the former Soviet Union. One bloc of Slavic nationalists joined with unreformed Stalinists and created a de facto red-brown alliance. Other Russians dallied with redesigned swastikas and created national socialist organizations. Paramilitary racists and skinheads, unrestrained by the conventions of civil society, filled a social niche of fear. Out of this mélange, Zhironovsky established himself at the juncture of anti-Semitism and Russian ethnic chauvinism. Zhironovsky's Liberal Democratic Party received 6.2 million votes for president in June 1991, and in December 1993 the party fielded 210 candidates for elective office, received 24 percent of the national vote, and won 59 seats in the new parliament.[15]

Zundel met with several of Zhironovsky's top aides, took stock of the party apparatus, and met privately with Zhironovsky at his dacha outside Moscow. He also met with national socialists critical of Zhironovsky's media-driven approach to electioneering. Zundel came home convinced that Zhironovsky was "intelligent" and a "clever tactician." Russians would "take revenge" because of what they had suffered from "Jewish Bolsheviks," he told the Holocaust-didn't-happen crowd. "I predict massive anti-Jewish pogroms in Russia." Zundel further decided that both "white Slavic Russians" and "white American nationalists" felt similarly about "minority racial and ethnic" groups in their midst. By contrast, Zundel spoke in glowing terms of the tall, blond-haired, blue-eyed Slavic population. "Every Russian I met with was, racially speaking, a beautiful specimen."[16]

Russia may now be weak, he argued in his concluding remarks. But it was still a "racially homogeneous nation" and would find a new form of government. Like journalist John Reed after his trip to revolutionary Russia in 1917, Zundel claimed to have seen the future. "It won't be an economic system like we have in the United States, dog eat dog capitalism. You know what it will be?" And then Zundel paused for dramatic effect. "National Socialism. Mark my words."[17]

No ambiguity blurred the meaning of Zundel's speech that evening. Russians hated the more darkly colored nationalities among them. They would soon kill lots of Jews and establish a national socialist regime. And at the end of his speech, Zundel received a warm and sustained round of applause, as if he had promised an early and bountiful Christmas.[18]

The conference ended. Mark Weber returned to the legal battle with Willis Carto and ultimately rebuilt the IHR as a smaller enterprise with significant connections to Holocaust deniers in the Middle East. Zundel returned to Canada, where he subsequently filed for citizenship. After that application was denied, he tried to establish legal residence in the United States. After all that failed, he was deported to his native Germany, where he faced charges related to his Holocaust denial activities.[19] But his trip to Russia had broken new ground. The establishment of permanent lines of direct communication between white nationalists in North America and their Russian counterparts would have been impossible before the end of the Cold War. As Russia and the former Soviet republics became an open market for the international trade in anti-Semitica, a string of publishers and activists from the United States, including David Duke, made money on the same ground where anti-Jewish pogroms had once been a fact of life. Meanwhile, in the United States the stratum of the electorate that Duke had aroused in Louisiana and that had then voted for Pat Buchanan showed itself again in the 1994 congressional elections.

Elections 1994: An Anti-immigrant Voting Bloc Emerges

November 8, 1994. After a nasty election season, in which Republicans campaigned against Bill Clinton as if the sitting president were the second coming of Satan, Democratic incumbents were pushed out of Congress like the fallen angels in *Paradise Lost*. The Democratic Party lost fifty-one seats in the House of Representatives and ceded control of that institution for the first time in forty years. It also turned over eight seats in the Senate and became the minority party there as well. The rout extended into state legislatures, and at the end of the day Republicans also controlled thirty governorships.[1] This was not an anti-incumbent "throw the bums out" election, however. Not one sitting Republican congressman, senator, or governor lost his or her seat.[2]

The big-print analysis argued that the Republican Party, by creating a compact known as the Contract with America, had successfully turned local and state races into a national referendum on the Clinton presidency. The small type showed an electorate divided by race and religion: Republican candidates for Congress drew 62 percent of white men and 55 percent of white women. (While a "gender gap" showed, a clear majority of white women voted alongside the men.) Democrats, by contrast, took 90 percent of black women. Further, of those who described themselves as "White born-again Christians," three out of four, 76 percent, voted Republican. Conversely, 78 percent of Jews voted Democratic. A clear sectional line was also evident: in the Midwest and South, 56 percent and 55 percent of voters polled Republican.[3]

The footnotes proved even more interesting, as a constellation of forces gathered on the Republican Party's right flank. In local and state races from Texas to Idaho to California, the Reverend Pat Robertson's Christian Coalition, the gun lobbies, and the Buchananite white wing each provided critical extra support to winning candidates and state referenda.[4] The Christian Coalition laid claim to victory in its monthly tabloid. Of the fifty plus new Republican seats, it said, "religious conservatives" won thirty-nine. "This was not just a Republican landslide," the coalition's executive director declared. "It was a landslide for a certain type of Republican."[5] The coalition believed that "type" was "pro-life" and antitax. According to this analysis, these new pro-life Republicans were replacing "liberal and moderate Republicans." The split inside the Republican Party's ranks was much noticed and discussed, even if not completely understood.[6]

A *National Review* article argued that those claimed as "religious conservatives" during the election were actually revolting against social and political elites—not exactly the usual stuff of "conservatives" per se. According to this report, these "elites" were government insiders, in the media and at universities, and Republicans as well as Democrats.[7] In this analysis, *National Review* failed to mention that this same opposition by white middle-class voters to "elites" was often accompanied by a parallel antagonism to the aspirations of dark-skinned people they considered "below" them on the social ladder. In fact, this constituency had grown significantly since Pat Buchanan's 1992 run at President Bush. Antiabortion politics and opposition to gay rights, à la the Christian Coalition, were not the only issues on its agenda. A segment proved to be protectionist on trade issues as well, isolationist in foreign policy, passionate about its supposed constitutional right to carry guns, and—most significant in 1994—opposed to immigration.

Washington State Senator Jack Metcalf's ascension to a seat in the U.S. House of Representatives was one among several examples of this new confluence of forces. Metcalf had been in and out of the Washington legislature, winning his first house seat in 1960.[8] In 1980 he was reelected to the state senate, and he soon began a campaign against the Federal Reserve Bank.[9] As a state senator Metcalf represented a district in northwestern Washington where commercial and sport fishing was more significant than commodity grain production. His campaign against the Federal Reserve proved less important to his voting constituents than his opposition to Indian tribal governments. In the legislature he opposed treaties and Supreme Court decisions that reaffirmed the sovereignty (and fishing rights) of tribes in the region.[10] Among other venues, he accepted an invitation to speak at the Washington State Populist Party's founding convention in 1984.[11]

Metcalf's speech in 1984 to a small meeting at a Christian Identity "library" near Velma, Oklahoma, provided a broader view of his actual political ideas. Although several people in the audience pushed him to talk more explicitly about Jewish banking combines, Metcalf was circumspect. "I'm going to give you a little lesson in practical politics. And I really think we in this movement should think about this," he told the group. "If you talk about a conspiracy coming to Congress—and we all know it was a conspiracy—if you talk about a conspiracy the average person is going to turn that off. I talk about a Special Interest. Everybody knows what a Special Interest is."[12]

Note that Metcalf left open the nature of this alleged conspiracy. It could have been a Jewish banking conspiracy or some other, but the salient point is that he argued for separating his own private beliefs in a "conspiracy" from his public explanation of the Federal Reserve. If voters chose not to decode his rhetoric, his movement aficionados certainly understood, and Metcalf was the subject of several puff profiles in *The Spotlight* during the mid-1980s.

Metcalf's age and tenure gave him a free ride with the press and the public. In 1992, he ran for the U.S. Congress. He won the Republican primary but lost the general election. When the Democratic incumbent retired in 1994, leaving the seat open, Metcalf took another turn. He ran as a fiscal conservative, a friend of the Christian right, and an opponent of "special privileges" for Native Americans. Despite his long tenure as a Republican ultraconservative, in this race Metcalf developed a following among environmentalists who also opposed Native Indian fishing rights. Suddenly Metcalf's long association with ideological anti-Semites and racists disappeared as a concern.

He sailed through the Republican primary and general election. And he received little negative press coverage. In fact, while a Seattle daily newspaper reminded its readers that Metcalf had "forged connections . . . with a right-wing organization [Populist Party] blasted by critics as anti-Semitic," the reporter also noted Metcalf's claim that such "connections" no longer existed. Then the paper's editors turned around and officially endorsed his candidacy.[13]

For its part, during the campaign, Liberty Lobby and *The Spotlight* acted as if their onetime favorite state senator did not exist. After the votes were counted on November 8, and Metcalf was borne into federal office on the shoulders of angry white men, the weekly tabloid changed tack and finally remarked on his election. *The Spotlight* claimed that the newly minted congressman would "undoubtedly" listen to its counsel "when decisions are being made."[14]

Jack Metcalf's transformation from a marginal anti–Federal Reserve state senator into a U.S. congressman was not particularly a sign of organizational strength by groups such as Liberty Lobby. Rather, it was one more sign of increased radicalization in a sector of the white populace. That change was even more evident with the anti-immigrant voting bloc that emerged in the Republican mainstream that year.

California Proposition 187

Listed on California ballots as "Save Our State," Proposition 187 mandated strict and punitive measures against undocumented or illegal immigrants. If it were enacted, entire families would be barred from receiving any public assistance, including routine medical care, and their children would be ineligible for public schooling. The initiative required teachers to screen their classrooms for students whose parents did not have papers. Similarly, medical personnel were to report any patients without documents. And the law promised to punish those caught in the production, distribution, or use of forged immigration papers with a stiff fine and prison. A federal court blocked the measure from immediate implementation, and ultimately its most stringent clauses were declared in violation of existing federal law.[15]

Yet Proposition 187 passed overwhelmingly, with 59 percent of the vote. Not surprisingly, the measure garnered little support among Latino voters, and less than one in four supported it. Asian American and black voters were almost evenly divided; 47 percent of each group came out in favor. With these numbers the proposition would not have passed if white voters had not overwhelmingly voted yes. According to exit polls, 63 percent of white voters, who were already an outsize majority of the electorate, supported the measure, demonstrating that by any count, a racial fault line separated most California voters.[16]

When considering the meaning of Proposition 187's popular support, *The Almanac of American Politics* described Californians as "marvelously tolerant" voters who had taken a turn toward "strong principles." They "just wanted the rules to be obeyed." Accordingly, "The important lesson here is that 187 was not a vote against immigration, but against illegal immigration."[17] Race and culture were not even mentioned in this commentary.

An alternative view, more common among liberals, decided: "Displaced workers, along with others who fear for their livelihood, are fertile ground in which to sow anti-immigrant sentiment, since angry and frustrated people often seek some target on which to blame their problems." In this view, "immigrants make a convenient scapegoat and a very tangible target for people's anger. [And] racial prejudice is often an encoded part of the message."[18] While this analysis recognized a racist component to the vote, it focused on economic fears as the most proximate cause of the proposition's passage. These "frustrations" were supposedly then transferred over to immigrants. In this context, scapegoating meant that voters had misplaced blame onto immigrants for other complaints, real or imagined, that had sources elsewhere. Immigrants were accorded the status of virtual bystanders, while most actual grievances were considered based in personal economic distress. Thus a vote for 187 was supposedly not a complaint against brown-skinned Spanish speakers as such but actually a misplaced protest of economic forces felt by the voters. It was a vote against job competition.

After social scientists ran the data from this election through statistical programs, other analyses were preferred.[19] One study was unequivocal, finding no evidence of a relationship between individual-level economic circumstances and opinions toward immigration: "Income and Personal Financial Situation—have no impact on the vote choice."[20] Another study parsed this question further. It also concluded that "personal finances" were not "statistically significant" in explaining (white) voter behavior, but that concern over the state of California's overall economic health "had an extremely strong, if not determining, effect."[21] At the time the California economy was unquestionably in a slump, and the state's revenues were problematic.

When scholars analyzed the data further, they found that what an individual voter thought was the solution to the state's fiscal difficulties was influenced by a combination of factors. These included the voter's ideological disposition—e.g., whether he or she regarded him or herself as liberal or conservative.[22] Conservatives were more likely to oppose government expenditures in general, and Prop 187 would have cut social service costs, and they voted for it at slightly higher levels than did liberals. By this account, a gubernatorial contest that ran concurrently with the referendum on Prop 187 also affected the vote. The Democratic candidate opposed 187. The victorious Republican incumbent emphasized the difficulties facing the state and urged voters to support 187 as a matter of fiscal responsibility. In sum, solidly middle-class white votes without individual economic stresses passed the anti-immigrant proposal as part of a larger fiscally conservative agenda.

But scholars found additional factors, such as social contact and political competition, that also proved to be decisive. As noted earlier, whites had voted for David Duke at higher ratios when they lived in counties and metropolitan areas with proportionately higher numbers of black voters. For white Louisianans, race had been the number one factor determining their vote. Political power was regarded as a zero-sum contest, seen in black-and-white terms. In California, however, the black-and-white divide was augmented by brown and yellow tones.

At an aggregate level, white voters living in counties with higher percentages of immigrants apparently voted yes on 187 in proportionately higher numbers.[23] When the data were broken down further, however, it became apparent that white voters did not react uniformly to all the different immigrant populations. When the new Americans were of Asian origin, for example, whites were more likely to favor immigration and vote against 187.[24] Similarly, when whites lived in communities where they had regular social contact with Latinos, they tended to vote against 187 in greater numbers. Conversely, when white voters lived in enclaves surrounded by high percentages of brown people but with little actual contact, they supported 187 in greater numbers. Regardless, the implication of all these analyses showed that no significant difference between "legal" and "illegal" immigrants mattered to white voters.

When all the votes were counted and all the numbers crunched, the voting patterns in California on 187 shared several characteristics with the Duke vote in Louisiana, although they were not identical. In both instances a majority of white voters acted as a distinct bloc. Once again, the concept of race showed itself at the center of the contest over the nature of American nationality. "What the vote for 187 tells us about whites is that they are now starting to vote for their own interests as a racial group, in opposition to the interests of other races," Sam Francis wrote in a particularly trenchant analysis of the 1994 elections. *The Washington Times* columnist predicted the election's effects would be felt far into the future. "If that trend continues, and there is every reason to believe it will, what it logically implies is the emergence of an overtly racial politics . . ." he concluded.[25] Although others expressed the same sentiments less forcefully, Francis's analysis anchored the views at his end of the political spectrum. Unfortunately for the Populist Party, these developments *within* Republican Party ranks virtually doomed any third party electioneering *outside* it.

The Populist Party Inches Toward Dissolution

The Populist Party could claim a number of accomplishments in its ten years of existence. During its first moments it had drawn together individuals from across organizations into one association, a necessary precondition for any independent electoral action. By casting itself as "populist," it had made a claim, however bogus, on a venerable American tradition. The party had served as a springboard for David Duke's election (as a Republican) to the Louisiana House of Representatives. David Duke's success had in turn pointed to the path subsequently taken by Pat Buchanan. The party had also given Bo Gritz a platform of potential significance.

Nevertheless, it ended this election year more irrelevant than a campus fraternity house during the Berkeley free speech movement. Populists had announced early that they would run fifty candidates for offices ranging from city supervisor to governor. But in one race after another, the party fell down. None of its past presidential candidates made even a guest appearance at a state convention.[26] The Populists' third party status created a raft of difficulties, particularly with ballot access. These obstacles need not have been insurmountable, except that other problems remained embedded within the larger white nationalist movement, militating against the Populist Party's success. Years of propaganda had targeted various forms of supposed Jewish control over society. And neither Willis Carto nor William Pierce argued that it was possible to "vote out" the "International Jewish Conspiracy." If Zionists (Jews) really did indeed control the government, as all believed, then gaining a seat inside occupied territory was a problem, not a solution. By this reasoning, supporting any candidates for office was not a rational option. On the other hand, spending your disposable income on another "assault" rifle, loading up on thousands of rounds of ammunition at a dollar a bullet, buying the latest camouflage fatigues, and joining a militia apparently were considered by many as the next best thing to sanity itself.

Certainly, 1994 had been a watershed year of new developments for white nationalists. A skinhead music enterprise had formed. Militia groups drew thousands of adherents to their cause. And the seed of a genuine white nationalist intelligentsia was planted. David Duke and Pat Buchanan had opened the door to the Republican Party for white-ist politics, and anti-immigrant initiatives had found a home there. A casualty to that success, the Populist Party never again mounted a serious election campaign. Its final moments went unnoticed and uncelebrated. Not so the life of Revilo Oliver, a major figure among white supremacists for four decades who died that year.

The Bell Curve: Legitimizing Scientific Racism

November 19, 1994. Although Revilo Oliver remained unknown outside white supremacist circles, his fingerprints showed up on virtually every far right tendency during the post–World War Two era. His status inside the movement was enhanced by his achievements in the academic world. A professor of classical philology at the University of Illinois at Urbana, he also taught Spanish and Italian and had received both Guggenheim and Fulbright fellowships. Born in 1908, he was a generation older than Carto and Pierce.

Oliver was on the original staff of *National Review* in 1955 but later broke completely with William Buckley and his brand of conservative thought. One of just twelve founding members of the John Birch Society in 1958, he had served on its executive council and as an associate editor of its *American Opinion* magazine. He was considered the person responsible for introducing the idea of a conspiracy by the Illuminati into Birch circles. But he was expelled in 1966 after a speech (as reported in the August 16, 1966, *New York Times*) in which he said: "If only by some miracle all the Bolsheviks or all the Illuminati or all the Jews were vaporized at dawn tomorrow, we should have nothing to worry about."[1]

He claimed to have advised Willis Carto's writing of the introduction to *Imperium*, although Carto denied it. Rumors had it that Oliver actually wrote the pages that Carto claimed as his own. He later broke with Carto over the fate of the National Youth Alliance (NYA) in 1969, excoriating Carto for acting with a "vindictive hysteria that seems odd in a person presumably not equipped with a uterus."[2] Neither his passions nor his vituperative language cooled in the years after. He signed on as an adviser to William Pierce's faction of the NYA in the 1970s, and

Pierce credited Oliver with the idea of writing a novel as a way to spread Aryan ideas. *The Turner Diaries* was the result.[3]

By the end of his life Oliver had written a half dozen books and more than 160 articles for the movement press, including pieces for Wilmot Robertson's high-toned monthly *Instauration*, but most for an explicitly national socialist bulletin entitled *Liberty Bell*.[4] Oliver also had provided, upon request, counsel to younger acolytes of the cause and by all accounts was a gracious host when they stopped by to kiss his ring.[5]

When Oliver died in 1994, Atlanta attorney Sam Dickson mailed out personal invitations to a memorial symposium in Urbana.[6] Not quite a funeral service, it was a bit more than just another talk fest. Several dozen souls gathered at a lodge to honor Revilo Pendleton Oliver. Dickson emceed the event, and at his request, the small assembly sang Sibelius's hymnlike *Finlandia*. They gave a standing ovation to his widow, Grace, as she sat in a wheelchair. One speaker after another rose and said they all were Oliver's "spiritual children" (even if he had produced no "biological" offspring). They remembered a genius that knew everything about everything—not just the Sanskrit and classical Greek of his profession. One, a fellow philologist from Oklahoma, reminded mourners of Oliver's creative use of pejoratives such as "slimy sheenies" to describe Jews and others. Dickson's colleague Martin O'Toole argued that militia-style conspiracy mongering would not solve the race problem and then sat down. National Alliance member Kevin Strom testified to the inspirational power of Oliver's personality. Strom, a figure of Pierce's organization, became the keeper of Oliver's movement writings, establishing a website for that exclusive purpose.[7]

Memory and memorials for Oliver aside, the most noteworthy aspect of this event was Sam Dickson's public apology to David Duke and Duke's own peroration on genetics and scientific racism. At his spot on the agenda, Dickson denounced "race traitors" such as former Supreme Court Chief Justice Earl Warren, who had crafted the initial *Brown* decision in 1954, and former President Jimmy Carter. "People are only remembered by the nation or race they served," Dickson argued. "Liberals will be forgotten." Racially conscious white people would look badly upon those who had broken ranks, he said. And in a phrasing that dripped with sarcasm and contempt he claimed that "no teary eyed little mulattos" will grieve for President Carter. On the other hand, he asserted that "if our race or civilization survives there will surely be monuments to Revilo P. Oliver." The Atlanta attorney worked himself into such a lather that his polite mask of discreetness slipped. "We look forward to the collapse of our rotten society" were his exact words.[8]

Then, as if the memorial symposium had thrust upon him the need for absolution, Dickson apologized forthrightly to David Duke. First, he praised Duke for being "widely recognized as the leading spokesman for our cause." Second, Dickson confessed that he had been at some undisclosed moment "too scathing" in his criticism of Duke. (Returning to his usual practice of understatement, Dickson also said he had made "uncharitable remarks" about the man who had once worn a swastika on his shirtsleeve and a white robe upon his back.) Nevertheless, Dickson believed Duke's response had been "broad-minded." Finally, Dickson was now "proud to be friends" with Duke, who had stayed true to the cause. Moreover, Duke's Louisiana campaigns had proved that "there is a chance for a change."[9] And that after all was what this small band of souls wanted even more than the chance to remember Revilo Pendleton Oliver's extraordinary genius.

For his part, Duke used the occasion to reprise many of the themes at the *American Renaissance* conference he had been excluded from six months before. "Optimism of our inevitable victory is in our genes," Duke claimed. So was everything else. Intelligence, ethics, personal politics, a penchant for technology, and even "what we are doing in this room," Duke listed as genetically determined. Genetic science had been unfairly "suppressed" after World War Two, he said, and for decades fundamental human characteristics had been falsely ascribed to "environment." But now "heredity" was making a comeback. Those who had argued that the "black intelligence deficit" was due to environmental factors—or even fifty-fifty environment and heredity—were being proved wrong. It was "all heredity," he said, even black "mating habits." For Duke the term was shorthand for the supposed inability of black families to stay whole with fathers who cared for their young. No touch of irony rang in the voice of this divorced father of two. No memory intruded of the black woman who raised him while his mother lay in a drunken stupor and his father flitted across the globe on business.[10]

Without missing a beat, Duke claimed that the "scientific community is moving in our direction . . . The ideas of *The Bell Curve* can't be suppressed anymore."[11]

The significance of *The Bell Curve*, published in October 1994 and exalted by David Duke at the Oliver memorial, should not be overstated. This eight-hundred-page text by Richard Herrnstein and Charles Murray, linking social standing and IQ measurements to heredity and genetics, was not the first in its field. As Stefan Kuhl demonstrated in his 1994 book *The Nazi Connection*,[12] eugenics had been a project of American elites long before Hitler claimed to improve Germany by getting rid of its Jews. Neither was Simon & Schuster the only reputable house publishing pages that claimed biology is destiny (and that genetics is biology). Pursuit of the Human Genome Project and deciphering DNA code had opened the door to a wholly new scientific arena, and the good, the bad, and the ugly had walked through.

Among those searching for biological sources of social behavior were National Cancer Institute scientists. They claimed to have found a "gay gene," a chromosomal imprint that caused homosexuality in men. Some gay rights advocates embraced the findings as proof that homosexuality was neither "sinful" nor a "choice," contrary to what Christian right ideologues asserted.[13] On a less genetic but more biological note, other scientists believed they had found a link between chemical imbalances in the neurological system and an individual's tendency toward criminal behavior and violence. When President George H. W. Bush announced the formation of a Federal Violence Initiative in 1991 to conduct further studies on the subject, however, the project ignited fears that the federal government was (once again) supporting punitive measures aimed at black youth under the guise of science, and the project was nominally killed. An article on the federal controversy, published in the prestigious *New Yorker* magazine less than six months after *The Bell Curve* first appeared, noted that "a vestigial feature of the American liberal mind" was "its undiscerning fear of the words 'genetic' and 'biological,' and its wholesale hostility to Darwinian explanations of behavior." Get over it, the reporter, Robert Wright, seemed to be saying. "It turns out, believe it or not," he opined, "that comparing violent inner-city males to monkeys isn't necessarily racist, or even necessarily right wing."[14] At a time when "nature" seemed to be retaking ground once lost in its debate with "nurture," *The Bell Curve* could have scored the final winning points. That did not prove to be the case, however.

Almost as soon as the book was released, *Newsweek* reported that it was based on a "deeply angry" perspective, that its "blunt declaration" of the intellectual inferiority of black people was "explosive," and that it "panders to white resentment." The reporter mustered opposing arguments, which challenged the book on its own scientific grounds.[15] Similarly critical newspaper reportage and opinion pieces gave the book, dense with data and charts, a respectable hearing but ensured that few beyond those already committed would automatically embrace its claims. A year later came a more accessible collection of essays, *The Bell Curve Debate*, challenging the claims—scientific, moral, and political—made by Herrnstein and Murray. Perhaps the most damning piece of evidence in that folio was a reprint of the entry for "The Negro" from the *Encyclopaedia Britannica*'s 1911 edition, written by a Cornell University professor who also served then as the chief statistician for the U.S. Census Bureau. Replete with claims that growth of the "Negro" brain was "arrested," the entry concluded that "the mental constitution of the Negro is very similar to that of a child, normally good-natured and cheerful, but subject to sudden fits of emotion and passion during which he is capable of performing acts of singular atrocity, impressionable, vain, but often exhibiting in the capacity of servant a dog-like fidelity . . ."[16] When we remember that this encyclopedia article once provided the baseline of information for schoolchildren of every hue and creed, perhaps the contemporary vestigial fears of racial liberals are better understood.

The Bell Curve was a grand commercial triumph, spending fifteen weeks on the bestseller list and selling three hundred thousand copies in hardcover.[17] But books don't change history; people do. No epochs turned over with the reintroduction of racial science into mainstream discourse in 1994. The success of *The Bell Curve* was not of the same order as events—the Soviet bloc's collapse and German unification—that ended the postwar period. Nor was Herrnstein and Murray's massive accumulation of data anything like the bravery and determination of those willing to fight Jim Crow and change the American racial order. Simply put, reading *The Bell Curve* by itself could not change the way most Americans thought about racial equality. In fact, two years after its first appearance, a National Opinion Survey found the percentage of white Americans willing to ascribe the existence of racial inequality to black people's inborn ability to learn continued to drop—in this count to under 10 percent.[18]

Nevertheless, the production and publication of Herrnstein and Murray's masterwork represented a most important break in conservative ranks. It also provided intellectual cover for those like Jared Taylor and his *American Renaissance* colleagues, who wanted to change the public discussion of race altogether. Much as Pat Buchanan's rejection of the Persian Gulf War signaled his turn away from global interventionism, Charles Murray's defection to the white side changed the balance of forces along America's racial fault lines. Herrnstein, a psychology professor at Harvard, had long been looking for links between race and IQ measurements, but Murray was new to the field. With degrees from Harvard and the Massachusetts Institute of Technology, he had spent decades studying social policy. First as a nonprofit program analyst in D.C. and then as an endowed fellow at the Manhattan Institute for Social Policy, he apparently grew increasingly critical of the welfare system and the "underclass" it supposedly created. In 1984, while still at the Manhattan Institute, he wrote a scalding critique entitled *Losing Ground: American Social Policy 1950–1980*. The federal welfare systems, he argued, promoted crime and dependency, among other ills, and should be abolished. Murray's book achieved Bible-like status in President Reagan's administration and underwrote the arguments of those already on the campaign trail excoriating "welfare queens" and their supposed Cadillacs, even as Murray then abjured explicit discussion of race.[19]

When Murray took a step toward a study linking race and social stratification with IQ, some of his erstwhile conservative colleagues became nervous. According to a report in *The New York Times*, the president of the Manhattan Institute said that Murray "had little to gain in terms of useful knowledge as a result of his inquiry and much to lose."[20] Murray and the institute parted company. The mainline Brookings Institute also turned down an opportunity to sponsor Murray's new research. The Cato Institute, a libertarian think tank highly regarded among economic conservatives, also passed. Finally, Murray landed at the American Enterprise Institute in 1990, carrying with him the same Bradley Foundation–endowed chair he had enjoyed at his Manhattan Institute perch. Business conservatives who had supported his earlier work on welfare switched sides after *The Bell Curve* appeared. "Biological determinism, which is what the Murray-Herrnstein book is all about, is anathema to the opportunity society," *BusinessWeek* magazine declared.[21]

Jared Taylor's *American Renaissance*, on the other hand, quickly embraced the book. It was simply restating ideas that it had promoted for years, the newsletter noted. It further believed that the controversy surrounding the book would help its cause. "The rules of dialogue may finally have changed," the Renaissancers hoped. Would it become possible to once again publicly defend segregation in housing or education, on the basis that black IQs didn't measure up? In one sentence that echoed David Duke's claim that he said in public what others thought in private, the newsletter averred that "the tumult over this book cannot help but legitimize what millions of Americans already think privately."[22] *The Bell Curve* might not immediately bring any new converts to its cause. But its appearance in suburban bookstores made it easier for those already convinced to express their ideas publicly. That process of legitimation, presumably, would eventually enable racially obsessed whites to win larger and more active followings.

The Oklahoma City Bomb and Its Immediate Aftermath

April 19, 1995. At 9:02 a.m., while elderly Social Security applicants waited for service and toddlers played in the day care center, the Alfred P. Murrah Federal Building collapsed in a jaggle of steel, concrete, and blood. Officials counted more than 500 wounded, many with life-changing injuries, and 168 dead, including 19 children. A rental truck, loaded with seven thousand pounds of fertilizer mixed with fuel oil in barrels, detonated by an arc of Tovex, had blasted apart the building, shattering all of downtown Oklahoma City and shaking Middle America's sense of safety and proportion.[1] At that moment this was the deadliest, most significant act of contemporary terrorism on American soil—incomprehensible in any commonsense terms. One initial response to the horror was to search for "Middle Eastern" terrorists, in part because of their use of truck bombs in the past.[2] But it soon became evident that the killers were Americans, born in the USA and bred on resentments circulating wildly in the terror zone where gun nuts met militias.[3]

Within hours of the blast, investigators located the vehicle identification number inscribed on the rear axle. They traced the truck back to a Ryder rental agency outside Junction City, Kansas. After questioning agency personnel, the FBI developed composite drawings of two men who had rented the truck, a fair-haired John Doe One and a darker John Doe Two. One clue to the perpetrators' motives became evident at that moment. To rent the truck, Doe One had displayed a North Dakota driver's license with a birthday of April 19, the date of both the bombing and of the FBI's final (and fiery) assault on the Branch Davidians in Waco. Agents then questioned area businesses and identified this Doe One as Timothy McVeigh, who had used his real name to rent a motel room. He had also listed a farmstead in Michigan belonging to James

Nichols as his home address. The FBI investigation moved to Michigan, and soon James's brother Terry Nichols was wanted for questioning. Just days after the bombing, the FBI found McVeigh in an Oklahoma county jail. He had been picked up for driving without a license plate, which had fallen off in the blast. Two hours after that, Terry Nichols turned himself in to FBI agents in Kansas. Ultimately, one other coconspirator was located in Arizona. The olive-complected John Doe Two, however, was never identified.[4]

Who were these people? Terry Nichols and his older brother James had spent several years circulating on the edges of the militia movement in Michigan. They attended meetings, experimented with explosives, and adopted the common law sovereign status in order to distinguish themselves from so-called Fourteenth Amendment citizens. Terry Nichols, who had married a Filipina, was an odd candidate for such white nationalist pretensions. After moving from Michigan, he had settled in Kansas, not far from where his former army buddy McVeigh had been stationed at Fort Riley, and eked a living out of the gun and military surplus trade at the bottom of the paramilitary subculture.[5]

Timothy McVeigh was a disgruntled veteran of the First Persian Gulf War. He too traveled the gun and survivalist circuit, buying, selling, and trading weapons and paraphernalia. But he was more directly enmeshed in the milieu's white nationalist undersprings. He carried copies of William Pierce's *Turner Diaries*, and he adopted the militia movement's public anger over Waco as his own cause. McVeigh used a telephone charge card issued by Liberty Lobby and made calls to known white supremacist outfits in the weeks before the bomb. And he had joined one of the many small Klan factions still taking memberships.[6]

By the time *Newsweek* issued its May 1 edition, with a color photo of a rescue worker cradling a bloodied baby in his arms, the public's vision was split in two. One eye fixated on the senseless death and barbaric destruction in Oklahoma City. The other focused on the milieu from which the perpetrators had sprung. For the first time since The Order had captured headlines with tales of murder and armored car robberies, popular magazines and television footage focused on a movement that had survived largely in the recesses of public uninterest. While federal agents looked for leads in phone records and fertilizer sales receipts, journalists spread out to collect and report on the groups and individuals now euphemistically referred to as the antigovernment movement. Gun lobbyists at the National Rifle Association were brought under renewed scrutiny. Congressional representatives friendly to militia groups during the 1994 election season were now looked at more sharply. "Secretive, paranoid, obsessed with guns and Waco, the militia movement may have 100,000 adherents," *Newsweek* concluded.[7]

As a result of this media exposure, many main street Americans recoiled in horror at the antigovernment furor. President Clinton emerged as a combination tough federal cop and compassionate national father figure. As Clinton, who had been badly damaged by the 1994 election results, (temporarily) regained the stature of his office, the long free ride ended for gunslinging militia propagandists, as well as *The Spotlight* subscribers, *The Turner Diaries* fans, and other members of the movement. They howled in protest, as public opprobrium rose around paramilitarists and their apologists.[8]

William Pierce and the National Alliance, however, did not complain too loudly. McVeigh's attachment to *The Turner Diaries*, and the similarities between a truck bomb in Pierce's novel and the bomb in Oklahoma City pushed the National Alliance back into view for the first time since The Order. Pierce took advantage of the publicity and projected the image of a cold-blooded, but well-reasoned, revolutionary. Instead of claiming that white nationalists should be held innocent of murder and mayhem, he argued that more was soon to come. In an address broadcast across a shortwave radio band ten days after the bomb, Pierce laid down the direction he wanted his troops to go. The "government" was certainly the biggest terrorist, he claimed. To bolster his argument that society was diseased, he reprised complaints against "career women" who worked outside the home, "homosexuals" who had escaped the closet, "minorities" buffered by "artificial equality," and of course the Jews. As such, he argued that it was natural for a few "normal people with healthy instincts" to respond to this so-called sickness with violence.

Pierce did not shrink from his conclusions: "Terrorism is a nasty business. Most of its victims are innocent people. Some of the office workers who died in the Federal Building in Oklahoma City may have been as much against the Clinton government as were those who set off the bomb. But terrorism is a form of warfare, and in war most of the victims are noncombatants." This was not a new line of thought for him. He had written the same thing two decades before in the pages of *The Turner Diaries*. And in a summary of Robert Mathews's Order, Pierce had argued that Mathews's actions were not wrong, but simply premature. Now he made a corollary case. The problem with the bombing in Oklahoma City, he said in this broadcast, was that it needed to be connected to a larger "plan." Absent such a plan, "we need to help people understand that a good bit, if not all, of the private terrorism we'll be seeing in the future will be a protest against the government's destruction of America."[9] In effect, Pierce embraced McVeigh and the bombing.

Not surprisingly, Willis Carto's Liberty Lobby took a different tack from Pierce's. Rather than consider the bombing the work of "healthy" individuals, *The Spotlight's* first headline considered it a "cowardly" act.[10] As April and May turned to June, however, the tabloid began recirculating claims that the bomb itself was not simply a truckload of fertilizer and fuel oil. As these imaginary bombs grew in technical complexity, so did speculation about the actual perpetrators, and the tabloid became a clearinghouse for competing conspiracy theories.[11]

Soon the main lines of logic had been extended by *The Spotlight* and virtually every other movement media: if Timothy McVeigh was in fact guilty of detonating the truck bomb, then a set of mysterious others had put the plot in motion and turned him into the fall guy. These "others" were often considered to be federal agents of one kind or another. By these accounts, and they were multiple in number, it was the government, not the militia, that was responsible for the carnage in Oklahoma City. Thus the government was involved in a big cover-up of its crime. John Doe Two could not be found because the feds didn't want to blow the cover off their story.[12] While few outside the paramilitary and white nationalist lines gave this reasoning much credence, it did serve those inside the ranks. A theory pinning the horror on the federal government rather than the "militia" kept those already within movement circles from jumping ship in disgust at the carnage. This new mantra was recited at every available opportunity after the bombing, while the identity of John Doe Two remained at the center of as many conspiracy theories as those of a second shooter on the grassy knoll.

Orlando Expo 1995

Six weeks after the bombing, movement events promoted long before April 19 went on as planned. A pro-gunners rally on June 4, in Washington, D.C., drew four hundred to the Lincoln Memorial. Kirk Lyons climbed that platform to tout his civil suit on behalf of the estate of one of the Waco Davidians.[13] Lyons had, at various times, filed four different lawsuits against individual government officials. Two made civil rights and tort claims, and the largest, *Misty Dawn Ferguson et al. v. Janet Reno*, had twenty-three Davidians as plantiffs.[14]

A week later, June 11, a slightly different assembly gathered at Kansas City to defend "constitutionalism" from New World Order destroyers. Camouflage-clad militiamen stood security and took tickets from more than three hundred attendees. Here former Arizona Governor Evan Mecham joined Colorado State Senator Charles Duke and California State Senator Don Rogers to defend states' rights and the Tenth Amendment alongside a bevy of marginal Christian patriot characters out of a Posse Comitatus photo album.[15]

The same weekend as the Kansas City meet, a preparedness expo opened at the Orlando convention center as if it were the main stage at Disney World. Over three days more than two thousand people parked in designated lots, dutifully rode the shuttle bus to the front doors, and gladly paid the six-dollar entrance fee. Much as at previous commercial survivalist events in Spokane, few seemed drawn by the chance to buy goods for such natural disasters as floods and hurricanes, although water purifiers, dried foods, and vitamins were for sale. Mylar ponchos stood in racks next to booths selling juice makers. Lectures on health issues drew a smattering of interest. But from the main stage and down the exhibition aisles a roll call of personalities from expos and militia-type meetings past stood end to end.[16]

Here again propaganda spielers campaigned against Fourteenth Amendment citizenship and advocated sovereign status, state citizenship, and militias. If you needed books on the Jews—from the ancient *Protocols of the Elders of Zion* to more contemporary examinations of the Federal Reserve System—they were available not far from the bomb-making manuals and stacks of (empty) ammunition boxes. John Trochmann's wife, Carolyn, distributed Militia of Montana literature from another table. Gun Owners of America executive Larry Pratt quietly sold memberships to his gun lobby like library cards for a Second Amendment reading room. When Pratt's turn at the podium came, he counseled the crowd not to be intimidated by any associations with the militia. "After all, every time you read the [country's] Founders they say something that makes them sound like they were a bunch of militia types," he continued, because "that's exactly what they were."[17]

At an oversize exhibition table, Bo Gritz sold "preparedness" merchandise: a sixty-five-dollar belt buckle with a hidden six-inch knife blade and sixty-dollar videotapes that taught lock picking and other skills. If you stood at his table long enough, Gritz would start talking about his "constitutional covenant" community in Idaho, the same one he had previously described as a "Christian covenant" community before the bomb blast had heightened media attention to such events as these. Gritz also took the main stage on several different occasions during the weekend. Each time a loyal crowd of five hundred partisans paid the extra five-dollar fee to hear him blast the government's flawed theory of the Oklahoma City bombing. More than any other speaker that weekend, Gritz contributed to a rearticulated sense that the movement was the real victim in this postbombing world. He also felt assured enough of his own status at this event that he spent most of one lecture promoting organizations and personalities other than his own.[18]

"Friends, it's time to stop talking and . . . start walking . . . I'm a life member of the NRA, but friends, that ain't nothing. You get out there where somebody's really doing something," he told the crowd. "I want you to go out there and make sure you're part of the Gun Owners of America."[19]

Post–April 19 Conspiracy Theories

In retrospect, the oft-asked question "Who really bombed Oklahoma City?" and the attendant conspiracy theories were almost naturally occurring events, like prayers for rain in a long drought. The sheer enormity of the crime created an almost knee-jerk disbelief in any simple explanation, whether offered by federal prosecutors or the FBI. Further, militia advocates, who hoped to influence the media and other pipelines to public opinion, were ever eager to pin the carnage back on the government, much as they had done with the Weaver case and Waco disaster. More, as part of a legal defense strategy, McVeigh's chief attorney spent years trying to find John Doe Two and "others unknown," often in off-the-track places such as the Philippines. And journalists, inquisitive and doubting by nature, found an embarrassing number of unanswered questions in the official explanations. These holes cried out to be filled, and reputable investigative reporters and disreputable poseurs alike rushed into the breach.[20]

The when, where, and how of the truck bomb's construction, for example, remained unresolved. The FBI verified the fact that Terry Nichols had helped secure and store the fertilizer used in the bomb. But the claim that Nichols (and only Nichols) helped McVeigh construct the bomb never satisfied all objections. If McVeigh helped unload dozens of bags of fertilizer, empty them into barrels in the back of the Ryder truck, and stir into the mixture multiple gallons of fuel oil, then why did the FBI never find any telltale residue of fertilizer dust on McVeigh's clothes?[21]

In another unsolved mystery, investigators had trouble learning the identity of the person connected to the remnants of a leg found at the bombing site, a leg clad in a military-style boot and camouflage boot blouse.[22] And as weeks turned into months after McVeigh's capture, the most enigmatic question remained: What had happened to John Doe Two, the dark-haired companion seen at the truck rental agency?

Much of the speculation about Doe Two (and possible Does Three and Four) swirled around Elohim City, the Christian Identity settlement in northeastern Oklahoma that had quietly survived the post-Order federal sweep. The related outpost in Arkansas, James Ellison's Covenant, the Sword and the Arm of the Lord (CSA), had disbanded ten years before, but Robert Millar's camp had prospered, supported in part by its own trucking company, a small sawmill, and livestock. And Elohim City had remained a safe harbor for movement cadres. After serving his federal prison sentence, Ellison had resettled there, marrying one of Millar's young granddaughters. It was the permanent burial ground for Wayne Snell.[23]

Although Snell had been declared innocent at the seditious conspiracy trial, his murder convictions for the deaths of a black highway patrolman and a pawnshop owner had stood. Snell's execution date had been scheduled for April 19 long in advance, and Robert Millar had ministered to the inmate at the end. Finally, just hours after the blast in Oklahoma City, Arkansas authorities put Snell to death. Afterward Millar drove the body from the prison in Texarkana to a hillside on the Elohim City property, and Snell was buried there.[24]

The possibility of a connection between Snell's execution and the bombing intrigued investigators of every persuasion, particularly after it was learned McVeigh had his own possible connection to Elohim City. Just days before the bombing, McVeigh made a call to Elohim City and asked to talk with a man known to his American friends as "Andy the German."[25] At home in Berlin, he was Andreas Strassmeir. The son of a prominent conservative politician, he had served in the *Bundeswehr*.[26] According to an affidavit circulated by Lyons, Andy first came to the United States in 1988, went home, and then returned months after the bombing. Lyons claimed he met Strassmeir during a reenactment ceremony of the Battle of Gettysburg and later made the arrangements for him to live in Elohim City. The German immigrant apparently lived there (off and on) from at least 1991 until the summer of 1995.[27]

He bought a trailer home from the locals and began a small-time business, buying and selling militaria at gun shows. After Waco he helped the camp's young men upgrade their weapons from hunting to assault rifles. When asked by reporters, he claimed that he didn't really know McVeigh, that the two had only a short-lived commercial exchange at a gun show. When asked why McVeigh at the time of his arrest had a Strassmeir business card in his wallet, Andy answered that he did not know. As for the phone call from McVeigh, Andy said he had not been able to talk because he was at a neighbor's working on a fence. He also claimed that he left Elohim City after a dispute with Millar over the latter's welcome mat for Jim Ellison. It was at that point that Lyons and associates stepped in again and helped him quietly leave the country.[28]

In addition to the speculation surrounding Strassmeir, reports surfaced that several members of a small group calling themselves the Aryan Republican Army spent considerable amounts of time at Elohim City. Dubbed by the daily press the Midwest Bank Bandits, they hit twenty-two banks in Ohio, Missouri, Kansas, Iowa, Nebraska, and Wisconsin, from October 1994 through December 1995. Forgoing the time-consuming work of opening vaults, they specialized in quick heists, jumping the teller counters, scooping the cash drawers, and leaving the premises within minutes. Typically, they left behind a diversionary device, such as a smoke grenade or a bomb look-alike, to assist their escape. They also wore a series of creative masks and costumes: a Santa Claus outfit at Christmastime, a Nixon mask on another robbery, and FBI ball caps and badges on a third. Despite the theatrical displays of deception, the net proceeds of this gang amounted to about $250,000.[29]

Led by Peter Langan and his principal partner, Richard Guthrie, the gang never included more than a half dozen bandits. They eluded law enforcement until Guthrie was captured in January 1996. Despite a friendship that dated back to their youth, Guthrie quickly led authorities to Langan, who was arrested in Ohio, after a brief shoot-out. From Langan, authorities recovered weapons, ammunition, and military ordnance. Disguises and the paraphernalia for creating false identifications were found. Among the guns, a small library attested to Langan's literary preferences. The titles: *Around the World with Kipling*, *The Celtic Tradition*, and *Bullfinch's Mythology*. Found too was the pamphlet *Our Nordic Race* and a book entitled *War Cycles, Peace Cycles*, both authored by propagandist Richard Kelly Hoskins. The authorities also recovered multiple copies of a videotape ostensibly produced as a recruiting tool. In the video, Langan, dressed in full gear, called himself Commander Pedro, waved a rifle, and spouted the usual rhetoric. The rest of the gang members were quickly arrested, and the Aryan Republican Army fell to stepped-up law enforcement operations after the Oklahoma City bombing. Guthrie confessed to nineteen of the holdups. He also handwrote a memoir while in jail, then hanged himself just days before he was slated to testify against the other bandits.[30]

During multiple trials in several states, an outline developed of the bank-robbing gang's activities, including the fact that several of those charged had spent a considerable amount of time at Elohim City. Among them was Mike Brescia, a skinhead recruited from Philadelphia, who had shared a trailer with Andreas Strassmeir off and on for almost two years. It stretches the imagination to believe that Andy the German did not know of his roommate's exploits. Several investigators, including a few militia types who wanted to pin the bombing on the Clinton administration, stepped off the paved road of known facts and ventured up a rockier path of unknown conspiracies. First they decided that Brescia, dark-haired and olive-complexioned, was John Doe Two. If that was true, they concluded, then the connection between McVeigh and Strassmeir had to have been more than just a simple gun show exchange. Some also believed that Strassmeir was some sort of intelligence operative, planted in the United States with the unwitting help of Kirk Lyons. By these counts, it seemed reasonable to conclude that the feds had prior knowledge of the Oklahoma City bombing and had done nothing to stop it. Regardless of Strassmeir's actual identity, however, this particular conspiracy theory hung by a single thin thread: Mike Brescia had to be John Doe Two. If Brescia was not Doe Two, or if Doe Two never existed, then the whole explanation fell apart.[31]

Years later, after McVeigh had been convicted at trial, his attorney, Stephen Jones, wrote a book on the case, titled *Others Unknown*, in which he recirculated several conspiracy theories that made his client look like a dupe rather than a fully aware perpetrator. A criminologist, Mark S. Hamm, in a book titled *In Bad Company*, argued strongly for the Brescia is Doe Two theory. These and other ideas recirculated later, when McVeigh and Nichols were tried in federal court.

"Mike Brescia is supposedly a dead ringer for John Doe 2," a *Village Voice* reporter said to Robert Millar in 1996. "And I'm Santa Claus," Millar replied. At the end all these theories required lots of speculation. And the speculation in this case went on without end.[32]

The Second Underground Collapses

December 14, 1995. The post–Oklahoma City bomb crackdown continued in Montana, where the U.S. attorney filed fraud and conspiracy
charges against twelve members of the Freemen. For the feds, the white
republic constructed in the minds of the Freemen was not an issue to be
adjudicated. The main charges revolved around wire fraud, the creation
of "worthless documents in the likeness of valuable and negotiable commercial instruments," essentially a fake check-writing scam, and the interstate transfer of stolen goods. The IRS was among the dupes, actually
accepting fraudulent checks written for more than the taxpayers owed.
The agency paid back the "overage" in real dollars, in one case sending a
check for fourteen thousand dollars to a California woman who owed
eight thousand in back taxes. The Freemen tried to buy guns and ammunition with one million dollars in phony checks. They also tried to buy six
trucks in Wyoming. Both the weapons and truck deals fell through.

The indictment's fraud counts described the Freemen's criminal
artistry. But an indelicate thuggery weighted other charges, including
the theft of camera equipment from a network news crew sent out to
film on location. More than a dozen other charges involved firearms.
And one of the overt acts cited in the conspiracy charge involved a late-
night convoy on September 28, 1995. Five Freemen leaders—several already fugitives from other charges—accompanied by others armed with
sidearms and assault-style rifles, had openly defied authorities and traveled from Musselshell County to Garfield County. Here, at a spot they
called Justus Township, the Freemen took their last stand.

To non-Freemen, this "township" consisted of a 960-acre wheat farm
and cattle ranch blessed with a natural spring, two fishponds, ranch-
style houses, log cabins, and outbuildings.[1] Long burdened by a debt in-

curred during the buy now, pay later land inflation boom of the 1970s, the farm had gone bankrupt in the agricultural crisis of the early 1980s. At that time the principal debtors joined the ranks of other farmers looking to Posse-style hucksters plying no-win medicine oils in the countryside. Predictably, the bad debt got only worse. After years of default, the bank sold the farm on November 16, 1994, with the proviso that the debtors had the right to redeem the property for a year after the sale.[2] By that time, however, the debtors had joined the Freemen and refused to vacate the land.[3] Instead, they turned the bankrupt acreage into a compoundlike setting as activists from other territories joined in.

A shifting assortment of two to three dozen men, women, and children hunkered down at Justus Township. In addition to the tools of their trade—computers, diskettes, and laser printers used for creating phony financial instruments—they stockpiled weapons. Whether cached away or worn on their hips, fifty-nine rifles, twenty-four handguns, eight shotguns, ammunition clips, and speed loaders made them a formidable armed force, even if most of the weapons were small caliber or bolt action.[4] They built "survival" bunkers and stockpiled food, and they sealed off a county road that passed through the property. In the main house, one large space was converted into a classroom, with old lawbooks and an encyclopedia set stashed in a cabinet near weapons and ammunition. A trailer set on the farmstead's perimeter served as the Freemen's guardpost, and they stood duty under an American flag.

They adopted an elaborate code of rules to live by that included compassion toward the "poor and needy," as well as proscriptions against "unclean animals unfit to eat." Included on that list were hogs, rabbits, catfish, shellfish, and camels. Among the "General Health Laws" was a rule that "garments worn by one who has a contagious disease are to be burned." Smoking cigarettes, however, was not outlawed, and the adults smoked constantly. These rules reflected how Christian Identity theology pervaded life decisions at Justus Township in Montana, just as it had motivated the Covenant, the Sword and the Arm of the Lord camp in Arkansas twelve years earlier. There were other similarities. The township, like the camp, had become a nodal point for like-minded activists, fugitives from the law and refugees from the routine of marginal middle-class lifestyles. Both compounds enjoyed immunity from law enforcement long after they had become centers of criminal activity. And the arrest and conviction of the ringleaders at the CSA effectively ended one period of clandestine resistance, just as the end of the Freemen saga signaled the effective conclusion of open defiance by militias and common law courts in the 1990s.

While the township was physically on a larger tract of land and more sparsely populated than the CSA camp had been (something like the difference between Montana itself and Arkansas), more than time and space distinguished the two compounds. The Covenant camp's leadership had been vertically structured, with James Ellison in a gurulike role at the top. By contrast, peer pressure, rather than a common obedience to a single leader, glued the Freemen characters one to the other. Perhaps for this reason, the FBI's capture of the principal leadership did not immediately result in the collapse of the group's will.

During the previous period, when the Freemen were building the larger common law court network, a federal agent succeeded in infiltrating the group. That agent attended one of the many classes, professed agreement, and began demonstrating his supposed support with contributions. At different times the agent bequeathed computers, a copy machine, and radio equipment to the township. The gifts bought him a measure of trust inside the group, and they also set up the FBI's coup de grâce. He brought a radio relay antenna to the farmstead and then persuaded two of the most senior leaders to leave the ranch house and help him erect a radio tower. When this trio was safely out of the sight line of those remaining behind, an FBI team moved in and quickly snared the two. They were whisked off to jail on March 27, 1996. The incident precipitated a siege lasting more than two months.[5]

During this standoff, the FBI's tactics were as flexible as the Freemen's were obstreperous. Instead of setting up barricades in plain view of the farmstead, agents remained virtually invisible to the fugitives, relying on numerous roadway checkpoints to control traffic and seal the area. No sharpshooters in black uniforms roamed the perimeter, as at Weaver's Ruby Ridge. No loud raucous music blasted at the compound, as had been done at Waco. The agency declined to electronically jam cellular telephone, television, or radio signals, leaving the Freemen relatively open channels to those off-site, through lines of communication that were quietly monitored. Instead of immediately shutting down power and utilities, the FBI waited until late in the standoff to cut electricity to the ranch. The nonconfrontational approach was clearly noticeable to the naked eye, and *The New York Times* tied the change directly to the criticism leveled at the agency following the debacles at Ruby Ridge and Waco.[6] No official wanted to give Louis Beam and John Trochmann and Pete Peters another set of martyrs to rally their troops behind. Also, when the Freemen refused to recognize that the FBI had jurisdiction in this case, the FBI enlisted one movement activist after another to negotiate on the government's behalf over an eighty-one-day period.[7]

Montana politicians and a state senator from Colorado were among the more than forty individuals who took turns meeting with the

Freemen. The most colorful was Bo Gritz, who flew into Garfield County in his own small plane with sidekick Jack McLamb and Randy Weaver in tow. The feds would not let Weaver past the checkpoint, but they gave Gritz and McLamb a grand reception. Trying to reproduce their success at Ruby Ridge four years earlier, Gritz spent five days talking with those still billeted inside. He commiserated over the financial difficulties farmers faced. He even resorted to a personal prayer with each person. "I took each person firmly by the hand, looked deep into their eyes, called their name and gave them a blessing that we would meet again in this same form," Gritz wrote of the session. All to no avail. Nevertheless, when Gritz finally left the area, he wrote an instructive seventeen-page intelligence assessment of the group and made it public. Among his conclusions: those Freemen still at the ranch wanted to communicate directly with one leader who had been arrested in the antenna sting.[8]

Enter then Kirk Lyons, Esquire. Lyons may have been married at the Aryan Nations campground in a ceremony conducted by Richard Butler, but his credentials northwest of the Mason-Dixon Line still needed burnishing. Randy Weaver, after all, had named Gerry Spence his attorney, not Lyons. And his contention that he was simply a "white separatist" who would gladly move to Sweden if someone just gave him enough money did not diffuse the "supremacist" and white nationalist politics he exuded. Early in this Freemen standoff, Lyons called the FBI and offered his services as a negotiator. After the collapse of Gritz's negotiations, and of others, the FBI called him back. Soon Lyons and two colleagues were on a plane to Montana, courtesy of the federal government.[9]

Lyons presented an unusual plan, but after deliberations the FBI accepted it. It guaranteed uninterrupted passage to one of the indicted fugitives, alongside attorney Lyons, from the farmstead to a meeting with the leader already in jail. After the two men deliberated, the FBI then allowed the same indicted Freeman to return unimpeded to the farmstead.[10] The Freemen wanted a surrender agreement that preserved their cache of multiple legal documents. The government gave Lyons the okay. Two days later, on June 13, 1996, all those still besieged surrendered to the FBI. Lyons watched as the papers in question were loaded on a truck. At an opportune moment he walked over to the Freemen's flagpole at the perimeter, lowered the American flag (which had been flying upside down for the past three weeks), and raised a Confederate battle flag. It was exactly the same gesture he had made at the courthouse in Fort Smith, Arkansas, in 1988, after the seditious conspiracy acquittals. Wherever Lyons stood, North or South, it appeared that his flag was still the Confederate war banner, and his core allegiances were unchanged.

He may have walked away from the bloodless surrender with his reputation buffed up a bit, but for those who were paying attention, the FBI got the major credit for preventing the arrests of a dozen fugitive check-writing scam artists from turning into another apocalyptic ball of fire. The FBI had finally won a round in the court of public opinion. The feds' softball tactics had also succeeded in splitting their militia opposition. During the standoff, several prominent militia figures had called for large-scale confrontations, including mobilizing at the Justus Township site itself, much as had been done at Weaver's Ruby Ridge and at Waco. John Trochmann's Militia of Montana, on the other hand, took an opposite tack in its newsletter: "Our position has been and will continue to be, as long as this operation remains peaceful . . . for patriots to remain in their own home." Instead, the Trochmanns proposed working with Montana legislators to defuse the situation, and they excoriated those few who attempted to create a stir.[11]

At the same time that the FBI was rising in the public's estimation, the Freemen were sinking. One movement personality after another had come to Montana sympathetic to their case. They usually left after several days with harsh words for the fugitives' intransigence.

The most accurate assessment of the situation was Chris Temple's. At Pete Peters's Estes Park meeting Temple had proposed a two-stage strategy to take advantage of the feds' incompetence during the Weaver debacle. At the time Temple still resided in Montana and regularly wrote commentary for a Christian Identity tabloid published in California. He had served successfully as cochair of the Weaver support committee, the United Citizens for Justice. And he had made his core national socialist beliefs a nonissue as he snuggled up close to the Robertson-style Christian right in the state. The Freemen "are at the center of the most significant clash between the . . . federal government and its citizens since Waco," Chris Temple wrote at the time of the siege. Nevertheless, he couldn't support the Freemen. They had stolen from regular everyday people, he complained, not just banks or government agencies. "Even local townspeople have been alienated deeply" by threats against some local officials, he lamented. The Freemen were simply greedy and had shown contempt for their neighbors.

Temple also recognized that the Freemen standoff had helped put a comma, if not a period, at the end of an era favorable to militia and common law court organizing. "Millions of people, after Ruby Ridge and Waco, started to seriously question their rulers for the first time in ages," Temple wrote. "The sad reality for the moment is that this conduct on the part of some of the Freemen has allowed the FBI to significantly rehabilitate itself in the eyes of the average American," he concluded.[12]

Crackdown After the Okahoma City Bomb

After the FBI and ATF quashed the Aryan Republican Army and concluded the Freemen siege, law enforcement authorities continued the post–Oklahoma City crackdown for several more years. A 1996 law called the Antiterrorism and Effective Death Penalty Act expanded the FBI's mandate, and two presidential directives in 1998 followed. As a result, FBI money specifically allocated for fighting terrorism doubled between 1995 and 1998—from $256 to $581 million—with a significant share of that going to snaring "domestic terrorists" such as those described above.[13]

The FBI's definition of "domestic terrorism" needs complete mention: "the unlawful use, or threatened use, of force or violence by a group or individual based and operating entirely within the United States or Puerto Rico without foreign direction committed against person or property to intimidate or coerce a government, the civilian population, or any segment thereof in furtherance of political or social objectives." Although this definition seems completely straightforward, its actual interpretation had long been subject to nuance and political gerrymandering. In the FBI's 1983 "Analysis of Terrorist Incidents in the United States," for example, thirty-one incidents were documented; they included eight "attempted bombings" alongside actual bombings, murder, and arson. Only one group from the white supremacist movement was cited, the Posse Comitatus, after Gordon Kahl shot two federal marshals in North Dakota. No Klan groups were listed. And none of the multiple bombings of medical clinics providing abortions was listed among the incidents—despite the perpetrators' indisputable attempt to "intimidate or coerce" a civilian population in furtherance of political objectives.

After 1995 the FBI's analytical emphasis shifted. At that point it decided the "face of domestic terrorism" had changed. It noted "an increase in activities associated with right wing groups," along with a decline in incidents from the left.[14] The militia and common law courts were now mentioned in its "risk assessment" of domestic terrorism. The agency shed any lingering hesitance about making difficult arrests. Preventing another Oklahoma City, not another Waco or Ruby Ridge, was now uppermost.

In one instance, a known fugitive in Montana, who had billeted himself away for three years at home, was finally served an old warrant for attempted murder.[15] In Ohio a militia "chaplain" was shot to death during a routine traffic stop.[16] In Oklahoma four people were arrested for planning a fertilizer and fuel oil bomb spree aimed at gay bars and civil rights groups.[17] In West Virginia seven arrests followed discovery of a plot to bomb an FBI building. In Arizona twelve militiamen were charged in a bomb plot, and in Georgia another three were arrested in a different plot.[18] Authorities now investigated ideologically motivated crimes more thoroughly. The army also launched an internal inquiry after a North Carolina–based skinhead soldier was charged with the random killing of black pedestrians.[19]

Law enforcement also arrested a gang of family members that called themselves the Aryan People's Republic. Commanded by twenty-two-year-old[20] Chevie Kehoe, this gang robbed a gun dealer in Arkansas, came back a year later and murdered him and his wife and little girl, kidnapped others, killed an erstwhile comrade, and shot it out with the police. The stolen weapons and loot were initially stored at Elohim City before being transported back to the Spokane, Washington, area. Some of the guns were later used by Peter Langan's Aryan Republican Army. The crime spree ended after Chevie's brother and coconspirator Cheyne turned himself in and informed the cops where his brother was hiding out.[21]

Nailed earlier in this extended crackdown was a group calling itself the Phineas Priesthood. It committed its first robbery in Spokane, Washington, in April 1996, while the Freemen siege was still under way. It set a pipe bomb at the local newspaper, *The Spokesman Review*, as a diversion, and robbed an area bank. During a second robbery of the same bank that July, it bombed a local Planned Parenthood clinic. On October 8, just six months after its first known robbery, FBI agents arrested three of its central figures: Charles Barbee, Robert Berry, and Verne Jay Merrell.

All three were socially stable, with long-term employment and marriage résumés without the kinds of abuses exhibited by the Kehoe men. Berry, age forty-two, ran an auto repair shop and had been married for eighteen years. Barbee, aged forty-four, had worked for twenty-two years at AT&T and been married for fifteen years with two young children. Verne Jay Merrell, age fifty, was neither blue collar nor economically distressed. Born into an upper-middle-class family in 1945, and raised in a Philadelphia suburb, he joined the navy in 1963 and spent twelve years working on nuclear submarines. After discharge he worked in private industry at four nuclear power plants. Merrell joined the Arizona Patriots in the early 1980s and left the power plant world behind. He resettled in Idaho in 1988, at a time when Aryan Nations and others were promoting a Northwest Republic. All three lived in northern Idaho's Panhandle and attended a Christian Identity church in the Sandpoint, Idaho, area.[22]

They were so thoroughly ensconced in their local communities that one jury found them difficult to convict. Only with a second trial, in 1997, did government prosecutors send the trio to jail. It wasn't their personalities or crimes that made this gang particularly noteworthy, however. Rather it was their invocation of a biblical character named Phineas that was most significant and requires some additional explanation.

The story of the so-called Phineas Priesthood had been popularized by the Christian Identity writer Richard Kelly Hoskins in a 1990 self-published book titled *Vigilantes of Christendom: The Story of the Phineas Priesthood*. Hoskins even developed a symbol for Phineas, an elongated capital letter *P* with a crossbar just under the semicircle. In 1996 the bank robbers left a note behind with the symbol on it and in another declared that "the high priests of Yahweh" were at work.[23] This small group was thus dubbed the Phineas Priesthood.

The Phineas story appears in Chapter 25 of the Book of Numbers, and occurs during a period where the twelve tribes are still wandering in the desert. According to the Hebrew Bible (in which the name is spelled with an additional *h*, Phinehas), unfaithful Israelite men had developed sexual unions with the women of neighboring tribes and had taken up the practices of Baal worship. As a result, the ancient Israelites suffered God's wrath and a plague. In order to expiate them of these sins, God commanded Moses to publicly execute the apostate ringleaders. Before Moses could carry out the command, however, Phinehas, a descendant of the priestly lineage through Aaron, noticed a prominent Israelite, Zimri, duck into an alcove to have sex with a Midianite princess named Cozbi. Phinehas grabbed his spear and stabbed them both to death while they were in the act. The plague against Israel was lifted. And Phinehas became a high priest. Rabbinical commentaries on this text in the millennia since have not treated Phinehas kindly, explicitly concerned that "he set a dangerous precedent by taking the law into his own hands."[24]

It was precisely this vigilante aspect of the story that attracted a stratum of the Christian Identity faithful. By Hoskins's telling, Phineas justifiably killed two people because they were engaged in "interracial" sex. (Actually, there are no "races" in the Hebrew Bible, and the differences between Israelites and Midianites are significant because of the Baal worship of the latter tribe. Moses of course most famously married a Midianite woman, Zipporah.)

In his book, Hoskins used the Phineas story to emphasize the theological justification for current-day violence. The title "priest" was an honorific earned in the defense of God's Law (as Christian Identity adherents understood it). These so-called priests "believe that their God has called them to their dangerous work," Hoskins wrote. "Anyone they consider to have violated any of the laws written in the Bible may become their quarry." The usual list of violations included interracial marriage (or sex), homosexuality, abortion, and usury, and the "dangerous work" to which Hoskins alluded involved the crimes of murder, bank robbery, and bombing clinics. He took his book on the road, selling it at Christian Identity meetings from Virginia to Idaho over the next few years.

The idea—and it was a concept rather than an organizational name at that point—found supporters.[25] Some movement activists wore the symbol as a belt buckle. A Posse Comitatus group in Ohio declared that a former White Patriot Party cadre was reputed to be a Phineas priest, without actually mentioning a name or the murderous act.[26] One Klan newsletter, published during the early 1990s, described the initial formation of the Klan after the Civil War as the surfacing of a Phineas Priesthood.[27] Further popularizing the story, a Pennsylvania skinhead group published a short-lived newsletter entitled *Phineas*.

Despite this spate of activity promoting vigilante murder, an October 1991 *New York Times* article noted that the Phineas Priesthood had "gone unnoticed by those who track white supremacist groups." Further, "among those contacted who said they knew little or nothing of the group were Klanwatch, the Department of Justice and the Anti-Defamation League of B'nai B'rith."[28] Until the 1996 Spokane robberies the Phineas name had not registered with the FBI either.

The anonymity of the Phineas Priesthood concept, however short-lived, underlined the complexity and contradictions of the situation after the bombing of the Oklahoma City federal building. Despite the heinous nature of the crimes in Oklahoma City, similarly focused vanguardist bands had multiplied, as if robbing banks were the same thing as picketing a shoe store. The Freemen had bilked their neighbors even as they claimed to build a white republic, separating themselves off from the surrounding community in the name of mass resistance. In the past, periods of heightened vanguardist activity such as this had pushed mainstreamers to the side, and vice versa. Not during the mid-1990s, however, as the usual lines demarcating the differences between the two strategic tendencies became blurred. While violence and mayhem abounded, the electioneering side of the movement grew also. This time it ensconced itself in the Buchananite wing of the Republican Party and developed an increased vibrancy represented best by the rebirth of the Council of Conservative Citizens.

(Re)Birth of the Council of Conservative Citizens

July 22, 1995. The FBI was still searching for John Doe Two when twelve hundred people gathered in the hamlet of Black Hawk, Mississippi, for an old-fashioned barbecue picnic and political rally. They listened to a seven-piece band playing country and gospel music, ate chicken, and heard from a list of almost three dozen politicians who ranged from state representatives to Governor Kirk Fordice. The event was sponsored by a bus company and the Carroll County chapter of the Council of Conservative Citizens, an unabashedly white nationalist organization with roots stretching back to the battles against desegregation in the 1950s. Carroll County had been one of its strongholds from the beginning. Located in north-central Mississippi, about 100 miles due south of Memphis, the county contained fewer than ten thousand people, and almost half, 45 percent, were black. White political hegemony had long rested on the disenfranchisement of black people. The county had more registered voters than residents in 1990, according to a report in *The Clarion-Ledger* (Jackson).[1] In this relatively poor and rural county, only 40 percent of the adult population had graduated from high school at the time data were collected for the U.S. Commerce Department's 1983 *Statistical Abstract*. Many of the county's white children attended private schools.[2] Preeminent among these was the Carroll Academy in Carrollton, established largely through the effort of the local chapter of the Citizens Councils of America, the precursor to the Council of Conservative Citizens sponsoring the picnic that day. From its inception as a regular event, the Black Hawk rally had been associated with that school and known as a gathering spot for segregationists and white supremacists. At this affair, Senator Trent Lott was the special guest speaker, introduced by the council's field organizer, Bill Lord, Jr.[3]

Elected to Congress in 1972 as a Republican, Lott was one of the first southern white politicians to have permanently left the state Democratic Party. He routinely voted against measures associated with civil rights, including reauthorization of the Voting Rights Act and recognition of Martin Luther King's birthday as a national holiday. He also repeatedly identified himself (and the contemporary Republican Party) with the Confederate cause. In one interview, Lott claimed "the fundamental principles" that Confederate President "Jefferson Davis believed in . . . apply to the Republican Party."[4] He was first elected to the U.S. Senate in 1988.

Lott had spoken at several council fests in the past. In May 1982, while still a congressman and serving as House minority whip, he had urged 200 banquet guests at the Carroll Academy to "fight for the principles of the Citizens Council program."[5] On April 11, 1992, Lott had once again graced the head table at a formal Council of Conservative Citizens dinner in Greenwood.[6] Standing alongside Bill Lord before a large COUNCIL OF CONSERVATIVE CITIZENS banner, Lott told the assembled diners: "The people in this room stand for the right principles and the right philosophy." For that occasion, Lott was introduced from the dais by his uncle, the Mississippi state senator Arnie Watson, who also served as a local Citizens Councils officer.[7] Arnie Watson was a brother to Trent Lott's mother, Ione Watson Lott, and he considered himself the U.S. senator's favorite uncle. "Trent is an honorary member" of the council, Watson told *The New York Times* in 1999. Lott's support for old-fashioned segregationist politics and his standing relationship with the councils later became points of public controversy. In 1982, 1992, and 1995, however, standing up for the Confederate battle flag and private white schools and the glories of Jim Crow segregation just seemed like the right thing to do.

The Citizens Councils of America was founded after the Supreme Court's *Brown* decision in 1954, and it became known as the white citizens' councils and the downtown Klan to civil rights activists. In several southern states, where they were intertwined with local businesses, state government, and law enforcement, the councils led the resistance to desegregation. The man credited with starting the "council" movement, Mississippi State Circuit Judge Tom Brady, wrote a manifesto supporting white supremacy and promising massive resistance to integration in the South.[8] Brady was a onetime delegate to the Democratic Party's National Convention, like many other southern segregationists during the Jim Crow era, and later became a state supreme court judge.[9]

At the Citizens Councils of America's height it claimed sixty thousand members, according to Neil McMillen in *The Citizens' Council: Organized Resistance to the Second Reconstruction, 1954–64.*

During the 1950s and 1960s, Willis Carto made repeated overtures to the organization and its leaders. He spoke at its meetings, won its formal approval when first starting Liberty Lobby, and put Judge Brady on an early advisory board. Carto also developed an independent correspondence and working relationship with Brady. The councils eschewed Carto's explicitly anti-Semitic rhetoric, however, and a few Jewish businessmen joined its ranks. The pages of its bulletin, *The Citizen*, continued to expound white supremacist theories until it closed down. Once the battle to defend state-sponsored segregation was decisively defeated, however, the organization's founders exhibited little more than regret for the lost past and little vision of a post–civil rights era future. And so it began a long slow decline during the 1970s.

During the Carter administration, when other elements of the white supremacist movement began to surge again, the Citizens Councils continued to shrink. The remaining centers of activity in Carroll County, Mississippi, St. Louis, Missouri, and Memphis, Tennessee, acted as hubs for other local chapters. Political and social activism, rather than propaganda or pure ideology, kept these groups alive. Besides electing their own officers, members continued fighting against school busing. They built support for private (all-white) academies. They campaigned for candidates for office—from school boards to county commissions to U.S. Congress. They held picnics and other social affairs, and one chapter even had its own women's bowling team. At the same time, these relatively innocuous activities continued to come wrapped in an undiluted rationale for the supremacy of those who deemed themselves white.

One of the most telling events occurred in 1979, when the Memphis council sponsored an appearance by the British national socialist John Tyndall, who was then traveling the United States much as he did again in 1991. Apparently, Tyndall so enthralled his Memphis audience that the council's tabloid, now called *Citizens Informer*, gave two-thirds of a page to speech excerpts. The editors capitalized all of what was obviously meant to be Tyndall's thunderous conclusion: "AND THE WHITE MAN WILL ONCE AGAIN MARCH VICTORIOUSLY THROUGH THE JUNGLES AND DESERTS OF THE WORLD AND STAMP HIS WILL AND HIS GENIUS ON EVERY CORNER OF THE GLOBE." Tyndall's unveiled call for white world supremacy evoked "enthusiastic clapping," according to the report on the meeting.

The *Citizens Informer* tabloid, published from St. Louis rather than Mississippi, occupied a unique place at the time. By providing affiliated local councils with news of one another's activities, it kept the organization together during its years of relative inactivity. In October 1980, the month before Reagan was elected president, it counted nineteen local and state councils on its list. Of those, three were state or regional in nature: Arkansas, the "Kentuckiana" area around Louisville, and southern Michigan. Three local councils had Kentucky addresses, three were in Illinois, one was in Florida, and one uniquely active council was in Greater Memphis. Six chapters spanned the state of Missouri. In Mississippi, the organization's birthplace, only one was a chapter formally associated with the St. Louis publication, but local councils remained active elsewhere in the state. Two regional "coordinators" kept local groups moving. Bill Lord, Jr., operated out of Mississippi. Gordon Baum practiced personal injury law in St. Louis. Both doubled as Citizens Councils officials.

Finally, when the Citizens Councils of America gave way to the association calling itself the Council of Conservative Citizens, both Bill Lord and Gordon Baum helped birth the new formation.[10] The full transition to the Council of Conservative Citizens occurred over a five- to seven-year period, beginning in March 1985 with the creation of two related nonprofit corporations in Missouri and ending in 1990 with the final dissolution of the old Citizens Councils of America. Baum became the chief executive. The *Citizens Informer* tabloid, still published in St. Louis by a third corporation, became the house organ of this reassembled amalgam of organizational faces.[11] And the new Council of Conservative Citizens (CofCC) inherited the dead organization's mailing list and membership.[12] The conversion occurred unevenly as local groups of the old Citizens Councils changed their names and formally affiliated with the Council of Conservative Citizens. In the new CofCC's hometown, St. Louis, for example, local affiliates still referred to themselves as Citizens Councils for some time after the formation of the new group. Slowly, one local organization at a time switched its self-reference from the old to the new. The Manatee County, Florida, group was typical in this regard. In 1990 it still referred to itself as a Citizens Council. By the following year, however, it had adopted the new name and formally become a Council of Conservative Citizens group. In the same fashion, long-standing Citizens Councils leaders—at the local level, as well as regional and national figures—became part of this growing new structure.

While the old Citizens Councils had been simply holding on, the new Council of Conservative Citizens began a period of rapid growth in the early 1990s. Rather than simply market its tabloid to new subscribers, as

Liberty Lobby's *Spotlight* did, or look for a few good men to turn into revolutionary cadres, as National Alliance did, it focused existing organizational resources on developing new local councils as a matter of policy.[13] Like any self-respecting Rotary or Kiwanis club, councils gave their best activists plaques and awards, as if supporting South African apartheid were a form of public service. They elected local boards of directors, held regular meetings, and created an internal organizational life that socialized and educated their members—without drawing them into the small cultlike groups that salted the Christian patriot movement in the Midwest and West. By building a stable foundation, rather than sending funds to a central headquarters, they enabled future growth and leadership development to occur organically.

Further adding to the CofCC's momentum, they maintained a nonsectarian policy toward other like-minded efforts. Members joined their local Republican women's clubs, promoted local antitax groups, and helped elect school board members. They also continued supporting and sustaining all-white private schools, particularly in Mississippi, much as Citizens Councils had in the past. And councils adopted a set of issues that paid significant organizational dividends, such as preservation of the Confederate flag and memorials. As a result, the CofCC could reasonably point to itself as uniquely embodying the unity of white nationalism and traditional southern conservatism. Sam Francis was among the first to extol this virtue. "By supporting and uniting the right to keep and bear arms, the right to life, tax reform, crime control . . ." he wrote, "the CCC actually works towards building a real national and unified coalition."[14]

For those weary of the competitive battles fought by Willis Carto and others, pragmatic collaboration was a safe port in factional seas. Further adding to its strength, CofCC members entwined themselves in the Republican Party's Buchananite wing like kudzu on an Arkansas hillside. The council's emphasis on working at the Republicans' grass roots had handsomely rewarded a relatively small investment. Witness the prominence of Mississippi State Senator Mike Gunn.[15] Like Sam Francis, Gunn had once served on the staff of North Carolina Senator John East. In 1990, Gunn won election to Mississippi's house of representatives, and in 1992 he took a seat in the state senate. Gunn proposed legislation requiring women receiving welfare to have a semipermanent contraceptive, Norplant, embedded in their arms. The measure failed. Nevertheless, the American Legislative Exchange Council named Gunn its "outstanding legislator of the year" at its 1993 annual meeting.[16] Gunn maintained a multifaceted relationship with other white nationalists. In addition to serving on the Council of Conservative Citizens' national board of directors, he ran a direct mail business. He did work for candidate David Duke in 1990 and 1991 and was paid ninety-five hundred dollars for designing a fund-raising solicitation.[17] When Pat Buchanan came to Mississippi in April 1995 to receive the support of Governor Kirk Fordice, Buchanan made a side trip to the Ross Barnett Reservoir, to speak at a fund-raiser for Mike Gunn. "Mike is a good friend of ours," Bay Buchanan told the local newspaper.

Sam Francis commented on these types of efforts in *The Washington Times*: "The result of the mainstream conservative strategy has been to dilute and disperse right-wing efforts . . . but since its main goal was fund-raising, who cared anyway? In contrast, the CCC goal is to make each cause work with and support the others, thus multiplying their impact on lawmakers and creating an authentic synthesis of the values and interests of Middle America."[18]

As a result of these policies and the growth they engendered, the Council of Conservative Citizens began to absorb activists from white nationalism's further corners. Most were from the second and third tiers of movement leadership. Their names, personalities, and immediate past activist histories, however, added to the CofCC's growing importance inside the movement. From David Duke's Republican campaigns in Louisiana emerged Hope Lubrano and Kenny Knight, among others. Knight brought his experience as Duke's campaign manager, and Lubrano had been a key organizer who later worked for Buchanan in the presidential primaries. From the Populist Party came A. J. Barker, the North Carolina siding salesman. Less than a year after joining, Barker became chair of the CofCC North Carolina affiliate. Also from the Populist Party's ranks came William Carter, a chiropractor who became the council's South Carolina state chair. As activists from a variety of groups enlisted, so too did a few well-placed cadres from William Pierce's National Alliance, who took up positions of influence and authority. Conspicuously absent in this growing formation was Liberty Lobby, and *The Spotlight* continued to ignore the council.[19]

Despite the presence of anti-Semites in its ranks, the CofCC shied away from explicit organizational expressions of anti-Semitism. The absence of conspiracy mongering and anti-Semitic "Jews run the world" rhetoric contributed to the CofCC's expansion, keeping it from diving completely off the political margins. Conspiracy theories typically turned every mundane occurrence into a grand metaphysical battle between good and evil. By contrast, the CofCC developed a surehanded, down-to-earth analysis of events. And without a nasty cloud of anti-Jewish rhetoric steaming up its meeting rooms, the CofCC persona more closely resembled that of everyday nondoctrinaire racism. Simply put,

CofCC activists lived and talked and acted much like many other white conservatives opposed to "special rights" for people of color. This policy on anti-Semitism enabled the most significant addition to the council's mix after 1994, as the leading figures of Jared Taylor's *American Renaissance* enterprise joined up. Both Taylor and Sam Francis were enlisted to the *Citizens Informer's* editorial advisory board, and several *Renaissance* contributors and conference speakers were invited to council meetings to make special presentations.

Taylor spoke at a gathering in Little Rock in April 1994 and then at a Georgia meeting alongside Sam Dickson and A. J. Barker that July. Again at council events honoring the Confederate dead, Taylor delivered his ideas on crime, the media, and flags. The council republished Taylor's defense of Confederate symbols: "The reason why the Confederacy is under such violent attack today is that it is a symbol not only of the white culture that the ethnic saboteurs wish to destroy, but is also seen—rightly or wrongly—as a symbol of a white culture that refuses to apologize. What better way to attack white America than to insult the last remnant of a *proud* white America [emphasis in original]."[20]

The *American Renaissance* grouping added intellectual heft to the council's grassroots activism, and over the next few years the two organizations became almost completely intermeshed. After *The Washington Times* threw Sam Francis out the window, his ties to the CofCC became even stronger.

The Washington Times Fires Sam Francis

September 29, 1995. *The Washington Times* published its last column by Samuel Francis, 868 words supporting an American soldier's refusal to submit to the New World Order and wear a United Nations helmet while on military duty in the former Yugoslavia. At that moment the disintegration of the Balkan state threatened to spread even further, and UN troops stood between competing ethnic-based nationalities. Francis argued in his usual bad-boy America-first style against any involvement in the region including multilateral efforts such as peacekeeping.

Although the *Times* considered itself a bastion for responsible conservatives in the country's capital, Francis's irresponsible ultranationalism had never been punished at the paper. But another event that week led to his submitting his resignation upon request.[1]

Getting fired is usually not news. Excessive absenteeism is a frequent cause for young workers for whom getting out of bed on Monday morning is too difficult, and middle-aged moms risk losing their jobs when their children get sick. Highly paid fifty-five-year-old professionals often "retire" early, to be replaced by those younger and lower on the wage scale. Salespeople who don't meet their quotas are routinely "let go." Whether or not they pay union dues, factory hands unable to keep pace with an assembly line producing sixty widgets an hour get "sacked." None of those above, however, would likely describe getting canned as "defenestration." Nor would they be able to excoriate former bosses in two installments in *Chronicles*, a national magazine of cultural criticism.[2] Nor would the average widget worker believe that the unyielding dogmatism of neoconservatives was the unspoken force behind the pink slip. But Sam Francis did. And he was right on all counts, including his usage of a Latinate term for getting thrown out a window.

Francis had not been just any ordinary editorialist, he would be the first to tell you. In nine years at *The Washington Times* he had served in multiple capacities, including editorial page editor and "nationally syndicated staff columnist." He had won awards more prestigious than any other received by a *Times* journalist. Despite his years of highly acclaimed service, he had been thrown out as if he were an obituary writer made redundant by a decline in the death rate.[3]

The most proximate cause of Francis's fall from conservative grace was a column he wrote attacking a Southern Baptist Convention's declaration that slavery had been a sin for which it asked forgiveness. As a matter of history, the Southern Baptist Convention needed to address the question of slavery, inasmuch as it had first been organized in 1845 as part of the southern defense of the peculiar institution. According to Francis, however, "neither 'slavery' nor 'racism' as an institution is a sin." In his defense, he argued, the apostle Paul had spoken in favor of "servants" obeying their "masters." Only with the Enlightenment, he wrote, did "a bastardized version of Christian ethics condemn slavery" and the "poison of equality" seep into the "tissues of the West."[4]

As Francis carefully pointed out, he was not guilty of theologically justifying slavery. He had simply called his readers' attention to the fact that the New Testament did not rule out slavery. And to buttress the point, he said that neither of his two immediate supervisors at *The Washington Times* had seen fit to pull the offending column before it ran or even make a preliminary editorial comment on its content. Nevertheless, the day after his column ran, Francis was summarily demoted in position and given a punitive cut in pay.

Three months later Francis's position deteriorated further after the rival *Washington Post* published a book excerpt on the first *American Renaissance* conference. It included a description of Sam Francis's call for an explicit white racial consciousness to defend the genetic material that had made America great. He was told to "resign." Just like that.[5]

Francis was abashed. Why had he been fired from a newspaper whose chief editor had once claimed to defend the Confederate flag? he asked. He concluded that a neoconservative cabal had been at least partially responsible. The *Times*, Francis claimed, was actually in the hands of fake conservatives, who (by Francis's reckoning) were really liberal wolves. In his mind, the "neos" wanted to drive "paleos" such as him out of positions of influence in Washington, D.C. [6]

Initially, neoconservatives were disappointed liberals who claimed they were driven into conservative ranks by the supposed excesses of the radical left in the 1960s. Through much of the 1970s and 1980s they retained a moderately conservative social agenda along with a fierce opposition to the Soviet Union and its sphere of influence. Before the Cold War ended, neoconservatives occupied key positions in several of the wellspring foundations and think tanks of the conservative movement. And they remained globalist and interventionist, in contrast with the nativism and isolationism that characterized paleoconservatives.[7] Paleoconservatives harkened back to the conservative movement as it existed prior to World War Two. They were traditionalists and social conservatives, unafraid of the tinge of racism and anti-Semitism periodically associated with their ideas. A deep schism between the two trends had emerged during the 1980s, when they fought over money and positions of power within the Reagan coalition.[8]

The split over foreign policy in 1990, when Pat Buchanan, regarded as a paleoconservative, opposed President Bush's drive for war in the Persian Gulf, was one piece of this larger dispute. At stake in September 1995, when Francis was fired, he claimed, were the "limits" that could not be transgressed when respectable conservatives discussed race. Francis's analysis had the ring of truth. He had crossed the border and been thrown out as a result.[9]

The erstwhile Heritage Foundation analyst and former senior aide to a U.S. senator, having been fired from the self-described conservative newspaper of record, now suffered no additional penalty from stepping even farther to the white side. When the Populist Party met for the last time on September 16, 1995—eleven years, one month, and one day after its founding convention—in attendance were Sam Francis and his colleague Jared Taylor from *American Renaissance*. They witnessed the formal vote taken to "suspend" operations of the entity called the Populist Party, as the party officially disbanded.[10] Francis's appearance at this event confirmed his trajectory out of the conservative establishment and into the leadership of the contra-establishment, the Council of Conservative Citizens.

As the council convened its semiannual board meeting and "national conference" in Birmingham the first week of December 1995, this gathering exhibited all the earmarks of organizational health. Two locally elected officials greeted the crowd. A small choir of preachers invoked Jesus' name and delivered grace. A Wetumpka city councilman pledged his opposition to gun control and support for the Confederate flag. Mississippi State Senator Mike Gunn added his name to the speakers' rostrum. Anti-immigrant activists from Alabama, Florida, and California, including a representative from the group that had spearheaded the

Proposition 187 campaign, warned of the dangers and prospects ahead. Also speaking that day were Jared Taylor, the American Renaissancer, and Judge Roy Moore, who was then making himself notorious by refusing to disassemble a courthouse monument to the Ten Commandments in a case that eventually wound its way to the Supreme Court. The *Citizens Informer* reported on Taylor's appearance at the Birmingham meet and published his photo on page one in a lineup that also included Judge Moore. On these pages, at least graphically, scientific racism joined Christian fundamentalism.[11]

Francis and Taylor, by eschewing conspiracy mongering and what they called "paramilitary infantilism," gave white nationalism greater potential access to the conservative mainstream.[12] While their emphasis on traditional culture and authority didn't create any new audiences among white power skinheads, the absence of bloodthirsty rhetoric kept away the bombers and shooters. And as Pat Buchanan prepared for his second run through the Republican primaries, the Council of Conservative Citizens developed the legs and lungs of a long-distance runner.

The years since 1992 had vindicated Pat Buchanan's initial campaign. He had tapped a nascent force that had grown into a full-scale "angry white man" syndrome, complete with a measurable distrust of government and the mass marshaling of militias. His anti-immigrant rhetoric had been followed by Proposition 187 in California. An insurgency had started that had not yet been quelled by the horror felt after the Oklahoma City bombing.

Buchanan had held his own forces together during these years with moneys developed by a nonprofit corporation bequeathed by an old friend from the Reagan White House. He renamed it The American Cause, installed himself as chairman, his wife, Shelley Buchanan, as vice chair, and his sister Bay as president. He added several former campaign aides to the payroll, keeping family and friends employed and available in off-election years. The corporation's nonprofit educational status allowed it to raise and spend money outside the purview of the Federal Election Commission while essentially maintaining the rudiments of a campaign apparatus. Between 1992 and 1996 it raised two and a half million dollars, much of that from direct mail solicitations to the campaign's contributor list.[13] A second related corporation received almost two million dollars from just one donor, Roger Milliken, an ultraconservative South Carolinian with a miniempire in the textile industry, an industry increasingly challenged during the 1980s and 1990s by low-wage competitors overseas.[14] With Milliken's money behind him, Buchanan spent four years thumping the anti–free trade drum, urging new tariffs to protect domestic industry.

Buchanan's friend and colleague Sam Francis had urged him to add the fight against gun control to the antiabortion and antigay agenda. Battles for cultural symbols such as the Confederate flag were as important as (if not more so than) promoting school prayer, he urged. Put opposition to immigration and free trade side by side at the top of the Middle American platform, Francis said, because these issues spoke directly to the "racial dispossession of the historic American people."[15] Buchanan listened and freely borrowed from Sam Francis's ideas during the 1996 primary campaign.

Elections 1996: Pat Buchanan Roils the Republicans

February 20, 1996. Pat Buchanan stunned the Republican establishment and placed first in the Republican Party's New Hampshire primary. During the campaign he had hit long and hard on low-cost foreign labor competition, but his concern for workers' wages and conditions did not extend as far as supporting trade unions. AFL-CIO leaders challenged Buchanan's newly found concerns. "Saying Patrick Buchanan speaks for workers is like saying the Ayatollah Khomeini speaks for priests and rabbis," the head of the trade union federation said. "Patrick Buchanan is a racist, he's anti-Semitic, he bashes women right along with labor and immigration, and he's a believer in supply-side economics."[1]

Nevertheless, Buchanan drew the highest percentage of New Hampshire voters concerned most about the economy and jobs, 33 percent. Exit polls also found that almost 60 percent of his constituency described itself as "very conservative," and almost as many considered themselves part of the religious right. In other words, "religious right" voters were also concerned about the economy, and Buchanan had a hard core of very conservative support.

During the course of his campaign, Buchanan pushed issues of American sovereignty and economic nationalism to the fore. He made the usual complaints about moral relativism's replacing "Judeo-Christian" values. But those themes were subordinated to stories about proud bread-winning workers losing their jobs to cheap imports and runaway factories. Early in the process, he signed Gun Owners of America executive director Larry Pratt as a campaign cochair. He also took other steps to broaden his appeal past the religious right throughout the primaries. In southern states he embraced the Confederate battle flag. In Arizona he waved rifles in the air and dressed like a Saturday night cowboy. And he hit at brown-skinned workers from Latin America wherever immigration was an issue. Yet Buchanan was a white Christian nationalist first and foremost, and his voters understood that.

According to a most remarkable exit poll of Super Tuesday primary voters in seven states, 54 percent of those who considered abortion the most important issue pulled Buchanan's lever. He drew 46 percent of those most concerned about immigration. He won 42 percent of those most fixated on foreign trade. On all three issues related to moral traditionalism and national sovereignty, Buchanan drew greater percentages than any other Republican. But of those most interested in jobs and the economy, he won only 18 percent. Any claim to "economic populism" had been secondary, derived from his rhetorical style rather than his political substance. Nevertheless, he represented a significant constituency, and by the end of the primaries he had polled a total of more than three million votes, almost three hundred thousand more than he had won in 1992.[2]

Much like the 1992 campaign, Buchanan's 1996 bid had been dogged by revelations of white nationalists and militia promoters in the campaign apparatus—only more so. Just days before the New Hampshire election, controversy erupted over his selection of Larry Pratt as a campaign cochair. The issue became Pratt's appearance with Aryan Nations figures at Pete Peters's post-Weaver meet in Colorado. Pratt had been a fickle cochair in any case as he had spent little time at the podium actually promoting Buchanan. Nor did Pratt's cochair spot keep him off the podium of a Taxpayers Party–sponsored conference. Newspapers and political pundits called for Pratt's removal; no person with white supremacist links should be a campaign official, was the argument. As a consequence, Pratt voluntarily decided to take a "leave of absence" as campaign cochair, while denying that he was either racist or anti-Semitic. "I loathe the Aryan Nations and other racist groups with every fiber of my being," Pratt told the press.[3]

During the same period early in the primary season, another campaign cochair, Michael Farris, was revealed to have (briefly) attended a banquet honoring those who had been convicted of shooting abortion doctors. Farris claimed to have left the dinner as soon as he learned its purpose, however, and managed to keep his post.[4]

Media reports also told of a troubling incident during the Louisiana primary campaign, where Buchanan supporters distributed propaganda attacking Texas Senator Phil Gramm for marrying a woman of Korean descent. This was not Buchanan campaign material, however, but *The Truth at Last*, published by Ed Fields. Written as if the publication's readers were Republican regulars rather than hard-core anti-Semites and racists, it read: "Many conservatives will not vote for him [Gramm] in the primary due to his interracial marriage. He divorced a White wife to marry an Asiatic!" Capital letters and exclamation points were all included.[5] Louisiana's primary had been reset to precede both the Iowa caucuses and New Hampshire, and Gramm had expected to do well there. Instead, that state, where David Duke had once received more votes than any other Republican, placed Buchanan second behind Kansas senator Bob Dole. In fact, *The New York Times* reported that "3 of the 13 delegates Mr. Buchanan won in Louisiana" had previously worked for Duke.[6]

Having knocked Phil Gramm out of the race and damaged Bob Dole, Buchanan pushed into the southern states, and more trouble followed. After it was revealed that Susan Lamb, his Jacksonville, Florida, county campaign chair, was a member of David Duke's National Association for the Advancement of White People, she was summarily dismissed.[7] Buchanan's South Carolina state chair, William Carter, was also fired after the press learned that he had chaired David Duke's 1992 campaign in that state.[8] What did not become news, however, was Carter's long movement history, including a stint as state chair of the Populist Party and his current status as chair of the state's Council of Conservative Citizens chapter.[9] Neither Lamb nor Carter was allowed to take the "leave" accorded Pratt.

These and other revelations prompted Kansas Senator Bob Dole to tell the press that Buchanan had "extremist" views.[10] A number of prominent conservatives, however, rushed to defend him. Ralph Reed, who then directed the Christian Coalition, and David Keene, the head of the American Conservative Union, both defended Buchanan, the person and candidate.[11] Like others who had initially argued that Buchanan was neither anti-Semitic nor racist, they effectively dismissed the evidence that his white and Christian nationalism was outside acceptable Republican discourse. Further, they did not want to alienate Buchanan's voters, particularly the so-called Reagan Democrats. Much like Louisiana Republican state leaders who had tabled criticism of David Duke while he was pulling former Democrats into the Republican voting column, Buchanan's defenders wanted to keep his voting constituency inside the party.

Thus the "Hands off Buchanan" call had less to do with Buchanan's personal politics than with maintaining a Republican base among the antiabortion zealots, anti-immigrant activists, gunners, economic nationalists, and Confederate flag wavers drawn to his campaign.

Also notable among those defending him from the charge of anti-Semitism was Seattle Rabbi Daniel Lapin, whose organization, Toward

Tradition, openly allied itself with the Reverend Pat Robertson's Christian Coalition. "There are good reasons to oppose Pat Buchanan for president and legitimate ways in which to do it," Rabbi Lapin argued, but "accusing him of anti-Semitism is not a good reason and vilifying his followers is not a legitimate way."[12]

Liberty Lobby Support for Buchanan

Underneath the general media's radar, Liberty Lobby and *The Spotlight* endorsed Buchanan with a special edition *Republican Voter's Guide.* This four-page tabloid-size insert predictably nailed the "powerful Special Interest Groups Behind Media Attacks on Buchanan." Who were they? Well, if the readers could wait as long as the second paragraph, then they would learn that "the wealthy and powerful American Jewish community (popularly known as 'the Jewish lobby' or 'the Israeli lobby') does not like Pat Buchanan." His "victory would constitute the greatest political revolution in history," the tabloid opined.[13] If you agreed, Liberty Lobby was eager to sell you a subscription.

Actually, Liberty Lobby liked Pat the nationalist more than Pat the Republican. By April 1 *The Spotlight* had begun pushing the idea of Buchanan as a third party standard-bearer. He stood "at the crossroads." The Republican elites would not nominate him. On the other hand, "a new party would immediately galvanize the millions of Americans who no longer have a home in the Democratic or the Republican Party."[14] If Buchanan decided to bolt from the Republicans, he could make history. While Liberty Lobby had supported Buchanan's Republican bid in 1992, it could not countenance his continued stay in the party after the 1996 primaries. Later it declared that he had used and abused supporters and "callously" led them "astray" by not leaving Republican ranks in 1996.[15]

In contrast with Liberty Lobby, the Council of Conservative Citizens neither made exaggerated claims nor used Buchanan's campaign simply as a marketing opportunity for its own ideological goods. Instead, council members, many of whom had once filled the Populist Party's leadership ranks, trudged through the election-year cycle like realpolitik soldiers. In 1995, soon after Buchanan announced his candidacy, council members in New York City had joined with several Populist Party officials to sponsor a fund-raiser in the Bronx. Then they helped collect thirty thousand signatures to put Pat on New York State's Republican primary ballot.[16] In Mississippi, Republican state senator Mike Gunn gave Buchanan a special boost.[17] And after the South Carolina council state chair William Carter was fired by Buchanan's campaign, there was little of the Willis Carto–style petulant thrashing by his former allies.

The council quietly stayed the course and focused on supporting the Confederate flag and opposing free trade agreements, pressing its case where it could.

At the second *American Renaissance* conference that May, attendees expressed support for Buchanan's nationalism and unhappiness about his campaign. One participant worried that Buchanan's attempt to appeal to various constituencies did not evoke a sense of white unity. Another tried balancing the effects of negative media exposure against the harm done by campaign missteps. The most informed critic, Sam Francis, argued that Buchanan lacked politically steady advisers and had lost direction. With the eye of an insider, he claimed that Pat's sister Bay, who managed the campaign, was unable to direct the bunch of kids "running things." Francis recounted his "defenestration" since the last meet. And during a question and answer session, Francis declared that the Republican Party must be destroyed, a sentiment certainly shared by many other Buchanan supporters in the room.

For his part, Jared Taylor reprised his attack on the pernicious appeal of social equality and "multiculturalism." During the past two years Taylor's personal visibility at white nationalist venues had increased sharply, and he had become a regular speaker at Council of Conservative Citizens events and Confederate flag revivals. For the council itself, Gordon Baum stood and repeated his entreaty for new members. Atlanta attorney Sam Dickson closed the proceedings once again, this time with a biting attack on race traitors—much like his closing at the memorial for Revilo Oliver.

The most marked change was by Wayne Lutton, the Institute for Historical Review intimate turned anti-immigration guru. As at the 1994 meet, Lutton used facts, figures, and anecdotes to weave together a fearful picture of a dark-skinned voodoo-worshiping future. But this time his speaking style was polished and emotional, rousing the crowd with invocations that "demography is destiny." Like Sam Francis, he accused the Republican Party of surrendering the continent to a "non-Western" invasion.[18] As the twenty-first century came into view, and the time when white people would lose their majority status loomed larger, Lutton and his anti-immigrant program became increasingly important.

In one postconference appraisal, published in Wilmot Robertson's *Instauration* newsletter, Lutton was credited as the only speaker with a sense of direction. The emphasis on IQ and crime, this writer averred, did not penetrate the enormity of the demographic tsunami facing Anglo-Saxondom. Particularly irksome to this participant was Jared Taylor's "appeal to a very broad racial category, which is commonly referred to as 'white.' In particular they have sought to enlist Jewish participation in their activities and to avoid any connection or association with anti-Semitism." Such an approach was deemed "counterproductive." A second attendee, by contrast, counted a possible alliance with Jews, deserving of "careful consideration."[19]

The debate about including Jews in the category of white people continued to swirl around *American Renaissance*, but it too faded as the Republican Party's convention came into view. Buchanan's forces teamed up with the Reverend Pat Robertson's Christian Coalition and seized control of the party's platform. They defeated Bob Dole's effort to soften the antiabortion language, and they included a strident anti-immigrant plank requiring a constitutional change to the Fourteenth Amendment. Capturing the platform committee was not the same as winning the nomination, however, and Bob Dole was loath to have a repeat performance of Buchanan's 1992 prime-time culture war speech. So Buchanan was given a spot and a time on the dais outside the limelight, charged with rousing the troops of the religious right, and ultimately pledged his loyalty to the party of Richard Nixon and Ronald Reagan. Nobody walked out.

Election Results 1996

November 5, 1996. Depending on who was listening, election night delivered different messages. For Democrats seeking to vindicate President Clinton, he trounced Senator Bob Dole, 49 to 41 percent. For Republicans, particularly conservative Republicans from the South, their continued dominance in the House and Senate brought Georgia Congressman Newt Gingrich back as Speaker of the House and Mississippi Senator Trent Lott in as Senate majority leader. For Ross Perot's loyalists, his slip from 19 percent of the vote in 1992 to 8 percent in this election signaled difficulties but not the effective end of the Reform Party. It would own several million automatic dollars from the Federal Election Commission, since it had pulled more than 5 percent. And for the myriad other less endowed third parties, right and left, the two-party oligopoly proved insurmountable.

Howard Phillips repeated his miserable 1992 vote-getting tally, receiving fewer than two hundred thousand votes as the Taxpayers Party's presidential candidate. And in the why-bother? category, former Nazi Party chief and Populist Party state chair Ralph Forbes got five hundred votes as the presidential candidate of Ed Fields's America First Party.

The electorate remained riven by race, religion, and gender: 53 percent of white Protestants voted for Dole, while 84 percent of blacks and 72 percent of Hispanics voted for Clinton. Asian Americans and whites both voted for Clinton at 43 percent, while Jews voted for the Democratic incumbent at 78 percent. The gender gap yawned at ten points: 38 percent of white men voted for Clinton, while he received 48 percent of white women's votes.[20]

Congressman Jack Metcalf, the longtime anti–Federal Reserve activist and anti–Native American treaty rights legislator from Washington State, won reelection to the House of Representatives after an extremely close vote count. Congresswoman Helen Chenoweth, the Republican from Idaho, breezed to a second term, her past support for militia and opposition to environmental regulation apparently resonant with voters and her back-door relationship with the John Birch Society not an issue. In another Texas district, Ron Paul reemerged from the libertarian far right to win election to Congress as a Republican. One of those few figures who routinely jumped back and forth across the border between respectability and zealotry, Paul had won three elections to Congress, lost badly as a Libertarian candidate for president, maintained a leadership position in the John Birch Society, and then reentered the Republican Party. His election underscored the one salient fact undermining the emergence of any third party on the Republican Party's right: there was still plenty of room inside the GOP for ideologues like Chenoweth and Paul and even for a white nationalist like Buchanan—as long as they did not run for president.

Farther down the tickets in state parties, an even bigger political space existed. Georgia State Senator Pam Glanton, a Republican with a record of association with militia supporters, for example, easily won reelection.[21] So did Mississippi State Senator Mike Gunn, the Council of Conservative Citizens leader who had benefited from that Buchanan-supported fund-raiser. Not all such Republican candidates succeeded, however. The council supported Dean Allen, who failed in a bid for state office in North Carolina. Sheriff Richard Mack, a militia circuit regular and darling of the gun rights lobby, lost his primary. And David Duke received only 10 percent of the vote in Louisiana's open primary for the U.S. Senate. The broadcast media paid him little attention, demonstrating once more that if a candidate continues to run and lose time and again, he eventually gets relegated to the class of also-rans.

Despite Clinton's victory, the institutional power of the Christian Coalition and the National Rifle Association, two pillars of the Republican right, remained unmatched by any parallel organizations loyal to the Democratic Party. Other groups were larger in numbers and could produce campaign funds and run ads. But none had the same power to mobilize its own membership to volunteer for campaigns and to vote.

Despite the growing strength of white nationalists, 1996 had been a disappointing year. Their troops were as likely to rob banks as run for office. They had no real candidate after Buchanan stopped running. "In the history of presidential politics, 1996 will go down as the year that Pat Buchanan cast away the political opportunity of a lifetime," one Ohio Klansman turned Populist Party wannabe said. "[He] raised and spent some $30 million. Yet, what is there—in the end—to show for all of this?"

The question was apt. Buchanan would never again win three million votes. If the Republican leadership could keep Buchanan's voters inside the party, then third parties would remain a difficult and ultimately frustrating pursuit time and again. The only alternative, a decided tendency of white nationalists believed, was outside the electoral process. Lack of access may help explain the popularity of the militia and other private armies more than any popular zeal for marching around in the woods with guns. Nevertheless, nonviolent extraparliamentary activity had its own frustrations. Sure, you could march by the thousands to keep the Confederate battle flag flying. You could eat, greet, and meet with fellow revisionists and scientific racists until your white skin sagged off your face. But that wasn't going to topple the New World Order establishment or end "race mixing."

Worse, the one mainstreaming movement chief with extra money, Willis Carto, allegedly kept hiding assets.

PART

Mainstreamers and Vanguardists at Century's End, 1997–2001

Willis Carto's thirty-year run as a movement godfather comes to an end. William Pierce's organization of cadres does not survive his death. Yet a new movement is looking to be born out of the old, even as its most important leaders have yet to fully emerge.

Carto Dispossessed

October 31, 1996. The judgment of history is not impartial. Whether future generations remember Willis Carto as an early godfather of an ultimately victorious white nationalism or his legacy is eventually lost in the backwaters of a white supremacy long stilled, only our great-grandchildren will be able to judge. If his testimony before the Honorable Rustin G. Maino, California Fourth Appellate District, Division One is considered at all, however, it will be a reminder that not all history depends on the victors. Some judgments depend simply on the law and the facts.

At this moment Judge Maino had a pedestrian decision to make: Did Willis Carto and his codefendants owe legion-IHR any money, and if so, how much? As the judge repeatedly told the court, his decisions would be the same regardless of the beliefs of the two contending parties.[1]

The new directors of the Legion for the Survival of Freedom now possessed the Institute for Historical Review's name, book stock, mailing lists, and such financial documents as Carto left behind. The content of future *Journal* articles was no longer the subject of shoe-stamping debate. The multimillion-dollar Farrel legacy, however, still remained beyond their grasp. Seeking to recover what it had lost, the legion-IHR had filed suit during the summer of 1994.[2]

Both sides decided to forgo a jury trial. The facts of the case were too complicated, all the lawyers agreed. The unstated corollary: neither Carto's dictatorial style nor the staff's revolt was likely to appear particularly sympathetic to a jury, even if the average Californian could forget that both plaintiff and defendant shared a common belief that the Holocaust was a hoax. As Judge Maino sat alone in judgment, he restrained emotionally charged rhetoric by the attorneys and sorted fiduciary truth from ideological fancy. He allowed greater latitude to elderly witnesses, who had traveled long distances to testify, and he repeatedly heard stories irrelevant to the decision at hand. If the nine-hundred-page transcript is any indicator, he also remained remarkably good-humored throughout the proceedings.[3]

The plaintiff's assertions were straightforward: after Jean Farrel died in Switzerland, her will had been contested. The legion-IHR's board of directors had appointed Willis Carto its "limited agent" to secure the legacy, and in 1990 Carto finally succeeded at winning 45 percent of the estate for the legion. Instead of directing the funds into legion accounts, however, Carto and codefendant Henri Fischer, an experienced international trafficker, had placed the assets in a separate corporation known as Vibet, Inc. With the funds outside the corporate control of the legion, Carto and Fischer had then distributed money, as they personally wished, to various "good causes," including to Liberty Lobby and its connected projects. Eventually discovering that Carto was treating the Farrel funds as his personal property, a new (and legitimate) board of directors terminated Carto's "agency" in 1993. Now the legion was trying to collect the entirety of the Farrel assets, a sum in excess of seven million dollars.[4]

Willis Carto's defense, by contrast, stretched and twisted around self-contradictory claims. On one hand, he contended that he still "owned" the Legion for the Survival of Freedom by virtue of his supposed status as its "substitute incorporator" in 1966. According to this argument, he legally controlled the legion and could dispose of its assets, including the Farrel millions, as he pleased. On the other hand, Carto also claimed that the legion's board of directors had formally met in March 1991 and officially decided to forfeit its ownership of millions of dollars and then had given the funds to him personally. In either case, Carto's defense contended the money was his.[5]

Paradoxically, Carto's testimony before Judge Maino, although clouded and unbelievable at points, projected critical moments of unadorned truth. For three decades Willis Alison Carto had avoided the truth about his various political and publishing projects. He had usually shunned long interviews with reporters. He kept his name off the masthead of *The Spotlight*, despite his actual role in setting its editorial direction. And he had hidden his relationship to the Institute for Historical Review under a blanket of pettifoggery. Nevertheless, Carto had produced a remarkable public record in the half dozen lawsuits he had pursued over the decades, volumes of courtroom testimony and evidentiary depositions more revealing than any two dozen media interviews.

This extensive court record must be read with care. In one and the same trial Carto could both unaffectedly tell a truth and hide a lie. He could claim in one deposition that he never wrote articles under another name and in another hearing rattle off a list of pseudonyms dating back to his first years as editor of *Right* magazine. He could claim he was not anti-Semitic and then testify endlessly about the nefarious ways of the Jews.

In one particularly revealing case from the 1970s and 1980s, Liberty Lobby had sued William Buckley's *National Review* magazine for libel. During this proceeding the magazine's attorney read a couple of paragraphs from *Imperium* into the record and questioned Carto about Francis Parker Yockey. "The soul of the Negro remains primitive and childlike in comparison with the nervous and complicated soul of western man" was one gem. "Primitive violence is natural to the Negro and the sense of social disgrace is lacking in him" was another. Did the witness consider this passage racist? the lawyer asked. "No, I don't consider it racist at all," Carto responded.[6] The answer told reams about the Liberty Lobby chief's actual worldview, and in all good common sense he must have known it undermined his claims for tort.

Yet during that same *National Review* trial he revealed much less when questioned about Liberty Lobby's relationship to the legion-IHR. In response to the question "Did Liberty Lobby ever have a connection with an organization called the Institute for Historical Review?," Carto replied with one word: "Never."[7]

That question had been asked time and again. Carto routinely insisted that Liberty Lobby was organizationally and ideologically separate from all his various enterprises on the West Coast; including Noontide Press and *Western Destiny* magazine in the 1960s and the Legion for the Survival of Freedom and Institute for Historical Review in the years after. Liberty Lobby was simply a patriots' lobby working the halls of Congress, providing testimony and educating the public, he claimed. Holocaust revisionism was not part of its platform. Neither was white supremacy or anti-Semitism, although he didn't mind telling everyone Liberty Lobby was "anti-Zionist." He was its "founder" and "treasurer" after all. At the same time, he claimed he was just a friendly volunteer when working on behalf of Noontide and the legion. When one opposing attorney, who had already discovered Carto's past membership on the Legion for the Survival of Freedom's board,[8] asked him why he had resigned from that post in 1969, Carto replied that he simply could not spend any more time on the project.[9]

When the same matter came before Judge Maino in the case at hand, Carto and his legal team completely reversed these previous claims. As the IHR staff noted in its own report on the trial, "time and again he impeached his previous testimony on virtually every substantive issue."[10]

Far from asserting that Liberty Lobby and the legion had never had a relationship of one to the other, for example, Carto's attorney most emphatically described them as one virtually seamless enterprise. "The evidence will show that all of the organizations work together for a common scheme to promote revisionism, among other topics, to the common public, to discuss constitutional issues," he averred in opening remarks. "And they were all in the same ball park, as the evidence will show, with respect to their editorials that included Liberty Lobby, who put out the *The Spotlight*."[11]

When asked in this trial about his resignation from the legion board, Carto quickly admitted that the resignation had been an attempt to conceal his real relationship to both Liberty Lobby and the legion. It was for show purposes only. Not being able to devote more time had nothing to do with it. "It was obvious that should I become public in my association with the Institute other than just giving it my personal approval, which I did . . . why this would be definitely contrary to the interests of Liberty Lobby as well as to the Institute," Carto testified under oath.[12]

His exact words need to be recorded here because Willis Carto was rarely as forthright as he was that day before Judge Maino. When the legion's attorney asked if his testimony before Judge Maino contradicted previous testimony in other cases, Carto's memory once again seemed to develop multiple problems. But with a little reminder he was able to remember.

Asked if had had ever made any statements under oath about having no position of authority with the legion, Carto replied that he didn't "think so." But the plaintiffs repeatedly produced documentary evidence of such statements. In a June 1989 letter, apparently written at a time when Carto was trying to court former California Republican Congressman Paul McCloskey, Carto had claimed that he had "no official position" with the legion-IHR.[13] When asked about a similar claim he had made in a 1993 letter to William Hulsey, then legion-IHR's lawyer, Carto once again told Judge Maino he could not remember such a letter . . . until it was produced to the court.[14] As had happened for over three decades, when questions hit too close to home, Willis Carto simply could not remember the facts. His problem in this court was that the plaintiffs did, in fact, remember. And they had the documents to prove it.

In previous trials he had claimed that he held no official position with the legion-IHR either because he did not want Liberty Lobby to be known for its support of Holocaust revisionism or because he was trying to keep litigation involving one organization from spilling over into another. In this case, he swore that he had always called the shots at the legion as its permanent "substitute incorporator," and as such the Farrel legacy was properly his to distribute to various "good causes," the largest of which was Liberty Lobby. And to prove that Liberty Lobby was a good cause, Carto's attorney avowed, in this instance, that the Lobby and IHR were ideologically inseparable.[15]

The legion's attorney, on the other hand, wanted to discredit these current claims. Thus he questioned Carto about past disavowals of a "position" with the IHR, demonstrating that Carto would testify to whatever was immediately expedient.[16]

Vibet and Fischer and Genoud

In addition to establishing the legion's claim to the Farrel money, its attorneys tried to use this trial to discover where Carto had stashed the funds. Weber's crew began this court session with the facts they already knew. During the period when Carto still controlled the legion, for example, several of the staff's paychecks were drawn on Swiss bank accounts for a corporation called Vibet, Inc. They had learned that Vibet, Inc. was a Bahamian corporation, initially established to hold the Farrel funds offshore. In addition, when Vibet's Swiss funds were wired into IHR accounts, the bookkeeper had recorded them as loans rather than as assets. This convoluted manner of accounting supposedly protected the legion-IHR from adverse court judgments during the period before the coup. After the coup, this system helped stymie the legion's new directors, as they searched for the Farrel funds.[17]

The legion's difficulties had been compounded, apparently, because of the ingenuity of Henri Fischer, named as a defendant along with Vibet. Fischer's reputation for international intrigue and double-dealing far exceeded any of Carto's own. Apparently born of French parents and raised in French Indochina, Fischer lived alternatively in Australia and California in the 1960s and 1970s. He also traveled internationally, including to destinations in the Arab Middle East and North Korea, and was rumored to be "connected" to one intelligence agency or the other, most probably the Central Intelligence Agency. According to Australian press reports, during the 1960s Fischer was part of an ultraright clique in that country's Liberal Party and published an internationally distributed anti-Semitic journal. The Australian Labor Party apparently deputized him in 1975 as its bagman in a deal with Iraq's Baathist Party. Laden with postelection debt, the Labor Party arranged for a five-hundred-thousand-dollar "contribution" from Iraq to be picked up in Japan by Fischer and brought to Australia. Fischer apparently did travel to Japan with two Iraqi officials and received five hundred thousand U.S. dollars, but he never delivered the money to the Labor Party. Instead, he ab-

sconded with the funds, losing a pair of "bodyguards" at a Singapore hotel in the process. His ex-wife contended several years later that he used
the money to buy a home in San Diego County, where he subsequently
settled.[18]

Fischer's home was actually a five-acre estate in Escondido, complete
with a full guesthouse and tennis court, surrounded by a chain-link
fence topped with barbed wire. Willis and Elisabeth Carto were rumored to have lived on this estate for more than two years, at the same
time as a man named Michael Brown, who had once been a bodyguard
for George Lincoln Rockwell, the American Nazi Party führer assassinated by one of his own men in 1967. When the Cartos needed their
own home, they acquired a multiacre estate of their own, also in Escondido. And when Carto needed assistance securing and then disposing
of the Farrel funds, according to the legion's lawsuit, he turned to
Fischer, who then helped set up Vibet, Inc., and made other arrangements for a tidy sum of two hundred or three hundred thousand dollars.
On the witness stand Carto could not remember how much his friend
had been paid.[19]

Eight months after the legion filed suit, but before the hearing in
Judge Maino's court, the Costa Mesa, California, Police Department
concluded that Fischer's estate on Pine Heights Way and the Carto
home on Quailridge Drive probably housed "bank records, correspondence, journals, ledgers and other documents showing the location and
amounts of LSF [legion] assets under their control." According to a
search warrant,[20] these assets had been "stolen" from the legion and
were subject to seizure. On March 22, 1995—three plus weeks before
the Oklahoma City bombing—police squads raided both residences and
carted off documents by the caseload. Liberty Lobby's *Spotlight* was enraged at the raid on Carto's home, and Carto wrote personally of the in-
dignities his wife, Elisabeth, endured during the raid, having her home
searched by a squad of police. But *The Spotlight* did not report on the
raid on Fischer's estate. Apparently, it would have been difficult to accuse Weber of being party to one conspiracy, while at the same moment
revealing that the object of that conspiracy was one Henri Fischer, an alleged bagman.[21]

Weber's attorney questioned Carto about the expenses incurred in securing the Farrel legacy. Lawyers had to be hired, and a host of details
handled in Switzerland. A huge sum, eight hundred thousand dollars,
was paid to a man Carto described as an "expeditor," Mr. François
Genoud. The legion's attorney began spelling the name for the record. "I

don't believe I gave the name," Carto interrupted, but the attorney continued. Despite prodding from both attorney and judge, Carto didn't want to discuss Genoud in open court, but he was forced to.[22]

> ATTORNEY: Now Mr. Genoud was a well-connected man?
> CARTO: Yes.
> ATTORNEY: And he's a well-respected banker, or was when he was alive?
> CARTO: Yes.
> ATTORNEY: Why did you choose Mr. Genoud to be your expeditor, sir?

Carto's attorney objected to the question, and the judge overruled.

> CARTO: Because in knowing him and discussing things with him and . . . and because he was available, I felt that he would be effective in performing the personal contact that he was capable of.
> ATTORNEY: Mr. Genoud was a personal friend of Adolf Hitler, correct? [23]

François Genoud was more than an aging, well-connected Swiss banker who once knew Adolf Hitler. In the immediate post–World War Two period, Genoud helped finance the escape of Nazi war criminals from Europe, acquired the literary copyrights of Hitler and two of his most significant adjuncts—Martin Bormann and Joseph Goebbels—and used a Swiss banking fortune to underwrite the nexus of wartime Nazis with a sector of postwar Arab nationalists. Most famously, he also helped the hijacking of a Lufthansa airplane in 1972, engineering the ransom demand by the Popular Front for the Liberation of Palestine.[24] Genoud's continued devotion to Hitlerian causes was well known to journalists and Nazi hunters. But his direct link to Willis Carto had never been made public before it became part of the transcript in California.

The Honorable Rustin Maino's final judgment eviscerated any legal claim Carto had to the Farrel legacy. He ratified the original Polis decision that the staff-friendly board was legitimate. He rejected "all 16 defenses proposed" by Carto's attorneys. He found that all "$7,500,000 belonged to the plaintiff" legion. And after deducting the costs from fighting Joan Althaus in court and other expenses, he found that the total converted by all the defendants—Carto, Fischer, Liberty Lobby, et al.—was

$6,430,000. That sum was owed to the legion, plus interest, starting January 1, 1993, the day after the first Polis decision.[25]

Separate from the formal decision awarding the funds to the legion, Maino wrote a letter explaining his view of the evidence. As a statement of informed opinion, it could have served as a virtual summary of Willis Carto's history in the courts: "I did not find him to be a witness who can be relied upon. His demeanor when he testified was evasive and argumentative. He could not follow the instructions of the court . . . I found that much of his testimony made no sense; much of his testimony in court was different than his previous testimony; much of his testimony was contradicted by other witnesses and documents. By the end of the trial I was of the opinion that Mr. Carto lacked candor, lacked memory, and lacked the ability to be forthright about what he did honestly remember."[26]

Evasiveness and lack of candor may have enabled Willis Carto to succeed during forty-five years as a white nationalist godfather. But these qualities did not sustain him in 1996 in a California court of American law. Now he owed millions of dollars to a group of relative upstarts, the first reversal of fortune, with several more to come. In addition, at this same moment across the white nationalist movement as a whole, the younger generations were grabbing center stage.

Resistance Records: Buying and Selling in the Cyberworld

April 9, 1997. On this tax raid, a multijurisdictional law enforcement task force wore bulletproof vests and kicked the door down with their weapons drawn. Inside a four-bedroom bungalow they found two men operating a few pieces of office equipment and approximately ten thousand compact discs. In a sleepy township outside Detroit, from this most ordinary place, operated the largest white power music distribution outfit in North America, Resistance Records. It had been under surveillance by a six-man team for more than two months. The cops watched the most mundane business activity. Delivery trucks came and went. Young men carried packages to the local post office. They managed customer lists and filled mail orders, as if selling woolen underwear to North Dakota farmers rather than copies of *Cult of the Holy War* CDs to suburban skinheads. Even the neighbors on this quiet country road had little idea what went on inside the house. The landlord, who told the local press that she was Jewish and would have never knowingly rented to a band of skinheads, said that this crew of hard-core national socialists paid their rent on time and had been trouble-free tenants.[1]

Resistance Records had grown quickly. During the past three years it had produced eight issues of a slick sixty-eight-page magazine and accumulated three hundred thousand dollars' gross annual sales of white power music, T-shirts, and paraphernalia. The business had not secured a license or paid sales tax, however, and through this opening the police rushed, hoping to shut this enterprise down. When the raiders came crashing through the door, they soon discovered that all the armaments were unnecessary. The staff surrendered quietly. No bullets were fired, and no hundred-day standoff ensued. Instead, the authorities spent six hours loading a rental truck with computers and about one hundred boxes of business records and merchandise. They also took the Resistance Records mailing list, five thousand names, including two hundred customers living in the Federal Republic of Germany.[2]

At exactly the same moment, Canadian provincial police raided the home of Resistance Records founder George Burdi in Ontario. They too confiscated business records and personal effects. Burdi was not home at the time, as he was in jail, having surrendered to authorities the previous February and begun serving a one-year sentence for assault. Upon release he did not return to the business, and eventually he left the movement altogether. He gave away his shares of Resistance Records stock, reconciled with his parents, fell in love with a Canadian woman of East Indian descent, and eventually made public his turn away from white nationalism. At the company he left behind, however, the remaining principals continued their trek.[3]

The Michigan authorities could find no criminal charges to post, so the company started selling music again six weeks after the raid, this time from a new location and with the proper business license secured. However, the staff did not begin republishing the magazine. In total, the skinhead subculture did not suffer the same crippling setback that armed militia and common law court groups experienced during this period. Militia-style groups had engaged law enforcement in an ill-fated contest of wills over control of the functions of government and the state, in a Gramscian war of maneuver. Although smaller than the militias, the white power music scene, by contrast, was waging a war of position. It sought the commanding heights of (white) youth subculture.[4] And on this side of white nationalism, Resistance Records, and the music scene of which it was a signal part, preserved many of the advances made by this generation during the previous three years.

Among the gains was a change in music venues. This generation had moved away from the cow pasture concerts, such as 1989's Aryan Nations fest in Tennessee, to sites such as the Westside Clubhouse in Detroit. Playing a regular gig at a weekend show in a barlike setting was infinitely more appealing to bands than standing in the back of a truck bed under the stars. The ability to play its own music and in its own halls ratified the schism between white power Oi and the larger punk music scene. Now that they were not competing for the same dance floors, the two subcults tended to ignore each other. And new groups of screaming and howling young white men were more apt to pick up guitars and blast away. Also, more U.S. bands joined their European counterparts on tours that cruised countries on both sides of the Atlantic. The Hammerskins' organization, present at Resistance Records' birth, continued multiplying and generated an increasingly mature indigenous leadership. As a result, an autonomous international white power youth network congealed.[5]

Nevertheless, the attempts by older movement leaders to suck money and energy out of the Generation Xers did not end with the failed blandishments of men such as Pete Peters, whose attempt to foist a set of biblical heroes upon skinheads had turned out so miserably. Although Ben Klassen had died and Tom Metzger had lost his leading role, new suitors vied for influence. William Pierce had achieved legendary status as the author of *The Turner Diaries.* And the National Alliance enjoyed growing prestige among skinheads because it had years before served as the organizational home of Robert Mathews, founder of The Order. After the tax raid, Willis Carto also stepped into this picture. And Carto and Pierce followed their twenty-five-year rivalry with a fight for control of the youth music business.

In this particular drama between Carto and Pierce, Jason Snow became the linchpin figure. A Canadian intimately familiar with the skinhead scenes on both sides of the North American border, Snow, age twenty-nine, was already a movement veteran and one of the three original incorporators of Resistance Records. Immediately after the tax raid, he had the controlling hand. He realized that the business needed a new capital infusion to survive, and early in 1998 he turned to a man he had already done business with, Todd Blodgett, an advertising broker for Carto's *Spotlight.* Snow asked Blodgett to arrange the sale of the company to Willis Carto.[6]

The transaction involved a complex set of money and stock transfers, made more complicated by the conflict with legion-IHR that troubled Carto's financial empire. Despite the fact that both Liberty Lobby and Carto personally had already declared bankruptcy, Carto figured out how to use the Foundation for Economic Liberty (FEL) to purchase thirty shares of the record company, at a thousand dollars a share. He also took a warrant to purchase thirty additional shares at the same price by the end of that year. As part of the deal, he gave Jason Snow a full-time job, with a thirty-thousand-dollar annual salary, working for Liberty Lobby. Blodgett, the advertising broker, agreed to purchase twenty-five of the shares. Thus at the end of the first round of buying and selling Carto controlled thirty shares through FEL, Blodgett had twenty-five shares, and Snow owned forty-five, with Carto promising to use one corporation or another to purchase an additional thirty from Snow. Resistance Records' impudent skinhead start-up had been swallowed whole by Blodgett and Carto, in an unsteady arrangement with Jason Snow.

For the moment it was one more corporation in the Liberty Lobby affiliated lineup.[7]

The record-selling operation moved from Detroit to a house in California, not too far from Carto's home in San Diego County. There a skinhead couple filled orders. Rather than restart the magazine, they sent *Resistance* subscribers six months of *The Spotlight*, a sure sign that Carto wanted the record company to pump up the subscriber base of his core publication rather than build a semi-independent business for the younger generation. By November 1998, just six months after the initial purchase, the whole deal unraveled. In a memorandum sent to Snow, Carto reneged on the agreement to buy the thirty additional shares. He demanded that Resistance Records pay back to FEL two "loans" totaling forty thousand dollars. At that point FEL controlled only twenty-one shares of stock. (Carto had given a skinhead named Eric Fairburn nine shares as part of a severance package from his employ at Liberty Lobby.) And he wanted to sell those twenty-one shares as soon as possible.[8] Willis Carto and hard rock did not fit together, and the aging moneyman wanted out altogether.

At this point William Pierce quietly stepped into the picture. He already understood better than Carto the significance of the white power music scene, how it attracted and retained young people and created a cultural milieu within which ideologues such as him could recruit. Several years before, he had established working relationships with the original Resistance Records crew. Pierce also knew that Carto wanted out, despite the fact that Resistance was then grossing about five thousand dollars a month. Plus the business possessed instant name recognition and cachet among white power youth. So the sixty-five-year-old former physicist plotted a hostile takeover against the seventy-year-old salesman, just as he had almost three decades before with the National Youth Alliance. Again the target was the youth market. Only this time Pierce took it slow, one step at a time.[9]

First, Jason Snow, the one stockholder left from the initial set of Resistance Records incorporators, purchased the twenty-one remaining shares from Carto's Foundation for Economic Liberty. That gave Snow sixty-six shares: the fifteen he kept during the first deal with Carto, the thirty shares Carto never purchased, and the twenty-one newly bought from FEL. Todd Blodgett, the unlikely merchandiser who had put together the earlier deal with Carto, now had thirty-four shares (the twenty-five he had purchased for $1,000 apiece, plus nine more purchased from Eric Fairburn for just a few hundred more). Then Pierce reincorporated Resistance Records in April 1999, as a limited liability corporation in Virginia. To complete the deal, he paid Snow $1,800 apiece for sixty-six shares, a total of $118,800. Carto and Snow were now out of the picture. Pierce owned two-thirds of the stock and controlled the company. Blodgett was still involved, however, on the basis of the thirty-four shares he owned in the old corporation. They were unlikely business partners, an unhappy and unsuccessful entrepreneur and a full-time white nationalist revolutionary, selling music that neither one of them listened to. Within a relatively short period, Pierce forced Blodgett out of the operation, began republishing *Resistance* magazine, and updated the business's website.[10]

The Internet Enters the Scene

In large measure, the Internet had already replaced the smaller zine-style newsletters that had once flourished across the skinhead subculture. Now the Internet allowed new businesses to pop up and sell music, vying for customers in the mass market. The World Wide Web had emerged in the mid-1990s, after a long incubation inside a complex of military and academic institutions.[11] Changes in technology and programming advances made a worldwide web of information sites available to the personal computer user; advanced software and commercial chat rooms provided a new and open field for young white nationalists. Among white supremacists, it was a cardinal belief that science and technology were their natural domain. They believed that it had been the so-called white gene pool that had conquered outer space. Now they had tackled cyberspace with a visible eagerness. With the advent of the Internet, Aryans of every type extended their reach beyond the computer bulletin boards set up by Louis Beam and Tom Metzger in the early 1980s.

The first movement website, Stormfront, had been established in 1994 by Don Black, the onetime Klan chief. After serving a prison sentence for his role in the abortive invasion of Dominica, and a brief period of Populist Party activism, he had found his own niche. Stormfront became an all-purpose site with its own discussion board and a sprawling set of Web publications. Eventually it featured pages in all the major European languages and links to a growing list of white nationalist, historical revisionist, and self-described racial conservative Internet sites managed by others.[12]

Here was evidence that cyberspace provided an almost perfect opportunity for the music marketeers at Resistance Records. They established their first website in August 1995, with a compact disc catalog and other information. A potential customer could listen to sample musical selections and order directly over the Internet using a charge card or with a check via the post. Other outfits did much the same, mimicking the larger commercial world's turn toward Internet marketing. Like a niche market taste in unusual olives or rare books, white power music established itself within a definable constituency. Organizations and individuals with the time, energy, and inclination created dazzling and attractive websites.[13]

The rapid proliferation of websites sparked a series of reports from human rights agencies, each seeming to outdo the other with predictions about how the Web would widen the exposure of white nationalist ideas to every schoolchild with an Internet service provider, enable groups to recruit untold numbers of new members, and lead to violence on the streets.[14] The Web was a deceptively flat medium, however, and almost none of these fear-laden predictions came true. Yes, students now gained access to materials that were once more difficult to get than a copy of *Playboy* magazine at the corner convenience store. But they also now read antiracist materials published in cyberspace, including those that criticized the racist Web materials. And no actual evidence emerged showing that any lone wolf killers entered the white nationalist world through an Internet portal. In fact, one profile of a World Church of the Creator member who shot ten and killed two people showed that he had joined the group after receiving an old-fashioned leaflet on his Illinois college campus.[15]

A limited study of Internet users conducted by Carnegie Mellon University professors produced results that undercut concerns about racists using the Web. Scholars found a correlation between increased levels of Internet use and decreased levels of social engagement. For each hour in cyberspace, they measured a corresponding jump in depression and social isolation. Rather than feel good about being engaged in a virtual community of friends, participants in the study experienced a decline in feelings of well-being. They were less likely to join with others in noncyberspace. Critics noted that the study was limited to the Pittsburgh area and did not include a large sample of users under forty years of age, those most familiar with and likely to use the Internet.[16] Nevertheless, the study pointed at a conclusion that many human rights observers did not expect: people who spend a lot of time surfing through white nationalist websites could be expected to . . . well . . . spend a lot of time surfing white nationalist websites, but the initial evidence did not show that they were any more likely to join and engage in real-time political activity.

What the Web did accomplish for the movement were the same things that it did for other sectors of society. It sped up and thus increased commerce and communications. Much like the advance of the fax machine over express mail, it changed next-day delivery to same-day delivery and then to same-moment delivery. Activists could use cyber-forums to chat or discuss ideas or just spread trashy rumors about one another—and they did all three. A teenage boy with a credit card could buy a white power music CD over the Web, instead of sending his dollar bills through the mail. Smart organizational administrators could gather their troops under one cyberroof. Probably the most singular benefit was the way the Internet broke down international borders and allowed white nationalists in several countries to talk to one another quickly and easily. A secondary result was that paper-and-ink publications such as *The Spotlight* became less important to the process of movement building, and paid subscriptions declined, just as they did for many daily newspapers.

In the end, however, the World Wide Web was a little bit like the wallpaper in your aunt Suzy's foyer: you knew it was there, but you didn't pay any particular attention to it. It was easy to ignore. Other things were impossible to forget, however, like the bombing of the federal building in Oklahoma City and the image of Timothy McVeigh dressed in a prison orange jumpsuit.

After the Oklahoma City Bomber(s) Are Tried, the Violence Continues

April 24, 1997. Two years after the Oklahoma City bombing, the trial of Timothy McVeigh started in a Denver federal courthouse. Memory of the deaths, maiming, and shattered lives remained raw at that point, and survivors and victims' families gathered at an Oklahoma site to watch the trial broadcast specifically to them. For the larger American public, McVeigh was still most remembered for the children murdered that day and for his seemingly complete lack of regret. Inside the white nationalist movement, conspiracy-minded journalists and paramilitary enthusiasts had tried to shift blame and public opprobrium away from the militia and onto the federal government. In the pages of magazines, tabloids, and cyberspace, and at gun rallies, constitution conferences, and survivalist expos, they had mustered an ever-changing assemblage of facts and fantasies about the still-missing John Doe Two.[1] The government's apparent decision to stop looking for the olive-skinned mystery man served to confirm those doubting the prosecution's claims. Add to the seemingly endless reserve of conspiracy theories Timothy McVeigh's court-appointed counsel, Stephen Jones, whose defense efforts worked this oil field like a two-hundred-foot jackknife derrick drilling with an eight-foot bit.

Convinced early that his client was guilty but did not act alone, Jones searched widely for Doe Two and "others unknown." He traveled to the Philippines in search of an "Islamic" connection to the bombing and spent time in the United Kingdom and continental Europe, investigating a possible German connection to the bomb and talking with antiterrorist bomb experts. And his defense team seemed to be enveloped in an aura of intrigue and double-dealing. FBI investigative materials, including the McVeigh phone logs, leaked into the ocean of journalists actively reporting on the case, virtually none of whom believed that all the perpetrators had been found. It was this doubt, more than any other, that Jones expressly sought to cultivate. Prior to trial, Jones submitted a 150-page brief contending that the bombing had been the work of either Iraqi terrorists or German neo-Nazis and pointing to a German national, Andreas Strassmeir, as the link in a nefarious conspiracy.[2] If the defense could prove that McVeigh had been just one cog in a much-larger terrorist machine, then presumably that would lessen his individual culpability and save the Desert Storm veteran from the death penalty.

Federal Judge Richard Matsch gave free rein to the defense prior to trial. Federal prosecutors considered Matsch a tough sell and not particularly friendly to government claims. In a twist of fate, Matsch had overseen one other significant trial involving white nationalists, the federal case brought against four members of The Order for depriving radio talker Alan Berg of his civil rights. In that trial, two were convicted, and two found innocent, seeming proof of Matsch's lack of favor to prosecutors.[3] Prior to McVeigh's trial, he had not only okayed spending for Jones's overseas travel but sealed his firm's expense records to protect its case from prosecutorial snooping.[4] The trial venue was also reset in Denver, a move that most pleased the defense. By any standard, Judge Matsch had provided Stephen Jones's team of lawyers every possible pretrial accord.

When the case finally went to court, the prosecution opened with a trim, hard-to-shoot-at case. Over four weeks the government presented witnesses claiming that McVeigh had been angry at the feds for the conflagration and death at Waco in 1993 and that he bombed the Murrah Federal Building in revenge. They showed McVeigh searching for bomb ingredients at fertilizer co-ops, racetracks, and gun dealers. The FBI had McVeigh's fingerprints on the receipt for purchasing two thousand pounds of ammonium nitrate. Phone company computer records identified the time, date, duration, and destination of hundreds of phone calls as twenty-seven witnesses explained dozens of these calls made on a telephone calling card issued by Liberty Lobby. A security camera in a McDonald's restaurant pictured McVeigh just moments before he rented the Ryder truck at a shop down the road in Junction City, Kansas. The owner of the shop identified McVeigh as the man who rented the Ryder truck used in the bombing. A security camera in the apartment building across the street from the federal building pictured the Ryder truck just minutes before the explosion.[5]

Despite all this, the case against McVeigh was largely circumstantial. As a consequence, prosecutors carefully presented the material evidence from the FBI. Before the trial the scientific integrity of the FBI's vaunted lab had been questioned when a lab supervisor claimed that evidence from dozens of cases, including the Oklahoma City bombing, had been mishandled. As a result, the prosecutor did not call any FBI witnesses connected to questionable lab practices. And he used a Scotland Yard scientist to confirm FBI testimony independently.[6]

The heart of the case rested on the testimony of a couple of fellow travelers, Michael and Lori Fortier. Michael Fortier had met McVeigh when both were in the service, and they had stayed friends while the Fortiers lived in Arizona. In addition to sharing in some of the prebombing criminal activity, the Fortiers had been privy to McVeigh's plans. He had shown them how to shape a truck bomb by arranging soup cans in their kitchen. The couple's credibility could reasonably be questioned. Their lives had been drenched in guns and drugs and other illegal activity. And they testified that they had lied to friends, families, and investigators to hide their prior knowledge of the bomb.[7] Plus they had undoubtedly been coerced into becoming witnesses.

Unlike James Ellison and other turncoats at the Fort Smith seditious conspiracy trial, however, the Fortiers held up well under defense cross-examination. When Jones tried to demonstrate that Michael Fortier had lied to the jury, for example, the government countered with a brilliant courtroom maneuver. The prosecutor asked Fortier to show the jury the alley where McVeigh had said in advance that he would leave the getaway car. The next day prosecutors called an FBI photographer, who testified that he had found the key to the Ryder truck at that exact same spot.[8] The effect reinforced the Fortiers' testimony. In the end the defense failed to discredit their story.

The government also presented uncontroverted evidence that McVeigh considered himself a militiaman. His sister Jennifer McVeigh read a letter by her brother to the American Legion: "We members of the citizen's militias do not bear our arms to overthrow the Constitution, but to overthrow those who PERVERT the constitution." The two siblings had regularly read Liberty Lobby's *Spotlight* as well as other movement publications. He sold copies of *The Turner Diaries* on the gun show circuit. And he had signed up with a Klan group.[9] Although prosecutors did not express it in these terms, they objectively proved that McVeigh was, in fact, more than just an ex-military man angry at government misdeeds at Waco. He was not simply an "antigovernment" activist. He was a soldier who had switched enlistments from the United States Army to the white nationalist underground.

What the prosecution did not do, however, was present evidence on who actually mixed the bomb ingredients. And except for chemicals common to both gun ammunition and detonation cord, there were no traces of bomb materials on McVeigh's clothes or in his hair or nostrils or anyplace else on his body. For some reason, Jones failed to take advantage of these weaknesses in the government's case. While Jones did cast doubt on some of the FBI's lab findings and showed that McVeigh's fingerprints were not found on the truck rental agreement, he was largely foiled during cross-examination by the prosecution's courtroom strategy. While defense witnesses did point toward the involvement of an unknown John Doe Two, McVeigh had never volunteered any information on the subject to his attorney. And after two years of globe-trotting and horse swapping with reporters, the defense failed to present an alternative theory of who actually constituted the bombing crew.

The possible involvement of "others unknown" did not lessen the guilt of Timothy McVeigh, the prosecution had argued. The jury agreed, and he was sentenced to death.[10]

Nichols at Trial

With Timothy McVeigh on death row, the question now presented itself: Would Terry Nichols soon join him? When that trial began the following October, the public's attention to bombing-related events had already dimmed. In part, the thirst for justice had been sated by McVeigh's conviction earlier in the year. In addition, Nichols's face and name were less well known than McVeigh's. Instead of a televised "perp walk" in a prison orange jumpsuit, Nichols had quietly turned himself into the FBI for questioning.

Nichols also presented himself much differently from McVeigh. He seemed almost like a hapless character, blown by the winds of fate. He had fathered several children and joined the army only after a failed marriage. He had remarried and settled down in the village of Herington, Kansas, where his relationship to white nationalism was conflicted. On one hand, after his first marriage failed he had married a dark-skinned woman born in the Philippines, a union that would have placed Nichols in William Pierce's "race traitor" category. On the other hand, Nichols had used the white citizenship theories of the Posse Comitatus and declared himself a "sovereign" citizen, in order to escape payment of a large outstanding debt. And like a Montana Freeman, Nichols had written a phony "fractional reserve check" when a court ordered him to pay the debt.[11] While McVeigh had little association with these Posse Comitatus–style doctrines, and Nichols had never joined the Klan, these were differences that only proved that the white nationalist movement was broader than any one organization and that both men could find a home in its ranks.

In contrast with McVeigh's attorney, Stephen Jones, who had never convincingly found a theme for his defense, Nichols's attorney, Michael Tigar,[12] stuck to a single refrain about the morning of April 19, 1995: Terry Nichols was absent from the scene of the crime. He was at home in Kansas, "building a life" with his new family, not in Oklahoma City, destroying the lives of others. It was a claim that Stephen Jones had not made about Tim McVeigh.[13] While Jones had argued volubly that Elohim City was at the center of the bombing conspiracy, he had never called a witness from there to testify. Michael Tigar's defense team called two, Joan Millar and Carol Howe.

The two women testified quite differently. Joan Millar, age fifty-six, mother of five, and a professionally trained nurse from Canada, had married into the family clan at Elohim City and remained a true believer in the particular blend of Christian Identity preached by the camp's patriarch, Robert Millar.[14] In contrast with Joan Millar's years of tough backwoods living, Carol Howe, age twenty-six, had grown up on the high side of Tulsa society. The daughter of a prominent CEO, she spent a couple of youthful years as a white power skinhead.[15] By Millar's account, Elohim City was a "village" that eschewed violence and hot "antigovernment" rhetoric. Howe, on the other hand, painted it as a "compound" seething with aggression.[16]

Millar told the court that she had received a call in early April 1995 from a male she did not know. She testified that the caller said that he had met some of the young men from Elohim City at a gun show and would be in the area within the next couple of weeks, and he wanted to know if he could come and visit. Joan Millar's testimony could have been the first to conclusively tie the Oklahoma City bombing to one of the many characters moving in and out of Elohim City. But it did not. According to phone records, the caller that day was definitely McVeigh. But if Joan Millar told the truth as she knew it, the two men had met in a gun show, a business card had exchanged hands, and that had been the end of it. The telephone records showed no other telephone contact between McVeigh and Elohim City.[17]

The defense also called Carol Howe, who told the jury that she had visited Elohim City on numerous occasions and had seen Tim McVeigh there in July 1994, talking with Andreas Strassmeir and one other man. If true, Howe's testimony could have changed the arrangement of all the known facts in the bombing and implicated Strassmeir as well as several of his known off-camp comrades in a criminal conspiracy with McVeigh. But cross-examination by government prosecutors threw significant doubt upon her testimony. For example, Howe acknowledged that law enforcement officials had shown her pictures of McVeigh on April 21, just two days after the bombing, but that she did not point to him as someone she had seen in any capacity and certainly not as a visitor to Elohim City. Three days later, however, after video footage of McVeigh had been burned into the national psyche, Howe told officials that she recognized McVeigh's face, this time from a Klan rally—not at Elohim City. Only much later, after she learned that a possible connection between McVeigh and Elohim City was being explored, did Howe testify that she had seen him at the camp. It looked as if Howe rechiseled the facts to conform to whatever theory would do the most harm to her former comrades.[18] Michael Tigar, like Stephen Jones before him, could not make a complete defense out of these tidbits of information.

The fifteen minutes of fame accorded Carol Howe pointed to a larger issue, the desperate need to fill the gaping holes in the federal prosecution of McVeigh and Nichols. John Doe Two had never been found. How the truck bomb had been constructed, as well as who helped mix the fertilizer and fuel oil, remained a mystery, as did other important parts of the bomb plot.[19] Nevertheless, the federal jury convicted Nichols of conspiracy and involuntary manslaughter, a charge often used to convict drunk drivers involved in mortal accidents. They found him not guilty on two crucial counts, murder and using a truck bomb for murder. He was sentenced to life in prison.[20] Terry Nichols would live, but Timothy McVeigh was executed at a federal penitentiary in Indiana on June 11, 2001.[21] Yet the multiple conspiracy theories about the Oklahoma City bombing did not die with him, nor would the violent subculture that had produced the bombing in the first place.

In November 1997, even as the Nichols trial was in progress, a set of murders were committed by skinheads in Denver: First a twenty-five-year-old from a financially successful home stole a car and led police on a thirty-mile chase, before shooting and killing a police officer and then himself. Just days later a nineteen-year-old skin shot a Mauritanian immigrant waiting to take a bus to work at a local hotel. When a woman standing by came to aid the dying immigrant, the nineteen-year-old shot her also, leaving that young mother partially paralyzed.[22]

Eric Rudolph Continues the Violence

In addition to the unrelenting violence of skinheads and militiamen, a wing of the antiabortion movement continued to take up arms against women's clinics and, in this case, gay people. On January 29, 1998, one week after the twenty-fifth anniversary of the *Roe v. Wade* Supreme Court decision, a bombing in Alabama repeated the malevolence, if not the size, of the murders in Oklahoma City. Placed outside the New

Woman All Women Health Care clinic in Birmingham, it blew a crater out at the entrance. A homemade antipersonnel bomb stuffed with nails, it killed an off-duty cop working as a security guard and permanently maimed a nurse. Unlike most of the anticlinic bomb attacks that preceded it, this bombing received extensive and prolonged media coverage. *The New York Times* called it "historic."[23] Doctors, nurses, and clinic personnel had already been shot to death in the war to end abortion, but this was the first fatal clinic bombing.

Federal agents immediately linked the Birmingham investigation to a set of cases in nearby Atlanta that remained painfully unsolved after almost two years. In July 1996 a forty-pound antipersonnel bomb had exploded in a crowded park during the Olympics. Nail shrapnel killed a bystander, another died soon after from heart failure, and another one hundred were wounded. The FBI completely bungled that investigation, falsely naming as a suspect a security guard who had volunteered some information at the time.[24] In January 1997 a bomb tore into a women's clinic in suburban Sandy Springs. No one was injured in the initial explosion, but a second device, loaded once again with nail shrapnel and timed for the arrival of police personnel, injured six. One month later, in February 1997, another bomb stuffed with nail shrapnel blasted an Atlanta nightclub favored by lesbian patrons and injured five. Investigators safely detonated a second bomb at the scene, aimed at rescue workers like those at the Sandy Springs clinic.

The first break in all four cases came in Birmingham. Passersby noticed a man leaving the area of the clinic take off a brown wig and drive away in a gray Nissan pickup truck with North Carolina tags. Authorities traced the truck to Eric Robert Rudolph, an otherwise unknown thirty-one-year-old. At the same time that agents were tracking Rudolph, regional media outlets received a letter purporting to be from a group calling itself the Army of God and claiming responsibility for the bomb.[25]

This letter closely resembled letters from the same putative Army of God that had been received in the Atlanta clinic and lesbian nightclub bombings. With its focus on abortion, a McVeigh-like invocation of Waco, and the call for death of the New World Order, this letter located its author at the juncture of white nationalism and antiabortion zealotry. Further, within days authorities found the truck, a trailer where Rudolph last lived, and a storage locker he had rented. Forensic evidence was also found, and the FBI named Rudolph a suspect in the Birmingham case within the week. Nevertheless, the FBI could not effect an arrest. Despite an intense manhunt involving one hundred agents, heat-seeking detection devices, helicopters, and all manner of technological wizardry, Rudolph eluded capture. Nine months later the feds indicted him in all three of the Atlanta cases as well, but they still could not find him.[26] After its successful conclusion of the Freemen siege in Montana in 1996, the FBI may have shed some of its image as "jack-booted" thugs, but the feds' inability to track Rudolph or crack the mystery surrounding his Army of God revealed the large holes in its post–Oklahoma City crackdown.

Eric Rudolph had been raised in a household thick with Christian Identity. Born in 1966, young Eric lived his first years with four brothers and one sister in southern Florida. After his father died, mother Patricia moved her children several times. One stop was western Missouri, where Eric and a younger brother lived for several months in the early 1980s on the Church of Israel settlement run by Dan Gayman, a Christian Identity leader. Gayman promoted the two seed theory that Jews were literally (and biologically) of the devil. His theological influence then extended to several members of Robert Mathews's Order, and Gayman received some of the stolen armored car money. Gayman eventually testified for the prosecution in the Fort Smith trial, and he returned ten thousand dollars of the loot. It is not known if Eric Rudolph actually met any of Mathews's gang at that time, but deeds of their exploits filled the air that the impressionable postadolescent teenager breathed. At one point he even dated one of Gayman's daughters for several months.[27]

Most of Eric's youth was not spent in Missouri, however, but in Cherokee County, North Carolina, a mountainous area abutting the Nantahala National Forest, where Georgia and Tennessee meet North Carolina in the heart of Appalachia. The family settled again near a Christian Identity outpost, this one run by Nord Davis. Davis distributed Posse Comitatus–type materials in the early 1980s, and he also directly assisted anti-Communist Nicaraguan contras through an outfit known as Civilian Material Assistance, run by a former Klansman.[28] Although Rudolph later claimed that he was not an Identity believer or a racist, his youthful immersion in the white supremacist movement undoubtedly helped him hear its call to arms.[29]

In 1986, Rudolph enlisted in the army, tried to qualify for the elite Special Forces but washed out, and was later discharged. He then returned to Cherokee County, worked part-time as a carpenter, and briefly trafficked in homegrown marijuana, according to ex-family members. Freed from the constraints of working a regular nine-to-five job, he also spent much of his time in the backwoods. He had hiked through the forests and explored caves and mountainsides while still a teenager. He obviously knew their secret places just the way an urban youth might travel the narrow alleyways of his own neighborhood. Rudolph lived quietly in this underground economy while apparently preparing to do death to the New World Order. After the Birmingham bombing, as federal agents sent bloodhounds up his trail, Eric Robert Rudolph simply disappeared.

The search for Rudolph in 1998 soon turned into its own drama. He became the subject of a couple of laudatory country music songs, residents started sporting bumper stickers reading "Run Eric Run," and the federals ran into a wall of silence.[30] With television and newspaper attention drawn to the region, Bo Gritz also marched into the forest with his own band of searchers, hoping to reprise his great adventure, negotiating the surrender of Randy Weaver six years before. He spent a week with his posse, unsuccessfully beating the Appalachian bushes, and then retreated, as he had after his unsuccessful foray onto the Montana Freemen's ranch.[31] For the next five years, Eric Robert Rudolph defied capture, until a local policeman caught him in 2003, rummaging through a grocery Dumpster in Murphy, North Carolina. He pleaded guilty and was sentenced to life in prison without parole.[32]

His crimes were included at the time on the FBI's annual assessment of the threat from terrorists. Also noted in the 1996 data were the Freemen, militia bomb plots in West Virginia and Washington State, and the Phineas Priesthood bank robbers—all crimes and conspiracies that would not have merited inclusion as incidents of domestic terrorism in the period prior to Oklahoma City. When the report for 1997 was published, it noted as "suspected terrorist incidents" the bombing of the Atlanta lesbian nightclub and the women's health clinic, crimes later attributed to Eric Rudolph.

These were also the first times a clinic bombing or an attack on gay men and lesbians had been included in the FBI's annual terrorism survey.[33] The 1998 report took the crimes against clinics one step farther up and recorded the Birmingham clinic bomb in its survey of definite "terrorist incidents." No such accounting had been done in 1993, when Dr. Gunn had been shot outside the clinic in Pensacola. The Clinton administration's Department of Justice had since created a Task Force on Violence Against Abortion Providers, however. It was run out of the department's Civil Rights Division, the same unit that had prosecuted skinhead violence during the early 1990s.

The existence of the task force notwithstanding, violence against abortion providers continued after Birmingham. Later that year, in October 1998, James Kopp shot and killed assassination style a gynecologist, Dr. Barnett Slepian. Slepian had just returned from synagogue to his home in Amherst, New York, when the sniper bullet came from a distance through his kitchen window. Kopp then escaped into an international underground that sheltered him for four years.

Similarly, the FBI crackdown on militia and common law court groups could not and did not stop white nationalist shooters, who popped up unannounced almost without interruption. The strategies of leaderless resistance and lone wolf attacks that had gained popularity in the mid-1990s remained in place.

The ferocity of the continuing violence belied the fact that the political space inside white nationalism for organized mayhem and murder had shrunk considerably since the Oklahoma City bombing in 1995. Further complicating the situation, the white nationalist movement as a whole had grown stronger. It seemed like a paradox. But it was not the vanguardists that were growing. Instead, it was the mainstreaming wing of the movement that developed increased influence, particularly around issues such as immigration and white southern veneration of the Confederate past. This was particularly evident with the growth of the Council of Conservative Citizens.

The United States Congress and the Council of Conservative Citizens

February 2, 1999. Two congressional Democrats introduced a resolution condemning the Council of Conservative Citizens and the racism it propagated.[1] Motivated by recent newspaper coverage of Senator Trent Lott's and Representative Bob Barr's attendance at council meetings in the past, the resolution was modeled on a similar measure passed in 1994 that condemned a Nation of Islam speaker.[2] It would have had no legislative power, except that of expressing congressional sentiment. Two clauses specifically mentioned the council by name:

> Whereas the Council of Conservative Citizens is an outgrowth of the segregationist "White Citizens Council," commonly known as the White-Collar Klan, which helped to enforce segregation in the 1950s and 1960s;
>
> Whereas the Council of Conservative Citizens promulgates dogma that supports white supremacy and anti-Semitism and maliciously denigrates great American leaders including Abraham Lincoln and Dr. Martin Luther King . . .

The House resolution gathered the support of 138 cosigners, including 9 Republicans. Nevertheless, the Republican House leaders, including Barr, refused to bring the measure to the floor for a vote. And in the Senate, where Lott reigned as majority leader, no companion resolution was even introduced. The imbroglio over congressional leaders and the Council of Conservative Citizens had actually started with media coverage the previous December, in the midst of a debate over whether or not to impeach President Bill Clinton. As chairman of the House Judiciary Committee, Barr was among the hard-liners pressing for impeachment.

Barr was first elected to Georgia's Seventh Congressional District in the 1994 Republican landslide, and his constituents stretched from Atlanta's northern suburbs west to the Alabama border.[3] During the 1980s those counties had been saturated with Klan activity and racist violence, and the voters there had elected a string of ultraconservatives in the past, including Larry McDonald, who did double duty as chairman of the John Birch Society.[4] Barr opposed gun control, abortion rights, and civil rights legislation. He also had agreed to keynote a Council of Conservative Citizens meeting in South Carolina in June 1998, after being asked by a council member who had a seat on the Republican Party's National Committee. Candidates for state superintendent of education and a South Carolina state representative also spoke at that meeting.[5] But it was Barr's attendance that caught *The Washington Post*'s notice.

When first asked about his attendance, Barr responded that the "accusations are unfounded and deplorable." Pressed further, Barr claimed that the council material he had been provided prior to speaking gave no indication of racism. If he had known about the group's real politics, Barr told the press, he would not have attended. Not so, council executive Gordon Baum told the *Post*: "He knew what we were all about before he spoke to us. We don't invite people and let them walk into the dark on us." Baum's counterpoint to Barr had the ring of truth. Another council spokesman seconded Baum by noting that prior to speaking, Barr had listened to a panel chaired by Sam Francis. And by any measure, Sam Francis's white nationalism was as subtle as an eight-pound hammer pounding on a twelve inch I beam. Other speakers at Charleston included attorney Sam Dickson and Jared Taylor, the *American Renaissance* editor. In the end Barr simply reiterated his denials.[6]

A similar sequence ensnared Senator Trent Lott. When first asked about his relationship to the council, Lott told the press he had "no first hand knowledge" of the group. Later, when a photo, originally published in the *Citizens Informer*, surfaced showing Lott with council leaders, the senator's office was pushed into a corner. It continued denying that he knew anything about the council other than its existence as a local grassroots group. And Lott's spokesman offered a pro forma statement about the council. "This group harbors views which Senator Lott firmly rejects. He has absolutely no involvement with them either now or in the future."[7] Lott's past support for the council was a matter of the printed record, however, and it was unlikely that he did not know about its core white supremacist beliefs. It is hard not to be familiar with your favorite uncle Arnie's true politics when you are likely to get a full blast of it over Thanksgiving dinner.

After the House resolution was introduced, the Republican Party chairman was forced to address the issue. "It appears this group does hold racist views," he told the press, and the party "rejects and condemns such views forcefully and without hesitation or equivocation."[8] In the aftermath of the statement, one national committeeman did resign from the council.[9] On the other hand, Mississippi Republican Governor Kirk Fordice, who had graced several council platforms himself, refused to criticize the group. They had good people with "good ideas," he said. Finally, after two months of deflection, the Republican leadership decided to quash the Democrats' first resolution. In its place they introduced a resolution by the party's lone black congressman, Representative J. C. Watts of Oklahoma. Watts's resolution condemned racism and bigotry in general, but did not mention the Council of Conservative Citizens specifically. Critics contended that his measure was aimed at keeping the Republican Party leadership off the hook. Nevertheless, three dozen Democrats voted with the Republican majority and passed the Watts resolution.[10] Critics responded to the vote with contempt. A *New York Times* editorial on the incident hit directly at the Senate majority leader. "The original resolution gave Mr. Lott a new chance to sever his connection with the council and ease doubts about his commitment to fairness as the leader of the Senate. Sadly, he declined."[11] Poet and novelist Ishmael Reed had said it most succinctly several weeks before: "White racism is suddenly in high fashion in the era of neo-Confederate chic . . ."[12]

The issue cooled as debate over the question of impeachment heated up, but Barr lost his seat in 2002, after congressional redistricting forced him into a primary fight against a fellow Republican conservative. Lott was entangled in a similar dispute after the 2002 election, when he waxed wistful about Strom Thurmond's 1948 archsegregationist campaign for president. If only the Dixiecrat had won, Lott said, the country would not have suffered the travails that had followed. It was a bald statement, which conjured up others he had made supporting segregation in the past. The national press restaged the drama regarding his relationship to the council. Finally, the Senate majority leader was forced to step down, seemingly chastened by the response to his remarks.[13] As for the Council of Conservative Citizens, the congressional debate didn't hurt it a bit. These were years of solid expansion.

Status of Council of Conservative Citizens Circa the Century's End

The council's relationship with *American Renaissance* had provided the organization with a new set of intellectuals and leadership. It now boasted six field offices, chapters in twenty-three states, and an advisory board of sixty stalwarts. It also claimed fifteen thousand members, including more than twenty Mississippi state legislators.[14] A meeting in North Carolina in November 1997 had attracted three hundred activists, twice the number who had attended similar meetings at the beginning of the decade. Winston-Salem's mayor-elect welcomed this crowd. A. J. Barker emceed the event in his capacity as a Council of Conservative Citizens state chairman, his stint as a Populist Party leader now well behind him. A panel of five attorneys talked about "civil rights and southern heritage," and another panel of preachers set out to save Christian civilization. Sam Francis and Jared Taylor took their now-permanent places on the council's podium. Kirk Lyons announced his latest organizational offspring, the Southern Legal Resource Center, and introduced five of the corporation's directors to the crowd. He claimed that fifty lawyers in eleven states had affiliated with his efforts. The crowd applauded Lyons when he said, "[T]he group we work best with is the Council of Conservative Citizens . . . because you are willing to put it on the line. You are willing to get out in the streets . . . You are willing to see your name in the paper and not shrink from your duties as Christians, as Southerners and as citizens."[15]

That year the council also added a discussion bulletin to its list of publications. In this forty-four-page booklet, a new voice in council circles, Robert DeMarais, argued the case against conservatism. Like five of the bulletin's six contributors, DeMarais held a Ph.D. from an accredited university. His inclusion was noteworthy, nevertheless, because of his staff position with William Pierce's National Alliance, where he served as "Marketing Manager for National Vanguard Books." DeMarais's article did not include any explicit anti-Semitism, but his presence among the bulletin's short list of authors served as a sign welcoming the National Alliance cadre into the ranks of the Council of Conservative Citizens. In a second edition of the bulletin, published in 1998, three of the five authors proposed that their movement's strategy should aim at breaking up the United States, through either the secession of states or the creation of white republics. Here the old Aryan Nations argument for enclave nationalism had migrated over from the vanguardist to the mainstreamer's side of the street. Only Sam Francis, rearticulating his thesis from a previous debate on the subject, argued persuasively for keeping the United States whole. But he also called once again for an explicit white nation and unchallenged racial dominance.[16]

At the same time, the council in Louisiana claimed victory when a Confederate banner was displayed by government edict. In one Alabama instance, members rallied against immigration. In another, they opposed a Birmingham sales tax. In a third, they continued to press for flying the Confederate flag atop the state capitol. The flag remained an organizing focus in South Carolina and Georgia as well. The council's leadership also made a foray north, holding a public meeting in Queens, New York, and later a Christmas party in a Manhattan East Village restaurant.[17]

In September 1998, a delegation went to France and attended a Front National event. At the time, the Front National had hundreds of locally elected officials,[18] attracted millions of voters, and maintained a strong presence in European politics. Known mostly for anti-immigrant politics, the front's chief, Jean-Marie Le Pen, also flirted around the edges of Holocaust revisionism and anti-Semitism. In the first round of multiple presidential elections, Le Pen usually drew between 10 and 20 percent of the vote. The Front National "festival" in Paris that year attracted tens of thousands, as well as sympathetic activists from Britain, Germany, South Africa, and Spain. During the fest, Jared Taylor, Sam Dickson, and Council of Conservative Citizens president Tom Dover met privately with Le Pen. As Taylor translated, Dover formally presented the Front National chief with a Confederate battle flag. "This flag represents an early blow to the hegemony of the United States," Taylor said in a supposedly humorous tone. Le Pen responded by saying, "We are sympathetic to the Confederate cause." The council's tabloid, *Citizens Informer*, reported on the exchange as if their leaders had met with the ghost of General Nathan Bedford Forrest rather than the absolutely corporeal Jean-Marie Le Pen.[19]

The meeting was one more sign that the borderline between the white nationalist movement and social and political convention was not fixed, and it had shifted significantly to the white side during the past decade. Further, the influence of the house intellectuals at *American Renaissance* pushed the organization's rank and file away from its sole preoccupation with refighting the Civil War and the battles of the civil rights era over to including a focus on twenty-first-century issues.

At national conferences and state meetings, on sidewalk picket lines and in the pages of its propaganda, the council contended that immigrants spread disease, committed crimes, lowered wages, and otherwise added to the dreaded "multicultural" (meaning multiracial) future. To help local activists, the *Citizens Informer* published an article on "The Nuts and Bolts of Immigration Reform Rallies." Paint your placards with white oil-based paint so that they would withstand any rainfall and use bold black letters, ran the advice. For photographs of themselves, "participants should squeeze together for a tight shot." Some of the suggested slogans had a post-9/11 theme, "Al Quaida Loves Open Borders"; others didn't: "Immigration Is a Cancer Now Swim Back" and "2 Million Illegals Voted Nov. 2000." Timing is everything, the article explained, and described how the St. Louis chapter had picked Cinco de Mayo as an attention-getting protest date.[20]

In addition, these protest events helped create local constituencies for more draconian public policies and the legislators to implement them. Councillors were long embedded as writers and editors for anti-immigrant periodicals and in leadership positions across the complex of so-called immigration reform organizations. And when the battle lines shifted to the ballot box, members of the council helped lead the way.[21] At the same time, the council was butting up against the limit of main-stream respectability. The vanguardists at the National Alliance were also growing stronger with every passing month during this period. The internal dynamics of the movement were changing. And the best new recruits were highly educated and young.

National Alliance Remakes Resistance Records

April 26, 1999. A dozen young women in Irish ethnic costumes danced traditional jigs. A Scots pipe and drum corps performed, as did a long line of teenage girls in Ukrainian folk outfits who danced to the delight of the audience. A Slovak folksinger and an ensemble in costume sang and danced their way into the hearts of the crowd. And when dinner was finished and the performances were over, the Stan Mejac Orchestra played music for any of the 335 attendees who wished to dance. At thirty-five dollars a couple, the European-American Cultural Society event at the German Central hall in Parma, Ohio, was a good time at a fair price. The event sold out two weeks before the show, and it made a little profit that year.[1] The success was due to the hard work of a local unit of the National Alliance, which produced the show, pocketed the proceeds, and created a broader and more sympathetic organizational periphery, thanks to the Alliance's local leader, Erich Gliebe.

Then in his mid-thirties, Gliebe was a first-generation American, steeped in the traditions of his father's native Germany. During World War Two, his father had fought on the eastern front for the Wehrmacht and after the war had immigrated to the white ethnic enclaves surrounding Cleveland, where he settled down and raised a family. As a youth Erich learned both the German language and folk dancing, and his father's wartime experiences became an integral part of his own personal history. When other students learned about the Holocaust at school, young Erich was told at home that it did not happen. After graduating from high school in 1981, he turned to boxing.[2] By his own account, boxing embodied the "manly" virtues he considered most important. A six-foot-four middleweight with a long reach and a powerful punch, he unabashedly adopted Aryan Barbarian as his moniker. First as an amateur with eighteen wins in twenty fights, and then as a professional who said he was undefeated in eight fights, Gliebe claimed discipline and hard work were as important as any natural abilities. He even concocted a racist theory about boxers: black boxers had "faster muscle twitch" and thicker skulls than whites, but white boxers had more "heart."[3] Gliebe also worked as a tool and die maker, a skilled craft much undervalued by those unfamiliar with its rigors. In his spare time, he volunteered endless hours for the National Alliance, which he had joined in 1990. He soon became its premier recruiter and was later considered by Pierce to be the organization's "most effective" member. A members' bulletin noted that Gliebe had bought an exhibit table at every gun show in his area, sold copies of *The Turner Diaries*, and solicited members. He became the "unit leader" in Cleveland, building it into the largest single local in the alliance, and then the regional coordinator for Ohio and parts of the surrounding states.[4]

In addition to holding yearly European-American Cultural Society festivals, Gliebe recruited out of the white power skinhead scene in the Great Lakes region. In the process, his Cleveland unit also became a must stop for several speakers traveling the National Alliance circuit. On three different occasions, Gliebe organized speaking events for David Irving, the British historical writer who made a profession out of denying Hitler's worst crimes.[5] David Duke spoke to a crowd of two hundred in 1997.[6] These events helped build and sustain a cultural and ideological milieu bigger than any *Bierstube* drink fest and more real than a cybersite forum. As a result, the National Alliance not only recruited new members for itself but came to dominate the white nationalist scene in Cleveland and to exert influence across the movement.

During this period, while Liberty Lobby was sliding into bankruptcy and prosecutors indicted militiamen, law enforcement left the National Alliance relatively unscathed. Even a court-ordered judgment of eighty-five thousand dollars against William Pierce did not slow the organization down. The judgment stemmed from an earlier lawsuit brought by the Southern Poverty Law Center against Ben Klassen's Church of the Creator. As noted earlier, one of Klassen's "reverends" had murdered a black sailor and the church had been held liable. As part of an effort to avoid payment, Klassen had quickly sold a piece of land to Pierce at below market value. Pierce then turned around and sold the parcel at a nifty profit, and a North Carolina judge ordered him to turn the profit over to the sailor's estate. After losing the court battle and an appeal, Pierce paid the judgment and continued operating, almost as if nothing had happened.[7] The accretion of members and resources continued apace, perhaps picking up speed and momentum.

Pierce kept a graph in his office, charting membership levels month by month. Late in 1998 he noticed a sharp spike upward that continued long into the following year. Searching for a reason behind the new and noticeable expansion, he ruled out several possible causes. It wasn't the onset of American bombing missions against Serbia, he decided, nor was it the current impeachment campaign against President Clinton. Nevertheless, he did believe that the Clinton administration was having a "salubrious effect on the recruiting climate." Neither did Pierce contend that any specific National Alliance activities were the cause. The organization was doing much the same as it had been in recent years, he noted.

In fact, the principal activity at the National Alliance headquarters remained mass media propaganda. Having slowed and then halted production of its slick high-cost, high-tone magazine *National Vanguard*, Pierce and staff instead started broadcasting a weekly radio program around 1991, buying time on local AM and FM stations, as well as on shortwave.[8] For those already committed to the cause, the radio communiqués provided regular commentary on world and national events. In both tone and argumentation, however, these messages were aimed at sympathetic listeners outside the organization's ranks. The national office also sold tapes of these broadcasts, along with a growing catalog of books and pamphlets. The alliance republished the commentaries again as part of a monthly periodical Pierce called *Free Speech*. The tapes and the publications were also available on the organization's Internet websites. Although he was sure that new people were listening to the radio broadcasts and reading the material, Pierce was reluctant to attribute the alliance's growth to this cause.

Instead, he decided that a change in political atmospherics was responsible. "People's hatred for the government has risen faster during the past year than their fear of the government," he wrote in a members-only bulletin.[9] This was an odd assessment for Pierce to make. The National Alliance did not fancy itself as a broad-based or ideologically diffuse organization, and it did not set out to capture new members on the basis of mass (white) sentiment. In addition, according to its own dogma, its attitude toward federal and local governments had always been secondary, derived from its approach to the more central and defining issues of race and the Jews. No one joined the National Alliance without understanding that the organization focused on Jews as Enemy Number One. If a prospective member wanted simply to join an "antigovernment" outfit, there were several score of those. Certainly, many groups that presented an antigovernment face to the public were at their core racist and anti-Semitic, John Trochmann's Militia of Montana and the Montana Freemen among them. But it was these militia-style and common law groups that were then suffering the most damage from the FBI. Neither increased "antigovernment" sentiment nor decreased "fear" caused the upward trend.

A more accurate assessment of the growth Pierce noticed during this period, by contrast, begins with a consideration of the by-product created by law enforcement's crackdown on militia and common law groups. Drained of members and money, these groups no longer competed with the National Alliance for new recruits. Ku Klux Klan groups during this period were also in eclipse, suffering from a never-ending battle of small dragons fighting among themselves for a decreasing piece of the white nationalist turf. On the explicitly national socialist side of the street, Aryan Nations had never fully recovered after Fort Smith, and Richard Butler was growing increasingly infirm. Tom Metzger continued to do business and maintain a presence, years after losing his house and everything else in the Portland civil case. But his White Aryan Resistance no longer operated as anything more than a personal soapbox. Skinheads, erstwhile Klansmen, and serious national socialists had few organizational options if they wanted to join a fully operational outfit with local chapters and a national structure. Among the narrow range of choices, Pierce's National Alliance stood the tallest and strongest.

Ironically, the National Alliance's visibility rested in part on mainstream media, as Pierce stopped boycotting journalists looking for a story. Magazines and newspapers anxious to uncover the truth about the onetime physics professor now featured him. Network television news crews interviewed him on the grounds of the headquarters complex. Pierce participated in talk radio programs via telephone hookup, like any author trying to sell books.[10] He endured ridicule and criticism on these shows, but the extended airplay also gave him an audience. Very few of those listening to these syndicated programs liked what Pierce said. Among those who did, however, were National Alliance recruits. Mainstream media visibility often conferred a definable respectability upon any organization it touched, regardless of its politics. And Pierce reaped the benefits.

Increased activity by rank-and-file units, like Gliebe's in Cleveland, also contributed to this growth period. The National Alliance had previously been constituted as a constellation of individual members around William Pierce. While units or chapters existed in a few geographic areas, they tended to be less essential. Most lacked both capable leaders and the kind of internal social environment that sustained long-term membership. Although a few exceptions existed, most units simply had meetings and distributed propaganda. After the organization's size reached critical mass in a number of locales, the increased numbers translated into a change in the quality of chapter life. Now units were able to sustain projects of their own. As noted, Cleveland promoted the most creative and substantial enterprises. Other areas proved themselves quite capable of spreading the message. In Fort Pierce, Florida, members distributed two thousand leaflets in three hours. A similar effort in Pittsburgh netted some (negative) mainstream media coverage, thus giving the alliance a two-for-one media hit. The Sacramento unit traveled to Reno, Nevada, and set up an exhibition table at one of the area's largest gun shows. And in several states, members participated in anti-NATO activities, as American bombing in Yugoslavia generated politically variegated protests. Other parts of the organization ventured into a more cultural and social realm. Maryland units, one in Baltimore and the other in Hagerstown, held a joint picnic. In North Carolina, the region sponsored a Confederate Memorial Day celebration.[11]

To this mix of factors—declining competition, increased media attention, and greater levels of internal socialization—add the changes at headquarters. The larger membership financed an increased number of paid staff working in central administration in West Virginia. In the process, the complex itself was slowly transformed. Unlike Richard Butler, whose Aryan Nations plot in Idaho remained essentially unchanged for twenty years, Pierce continually added buildings and upgraded his compound's infrastructure. At the same time, the middle management grew in both numbers and organizational skill.[12]

Nevertheless, Pierce still ran the National Alliance as a one-man dictatorship. He appointed every unit and regional leader, decided what the leaders could say and do on behalf of the organization and what they could not say and do. To further his process, Pierce instituted a biannual leadership meeting in West Virginia. Approximately sixty handpicked members attended a session, lasting several days, where they got the chance to interact directly with their ideological master. Pierce used these occasions as an opportunity to cull the group for new leaders, promoting a few to middle management positions.[13]

Almost twenty-five years after he had incorporated the National Alliance and begun publishing the first serial installments of *The Turner Diaries*, William Pierce finally possessed a sizable, stable, professionally administered, and increasingly active organization of white nationalist revolutionaries. It was still primarily a propaganda outfit, not a party vying directly for political power, but it had other credits to its name. It had spun off or inspired killers and bombers from Robert Mathews to Timothy McVeigh. It had influenced other organizations and personalities, from David Duke's Knights of the Ku Klux Klan to George Burdi and the Hammerskin Nation.

With Resistance Records now fully transferred into his possession, Pierce turned toward recruiting the twenty-somethings that populated the white power music scene. He acquired Nordland, a Scandinavian music enterprise that had mirrored Resistance Records in style and substance.[14]

Pierce arranged for publication of *Resistance*, no. 9, the first issue to appear since before the Michigan tax raid in 1997.[15] He wrote the lead editorial and praised music to which he did not listen as the stuff of "rebirth and renewal." An ad for the National Alliance and other less obvious blandishments filled those pages not assigned to puff reviews and band promotions. Oddly, several articles insulted skinheads for their tattoos and lack of discipline, but otherwise the magazine looked much like previous issues. In retrospect, perhaps the most important piece was an interview with Erich Gliebe. At that moment Gliebe still served as the alliance's Ohio regional coordinator. Pierce soon promoted him to a full-time position as Resistance Records' manager and editor of its magazine. Gliebe still preferred ethnic folk dancing to mosh pit thrashing. "While moshing is a great way to relieve stress and can be fun," he told *Resistance* magazine, "it is a much manlier thing to lead a lady in your arms across the dance floor than running into some sweaty drunk in the mosh pit."[16] Despite this gap in musical tastes, Pierce hired him to edit the magazine, and Gliebe was glad to do it.

Resistance's skinhead readership, however, took umbrage at Gliebe's remarks about manhood. They undoubtedly admired his "Aryan Barbarian" side, but otherwise he seemed out of sync with many of the subculture's other values. This tension between the National Alliance's straitlaced lifestyle and the wild-in-the-streets attitudes of the young white powerniks continued to bedevil Gliebe. As the company's manager and the magazine's editor he soon apologized for not understanding the "subtle nuances of the skinhead subculture."[17] At that point Gliebe had to act as if he cared. Simply put, he could not impugn the tattooed beer-soaked norms of skinheads and successfully sell them hundreds of thousands of dollars in music and paraphernalia at the same time.

Gliebe was also forced to make further amends after the appearance of an article critical of Bob Mathews and The Order. Mathews was still considered a heroic martyr more than a dozen years after he had been killed in an FBI shoot-out, particularly by those who read this particular magazine. The author of that article, a top National Alliance cadre and former Special Forces officer, argued that The Order had violated every law of clandestine warfare and committed several major political mistakes as well. After publication, a stream of protests arose from readers, and most problematic of all, members of The Order wrote the magazine from their prison cells, demanding a retraction and an apology. Gliebe provided both. "We realize that we are not going to win anybody's support by criticism and name-calling," he wrote in an editorial response.[18]

Despite this rocky beginning, Gliebe settled into the job while working from his home in Ohio. The music distribution business grew like a Silicon Valley start-up, and over the next three years increased sales, combined with an expanding National Alliance membership dues base, funded an expansion at headquarters in West Virginia. New staff was hired, and a new building constructed. Resistance Records focused on its task: reaching postadolescent males, fifteen to nineteen years old. For three decades Pierce's yearly organizational budget had lagged far, far behind Carto's. Now Pierce, Gliebe, and company were successful enough that the National Alliance's rising economic fortunes more closely rivaled the Liberty Lobby complex's declining assets.

Liberty Lobby in Bankruptcy Court

July 1, 1999. Room 24 in Washington, D.C.'s Federal Bankruptcy Court looked spare, bleak, and bureaucratic. Behind a well-worn double gate sat six spectator benches. Instead of a jury box, a dozen seat stumps stood like silent sentinels truncated by debt and misfortune. A witness stand was fixed in front of two glass-topped tables—on one side the debtor, on the other the creditors. At the front of the long, narrow room sat Judge Martin Teel, the third judge to rule upon the fate of Willis Carto and Liberty Lobby on one side and Mark Weber and the Legion for the Survival of Freedom–Institute for Historical Review on the other. Teel's purpose that day was to hear a motion to fix a bankruptcy court's special trustee over Liberty Lobby's day-to-day finances.[1]

Understanding Liberty Lobby's route to Courtroom 24 is a somewhat difficult task, requiring a fair amount of knowledge of the twists and turns taken since Carto tried to relitigate issues decided first by Judge Polis in 1993 and again by Judge Maino in 1996. In a lawsuit filed in Texas, where the IHR's parent Legion for the Survival of Freedom had first been incorporated, Carto once more unsuccessfully alleged that his status as the legion's "substitute incorporator" gave him virtual ownership of the IHR. He filed another lawsuit in D.C., alleging that Mark Weber and others had engaged in racketeering. At each point, Judge Maino's ruling stood. Carto and his codefendants still owed legion-IHR the balance of the Farrel estate money, over six million dollars.[2]

Meanwhile, Weber's legion-IHR pressed for a court-appointed receiver to speed collection of money it was owed. Finally, on March 27, 1998—eighteen months after his initial decision—Judge Maino had ordered a receiver to begin collection.[3] The pace of events quickened after the receiver began seizing Liberty Lobby's mail, which contained its lifeblood—contributions, subscriptions, and other income, funds that the judge had decided now belonged to legion-IHR. In response, Liberty Lobby filed a bevy of new motions aimed at stopping the receivership. All failed. If it did not want to lose control of its own mail (and income), only two options were tenable: either begin payments to legion-IHR or declare bankruptcy. On May 13, 1998 Liberty Lobby filed in D.C. a Chapter Eleven reorganization bankruptcy. Willis Carto filed personally in California a Chapter Seven liquidation bankruptcy. Liberty Lobby hoped to continue operating while it supposedly paid off its debts. Carto wanted to escape the judgment altogether. After these filings, Judge Maino's collection process came to a temporary halt.[4]

The years of litigation had taken a toll on both Willis Carto and Liberty Lobby. After keeping his personal and business affairs out of the public domain during a lifetime of litigation, his most intimate financial arrangements were now subject to intense examination. Carto dragged and delayed in every venue. At one point he invoked the Fifth Amendment in a disclosure hearing because, he said, of a pending criminal investigation in Switzerland. Another time he wouldn't tell the court who or what owned the house he lived in or what his wife's middle name was.[5]

For its part, Liberty Lobby's annual income slipped from about four million dollars before Weber's coup to eight hundred thousand five years later. *The Spotlight* subscriptions fell (further), from 90,000 to 60,000. It was a paradoxical situation. Liberty Lobby still maintained the biggest list of supporters among white nationalist outfits. But the whole operation was becoming smaller and less salient. When the Populist Party had been formed in 1984, for example, *The Spotlight* claimed 150,000 subscribers. Now Liberty Lobby had neither an electioneering adjunct to call its own nor a stable market for its merchandising. Only its *Barnes Review* magazine seemed to thrive.[6]

Rather than end the collection process, bankruptcy pushed affairs from bad to worse. Chapter Eleven is a reorganization bankruptcy, in which a United States trustee develops a court-approved plan in conjunction with the creditors and the debtor. Presumably, the plan allows the debtor to continue operating. But it also requires complete disclosure by the debtor, which must file monthly reports of its financial activities, hold supervised meetings with its creditors, and adhere to the plan—once it is approved.

As part of the process, the court convened a meeting at which Liberty Lobby's comptroller, Blayne Hutzel, answered questions. In contrast with Carto, Hutzel was direct and forthcoming. At least four different corporations employed twenty-five people at the Independence Avenue headquarters: Liberty Lobby, Inc., Government Education Foundation, Foundation for Economic Liberty, and Foundation to Defend the First Amendment. These four corporations were not the only ones that Carto operated, but they were the most important. Liberty Lobby paid rent to the Government Education Foundation, which owned the office building (and the computers and other office equipment). The rent was not a fixed amount; it varied from month to month, depending on Liberty Lobby's revenue. Similarly, the employees all supposedly worked varied amounts of time for the four corporations, but all received their payroll checks from Liberty Lobby, which then allocated the payments on the books of the four corporations. Like the rent, the allocations were neither fixed by prior agreement nor determined by the numbers of hours worked for each entity. Instead, payroll allocations varied according to the revenues received by each corporation.[7]

Book sales were handled in a similar fashion. A department of Liberty Lobby ostensibly sold the books. But the books were actually owned by the Government Education Foundation, which then supposedly paid Liberty Lobby a commission for its role as the merchandiser. No cash ever actually changed hands. Hutzel's description of the accounting was no doubt honest, but it was still virtually indecipherable. "At the end of the month book sales are debited and the loan account for GEF is credited to the book sales," he testified. "On GEF's records, the loan account with Liberty Lobby is debited and book sales show up in GEF. That is done by journal entry." While this system may have made perfect sense to Willis Carto, it ensured that an outside observer would never find the pea under the shell. Only the most accomplished accountant could penetrate the bookkeeping maze. This method also maximized the debt standing on Liberty Lobby's books, while minimizing its assets.[8]

At that point, Liberty Lobby and legion-IHR had still not agreed on a bankruptcy payment plan. While Liberty Lobby tried to avoid paying the judgment debt, the courts slowly shut down its avenues of escape. Each month that Liberty Lobby filed a financial report brought the day of reckoning closer. Finally, on June 11, 1999, the United States trustee petitioned for appointment of a special Chapter Eleven trustee to take over Liberty Lobby's day-to-day finances. According to the motion, the shell game of moving money from one entity to another had not been properly reported. "This prevents creditors from having sufficient financial information to make an informed decision in voting on the plan," according to the trustee's motion. And the debtor's conduct "raises serious questions concerning the veracity of the information" already reported.[9]

Judge Teel called the hearing in Room 24 on July 2 to resolve the matter. The long road appeared (although appearances can be deceiving) to have come to an abrupt end. Once again Liberty Lobby asked for a delay, as its bankruptcy attorney tried to withdraw from the case. The request was denied. Liberty Lobby's attorney then argued against appointment of a special trustee. He acknowledged that the relationships between the various corporate entities might not be "pure." Still, his clients did not want an outsider looking at their books. In any case, he said, the bookkeeping bungling did not constitute fraud.[10]

The counterargument belonged to legion-IHR, whose attorneys aimed at demonstrating fraud in Liberty Lobby's finances. If the judge concurred, the appointment of a special Chapter Eleven trustee was virtually guaranteed. Collecting the Farrel estate millions would presumably be one step closer. IHR's first witness was Todd Blodgett, the advertising huckster who negotiated the sale of Resistance Records to William Pierce. Blodgett told the court that he had sold advertising for *The Spotlight*, bought and sold mailing lists, and raised funds from large contributors. He worked both in-house, he said, and at his own agency up on Connecticut Avenue. He testified that Carto directed large donors to make their checks payable to the Foundation for Economic Liberty or the Foundation to Defend the First Amendment, rather than to Liberty Lobby. Both were nonprofit corporations, and donations were tax-deductible, according to the IRS. Some donors also received advertising space in *The Spotlight* for their supposed tax-deductible contributions, Blodgett said.

During this period, Blodgett said, he made a deal to purchase the Liberty Lobby mailing list for his own use and agreed to pay Liberty Lobby eighty-five thousand dollars. He still owed twenty-five thousand on the contract at the time Liberty Lobby filed bankruptcy, on May 13, 1998. Blodgett testified that he had paid the twenty-five thousand dollars on the Memorial Day weekend following, handing Carto 250 one-hundred-dollar bills in cash, while they both were in Phoenix attending a conference for Identity believers. Carto brought a special heavy-duty metal valise to carry off the funds.[11] If paying twenty-five thousand dollars in cash did not look to Judge Teel like a Hollywood-style off-the-books drug deal, closer examination of Liberty Lobby's monthly financials to the bankruptcy courts would easily determine if the sums had been properly reported. But before Blodgett was cross-examined by Liberty Lobby's attorney, the court adjourned. The next session was scheduled for a month later.[12]

The hearing, particularly Blodgett's testimony, apparently convinced Carto that his best path was to avoid the reporting that bankruptcy court required. Within the next month earnest negotiations with Mark Weber began, and an agreement was reached and ratified by Judge Teel. It required that both parties refrain from further litigation, and it provided legion-IHR with several lump-sum payments and regular monthly payments. The total sum Liberty Lobby would ultimately have to pay would depend upon how much interest was accumulated, but the baseline figure negotiated stood at $1 million two hundred thousand plus additional $100,000 payments at six-month intervals. It was a sum less than half the original Farrel settlement, but enough for Weber's crew to hire staff and reinvigorate the IHR. The first check to legion-IHR for $200,000 was paid that August. It looked as if six years of litigation between the two parties might finally be coming to an end. If the agreement was breached, however, the entirety of Judge Maino's original judgment (plus interest) would once again be due.[13]

Predictably, *The Spotlight* told its readers that paying a settlement it had tried to avoid was actually a victory. The headline read: "Good News for Liberty Lobby; Bad News for Our Enemies."[14] For more than two decades, *The Spotlight* had been maintaining that down was really up: that Gordon Kahl was simply a tax-protesting farmer rather than a trigger-happy Aryan warrior; that David Duke was a controversial candidate rather than a white supremacist imbued with national socialist principles; and that men like Don Wassall and Mark Weber were the equivalent of Mossad agents rather than just factional opponents working in the same political movement. At that point, Liberty Lobby was sliding down a steep hill, heading for a crash. Declaring otherwise was a little bit like claiming the world was going to come to an end after December 31, 1999.

The Millennium Changes

January 1, 2000. 23 Tebet 5760. The Year of the Dragon. The sun's surface burned at ten thousand degrees Fahrenheit. The moon rose in the east and settled in the west. The earth flew through the Lord's heavens at 66,600 miles per hour. Volcanic activity steamed as usual. The oceans slept quietly. And most rivers (the Nile excepted) continued flowing toward the equator. On seven continents six billion people continued living as they had before. Most of them were ill fed, but hunger and poverty were chronic conditions and not particularly of the moment. In New York City, three million happy souls gathered in Times Square for a midnight celebration. In Washington, D.C., William Jefferson Clinton presided over a nation at peace and Alan Greenspan chaired the Federal Reserve Board. For the public, this was the turn of the millennial clock. The world did not end. Computers did not crash. The lights stayed on, and automatic teller machines spit out cash just like the day before.

Years of public worries had predicted a different change at the millennium. Power grids and banking systems, communications and transportation, local economies and world commerce, political stability and individual safety—all were thought vulnerable to the Y2K bug. Described almost as if it were a computer virus, this bug was supposedly a problem left over from decades before, when computer memory had been scarce. To save space, programmers wrote codes with dates represented in eight digits, not ten. December 31, 1999, became 12-31-99. But with one turn of a calendar page a potential danger emerged. At 01-01-00, January 1, 2000, could be mistaken for January 1, 1900. Things computer driven might come to a grinding halt. Planes would fall from the sky. Cities might succumb to rioting mobs looking for light, heat, and food. Civil society and civilization could disappear entirely.

Much of popular culture seemed to stand at century's end on an apocalyptic brink. To the cyberdoomsday scenario, add a particular set of Christian beliefs about the End of Time. In the mainstream media, *Newsweek* drew together several strands in a nine-page spread entitled: "Prophecy—Millennial Visions. What the Bible Says About the End of the World."[1] Large full-color outtakes of Renaissance-era paintings depicting apocalyptic and other biblical themes decorated the text. Survey data highlighted much of the story: "40% of U.S. adults believe the world will end as foretold: in a Battle of Armageddon between Jesus and the Antichrist . . . 19% of Americans . . . believe that the Antichrist is on earth now." A similar number believed "Jesus will return to the earth during their lifetimes."[2] The perception of the world's end, by either computer glitch or eschatological design, was said to be inspiring a range of survivalist and paramilitary activity, from Joe Doe Militiamen storing food and fuel to sects waiting with arms and ammunition for the hard times ahead. Some were sure to start shooting just to help events along, a bevy of so-called experts predicted.[3]

Not everyone cited by the magazine was convinced that white supremacists or Christian zealots were slouching toward Armageddon. J. Gordon Melton, an academic with a special interest in religion, added *Newsweek*'s caveat: "Yet among Christian communities, the coming millennium has inspired a surprisingly low count of doomsday survival cults."[4] Before nothing happened, a few voices asserted that nothing was going to happen.[5] Other scholars, particularly those with an interest in millennial studies, as well as government agencies, acted as if they thought otherwise.[6]

To forestall any future problems, the U.S. Senate had established a Special Committee on the Year 2000 Technology Problem several years before Y2K computer concerns hit the media. In February 1996 the committee reported that some local and state governments might not make the necessary computer program upgrades to bridge the date change successfully. It also posited a possibility for "urban unrest" as a result. In 1999 the Federal Bureau of Investigation produced a report, *Project Megiddo*, named after a hill in northern Israel from which the term "Armageddon" was derived. One version of the report was solely for internal agency use. A second was made available to the public. It focused on the threat posed by those who believed the year 2000 marked the end of the world and who might use violence. The FBI specifically ruled outside its analytical parameters those "domestic terrorists" for whom the year 2000 was not a trigger. Despite a passing mention of a group called Black Hebrew Israelites, the report's main target was the phenomenon it called "right-wing extremism."[7]

Almost immediately critics assailed the FBI report. One liberal analyst warned that the report's release had led to a "hysterical atmosphere," increasing the likelihood that cops would overreact. "This is potentially disastrous," he concluded.[8] Most of the fire against the FBI's report came from the conservative end of the spectrum, however. Phyllis Schlafly and Paul Weyrich complained that only the "right wing" was referenced in the report. Why wasn't the "political left" targeted? they asked in a letter to Republican congressional leaders.[9] Sam Francis, now ensconced in his role as Council of Conservative Citizens counselor, amplified the criticism in a syndicated column. Francis's first concerns were political and cultural power, and he admitted that he had never gotten "excited about Y2K." Nevertheless, he claimed that "an entire dissident political and religious subculture" had been "demonized" by the FBI.[10]

Compounding legitimate criticism of the FBI's conclusion with a bit of anti-Semitic hysteria, commentators from Pete Peters to Willis Carto's *Spotlight* issued a unanimous verdict: the FBI's *Megiddo* report simply rewrote similarly scurrilous reports by those conspiratorial string pullers at the Anti-Defamation League. It smeared all "patriots," they reported.[11]

In actuality, the FBI believed that the danger came from two directions. The first was from those who believed secular conspiracy theories about the New World Order. In these theories the Y2K computer problem would supposedly start a sequence of events leading to cataclysm and a United Nations–New World Order takeover of the United States. To thwart this imaginary occupation, guns and ammunition and all manner of survival gear were needed.[12] The FBI did seem to miss the fact that this particular iteration differed little in form or substance from those conspiracy theories that had preceded it, including militia-style ramblings about black helicopters in the mid-1990s. In fact, it wasn't the end of the world that worried these people, but a loss of (white) national hegemony. The second hypothetical threat allegedly came from those motivated by religious doctrine and the belief that the millennial change signaled the End Times or the Second Coming of Christ. Here the FBI directed most of its analysis at Christian Identity believers. Identity doctrine, the FBI stated correctly, regarded the battle of Armageddon, the final battle between good and evil, as a race war. As evidence, the report cited several high-profile racially motivated murders.[13] As it happened, none of those crimes was actually committed with the calendar change in mind. The FBI's *Project Megiddo* failed to understand the specific Identity conception of Armageddon, which is not linked to the Year 2000 or any other distinctive date. And in this mistake the FBI was not alone. A number of watchdog organizations misjudged the response by Christian Identity adherents and other white nationalists to the calendar change.[14]

Certainly, a few Identity voices made a lot of noise, and one or two Aryan loudmouths, eager to grab headlines, made all sorts of threats they had no ability (or actual desire) to fulfill.[15] But the most significant response to the impending calendar change came briefly in the late 1990s from survivalist marketers. The most creative sales effort belonged to Bo Gritz, who had changed directions after the November 1992 elections. He quickly abandoned the electioneering wing of the movement in favor of the commercial side of paramilitary "preparedness." He began selling tickets to survivalist trainings as if they were ice cream on a hot afternoon in the city. At venues across the western states, he enlisted a shifting assortment of former military men, ex-cops, and con artists to teach "combat medicine," lock picking, weapons handling, radio transmission, and other skills. Self-proclaimed patriots paid money to attend and then more money if they wanted to buy videotapes of the presentations. Gritz called these classes on breaking and entering SPIKE (Specially Prepared Individuals for Key Events) trainings. Here the key word was "individual" preparedness. No groups of men slogging in formation through the woods.[16] Someone else would have to teach that. Much like Gritz's seamless transition from presidential candidate to survivalist merchant, the trainings then had turned effortlessly in the mid-1990s into a commercial land venture he called Almost Heaven.

A several-hundred-acre land tract outside Kamiah, Idaho, it abutted the Nez Perce Reservation. Gritz promoted it as a safe haven, a so-called ark in a time of Noah, bound together by shared beliefs. This "covenant community" was actually structured like a smart real estate enterprise, with business trusts as the medium of control. The remote wooded and rolling central Idaho land attracted an assemblage of 160 souls, who built a variety of structures. One man created a hut of hay bales and plastic batting. Another pulled a double-wide trailer onto his lot. A third built a six-sided cabin in the woods. Each was lured by the promise of living off the grid.[17]

By moving in this direction, Gritz followed a course headed 180 degrees away from his days as a Populist Party candidate. Instead of pulling his constituents into the system, he was following them into dropping out. Instead of urging them to register and vote, he repeated various Christian common law notions, including the old Posse Comitatus distinction between organic sovereigns and federal citizens.[18] Strategy always came in second or third for Gritz, however, behind patriotic profiteering. In this run-up to the millennial change he was joined by others making money on the preparedness expo circuit. The traveling expo road shows that had drawn Louis Beam to Spokane in 1992 and Larry Pratt and Bo Gritz to Orlando after the Oklahoma City bombing had continued apace. Each year a supposed threat had been conceived a little differently. In 1997, for example, the main danger to national sovereignty came from the gun grabbers at the United Nations, but as at every expo, vendors sold water purifiers and dried foods as the cure. In 1998 the sales effort shifted to Y2K-specific preparedness. The gold and silver dealers therefore switched tack. Rather than warn of a gun grabber takeover, they told audiences to buy gold because the Y2K computer bug was going to shut down banks and banking systems.

However, the preparedness market became saturated long before the calendar was set to change, particularly in the Midwest, where expos had been a continual presence since the early 1980s and the total number of survivalists remained relatively limited. In 1999 one vendor candidly said he was still selling water purifiers in California, but sales in Kansas City had slowed to a halt.[19] As early as December 1998, a full year before any millennial disasters would supposedly hit, *The Spotlight* told its declining number of subscribers that "scaremongers" were pumping up public panic for private profit. "Don't Be Fooled on Y2K," the tabloid opined.[20] After the doomsday date came and went without incident, *The Spotlight* took the opportunity to say, "Told you so." The tabloid called to account one scaremeister popular among John Birch Society types, Gary North, for deciding that the calendar change might provoke the "biggest problem" in modern history. Another *Spotlight* target was Don McAlvaney, who had spent years speaking at preparedness expos that also featured Bo Gritz.[21]

Nevertheless, Liberty Lobby could not itself resist the pull of the Y2K market. It published several special *American Family Preparedness* tabloid-size inserts for subscribers that were distributed free at these expos. The inserts featured a few print articles about buying guns and preparedness and lent the enterprise an authoritative look. The tabloid's representatives sold "Liberty Library" book stock. And Liberty Lobby garnered additional advertising revenue by selling display ads to other outfits drilling the same landscape. By any measure, *The Spotlight*'s merchandising was opportunistic, not ideological.[22]

By contrast, Pete Peters opposed the Y2K salesmen as a matter of doctrinal certainty. The expos, he wrote, were, "in reality, patriots' flea markets where Kosher Conservative speakers . . . scare . . . the audience who then go through the flea market to buy everything from gold and silver to generators and food storage."[23]

Peters had kept much of his following throughout the 1990s despite a few setbacks, including the death from cancer of his wife, Cheri, and a subsequent rift with his children when he remarried.[24] In fact, Peters still represented a definable camp of Christian Identity preachers and their respective flocks. More significant, his critique of the Y2K scare-mongers was thoroughly grounded in a specific Christian Identity eschatology. "We have been called to be more than survivors," he argued to his flock. "We have been called to be overcomers and to wage spiritual battle against our enemies."[25] Peters's refusal to fan the Y2K flame should have weighed more than the opportunism of a few visible cranks in any assessment of the millennial change.

It was Peters's analysis that was the most important missing ingredient in the FBI's *Project Megiddo* report. Further, an analysis of the Identity-specific theory of the End Times was absent from the predictions by those academics and other experts who guessed wrong about what would happen on January 1, 2000. Much like the distinction between one seed and two seed adherents inside the Christian Identity camp, on this piece of eschatological arcana rests an entire doctrinal superstructure.

Christian eschatology has to do with doctrines related to the End Times, the associated Second Coming of Christ, and the establishment of God's Kingdom. Most Christian believers fall into three camps: amillennialism, postmillennialism, and premillennialism. In this case, "millennialism" refers to the period when Christians believe their Lord will rule the earth. The first group holds no particular set of ideas about when Christ will return to earth and how God's Kingdom will be instituted. Premillennialists believe that Christ returns *prior* to the thousand-year kingdom, which is established through his agency (and his agency alone). Most Christian fundamentalists, those who believe in a literal interpretation of their Bible, are premillennialists.

One of the hallmarks of premillennialism is the notion of dispensationalism, a specific ordering of events (including world events) by the Lord. A dispensation, then, is a specific period of time that begins with a revelation and ends with a divine judgment. The period before the Second Advent of Christ is considered a dispensation unto itself, a particular period of time that opens in prophecies and signs so that it can be known to the faithful. It ends with Christ's judgment of all. On the exact nature of this last dispensation, known popularly as the period of the End Times, all premillennialists do not agree. But if any millennial-associated violence aimed at quickening the arrival of their Christ, it might have come from this theological camp. In any case, nothing happened.[26]

Postmillennialists, on the other hand, believe that the Kingdom of God will be brought about through human agency, essentially through the work of the church. After a thousand years of this kingdom, Christ is supposed to return to earth, hence the name postmillennial. Christ's return ends all time and begins the hereafter known as eternity. Liberal and mainstream Protestant denominations make up the greatest number of postmillennialists. But Christian Identity—with its emphasis on human action and a prolonged race war—falls within a postmillennial-like worldview.[27] Simply put, Christian Identity adherents were not preparing for Y2K-specific End Times. And law enforcement officials and religious scholars who rang an alarm about end-of-the-century violence by Identity adherents proved manifestly mistaken.

The Racial Millennium

While all this speculation about the meaning of the calendar change was going on, white nationalists were actually preparing for a different period of great transformation and tumult, what might be called a racial millennium. According to the U.S. Census Bureau, the total population of the United States in 2000 was 281,421,906.[28] Of that total population, 11 percent was counted as "foreign born." Over 69 percent was considered "white, non-Hispanic." Over 12 percent was counted as black. Another 12.5 percent (35,305,818) was counted as "Hispanic," and 3.6 percent "Asian and Pacific Islander." The numbers shifted significantly in predictions for the year 2050, when those children born during the year 2000 might be becoming grandparents. At that point, 13 percent of the population was expected to be foreign born. The number that most alarmed white nationalists, however, was the relationship of "white, non-Hispanics" to the total: 53 percent, a drop of almost twenty points from their majority status in the year 2000. The black population was expected to remain at around 13 percent of the total while those counted as "Asian and Pacific Islander" would double to almost 9 percent, and those counted as "Hispanic" were expected to take the largest jump, to 24 percent.

By the year 2070, the Census Bureau predicted, "white, non-Hispanics" would decline to 47 percent of the total. The change in the demographic character of the population was expected to happen faster in some states and cities than in others, of course. But the essential fact remained: in about the same number of years that elapsed between World War Two and the year 2000, white nationalists could expect to lose the powers and privileges of majority status. Thus those who conflated nation with race expected to lose what they regarded as the "genetic basis" for Western Civilization.

In the white nationalist mind, becoming a racial minority is only one step away from racial extinction. And fear of racial extinction has animated white supremacists since before the first antimiscegenation laws were passed. When white supremacy reemerged as a distinctive movement in the 1970s, its leaders and publicists railed against any number of contemporary events and changes that they regarded as infringements upon "white rights." At the same time, however, they remained animated by a fear that the white race would disappear. David Duke's Knights of the Ku Klux Klan, for example, published a special recruitment tabloid under the banner headline of "A New Racial Minority," featuring a picture of a pale-skinned infant. Future babies, Duke warned, would not be this color. In the early 1980s, Aryan Nations published a three-color map with boldly drawn arrows showing the waves of brown-skinned immigration it expected to swamp the white heartland. This fear for the racial future, posed as a concern for white children, became part of the movement's core ritual observances. When Bob Mathews first organized his group of Order bandits, for example, they pledged their eternal fealty in a circle with a white baby in the middle. And Order member David Lane turned his famous "Fourteen Words" into a virtual religious mantra: "We must secure the existence of our people and a future for White children." Skinheads who joined the movement long after Lane had been imprisoned knew and repeated this slogan from California to Michigan and from Toronto to Stockholm. To hear this movement tell it, white people were an endangered species, akin to the white wolf.

After the transformation of white supremacy into white nationalism, a broader stratum of thinkers and activists began to consider the future of the American polity in specifically racial terms. Pat Buchanan's focus changed from combating communism to worries about the possibility of assimilating "Zulus" to a final declaration that declining white birthrates (coupled with increased numbers of brown-skinned, Spanish-speaking immigrants and high "nonwhite" birthrates) signaled the end of Western Civilization itself. Even white power skinheads, not yet old enough to matriculate high school, claimed that fear for the future of their yet-to-be-born children motivated their desire to get drunk and knock some dark-skinned stranger on the head.

Less brutishly, the Council of Conservative Citizens talked about race, immigration, and the future, while its members marched to preserve monuments to the Confederate past. One monthly tabloid allied with this wing of the movement, *Middle American News*, used its back page to publish a large picture of a white baby with the headline "By the Time She Retires, Will the U.S. Be an Overcrowded Country?" Without using the words "white" or "race" the pictures and text conveyed a white racial story: "Because of immigration policies adopted by Congress, America's population will grow from 281 million today to more than 500 million by 2050, according to the U.S. Census Bureau. The millions of newcomers are radically changing the U.S. into a multicultural society. Is this the future we want?"[29]

American Renaissance too made the prospective future of the white race a key element of its program. Jared Taylor repeatedly claimed that racial diversity was a horror, "so obviously stupid that only very intelligent people could have thought it up." Diversity and multiculturalism provoked wars among peoples, caused white people to move from their neighborhoods to the suburbs, and was about to turn North America into a "pesthole." Only Europeans and Asians, he opined, could build successful societies. And if the present looked grim to Taylor, the future was certain to be worse. "What we are witnessing is one of the great tragedies in human history," he claimed. "Powerful forces are in motion that, if left unchecked, will slowly push aside European man and European civilization on this continent. If we do nothing, the country we leave to our grandchildren will be a grim Third-World failure, in which whites will be a minority."[30]

As a ray of white hope, Taylor believed that white people tended to lead segregated lives by natural instinct. Certainly he was right that housing segregation, for example, had not changed significantly since the passage of the open housing laws. In fact, there was evidence that growing numbers of young white people, the generation that would become the great-grandparents of the year 2050, were tending to regard "separate but equal" as a legitimate doctrine in the twenty-first century. A 1999 poll conducted by Zogby International found a definable drift away from integration and toward a "separate but equal" doctrine among younger people age eighteen to twenty-nine. Asked if "it's OK if the races are basically separate from one another as long as everyone has equal opportunities," 50.3 percent of survey respondents agreed.[31]

The separate but equal doctrine had been described as inherently unequal by the Supreme Court in 1954. If this simple fact of life could be successfully ignored in 1999, less than fifty years later, the argument for racial partition would have greater salience, some Renaissancers believed. Others wanted to eviscerate the Fourteenth Amendment now. Survivalist tactics such as establishing so-called covenant communities and keeping stocks of food and rifles would not alter immigration and birthrates. All agreed that the coming permanent racial transformation of the United States posed a long-term danger to white nationalists, greater than any damage computer bugs could do by shutting down the banking system. For mainstreamers and vanguardists alike, the cultural war was not a war for control of a single culture. Rather, it was a war between cultures for dominance over a single piece of North American real estate. It was a battle for the future. And it often began with combat over the past.

Elections 2000: The Neo-Confederate Resurgence

January 8, 2000. The new millennium began in South Carolina with a ceremonial remembrance of the past. After reading of the names of Confederate war dead, men dressed as Civil War reenactors, wearing gray uniforms and carrying muskets, marched ahead of a throng six thousand strong singing "Dixie" through the streets of Columbia, the state capital. Dwarfed by a sea of rebel battle flags, a shrunken ninety-three-year-old woman, said to be the last surviving widow of a Confederate veteran, was wheeled in her chair to the front. An oversize Confederate battle flag hung behind a speakers' dais that included six state representatives and a state senator. All intended to protect the banner's pride of place on the capitol's flagstaff, where it had been flying beneath both the Stars and Stripes and South Carolina's state flag since 1961. Vitriol flowed from the platform that day like undigested bile, much of it directed at the NAACP, which had been campaigning to remove the Confederate banner from its state-sanctioned position. One state senator called the NAACP the National Association of Retarded People. Another elected representative screamed, "If they keep trying to bring it down, they're going to find out why they call it a battle flag."[1]

In addition to elected officials and Sons of Confederate Veterans members, organizations such as the League of the South, which promoted its own brand of southern nationalism, mobilized their membership to march alongside newly prominent neo-Confederate groups, such as the Southern Party and the Heritage Protection Association. Council of Conservative Citizens and National Alliance members joined the crowd, as did Kirk Lyons, who had recently started yet another nonprofit corporation called the Southern Legal Resource Center and developed a new law practice focused on Confederate-related issues.[2]

The Confederate battle flag had been resurrected in the 1950s by segregationists, who hoisted it atop state capitols to show their defiance of federal authority. In Georgia, for example, the state legislature had incorporated the Stars and Bars into the state flag in 1956. After decades of protest against the flag's public display, the NAACP mounted a campaign to remove the Confederate symbol from the Georgia flag, culminating in a compromise in 2001 that gave it a less significant placement in a new state flag.[3]

White nationalists continued using Confederate imagery and memorials as statements of group identity. Rebel flags had infused the white riot in Forsyth County, Georgia, in 1987, for example, and Aryan Nations had rallied its skinhead contingents at the foot of a Confederate war memorial in 1989. Kirk Lyons had raised the battle banner on a federal flagpole in Arkansas to celebrate the Aryans' victory in the seditious conspiracy trial, and he had repeated the performance in Montana after surrendering the Freemen.

In South Carolina the NAACP had started an antiflag campaign in 1994. Pro-flag forces began rallying their own troops across the state in response. Led at that time by the South Carolina state chairman of the Council of Conservative Citizens, William Carter, they brought their Confederate banners to the Lexington County Peach Festival parade on the July Fourth weekend and to Hilton Head on Labor Day and held a string of meetings that year in Myrtle Beach, Barnwell, Orangeburg, and Greenwood.[4] The pro-flag forces also had a hand in electing Republican David Beasley governor. Once elected, however, Beasley took steps to remove the flag as a point of contention and sought a compromise with the NAACP. Angered at Beasley's perfidy in this contest of political wills, pro-flaggers had enough power to let him go down to defeat in the 1998 elections.[5] As the fight progressed, the CofCC's ideological position and influence grew within the broader neo-Confederate movement. And the state of South Carolina, birthplace of the Confederacy, continued flying the banner into the new millennium.

While some Confederate flag wavers claimed they were promoting their heritage and not what they called "hate," they denied that racist domination was an integral part of that history. They contended that Confederate nationalism should be considered separately from both chattel slavery and the Ku Klux Klan. For Council of Conservative Citizens leaders, by contrast, the flag was an unabashed symbol of whiteness. In an article written for a local Sons of Confederate Veterans newsletter, Jared Taylor wrote: "The reason why the Confederacy is under such violent attack today is that it is a symbol not only of the white culture that the ethnic saboteurs wish to destroy, but it is also seen—

rightly or wrongly—as a symbol of white culture that refuses to apologize. What better way to attack white America than to insult the last remnant of a *proud* white America [emphasis in original]?"[6]

A set of studies conducted at southern universities found evidence that supported Jared Taylor's argument, rather than the "heritage, not hate" claim. These scholars described a group of white people who were self-conscious of their whiteness as a badge of ethnic identity and at odds with multiracialism and egalitarianism. More important, pollsters found higher levels of support for the Confederate flag among young whites.[7] As these young whites thought of themselves as a "dispossessed majority," projected by census takers to become a racial minority in a nation of minorities by the mid-twenty-first century, they prepared themselves for the future by wearing the battle flag on T-shirts and ball caps. Their T-shirt slogan was "You Wear Your X and I'll Wear Mine," a reference to the ball caps memorializing Malcolm X that were popular among a segment of black youth. These competing ball caps were not celebrating the past as much as symbolizing current racial identity.

Further evidence that the battle flag was not strictly a symbol of regional remembrance came from a California protest aimed at brown-skinned, Spanish-speaking day laborers. When the picket ran into counterprotests by immigrant rights activists, several of the younger white nationalists could no longer restrain themselves. They unfurled a Confederate battle flag alongside a swastika banner and Old Glory's red, white, and blue. The incident sparked a cyberspace discussion. One character named "Valhalla" asked, "Why did you let people bring Nazi flags? While 80% of whites are opposed to illegal immigration, probably 99% are opposed to Nazism." To which someone going by the moniker "baldy" replied: "The commies were chanting 'Nazis Go Home' for hours . . . so I and everyone present on the street in the hot sun, facing hostile commies, browns and who-knows-what greenlighted the flag idea. We will stand behind our decision."[8] Here was a true contest of ideas, and the Confederate battle flag was raised as an emblem of white domination to come.

For his part, Pat Buchanan still regarded the contemporary battles over the flag as a defense of the past. "What kind of timidity and cowardice are today gripping South Carolina that so many of her sons will not defend the battle flag of kinsmen who fought and died," the son of Confederate veterans editorialized.[9] Buchanan had become the spokesman for a definable segment of white nationalist sentiment after his two runs for president in 1992 and 1996. As he prepared for yet another bid in the year 2000, however, his electioneering proved to be as out-of-date as his theories of the flag.

Pat Buchanan and the Reform Party

March 3, 2000. Texas governor George W. Bush was checking off the presidential primaries in preparation for a contest with Vice President Al Gore when Reform Party candidate Pat Buchanan appeared at a state convention in Greenbelt, Maryland, that was open to the public. One hundred and fifty people attended. Buchanan told them that the Reform Party could break up the two-party monopoly over the elections and he wanted their nomination to run as president. If elected, he said, "at that very moment their New World Order comes crashing down." As he had in several other states, Buchanan swept the nominators' selection process that day, winning all eleven delegates to a future national convention. During the meeting he was buttonholed by a Liberty Lobby official for a photograph handing a *Spotlight* special edition supporting Buchanan's candidacy to the man himself. *The Spotlight* reported on the exchange, claiming Buchanan replied, "I've already read it. I've got a copy at my house." Sixteen years after launching the Populist Party, a failed effort to establish a third party to the right of the Republicans, Willis Carto and Liberty Lobby thought they had found it in Buchanan's Reform Party.[1]

The Reform Party was founded as a personal vehicle for Ross Perot, a multimillionaire with a Texas twang and a knack for cornball quips. Perot financed his own independent campaign for president in 1992, calling for fiscal restraint and a balanced budget, and emphasizing the fact that elected officials worked for the taxpayers. "You are the boss," he told the public. The message resonated with a segment of voters. His money and celebrity pushed him into the nationally televised debates, and he won a striking 19 percent of the popular vote in the general election.[2]

In the run-up to the 1996 election cycle, Perot created the Reform Party as a stand-alone political party. It subsequently received almost thirty million dollars in Federal Election Commission matching funds. This time around, however, Perot was kept out of the nationally televised debates, and his support dropped to 9 percent of the vote. Nevertheless, because it had received more than 5 percent of the national vote, the party remained eligible for federal matching funds in the next contest for president.[3]

As the party approached the 2000 election cycle, a changing body of governing rules and a shifting set of personnel at the helm resulted in an unsteady leadership and a membership rendered inert by the factional fighting. Further exacerbating the instability, the Perot loyalists still populating the Reform Party lacked a viable presidential candidate of their own. Into this vacuum Pat Buchanan stepped boldly and decisively.

Reform Party rules prescribed a two-track route to nomination. The first was through state conventions, where party officers, national committee members, and delegates to the national convention were selected. In effect, these statewide meetings were much like Republican and Democratic Party caucuses. The second track was through a mail-in ballot. This was akin to a national primary, only more convoluted. Mail-in ballots were sent to all 250,000 Reform Party members. The would-be candidates could also request that ballots be mailed to those supporters who met the party's eligibility guidelines. Unlike a primary vote, however, the mail-in ballots were advisory only, and no convention delegates were selected on this track. Instead, it was the convention that would formally nominate the party's candidate.[4]

Pat Buchanan and his sister Bay, acting as campaign manager, easily mastered this state-by-state process. After two runs through the Republican presidential primaries, they possessed a core group of followers in the person of the Buchanan Brigades. They won state leadership posts away from the Perotistas in the Reform Party, often packing otherwise sparsely attended meetings in the process. Then the brigadiers got themselves selected as delegates to the national convention, much as they did in Maryland. Adding to the brigades' firepower in this election cycle were cadres from the white nationalist movement who decided to aid Buchanan's bid on their own terms. Vanguardists and mainstreamers alike believed they had a chance to find a place in the leadership of a mass revolt by angry white people. *Spotlight* readers and Liberty Lobby were notable in this regard.[5]

White Nationalist Support in the 2000 Campaign

Liberty Lobby's support for Pat Buchanan had not been particularly steadfast. After the 1996 election, *The Spotlight* had published articles claiming his failure to leave the Republican Party had turned him into a liar who used and abused his supporters.[6] As a consequence, when Buchanan announced early in 1999 that he was preparing yet another Republican bid, Liberty Lobby ignored him. After his decision to run on the Reform Party ticket, however, the Lobby embraced him gladly. It claimed that its board of policy members "favored" Buchanan over all others by 60 percent in a mail-in vote. *The Spotlight* began regular favorable reports on his candidacy, defended him against charges leveled in the general media, and recounted his views on immigration and other relevant topics.[7] Similarly, it printed pages of local and state contacts for the campaign and urged its readers to get directly involved.

The special insert handed to Buchanan at the Maryland meeting was entitled "Buchanan 2000: The People vs the Big Media, the Big Money & the Global Elite." Thousands of copies were distributed at every possible venue, creating a small stir in the world outside Buchanan supporters. When asked on *Meet the Press* about Liberty Lobby, Buchanan acknowledged the tabloid insert's existence. "I have not read the publication, but apparently it is inoffensive in and of itself," he said.[8] *The Spotlight* begged to differ, as noted above.[9]

Whether or not Pat Buchanan admitted he had read a piece of Liberty Lobby propaganda was not of any genuine import. Nevertheless, the relationship of white nationalists to his 2000 campaign remained, as in 1992 and 1996, a point of genuine consequence.

Council of Conservative Citizens members also joined the brigades. By the time the Reform Party race began, Sam Francis was firmly ensconced as the editor in chief of the council's periodical, the *Citizens Informer*.[10] While Buchanan's old friend and colleague ensured that the quarterly tabloid preferred Buchanan to any other candidate, the council itself avoided an explicit endorsement.[11] Its Mississippi council members were particularly loath to leave Republican ranks. Despite equivocations elsewhere, in Chicago one of the council's chief representatives, Father Dennis Pavichevich, played a key role in a fund-raiser for Buchanan. In addition to supporting Buchanan, Pavichevich did double duty as priest of the Holy Resurrection Serbian Orthodox Church and as vice chair of the council's northern Illinois chapter. A decidedly different kind of Chicagoan, he flew both a Serbian flag and one of the many permutations of the Confederate States of America national flag. He also served as host for a group calling itself The Coalition for

Peace in the Balkans, which held a hundred-dollar-a-plate fund-raising luncheon.[12]

In keeping with his America first–style isolationism, Buchanan had long advocated American disengagement from the Balkan wars of the 1990s. It was a position that resonated with certain sections of the Serbian community, particularly as President Clinton bombed Serbia's positions, first in its conflict with Croatia over the Dalmatian coast and later when the battle for control of Kosovo turned bloody. And this Chicago event drew largely from the local Serbian-ethnic community. Add to this conjunction personnel from the flagship institution of the paleoconservative movement, the Rockford Institute, located in Rockford, Illinois. Both Tom Fleming, editor of the institute's glossy monthly *Chronicles* magazine, and its foreign affairs editor, Srdja Trifkovic, played key roles alongside Pavichevich during the fund-raiser. Fleming, a native Carolinian with a long southern nationalist pedigree, introduced Buchanan to the roomful of Serbs, and Trifkovic whispered in the candidate's ear during a question session where the answers required an intricate knowledge of the Yugoslav civil wars.[13]

After the speeches, Buchanan signed copies of his most recent book, *A Republic Not an Empire*, and the Council of Conservative Citizens activists in the room passed out *The Spotlight's Buchanan 2000* insert.[14] It was an ecumenical, even interfaith event, worthy of a genuine candidate. By the usual standards of small third parties, collecting one hundred supporters at a hundred dollars a plate was a grand success. But the highly visible presence of white nationalists in the campaign machinery was like oiling the gears with sawdust and sand grit. And for a brief moment it almost ground the works to a halt at headquarters.

A British national living in the D.C. area named Mark Cotterill had been raising funds for the British National Party among white nationalists in the States, building a network of supporters among Council of Conservative Citizens activists, National Alliance members, and prominent individual operators such as David Duke. He was also spending time doing volunteer work in the Buchanan headquarters in Vienna, Virginia, and recruiting others to do the same, writing in his newsletter: "Many of our members are already helping out the Buchanan campaign . . . as the campaign heats up they need all the extra help they can get . . ."[15] Soon after a printed account of Cotterill's activities surfaced, campaign manager Bay Buchanan "fired" him from his headquarters position and threw out about another twenty volunteers as well. The move intended to demonstrate the campaign's disavowal of racists and anti-Semites but only proved the accuracy of a *Washington Post* story on Buchanan's transformation of the Reform Party.[16]

The coverage caught the Buchanan camp at a particularly vulnerable moment. Anti-Buchanan elements in the Reform Party had finally awakened to the fact that the party that they had originally built was no longer in their hands. The revelations added an edge of desperation to the anti-Buchanan camp, and it once again threatened to tar the candidate as a bigot. If voters had forgotten about the revelations from campaigns past, if they had missed the discussion of Buchanan's views of World War Two, or if they agreed with him on immigration or trade but did not want their neighbors to think they voted for "haters," a new group of reformers now stood ready to remind them.

Nevertheless, Pat Buchanan's brigades had already ground their way through the party, state convention by state convention. Perot loyalists were unable to offer any substantial resistance. The remaining anti-Buchanan forces finally rallied behind John Hagelin, a physics professor at Maharishi University of Management in Iowa. Hagelin also served in the 2000 election as the candidate of the Natural Law Party, a group every bit as obscure as its name implied. When it came time to send out "primary" ballots, Hagelin brought a list of twenty-four thousand to the party to receive mail-in ballots. Buchanan, by contrast, provided a list of five hundred thousand names. His two runs through the Republican primaries had left him with a residual hard-core base of supporters. Campaign manager Bay Buchanan knew how to master the rules and marshal the troops. With the additional backing of white nationalists, Buchanan easily commanded the most formidable force in the party, more powerful even than Perot. Also, Buchanan did not shirk from a crass bit of organizational opportunism when the situation demanded it.[17]

At the last minute the Reform Party executive committee, the one body still largely in the hands of Perot loyalists, tried to stem Buchanan's brigadiers. Meeting in Dallas, the committee voted to disallow Buchanan's mail-in ballots.[18] His list included an unknown number of ineligible names, it charged. As the Reform Party convention in Long Beach, California, loomed, the conflict within the Reform Party and the public's association of Buchanan with racism threatened to undo his candidacy.[19]

Reform Party Convention in Long Beach

The Reform Party convention opened with 150 Hagelin supporters marching behind their candidate from a hotel to the convention center, chanting, "Go, John, go." At the second floor entrance to the delegate hall they ran into a line of tables and security guards blocking the entrance. The chant changed to "We want in, we want in," until they decided to leave and hold their own rump convention. They may have controlled the executive committee in Dallas, but in Long Beach the Buchananites controlled the credentials committee. For the moment Hagelin's crew met at the Performing Arts Center and pinned their hopes on the mail-in "primary" ballot. They paid for an outside auditor to count votes. The announcement upset Hagelin's claim to legitimacy, however. Of the 887,000 ballots mailed out, less than 10 percent were returned. Of those, Buchanan took 49,529, or more than 63 percent; Hagelin won 28,539, or almost 37 percent. Two to one, Buchanan had it. Undeterred, the rumpers voted to disqualify Buchanan from the ballot and then nominate Hagelin. The physics professor from Maharishi University said: "I accept with pride the mantle of H. Ross Perot."[20]

Over at the convention center, the fighting shifted from the front door to the seating of competing state delegations. Buchanan's team was the only one with a floor operation, individuals strategically placed around the hall wearing orange ball caps and waving them to instruct voting. From Wisconsin and a few other states more than one group claimed official status, and the Buchanan forces managed to vote their opposition out of the room. Among those who did have sanctioned seats were Christopher Bollyn, a Liberty Lobby official who was a member of the Illinois delegation.[21] In the California delegation a white power musician named Eric Owens stood out. William Grutzmacher, the Reform Party's state campaign chair in Nevada, had run for mayor in the Chicago primaries five years before and was known in that city for writing: "It is a fact of recorded history that while my ancestors were building cathedrals and composing symphonies, the Orientals were feeding their babies to the pigs and the blacks were eating each other."[22] And when the chief of the California delegation gave the opening remarks and said this is a "national convention that doesn't have to be held hostage to Political Correctness," an overhead video screen fixed on a man wearing a ball cap emblazoned with a Confederate battle flag. The delegate was not from South Carolina.

Late on the first day the conventioneers watched a video from Buchanan's 1996 Republican campaign. The segment that won the biggest applause was his infamous culture war speech from 1992. On day two an almost audible gasp escaped from the pool of reporters after Pat Buchanan announced his vice presidential candidate, Ezola Foster.[23]

A churchgoing sixty-two-year-old black woman, born in Louisiana but long active in California's anti-immigrant politics, Ezola Foster had grown up under Jim Crow segregation. She had attended all-black schools through college. While Pat Buchanan was writing Republican speeches for President Nixon, Foster was voting Democratic. She switched to the Republican Party during the Reagan era and began a long, lonely trek to the far right. She taught typing in Southern California until 1996, when she applied for workers' compensation on the basis of a mental condition. (She alleged that she suffered emotional distress at the hands of her students.) Although she could no longer handle the stress of teaching in the public schools, Buchanan apparently believed Foster's political pedigree rendered her a suitable candidate for vice president. She had joined the John Birch Society in the mid-1990s and was familiar with the entire panoply of issues animating the far end of the right wing, including the Confederate battle flag. It was a symbol of heritage, she told reporters in South Carolina. And she had given a platform speech at the same Buchananite American Cause meeting where Sam Francis had invoked Gramsci as a guide for race-conscious white politics.[24]

During her acceptance speech at the convention she excoriated the opposition. "Well, you hear these two parties talking about reaching out to minorities. That's a code word. Let's break it down to what it means. It means giving black leaders affirmative action and reparations for slavery. It means giving Latino leaders an open border policy and saying to the world, come on the price is right, the American taxpayers will pay." She also gave her running mate a rousing endorsement: "If anybody knows a racist, I do. Pat Buchanan ain't no racist." When answering questions from the press, she was asked, Isn't this a white party? Her concerns were more with ideology than the color of skin, she replied. Across the convention center, some of the sentiment echoed hers. Some didn't.[25]

At the *Reform Party News* booth the response was: "Buchanan made a bold and positive move." Over at the T-shirt vendor, one of the remaining Perotistas said Foster "helps show we're inclusive." At a table stuffed with pamphlets from the California Coalition for Immigration Reform, they remembered Foster from the Proposition 187 election. She was smart and ethical and "loves America," they said. At a table for the Missouri Reform Party the reply was short and not sweet: "I don't know anything about her." At the *Spotlight* table, which doubled as an outpost for the Maryland Reform Party, Willis Carto didn't want to talk much about Foster.[26]

Outside the convention center, each white nationalist camp reacted in its own way to Buchanan's selection of Foster. Jared Taylor at *American Renaissance* felt neither disappointed nor betrayed by Buchanan because he had never believed that the former Republican understood the biological underpinnings of "European character and traditions."

Buchanan might be good on issues such as immigration and crime, Taylor reasoned. And he might have once said that Englishmen assimilated more quickly than Zulus. But "Mr. Buchanan appears to base these positions on his conception of conservative principles rather than because he has a clear racial identity," Taylor wrote in an analysis posted to the newsletter's website.[27]

Taylor opposed Ezola Foster's candidacy simply because she was black. He could countenance a few men of Jewish descent on his conference podium, but he did not believe that Foster's face could promote the Reform Party, not if it was going to be the "organized political voice" of white people. Clearly it wasn't. Taylor also contended that Buchanan was just another candidate. "Those who saw his campaign as an expression of racial identity have quite properly withdrawn their support."[28]

In contrast with Taylor's assessment, Liberty Lobby finally expressed in print some mild disappointment that Buchanan had chosen a black woman as his running mate, but it supported the Reform Party in much stronger terms. Liberty Lobby reasoned that Buchanan's selection had been "designed to mitigate the media's inevitable attack on him as a racist and anti-Semite." It had not worked, however, and had only driven away those (like Taylor) who could not countenance her face on their propaganda. *The Spotlight* would have preferred that Buchanan had chosen a white family man from the ranks of labor, not a "labor boss," it editorialized, but someone who could draw white working-class votes to the Reform Party.[29] At the end of the campaign, just as it had been at the beginning, Liberty Lobby remained most concerned with creating a viable third party. The purity of its politics could wait until later.

Willis Carto personally reinforced this view two days before the election. Thinking back on the time, more than thirty-five years before, when he had pursued a strategy of building a faction within the Republican Party, he now deemed it unfeasible. "The big money crowd has its tentacles into every moving part of the Republican Party," he argued. The idea of grafting racially conservative southern Democrats onto the northern Republican tree, which he had advocated in the 1950s, was now an accomplished fact. But the realignment had not brought all the changes he wanted. Now he believed that there was "no getting around" the creation of a third party. "America is trending toward a Third World status right now," he argued.

"Any so-called patriot or so-called conservative leader or publication not supporting the Reform Party is too corrupt or stupid to have your support," Carto told *Spotlight* readers. "People tell me that advocating support for the Reform Party and its activities will undermine Liberty Lobby, but I don't care," he continued.[30]

Carto talked as if his personal financial affairs were under his full control, not in the hands of a bankruptcy court. From his conduct at the Reform Party convention, no one would have known that Liberty Lobby was a year away from dissolution. Or that George W. Bush would win more votes from confirmed racists that November than Patrick Buchanan and his entire third party team.

November 7, 2000

On election night Al Gore received a half million more votes than George W. Bush: 50,999,897 to 50,456,002. While the popular vote's results were unequivocal, the race was far closer in the electoral college. In that count, Pat Buchanan's placement on the Florida ballot apparently contributed to George Bush's ascendancy to the presidency. On the first count, Buchanan received 3,407 votes in Palm Beach County, Florida, a liberal Democratic stronghold with large numbers of elderly Jewish voters. Local Reform Party officers knew the total was greatly inflated. And their candidate believed that only 300 to 400 of those votes were actually his. "The rest, I am quite sure, were Gore votes," Buchanan told John Nichols, author of *Jews for Buchanan*, a detailed story of the postelection voter count mayhem in Florida.[31] The butterfly ballot form apparently confused some voters, and recounts were demanded and rebuffed by Florida's secretary of state (who also served as a Bush campaign cochair). The process went into the courts. After a final decision by the United States Supreme Court that halted the recounts, the federal election was finally decided—five weeks after election night.[32] The 3,000 votes that Buchanan reckoned were not his were counted in his column nevertheless. This decision pushed George W. Bush ahead in Florida by about 500 votes. Like a set of tumbling dominoes, this gave Florida's twenty-five electoral votes to Bush and then won him a four-vote margin of victory in the electoral college.

Unlike in 1992 and 1996, when Ross Perot polled significant numbers of votes, the so-called third parties failed miserably in this election. In fact, each third party's count was more miserable than the next. The combined total of votes for all ten small parties did not reach even 5 percent of the electorate. As a Reform Party candidate, Buchanan received just 448,895 votes, 2.5 million votes fewer than he had received in the 1996 Republican primaries.[33] Consider by comparison the Populist Party in 1992, when militiameister Bo Gritz won almost half as many votes as Buchanan did in 2000, but with only one-twentieth of the financial support. Further, by failing to pull the required 5 percent, Buchanan even lost the Reform Party's future chance at automatic Federal Election Commission funding, the sine qua non of a viable third party.

Several factors contributed to this abysmal drop in support, including the fact that Buchanan underwent gallbladder surgery after the convention and was forced to slow his campaigning.[34] But the fight inside the Reform Party proved even more decisive, bloodying Buchanan to an extent from which he never recovered. The opposing Reform Party camp went to court after the convention, attempting to deny Buchanan the party's federal matching funds. Although he eventually won the court case and received the money, the legal suit stymied his campaign until after Labor Day.[35] He had planned to use a significant portion of the FEC funds to buy television advertising and thereby push his name up in the polls. With a significant enough standing in the polls, he believed he could win a place in the nationally televised debates. With years of television experience on his résumé, Buchanan reasoned that he would fare well in the debates. Instead, he sank to invisibility in the polls, and the debate sponsors deemed him a minor candidate and did not include him.

As a result, white nationalists came out of the election empty-handed. They had spent twelve months trumpeting Buchanan and volunteering for his brigades, hoping at least to inherit a viable third party apparatus. Instead, they received Ezola Foster. The election's results begged for a sharp retrospective look by white nationalists who had worked hard on his campaign.

The Council of Conservative Citizens complained that a "liberal, country-club Republican rode to victory on the strength of conservatives." If Buchanan had once represented a chance to construct a viable alternative to the Republicans, that possibility was gone for now, the *Citizens Informer* tabloid editorialized.[36]

The tabloid was then under the direction of Sam Francis, the one member of Buchanan's inner circle who had most steadfastly promoted the idea of a third party campaign. Just a year before, he had described Buchanan as a courageous, effective, and articulate warrior. Francis did not shrink from his conclusions now. Writing under his own name in two different periodicals—the white nationalist newsletter *American Renaissance* and the paleoconservative monthly *Chronicles*—Sam Francis drew two slightly different, but related, sets of conclusions: For the Renaissancers, he faulted Buchanan personally for not appealing directly to the resentments of white working people. The candidate had emphasized trade and foreign policy issues, rather than the red meat of race and immigration. Plus Francis found the selection of Ezola Foster inexplicable. Both moves sent signals to white nationalist sympathizers that Buchanan was a candidate much like any other candidate, willing to trade away his principles for the supposed acceptance of mainstream conservatives. As a result, these voters had been confronted with no real choice that November.[37] To *Chronicles* readers, Francis contended that it was the masses of white people rather than simply the candidate himself who lacked the necessary racial consciousness to vie successfully for power. As proof, he cited the split votes by white men and white women, the gender gap, showing that white men usually vote for racially conservative candidates and issues in greater percentages than women do. If white people would only vote as a unified bloc, he believed, they could reclaim the culture and the Constitution for themselves alone. Francis restated his constant refrain: a direct appeal to race was needed to awaken this sense of white self-consciousness.[38]

Absent such a call by a credible political figure, he believed, white nationalism would likely remain a nonmajoritarian movement, without the ability to contest directly for governmental power. At election time it would remain a hidden force within the two-party system; although primarily located in the Republican Party, it was likely to remain subordinated to economic conservatives in the party. Outside of party politics, it expressed itself in civil society: in the conflicts between church and state, in policy debates about gun control and Confederate monuments and symbols, and in the growing angst over immigration and the fact that white people will become a demographic minority in a nation of minorities at mid-century.

Despite Sam Francis's description of the Republican Party as the "Stupid Party," most of the voters who supported one aspect or another of white nationalist politics decided not to vote for an ultimately inconsequential third party—whether or not that party represented their most deeply held beliefs. Consider the evidence from South Carolina. In that state Buchanan received only thirty-five hundred votes. Yet just the previous January, almost double that number had rallied to defend the Confederate battle flag's flying at an official state site, meaning that most of the Confederate flag wavers had either not voted at all or pulled George Bush's Republican lever. (They were unlikely to have voted for the Democrats.) North Carolina too had long been abuzz with prominent organizations such as the Council of Conservative Citizens, National Alliance, and Christian Identity churches. Wilmot Robertson, Kirk Lyons, Ben Klassen, and Eric Rudolph all had lived there. Yet when voting day came, Buchanan received fewer than nine thousand votes in that state. George Bush, on the other hand, beat Al Gore among North Carolinians by a landslide of thirteen percentage points. In the Deep South, as in the rest of the country, the largest slice of white-wing voters belonged to the Republicans.[39]

In this regard, the numbers in Alabama were even more instructive. A referendum proposing to amend the state's constitution to abolish the prohibition of interracial marriage had been on the ballot.[40] Written in 1901, the proscription had been rendered unenforceable by civil rights legislation and the 1967 Supreme Court decision in *Loving v. Virginia*. The ban was removed from the state constitution in 2000, when 801,725 Alabamians voted yes on a referendum to delete it. It should be noted, however, that 545,933 voted to keep the language in place.[41]

Two social scientists, Micah Altman and Philip Klinkner, conducted a study of those no voters and found that 49 percent of whites and about 8 percent of blacks voted to keep the (unenforceable) exclusionary language in place. "[M]ost Alabamians understood the ballot language," they wrote, and concluded that "support for keeping the anti-miscegenation provisions is difficult to explain absent of racial bias."[42]

In other words, on the basis of this referendum vote alone, Pat Buchanan might have expected to receive hundreds of thousands of votes. Yet he won a mere 6,364 votes instead. Where did the other votes go? Bush received 944,409 votes in Alabama to Gore's 695,602.

Whether or not George W. Bush spoke Spanish or had kin with brown skin, he was the candidate who pulled the largest number of votes from white people opposed to interracial marriage (and other forms of integration). Similarly, those "racial conservatives" who supported the official display of Confederate colors did not waste their votes on a third party candidate.

For its part, *The Spotlight* responded to Buchanan's failure at the polls as if it had never happened. After the election the three-time candidate disappeared from the tabloid's pages as fast as he had (re)appeared the year before. A self-reflexive second thought never graced its pages: not about Pat Buchanan, or about the Populist Party or any other of a half dozen similarly forgotten projects and certainly not about the years of needless litigation that now brought Liberty Lobby itself to the verge of extinction.

The Liberty Lobby Fortress Crumbles

July 9, 2001. Forty-six years after Willis Carto had founded Liberty Lobby in his San Francisco apartment, it went out of business. This had been his central fortress, the one he had protected above all others, but it finally collapsed under the weight of the multiple deceits he had purveyed in its defense. Twenty-six years after *The Spotlight*'s first edition, the headline announced the end in ninety-point bold type: "FINAL EDITION! A Federal Judge Has Ordered This Populist Newspaper Shut Down."[1]

The headline and accompanying story were half right. A short set of turns in the road had led to the last *Spotlight* tabloid. After the July 1999 bankruptcy hearing, Liberty Lobby had quickly settled out of court with the legion-IHR rather than face a trustee appointed by a judge. A forbearance agreement was signed that included two major points: Liberty Lobby was to pay a reduced sum over time, and neither party was to engage in any more lawsuits. Payments began, and Liberty Lobby remitted more than a million dollars to the legion. It looked as if the matter would finally be resolved. Except that Carto and Liberty Lobby had not kept the bargain. They reneged on payments and filed another in their long line of lawsuits. In response, Weber and the legion had gone back to court. On December 15, 2000, a judge ruled that the agreement had been breached. Six weeks after the election, both Carto and Liberty Lobby were once again liable for the entire original judgment, throwing the case back into bankruptcy court, where it awaited resolution.[2] The bankruptcy judge then dismissed Liberty Lobby's Chapter Eleven filing, closing the last remaining legal loophole.[3] Either Liberty Lobby paid off its remaining debt to the Legion for the Survival of Freedom–Institute for Historical Review, or it would be forced into dissolution and its assets seized. The choice had been Liberty Lobby's to make. Nobody "ordered" *The Spotlight* to cease publication. But thirty lawsuits and countersuits had finally come to an end. Liberty Lobby closed its doors, simply refusing to pay off those it regarded as upstarts and usurpers in California. Step by step, it had boxed itself into a legal corner. Now, it was truly history. The end was anticlimactic. Only the parties directly involved seemed to notice.

In retrospect, *The Spotlight* had represented a significant advance for Liberty Lobby. In addition to becoming the organization's chief propaganda outlet, it had generated revenue like a mail-order catalog, advertising every kind of Liberty Lobby merchandise, from coins to books and pamphlets. It also reinforced other fund-raising efforts by the organization, including direct mail solicitations. At the moment of conception and for a number of years thereafter, *The Spotlight* and the revenue it generated turned Liberty Lobby into the largest (and thereby dominant) force in its movement. And the tabloid's propaganda outreach had enabled Carto to spin off other projects, such as the Institute for Historical Review and the Populist Party.

At the same time, *The Spotlight* had been indispensable to the white supremacist movement as a whole—particularly during its first decade of publication. Organizations and causes as diverse as David Duke's Knights of the Ku Klux Klan in 1975, the defense of the shooters at Greensboro after 1979, and Gordon Kahl's 1983 gun battle with federal marshals had benefited from the tabloid's coverage. As late as the Randy Weaver incident in 1992, publicity in Liberty Lobby's house organ had been central to generating sympathy and support. It helped turn a serial aggregation of organizations and individuals into a single movement, reading a common literature and self-conscious of its unique identity. Liberty Lobby had been the largest and most significant voice for the mainstreaming tendency; it had also been an essential part of the infrastructure for the entire movement. But its position and influence had been declining for years.

Liberty Lobby's response to George W. Bush's ascension to the presidency was decidedly less significant than it would have been twenty or thirty years before. Unlike in the period when Carto's outfit successfully courted segregationist congressmen, it now commanded little attention on Capitol Hill. The new president was not going to select for any high-level post someone publicly associated with Liberty Lobby, as the newly elected President Ronald Reagan had done in 1981. Just as the days were gone when Liberty Lobby had exerted some influence outside white supremacist circles, so too was the time over when it could make or break an issue or an organization within the movement. Just ten years before, David Duke had bought the *Spotlight* mailing list as a first step toward generating significant nationwide support for his election campaigns. Now the weekly's circulation figures had reached a twenty-five-year low. Longtime subscribers from Carto's World War Two generation were dying off, and the attempt to bring Generation X readers into the fold (by adding Resistance Records subscribers to *The Spotlight*'s list) had largely failed.

Carto's longtime rival William Pierce, on the other hand, had mastered a variety of media outlets intended to reach new generations of young people. The National Alliance broadcast a weekly radio program via shortwave, and its active Internet sites and successful music business provided powerful alternatives to print-only publications. In fact, the Internet's role inside the movement had grown in parallel to its impact on general society, undermining established media outlets, reinforcing niche markets, and desocializing interactions in physical space even as it resocialized them in cyberspace. As noted earlier, white nationalists set up chat rooms, sold merchandise, and published on the Internet, using it to facilitate communication across the globe. The same Internet that enabled young people to establish their own cybernetworks also pulled them out of contact with older movement veterans and organizations, such as Willis Carto and Liberty Lobby, that did not easily adapt to the new medium. Simply put, they did not need *The Spotlight*'s classified ads to sell white power music. They could advertise themselves on the Net. The multiplicity of sites tended to undercut the hegemony of any single-source outlet, including Liberty Lobby's mash of tree pulp. By 2001, *The Spotlight* had dropped to 60,000 subscribers from the 150,000 it had had when Bob Weems had spoken fifteen years earlier in an Arkansas meeting hall.[4]

During the first half of 2001, Carto had used *The Spotlight*'s remaining pages to heap verbal abuse upon Mark Weber and anyone associated with him. The tabloid reasserted its claim that Weber et al. were agents of the Mossad or the FBI or the Anti-Defamation League or all of them at once. It also charged Weber with mistreating his wife and stealing from her grandmother. Moreover, the tabloid accused Weber of being Jared Taylor's friend. Weber had met Taylor in Ghana in 1970, and *The Spotlight* informed its readers that the African country was then under the thumb of the Israeli Mossad. Plus Taylor had subsequently worked in international banking, which only heightened suspicions. If that was not proof enough of Weber's treachery, well, there was that moment documented by *The Spotlight* when "Taylor and his future wife received a call from Irwin Suall."[5] Weber denied these claims.

Institute for Historical Review Survives Liberty Lobby

The attempt to pillory Weber and drive the Institute for Historical Review out of business did not work. With little extra cost, the Internet allowed the IHR to match or exceed every published pronouncement in *The Spotlight* with a statement and documentation of its own. The IHR's website kept constantly updating news of the court cases, including postings of relevant testimony and judgments.[6] Mark Weber matched Willis Carto's dogged tenaciousness with his own, and he kept the Institute for Historical Review operating for a decade on a much-reduced scale.

Rewriting the Holocaust was a decidedly different project in 2001 from twenty years earlier. It had become an article of faith within Klan, national socialist, and later white power skinhead circles that the Jews had invented the Holocaust. It was now common knowledge outside the movement that some people somewhere denied the worst of Hitler's crimes, even if it was not common knowledge precisely who those people were. And a measurable stratum of American society tended to believe the IHR's claims on that point. At the same time, forty-five years after *Brown v. Topeka Board of Education*, much of the public debate had shifted, and now numbers of the white populace felt as if *they* were the victims of racial discrimination, not people of color. That change in white sentiment had occurred without anyone's necessarily accepting the early argument made by Willis Carto and William Pierce that it was first necessary to break the link between knowledge of the Holocaust and support for racial egalitarianism.

In Germany, rewriting this history had become ensnarled in a debate on German national identity. Sectors of the Arab and Islamic world now promoted Holocaust denial as part of the conflict with the state of Israel.[7] Holocaust denial had failed to establish itself as a scholarly pursuit in the Anglo-American world, however, and its best-known practitioner, David Irving, lost a libel case in British courts, after an American author described him as a "Holocaust denier." He subsequently was sentenced to three years in jail by an Austrian court after pleading guilty to charges that he had in fact denied Hitler's Nazis' deliberate attempt to exterminate the Jews of Europe.[8]

In this changed context, Weber did not change the IHR's course entirely. When he convened the institute's thirteenth conference about fifteen months before Liberty Lobby's final dissolution, he had invited many of the same characters who had attended previous meetings. Definite changes in approach were evident, however. A professor known for his genetic determinist views of race was borrowed from the *American Renaissance* stable of speakers, and race was explicitly part of the IHR conference agenda for the first time. And former California Republican Congressman Pete McCloskey appeared in this scholarly confab, giving Weber and co. a glimpse of the respectability they had been seeking since the beginning. McCloskey told the gathering, "I don't know if you are right or wrong about the Holocaust," according to the IHR's own account of the meeting, but he apparently wished everyone well.[9]

The most significant shift was not in the persons who spoke or the topics they covered but in the relative openness of the meeting. Gone were Carto's furtiveness and the secretness within which the meeting place had been shrouded. At Weber's IHR gathering, a *Los Angeles Times* reporter attended almost all the sessions, and various other media were given access; the speeches were broadcast live via the Internet. Here Weber borrowed heavily from Jared Taylor, who did not shrink from publicly advertising the location of his *American Renaissance* conferences or keep reporters and video cameras at bay.

Despite the changes in tone, the IHR still faced the same obstacles as before. Plus, as noted earlier, *American Renaissance* had replaced it as the premier think tank for the white nationalist movement as a whole. More, the market for publications rewriting the Holocaust was saturated in the United States, and the institute was looking farther and farther afield. In December 2000 the IHR had announced that it was supporting a conference on "Revisionism and Zionism," set for Beirut the following spring. The principal organizer was a Swiss "revisionist" who had moved to Iran, and by March 2001 registrants from the United States and Europe were planning to meet with their counterparts from Japan as well as from Iran, Lebanon, and Egypt. Speeches were to be given in Arabic, French, and English. That particular conference was canceled, however, as the Lebanese government threatened to close the gathering down.[10] Nevertheless, the direction was set for the first years of the twenty-first century. And a conference similar to the canceled Lebanese event was successfully held in Teheran in 2006.[11] The principal growth areas for rewriting the Holocaust would be the former Soviet Union and the Middle East.

PART

seven

Prolegomena to the Future, 2001–2004

The events of September 11, 2001, brought together Americans in grief and determination. People celebrated the bravery of the citizens of New York City and those who had fought their captors in the skies over Pennsylvania. Everything did not change, however. The post–Cold War battles over race, culture, and national identity reemerged in an anti-immigrant movement spanning the distance between Republicans and Buchananites to vigilantes and white power skinheads. As the oldest generation of white nationalists leave the stage, a new cast of characters promises to fight well into the future.

56

After September 11, 2001

September 11, 2001. If you did not see it at 9:03 a.m., when television news cameras caught the second plane crashing into the World Trade Center, you certainly watched the attack on the evening television news. And in the weeks and months that followed you may have watched it again (and again) until your retinal memory burned with smoke and fire and the shudder of fallen buildings and crushed lives. You knew many of the details long before the dead had been counted. A band of hijackers commandeered a passenger plane from Boston and crashed it into the north tower, instantly killing themselves and all aboard. A second gang simultaneously captured another plane from Boston and aimed it at the south tower. The burning jet fuel weakened the floor trusses until the top floors crashed down one upon the other. The entire structure collapsed, essentially vaporizing hundreds and spewing a poisoned fog across southern Manhattan.

Within the hour a third plane slammed like a ballistic missile into the Pentagon. This one had departed from Dulles Airport outside Washington, D.C., and changed course over West Virginia. The passengers, crew, and Defense Department employees were killed. Passengers on a fourth airplane, after learning via their cell phones of the other attacks and being hijacked themselves, decided they would die fighting rather than let their plane become another weapon in the hands of terrorists. In words that now haunt your memory one passenger bellowed, "Let's roll," as they rushed their captors, crashing the plane into a Pennsylvania meadow before it reached a target. All aboard died as heroes. You saw the ruins after the fact and read the reports but still had trouble believing the enormity of these attacks.

The heroism of ordinary people caught in extraordinary circumstances remains one of the enduring memories of this day. Hundreds of New York City firefighters rushed into the World Trade Center in an attempt to save lives but were lost in the crush of concrete and steel. Stockbrokers shepherded their fellow employees down darkened and dangerous staircases. Many others unnamed and unheralded rallied a distinctive American pride. In New York City, police and firefighters became instant heroes in communities where conflict with overbearing law enforcement personnel had previously ruled. In the Midwest and South, decades of cultural distance from New York turned into an emotional bond with that most cosmopolitan and polyglot of urban centers. Thousands gave blood in their local communities, construction workers volunteered for rescue efforts, and American flags appeared on bumper stickers and car antennas, in cornfields and on windowpanes, and at every public gathering to mourn the dead. Art displays and music, literature, and cultural invention expressed grief and anger, pride and bravado. Among other indicators of popular sentiment, the playlist on country music stations became inflated with ballads recalling the heroism of firefighters and policemen. Even rocker Bruce Springsteen, whose anthem "Born in the USA" mourned the losses suffered by Vietnam vets, launched his next concert tour in the conscious shadow of September 11. A raw and edgy American nationalism and patriotism showed itself across the country.

As a new "us" stood up, we pointed our collective finger at "them." Unlike Oklahoma City, when the first impulse proved wrong, now the enemies were in fact foreign terrorists. Within days, eighteen hijackers had been identified, an overwhelming majority Saudi Arabian nationals. President George W. Bush declared war. "This will be a monumental struggle of good versus evil," he told the cabinet.[1] Administration officials repeatedly told foreign leaders and the American public that there would be no middle ground in this war against terrorism.

President Bush counted "freedom and democracy" on his side of this battle. On the other side, the foe was more ambiguous. Various enemies were named: terrorists, states that supported terrorism, and a new axis of evil—Iraq, Iran, and North Korea. Unofficially, the list was longer and included Islamic fundamentalism in its several permutated forms. Unlike the Cold War, which pitted the United States and its Western European allies against the Soviet Union and communism, the enemy in this new war was not territorially specific and its ideological center not clearly defined. American allies also seemed less definite.

Further complicating this new war of "us" against "them," the possibility existed that some of us might actually be some of them. Within weeks of September 11, a number of anthrax attacks left five dead and paralyzed the postal service. Originally a cattle disease, anthrax had long before been "weaponized" as part of an American biological warfare program. Spores are cultivated in laboratories and then ground into a fine powder that can become a lethal airborne weapon. Letters containing anthrax were sent to the offices of two United States senators and to a Florida-based media business. As concern over these incidents of bioterrorism increased, threats of anthrax attacks overwhelmed the number of actual incidents. Planned Parenthood offices and clinics, for example, reported receiving more than five hundred threats during the period immediately after September 11. The FBI's stated belief that the spores were domestic, rather than foreign, in origin heightened feelings of unease and fear. Yet no one was charged in these crimes.[2]

In this climate, Congress quickly passed and President Bush signed legislation granting federal and local authorities new police powers that raised significant constitutional and civil liberties complaints. One federal judge, a Reagan-era appointee, complained immediately of changes sought in the jury system: "This is the most profound shift in our legal institutions in my lifetime and—most remarkable of all—it has taken place without engaging any broad public interest whatsoever."[3] A plan floated by Attorney General John Ashcroft's Justice Department called for a nationwide spy-on-your-neighbor program whereby postal carriers, meter readers, and others who casually gained access to an individual's home would be encouraged to report "suspicious activities" to the authorities. That idea was dropped before it became legislation, but other measures were adopted as law.[4]

Further adding to the sense of siege within American borders, approximately 1,200 aliens and citizens were detained for questioning in the attacks, and 762 aliens were jailed. The Justice Department contended that those wanted as potential "material witnesses" could be held indefinitely in jail while waiting to testify before investigative grand juries. Many waited for months before being given legal representation. A later report by the Department of Justice's inspector general found "significant problems" in the detainments, including a pattern of abuse.[5] Some steps were taken later to curtail a few of the worst infringements. The message in the weeks after September 11, however, was unambiguous: trampling on a few civil liberties in the fight against terrorism was the price Americans would have to pay for feeling safe. One Republican congressman, in a fit of unapologetic chauvinism, told listeners on a radio talk show that racial profiling was needed to apprehend terrorists: "If I see someone comes in that's got a diaper on his head and a fan belt wrapped around the diaper on his head, that guy needs to be pulled over."[6]

For some, the September 11 bloodletting seemed to let loose stored-up demons. The Reverend Jerry Falwell, speaking on the Reverend Pat Robertson's television program, was almost completely candid in his accusations: "I really believe the pagans and abortionists, and the feminists and the gays and the lesbians who are actively trying to make that an alternative lifestyle, the ACLU, People for the American Way, all of them who have tried to secularize America, I point the finger in their face and say, 'You helped this happen.'"[7]

One *National Review* columnist took a different approach to Arab and Muslim countries and opined: "We should invade their countries, kill their leaders and convert them to Christianity."[8] That journalist lost that particular roost, but the sentiment was widespread. A brutal violence sprang spontaneously forth, with no distinction between terrorists and Muslims or between Muslims and anyone else visibly dark-skinned and "foreign" in appearance. According to *Los Angeles Times* reporter Richard Serrano, federal investigators opened 350 investigations into hate crimes directed at those perceived to be Arab during this period. State and local authorities were looking at an additional 70 cases. A number of these were murders, including that of a Sikh cabby in San Francisco whose brother had been killed earlier in a hate crime in Mesa, Arizona.[9]

In one of the odd twists following the trade center's destruction, a bat's nest of anti-Semitic conspiracy theories flew up out of the ashes. A rumor that Jews had been warned in advance that the trade center would be destroyed and consequently stayed home from work on the fated day was repeated as truth at both ends of the political spectrum. Although the meaning of opinion survey data is contested, an estimated thirty-five million Americans—17 percent of those polled—held significantly anti-Semitic views in the period after September 11. Fully one out of five "blame[s] America's support for Israel for the attacks."[10] Never mind the nature of Wahabi ideology motivating Al Qaeda or American troops in Saudi Arabia guarding the gates of oil.

In this hurricane of horrors, the response to September 11 by white nationalists might seem like a tablespoon of rain. Who needed the militia to supposedly defend American sovereignty after President Bush declared "war" on any number of enemies? How many foolish white nationalists would mix fuel oil and fertilizer when the entire law enforcement establishment was mobilized to fight "terror"? Somebody somewhere was sending envelopes of anthrax through the mail, but there was no material evidence that it involved any lone wolf Aryans. And where would the bruised and battered sympathies of Middle Americans lie now if a Randy Weaver type decided to shoot it out with the cops? Law enforcement officials were heroes now, not black-booted thugs. For a brief period, the domestic atmospherics and international tensions more closely resembled the early years of the Cold War, rather than that of the postwar New World Order.

Facing this complex of nasty weather, white nationalists nevertheless ventured forth.

At the vanguardist end of the movement, a few voices cheered the deaths and destruction at the World Trade Center and lamented only that there were not enough white men willing to do the same.[11] Their words served as a reminder that organized violence and mayhem might be temporarily put on hold but the potential to re-create a group like Bob Mathews's Order remained. Instead of actually calling upon his own members to commit murder, however, William Pierce used the occasion to drill an ideological lesson into the young men and women in and around the National Alliance. In a radio broadcast just days after September 11, Pierce laid the blame for the attack squarely on Jews and Israel. "We were attacked," he said, "because we have been letting ourselves be used to do all of Israel's dirty work in the Middle East." If the United States wasn't pushing "Jewish fashions and our Jewish television and our Jewish attitudes" into the Middle East, then the United States would not be attacked, he argued. Otherwise, "patriots and religious fundamentalists" would leave this country alone.[12] In pointing his finger at Jews rather than Falwell's long list of secularists, Pierce outlined in sharpest detail the difference between his version of white nationalism and Falwell's Christian right.

Just as noteworthy as Pierce's emphasis on Jews was his failure to mention immigration, lax border controls, and the supposed anti-Americanism of Islamic fundamentalism—all issues targeted by other sectors of the white nationalist movement. In fact, as the National Alliance member bulletin proudly noted, the entirety of Pierce's radio talk, entitled "Who Is Guilty?," appeared in the October 5 edition of *Muslims*, which the bulletin described as "the largest English-language Islamic newspaper published in the United States."[13]

Pierce recognized the power of old-fashioned Stars and Stripes patriotism after September 11. Rather than operate under its umbrella, however, he wanted to harden his following against its pull and widen the gulf between white nationalists and middle-of-the-road white Americans. He described those following President Bush as "lemmings," willing to rush off a cliff in a mass suicide. "Patriotism," Pierce declared, "is a sentiment which will be in fashion again for a few months."[14] In that one sentence he laid the basis for a strategy during the period ahead. After a "few months," a broader constituency would be willing to blame Israel and the Jews. He hammered the point in preparation.

By the end of 2001 William Pierce had decided that he saw a subtle shift of opinion among that slice of white people he regarded as his potential constituency. They had not previously agreed with his "blanket condemnation of Jewish influence," he wrote. Now those same people finally agreed with him. Accordingly, he believed they finally understood that "we must act to end the overall Jewish influence, the collective Jewish influence . . ."[15] It was "remarkable," he wrote in the November 2001 members' bulletin, how many white people "are facing at least part of the truth." The Jews "have never been more exposed," he claimed. This presented the National Alliance with a "new opportunity," he said.[16] Regardless of the actual status of the political environment at that moment, his organization had never been more prepared to act upon it.

The West Virginia headquarters complex had been built up and now included two office buildings and a warehouse for music and book distribution. The headquarters staff had grown over the decades from William Pierce and one secretary to almost twenty persons carrying out a variety of tasks.[17] Every week it broadcast a shortwave radio program entitled *American Dissident Voices*, providing a growing audience across the globe with the alliance's view of topical issues. Each month it published a members-only bulletin and a newsletter entitled *Free Speech* for wider distribution. Periodically *National Vanguard* magazine appeared with more in-depth treatments of ideological issues. In addition to selling music, Resistance Records continued publishing *Resistance* magazine, drawing young white power music fans into the National Alliance's orbit. A couple of professionally managed websites glued the entire enterprise together in cyberspace.[18]

The membership had grown close to two thousand and was now concentrated in forty-three units and proto units in twenty-six states, with another five units in Canada.[19] While not large enough by themselves to constitute a mass movement, by the standards of tight-knit, highly disciplined Leninist-style vanguard organizations the National Alliance had become a formidable force.

The previous July it had held a protest at the German Embassy in Washington, D.C., opposing the criminal extradition of a German comrade who was wanted for murder in his homeland. About fifty pickets, many of them skinheads from the D.C. area, walked that day. One of the alliance leaders got bloodied in a scuffle with antiracists, but they counted the event a success nonetheless.[20] Then on November 10, two months after 9/11, as American airpower struck Taliban forces in Afghanistan, the National Alliance led a group of seventy protesters outside the Israeli Embassy. Although many of the participants had recently graduated from the white power music subculture, this was not a skinhead-style event. No one shouted "Sieg Heil," as had been done at Klan and Aryan Nations rallies in Georgia and Tennessee. No swastika flags flew that day. This crowd dressed for success: dark suits for many; ties and long-sleeved dress shirts for those with tattoos peeking out from behind their collars. The few young women on the street dressed like secretaries, not flight-jacketed skin molls. Typifying the change in fashion, one middle-aged activist from Virginia, who had spent much of the mid-1980s marching around in camouflage fatigues, wore a dark suit and power tie and carried himself like a middle manager instead of a lieutenant in a white power army.[21] The picket signs reflected the National Alliance's approach to the post–September 11 world: ISRAEL THE ORIGINAL TERRORIST STATE, FIGHT YOUR OWN WAR, NO JEWS NO WAR, and ZIONISM IS RACISM.[22]

In contrast with the National Alliance's laserlike focus on Jews, after 9/11 the Council of Conservative Citizens continued its broader approach, which paired protecting the icons of the Old Confederacy with targeting new dark-skinned immigrants. On the same November day that the National Alliance picketed Israel's embassy, the council rallied against immigrants in Conover, North Carolina, a small town of fifty-five hundred on Interstate Highway 40. They repeated the performance the following January in Yadkinville, a still-smaller town outside Winston-Salem. Several dozen middle-aged men in ordinary street clothes held signs reading NORTH CAROLINA MEXICO'S NEWEST COLONY, MEXICANS NOT WELCOME, and DEPORT ALL ILLEGALS. A handful of speakers denounced immigrants and the companies that hired them. Among the speakers at both rallies was A. J. Barker, the onetime Populist chairman now ensconced as the council's Southeast regional coordinator.[23] The council confirmed its new place in the white nationalist heavens during these months. It had not suffered any loss of prestige *within* the movement after the Trent Lott affair, even if it was now avoided publicly by all but the most unreconstructed southern politicians. Most of the council's activities were concentrated in the South and border states. With Liberty Lobby now gone as a trade name, and Willis Carto's remaining publications declining in both circulation and significance, the council became the central address for a twenty-first-century mainstreaming strategy. Its leadership had become thoroughly intertwined with the intellectuals and Ph.D.'s connected with *American Renaissance*, a complementary pairing that enhanced the pull power of both organizations. And unlike Carto's Institute for Historical Review and Liberty Lobby, both *American Renaissance* and the Council of Conservative Citizens refrained from overt expressions of anti-Semitism. After September 11, however, several of the council's officials did join the chorus blaming the terror attacks on American support for Israel.[24] That small shift of organizational positioning proved William Pierce at least partially correct about a post-9/11 turn toward his direction. The council's version of anti-Semitism was not the same as the Hitlerism promoted by the National Alliance. Instead, the council largely adhered to an America first model of white nationalism.

Has Everything Changed?

The preoccupations of the National Alliance and the Council of Conservative Citizens underscored the continuity between their worldviews before September 11 and after. By the white nationalist reckoning, nothing much had changed. Elsewhere in the American political universe, however, the mantra was the exact opposite: 9/11 had changed everything.

If September 11 had in fact "changed everything," then the political alignments that had developed after the collapse of communism and the end of the Cold War would shift once again, this time to reflect a new conflict, a war against terrorism.

As discussed earlier, the end of the post–World War Two era had changed white supremacy's prospects. After the crackup of the anticommunist consensus, a slice of conservatives had effectively allied themselves with a newly realigned white nationalism. Pat Buchanan ran through doors opened up by David Duke. Dissent over the Persian Gulf War in 1991 had turned into an America first isolationism. The militia movement in the mid-1990s won a place for a nationalist resistance to both the multiracial American state and the globalized New World Order. Here opposition to foreign interventions was considered de rigueur.

If a second realignment had occurred after 9/11, then Buchanan's paleoconservatives would be expected to fall back within a broader conservative movement, as they had during the Cold War. And they would support foreign interventions, for example. If a clash of civilizations did pit the West against Islam, then white nationalists would be forced to subsume their efforts under the rubric of the American (multiracial) state. Racism and discrimination would persist, but white nationalism as a distinctive opposition to the status quo would be driven out of the mainstream.

For a few years after 9/11, it looked as if the new war against terrorism might play during the first decades of the twenty-first century much the same role as anticommunism had after World War Two.

Americans felt vulnerable as never before. The oceans that had previously separated them from wars in Europe, Asia, and Africa now seemed to have evaporated faster than the blink of an airplane's safety lights. For the moment at least, the swell of patriotic flag waving seemed to bring a new sense of national unity. "The events of September 11 have affected public opinion more dramatically than any event since World War II," the Pew Research Center concluded after taking a poll. Pew cited a change in attitudes toward the federal government, which had sagged with disapproval during most of the 1990s. In October 2000 only 54 percent of the public viewed the government favorably. A year later, in November 2001, that number jumped to 82 percent.[25] The overwhelming support for the fight against international terrorism seemed to squeeze out the space for any legitimate dissent.

A few opinion makers at the center of the conservative movement articulated what seemed like the emerging mainstream consensus: they regarded the ten years between the end of the Cold War and September 11 as an interregnum, a short historical hiccup before a new geopolitical alignment took shape. In this short decade the United States had become the only remaining superpower, and its hegemony had been unquestioned. Now "radical Islam" was challenging the power of the United States, and past antagonists such as Russia and India were lining up in mutual opposition to Islamic terror. The notion seemed unquestioned that the world was divided into competing "civilizations," and that Western Civilization and Muslim Civilization were now locked in a struggle similar to the past Cold War, when capitalist states in the West battled communist states in the East.[26]

President Bush launched a war in Afghanistan, toppling the Taliban government, and put the major figure behind the 9/11 attacks, Osama bin Laden, on the run. He also invaded Iraq, taking up where the first president Bush had left off. American military forces quickly removed Saddam Hussein, but the goal of creating a stable new regime remained undone. As the first decade of the twenty-first century progressed, however, a growing body of evidence undermined the notion that everything had changed.

Cracks and fissures along lines of race, ethnicity, and religion reappeared at pre-9/11 levels. On the simple question of military service, for example, a Pew poll in 2003 showed that 55 percent of white people believed that everyone has an obligation to fight, even when the United States is wrong. By contrast, only 30 percent of black people held a similar opinion, contravening the idea that one unified American people stood boldly against foreign enemies. The electorate divided into partisan camps, defined largely by demography and race. The Republican Party cemented its hold on white Protestant evangelicals, while the Democratic Party remained the home for black people and Jews. On questions of foreign policy, Democrats were more likely than Republicans to favor international cooperation and less likely to support go-it-alone measures.[27]

As the war in Iraq ground on, a significant spike occurred in what the Pew Research Center called "isolationist" sentiment, most tellingly, at "levels not seen since [the] post–Cold War 1990s and the post-Vietnam 1970s." After Hurricane Katrina destroyed the Gulf Coast and much of New Orleans, images of homeless black people left stranded by government inaction competed for public attention with the memory of the burning World Trade Center. For black people in particular, Katrina became *the* disaster—man-made or natural.[28] Further eroding the popular social consensus, a series of scandals and missteps undermined favorable views of the federal government, slashing it to pre-9/11 levels at 44 percent. Although individual opinion polls go up and down over time, this change in the gestalt of vernacular thought signaled an end to the consensus once wrought by the events in September 2001.

The war against terrorism increasingly looked like a partisan endeavor. The clash of civilizations thesis looked more like a narrow piece of intellectual property and less like a wide plank in the American psyche. Within a few short years it appeared that much of the political environment immediately after 9/11 had been eroded. Like prophecies that the turn of the millennial clock would produce apocalyptic violence and Y2K mayhem, those who predicted that "everything had changed" were simply proved wrong.

Paleoconservatives opposed President Bush's "war against terrorism" abroad and the draconian assault on civil liberties at home with the same vigor that they had opposed the First Persian Gulf War.[29] Neither Council of Conservative Citizens activists nor National Alliance cadres signed up to protect President Bush's version of Western Civilization. And Sam Francis articulated the white nationalist opposition to the new national security state with the same precision that he had once used to argue an interventionist view at the Heritage Foundation.

Francis argued that both before and after September 11, President Bush & Company favored low-wage brown-skinned immigration as a necessary fact of economic life. Further, he wrote, "in the minds of the ruling class, there is little practical and virtually no moral difference between American militias [like Trochmann's Montana Militia] . . . and the Islamic mass murderers of Al Qaeda." Francis contended that the "rhetorical and analytical fog" promoted by those arguing that everything had changed after September 11 was intended to "assist in the legitimatization and consolidation of ruling class hegemony and the global regime it is constructing."[30] Francis's unadorned call for opposition to the status quo, couched in the analytical language of the Italian communist Antonio Gramsci, was the clearest statement of its kind from any political quarter.

The white nationalist genie was not going back into the Cold War–style interventionist bottle. White power skinheads were not going to start playing Barry Statler songs at their concerts. Neo-Confederates would still wave the Stars and Bars, even as black soldiers bled and died in Afghanistan and Iraq. Renaissancers and councillors, mainstreamers and vanguardists, militiamen and Aryanists—none was willing to give back the gains won in the 1990s. They knew that the next thirty years would be more important to their cause than the last thirty. It wasn't Osama bin Laden who would render white people a minority in the supposed land of their forefathers.

The Anti-immigrant Movement Blossoms

February 21, 2002. Six months after September 11, the changing racial demographics in the United States stood at the center of white nationalists' attention.[1] At *American Renaissance*'s conference of 250 near Dulles Airport, President Bush's war against terrorism in Afghanistan and Iraq was of less concern than the fight brewing on the border with Mexico. Here Pat Buchanan's book *The Death of the West* was well received.[2] It predicted the end of civilization as the attendees had known it. Buchanan started his book with the claim that "[i]n half a lifetime, many Americans have seen their God dethroned, their heroes defiled, their culture polluted, their values assaulted, their country invaded, and themselves demonized as extremists and bigots for holding on to beliefs Americans have held for generations."[3] Although Buchanan used terms such as "faith" and "values," the gist of this book centered on the idea that population was destiny. The West, he wrote, was dying from low birthrates among white "European" peoples and higher levels of fertility by people of color, most particularly brown-skinned immigrants. In his talk that day, Sam Francis told the crowd that he had read a draft of the book when it was still called *The Death of Whitey*.[4]

That weekend Francis declaimed on the supposed national security dangers posed by immigration, thus connecting the administration's war against terrorism to his battle against brown-skinned immigrants from south of the Rio Grande. To elaborate on this point, *American Renaissance* invited an anti-immigrant activist from California, Glenn Spencer, to make a presentation. Spencer had been active in the Proposition 187 campaign in 1994, and press reports credited him with personally collecting forty thousand signatures to help put that measure on the ballot. He was well known for rhetoric that denigrated Mexican people, and that day he warned that Mexicans were setting out to demographically reconquer the Southwest, land that the United States had seized 160 years before in the war with Mexico. Spencer claimed to have evidence of this *reconquista* conspiracy procured from "secretly recorded" meetings of Mexican Americans.[5] Regardless of its truth, the reconquista theory had become a staple idea among anti-immigrant groups. At that time a border fence in California pushed immigrants into crossing in the Arizona desert, and the focus of anti-immigrant organizing was shifting from California to Arizona. In August 2002, six months after his turn at the *American Renaissance* podium, Spencer moved to Arizona and set up an outfit he called American Border Patrol.[6]

A new set of activists got involved in a vigilante effort to curb "illegals." They included militia-style organizations such as Ranch Rescue and Chris Simcox's Civil Homeland Defense. Simcox was another transplant from California to Arizona, where he bought ownership of the tabloid *Tombstone Tumbleweed*, which he used to promote his anti-immigrant politics. At first, members of Simcox's outfit were required to have permits to carry concealed weapons, and they trolled the area, weapons in hand, looking for "illegals." Later they morphed into a national organization called the Minuteman Civil Defense Corps.[7]

As Arizona became a flashpoint, a local organization called Protect Arizona Now (known by its acronym, PAN) collected signatures to put a referendum on the 2004 ballot. Modeled on California's Prop 187 ten years before, Arizona's Prop 200 required proof of citizenship for people registering to vote or seeking state services such as welfare.[8] By design, the measure aimed at making life in the United States difficult for immigrants—with or without documents. The initial petition-gathering process stalled, however, during its first months. But the effort was saved by the D.C.-based Federation for Immigration Reform, which stepped in with six hundred thousand dollars in contributions to PAN.[9] The money paid for professional signature gatherers, and enough names were submitted to guarantee the measure a place on the ballot.

During this campaign, PAN created a national advisory board and named as its chair Virginia Abernethy, a sixty-nine-year-old emeritus professor at Vanderbilt University's School of Medicine. With a Ph.D. from Harvard and a publications list on topics connecting health, the environment, and population growth, she also chaired a D.C.-based nonprofit called Carrying Capacity Network that aimed at sharply reducing immigration into the United States. She was also a member of the Council of Conservative Citizens and one of the dozen Ph.D.s whom Sam Francis used to plump up the *Citizens Informer*'s editorial advisory board. She was a frequent speaker at council events in the

South, and her Carrying Capacity Network was one of the few regular advertisers in its tabloid's pages.[10] More, she sat on the editorial board of one of the white nationalist movement's newest periodicals, *The Occidental Quarterly*, started in 2001. Among the *Quarterly*'s stated principles: "The European identity of the United States and its people should be maintained. Immigration into the United States should be restricted to selected people of European ancestry." Its policy toward the descendants of Africans first brought to the Americas long before most Europeans was summed up in the statement that "equality . . . is not a legitimate political aspiration."[11]

When reports of Abernethy's affiliations first emerged during the Prop 200 campaign, it created a stir in the press. The Federation for American Immigration Reform described her views as "repugnant" and "divisive," although the D.C. outfit did not mention the Council of Conservative Citizens members in its own ranks.[12] For its part, PAN's leader described Abernethy as the "grand dame of the anti-illegal immigration movement." When asked about her views, Abernethy denied that she was a racist. When questioned by Arizona newspapers, she replied: "I'm in favor of separatism . . ." She added, "We're saying that each ethnic group is often happier with its own kind."[13]

During the 1960s there would have been no questions about such a view, and it would have been accurately described as "segregationist." The Supreme Court's decision in *Brown* that "separate . . . was inherently unequal" was still fresh in the public mind. In the first decade of the twenty-first century, Abernethy's disavowal did not shake her place in the white nationalist movement any more than David Duke's assertion that he was simply a white civil rights activist or Randy Weaver's claim of ideological innocence.

In any case, the vast majority of white voters remained unconcerned by this storm. They overwhelmingly passed Proposition 200, turning it into law. A postelection survey found that supporters of the measure were primarily motivated by "negative feelings towards illegal immigrants . . ." and that "nearly 60% of voters knew how they would vote when they first heard about it." In fact, "most respondents did not link provisions in the initiative to their support or opposition . . ."[14] They wanted to send a message, and Virginia Abernethy helped make it happen.

As the anti-immigrant phenomenon flared in Arizona, a cross-country movement stretched from the vigilantes on the border to policy makers in the states of the Midwest and Southeast to think tanks and political action committees in Washington, D.C. In this movement, differences between legal and illegal immigrants faded into a generalized belief that a brown-skinned, Spanish-speaking tidal wave was swamping the white-skinned population of the United States. The attempt to stop un-documented workers at the borders morphed into a campaign to end immigration altogether and to save a supposedly white nation from de-mographic ruin. As Representative Tom Tancredo, a Republican from Colorado's Sixth District, said, "if we don't control immigration, legal and illegal, we will eventually reach the point where it won't be what kind of a nation we are, balkanized or united; we will have to face the fact that we are no longer a nation at all . . ."[15]

Tancredo had been associated with the Christian right side of the Re-publican Party in the 1970s and 1980s. In the twenty-first century he was chief of a congressional immigration reform caucus of more than ninety members that promoted legislation to reduce legal immigration, plug the borders, and, in its own words, "address the widespread prob-lem of voting by illegal aliens." It also promoted legislation denying citi-zenship to children born in the United States if their parents were undocumented residents. This goal is explicitly contradicted by the Constitution's Fourteenth Amendment, which declares that any person born in the United States is a citizen. This is the same Fourteenth Amendment that has been under attack by white nationalists from the Posse Comitatus and Montana Freemen to Aryan Nations.[16]

During the first years of the twenty-first century, almost all the growth in the white nationalist world occurred inside the anti-immigrant move-ment. Hundreds of thousands of people contributed millions of dollars to several dozen organizations.[17] And as the "racial millennium" ap-proached, the contest over national identity and the dominance of white people promised to continue unabated and to feed the anti-immigrant movement for still another generation. The fates of Willis Carto and William Pierce, by contrast, were soon decided.

Willis Carto and William Pierce Leave the Main Stage

March 19, 2002. Nine months after the final collapse of Liberty Lobby, the California home of Willis and Elisabeth Carto was sold at sheriff's auction. The buyer, not by coincidence, was the Legion for the Survival of Freedom, doing business as the Institute for Historical Review.[1] In this long mutual siege, Mark Weber prevailed at the end. The onetime acolyte of William Pierce in effect repaid the calumny that Carto had heaped upon the former physics professor during the fight over the National Youth Alliance thirty years before. Weber may not have gotten his hands on all seven and a half million dollars of the Farrel funds, but he squeezed enough out of Carto to restart the Institute for Historical Review and knock Liberty Lobby out of operation. Carto ended up much as he had started out, trying to keep the full range of his activities from reaching the scrutiny of the courts. The California bankruptcy court that handled Carto's personal disposition was far more revealing than any of his previous legal entanglements.

After a judge declared Willis and Elisabeth Carto (along with the Furrs, Liberty Lobby, and former bagman Henri Fischer) liable for the money fraudulently conveyed to their own causes, the Cartos faced an accounting for the funds. Declaring personal bankruptcy had delayed the day of reckoning. But like the bankruptcy at Liberty Lobby, it could not put off a final judgment forever.[2]

In these debtors' hearings, the details of the Carto family's finances became a matter of record. As in proceedings past, Willis Carto was asked about the multiple pseudonyms he had used, including the infamous "E. L. Anderson," which dated from the 1950s. Unlike those who had taken other depositions, the lawyer asking the questions had the benefit of Mark Weber's prior knowledge, gained from the years he had worked closely with Carto. At times during the examination, Willis Carto employed his powerful ability to forget. He did not know the whereabouts of the man who had allegedly helped hide the Farrel funds in Swiss accounts. Neither did he know the party to whom Liberty Lobby paid thousands of dollars a month in rent for its office building in D.C. On other matters, however, Carto revealed what he had to. Yes, he was treasurer of Liberty Lobby, a position he had never denied in four decades of litigation. No, he had not paid income tax in twenty years. Liberty Lobby had paid him only one dollar a year, and he received veterans and Social Security benefits. Otherwise he lived by the grace of his wife's income. She had pulled down thirty-two thousand dollars a year as a "supervisor" at Liberty Lobby. No, he did not own a car, or any other assets for that matter. A separate nonprofit corporation owned both his car and his wife's car. He wasn't sure who paid the car insurance, but he didn't. Liberty Lobby had paid for the gas, his health insurance, and a retirement plan.[3]

Then Willis and Elisabeth were questioned about their home in Escondido, California. It was a substantial house by any standard: three bedrooms, three bathrooms, and a hillside pool on ten acres of land, a mansion in comparison to the mountainside trailer that William Pierce inhabited in West Virginia. The house was the couple's largest and most available personal asset. Understandably, Willis and Elisabeth did not want to give it up, and so they claimed the home should be exempt from the court judgment. It was not theirs to surrender, they argued, stating that a company known as Herford Corporation, headquartered in Panama, actually owned it. Ultimately, the courts deemed otherwise. Hereford Corporation and the Cartos were essentially one and the same, the judge ruled.[4] Thus Willis and Elisabeth Carto were forced out of their home, so that a sheriff's sale could be held to satisfy the judgment.

Weber and the remaining legion-IHR staff had a bit of tongue-in-cheek fun at the expense of their former boss. They used a website to advertise the sheriff's sale and described the house as "The Carto mansion—aka 'Berchtesgaden West,'" using a reference to Hitler's onetime personal mountain retreat. Perhaps his former staff had known Willis better than anyone. Along with the house and lot listing they added: "The portrait of Willis Carto, hand over heart, in front of the Nazi flag, is not included in the sale." After paying $350,000 at the sheriff's sale, the legion-IHR turned around and put it on the market. The asking price: $600,000.[5]

Losing your home in a bankruptcy sale at any age is a miserable business. Forced eviction at the age of seventy-six is tougher yet. Carto showed no signs of remorse, however, only anger at his former underlings and an apparently sincere belief that ultimately he had been brought down through the machinations of an Israeli intelligence agency rather than by his own unwillingness to abide by the courts' decisions after 1993.

Like a Confederate cotton trader unable to grasp the full meaning of the Thirteenth Amendment, Carto picked up after bankruptcy and carried on as before. He published *The Barnes Review* to replace the Institute for Historical Review. The *American Free Press* substituted for *The Spotlight*.[6] Cotton was no longer king, however, and Willis Carto's three decades of primacy in the white nationalist firmament were over. Carto had done more than any other individual to birth a movement in the post–George Wallace, post–civil rights era, and his Liberty Lobby and *The Spotlight* had provided much of its core infrastructure. Yet that same infrastructure had been paradoxically undercut by his constant displays of sectarian pique and his legal wars with former colleagues. Decades of litigation with a dozen different opponents had drained precious resources out of the movement, and he had destroyed as many reputations as he had helped build.

In the end Willis Carto was a merchant, in the business of selling white supremacy and anti-Semitism; his own concerns always focused on the next sale, rather than the next generation. Nevertheless, his accomplishments have continued standing after he walked off the main stage of action. He had turned the defeat of Hitler and Hitlerism into a phony revisionist history, in which Nazi gassings were a myth and the Holocaust was a hoax. He had constructed a mainstreaming tendency in the movement, jettisoning the white sheets and brown shirts. In the process he created a vernacular coded language in which white supremacy was called populism and anti-Semitism was simply anti-Zionism. More than any other individual in his time and place, he built the infrastructure and generated the resources supporting a long-standing white supremacist political movement. So it is only appropriate that in order for a white nationalist movement to grow in the future, a fellow like Willis Carto must have existed in the past.

The Death of William Pierce

William Luther Pierce was another story. On July 23, four months and four days after the Cartos' house sold at the sheriff's sale, Pierce died quietly in West Virginia.[7] His illness and death at age sixty-nine were unexpected. He had enjoyed good health all his life and visited doctors for checkups only rarely. As a result, he did not notice his cancer until it was too late. Unlike the years it had taken to topple Carto, Pierce went quickly. He had surgery in Beckley and for a brief moment thought he might have a full recovery. But it soon became evident that cancer was spreading. Faced with the prospect of a long-term disability that required daily dialysis and left him unable to work, he decided against any further treatment. He signed a will, quickly assembled a small group of his most trusted leaders, and over several days gave his last instructions from his deathbed. After his death the body was cremated.[8]

News of Pierce's death drew little reaction from Willis Carto, who barely acknowledged that his old nemesis had ever lived. Carto just wondered about the future direction of National Alliance supporters. "Dr. Pierce was not an associate," Carto told an inquirer. "I knew him many, many years ago, but I never had any sort of relationship with him. As far as his organization goes, I'm looking with great interest to see who takes it over. He was an outspoken publicist and has a lot of followers around the country."[9]

David Duke, by contrast, openly acknowledged his intellectual debt to Pierce. "I really think that Dr. Pierce made a tremendous contribution to our cause. He helped people think straight about the Jewish Question and the other vital realities of race. After having read almost every word he wrote, I feel once more as though a family member was lost. I have been experiencing that a great deal recently! He was one of us. I learned a great deal from him, and it is very depressing to think that his voice is stilled."[10]

The New York Times published a twenty-inch obituary above the fold, a sure sign that the former physics professor had indeed achieved a modicum of fame and notoriety. The *Times* quoted a National Alliance spokesman before any critics. Pierce was not motivated by hatred of other races, the spokesman said, but by "a love for his own people."[11] Pierce's love apparently had trouble extending as far as his twin sons. Only one attended the memorial service in West Virginia. The other stayed away.[12] And Pierce bequeathed nothing to either of them. "I declare that I am now divorced and that I have two children, namely Kelvin Pierce and Erik Pierce," read article one of the last will and testament. That was it. The will did appoint an executor, a middle-aged, mechanically gifted comrade who had lived on the compound for years and had contributed to the improvement of its physical plant. The executor personally received all of Pierce's trucks, tractors, and other vehicles. The rest of Pierce's property—land, stock, copyrights, and cash—was bequeathed directly to the National Alliance.[13]

The pending issue at the end was not who would inherit a used car. Rather, the questions revolved around who would be named the next National Alliance chairman and whether that person would be able to hold a large organization together through the factional rivalries that were sure to come. In the most immediate aftermath, it appeared as if all the institutions that Pierce had built might remain stable and coherent. The leaders left behind appeared in agreement over the future course of the organization and chose thirty-eight-year-old Erich Gliebe as their new chairman.[14] Although Gliebe was not a rocket scientist like his predecessor, he had been the alliance's top recruiter and ran Resistance Records as if it were a money machine. For the moment at least, he commanded the loyalty of the membership as well as those leaders who might have immediately contended for the top spot. Gliebe's reputation as Pierce's favorite gave him a short "honeymoon" period, when his decisions were rarely questioned and he had sense enough to lean on others. Yet holding the National Alliance together soon became impossible.

The Penultimate Moment

August 24, 2002. It was the largest event of its kind in D.C. since before World War Two. One month after Pierce's death, the National Alliance organized a demonstration in Washington, D.C. This event was ostensibly aimed at protesting government support for the state of Israel, and the marchers used the alias "Taxpayers Against Terrorism" for this occasion. The contention that they were "against terrorism" was an irony compounded by FBI testimony that counted the National Alliance as a "domestic right-wing terrorist group."[1]

Terrorists or not, police three columns deep—many dark-skinned under their blue uniforms—lined Delaware Street in the nation's capital, shielding 750 white nationalists from the taunts and chants of several hundred antiracist protesters. The antiracists dogged the parade from beginning to end. At times the conflict between the two opposing groups seemed like a replay of the dance floor battles between skinheads and punk rockers almost twenty years before.

As the white-ists paraded from the Union Station parking lot toward the Capitol's West Lawn, they chanted in call and response: "What do we want?" the megaphones screamed. "Jews out!" the crowd answered. "When do we want it?" they continued. "Now!" was the exclamation point. Their signs amplified the message: NO MORE INNOCENT BLOOD FOR ZIONISTS and DIVERSITY IS GENOCIDE FOR THE WHITE RACE.

National Alliance members, under the direction of deputy membership coordinator Billy Roper, wore coats and ties and ordinary summer street clothes. They carried flags and banners emblazoned with a life rune and oak leaf wreath, the symbol most associated with their organization. Although they considered the event a memorial for William Pierce, his name was not printed on any of the placards, and Erich

Gliebe was not visible in the crowd that day. In effect, this was a "coalition" affair involving a half dozen other organizations, with each non–National Alliance group carrying its own signs.

Confederate battle flags flew. Clumps of thick-shouldered men with shaved heads and heavily inked forearms walked together, their black T-shirts emblazoned with the names of bands or with the word "Panzerfaust," a record company competing with Gliebe's Resistance Records. A few young women marched interspersed among the men. Small squads with swastika flags stopped and mugged for reporters' cameras, giving stiff-armed salutes and chanting, "Sieg Heil," with the Capitol's dome top in the background.[2]

The presence of the swastika set proved difficult for the National Alliance. William Pierce had opposed dressing up in fake uniforms and wearing swastika armbands since before he quit the National Socialist White People's Party. And the National Alliance historically had scowled on those acting like a Nazi caricature. In an e-mail exchange afterward, alliance coordinator Roper complained that "Sieg-Heiling" and "waving swastika flags make[s] my job more difficult and eventual White victory less likely."[3] He was in a bind, torn between two loyalties: the new regime led by Gliebe and the excitement in the streets. It did not take long for Roper to abandon the National Alliance and establish one of the many small organizations populating the national socialist universe.

From that perspective, the march that August was not a memorial. Instead, it turned out to be the first in a series of events leading to the unraveling of the National Alliance. Gliebe was a particularly bad manager. He turned every murmur of dissent within his ranks into a cause for expulsion. Every discharge required him to reshuffle the organization's leadership structure and hire new staff at headquarters. Revenues from dues fell as membership numbers declined. Rival music distribution outfits siphoned off funds previously monopolized by Resistance Records, which suffered additional problems because its magazine was not published regularly. The pool of ex-members grew.[4]

A bloc of ex-members associated with Kevin Strom charged Gliebe with both graft and incompetence. They cited his failure to finish routine tasks and his unwillingness to brook criticism. But the capstone problem was money. They charged that Gliebe raised funds for a permanent memorial to Pierce and then did not build it. He wasted money on frivolous projects (including purchase of thousands of boots with swastika-shaped soles from China). The Alaska regional coordinator demanded an audit. "I think it's important to emphasize that the money spent and squandered by Mr. Gliebe was Dr. Pierce's SAVINGS," the Alaskan wrote with the emphasis included. "Much of this money was donated and entrusted to Dr. Pierce and the rest of us to make a better life for our children. Not to get a first class upgrade for a stripper's plane ticket. Not for a brand-new luxury SUV with heated leather seats and a power sun-roof."[5] These complaints appeared on several white national-ist websites, turning the organization's disintegration into a twenty-first-century debacle, broadcast live in cyberspace.

Gliebe's personal characteristics by themselves were not the only cause of the problems facing the National Alliance after Pierce's death. The difficulty of anointing an organizational heir had plagued this move-ment since before George Lincoln Rockwell died at the hands of a dis-gruntled American Nazi Party member. In this sense Willis Carto's dispossession by legion-IHR staffers had kept that tradition alive. In a movement where every man is his own führer, differences over strategy and program are exacerbated by personality and power. Robert Miles never found someone to successfully inherit his Mountain Church. Richard Butler appointed and reappointed a string of Aryan Nations per-sonalities, as did Ben Klassen at his Church of the Creator, but none of those selected could do the job. At root, these elder Aryanists never managed to build an infrastructure separate from their personalities.

At Pierce's end, the organization he built turned out to mean less than the people he left behind. The buildings and real estate at the West Virginia headquarters turned into a virtual empty shell, as case-hardened National Alliance cadres scattered across the white nationalist landscape. Over the course of thirty years twenty thousand individuals had enlisted in William Pierce's outfit and stayed members for an aver-age of seventeen months. At the time of his death almost twenty-five hundred had been paying dues.[6] These thousands of activists became William Pierce's legacy. Schooled in a philosophical outlook and ethos, they continued operating behind the racial divide in American life. Still, several of the most prominent of former National Alliance members lost their way. Kevin Strom, for example, who had been the organization's voice on many of its radio broadcasts, promised to become the "house intellectual" for one of the alliance's spin-offs, only to have his career cut short by his arrest and jailing on child pornography charges.[7]

The death of William Pierce and the bankruptcy of Willis Carto marked an end point in the generational life of the movement, even if it did not mark the actual end. An accounting of activists and leaders across the years revealed that other leaders of the previous generation, both vanguardists and mainstreamers, had also faded into the back-ground during the first moments of the twenty-first century. Louis Beam and Tom Metzger, for example, found their own routes to semiretire-ment. In years past, their imprecations to violence and mayhem were made in the public square. Metzger, who had gained notoriety for his cultivation of white power skinheads, continued to operate a small-time propaganda mill. But he eventually left Southern California and moved back to Indiana.[8] Beam became a ghostlike figure, absent the Klan-style paramilitaries and underground guerrilla armies that he had promoted. After a contentious divorce from Sheila Toohey in 1997, the woman he had once praised for shooting it out with Mexican authorities, Beam quietly remarried and began raising yet another family. He posted messages on his personal website but otherwise kept himself out of view.[9]

The jailed Order soldiers who had been Beam's codefendants at Fort Smith were all but forgotten as individuals, even as the myth associated with Bob Mathews's Order continued. "There is no mail & no assistance at all," Bruce Carroll Pierce wrote from jail. "Frankly, it hurts to see mongrel drug dealers, pimps & the ungodly receive more attention."[10] Only David Lane remained a presence outside the walls.[11]

Of the militia-era personalities, Bo Gritz had shot himself, apparently in response to a divorce petition by his wife, Claudia. He survived—the wound was not life-threatening—but left his Almost Heaven community behind.[12] Randy Weaver moved quietly back to Iowa after spending some time in Montana.[13] Chris Temple, who had articulated the post–Ruby Ridge shoot-out strategy so clearly at Estes Park, became involved in an extended series of muddy money schemes before going to jail in 2004 after defrauding his investors.[14] John Trochmann was reportedly expelled from his own Montana Militia by his brother.[15]

Other men who figured prominently during the previous decades kept going, even if at a reduced pace. Thom Robb continued to operate his Ku Klux Klan outfit much like a family business, and his children were ready to inherit whatever mailing list and dues payers survived.[16] Competing Klan factions rose and fell according to the length of time their leaders stayed out of jail. Pete Peters maintained his Christian Identity ministry from Colorado and continued to attract young families with children to periodic Bible camps. Nevertheless, he increasingly relied on Internet broadcast technology to get out his message, which he began referring to as "Anglo-Israelism."[17]

Still other organizations continued to thrive much as they had in the decade before. Kirk Lyons, the peripatetic attorney, reinvented himself as an attorney for Confederate causes large and small and became a leading figure in the Sons of Confederate Veterans.[18] The Council of Conservative Citizens prospered after 9/11, pushing anti-immigrant politics throughout the South. A. J. Barker and other luminaries from the Populist Party's past, including those from the Don Wassall faction, entered the new century ensconced in the council. Jared Taylor continued publishing *American Renaissance* and holding conferences to promote the scientific side of white nationalism. Other intellectual enterprises such as Mark Weber's Institute for Historical Review and the new periodical titled *The Occidental Quarterly* found their niche comfortable but not expansive. Don Black's Stormfront website, with its reflections in German, French, Serbian, and other European languages, remained the preeminent forum for discussions among white nationalists, as well as a purveyor of propaganda, news, and links to other sites. Thousands of activists visited the site every day, and by 2005 the site was claiming a "membership" of forty thousand plus.[19] Sam Francis died early that year from a heart attack, and his place in the white nationalist firmament would not be easily filled.[20]

At this point, white nationalists still did not control a genuine third party apparatus, and ballot access in all the states remained an elusive goal. Without a widely distributed weekly newspaper or monthly magazine to promote their cause, organizations and individuals had turned to cyberspace as their primary communications link with one another. With the Internet, one person selling a carton of music CDs could declare himself king of the white power scene. The tendency to schism, so prevalent in the past, remained unchecked.

Nevertheless, white nationalists had exhibited both remarkable resilience and financial strength. Liberty Lobby had raised and spent approximately four million dollars year after year and distributed 150,000 copies of its tabloid every week. The Institute for Historical Review typically spent another $250,000 a year, as did *American Renaissance* after its founding. The white power music industry sold CDs and poured money into a growing subculture. Christian Identity ministers bought broadcast time on AM radio, and militiameisters made money at survivalist expos and gun shows. David Duke spent another two million plus running for office in Louisiana. The movement had received free publicity for one-off leaflet drops and well-planned stunts like the Klan's border watch events. After 9/11, anti-immigrant politics shoveled money back into the movement like a coal conveyor feeding fuel into a power plant. And the accounting of funds must include the money stolen in bank robberies and spent surreptitiously on movement causes.

Vanguardists had survived police crackdowns, multiple criminal prosecutions, civic opposition, and legal challenges. They had congealed a "culture of resistance," a term usually reserved for movements of the "left." By keeping the ideas of national socialism alive, they had also created a usable past for any similar movement in the future.

Mainstreamers redeemed racism and anti-Semitism, resurrecting a set of beliefs that had been otherwise discredited during the post–World War Two era. While these ideas and practices were already present within the civic culture and political mainstream, the movement gave the sentiments and prejudices of ordinary racists a seeming coherence.

In its aggregate form, white nationalism expressed grievances real and imagined, providing a language for prerational thoughts and feelings previously caught in the throats of a stratum of white people. White nationalists had only partially succeeded at creating a movement qualitatively different from the old white supremacist movement out of which it had grown. The transformation of white supremacy into white nationalism, however incomplete, changed the movement's gestalt. By raising the question of which nation they belonged to, white nationalists created a self-identified group with the rudiments of a distinct ethniclike identity. They vied as a race for cultural and political dominance within the United States and laid the basis for a future claim on a nation-state of their own.

By any measure, the white nationalist movement had possessed significant resources during the previous three decades and used them to great effect. Movement activists had influenced a larger white constituency and set up a visible camp on the far right edge of the Republican Party. They had created a white nationalist opposition to the status quo that *will not* go away in the near future.

60
The Future

Memorial Day weekend, 2004. Across the country a hard-fought presidential election dominated discussion. Backroom strategists plotted ad campaigns, and phone banks trolled for voters. Debates flared about war and terrorism abroad. State referenda promised to squash the possibility that gay men and lesbians could be legally married. Candidates rallied about the economy, gun rights, and abortion. In Congress, a Republican-dominated caucus opposed its president's proposal for a codified guest worker program and promoted anti-immigrant solutions to the continuing chaos on the border. For many voters, the fate of the United States hung in the balance.[1] They had largely forgotten that a white nationalist movement existed. But at a meeting in a New Orleans hotel ballroom, David Duke had gathered 250 activists from several different organizations for a "unity conference."[2]

Duke's route to this meeting had passed through Louisiana to the former Soviet Union, the Arab Middle East, and a federal penitentiary in Texas. After his ill-fated presidential primary bid in 1992, Duke had again lost a race for the U.S. Senate in 1996 but won a seat on a local Republican Party council in 1997. Two years later he lost a congressional primary.[3] As the money and votes in mainstream politics dried up, he wrote *My Awakening*, a seven-hundred-page tome he self-published in 1998.[4] As a piece of literature, the book was something akin to *Mein Kampf*. Part memoir and part Aryan primer, it was a commercially successful product he sold while on the speaking circuit.

In 1999 federal authorities began a mail fraud investigation of Duke,[5] which he implicitly acknowledged in a fund-raising letter dated October 17, 2000. "Your gifts," he wrote of the past money he had received, "have given me a decent living . . . and even enabled me to relax away from the pressure sometimes."[6] Translated into plain talk: donors gave Duke money, and he spent it on everything from groceries to gambling—and not just on the white nationalist struggle, as he had previously pretended. Meanwhile, the federal inquiry continued, and on November 16, 2000, the feds raided Duke's home and office. The affidavit the authorities filed for the search said that Duke had misused more than two hundred thousand dollars in contributions from his supporters, much of it gambling at local casinos.[7]

At the time of the raid, Duke was in Russia—for his fourth visit since 1995.[8] Rather than come home and defend himself, he spent the next two years traveling across Europe (east and west) and the Arab countries of the Middle East. In France, Duke had his picture taken with Jean-Marie Le Pen. In Russia he turned his 1995 meeting with Zhironovsky into a spot at a 2002 "anti-Zionist" conference in Moscow. In Kiev in August 2002 he received an honorary doctorate from the National Academy of Management. That same month he attended a convention of a white nationalist party in Germany. The following November he spoke at a meeting in Bahrain.[9] During these years abroad, Duke sold racism and anti-Semitism the way any other American businessman might sell hamburgers and Mickey Mouse.

Less than six weeks later, on December 18, 2002, Duke reappeared in Louisiana and signed documents pleading guilty to mail fraud and tax evasion. He admitted bilking his supporters and lying about his income to the feds. He was sentenced to fifteen months in prison and paid a ten-thousand-dollar fine, before going to prison in April 2003.[10] He served his sentence at the federal prison in Big Spring, Texas, the same jail that had once held his buddy Don Black after the Dominica fiasco.

When Duke was released a year later, he picked up where he had last left off. At the unity conference, his charisma and gift for public oratory set him apart from the other speakers. He cast adherence to the white nationalist cause as the most selfless devotion to humanity, and he captured the gut anxieties of average racists like no other person of his generation. And when Duke introduced fifty-seven-year-old Sam Dickson, the acerbic attorney from Atlanta, it became obvious that both men felt they were preparing for the next generation.[11]

Dickson revisited the white nationalist movement's underlying assumptions. "Our race needs a homeland where we can be by ourselves," he said, unpopulated by Muslims, Jews, those he called "Negroes," and other unspecified people of color. Liberals, specifically white liberals, stood in the way now. Then Dickson changed course and began listing reasons for hope in the future.

One was the September 11, 2001, terrorist attacks. They had lifted the lid on the "Jewish issue," he said. For the first time anti-Semites could talk openly. Racial liberalism among whites, he argued, with its "Camelot" and "hootenannies" and Peace Corps, was a thing of the past. Those people thought they were going to turn "Ghana into Norway," he said in a quick turn of phrase, but "nobody believes it anymore." Public opinion polls may show white support for "diversity" and desegregation, he told the crowd, but polling is about "public opinion," what you are willing to tell a stranger over the phone. Actual, privately held beliefs are more evident in the way people live. And white people will "pay $300,000 for a $75,000 home, just so they can live with other white people." Deep down, he claimed with a certain glee in his voice, they all realize "black people are hopeless."[12]

Racial egalitarianism, according to his analysis, had rested on the prospect of seemingly unlimited economic expansion during the decades following World War Two. But the good times were over. Now he argued, "The worse the better, let the bad times roll." Other factors were also changing. Television had once given liberalism a "media monopoly." Now the Internet provided open access to ideas of every kind. The liberal monopoly had ended, he proclaimed.[13]

The most important change he noted that day was generational. The war against Hitler had once led white people to associate what he called "normal racial values" with Nazis, and they had been America's enemy. "The World War Two generation is being gathered unto their fathers," he declared in triumph. With their deaths, he believed, remembrance of the fight against Hitlerism would fade. The postwar period would finally and completely end. And after stating the case for a brighter whiter future, the attorney sat down to deep and grateful applause.[14]

In his talk that day, Dickson succinctly summarized the white nationalists' case (as they understood it) for the twenty-first century. After thirty years of grassroots organizing, they had learned several of the more unsavory facts in American life. A significant number of white people, for whatever set of reasons, continue to buy overpriced houses just so they can live in all-white neighborhoods. Survey respondents *are* often less than forthright, particularly when responding to sensitive questions about race-related matters.[15] Some white people *will* use racial slurs and tell jokes when talking with other white people but *will not* use them when talking within earshot of black people. The terms of public discussion changed sharply after World War Two and the civil rights revolution, and overt racism and anti-Semitism were no longer considered socially acceptable. Throughout the events described in this book, white nationalists aimed at transforming this social (and racial) discourse. And to the degree already discussed, they partially succeeded. In sum, a number of white nationalist leaders had a fairly accurate sense of the future direction of a sector of the white populace. And from this group the mainstreamers of the twenty-first century will continue to develop.

At the same time, white nationalists consistently misunderstand the larger world around them. A significant number of white people remain determined to live and live happily in a multiracial, multicultural United States. And they do not regard themselves as "race traitors." Perhaps even more significant, black people and other people of color are not passive objects of history. They are historical subjects in their own right. African Americans in particular had changed American life at every one of its critical junctures since the advent of New World slavery. Ideological thinkers on the white-ist side of politics remain completely blind to this aspect of the twenty-first century. And from this failure, vanguardists and Aryan killers will continue to pop up, at odds with the direction of American life.

The generations after the postwar boomers have yet to fully take the stage. From this juncture, those now twenty plus years old will determine the future direction of the white nationalist movement. They are tech-savvy and well educated. Having not lived through World War Two, they will not be chastened by the horrors of Hitlerism. Having never experienced Jim Crow and the struggles against it, they will be unburdened by its memory. Their only uniform will be their white skins in a country where white people are increasingly a demographic minority among minorities. The prerogatives now accruing to majority status will be challenged, as black, brown, and yellow faces increasingly populate the halls of economic and political power. The presidency of Barack Obama only confirms their notions of white dispossession. And in the decades to come, the next generations of activists will seek to establish a white nation-state, with definable economic, political, and racial borders, out of the wreckage they hope to create of the United States. Some will kill and bomb and shoot their supposed racial enemies. Some will run for elected office and win. They will fight for local (white) control. Failing a complete victory, they will continue the cultural battle over symbols from the past and the history of the future. And they will draw on the legacy of those who resurrected white supremacy as an autonomous movement in the 1970s and brought it into the twenty-first century.

Notes
Acknowledgments
Index

NOTES

Preface

1. Erich Fromm, "Foreword," in Edward Bellamy, *Looking Backward* (originally published 1888; Signet Classics New American Library, 1960), p. v (46 utopian novels between 1889 and 1900).
2. John L. Peak, "'Yellow Peril' Threatens World With Disaster"; "A Preacher's Gloomy View, Dr. Combs Sees Many Perils Facing the Republic"; Rev. Stephen Northrop, "Universal Rivalry to Lift One Another Up"; *The Kansas City Times*, January 1, 1901.
3. Allan Chase, *The Legacy of Malthus: The Social Costs of the New Scientific Racism* (Urbana: University of Illinois Press, Illini Books Edition, 1980), pp. 138–75, 274–301.
4. Leonard Zeskind, "Saving Grace or Human Race," *Kansas City Star*, December 26, 1999.
5. Leonard Zeskind, *It's Not Populism: America's New Populist Party a Fraud by Racists and Anti-Semites*, writing and research assistance by Ken Lawrence, published by the National Anti-Klan Network and Southern Poverty Law Center, 1984.
6. Counting white supremacists is not a precise science. I count the number of distinct organizations, Identity churches, publications, etc., and then extrapolate. Exact numbers can be derived from court documents, postal circulation numbers, or website memberships. Klan members are gathered by closely monitoring rallies and other semipublic activity. The best numbers on white power skinhead groups often come from antiracist skinheads or punk groups. Militia membership separates into hard-core individuals who train with weapons and go to private meetings, and the much larger numbers who go to public affairs. By aggregating these totals and then subtracting overlaps, the best estimate is made.
7. Robert S. Griffin, *The Man of a Dead Man's Deeds: An Up-Close Portrait of White Nationalist William Pierce*, first published on the Internet in 2000, also published in paper, 1st Books Library, 2001 (an extremely sympathetic portrait of Pierce's ideas and person, this book fails to locate Pierce in a movement environment or make a critical assessment of his ideas); George Michael, *Willis Carto and the American Far Right* (Gainesville: University Press of Florida, 2008); Frank P. Mintz, *The Liberty Lobby and the American Right: Race, Conspiracy and Culture* (Westport, Ct.: Greenwood Press, 1985). Both Michael's and Mintz's accounts are narrowly constructed and suffer from failing to fully access the long track record Carto left in the courts.
8. Darko Zubrinic, "The Sarajevo Haggadah," 1995, www.croatianhistory.net/etf/hagg.html.

1. The Apprenticeship of Willis Carto

1. David Duke, "Introduction of Willis Carto," International European American Unity and Leadership Conference, May 30, 2004, Airport Plaza Hotel, New Orleans, Louisiana, transcript of www.davidduke.com/conference/audio/.
2. Willis Carto, "Supplementary Answers to Interrogatories," filed June 10, 1963, *Willis Carto v. Giant Food, Inc.*, United States Court for the District of Maryland, Civil Action 14419.

3. Willis Carto, "Plaintiff's Answers to Interrogatories," filed October 25, 1963, *Carto v. Giant Food*.

4. Elisabeth Carto, "Judgment Debtor Examination of Elizabeth W. Carto," June 13, 2001, pp. 3–12, *Legion for the Survival of Freedom, Inc. v. Willis Carto*, California State Court San Diego, M 64584.

5. Willis Carto, letter to Norris Holt, January 19, 1955, "You are looking at the first letter ever sent on a letterhead of the JCR."

6. E. L. Anderson, Ph.D. [Willis Carto], "Cultural Dynamics I, II and III," *Right*, November 1959, March 1969, and June 1960. Reprinted by Noontide Press and by *Western Destiny*.

7. "Liberty Lobby Being Formed," *Right* 23 (August 1957): 1. He projected an initial budget of $119,500.

8. Willis Carto, "Introduction," in Ulick Varange [Francis Parker Yockey], *Imperium* (Noontide Press, April 1983), p. xix.

9. Willis A. Carto, "A Liberty Lobby Is Needed," *Right*, September 1957. At a September 1957 meeting of a Chicago-based organization known as "We The People," one thousand conventioneers unanimously endorsed a resolution supporting the creation of a "Liberty Lobby."

10. Willis Carto, "Supplemental Answers to Interrogatories," filed June 10, 1963, *Carto v. Giant Food*. "From June to September 1960 I was in Boston helping to organize the John Birch Society, an American anti-communist organization." In a September 25, 1979, deposition in *Liberty Lobby, Inc. v. Anti-Defamation League of B'nai B'rith*, Carto said he worked for the Birch Society in 1959 and gave several conflicting accounts of events during this period.

11. *Right*, March 1960.

12. Curtis Dall, "Statement of Curtis Dall, Chairman, Board of Policy, Liberty Lobby, Washington, D.C. Given before the Senate Finance Committee on August 10, 1962, in opposition to H.R. 11970"; Drew Pearson and Jack Anderson reported on Dall's statement in "The Reappearance of Curtis Dall," *The Washington Post*, June 1, 1963. The article became the subject of a libel suit, *Curtis B. Dall v. Drew Pearson et al.*; in case no. 921, October 1964, the Supreme Court published Dall's testimony as part of its decision on a writ of certiorari. Dall did not prevail in his libel suit; Drew Pearson, "To Washington Merry-Go-Round Editors," April 28, 1965, syndicated column.

13. Willis Carto, "Deposition of 'Willie' Allison Carto," April 25, 1963, *Carto v. Giant Food*.

14. Ibid.

15. "Deposition of Joseph E. Roberts," December 21, 1963, p. 7, *Carto v. Giant Food*.

16. Giant Food "Answers to Interrogatories," filed October 25, 1963, p. 9, *Carto v. Giant Food*.

17. "California Man Fined for Cursing in Market," *The Washington Post*, November 21, 1962.

18. "Complaint," filed February 10, 1963, *Willis A. Carto v. Giant Food*.

19. "Interrogatories," filed by Giant Food March 15, 1963, *Carto v. Giant Food*.

20. "Excerpt from Transcript of Proceedings Before Hon. Harrison L. Winter, Judge," February 2, 1965, *Carto v. Giant Food*.

21. "Looking Forward: A study of the new trend with the conservative movement," first published by Liberty Lobby as "The Conservative Victory Plan" in March 1965. Leaflet for labor unions reproduced on pp. 24–25.

22. W. B. Hicks, Jr., "Special Tenth Anniversary Report," June 18, 1965.

23. "Looking Forward," p. 14.

24. Ibid., p. 22.

25. Ibid., p. 23.

26. John C. Obert, "Yockey: Profile of an American Hitler," *The Investigator*, p. 24, October 1981, publisher Jack Anderson; C. H. Simonds, "The Strange Story of Willis Carto," *National Review*, September 10, 1971; Kevin Coogan, *Dreamer of the Day, Francis Parker Yockey and the Postwar Fascist International* (Brooklyn: Autonomedia, 1999); "Department of the Army memo," G-2 SPS Halloran/mkm/gch/56419/grj, November 9, 1953, Yockey, Francis Parker: "He was honorably discharged on 14 July 1943 at Hq. Camp Gordon, Ga., by reason of Certificate of Disability due to dementia praecox, paranoid type, cause undetermined."

27. Kevin Coogan, *Dreamer of the Day*, pp. 468–77.

28. Ulick Varange [Francis Parker Yockey], *Imperium: The Philosophy of History and Politics* (The Noontide Press, 1983). The quote about Jews is on p. 418.

29. Anderson [Carto], "Cultural Dynamics," republished in *Western Destiny* IX, no. 3 (August 1964): 10–13.
30. Anderson [Carto], "Cultural Dynamics."
31. Willis Carto, "Introduction," in Yockey, *Imperium*, p. ix.
32. Willis Carto, "Introduction," in Yockey, *Imperium*, p. xiv.
33. John C. Obert, "Yockey: Profile of an American Hitler."
34. Willis Carto, "Introduction," in Yockey, *Imperium*, p. xix.
35. Willis Carto, "Introduction," in *Imperium*, p. xlii.
36. E. L. Anderson (aka Carto), "Cultural Dynamics."
37. "The Virtue of Tolerance," *Western Destiny*, August 1964, p. 3.
38. E. L. Anderson [Carto], "Dear Subscriber" letter of May 17, 1966, *Western Destiny*.
39. David Duke, introduction of Willis Carto, Memorial Day weekend 2004.
40. Wilmot Robertson, "Man, the Racist Animal," *Western Destiny*, April 1966; Robertson, "Art and Aristocracy" Parts I & II, *Western Destiny*, January and February 1966; Richard Kelley Hoskins, "Organic Civilization," *Western Destiny*, August 1965; Hoskins, "Two Controversial Ideas: A Glance at Yockey," *Western Destiny*, July 1964.
41. Don Warren, personal communication to author.
42. Wilmot Robertson, *Dispossessed Majority* (Cape Canaveral, Fla.: Howard Allen Enterprises, 1976), pp. 79–80.
43. Ibid., p. 16.
44. Willis Carto, "Deposition of W. A. Carto," *Liberty Lobby Inc. v. Dow Jones and Company, Inc.*, vol. 2, August 7, 1985, pp. 336–50.
45. "Roger Pearson to Tour United States," *Right*, June 1959, p. 1; Roger Pearson, foreword, *Eugenics and Race* (The Noontide Press, 1966), "This booklet comprises a selection of articles from the pages of Northern World."
46. Stephen Langton [Roger Pearson], "Judeo-Communist Influences in Western Art," *The New Patriot* 9, no. 1 (March 1967): 33.
47. Scott Anderson and Jon Lee Anderson, *Inside the League*, Dodd, Mead & Company, New York, 1986.
48. "The 1963 Inaugural Speech of Governor George Wallace," January 14, 1963, ADAH Alabama Department of Archives & History.
49. Dan T. Carter, *The Politics of Rage: George Wallace, the Origins of the New Conservatism, and the Transformation of American Politics* (New York: Simon & Schuster, 1995), pp. 195–225; Jody Carlson, *George C. Wallace and the Politics of Powerlessness* (New Brunswick, N.J.: Transaction Books, 1981).
50. Carter, *Politics of Rage*, p. 297.
51. Ibid., p. 295.
52. Asa Carter was Wallace's speechwriter; Klansman Robert Miles was the Michigan state chairman; William K. Shearer in California, White Citizens Council leader William Simmons, Kent Courtney, and Leander Perez were all part of the inner circle; see Carter, *Politics of Rage*.
53. Seymour Martin Lipset and Earl Raab, *The Politics of Unreason: Right-Wing Extremism in America, 1790–1970* (New York: Harper & Row, 1970); "no ideological racism" on p. 351; Gallup data on youth vote on p. 367; Yankelovitch data on class nature of vote on pp. 365–69.
54. Michael D. Russell, "Deposition of Michael D. Russell," *Liberty Lobby Inc. vs. American Lobby Inc. et al.*, Civil Action no. 1286-70, December 21, 1970.
55. Frank P. Mintz, *The Liberty Lobby and the American Right: Race, Conspiracy and Culture* (Greenwood Press), p. 129.
56. John Accord, "Affidavit of John Accord," signed May 14, 1969.
57. Ibid., p. 6; Dennis C. McMahon, "Affidavit," May 10, 1969; Accord and McMahon, "Neo-Nazi Movement Revealed as Dangerous Threat," June 18, 1969.
58. C. H. Simonds, "The Strange Story of Willis Carto," *National Review*, September 10, 1971.
59. Western Destiny Bookstore, n.d. (booklist from this period lists "Imperium by Francis Parker Yockey, Paperback"); Paul W. Valentine, "The Student Right: Racist Martial," *The Washington Post*, n.d. ("reproduced from . . . Special Collections Knight Library, University of Oregon").
60. Revilo Pendleton Oliver, "Dear Colonel Dall" letter, December 17, 1970.

2. William Pierce, National Socialism, and the National Youth Alliance

1. W.L.P. [William Pierce], "The Radicalizing of an American," *Best of Attack! and National Vanguard Tabloid* (National Alliance, 1984). William Pierce, "Interview with James Ridgeway for MSNBC-Edgewise," n.d., Media Transcripts, Inc.; Will Blythe, "The Guru of White Hate," *Rolling Stone*, June 8, 2000; Roger S. Griffin, *The Fame of a Dead Man's Deeds: An Up-Close Portrait of White Nationalist William Pierce*, copyright 2000, pp. 26–32, originally available via Internet download.

2. "The Radicalizing of an American," *Best of Attack! and National Vanguard Tabloid*, pp. 124–26, from no. 61, 1978.

3. FBI 157-1673, Richmond Field Office File, "William Luther Pierce," January 30, 1967; the FBI developed a detailed profile of Pierce's education, employment, and residential history; W.L.P. [William Pierce], "The Radicalizing of an American," *Best of Attack! and National Vanguard Tabloid*; Griffin, *Fame of a Dead Man's Deeds*, pp. 26–36.

4. W.L.P., "The Radicalizing of an American," p. 124.

5. Ibid.

6. FBI 157-1673, William Luther Pierce, November 21, 1966; FBI 157-1673, January 30, 1967, p. 6–8, "Employment" (new material was appended to this file over time).

7. FBI 157-1673, January 30, 1967 (describes Pierce's attachment to Rockwell and national socialism, as well as his absence from American Nazi Party activities. Includes the move to Virginia).

8. William Pierce, "Deposition," September 22, 1995, *Connie Mansfield, Personal Representative of the Estate of Harold Mansfield, on behalf of herself and the Estate v. William Pierce*, U.S. District Court for the Western District of North Carolina Bryson City Division Civil Action No. 2: 95CV62, pp. 12–21; Southern Poverty Law Center filed this lawsuit after a white supremacist murdered a black sailor in Jacksonville; *The New York Times*, May 20, 1996. Ms. Mansfield was awarded $85,000.

9. Dennis Roddy, "Hate was in his blood but not in his genes," *Pittsburgh Post-Gazette*, August 28, 2002, "His family was of no importance to him," [son] Kelvin Pierce [said].

10. FBI 157-13485, "William Pierce," September 21, 1972, "PIERCE SHOULD BE CONSIDERED POSSIBLY ARMED AND DANGEROUS [caps in original]"; FBI 157-13485, "William Luther Pierce," April 23, 1970, pp. 19–20; NS Arms was registered with ATF but business had "practically folded up due to recent legislation."

11. George Simonelli, *American Fuehrer: George Lincoln Rockwell and the American Nazi Party* (Urbana: University of Illinois Press, 1999), pp. 104–40; William H. Schmaltz, *Hate: George Lincoln Rockwell and the American Nazi Party* (Washington, D.C.: Batsford Brassey, 1999).

12. FBI 157-13485, "William Luther Pierce," May 16, 1971, "Summary of Subject's Propaganda Activities," pp. 6–14; "Nazi Lecturer Urges: Shoot the President," April 10, 1970; FBI memo from Director to U.S. Secret Service, "William L. Pierce, Threat Against the President," April 12, 1970.

13. John Tyndall, "Letter to William L. Pierce," March 23, 1967.

14. FBI 157-13486, "William Luther Pierce," May 18, 1971, pp. 12–14, selections from Pierce's "Prospectus for a National Front," August 31, 1970.

15. "Mailing List Theft Laid to Lobbyist," *The Washington Post*, October 1, 1971.

16. FBI 157-13485, "William Luther Pierce," August 19, 1975; National Youth Alliance incorporated in Virginia on October 14, 1970, charter no. 128608.

17. William Pierce, "Since December of last year a determined and intensive campaign has been waged to destroy the National Youth Alliance . . . our response . . . civil action 475-51 in I.S. District Court for the District of Columbia," n.d.

18. "A Few Facts about Willis A. Carto," *News from the National Youth Alliance* [Pierce Faction]. This ten-page mailing contained "Exhibits A–H."

19. "A Few Facts About Willis Carto." Exhibit B showed a portion of the "Deed of Trust."

20. "News from the National Youth Alliance," n.d.

21. C. H. Simonds, "The Strange Story of Willis Carto," *National Review*, September 10, 1971.

22. *Liberty Lobby, Inc. vs. National Review, Inc.*, U.S. District Court District of Columbia, Civil Action 79-3445; *Los Angeles Times*, November 26, 1986. Judge Robert J. Ward dismissed the libel suit.

23. National Youth Alliance, *Action* newsletter, March 1971, April 1971, May 1971.

24. FBI 157-6353, "William L. Pierce," February 11, 1972; files include clips from George Washington University, *The Hatchet*, February 7, 1972, "Ex-Nazi Assailed by Eggs, Stinkbomb"; "Award of Damages," *The Washington Post*, April 25, 1973, p. A-34.

25. Robert Lloyd, National Organizer, "Open Letter to a Student Activist," National Alliance *Action* newsletter, March 1971.

26. William Pierce, *National Alliance Bulletin*, February–March 1978, p. 1.

27. "Revolutionary Notes," *Attack!*, no. 12 (1972), reprinted in *The Best of Attack! and National Vanguard*, p. 13.

28. "Why Revolution," *Attack!* no. 6, 1971, reprinted in *The Best of Attack! and National Vanguard*, pp. 9–10.

29. Revilo Pendleton Oliver, "Dear Colonel Dall" letter, December 17, 1970.

30. George Thayer, *The Further Shores of Politics: The American Political Fringe Today* (New York: Simon & Schuster, 1967).

31. Randall Williams, ed., "Comparative Klan Strengths," *The Ku Klux Klan: A History of Racism and Violence*, Klanwatch Project of the Southern Poverty Law Center, 1981, p. 23. The data in that report was from the U.S. Justice Department figure and the Anti-Defamation League. In 1971 it counted 4,500 Klansmen, in 1974 there were 1,500; Neil R. McMillen, *The Citizens' Council: Organized Resistance to the Second Reconstruction, 1954–64* (Urbana: University of Illinois Press, 1994); Benjamin R. Epstein and Arnold Forster, *The Radical Right: Report on the John Birch Society and Its Allies* (New York: Random House, 1967).

32. FBI 157-13485, "William Luther Pierce," August 19, 1975, National Alliance was incorporated on February 26, 1974.

33. "National Alliance: New Superstructure for Movement,"*Attack!* February 1974, p. 4.

34. Nick Camerota, "Nick's Observations-Requiem for the Right," *Attack!* no. 46, 1976, reprinted in *The Best of Attack! and National Vanguard*, p. 75.

3. *The Turner Diaries* and Resurgence

1. "Does America Deserve to Live?," *The Best of Attack! and National Vanguard*, p. 57; "Jews, the USSR, and Communism," *The Best of Attack! and National Vanguard*, p. 64.

2. Author, recollection of the first edition, standard pocketbook-size paperback, 200 pages; *The Best of Attack! and National Vanguard*, p. 81; Charles Ashman, "The American Nazi Floating Crap Game," *St. Louis Today*, July 26–August 10, 1974, p. 9.

3. Andrew Macdonald [William Pierce], *The Turner Diaries* 2nd ed. (National Alliance, September 1980).

4. "Sexuality in a Sick Society," *National Vanguard*, January 1983, p. 17; "A Search for Values: Toward a White Ethic," *National Vanguard*, August 1982, p. 13; an author is not listed on either piece, but both bear the unmistakable imprints of Pierce's writing style during those years. "Feminism," *Membership Handbook for Members of the National Alliance* (National Vanguard Books, 1993), pp. 39–42.

5. *Soldier of Fortune*, January 1981, March 1981.

6. National Vanguard Books, Catalog no. 8, June 1984, p. 9; "Books," *The White Patriot*, Knights of the Ku Klux Klan, no. 55, January 1983, p. 16.

7. Barricade Books, Lyle Stuart. At the time Lyle Stuart bought the rights, *The Turner Diaries* had already sold 200,000 copies, Pierce told MSNBC interviewer James Ridgeway; the 500,000 number was reported, among other places, by John Sutherland, *The Guardian*, July 29, 2002.

8. *National Alliance Bulletin* [Members Only], February–March 1978, p. 3.

9. *National Alliance Bulletin*, activities were reported in issues for January 1980, March–April 1980, May 1980, June 1980, September 1980.

10. "Hear Untold Truths Every Day," *The National Spotlight* 1, no. 1 (September 17, 1975). A list of Liberty Lobby radio programs on over 175 stations in 41 states; "How *Spotlight* Became Nation's No. 1 Weekly Newspaper," *The Spotlight*, June 4, 1979, p. 8.

11. "*The National Spotlight* is born today," *The National Spotlight* 1, no. 1 (September 17, 1975); "Statement of Ownership, Management and Circulation," *The National Spotlight* 1, no. 3 (October 1, 1975), p. 5, "total paid circulation 151,254."

12. "Aid in instilling unity of thought and action to good citizens everywhere," *The National Spotlight* 1, no. 1.

13. Editorial, *The National Spotlight* 1, no. 1 (September 17, 1975): 9.
14. "Dear Friend," Liberty Lobby promotional letter, signed by Curtis B. Dall, Robert M. Bartell, Carol M. Dunn, James B. Tucker, dated September 28, 1979.

4. David Duke and a New Klan Emerge

1. "Klan Leader Egged During Tour" and "Arrest Protest in Klan Incident," UPI, October 16, 1977, reprinted in *The Crusader*, no. 27, Klan Border Watch edition, official publication of the Knights of the Ku Klux Klan, Metarie, Louisiana.
2. John Hammerly, "KKK's Same Spiel: America for Whites" (staff writer for publication unknown), reprinted in *The Crusader*, no. 27.
3. David Duke, "personal account of some of the California activities"; "Protestors Break Down Hotel Door: KKK Members Meet with Lt. Gov. Dymally," UPI; both articles reprinted in *The Crusader*, no. 27.
4. "Border Watch Continues," *The Crusader*, no. 28, p. 1.
5. "Klan Border Watch Edition," *The Crusader*, no. 27, p. 3.
6. Ibid., p. 12; Tyler Bridges, *The Rise of David Duke* (Jackson: University Press of Mississippi, 1994), pp. 66–69. Devin Burghart drew my attention to the importance of this Klan border watch.
7. Patsy Sims, "David Duke: The Image Maker," *The Klan* 2nd ed. (Lexington: University Press of Kentucky, 1996), pp. 152–96; Wyn Craig Wade, *The Fiery Cross: The Ku Klux Klan in America* (New York: Simon & Schuster, 1987), pp. 368–75; Bridges, *The Rise of David Duke*, pp. 3–14.
8. Karl Hand, "David Duke for President?" *NSLF Movement Notes*, n.d.; Hand wrote, "Don't leave your wife, your girl friend or your daughter alone with this guy"; Karl Hand, former national organizer, Knights of the Ku Klux Klan, "Why not David Duke," flyer, n.d.
9. Sims, *The Klan*, p. 159 (*The National Socialist Bulletin*, August 1, 1970, published by the NSWPP, refers to "National Socialists led by David Duke" at LSU); the 1970 picture of Duke in a brownshirt uniform has circulated widely.
10. Bridges, *The Rise of David Duke*, pp. 31–32.
11. FBI 157-1406-8, April 2, 1971, "National Socialist White People's Party"; FBI 157-14016-16, July 7, 1971, "White Youth Alliance"; FBI 157-14016-49, January 25, 1972, "The National Party has replaced the WYA with many former WYA members joining the National Party"; FBI 157-14016-50, January 25, 1972, White Youth Alliance, Airtel, "Agents to whom DUKE furnished information contained in enclosed LHM are SAS [redacted]"; FBI 157-14016-51, dictated February 7, 1972.
12. Leonard Zeskind (unsigned), "Duke Takes Lumps After Defeat at Polls," *The Monitor* 25 (May 1992), Center for Democratic Renewal (typo in this article erroneously has Duke arrested on January 28, 1972; he was arrested on January 18).
13. Sims, *The Klan*, p. 184.
14. David Mark Chalmers, *Hooded Americanism: The History of the Ku Klux Klan* 3rd ed. (Durham, N.C.: Duke University Press, 1987), pp. 8–21; Wyn Craig Wade, *The Fiery Cross*, pp. 40–41.
15. www.waymarking.com/waymarks/WMAZE (accessed on February 6, 2008); www.tennessee.go/environment/parks/NBForrest (accessed on February 6, 2008).
16. W.E.B. Du Bois, *Black Reconstruction in America* (New York: Atheneum, 1979), p. 190; Eric Foner, *Reconstruction: America's Unfinished Revolution 1863-1877* (New York: Harper & Row, 1988).
17. David Duke, "We Must Build a White Political Machine," editorial, *The Crusader*, no. 1 (Fall 1973).
18. Nicholas Lemann, *Redemption: The Last Battle of the Civil War* (New York: Farrar, Straus and Giroux, 2006); Eric Foner, *Reconstruction: America's Unfinished Revolution 1863–1877* (New York: Harper & Row, 1988), pp. 564–600.
19. *Knights of the Ku Klux Klan Handbook*, David Duke signed the "Preface," n.d., no page numbers, all quotes in this paragraph are from the *Handbook*.
20. Ibid.
21. Chalmers, *Hooded Americanism*, p. 291. Chalmers provides an excellent state-by-state guide to the successes and failures of the Klan during the 1920s.

22. Ibid., p. 26.

23. Johnson-Reed Act of 1924; Allan Chase, *The Legacy of Malthus: The Social Costs of the New Scientifc Racism* (Urbana: University of Illinois Press, Illini Books Edition, 1980), p. 9; Matthew Frye Jacobson, *Whiteness of a Different Color: European Immigrants and the Alchemy of Race* (Cambridge, Mass.: Harvard University Press, 1998), pp. 82–85; John Higham, *Strangers in the Land: Patterns of American Nativism 1860–1925* (New York: Atheneum, 1965), p. 321.

24. Leo P. Ribbufo, *The Old Christian Right: The Protestant Far Right from the Great Depression to the Cold War* (Philadelphia: Temple University Press, 1983), pp. 25–79 on Pelley and pp. 80–127 on Winrod; Donald I. Warren, *Radio Priest: Charles Coughlin, the Father of Hate Radio* (New York: The Free Press, 1996); Leonard Mosley, *Lindbergh: A Biography* (New York: Doubleday & Company, Inc., 1976), pp. 274–302 (chapters on America First and Des Moines).

25. Chalmers, *Hooded Americanism*, p. 299.

26. Ibid., p. 343.

27. Ibid., pp. 256–65; Diane McWhorter, *Carry Me Home: Birmingham, Alabama: The Climactic Battle of the Civil Rights Revolution* (New York: Simon & Schuster, 2001), pp. 519–30.

28. "Reporter Broke Case Open," *Times Colonist* (Victoria, British Columbia), June 13, 2005; Marcel Dufresne, "Exposing the Secrets of Mississippi Racism," *Washington Journalism Review*, October 1991; Jerry Mitchell, "Activist Recalls Jailhouse Lie," *The Clarion-Ledger*, June 21, 2002.

29. "White Self Hatred—Master Stroke of the Enemy," *Attack!*, no. 37 (1975); "Why We Fight: The Motivation of a True Klansman," *The Crusader*, official publication of the Knights of the Ku Klux Klan, no. 1 (Fall 1973), article credited to Pierce's publication *Attack!*, which originally published it in 1972; "Who Rules America?" National Alliance, n.d.

30. William Pierce, "The Real Enemy," *The White Patriot: World Wide Voice of the Aryan People*, Don Black, publisher, no. 55, January 1983, p. 13; Evelyn Rich, "Ku Klux Klan Ideology 1954–1988," Ph.D. dissertation, 1988, University Microfils International Dissertation Information Service, p. 180.

31. "Mightier Than an Army," *National Vanguard*, no. 94 (April 1983).

32. "Why Is the Klan Opposed to Jews?," *The White Patriot*, no. 55 (January 1983), p. 12.

33. FBI 157-2396-461, "Information RE: Dr. William L. Pierce and [redacted]," November 24, 1975; Nick Camerotta, associate editor of *Attack!*, "The Last Hurrah," *The Crusader*, no. 5, p. 17.

34. "Why We Fight," *Attack!*, no. 16, November 14, 1972; "Why We Fight," *The Crusader*, no. 1 (Fall 1973).

35. "Who Rules America," *Crusader: The Voice of the White Majority*, no. 23, Special Introductory Issue.

36. Howard Schuman, Charlotte Steeh, Lawrence Bobo, Maria Krysan, *Racial Attitudes in America: Trends and Interpretations* rev. ed. (Cambridge, Mass.: Harvard University Press, 1997), pp. 184–89.

37. "Klan No Longer 'Invisible Empire,' Issues Aired Publicly," *The National Spotlight*, October 31, 1975.

38. Kathleen Blee, *Women of the Klan: Racism and Gender in the 1920s* (Berkeley: University of California Press, 1991), pp. 1–4, 103–12.

39. Ben Bradlee, Jr., "David Duke Revitalizes Klan," *Los Angeles Herald Examiner*, republished in *The Crusader*, no. 79 (for women percentage); Robert Miles, "Aryan Women: Racial Comrades in Arms," *The Crusader*, no. 33 (September 1978).

40. "The Klan Today," *The Ku Klux Klan: A History of Racism and Violence*, Special Report, Southern Poverty Law Center, 1981, p. 49.

41. Bill Stanton, *Klanwatch: Bringing the Ku Klux Klan to Justice* (New York: Grove Weidenfeld, 1991), pp. 3–9; "Final Order Approving Consent Decree," November 21, 1989, *Bernice Brown et al. v. The Invisible Empire Knights of the Ku Klux Klan*, U.S. District Court Northern District of Alabama Southern Division, 80-HM-1449-S (originally filed November 3, 1980).

42. Elizabeth Wheaton, *Codename Greenkil: The 1979 Greensboro Killings* (Athens: The University of Georgia Press, 1987); Dr. Michael Nathan, Dr. James Waller, Sandi Smith, Cesar Cauce, and Bill Sampson. Another nine were wounded, several of those seriously.

43. Wyn Craig Wade, *The Fiery Cross*, pp. 347–62; Gary May, *The Informant: The FBI, the Ku Klux Klan, and the Murder of Viola Liuzzo* (New Haven: Yale University Press, 2005).

44. "Klan Leader Reportedly Informed for F.B.I.," *The New York Times*, August 31, 1981, article cited report in Nashville *Tennessean*.

45. Wade, *The Fiery Cross*, p. 391 (women shot in Chattanooga win damages from members of the Justice Knights); Chris Lutz, *They Don't All Wear Sheets: A Chronology of Racist and Far Right Violence 1980–1986*, Center for Democratic Renewal, published by the Division of Church and Society of the National Council of Churches of Christ in the USA, 1987.

46. David Duke, Interviews with Evelyn Rich, La Quinta Motor Inn, Metairie, Louisiana, March 18 and March 20, 1985.

47. Bridges, *The Rise of David Duke*, pp. 81–82.

48. Ibid., pp. 85–88.

49. "Klan Moves Forward: Under New Grand Wizard," *Crusader: Voice of the White Majority*, no. 51, January 1981. Don Black became the new Grand Wizard, but was displaced after he went to prison.

5. The Election of 1980: The Klan and Ronald Reagan

1. "Klan's Metzger Enters U.S. Congressional Arena," *California Klan News* 3 no. 1, n.d.; Metzger for Congress, Committee No. 093122, Federal Election Commission filing, June 30, 1980 (FEC records show Metzger's committee reporting about $26,000 in expenditures through December 31, 1980); Al Martinez, "Metzger Says KKK Seeks to Fill Vacuum," *Los Angeles Times*, June 16, 1980; "Oceanside's Day of Infamy," *California Klan News* 3 no. 1, pp. 6–8 (Metzger republished newspaper articles and photos and added commentary on the March 15 riot); Doug Seymour, interview with author, May 1986 (Seymour was a San Diego Police Department reserve officer on undercover assignment in Metzger's Klan and was present at the Oceanside events). On April 4 following, Metzger participated in a candidates' forum at San Diego State University.

2. Elinor Langer, *A Hundred Little Hitlers: The Death of a Black Man, the Trial of a White Racist, and the Rise of the Neo-Nazi Movement in America* (New York: Metropolitan Books, 2003), pp. 108–36 and 141–49 (for Metzger background); Doug Seymour, interviews with author, May 1986; Leonard Zeskind (unsigned), "Metzger Begins Move to the Top," *The Monitor*, May 1988; Leonard Zeskind (unsigned), "Peddling Racist Violence for a New Generation: A Profile of Tom Metzger and the White Aryan Resistance," Background Report no. 5, Center for Democratic Renewal.

3. "Voters Ready for Change," *The Spotlight*, September 1, 1980, p. 6.

4. Michael Goldfield, *The Color of Politics: Race and the Mainsprings of American Politics* (New York: New Press, 1997), p. 314; Bob Herbert, "Righting Reagan's Wrongs?" *The New York Times*, November 13, 2007.

5. Marjorie Hyer, "Evangelist Reverses Position on God's Hearing Jews," *The Washington Post*, October 11, 1980; Clyde Wilcox, *God's Warriors: The Christian Right in Twentieth Century America* (Baltimore: The Johns Hopkins University Press, 1992), pp. 95–142; Sara Diamond, *Spiritual Warfare: The Politics of the Christian Right* (Boston: South End Press, 1989), pp. 45–110.

6. Thomas Byrne Edsall with Mary D. Edsall, *Chain Reaction: The Impact of Race, Rights, and Taxes on American Politics* (New York: W. W. Norton, 1992), pp. 129–31 (for tax vote).

7. Ibid., p. 138.

8. Bill Grimstad, "Reagan: A New Beginning?" *Crusader: The Voice of the White Majority* 51 (January 1981): 1.

9. Editorial, *The Spotlight*, February 2, 1981, p. 1.

10. "*Spotlight* Notes One-Third Million Circulation Plateau: Friends Help Celebrate at Washington Gala," *The Spotlight*, February 23, 1981. *Spotlight* subscriptions reached 305,000, according to Liberty Lobby documents.

11. Editorial, *The Spotlight*, February 2, 1981.

12. "Richardson Denounces Liberty Lobby, Withdraws as Nominee," *The Spotlight*, May 11, 1981, p. 19; Fleming Lee, "Galileo Tortured into Saying Earth Is Flat; Does Richardson Believe His Own 'Confession'?" *The Spotlight*, May 11, 1981, p. 18.

13. Spencer Rich, "Withdrawal by Richardson Saves Administration Unpleasant Fight," *The Washington Post*, April 26, 1981; Lynn Rosellini, "Health Post Choice Withdraws amid Controversy," *The New York Times*, April 26, 1981.

14. James P. Tucker, Jr., "Establishment Media Smears Liberty Lobby," *The Spotlight*, May 4, 1981, p. 4.

15. Lee, "Galileo Tortured," p. 18.

16. Willis A. Carto, ed., *Profiles in Populism* (Old Greenwich, Conn.: Flag Press, 1982), pp. 199–200 (from "A Populist Glossary," first published as a serial in *The Spotlight* during 1980 and 1981).

17. Evelyn Newman, "Klan Victims Sue Federal Gov't," *National Anti-Klan Network Newsletter*, Fall 1983 (includes quotes from Reynolds to Crumsey).

18. Philip Shenon, "U.S. Rights Official Discounts Tension," *The New York Times*, February 7, 1987.

19. Drew Days, *Harvard Civil Rights-Civil Liberties Review*, 1984, cited in Edsall and Edsall, *Chain Reaction*, p. 190.

20. Edsall and Edsall, *Chain Reaction*, pp. 172–97.

21. David C. Savage, *Turning Right: The Making of the Rehnquist Supreme Court* (New York: John Wiley & Sons, 1993), p. 9.

22. Edsall and Edsall, *Chain Reaction*, pp. 187–88.

23. George Nicholas, "Arabs Cite 29 Foreign Agents Close to Reagan," *The Spotlight*, June 22, 1981, p. 1; Henry Thompson, "Reagan Knew Iraq No Threat While Defending Israeli Raid," *The Spotlight*, July 6, 1981, p. 1; Harrison Horne, "Reagan Preaches Populism, Practices 'Politics as Usual,'" *The Spotlight*, September 13, 1982, p. 1; Harrison Horne, "Reagan's Tax Hike Takes Bite from Most Ardent Supporters," *The Spotlight*, September 27, 1982, p. 6.

24. According to Liberty Lobby documents, *The Spotlight* January 5 and 12, 1981, had a paid circulation of 268,423 subscriptions, 22,021 pledge, and 53,364 bulk for a total paid of 343,808. *The Spotlight* December 3, 1984, had a paid circulation of 108,725 subscriptions, 24,427 pledge, and 21,694 bulk for a total paid of 154,846.

25. *Liberty Lobby, Inc. et al. v. Jack Anderson*, United States District Court for the District of Columbia, Civil Action 81-2440; *Liberty Lobby, Inc. et al. Appellants v. Jack Anderson et al.*, United States Court of Appeals, District of Columbia Circuit, 83-1471.

26. *Howard Hunt, Jr. Appellant v. Liberty Lobby, Inc.* United States Court of Appeals District of Columbia Circuit, 821787; *E. Howard Hunt, Jr. Plaintiff-Appellee, v. Liberty Lobby, a D.C. Corp., Defendant Apellant*, United States Court of Appeals, Eleventh Circuit, 82-5321; *Mel Mermelstein v. Institute for Historical Review, Legion for the Survival of Freedom*, Superior Court of the State of California for the County of Los Angeles, C356542.

6. Denying the Holocaust

1. Reporter's transcript, October 9, 1981, before Hon. Thomas T. Johnson, *Mel Mermelstein v. Institute for Historical Review, Legion for the Survival of Freedom*, Superior Court of the State of California for the County of Los Angeles, C356542, p. 36; Judgment in case no. 356542 filed by county clerk on August 5, 1985; Myrna Oliver, "Holocaust Doubters Settle Auschwitz Survivor's Suit," *Los Angeles Times*, July 25, 1985.

2. "Booklist," Institute for Historical Review, Winter 1982/83 ("#335 *Anne Frank's Diary: A Hoax*, by Ditlieb Felderer"); "A few facts about the Institute for Historical Review," Subscription flyer, n.d. (books listed include *The Auschwitz Myth*, by Wilhelm Staglich); "Revisionist Report," (resolution passed unanimously at the first IHR conference), *The Spotlight*, September 24, 1979.

3. Frank Tompkins, "$50,000 Offered for Proof Nazis Gassed Jews," *The Spotlight*, September 24, 1979, pp. 6–7; Michael Collins Piper, *Best Witness: The Mel Mermelstein Affair and the Triumph of Historical Revisionism* (Washington, D.C.: Center for Historical Review, 1994), pp. 29–32.

4. "Special Holocaust Edition," *The Crusader*, no. 49, n.d. (Metairie, La.: Patriot Press); "The Great Holocaust Debate," *The Spotlight*, September 24, 1979.

5. Harold Ellington Cabot, "$50,000 Reward for Substantiating Holocaust Unclaimed," *The Spotlight* September 1, 1980, p. 14.

6. Lewis Brandon [David McCalden], letter to Mel Mermelstein, November 20, 1980, "We will re-open the reward so that you can apply"; Keith Stimely, "Nazi Gassings a Myth?" special report published by the Institute for Historical Review, n.d.

7. Mel Mermelstein, *By Bread Alone: The Story of A-4685* (Los Angeles: Crescent Publications, 1979); Turner Network Television, *Never Forget*, starring Leonard Nimoy, aired April 8, 1991; Mark Belinghof, "Docudrama Focuses on Man's Fight Against Revisionists," *Kansas City Jewish Chronicle*, March 29, 1991.

8. David McCalden, *David McCalden Revisionist Newsletter*, no. 2 (1981).

9. *Mel Mermelstein v. Institute for Historical Review, Legion for the Survival of Freedom*, C356543, court reporter's transcript of October 9, 1981, hearing, p. 15.

10. Willis Carto, videotape of deposition, February 25 and 26, 1985, in Washington, D.C., *Mel Mermelstein vs. Institute for Historical Review*, Legion for the Survival of Freedom, Superior Court of the State of California for the County of Los Angeles, C356542.

11. *Mel Mermelstein v. Institute for Historical Review*, California Superior Court, C356542; *Willis Carto v. William Cox, Melvin Mermelstein, Herbert Brin, Heritage Publishing Company, Auschwitz Study Foundation, Inc.*, United States District Court for the District of Columbia, Civil Action no. 83-1788; *Mel Mermelstein v. Legion for the Survival of Freedom*, California Superior Court, C629224; *Mel Mermelstein v. Legion for the Survival of Freedom*, California Court of Appeals, Second Appellate District, Division Two, B064033.

12. LaVonne Furr, deposition, March 14, 2000, *Legion for the Survival of Freedom, Inc. v. Lewis Furr and LaVonne Furr*, 97-221, in the Chancery Court of Garland County, Arkansas, March 14, 2000, pp. 12–17.

13. LaVonne Furr, deposition, *Legion for the Survival of Freedom, Inc., v. Lewis Furr and LaVonne Furr*, pp. 12–17 (helped husband and Mathews), pp. 40–41 (met Carto in D.C.).

14. Legion for the Survival of Freedom, "By-Laws," signed by LaVonne Furr as secretary, June 16, 1966; LaVonne Furr accurately described the reincorporation during the deposition cited above, but gave an incorrect date (1967).

15. LaVonne Furr, deposition, *Legion for the Survival of Freedom, Inc., v. Lewis Furr and LaVonne Furr*, pp. 44–47, pp. 36–37, pp. 48–49.

16. *American Mercury* 536 (Spring 1980), ("Since June, 1966, it [A.M.] has incorporated RIGHT, WESTERN DESTINY, FOLK, and NORTHERN WORLD").

17. Austin J. App, Ph.D., "That Elusive Six Million," *American Mercury*, 481 (June 1966).

18. Teressa Hendry, "Was Anne Frank's Diary a Hoax?," *American Mercury* (Summer 1967).

19. Hans von Thenen, "The Truth About Dachau Concentration Camp," *American Mercury* (Spring 1976), pp. 26–27.

20. Benito Mussolini, "Church, State and Sex," *American Mercury* (Fall 1976, reprinted from a 1931 edition of an English-language magazine, *Liberty*).

21. Manfred Roeder, "Germany Alive!" *American Mercury* (Summer 1975), p. 34.

22. Willis Carto, deposition, *Liberty Lobby, Inc., v. Dow Jones and Company*, June 19, 1985, p. 96.

23. *American Mercury* 483 (Winter 1966), State of Circulation, Line C, Paid Circulation of Issue Nearest, 7,087; 487 (Winter 1967), Line C, 6,123; 491 (Winter 1968), Line C, 7,039; 495 (Winter 1969), Line C, 9,561; 499 (Winter 1970), Line C, 11,646; 511 (Winter 1973), Line C, 14,308; 515 (Winter 1974), Line C, 18,640; 523 (Winter 1976), Line C, 11,385; 527 (Winter 1977), Line C, 10,655; 531 (Winter 1978), Line C, 8,322; 535 (Winter 1979), Line C, 7,767.

24. David McCalden, *David McCalden Revisionist Newsletter*, no. 2 (December 1981); during the winter of 1977 Noontide distributed H. K. Thompson, Jr., *Doenitz at Nuremburg: A Reappraisal* (New York: Amber Publishing Co.), among others.

25. David McCalden, deposition, June 12, 1981, p. 72, *Mel Mermelstein v. Institute for Historical Review, Legion for the Survival of Freedom*, C356543.

26. Willis Carto, letter to Lavonne Furr, September 12, 1993.

27. E. L. Anderson, Ph.D. [Carto], "The Way It Might Have Been," *American Mercury* (Summer 1973); LaVonne Doden Furr is listed as managing editor; both E. L. Anderson and Lee Roberts are listed as contributing editors on p. 8.

28. Wilmot Robertson, *Dispossessed Majority* 2nd rev. ed. (Howard Allen Enterprises, Inc., 1976), p. 14; Robertson made a subtle but significant change in a later edition, changing

the referenced sentence to "after the inventory of Hitler's racial **policies** was published" (author's emphasis) (3rd rev. ed., 1981).

29. C. Vann Woodward, *The Strange Career of Jim Crow* (New York: Oxford University Press, 1955); Eric Hobsbawm, *The Age of Extremes: A History of the World 1914–1991* (New York: Pantheon Books, 1991), p. 239.

30. "The Holocaust Problem," *National Vanguard*, Newspaper of the National Alliance, no. 84, November 1981, p. 14 (this editorial was unsigned, but William Pierce wrote all of the National Alliance editorials, and this one bears the marks of his writing style).

31. "The Holocaust Problem," *National Vanguard*, pp. 8 and 14.

32. Ibid., p. 14.

33. Ibid., p. 8.

34. A. R. Butz, *The Hoax of the Twentieth Century* (Surrey, UK: Historical Review Press), n.d.; A. R. Butz, *The Hoax of the Twentieth Century: The Case Against the Presumed Extermination of European Jewry* (Torrance, Calif.: Institute for Historical Review, first U.S. printing May 1977).

7. Survivalism Meets a Subcultural "Christian Identity"

1. Author, notes from the survival expo in Kansas City; Leonard Zeskind (unsigned), "National Survivalist Expo in Kansas City," *The Hammer* 1 (November 1982); Mary Lou Nolan, "Survivalists' Exhibits Offer Food for Thought and Holocaust," *The Kansas City Star*, September 24, 1982.

2. James William Gibson, *Warrior Dreams: Paramilitary Culture in Post-Vietnam America* (New York: Hill and Wang, 1994).

3. Author attended many different "Gun & Knife Shows" in Kansas, Missouri, Georgia, and Arizona during the years 1981–2001.

4. *The C.S.A. Survival Manual*, The Covenant, the Sword and the Arm of the Lord, Spring 1982, p. 34.

5. Deborah Singer and Roger Moore, "Of Families, 'Supremacy' and Survival," *The Kansas City Star*, July 25, 1982; "C.S.A. Survival Training School," *C.S.A. Journal* 7, n.d.; James Coates, *Armed and Dangerous: The Rise of the Survivalist Right* (New York: Hill and Wang, 1987), pp. 137–38.

6. Leonard Zeskind, *The "Christian Identity" Movement: Analyzing Its Theological Rationalization for Racist and Anti-Semitic Violence*, Division of Church and Society of the National Council of Churches of Christ in the U.S.A., October 1986.

7. David Brion Davis, *Inhuman Bondage: The Rise and Fall of Slavery in the New World* (New York: Oxford University Press, 2006), pp. 64–70 and 186–90 (Davis's authoritative account demonstrates both the importance of the Biblical story of Ham in justifying slavery and the use of that justification by Christians, Muslims, and Jews); Elaine Pagels, *The Origin of Satan* (Vintage, 1996) (the origin of the Devil Jew in Christian thought).

8. "What We Believe," *CSA Journal* 7, "We believe that God is raising up a remnant . . . who will rule and reign as his Elect."

9. J. William Buford, Bureau of Alcohol, Tobacco, and Firearms, "Affidavit," April 3, 1985, p. 3.

10. Joe Scales, "A Fortress in Arkansas Mines Weapons Bunkers Found at Camp: Covenant Group's Arsenal Extensive," *The Kansas City Star*, April 24, 1985.

11. "Ozark Survivalists Train for Chaos," Associated Press, November 24, 1981.

12. "Survivalist Tied to Oklahoma Murder," Associated Press, April 25, 1985; Scales, "A Fortress in Arkansas."

13. "Alliance Member Gerhard Stalhut (with rifle) gives instructions in house to house combat," photo with cutline, *National Alliance Bulletin*, July 1982. "Survivalism: Response to Racial Chaos," *National Vanguard* 83 (August 1981), pp. 2, 4, 12.

14. James Ellison attended seminary in Illinois and later became a Church of Christ minister in San Antonio, Texas.

15. James Ellison, "Video Interview by U.S. Marshals Service District of Columbia," transcript, July 24, 1995; Kerry Noble, *Tabernacle of Hate: Why They Bombed Oklahoma City* (Prescott, Ont., Canada: Voyageur Publishing, 1998), pp. 25–66 (Noble was the number-two person after Ellison).

16. William Samuel Thomas, "Interview with Jack Knox FBI et al.," Sebastian County Jail, May 3, 1985; ATF Special Agents Sheila Stephens and Joe Long, "Summation of Interview," April 26, 1985 (interviewed eighteen CSA members and six former members).

17. Bruce Gibson (former CSA member) interviewed by Sgt. Gene Irby, Arkansas State Police, Jack Knox, FBI, Bill Hobbs, FBI, May 7, 1985 (cites Ellison taking two wives); James Ellison, "Transcript of testimony," *United States v. Robert E. Miles et al.*, 87-20008, pp. 404–406.

18. Evelyn Rich, communication to Center for Democratic Renewal, n.d., "Duke . . . starts talking about the Bhagwan. Duke and Warner very into the Bhagwan. He has the right ideas because he does not waste his time on the poor. . . . Warner and Duke try to figure out how they can cash in on the Bhagwan" (notes from February 1986 IHR conference in Culver City, California).

19. James Ellison, "Transcript of testimony," 87-20008, pp. 584–90.

20. Singer and Moore, "Of Families, 'Supremacy' and Survival."

21. "Christian Patriots Discuss Survival in a Time of Crisis," *The Spotlight*, October 29, 1979; Christian-Patriots Defense League, "Survival Conference and Citizens Emergency Defense System Seminar at Mo-Ark Camp near Licking, Missouri," invitation and registration packet, n.d.; Monte Plott, "Right-Wing Militancy Growing," *St. Louis Post-Dispatch*, January 27, 1981.

22. Pete Miller, "U.S. Citizens Must Learn How to Protect Themselves" and "Gathering by Patriotic Survivalists," *The Spotlight*, August 30, 1982, p. 13; included photograph of two men posed while dressed in camouflage (with CSA patches) and sighting their rifles.

23. "Dear Paul Revere Club Member," newsletter, November 1982, p. 2 (Paul Revere Club was an arm of the Christian-Patriots Defense League).

24. Jim East, "Veil of Seclusion Anonymity Pierced," *The Tulsa Tribune*, April 2, 1985; Judy Thomas, "We Are Not Dangerous, Leader of Separatists Says," *The Kansas City Star*, March 17, 1996; author, notes from visit to Elohim City, March 1996; Robert Millar, interview with author and James Ridgeway, March 1996.

25. "Survivalism: Response to Racial Chaos," *National Vanguard* 83 (August 1981).

26. Ibid.

27. Contra James Coates, who describes William Pierce as "another charismatic denizen of the Survivalist Right," *Armed and Dangerous*, p. 48.

28. "A Search for Values Toward a White Ethic," *National Vanguard* 89 (August 1982): 13–18 (quote on p. 13).

29. Ibid.

30. FBI PG 100A-18698, National Alliance aka Cosmotheist Community, Mill Point, Pocahontas County, West Virginia, May 1, 1987 ([Pierce] "is utilizing the Cosmotheist Church in effort to gain tax exempt status"); the Church apparently won federal and state tax-exempt status for all of his land in West Virginia, but then lost state exempt status except for 60 acres; William Pierce, "Investment of Powers of Trusteeship," for an unincorporated church, filed April 7, 1986.

31. "A Search for Values Toward a White Ethic," p. 13.

8. Nation and Race: Aryan Nations, Nehemiah Township, and Gordon Kahl

1. "Nehemiah Township Charter and Common Law Contract," notarized July 11, 1982, filed State of Idaho County of Kootenai, July 12, 1982; signatories included Richard Butler, Thom Robb, Edward Arlt, Roy B. Mansker, and Robert E. Miles.

2. Paul Arras, "Danger from the Extreme Right," April 9, 2001, web.syr.edu/~paaras/right.html.

3. "Nehemiah Township Charter and Common Law Contract," p. 4, no. 22; Daniel Levitas, *The Terrorist Next Door: The Militia Movement and the Radical Right* (New York: Thomas Dunne Books, 2002), p. 349.

4. "Announcing the Special Session Aryan Nations Congress," July 1986, agenda listing the variety of topics to be discussed; Floyd Cochran, interview with author, August 19–20, 1992, Kansas City, Missouri (Cochran had previously been an Aryan Nations officer and lived in the bunkhouse and worked in the offices); the first Aryan Nations Congress was in Hays, Kansas, on April 11, 12, and 13, 1980, per "Congress of Aryan Nationalists" brochure and Howard Richards, letter to the Hays newspaper, n.d., describing his "recording service" for the meeting.

5. Author, visit to Aryan Nations campground site with Kootenai County Undersheriff Larry Broadbent, 1986.

6. Floyd Cochran, interview with author, August 19–20, 1992, Kansas City, Missouri.

7. "Announcing the Special Session Aryan Nations Congress," July 1986, agenda listing the variety of topics to be discussed; "Announcing the Special Session Aryan Nations Congress," July 1987, agenda listing nine speakers with eight organizational affiliations; Hylah Jacques, reporting on the 1986 congress, August 1986.

8. Levitas, *The Terrorist Next Door*, pp. 7–8 (for origin of Posse), pp. 10–20 (Gale descended from Jewish parentage).

9. Levitas, *The Terrorist Next Door*, pp. 108–12, pp. 299–300; Leonard Zeskind (unsigned), "Background Report on Racist and Anti-Semitic Organizational Intervention in the Farm Protest Movement," n.d., Center for Democratic Renewal.

10. FBI MI 157-2768, "Sheriff's Posse Comitatus," Milwaukee, October 4, 1974; FBI 157-33487-32 (and other files in the 157-33487 series), "Sheriff's Posse Comitatus Marathon County Chapter Extremist Matters," December 19, 1974, FBI 157-33487.

11. Levitas, *The Terrorist Next Door*, 127–29 (emergence of Wickstrom), pp. 168–242 (shift to the Farm Belt Midwest).

12. Kevin Ristau and Mark Ritchie, "The Farm Crisis: History and Analysis," *Shmate: A Journal of Progressive Jewish Thought* 16 (Fall 1986): 10–20; "Crisis in Agriculture," www.nebraskastudies.org/1000/stories/1001_0100.html.

13. Osha Gray Davidson, *Broken Heartland: The Rise of America's Rural Ghetto* (New York: The Free Press, 1990), p. 17; U.S. Congress, Senate Committee on Governmental Affairs, Subcommittee on Intergovernmental Relations, 1986, "Governing the Heartland: Can Rural Communities Survive the Farm Crisis?" 99th Congress, 2nd Session, Draft Committee Print.

14. "Responding to the Rural Radical Right," *When Hate Groups Come to Town: A Handbook of Community Responses* rev. 2nd ed. (Center for Democratic Renewal, 1992), pp. 118–27.

15. Prairiefire Rural Action, "Rural Crisis Fact Sheet," n.d., prepared for the United Church Board for Homeland Ministries.

16. Levitas, *The Terrorist Next Door*, see in particular pp. 168–82, pp. 210–16.

17. James Wickstrom, *The American Farmer: 20th Century Slave*, n.d., Wisconsin Posse Comitatus; James Wickstrom, *Posse Noose Report*, March 1981; Donald E. Zabawa, "Statement," witnessed by KBI agents, May 23, 1984; Daniel Resnick, "Commission Urges FCC to Deny KTTL-FM License Renewal Request," *The Docket* 14, Newsletter of the Kansas Commission on Civil Rights (Summer, Fall 1983); William Potter Gale, "Remarks Advocating Violence," transcript compiled from National Identity Broadcast on station KTTL-FM, Exhibit 6.

18. Kansas Bureau of Investigation, "Testimony of Thomas E. Kelly, Director, Before House Judiciary Committee," February 21, 1983; Anonymous, "Report," K.B.I. Ref. no. 99-55879, March 29, 1982; Roger Verdon, "Weskan Training School Taught 'Killer Team' Tactics?" *The Salina Journal*, February 20, 1983.

19. William R. Ritz, "Farm Militants Study Bomb-Making," *The Denver Post*, February 13, 1983 (cites Eugene Schroder as the organizer); author, notes on Schroder presentation, "Mid-America Constitution Conference, America 96," June 9, 1996; "Grand Jury Convenes in Wichita, Kansas," *American Agriculture Movement Newsletter* 1, no. 1 (July 1995), (published by a group that claims to be the AAM office in Campo, Colorado); Carrie Fleider, "Minister of Propaganda: Eugene Schroder is a tireless promoter of common-law court theories," *Intelligence Report*, Spring 1997, pp. 15–17; Thomas A. Burzynski, "Is the Constitution Suspended?," *The New American*, February 5, 1996 (critique of Schroder from a Birch Society perspective).

20. William R. Ritz, "Farm Movement Sows Bitter Crop," "56 Received Instruction on Warfare," *Denver Post*, February 13, 1983.

21. Gordon Kahl, "I Gordon Kahl," handwritten sixteen-page letter, n.d.; this letter was typed and distributed by Aryan Nations with a "commendation" submitted from Nathan Bedford Forrest [Louis Beam], February 25, 1983; "Self-Described Christian Patriot Tells Story the Establishment Media Ignored," *The Spotlight*, June 20, 1983.

22. James Corcoran, *Bitter Harvest: Gordon Kahl and the Posse Comitatus, Murder in the Heartland* (New York: Viking Penguin, 1990), pp. 97–100.

23. Kahl, "I Gordon Kahl"; Corcoran, *Bitter Harvest*, p. 100.
24. Yorie Kahl, interview transcript beginning: "I'm in Lewisberg Penitentiary," www
.taoslandandfilm.com/Yorie.html.

9. Christian Patriots After Gordon Kahl

1. Author, notes and photos from personal observation of rally; "Datebook," *The Spotlight*, August 15, 1983, p. 21, advertisement for Gordon Kahl Memorial Arts and Crafts Festival; Joseph B. Verrengia, "Kansas Rally a Tribute to Slain Tax Protestor," *The Kansas City Times*, August 21, 1983; Jake Thompson, "Organizers of Kahl Rally See Themselves as Patriots," *The Kansas City Times*, August 18, 1983.
2. RGB (Richard Butler), "Announcement of Gordon Kahl Booklet," n.d., distributed on Aryan Nations letterhead; Len Martin, talk at Cheney Lake rally.
3. Ibid.
4. Author, notes and photos from rally, including "Memo on the Gordon Kahl Memorial Rally."
5. "Real Owners of Federal Reserve," Shive handout, no author, n.d. Handouts also included flyers for "Farmers Liberation Army," Halstead, Kansas.
6. Author, notes and photos from rally.
7. Ibid.
8. Ibid. Libby also handed out flyers for his pamphlet, with a Wichita postal box as a contact address.
9. Chief Justice Roger Brooke Taney, *Opinion of the Court in Dred Scott, Plaintiff in Error v. John F. A. Sandford*; Paul Finkleman, *Dred Scott v. Sandford: A Brief History with Documents* (New York: Bedford Books/St. Martin's, 1997). Judge Taney held that no black person—free or slave—could be considered a citizen of the United States.
10. "The Illegitimacy of the 14th Amendment," *Secessionist* no. 5, American Secessionist Project, www.secessionist.us/secessionist_no5.htm; "To Lose Our Sovereignty: Of the Dismantling of a Christian Nation," Republic vs. Democracy, n.d. ("Adoption of the Fourteenth [Amendment] was secured by military occupation of the Southern States").
11. Levitas, *The Terrorist Next Door*.
12. Robert W. Wangrud, "The Silent Roar," *Behold!* 2, no. 7 (July 1987); Robert W. Wangrud, "Martial Law or Law Martial," *Behold!* 5, no. 3 (March 1990); "To Lose Our Sovereignty: Of the Dismantling of a Christian Nation," Republic vs. Democracy, n.d.
13. "To Lose Our Sovereignty: Of the Dismantling of a Christian Nation," Republic vs. Democracy, n.d.
14. Russell Carollo, "A Look Back at Suspect's Lifestyle," *Texarkana Gazette*, November 17, 1982, reprinted July 2, 1984; Lyle McBride and Bill Webb, "Suspect in Shooting Described as Survivalist," *Texarkana Gazette*, July 1, 1984; "Mary Snell . . . A Woman of Valor," *The Jubilee*, May/June 1995 (Richard Wayne and Mary Jo Snell married May 31, 1948).
15. Arkansas State Police 49-997-84, Sergeant Mike Fletcher to Lieutenant Finis Duvall, July 4, 1984, re: Richard Wayne Snell: "He was a courier for Gordon Kahl . . ."; Alert Recovery, Inc. 3R8-51, 52, 53, report by Don Thornton on August 15, 1983, invoice to Farmers First National Bank; Arkansas State Police ASP-3-A, "Investigator's Notes," Inv. Charles Lambert, dictated July 2, 1984 (three felony warrants from Stephenville, Texas); Arkansas State Police ASP-3-A, Inv. Russell Welch, "Interview of Suspect," August 30, 1984.
16. ATF 53430 83 2006 H, Special Agent Bill Hobbs, "Report of Interview with Bill Thomas," May 3 and 5, 1985; Levitas, *The Terrorist Next Door*, pp. 220–22; Kevin Flynn and Gary Gerhardt, *The Silent Brotherhood: Inside America's Racist Underground* (New York: The Free Press, 1989), pp. 260–61.
17. ATF 53430 83 2006 H, Special Agent Bill Hobbs, "Report of Interview with Bill Thomas," May 3 and 5, 1985.
18. Arkansas State Police, ASP-4, Criminal Investigation Divisions Status Report, Final Disposition, "November 2, 1984, Wayne Snell was found guilty . . . of the crime of Capital Murder."
19. Lynn Mills, "Give me Liberty . . . or . . . ," *The Jubilee*, May/June 1995, "Snell was pronounced dead at 9:16 pm" (article includes a list of Snell's murder convictions).
20. Arkansas State Police CRL-49-997-84, State Bureau of Investigation Agents Kim Carter and Greg Glenn, "Inventory of Cream Colored Van," July 1, 1984.

10. Birth of the First Underground

1. *The Hammer: Anti-Racist, Anti-Fascist News and Analysis* 4 (August 1983), Institute for Research & Education on Human Rights, Inc., Kansas City, Missouri.

2. "White Separatist or Aryan Seditionist," *The Mountain Kirk*, n.d., includes "Biographical Chronology" (member of the "Youth Battalion of the White Russian VRNP" in 1936, recruited and trained volunteers for anti-Soviet Ukrainian field forces 1947 to 1970); James Ridgeway, *Blood in the Face: The Ku Klux Klan, Aryan Nations, Nazi Skinheads, and the Rise of a New White Culture* (New York: Thunder's Mouth Press, 1990), pp. 81–85; author, notes on multiple issues of Miles's newsletter, *From the Mountain*, 1981–91, which included autobiographical references.

3. Bob Miles, *From the Mountain*, January–February 1990 (includes pictures of Miles in Free French and other uniforms).

4. Bob Miles, "A Personal Update From the Mountain," January 2, 1991. In this one-page letter Miles acknowledges that many rumors exist.

5. Ridgeway, *Blood in the Face*, pp. 81–83.

6. Ridgeway, *Blood in the Face*, p. 83, quoting Tom Turnipseed, a campaign director for Wallace in 1968 who became a board member of the Center for Democratic Renewal and made similar comments to the author during their multiple conversations.

7. Robert E. Miles, "Letter to Robert Shelton, Imperial Wizard, United Klans of America," December 12, 1971, republished in *From the Mountain*, July 1972. Miles signed the letter as "Imperial Kludd" of the UKA.

8. "Klan Chaplain Held in Michigan Assault," UPI, published in *The Washington Post*, June 23, 1972; Jeffrey Hadden, "Former Klan Leader Miles Is Sentenced to 9 Years," *Detroit News*, October 27, 1973; Dorothy Miles, "Dear Friends" letter, *From the Mountain*, July 1972; Robert Miles, "What Feathers Do You Deserve," *From the Mountain*, July 1972.

9. Miles, "Dear Friends" letter.

10. Robert E. Miles, 33/5, printed and bound by the Mountain Church of Northern Ohio, 1983, (sixty-plus page booklet).

11. Robert E. Miles, 33/5, pp. 3–4.

12. Robert E. Miles, 33/5.

13. Robert E. Miles, *From the Mountain*, September–October 1987, p. 1 (description of Samhain in October as the "White Race's Holiday"; each spring a meeting coincided with the weekend nearest Hitler's birthday anniversary, April 20).

14. The Center for Democratic Renewal in Atlanta and the Southern Poverty Law Center's Klanwatch Project in Montgomery closely monitored the Georgia rallies during the period between 1986 and 1992, and usually reported on them in their respective publications, *The Monitor* and the *Klanwatch Intelligence Report*; Aryan Nations, "Announcing the Special Session Aryan Nations Congress, A.D. 12–13 July 1986" (invitation leaflet listing speakers, including "Robert Miles, Pastor, Mountain Church; Aryan Nations Ambassador").

15. Louis Beam often used the pseudonym Nathan Bedford Forrest, after the Confederate general who first led the Klan.

16. FBI, "Wanted By FBI Louis Ray Beam," Identification Order 5D40, June 17, 1987.

17. Louis Beam, *Essays of a Klansman* (Hayden Lake, Idaho: A.K.I.A. Publications, 1983), p. 36.

18. Ibid., p. 37.

19. Ibid., p. 39, "American political leaders committed us to a war they were determined to lose . . . When in spite of all their restrictive rules the American soldier still won on the battlefield—a political defeat was arranged to achieve the desired results."

20. Louis Beam, "Opening Statement," Seditious Conspiracy Trial in Fort Smith, February 17, 1988 (author notes at court).

21. Louis Beam, *Essays*, p. vi.

22. J. B. Campbell, "Louis and Sheila," *The Jubilee*, May/June 1994; Randall William, ed., *The Ku Klux Klan: A History of Racism and Violence* (Klanwatch Project of the Southern Poverty Law Center, 1981), p. 60 (profile of Louis Beam, includes 1981 conviction for paramilitary training in Texas); Morris Dees with James Corcoran, *Gathering Storm: America's Militia Threat* (New York: Harper Collins Publishers, 1996), p. 35.

23. "Secrecy Prevails in Klan [Border] Watch," *The Crusader*, 28 (photo cutline describes Beam as a Great Titan, a statewide title); *Vietnamese Fisherman's Association v. Knights of the Ku Klux Klan*, U.S. District Court Southern District of Texas, H-81-895, permanent injunction 1982, www.splcenter.org/legal/docket/files.jsp?cdrID+40&sortID+0; Grand Dragon Beam resigned from the Knights in 1981.

24. Photo of Louis Beam with cutline: "Beam forcibly removed the child from the mother's home," *Poverty Law Report*, March–April 1982, Southern Poverty Law Center; Bill Morlin, "One of the nation's leading racists . . . attempts to win joint custody," *The Spokesman-Review*, February 3, 2002 (ex-wife Kara Mikels dropped charges in the 1982 case).

25. Louis Beam, *Essays*, p. 8.

26. Louis Beam, "Interview with journalist at Christian Patriots Defense League Survival Conference," transcript forwarded to author, June 24, 1984.

27. Louis Beam, *Essays*, p. 15.

28. Ibid., p. 8.

29. Ibid., p. viii.

30. John C. Calhoun and Louis R. Beam, "The Perfected Order of the Klan," *Inter-Klan Newsletter and Survival Alert* 5, p. 5; John C. Calhoun, "Of Man, God, and War—Thoughts from the Fifth Era," *Inter-Klan Newsletter and Survival Alert!* 5, p. 10. Calhoun, who often coauthored articles with Beam, signed the article.

31. Louis R. Beam, Jr., "Klankraft and Klan History," in *Essays of a Klansman*, p. 17; Robert E. Miles, "Pull Away, Brethren, Pull Away," *Calling Our Nation*, 43.

32. Louis Beam, *Essays*, p. 17.

33. Robert Miles, 33/5, p. 10.

34. Louis Beam, "Leaderless Resistance," *Inter-Klan Newsletter & Survival Alert*, n.d. (1983).

35. Ibid.

36. "Leaderless Resistance" was republished on multiple occasions, but it was first written and published in the *Inter-Klan and Newsletter Alert* in 1983.

37. Carl Franklin, "One Army," *Calling Our Nation* 36, published by Aryan Nations–Teutonic Unity.

38. Ken Lawrence, "Behind the Klan's Karibbean Koup Attempt Parts I and II," *Covert Action Information Bulletin* 13 and 16 (July–August 1981 and March 1982); Warren Kinsella, *Web of Hate: Inside Canada's Far Right Network* (New York: HarperCollins Publishers, 1994), p. 204; Wade, *Fiery Cross*, pp. 372–73.

39. "Klan Moves Forward, Under New Grand Wizard," *Crusader: The Voice of the White Majority* 51 (January 1981), includes background on Don Black; Don Black, interviews with Evelyn Rich, March 12 and March 24, 1985.

40. "Grand Wiz'rd Imprisoned," *The White Patriot* 55 (January 1983): 5; Leonard Zeskind (unsigned), "Split in the Knights of the KKK, Black and Robb Vie for Power," *The Hammer: Anti-Racist, Anti-Fascist News and Analysis* 3 (May 1983). The Don Black faction published issues of the *White Patriot* and one issue called *White Knight* from Metairie, Louisiana; the Thom Robb faction published issues of the *White Patriot* from a Tuscumbia, Alabama, address.

41. Kevin Flynn and Gary Gerhardt, *The Silent Brotherhood* (New York: The Free Press, 1989), pp. 88–91.

42. NOFIT flyer from 1983. "NO MORE OF THE BANKER'S AND POLITICIANS' LIES. WE TRIED THE BALLOT BOX . . . IT'S TIME FOR A NEW 'BOSTON TEA PARTY.'"

43. "Farmers Join Truckers in Protests; Call for Massive Foreign Aid Cuts," *The Spotlight*, February 14, 1983; "No More Talk Say Farmers, Truckers," *The Spotlight*, March 31, 1983, p. 4.

44. Flynn and Gerhardt, *The Silent Brotherhood*, pp. 78–90.

11. Enclave Nationalism and The Order

1. Untitled article beginning "The Sixth General Convention will be held Saturday September 3," *National Alliance Bulletin*, February 1983, "Love at First Sight," photo cutline, *National Alliance Bulletin*, October 1983.

2. Robert Mathews, *A Call to Arms*, audiotape of 1983 speech (National Vanguard Books, 1991).

3. Ibid.

4. Robert Mathews, "To the Editor," letter explaining Mathews's views and the shoot-out involving Gary Yarborough, n.d., received at Aryan Nations headquarters, December 8, 1984, also reprinted in *The Secret Army or Wenn Alle Brüder Schweigen*, compilation by Fafnir [Robert Miles], Followers of the Way, Fowlerville, Michigan, 1985.

5. Ibid.: "Thus I have no choice. I must stand up like a white man and do battle."

6. "What It Will Take," unsigned editorial, *National Vanguard* 103 (January/February 1985): 2; "Political Justice," *National Vanguard* 106 (January/February 1986): 7; *The Secret Army or Wenn Alle Brüder Schweigen*, compilation by Fafnir [Robert Miles].

7. Wayne King, "23 in White Supremacist Group Are Indicted on Federal Charges," *The New York Times*, April 16, 1985; "Trooper Killed by Suspect," Associated Press, *The New York Times*, April 16, 1985; *United States v. Bruce Pierce, Gary Lee Yarborough, Randolph George Duey, Andrew Virgil Barnhill, Denver Daw Parmenter II, Richard Harold Kemp, Richard E. Scutari, David Eden Lane, Randall Paul Evans, Robert E. Merki, James Sherman Dye, Sharon K. Merki, Frank Lee Silva, Jean Margaret Craig, Randall Eugene Rader, Kenneth Joseph Loff, Ronald Allen King, David Tate, Thomas Bentley, Ardie McBrearty, Jackie Lee Norton, George Franklin Zaengle, William Anthony Nash*, U.S. District Court Western Washington at Seattle, CR85-001M, April 12, 1985.

8. *United States v. Bruce Pierce, Gary Lee Yarborough, et al.*; Kevin Flynn and John Gerhardt, *The Silent Brotherhood*, pp. 167–70, 203–207.

9. Flynn and Gerhardt, *The Silent Brotherhood*; Tom Martinez with John Guinther, *Brotherhood of Murder* (New York: McGraw-Hill, 1988); Stephen Singular, *Talked to Death* (New York: William Morrow, 1987).

10. Corcoran, *Bitter Harvest*, p. 245.

11. *United States of America v. Bruce Carroll Pierce, Gary Lee Yarborough, et al.*

12. *USA v. Pierce et al.*, Cr85-001M, transcript of opening statements.

13. "What It Will Take," editorial, *National Vanguard* 103 (January/February 1985): 3.

14. Robert Miles, *From the Mountain*, March/April 1985.

15. Ibid.

16. Benedict Anderson, *Imagined Communities: Reflections on the Origin and Spread of Nationalism* (London: Verso, 1991). Author thanks Chris Lutz for information about this book.

17. Robert E. Miles, "The Birth of a Nation: A Declaration of the Existence of a Racial Nation Within the Confines of a Hostile Political State," statement published by Mountain Church, n.d.

18. "Operations Report," and "Business Report," *NSV Report: A Quarterly Overview of the National Socialist Vanguard* 3, no. 3 (July/September 1985), The Dalles, Oregon.

19. Leonard Zeskind (unsigned), "Drive for 'Aryan Republic' Stalled," *The Monitor* 9 (November 1987), (notes Kim Badynski had moved); in November 1985, author informed participants in an Interstate Task Force on Human Rights meeting in Spokane about Miles's proposal.

20. "Declaring a Territorial Sanctuary," agenda item, Aryan Nations Congress, July 12–13, 1986; Richard Butler, "Dear Kinsmen," *Aryan Nations Newsletter* 63 (June 9, 1986): 2; *Calling Our Nation*, 53 (Aryan Nations): 1–2.

21. William Pierce, "A National Alliance Report," transcript of audiotape made by Russ Bellant, Free Association Forum, Cohoctah, Michigan, April 19–20, 1986.

22. "Living for Fitness," editorial, *National Vanguard* 106 (January/February 1986).

23. "Where Will It End," NAAWP News, no. 34, p. 10.

24. "Where Will It End," NAAWP News, no. 34. "It can end in racial civil war, in mongrelization, or it can end only to make way for a new beginning, the beginning of an all-white nation on this continent," Duke's National Association for the Advancement of White People concluded.

12. Origin of the Populist Party and the Break with Reaganism

1. Dardanelle, Arkansas, www.arkansas.com/city-listings/city_detail/city/Dardanelle; *Arkansas, Kansas, Missouri & Oklahoma Tourbook*, AAA, 2008, p. 37.

2. R. K. Travler, "Christians Laud New Party; Plan National Day of Prayer," *The Spotlight*, April 2, 1984, p. 26.

3. "Forbes Joined by Whites in Battle re Integration," *The National Chronicle* 20, no. 9 (March 18, 1971), includes pub box title "The Supremacy of the White Man Must Be Upheld," states that Forbes was active in the American Nazi Party from 1961 through 1968; Ralph Forbes, *Straight Shootin', The Chaplain's Report to White-Christian-America*, January 1983.

4. "Mrs. Stucki, Keys of Heaven—Ralph Forbes, Why we need a populist party by Bob Weems, Mt. Nebo, Arkansas, April 21, 1984," videotape.

5. Leonard Zeskind (State of the Union), "Klan and Skins Rally in Georgia," *Searchlight*, October 1989. Includes photo taken by author on September 2, 1989, of Weems in a Klan robe holding a sign reading "NAACP Planet of the Apes, One Nation Under ZOG."

6. "Klan Rally in Jackson, Mississippi," *The White Patriot: Worldwide Voice of the Aryan People* 2, no. 2 (March 1982): 2; Leonard Zeskind (unsigned), "When is a 'Populist' Really a Klansman?," *The Hammer* 7 (Summer 1984): 14–15; "Klan chaplain offers as candidate for the Fourth District seat," *Daily Herald* (Biloxi-Gulfport, Mississippi), April 20, 1981, "Robert Weems of Florence, the grand chaplain of the Invisible Empire, Knights of the Ku Klux Klan in Mississippi."

7. Robert Weems, "Why we need a populist party," April 21, 1984, from videotape.

8. Ibid.

9. Ibid.

10. Richard A. Viguerie, *The Establishment vs. The People: Is a New Populist Revolt on the Way?* (Chicago: Regnery Gateway, Inc., 1983).

11. Robert Allen, *Reluctant Reformers: The Impact of Racism on American Social Reform Movements* (Washington, D.C.: Howard University Press, 1974), pp. 49–79.

12. Michael Kazin, *The Populist Persuasion: An American History* (New York: Basic Books, 1995). Kazin is not without his critics, including Lawrence Goodwyn, author of *The Populist Moment: A Short History of Agrarian Revolt in America*. Nevertheless, all of Kazin's critics, by pointing to the varying and much different definitions of "real" populism, actually prove Kazin's point that "populism" is by itself an elastic term, devoid of specific ideological content.

13. "Report—Populist Convention, Nashville, TN 8/18–19. 1984."

14. Ibid.; "Report on the 1984 Populist Party Convention in Nashville, Tenn., August 17–19," communication forwarded to author.

15. Seymour Martin Lipset and Earl Raab, *The Politics of Unreason: Right-Wing Extremism in America 1790–1970* (New York: Harper & Row, 1970), p. 353. Cites Shearer as an AIP California factional spokesman in 1968 and leader at that time of the White Citizens Council of California.

16. Thomas James, "Ideological Merger Is Good for You," *The Spotlight*, April 9, 1984, p. 17; Populist Party, "National Convention August 17–19, 1984," agenda item, "Sunday August 19, 10:35 a.m. School of Politics, Dean William K. Shearer, Asst. Dean Willis A. Carto"; "Populist Party Executive Committee Looks to Future," *The American Independent*, William K. Shearer, publisher, January 1985.

17. Joe Brennan, "Populists Tap Richards and Salaman," *The Spotlight*, September 3, 1984; Kristine Jacobs, "The Populist Party, Liberty Lobby Merges with American Independence Party," *Interchange Report* 5, no. 2 (Fall 1984). Cites differences between Bob Richards and Willis Carto.

18. "Candidates Espouse America First," *The Spotlight*, September 3, 1984, pp. 1–3.

19. "Report—Populist Convention, Nashville, TN 8/18–19. 1984," communication to author. Report misspells Keith Shive's name as "Scheib," because the reporter only heard the name rather than saw it in print.

20. "Report on the 1984 Populist Party Convention in Nashville, Tenn., August 17–19," p. 3.

21. Randall Williams, letter to Lynn Wells, October 25, 1985; Richards registered his own political action committee; Kristine Jacobs, "The Populist Party, Liberty Lobby Merges with American Independence Party," *Interchange Report* V, no. 2 (Fall 1984).

22. *The American Independent*, William K. Shearer, publisher, January 1985 (for debt); Federal Election Commission records show the Populists receiving 66,241 votes; Michael Collins Piper, "Populist Party Showing Fast Growth," *The Spotlight*, January 7 and 14, 1985 (cites vote total at 63,864).

23. Leonard Zeskind, "It's Not Populism: America's New Populist Party a Fraud by Racists and Anti-Semites," Ken Lawrence, writing and research assistance, National Anti-Klan Network and Klanwatch Project of Southern Poverty Law Center, 1984.

24. William Shearer, *The American Independent*, November 1984, p. 4; William K. Shearer, "Populists for American First Ignore Irresponsible Attacks," *The Spotlight*, December 17, 1984, p. 2.

25. William K. Shearer, "Political Parties Have Duty to Present Responsible Image," *The California Statesman*, January 1986, p. 3.

26. "Populist Party Demands Accounting of Funds from Wily Willis Carto, He Responds by Trying to Destroy the Party," *The California Statesman*, April 1986; "No, Mr. Carto, Populists Are Not Republicans, Democrats, or Nazis," *The American Independent*, May 1986; William K. Shearer, "Liberty Lobby v. Shearer," *The California Statesman*, March 1991: "In early June 1987, I resigned as a member of the Populist Party's executive committee."

27. Richard Butler, "Editorial: At WAR," *Calling Our Nation* 45:2.

28. "Rolland Victor, the Populist Party's national vice-chairman for agriculture," photo cutline, *The Spotlight*, July 22, 1985, p. 22.

29. *Populist Party of Iowa, a non-profit corporation, plantiff v. Federal Reserve Board, defendant*, United States Court for the Southern District of Iowa, 85-626-B, filed August 2, 1985; "Harvesting Fear," *Iowa Illustrated* television program, KWWL-TV, Waterloo, Iowa, November 10, 1985.

30. Leonard Zeskind and Daniel Levitas (for Prairiefire Rural Action), *Far-Right Racist and Anti-Semitic Organizations Active in the Middle West and Iowa* (Center for Democratic Renewal, 1985), p. 12.

31. Sheldon Emry, *Billions for the Bankers, Debts for the People*, 30-page pamphlet, America's Promise, Phoenix, Arizona, n.d.

32. James Ridgeway, conversation with author, February 1986.

33. Lou Harris and Associates, Inc., "A Study of Anti-Semitism in Rural Iowa and Nebraska," conducted for the Anti-Defamation League of B'nai B'rith, February 1986, p. 7.

34. Author, notes and documents on mainstream liberal farm-related trainings, meetings, and other events between 1983 and 1988; Levitas, *The Terrorist Next Door*, pp. 278–83.

13. Europeans and Southerners at the Institute for Historical Review

1. Joseph Smith, "Revisionists Hold 7th Annual Conference Despite Opposition," *The Spotlight*, March 3, 1986; Michael Collins Piper, "Revisionists Slate 1986 Conference," *The Spotlight*, January 17, 1986; Russell Bellant, *Old Nazis, the New Right and the Republican Party* (Boston: South End Press, 1988, 1989, 1991).

2. Label Vitterman, communication to author describing the proceedings of the IHR conference, February 26, 1986; William Morrison from Angriff Press and World Service Library (video distributor) attended the conference, Russel Veh of the National Socialist League showed up, but stayed on the meeting's perimeter.

3. Evelyn Rich, communication to Center for Democratic Renewal, Joe Fields with pin.

4. Label Vitterman, communication with author, February 26, 1986.

5. "Joseph Moldiano," IHR Screen, memo-letter dated January 31, 1986; "Statement for Admission to Private Meeting," January 31, 1986.

6. Label Vitterman, communication to author.

7. Don Warren, communication to author, October 15, 1987 (Remer and Klapprott attended IHR's 1987 conference); "State Department Censorship Can't Scuttle 8th Conference," *IHR Newsletter*, October/November 1987.

8. "State Department Censorship Can't Scuttle 8th Conference": "Klapprott was indicted and tried in the notorious Sedition Trial of 1944," but not convicted.

9. Sam Dickson, *Shattering the Icon of Abraham Lincoln*, Institute for Historical Review, July 1993, "This paper was presented to the Seventh International Revisionist Conference, 1986 . . . ," (Lincoln like FDR, p. 17; crafty politician, p. 3; Northern sectionalist, p. 4; "opponent of slavery" and "committed to Negro equality at the inception of his career," p. 5; opposed Polk's war, p. 5).

10. Sam Dickson, *Shattering the Icon of Abraham Lincoln*, p. 7.

11. Who's Who in American Law, 1979 edition; Sam Dickson, transcription of June 19, 1986, program on WGST-Radio (the Atlanta program featured Sam Dickson and Lynn Wells as guests); Dickson repeatedly denied being a "white supremacist," despite the fact that he sneered at the notion of racial egalitarianism at every possible venue.

12. Sam Dickson, WGST-Radio ("As to my being against democracy," he claimed, "the founders of this country were against democracy"); Charles W. Griffin III, "Outside the Mainstream, at Home in Cobb County," *Fulton County Daily Report*, August 7, 1991.

13. "Consolidated Vote State Democratic and Republican General Primary Election August 8, 1978." Compiled by Ben W. Forston, Jr., secretary of state, Atlanta, Georgia; Sam Dickson, "Campaign Financing Disclosure Report," filed August 22, 1978.

14. Sam Dickson, WGST-Radio, "Dear Friend" invitation letter for Georgia Weekend on October 27, 1985, n.d., signed "Sincerely, Sam G. Dickson."

15. Sam Dickson, WGST-Radio.

16. Ibid.

17. Dr. E. R. Fields, "My Awakening," n.d. (Fields describes his education, his participation in various anti-Semitic enterprises, and the founding of the NSRP); "The History of the *Thunderbolt*," n.d., no author listed (but this four-pager bears the unmistakable style of Ed Fields), includes description of Fields as editor of a publication for the Columbians called *The Thunderbolt*; a 1984 split in the NSRP left Jerry Ray (brother of assassin James Earl Ray) in charge of the remains of the NSRP, and Fields held on to *The Thunderbolt*; Jerry Ray, letter with attachments to Lynn Wells, September 5, 1984.

18. Author, personal observation of Ed Fields at multiple Labor Day weekend Klan marches in Gainesville and other north Georgia communities from 1986–1991.

19. Frederick J. Simonelli, *American Fuehrer: George Lincoln Rockwell and the American Nazi Party* (Urbana: University of Illinois Press, 1999); Patsy Sims, *The Klan* 2nd ed. (Lexington: University Press of Kentucky, 1996); Evelyn Rich, communication to Center for Democratic Renewal, n.d. (February 1986).

20. Evelyn Rich, written communication with Center for Democratic Renewal, verbal communication with author, February 21, 1986.

21. Ibid.

22. Sam Dickson, *Shattering the Icon*, p. 2.

23. Wilmot Robertson, *Dispossessed Majority* (Howard Allen Enterprises, 1987), p. 14. Robertson cited Stephens from Charles and Mary Beard in *The Rise of American Civilization*; an Internet version of Stephens's speech has different punctuation.

24. Ibid., p. 77.

25. Ibid., p. 78.

26. Wilmot Robertson, *The Ethnostate* (Cape Canaveral, Fla.: Howard Allen Enterprises, 1992), p. 13.

27. Robertson, *Dispossessed Majority*, p. 151.

28. Ibid., pp. 14–15; Ted O'Keefe, "Mead, Freeman, Boas: Jewish Anthropology Comes of Age in America," *National Vanguard*, June 1983.

29. "The IHR Radio Project," *IHR Newsletter*, April 1986; "The IHR Radio Project," *IHR Newsletter*, July 1986 ("The Radio Project as a source for radio news journalists to get the 'other side' of the holocaust"); Label Vitterman, personal communication to author, February 1986.

30. "Farrakhan Says Libyan Leader Will Address Convention," United Press International, February 23, 1985; Mattias Gardell, *Countdown to Armageddon: Louis Farrakhan and the Nation of Islam* (London: C. Hurst and Company, 1996).

14. White Riot in Forsyth County on King Day

1. Jesse Helms, "Remarks of Senator Jesse Helms," *Congressional Quarterly* 129, no. 130 (October 32, 1983), S13452–S13461, republished and distributed as a pamphlet; Dr. E. R. Fields, "Martin Luther King's Communist Record," *White Patriot*, April 1986, p. 2; "A Report on the King Holiday Protest March and Rally," *White Patriot*, April 1986, p. 1.

2. Dr. Martin Luther King, Jr., of course, was not solely responsible for creating a post–Jim Crow U.S., any more than George Washington was the single founder of the country. But

the holiday named in his honor has become, for many, a time for celebrations of the country's "diversity" and for recollection of the civil rights struggles of the past.

3. Dean Carter, letter to *Forsyth County News*, May 3, 1987, "There has been a great deal of misunderstanding surrounding . . . the walks for brotherhood I organized in your community."

4. Abby L. Ferber, *White Man Falling: Race, Gender, and White Supremacy* (Lanham, Md.: Rowman & Littlefield Publishers, 1999), pp. 85–95; Grace Elizabeth Hale, *The Making of Whiteness: The Culture of Segregation in the South* (New York: Vintage Books, 1998), pp. 227–39.

5. "White Power Rally Begins at 9:30 a.m. Saturday, January 17, 1987," leaflet distributed in north Georgia, Committee to Keep Forsyth and Dawson Counties White.

6. *Hosea Williams, individually and on behalf of all black citizens of the State of Georgia, Plaintiffs v. Southern White Knights, Knights of the Ku Klux Klan, et al.*, U. S. District Court Northern District of Georgia, Atlanta Division, Civil Action no. C87-565A, filed March 24, 1987 (this was a class-action case pursued by Southern Poverty Law Center lawyers); as the case went to the jury it was renamed because of a change in the primary plaintiff, *James E. McKinney v. Southern White Knights et al.*; "Judgment," Civil Action no. 1:87-cv-565-CAM, October 25, 1988.

7. "Weekly Update," Center for Democratic Renewal, January 18, 1987 (a participant-observer reported, "It was a lynch-mob . . . it was planned and organized"); "Thousands Respond to Klan Violence," *The Monitor* 6 (March 1987): 2, Center for Democratic Renewal; John Brady and Joe Earle, "Violent Protestors Disrupt Forsyth March," *The Atlanta Journal-Constitution*, January 18, 1987.

8. "Weekly Update," Center for Democratic Renewal, January 18, 1987; "Thousands Respond to Klan Violence," *The Monitor* 6 (March 1987): 2; "Is This North Georgia's Future," *The Monitor* 7 (August 1987).

9. Sheriff Wesley Walraven, testimony September 21, 1988, notes by Mark Alfonso, *Hosea Williams, individually and on behalf of all black citizens of the State of Georgia, Plaintiffs v. Southern White Knights, Knights of the Ku Klux Klan, et al.* Walraven testified that the brotherhooders walked 2,251 feet from the Bethelview Rd. intersection before they were forced to end the march.

10. Brady and Earle, "Violent Protestors Disrupt Forsyth March": "After the march, nearly 1,000 Klansmen and sympathizers assembled at the Forsyth County Courthouse"; Wade, *The Fiery Cross*, p. 302 (for Stoner).

11. Carter, *Politics of Rage*, p. 216.

12. Mabelle Segrest, affidavit, *Williams et al. v. Southern White Knights et al.*, November 10, 1987; Daniel Carver, telephone message, January 18, 1987, transcript by Mark Alfonso.

13. "A Confederate Battle Reenactment: Forsyth County, Georgia, Jan. 17," photos by Dr. Fields, *The Thunderbolt* 316:3.

14. Wali Muhammad, "Forsyth County Outrage: Story of Black Expulsion," *Atlanta Voice*, January 31, 1987 (credits C. B. Hackworth 1986 story in *Creative Loafing*).

15. Mike Christensen, "Rape, Lynching of 1912 Bitter Legacy in Forsyth," *The Atlanta Journal*, January 20, 1987; Wali Akbar Muhammad, "How African-Americans Were Forced Out of Forsyth County, Ga.," *The Brandon Institute for International Studies and Commerce News*, January 1987 (cites *Dahlonega Nugget*, October 11, 1912); Debbie McDonald "Why Forsyth is White," *Gainesville Times*, n.d.

16. Herbert Shapiro, *White Violence and Black Response: From Reconstruction to Montgomery* (Amherst: The University of Massachusetts Press, 1988). NAACP advertisement in *The New York Times*, November 23, 1922, reproduced after p. 304.

17. Shapiro, *White Violence and Black Response*, p. 98.

18. Ibid., p. 99.

19. George M. Fredrickson, *White Supremacy: A Comparative Study in American and South African History* (New York: Oxford University Press, 1981), pp. 226–27; Michael D'Orso, *Like Judgment Day: The Ruin and Redemption of a Town Called Rosewood* (New York: Boulevard Books, 1996); Shapiro, *White Violence and Black Response*, pp. 107, 115–17, 155–52, 180–85.

20. James Baldwin, "On Being 'White' . . . and Other Lies," in *Black on White: Writers on What It Means to Be White*, David Roediger, ed. (New York: Schocken Books, 1998).

21. Scott Thurston and Ron Taylor, "Forsyth Violence Provides Rallying Cry for Participants, Crowd in King Parade, *The Atlanta Journal*, January 20, 1987; "On the March for Human Rights: UAW Members Brave the Klan's Threats as They Walk Peacefully Through Forsyth County Georgia," *Solidarity* 30, no. 1 (February 1987): 8.

22. "Weekly Update," Center for Democratic Renewal, February 1, 1987 (cites rallies in Easton, Maryland; Louisville, Kentucky; St. Louis University, and canceling of two sports games involving the Forsyth County High School team). Author was working in Atlanta for the Center for Democratic Renewal at the time, notes and multiple reports, national and international television news covered the Forsyth County events.

23. Mike Christensen, "20,000 march on Forsyth County," *The Atlanta Journal-Constitution*, January 25, 1987; Dudly Clendinen, "10,000 in March for Civil Rights Jeered by Klan in Georgia Town," *The New York Times*, January 25, 1987; staff reports by participant-observers, Center for Democratic Renewal.

24. "White Power Rally Begins at 9:30 a.m. Saturday January 24, 1987," leaflet, the Committee to Keep Forsyth and Dawson Counties White, n.d.; "Debriefing of Thaddeus after the Forsyth County Brotherhood II March on January 24, 1987," Center for Democratic Renewal, p. 4.

25. "3,000 White Patriots March in Forsyth," *The Thunderbolt* 316, Ed Fields, ed. (describes the white supremacist march); Ed Fields, "Forsyth White Uprising Inspires Nation," newsletter, February 1987; "Debriefing of Thaddeus . . . January 24, 1987," p. 5 (saw Duke, Black, and Ed Fields speaking to the crowd).

26. "Grand Wizard Freed! Don Black Returns," *White Patriot, Worldwide Voice of the Aryan People* 61, n.d. Black was released from prison in January 1985.

27. "3,000 White Patriots March in Forsyth," and "Police Brutality Charged GBI in Forsyth," *The Thunderbolt* 316, Ed Fields, ed., pp. 1, 5 (describes arrest of David Duke, Don Black, and Frank Shirley); Charles Walston and John Brady, "56 People Charged in Forsyth County, but None Were Civil Rights Marchers," *The Atlanta Journal-Constitution*, January 26, 1987; Tyler Bridges, *The Rise of David Duke*, p. 130 (on June 27, 1987, Duke pleaded "no contest" to blocking a roadway).

28. "Debriefing of Thaddeus . . . January 24, 1987," Center for Democratic Renewal, p. 9; Bill Montgomery, "Huge Size of 'Army' Stuns Foes," *The Atlanta Journal-Constitution*, January 25, 1987.

29. Thom Robb, "Gas Gays," *The Torch* 9, no. 3 (July 1977).

30. Thom Robb, "It's Their Government," *The Torch* 119 (October 1983).

31. "Grand Wiz'rd Imprisoned," *The White Patriot* 55 (January 1983).

32. "White Nationalists Bounce Back," *Frontline* (publication of the Southern National Front) 2, no. 2 (March 1987): 8–9 (describes march through Raleigh on January 18); Cecil Cox, "A letter from Cecil Cox to Members of the White Patriot Party," n.d. (announces formation of the Southern National Front); Judge W. Earl Britt, "Order," *Bobby Person v. Carolina Knights of the Ku Klux Klan, Glen Miller, et al.*, U.S. District Court for Eastern District of North Carolina, Raleigh Division, 84-534, January 18, 1985 (case pursued and won by the Southern Poverty Law Center).

33. "'Democracy Never Works' Says WPP at January Convention in N.C.," *The Monitor* 1, no. 1 (January 1986); "Thousands of Southern White Patriot Soldiers Are Marching and Rallying Across Dixie," and Glen Miller, "Our Plan," *The Confederate Leader*, Special Introductory Issue, n.d.

34. "White Patriots and the Southern Poverty Law Center," *1986 Report: Bigoted Violence and Hate Group Activity in North Carolina*, North Carolinians Against Racist and Religious Violence; "Miller, Patriots Convicted of Contempt," *Newsletter* 4 (Fall 1986), North Carolinians Against Racist and Religious Violence (articles include summary of testimony about weapons, paramilitary training, etc., contempt trial in September 1986).

35. "White Nationalists Bounce Back," *Frontline* 2, no. 2 (March 1987): 8–9, publication of the Southern National Front (describes march through Raleigh on January 18).

36. "3 Killed in Adult Book Store," "Officers Believe Store Linked to Organized Crime," *The Shelby* (N.C.) *Star*, January 19, 1987.

37. Pat Reese, "White Supremacists Suspects in Killings," *The Fayetteville Observer* (Fayetteville, N.C.), September 4, 1987; Mab Segrest, "Background Memo on the Shelby Bookstore Murders and Possible Neo-Nazi Involvement," North Carolinians Against Racist and Religious Violence, n.d.; "White Patriots Indicted in Carolina Execution-Style Killings," *The Monitor*, January 1988.

38. Mab Segrest, *Memoir of a Race Traitor* (Boston: South End Press, 1994), pp. 149–64. Segrest worked at North Carolinians Against Racist and Religious Violence at the time.

39. "Summary of Trial of Douglas Sheets for Shelby III Murders," May 1989, from *Shelby Star*, *Charlotte Observer*, and *Monitor*'s notes," file memo from North Carolinians Against Racist and Religious Violence.

40. *Anti-Gay Violence and Victimization in 1985*, a Report by the Violence Project of the National Gay and Lesbian Task Force; *Anti-Gay Violence and Victimization in 1986*, a Report by the National Gay and Lesbian Task Force; Mab Segrest and Leonard Zeskind, *Quarantines and Death: The Far Right's Homophobic Agenda*, Center for Democratic Renewal, 1989.

41. Segrest and Zeskind, *Quarantines and Death*.

42. Leonard Zeskind (unsigned), "Identity Group Defeats Anti-Discrimination Ordinance," *The Monitor* 15 (May 1989).

43. David Duke, *My Awakening* (Covington, La: Free Speech Press, 1998), p. 610.

15. David Duke, the Democratic Party Candidate

1. David Duke, speech at Populist Party National Committee, Sewickly, Pennsylvania, March 7, 1987; Marek Lumb, communication to author (included audiotapes of the proceedings, March 1987); "Is This North Georgia's Future?: Racist Organizing Follows Brotherhood March," *The Monitor* 7 (August 1987).

2. "More to March Than Meets the Eye," *The Spotlight*, March 16, 1987, p. 23.

3. Joe Brennan, "FEC Slaps Down Shearer," *The Spotlight*, March 23, 1987, p. 1.

4. "Groundswell Building for Hansen to Run for President," *The Populist Observer* 13 (February 1987): 2.

5. Joe Brennan, "Populists Meet in Washington, Vote to End Era of Boss Rule," *The Spotlight*, February 16, 1987; "McIntyre Named Party Chairman," *The Spotlight*, "Rarick Rebukes Californian," *The Spotlight*, February 16, 1987, pp. 12–13; "Statement to Be Filed with the FEC," *The Spotlight*, August 25, 1986, p. 5.

6. Brennan, "Populists Meet in Washington" (sets meeting date in Sewickly); the Shearer group met that same day in Dallas, Texas.

7. Marek Lumb; communication to author; Michael Collins Piper, "Populist Party Rises from the Ashes," *The Spotlight*, March 23, 1987, p. 5.

8. Marek Lumb, "McIntyre Named Party Chairman," *The Spotlight*, February 16, 1987, p. 12.

9. Marek Lumb, communication to author, March 1987.

10. Marek Lumb; Piper, "Populist Party Rises from the Ashes."

11. "Hansen, George Vernon, (1930–)," *Biographical Directory of the United States Congress*, bioguide.cingress.gov.

12. "Ex-Rep. Hansen Is Arrested in Omaha Airport," Associated Press, *The Des Moines Register*, April 16, 1987.

13. Christopher Smith, "Idaho's George Hansen Takes on Another Cause," *The Idaho Statesman*, December 7, 2007 ("the Supreme Court vindication" on the ethics conviction in 1984).

14. Mrs. Connie Hansen, "Dear Friend of Liberty Lobby and *The Spotlight*," n.d.

15. Michael Collins Piper, "Hansen Speaks Freely," *The Spotlight*, January 5 and 12, 1987; Michael Collins Piper, "Hansen Compares Himself to Political Prisoners Elsewhere," *The Spotlight*, January 19, 1987; Michael Collins Piper, "Hansen Faced 'Catch-22' in Fund-Raising Reports," *The Spotlight*, January 26, 1987.

16. "Groundswell Building for Hansen to Run for President," *The Populist Observer* 13 (February 1987), pp. 1–2.

17. Communication to author, audiotapes made by a meeting attendee, March 7, 1987; Piper, "Populist Party Rises from the Ashes": "Hansen graciously informed . . . he was willing to serve as the party's stand-in candidate."

18. Author, personal observation, June 8, 1987 (as Dickson strolled by with Don Black and

Evelyn Rich, he smiled and waved his hand and said "Shalom Shalom" to author and Mark Alfonso).

19. Mark Alfonso, "Report on Duke Meeting," Center for Democratic Renewal, June 8, 1987; author, photos and notes; "More to March Than Meets the Eye," *The Spotlight*, March 16, 1987 (mentions Shirley's arrest).

20. James Yarborough, conversation with author, Marriott Inn, Marietta, Georgia, June 8, 1987.

21. Robert Morrow, "Nationalist's Campaign Bid Seen Shaking Democrats," *The Spotlight*, May 25, 1987, p. 10.

22. Leonard Zeskind (unsigned), "Watch for Far Right to Try a Larger Strategy in '88 Elections," *The Monitor* (August 1987); "Duke Will Run For President," *NAAWP News* 46, published by the National Association for the Advancement of White People; David Duke, "Dear Friend," letter about campaign funds insert in *NAAWP News* 46.

23. Paul C. Peterson, "Duke May Run For President, David Duke vs Jesse Jackson," *NAAWP News* 45; "Weekly Update," Center for Democratic Renewal, October 19, 1987.

24. Democratic National Committee, "Chairman Kirk Disavows Ku Klux Klan President Candidacy: Alerts State Parties," *Democratic News*, June 9, 1987.

25. "Populist Party: We Want Hansen! Convention Big Success," *The Populist Observer* 21 (October 1987): 1–7, Marek Lumb, verbal communication to author; Bob Jay, verbal communication to author.

26. "Weekly Update," Center for Democratic Renewal, September 8, 1987 (CDR staff and volunteers closely monitored this event).

27. "Populist Party: We Want Hansen," October 1987, no. 21, p. 2 (for McIntyre quote); Marek Lumb, "Populist Party Convention September 4–6, 1987, St. Louis Holiday Inn Airport North," report communicated to author.

28. "Populist Party: We Want Hansen! Convention Big Success," *The Populist Observer*; Marek Lumb, verbal communication to author, September 7, 1987.

29. "Populist Party: We Want Hansen! Convention Big Success"; Tom McIntyre, "To Be or Not to Be? Hansen Mulls Over Populist Party Nomination," *The Populist Observer* 22 (November 1987): 1–2.

30. Bob Jay, verbal communication to author, September 6, 1987; Marek Lumb, verbal communication to author, September 7, 1987.

31. "Violent Incidents Continue in Georgia," *The Monitor* 8 (September 1987).

32. "Far Right Youth Recruitment Serious Long Term Threat," *The Monitor* 8 (September 1987).

33. Joseph Sobran, "The Use and Abuse of Race," *National Review*, March 27, 1987.

34. "Weekly Update," March 22, 1987 (cites Wallace Warfield as acting director, testimony on February 24, 1987).

35. "Weekly Update," February 7, 1987.

16. Crackdown and Indictment at Fort Smith

1. Sheila Beam, "Affidavit of Sheila Marie Toohey Beam," signed and notarized December 17, 1987, Harris County, Texas; J. R. Campbell, "Louis and Sheila," *The Jubilee*, May/June 1994, pp. 12–15; Bill Minutaglio, "Biography of a Hatemonger," *Dallas Life Magazine*, May 22, 1988.

2. Sheila Beam, "Affidavit of Sheila Marie Toohey Beam."

3. FBI, "Wanted By FBI: Louis Ray Beam," Identification Order 5D4D, June 17, 1987.

4. "White Supremacist," Associated Press, November 24, 1987; "Beam-Chiropractor," Associated Press, November 25, 1987.

5. Louis Beam, audiotape number RMR05, Scriptures for America Ministry, recorded at "Meeting of Christian Men," in Estes Park, Colorado, October 23–25, 1992.

6. "Beam," Associated Press, November 19, 1987; "Beam Moved," Associated Press, November 20, 1987. Beam went on a hunger strike and was transferred to Springfield Federal Penitentiary.

7. The Southern Poverty Law Center pursued lawsuits against violence by white supremacists, including: *Brown v. Invisible Empire of the KKK*, *Association of Vietnamese Fishermen v. Knights of the KKK*, *Beulah Mae Donald v. United Klans*, *Benahu v. Metzger*, *Mansfield v. Church of the Creator*.

8. T. R. Reid, "2 Neo-Nazis Convicted in Radio Host's Murder," *The Washington Post*, November 18, 1987; author interviews with Colorado authorities conducted December 1995.

9. *United States of America vs. Robert Edward Miles, Louis Ray Beam, Jr., Richard Girnt Butler, Richard Joseph Scutari, Bruce Carroll Pierce, Andrew Virgil Barnhill, Ardie McBrearty, David Eden Lane, Lambert Miller, Robert Neil Smalley, Ivan Ray Wade, Richard Wayne Snell, David Michael McGuire*, United States District Court, Western District of Arkansas, Fort Smith Division, Criminal no. 87-20008-01-14.

10. Farris L. Genide, FBI special agent, "Affidavit," *In the Matter of the Application of the United States of America for an Order Authorizing the Interception of Wire Communications*, United States District Court, Western District of Michigan, Southern Division, Misc. no. 86-0343, p. 9.

11. Unlike other commanders, however, Mathews participated personally in everything from bank car robberies to recruiting—exposing him to just the kind of potential informant that toppled him and then the group.

12. "Sedition, Subversive Activities and Treason to Shipping," *American Jurisprudence: A Modern Comprehensive Text Statement of American Law*, 2nd ed., vol. 70 (The Lawyers Co-operative Publishing Co. and Bancroft Whitney, 1987), p. 13.

13. Stephen M. Kohn, *American Political Prisoners: Prosecutions Under the Espionage and Sedition Acts*, (Westport, Conn.: Praeger Publishers, 1994), p. 14.

14. "Sedition, Subversive Activities and Treason to Shipping," *American Jurisprudence* 2nd ed., vol. 70, p. 12.

15. Ibid. (on the actual status of these laws the literature seemed to be contradictory).

16. Kohn, *American Political Prisoners*, pp. 8–21.

17. The Smith Act is 18 USCS S 2385.

18. Leo P. Ribuffo, *The Old Christian Right: The Protestant Far Right from the Great Depression to the Cold War* (Philadelphia: Temple University Press, 1983), p. 194; John Edgerton, *Speak Now Against the Day: The Generation Before the Civil Rights Movement in the South* (Chapel Hill: The University of North Carolina Press, 1994), p. 503; Kohn, *American Political Prisoners*, p. 21.

19. Edgerton, *Speak Now Against the Day*, pp. 221–22.

20. Lawrence Reilly, *The Sedition Case* (Metairie, La.: Sons of Liberty, first printing 1953, third printing 1985), p. 31.

21. Reilly, *The Sedition Case*, p. 42; Justin Raimondo, "Reactionary Radicals, Radical Reactionaries: Tales of a "Seditionist," The Story of Lawrence Dennis, *Chronicles*, May 2000, pp. 19–22; Ribuffo, *The Old Christian Right*, pp. 198–215.

22. Albert J. Lima, "The Smith Act: An Inside Look," *The Guild Practitioner* 38, no. 1 (Winter 1981), Lima cites *Dennis v. United States*, 341 US 494, 1951; Mr. Justice Black dissenting, www.tourolaw.edu/patch/Dennis/Douglas.html (accessed September 13, 2000).

23. Peggy Dennis, *The Autobiography of an American Communist: A Personal View of a Political Life, 1925–1975* (Westport, Conn.: Lawrence Hill & Co., 1977), pp. 172–215; Al Richmond, *A Long View from the Left* (New York: Dell, 1972), pp. 298–366; Kohn, *American Political Prisoners*, p. 21 (a total of 185 Communist Party and Socialist Workers Party leaders were indicted under the Smith Act).

24. Bradley T. Winter, "Invidious Prosecution: The History of Seditious Conspiracy—Foreshadowing the Recent Convictions of Sheik Omar Abdel-Rahman and His Immigrant Followers," *Georgetown Immigration Law Journal* 10, no. 2, 191.

25. Katherine Bishop, "U.S. Dusts Off an Old Law," *The New York Times*, March 27, 1988; Winter, "Invidious Prosecution," pp. 191–202, 206.

26. Winter, "Invidious Prosecution," p. 206.

27. "Government's Pre-Trial Memorandum," *United States of America v. Robert Miles et al.*, United States District Court, Western District of Arkansas, Fort Smith Division, Criminal no. 87-20008, filed February 9, 1988, pp. 13–14.

28. Anderson, *Imagined Communities*.

17. Before the Trial Begins

1. Leonard Zeskind, "Sedition Trial Reveals Inner Workings of Racist Underground," *The Monitor* 11 (April 1988), (includes photo of march with banner); notes and photos sent to author of February 13 march; Cheri Peters, producer, *Sedition USSA-Style*, Video Truth Network, Scriptures for America (includes some footage from the march).

2. Joe Grego, "The Klan Blitz Through Arkansas," *White Patriot* 76 (this entire issue recounted the various rallies); "Arkansas," 1988 activity report, *White Patriot* 77; "Thom Robb's Street Action Defense Plan," *The Thunderbolt* 326.

3. Founded by Gerald L. K. Smith, well known for his anti-Semitism and racism, the Great Passion Play Theme Park outside Eureka Springs, Arkansas, features a sixty-seven-foot tall "Christ of the Ozarks" statue. The park is now under new management.

4. "Sedition Trial—Sedition Tour," Oklahoma White Man's Association newsletter, n.d. Joe Grego and John Clary had helped Thom Robb with the rallies, but later aligned themselves for a short while with Tom Metzger's White Aryan Resistance.

5. "Sedition Trial—Sedition Tour."

6. Thom Robb, "A Statement to the Media," April 27, 1987, reproduced in *White Power*, n.d., p. 2.

7. "Important! Read this Paper! Butler and Miles Indicted!" and "Be Honest," *White Patriot*, n.d.

8. "Race: Our Own Television Talkshow," *WAR '84* 3, no. 5, White Aryan Resistance, ed. Tom Metzger; "Aryan Entertainment," videotape "No. 304 Ku Klux Klan—P.O.W. Frank Silva," *WAR* 8, no. 3.

9. "Welcome to the White American Resistance Information Network," SYSOP Alex Foxe, July 15, 1985, printout of computer bulletin board log-on session, includes listings for five other bulletin board phone numbers, three pages of names and addresses of white nationalist organizations, a catalogue of "Race and Reason" videotapes, and a list of cable stations that broadcast that program.

10. Tom Metzger, "Dear Racial Comrade," letter, February 22, 1988; "Sedition Trial Reveals Inner Workings of Racist Underground," *The Monitor* 11 (includes photo of Metzger with armband).

11. "Sedition Law Threatens Free Speech," *The Thunderbolt* 324, ed. and publisher Ed Fields.

12. Ibid.

13. Larry Lee, "Request for Acquittal Denied," *Southwest Times Record*, March 26, 1988.

14. "Why Bob Mathews Fought to the Death," "Public Idolized Bob Mathews," "Bob Was a Very Special Man—We Were Always in Love," Ed Fields interview with Mrs. Bob Mathews, "Watch for this Arch-Traitor" (about Tom Martinez), *The Thunderbolt* 302, "Special Bob Mathews Memorial Edition."

15. Thom Robb, "To Those Who Didn't Understand," *White Patriot* 76, p. 6.

16. Tom Metzger, recorded phone message, War Hotline; similar ideas are found in Tom Metzger, "Ft. Smith Inquisition," *WAR '88* 7, no. 2, p. 1.

17. Richard Butler, "RE: Sedition Alert," letter sent to Aryan Nations list, December 16, 1986.

18. Robert Miles, *From the Mountain*, March/April 1987, p. 1.

19. Dorothy Miles, letter, n.d.

20. "Sedition—To Be or Not To Be?," *Aryan Nations Newsletter*, 67.

18. Seditious Conspiracy Goes to Trial

1. Author, notes, observations and court documents, February 15–19, 1988; J. Michael Martinez and Robert M. Harris, "Graves, Worms and Epitaphs: Confederate Monuments in the Southern Landscape," eds. J. Michael Martinez, William D. Richardson, and Ron McNinch-Su, *Confederate Symbols in the Contemporary South* (Gainesville: University Press of Florida, 2000); Patricia L. Faust, *Historical Times Illustrated Encyclopedia of the Civil War* (New York: Harper & Row, 1986), pp. 22, 278.

2. Author notes, February 16, 1988; Rodney Bowers, "Jury Seated in Sedition Case," *Arkansas Gazette*, February 17, 1988; Larry Lee, "All-White Jury to Hear Sedition Case," *Southwest Times Record*, February 17, 1988.

3. Larry Lee, "Evidence Leads to Threat of Mistrial," *Southwest Times Record*, March 11, 1988; Larry Lee, "Government Case Takes It on the Chin," *Southwest Times Record*,

March 18, 1988; Larry Lee, "Act II of Sedition Trial to Begin," *Southwest Times Record*, March 20, 1988: "Government attorneys have been stung by Arnold's multiple rulings suppressing numerous pieces of evidence."

4. Author, notes on Hoffmeister's opening statement, February 17, 1988; "Chris Notes," Center for Democratic Renewal staff observations, February 17, 1988.

5. Larry Lee, "Attorney Tells Strange Story," *Southwest Times Record* (Fort Smith), April 6, 1988, p. 7A.

6. Ben Stocking, "Hate Groups Have an Ally in Lawyer," *Raleigh News & Observer*, April 19, 1992, p. 15A.

7. James Ridgeway and Leonard Zeskind, "Can Timothy McVeigh Beat the Death Penalty," *The Village Voice*, April 9, 1996. During an interview with Ridgeway and Zeskind, Elohim City chief Robert Millar confirmed Lyon's 1988 stay.

8. Author's notes on Pierce's demeanor from personal observation at the Seattle RICO trial and the Fort Smith trial; Flynn and Gerhardt, *The Silent Brotherhood*, p. 396 (Pierce sentenced to 100 years in Seattle and an additional 150 years in the Berg civil rights trial in Denver).

9. Flynn and Gerhardt, *The Silent Brotherhood*, p. 395 (Lane sentenced to forty years in Seattle and an additional nonconsecutive 150 years in the Berg civil rights trial in Denver).

10. Flynn and Gerhardt, *The Silent Brotherhood*, p. 397 (Scutari sentenced to forty years for racketeering and twenty years for the Ukiah robbery).

11. Flynn and Gerhardt, *The Silent Brotherhood*, p. 392 (Barnhill sentenced to forty years for racketeering).

12. Flynn and Gerhardt, *The Silent Brotherhood*, p. 395 (McBrearty sentenced to forty years for racketeering).

13. Flynn and Gerhardt, *The Silent Brotherhood*, p. 398 (Smalley was sentenced to five years in a previous gun case).

14. "Government's Pre-Trial Memorandum," *United States of America v. Robert E. Miles et al.*, U.S. District Court for Western Arkansas Fort Smith Division, Criminal no. 87-20008, pp. 16–19.

15. Robert Miles, "Mrs. Snell," *From the Mountain*, May–June 1988; "The Clock Is Ticking for Death Row Captive Richard Snell," *The Jubilee*, January/February 1995; *The Last Call Bulletin*, November/December 1989; Mary Snell, publisher, The Last Call Ministries, letter to subscriber, July 11, 1990.

16. Author, notes taken during prosecution's opening statement, February 17, 1988.

17. Author, notes on Beam's opening statement, February 17, 1988.

18. Beam, *Essays*, p. vi.

19. Author's notes.

20. "Sedition Trial," Associated Press, February 9, 1998 (judge throws out evidence on Beam).

21. Robert Miles, "Introduction of Glen Miller," transcription of tape recorded by Russell Bellant, April 19–20, 1986, meeting on Miles's homestead.

22. Larry Lee, "Training Target Questioned," *Southwest Times Record*, March 12, 1988.

23. Bob Miles, *From the Mountain*, September/October 1987, "F. Glenn Miller . . . failed to lead when the acclaim and laurels turned to thorns. No man should lead if he cannot face the stake and the fire"; Bob Miles, "Aryan Update" phone message recorded by author, March 13, 1988 (Miller was a "turncoat, a pancake which was flipped up on its end").

24. Author, notes on testimony by Peter Lake on February 18, 1988; Rhonda Fears, "Beliefs Come Out in Trial," *Southwest Times Record*, February 20, 1988; James Ellison, transcription of testimony tape in 87-20008, pp. 85–87.

25. James Ellison, transcription of testimony, p. 120.

26. Ellison, transcription of testimony about weapons, pp. 173–93.

27. James Ellison, transcription of testimony, p. 142.

28. Ibid., p. 100.

29. Ibid., p. 426.

30. James Parker, question to James Ellison, transcription of testimony, p. 427.

31. James Ellison and Louis Beam, transcription of testimony at pp. 346–47.

32. FBI FD 302, Bruce Carroll Pierce, "Statement taken by SA Thomas J. McDaniel and SA Wayne F. Mannis," April 1 and 2, 1985, Atlanta, Georgia, transcription on April 22, 1985. This affidavit had been admitted into evidence during The Order's Seattle RICO trial.

33. Larry Lee, "Accused Says He Will Change Sedition Plea," *Southwest Times Record*, March 9, 1988; Larry Lee, "Defendant Will Not Give Guilty Plea," *Southwest Times Record*, March 10, 1988. After the trial, Miles also commented favorably in his *From the Mountain* newsletter about Bruce Pierce.

34. Larry Lee, "Arnold Suppresses Confession," *Southwest Times Record*, March 17, 1988; Larry Lee, "FS Defendant Acquitted," *Southwest Times Record*, March 19, 1988.

35. UPI, "Trial of White Supremacists Is 'McCarthyism,' One Says," *The Atlanta Journal-Constitution*, April 3, 1988.

36. Larry Lee, "Bills for Sedition Trial Mounting," *Southwest Times Record*, April 13, 1988.

37. Larry Lee, "Beam's Scorn not Disguised—Attorney Hoists Confederate Flag," *Southwest Times Record*, April 8, 1988.

38. David Lane, *Autobiographical Portrait of the Life of David Lane & the 14 Word Motto* (St. Maries, Idaho: 14 Word Press, 1999). While in prison Lane married Katya Maddox, who operated a newsletter and published his writings; David Lane, "Vengeance Now!," *WAR* 13 (March 1994); David Lane, "If Federals Don't Succeed, They Will Try and Try Again," *The Spotlight*, June 5, 1995; "Getaway driver in radio talk show host murder dies in prison," KUSA-TV, Terre Haute, Indiana, May 29, 2007.

39. Rodney Bowers, "Juror, Accused in Love," *Arkansas Gazette*, n.d.; Associated Press, "Juror in Sedition Case to Marry Defendant," *Dallas Morning News*, September 13, 1988; author's notes, December 14, 1994, phone call to McGuires confirmed their marriage.

40. "Juror Admires Defendant," Associated Press, *Southwest Times Record*, April 27, 1988; "Impartiality of Some Jurors in Sedition Trial Is Questioned," *Klanwatch Intelligence Report* 41 (December 1988), Southern Poverty Law Center.

41. Robert Miles, "Fable of the Rams," *From the Mountain*, January/February 1988.

42. Robert Miles, "Monday AM Q-B Views," and "'Nuff Sed," *From the Mountain*, May/June 1988. Miles also described the entirety of the trial in the January/February and March/April 1988 editions of *From the Mountain*.

43. "Subpeona to Testify Before Grand Jury," United States District Court—North Dakota, May 8, 1991, reproduced in *From the Mountain*, June 1991; Bob Miles, letter to Jim Ridgeway, June 30, 1992.

44. "In Memory of Robert Edward Miles," memorial service announcement for death on August 16, 1992; "From Pastor and Mrs. Miles Daughter," *From the Mountain Final Newsletter*, April 1993.

45. "From Pastor and Mrs. Miles Daughter," *From the Mountain Final Newsletter*, April 1993: "I believe he loved my mother so much he did not wish to remain here without her."

46. Robert Miles, *From the Mountain*, July–August 1990 (Miles summarizes his own history and the overall situation for his movement at that time); Robert Miles, *From the Mountain*, March/April 1988, for quote "movements yet to be born."

19. Pete Peters's Family-Style Bible Camp for Identity Believers

1. James A. Aho, *The Politics of Righteousness: Idaho Christian Patriotism* (Seattle: University of Washington Press, 1990), pp. 135–63.

2. Ann Burlein, *Lift High the Cross: Where White Supremacy and the Christian Right Converge* (Durham, N.C.: Duke University Press, 2002), pp. 35–37.

3. Cheri Peters, "The Masculinized Female," For Women Only, *Scriptures of America Newsletter*, March 1987, p. 7. Cheri Peters's For Women Only page appeared in almost every issue of the newsletter.

4. Kathleen Blee, *Inside Organized Racism: Women in the Hate Movement* (Berkeley: University of California Press, 2002), pp. 122–38.

5. Peggy Christensen, "The Wife Secret Behind Man's Courage," Scriptures for America videotape no. RMR 88-19; Peggy Christensen, publisher, *The Correspondent* 8, no. 7 (July 1989).

6. "Mystery Speaker/W. A. Carto, Publisher of the Spotlight," photo of Carto, *1994 Scriptures for America*, 10th Anniversary Rocky Mountain Family Bible Camp; Louis Beam, "Break

the Sword, Overcoming Fear, Inaction And Doubt," tape no. 9301, *Scriptures for America*, 1993 Rocky Mountain Family Bible Retreat, audio- and videotape list; Kirk Lyons, *Scriptures for America*, 1988 Rocky Mountain Family Bible Retreat, audio- and videotape list.

7. Ed Cohen, "Hoskins Advisory: It's Not a Typical Investment Letter," *The News & Daily Advance* (Lynchburg, Va.), August 23, 1981.

8. Lib Wiley, photo with cutline, "At Hoskins Home," *Lynchburg Daily Advance*, December 17, 1959.

9. Robert Woodrum, "City Man's Extremist Writings Crop Up in Civil Rights Case," *The News & Daily Advance* (Lynchburg, Va.), November 1, 1991.

10. Richard Kelly Hoskins, *Our Nordic Race* (publisher not listed, 1959); Richard Kelly Hoskins, *Our Nordic Race*, 7th ed. (1975), pp. 7–8.

11. Richard Kelly Hoskins, *Vigilantes of Christendom: The Story of the Phineas Priesthood* (The Virginia Publishing Company, 1990), p. 383 ("I notified Senator Harry Byrd, Senator Willis Robertson, and half a dozen Virginia congressmen who were members of the Defenders").

12. Richard Kelly Hoskins, "Two Controversial Ideas," *Western Destiny*, July 1964, p. 5; Richard Kelly Hoskins, "The Unique West," *Western Destiny*, October 1964, p. 6; Richard Kelly Hoskins, "Organic Civilization," *Western Destiny*, August 1965, p. 7: "Wherever a sizeable number of alien cells gather they form a tumor . . . In each of our larger cities these alien tumors tend to blight the area which they occupy, and following the habit of tumors they have a high demand for body nutrients, poor efficiency and always take more than they give."

13. Gene Gunn, "Hoskins: Understanding and Knowledge Are Not the Same Thing," *The Justice Times*, June 1987, p. 1, cont'd p. 4 ("Hoskins said he was an alcoholic in the early 1960s"; the quote about "couldn't work . . . no money" is also from this article).

14. Richard Kelly Hoskins, *War Cycles, Peace Cycles* (Lynchburg: The Virginia Publishing Company, 1985), p. 244.

15. *Scriptures for America*, newsletter, vol. 5 (1988), p. 33.

16. Ibid., p. 32.

17. "The Anglo-Saxon-Celtic Israel Belief," *Destiny* magazine, January 1941.

18. Howard Rand, ed., *Destiny*, second quarter 1969, pp. 218–19. This publication was a preeminent source for British Israelism in North America during the 1920s–1940s.

19. Michael Barkun, *Religion and the Racist Right: The Origins of the Christian Identity Movement* (Chapel Hill: The University of North Carolina Press, 1994). This book (mistakenly) precluded considering one seeders like Pete Peters from Christian Identity ranks; author conversation with Michael Barkun in New York at American Jewish Committee meeting.

20. Dan Gayman, "Parable of the Tares of the Field," *The Watchman* 13, no. 2 (Spring 1990): 37.

21. *The Holy Bible*, Authorized King James Version, 1985 edition, The Gideons International.

22. Pete Peters, "The Way of Cain," Parts One and Two, Scriptures for America, Tapes 600 and 601.

23. *The Holy Bible*, King James Version, 1985 edition, The Gideons International, Genesis 27:29.

24. Author, interviews with Mark Thomas, May and June 1996. Thomas, an Aryan Nations leader and convicted felon, had an excellent grasp of the various permutations of Christian Identity.

25. Contra James Aho, *The Politics of Righteousness*. This book counts a breed of "non-racist" Identity believers, and contends that men such as Dan Gayman are not anti-Semitic (pp. 93–94).

26. Charles A. Weisman, *Who Is Esau-Edom?* (Weisman Publications, 1991), p. 49.

27. Ibid., p. 55.

28. Weisman claims that so-called physical differences between Jews and white Europeans are "primarily a result of their genetic differences," p. 56.

29. Weisman, *Who Is Esau-Edom?* p. 22.

30. Ibid., pp. 63, 113: "It is a genetic function of the Jew's existence to do the works of their ancestor, Esau, by destroying the white Adamic race."

31. Ibid., p. 27, "It is the Jews' fate, as bearers of the blood and characteristics of Esau-Edom, to lack the essential attributes needed to create and build a civilization of their own."

32. Pete Peters, *A Scriptural Understanding of the Race Issue* (Scriptures for America, 1990), p. 1.

33. Pete Peters, "Inter-racial Marriage Pt. 2" (Scriptures for America), audiotape no. 171 (B side).

34. Peter J. Peters, *Death Penalty for Homosexuals Is Prescribed in the Bible* (Scriptures for America, 1992).

35. *Attitudes About Homosexuality and Gay Marriage*, American Enterprise Institute, June 3, 2008. Gallup asked: "Do you feel homosexuality should be considered an acceptable alternative lifestyle or not?" This question was asked over two decades. In 1982, 51 percent said not acceptable. In 2008, 40 percent said not acceptable.

20. Elections 1988: David Duke and Pat Robertson Out on the Hustings

1. Clyde Wilcox, *God's Warrior: The Christian Right in Twentieth Century America* (Baltimore: The Johns Hopkins University Press, 1992), pp. 145–47; "Super Tuesday Primaries: The Results," *The New York Times*, March 10, 1988, p. 11. Robertson's aggregate vote on Super Tuesday was 589,594.

2. Alec Foege, *The Empire God Built: Inside Pat Robertson's Media Machine* (New York: John Wiley & Sons Inc., 1996), p. 38.

3. Ibid., pp. 15, 27, 28 (for American Center founding) and pp. 28, 184–85 (for Regents University); Pat Robertson, *The New Millennium*, 1990; Robertson, *The New World Order*, 1991; Robertson, *The Secret Kingdom*, 1992; all three published in one volume by Inspirational Press, 1994.

4. Jerome L. Himmelstein, *To the Right: The Transformation of American Conservatism* (University of California Press, 1990), pp. 200–204.

5. Senator A. Willis Robertson, signatory, "The Southern Manifesto," *Congressional Record*, 84th Congress Second Session, vol. 102, part 4, March 12, 1956, Government Printing Office 4459–4460. The Southern Manifesto promised to reverse the Supreme Court decision in *Brown*.

6. Vicki Kemper, "Looking for a Promised Land," *Sojourners* magazine, June 24, 1988.

7. Robertson, *The New World Order* (Dallas: Word Publishing, 1991), pp. 68–74; Michael Lind, "Rev. Robertson's Grand International Conspiracy Theory," *The New York Review of Books*, February 2, 1995; Gustav Niebuhr, "Pat Robertson Says He Intended No Anti-Semitism in Book He Wrote Four Years Ago," *The New York Times*, March 4, 1995; Daniel Levitas, "A.D.L. and the Christian Right," *The Nation*, June 19, 1995.

8. Robertson, *The New World Order*, pp. 120–28; "Pat Robertson: Extremist," People for the American Way, n.d., p. 13; Skipp Porteous, "The World According to Pat Robertson," *Reform Judaism*, Spring 1993.

9. Editorial, *The Spotlight*, May 12, 1983 (described in detail Liberty Lobby's differences with Robertson); Cornelius Vanderbreggen, "Christian Scholar Interprets What Bible Says About Israel," *The Spotlight*, July 4, 1983 (and Vanderbreggen articles in the July 11, July 18, July 25, August 1, August 8, and August 15, 1983, editions).

10. Joe Brennan, "Televangelist Might Be Wild Card in GOP Primaries," *The Spotlight*, August 31, 1987, pp. 10–11.

11. Ibid.

12. Ibid.; Editorial, *The Spotlight*, May 12, 1983.

13. Michael Collins Piper, "Third Party Chairman Notes Encouraging Victories," *The Spotlight*, February 8, 1988, pp. 16–18.

14. David Duke for President Committee, ID no. C00215426, FEC Form 3P (2/83) Schedule B-P, January 29, 1988, p. 2, paid Howard Allen Enterprises $2,237; paid Cordite Fidelity (*The Spotlight*) $3,937; p.1, BC&E $3,000; ID no. C00215426, filing received March 8, 1988, p. 4, paid Liberty Lobby for list rental $3,212; ID no. C00215426, filing received April 25, 1988, p. 5, paid *The Spotlight* $3,626 for ad.

15. David Duke for President Committee, ID no. C00215426, FEC Form 3P (2/83) Schedule B-P, filing for March 8, 1988, p. 6, paid Wm Rhodes $850 for labor; ID no. C00215426, filed April 25, 1988, Itemized Disbursements, p. 1, Matt Anger, $1,200; Allen Baylough Quakerstown, PA, $503; p. 3, Ralph Forbes $500 and $3,075; "Alan Baylough of the Eastern Pennsylvania Unit," *National Alliance Bulletin*, May 1980; Matt Anger (writing under the alias Matt Malone), "Flawed from the Beginning," *The Nationalist* 3, no. 1

(February 1987), publication of the National Democratic Front; "Populist Party State Chairman, Arkansas Ralph Forbes," *The Populist Observer*, October 1988; Floyd Cochran, interview with Leonard Zeskind, August 1992 (describes William Rhodes's stint as an Aryan Nations videographer); Leonard Zeskind (unsigned), *Ballot-Box Bigotry: David Duke and the Populist Party*, Center for Democratic Renewal Background Report no. 7, p. 6.

16. "Weekly Update," February 1, 1988 (includes Philadephia meeting; S. Miller, personal communication to author, described question to Duke about Metzger).

17. Joe Kirby, "Duke to Seek Presidency; Blasts IRS, Welfare at Rally," *Marietta Daily Journal*, n.d., republished in *NAAWP News* 46:2.

18. "Elections Division Race Summary Report," The State of Texas, Office of the Secretary of State, 1988 Democratic Primary Election, 04/04/88; "Percentages for 1988 Democratic and Republican Presidential Preference Primary," Georgia Secretary of State, Elections Division, March 8, 1988.

19. "Super Tuesday Primaries: The Results," *The New York Times*, March 10, 1988, p. 11, votes for candidates in Louisiana; David Duke, speech before the Washington State Populist Party Convention, July 23, 1988, reproduced on videotape. Duke talked about his half-hour TV advertisement and noted that he had "won a majority of white votes" in several parishes.

20. Willis Carto, "1988 and Beyond," *The Populist Observer*, December 1987, p. 3.

21. Paul Richert, "It's Duke and Rambo," *The Populist Observer*, April 1988, p. 2.

22. Joe Brennan, "Populists Select Duke and Gritz," *The Spotlight*, March 28, 1988; "Parker Replaces Gritz on the Populist Party Ticket," *The Populist Observer*, May 1988, p. 4 (includes text of Gritz's resignation letter); Merle Naylor, "Genuine American Hero Will Speak at LL Banquet," *The Spotlight*, August 31, 1987.

23. David Duke, "Duke Excerpts," *The Populist Observer*, April 1988, p. 5.

24. Paul Richert, "Overflow Crowd Attends New Jersey Convention," *The Populist Observer*, May 1988, p. 3 ("immigration most important issue"); Jonathan Marcus, *The National Front and French Politics: The Resistable Rise of Jean-Marie Le Pen* (New York: New York University Press, 1995), pp. 61–67; Leonard Zeskind, "Success of French Fascists Inspires Counterparts in the United States," *The Monitor*, July 1988 (author attended FN May Day march in Paris in 1988).

25. "David Duke for President . . . Vote Populist Party," brochure with Ten Point Program, 1988.

26. Cartoon-illustration, *NAAWP News* 45:2.

27. Leonard Zeskind (unsigned), "White Supremacists Plan to Exploit Stock Market Decline," *The Monitor* 11 (April 1988).

28. "Here's Where David Duke and the Populist Party Stand on the Issues," "Protect American Farmers and Workers . . . by instituting protective tariffs," Populist Party campaign brochure with Duke on cover, n.d.

29. Willis A. Carto, "Introduction," *Profiles in Populism* (Washington, D.C.: Flag Press, 1982), pp. xiii–xiv. Carto wrote this book's introduction and conclusion.

30. Leonard Zeskind, "White Supremacists Plan to Exploit Stock Market Decline," *The Monitor* 11 (April 1988).

31. David Duke, speech at Washington State Populist Party Convention, July 23, 1988, reproduced on videotape.

32. "McIntyre Reelected as National Chairman," *The Populist Observer*, April 1988, p. 7.

33. Ibid.

34. Cheryl Ronan, interview with author, March 1989 (Ronan was director of Civil Rights for Individuals in Fort Collins and provided author a complete overview of events); Leonard Zeskind (unsigned), "Identity Group Defeats Anti-Discrimination Ordinance," *The Monitor* 15 (May 1989); LaPorte Church of Christ's Brief, Colorado Court of Appeals, 91 CA 1024, n.d. (includes exhibits).

35. "Agreement for Political Broadcasts" and "Citizens of Fort Collins," republished by Scriptures for America as "Exhibit One," in *People . . . v. LaPorte Church of Christ*, Colorado Court of Appeals, 91 CA 1024; leaflets entitled "Human Rights or Special Rights," "What Are the Goals of Homosexual Activists," and "How Homosexual Legislation Could Affect": all three concluded with "Vote No on Prop. #106," n.d.

36. *People . . . v. LaPorte Church of Christ,* Colorado Court of Appeals, 91 CA 1024.

37. Cheryl Ronan, interview with author.

38. "Third Party Candidates Got Less Than 1 Percent of Vote," Associated Press, November 22, 1988. Duke received 44,135 votes, or .04 percent of the vote.

21. Populist Party Meets in Chicago After David Duke Wins a Legislator's Seat

1. David Duke, fundraising letter sent to members of the Forsyth County Defense League, postmarked New Orleans, February 8, 1989.

2. Leonard Zeskind (unsigned), "David Duke's Louisiana Victory Is Reflection of a National Strategy," *The Monitor,* May 1989.

3. David Duke, *My Awakening,* pp. 609–12: "I learned that the psychology of victory becomes easier under the banner of a major party."

4. Howie Farrell, fund-raising letter, postmarked January 2, 1989.

5. Bridges, *The Rise of David Duke,* p. 152.

6. "The Unmasking of David Duke: Part One," and "The Unmasking of David Duke: Part Two—A Tale of Two Young Men," paid for by the John Treen Campaign Committee.

7. Lance Hill, communication to author on multiple occasions.

8. Michael Hoffman, *Research Magazine,* March 1989.

9. Ed Fields, "Ring the Bells, Herald the Good News," *The Truth at Last* 333 (1989).

10. John Frankowski, "David Duke . . . State Legislator," *The Populist Observer,* March 1989, p. 2.

11. Leonard Zeskind (unsigned), "Ballot-Box Bigotry: David Duke and the Populist Party," Center for Democratic Renewal Background Report no. 7, p. 12. The Populist Party raised and spent $136,172 on Duke's bid for president on their ticket; Duke raised and spent $406,569 on that campaign in 1988.

12. Russ Bellant, "Populist Party National Executive Committee Meeting and David Duke Press Conference," n.d.

13. Michael Collins Piper, letter to Liberty Lobby Board of Policy Members, n.d., republished in "Wassallgate: The Pillaging of the Populist Party," a Special Report from *The Spotlight.*

14. Willis Carto, "Letter to the Members of the Executive Committee," March 2, 1989, reproduced in "Wassallgate": "In my view, the present problem has been caused by Don's rejection of former liberal senator Gene McCarthy, who I had scheduled to come for nothing."

15. Willis Carto, letter "To the Members of the Executive Committee," March 2, 1989.

16. Paul Richert, "Vindication! Pittsburgh Jury Finds That Willis Carto and Liberty Lobby Libeled the Populist Party and Don Wassall," reprint from the November/December 1997 issue of *The Nationalist Times.*

17. Communication to author, report on Populist Party national committee meeting in Chicago, March 1989.

18. David Duke, "Duke Gives Rousing Speech to Populists at Chicago Convention," *The Populist Observer,* April 1989, p. 7.

19. Leonard Zeskind, "Ballot-Box Bigotry," pp. 12–13.

20. Duke, "Duke Gives Rousing Speech," p. 1.

21. Lawrence N. Powell, "Slouching Toward Baton Rouge: The 1989 Legislative Election of David Duke," in *The Emergence of David Duke and the Politics of Race,* ed. Douglas D. Rose (Chapel Hill: The University of North Carolina Press, 1992).

22. Beth Rickey, a Louisiana Republican Party Central Committee member, in multiple discussions with author 1989–1991. Also see Elizabeth A. Rickey, "The Nazi and the Republicans: An Insider View of the Response of the Republican Party to David Duke," in *The Emergence of David Duke and the Politics of Race.*

23. Duke, "Duke Gives Rousing Speech," p. 9.

24. "Bill Elder's Journal," WWL-TV New Orleans, April 2, 1989, from videotape of program.

25. Beth Rickey, discussions with author.

26. Lance Hill, insight, recollections, and writings shared with author.

27. Don Morgan, "Eliminating David Duke," *Avant!,* March 23, 1990, published by Tulane University.

28. Chalmers, *Hooded Americanism,* pp. 314–16.

29. Louisiana Coalition Against Racism and Nazism, opinion poll conducted during July 1989, questions no. 82 and 83.

30. David Duke, "Bill Elder's Journal," WWL-TV, April 2, 1989.

31. Lance Hill, "The Influence of National Socialist Political Theory in the Contemporary Political Thought of David Duke," n.d. This document was circulated by LCARN as part of a resource packet and rewritten and published as "Nazi Race Doctrine in the Political Thought of David Duke," in *The Emergence of David Duke and the Politics of Race*, ed. Douglas D. Rose.

32. Beth Rickey, "The Nazi and the Republicans: An Insider View of the Response of the Republican Party to David Duke." Rickey provided author with a draft copy of the resolution.

22. Skinhead International in Tennessee

1. Mark Alfonso, photos and notes, Center for Democratic Renewal. The walkie-talkies were from a group calling itself "SS of America," headquartered in Charlotte, North Carolina.

2. "Aryan Americans, Awake," flyer honoring Sam Davis and promoting October 7, 1989, march in Pulaski, Aryan Nations, mailed bulk rate from Idaho, n.d.; "Aryan Nations a Gathering of Will," lists bands for the Pulaski events: Up Front, Bound for Glory, Doc Martin, Arresting Officer, Bobby Norton, Aryan Nations Southern Leader; Leonard Zeskind (unsigned), "Tennessee Aryan Nations March Opposed," *The Monitor* 17 (December 1989) (described the march in detail).

3. Connie Craig, "Aryan March," Associated Press, October 3, 1989 (for orange ribbons); Zane Hughes, "Stay Off Square Saturday," *The Giles Free Press*, October 5, 1989.

4. Joe Collins, "Strange Times for a Small Town," *The Giles Free Press*, October 5, 1989, p. 1.

5. Louis Beam, "Sam Davis Speech," taped by Mark Alfonso, Center for Democratic Renewal, October; Mark Alfonso, comment on Kirk Lyons, communicated to author, 1989.

6. Pete Peters, "Skinheads, The S.O.S. Troops of the Right," Scriptures for America, audiotape no. 433 (sermon Peters gave to his congregation in Colorado after attending the Pulaski events).

7. Pete Peters, "A Close Shave with the Skinheads," Scriptures for America, audiotape no. 432 (includes some recording of Beam's speech during Peters's sermon to his congregation in Colorado).

8. Peters, "Skinheads, The S.O.S. Troops of the Right."

9. Joe Drape, "Hard-Core Hatred: Skinheads' Racism Violence Alarms Civil Rights Leaders and Lawmen," *Dallas Morning News*, March 21, 1988.

10. Author, personal observation, September 2, 1989; Leonard Zeskind (unsigned), "Labor Day Rally in Georgia Reflects Changes in Klan," *The Monitor* 16 (October 1989) (describes Klan-skinhead tension).

11. Dick Hebdige, *Subculture: The Meaning of Style* (London: Methuen & Co. Ltd., 1979). Skins, like "punk rockers, hippies, crips, [and] bloods . . . challenge power relations within our society through their distortion, alteration, and ironic use of common everyday symbols and styles."

12. Nick Lowles and Steve Silver, "From Skinhead to Bonehead—The Roots of Skinhead Culture," and Steve Silver, "Blood and Honour: 1987—1992," in *White Noise: Inside the International Skinhead Scene* (Ilford, UK: Searchlight, 1998); author, notes taken while watching a tape of a Skrewdriver concert.

13. Eric Andrew Anderson, "Skinheads: From Britain to San Francisco via Punk Rock" (thesis submitted for a Master of Arts in anthropology, Washington State University, December 1987). The Ramones' first concert was in 1974, and they first toured London in 1976.

14. Ibid., p. 64.

15. Nick Camerota, "Nazi Chic," *Attack!* 57 (1977), republished in *The Best of Attack! and National Vanguard Tabloid*.

16. "Nazi Youth Gangs Inspire Alarm," *The Monitor* 3 (June 1986) (quotes letter to *Maximum Rock n Roll*, 1986). At first the editors of *Maximum Rock n Roll* were unsure about how to respond (communication from Tim, editor), but by 1989 the magazine was publishing articles such as "Racist Skins Attack Gig," *Maximum Rock n Roll*, January 1989.

17. Mike O'Keefe, "Triumph of the Swill," *Westword*, May 22, 1991; Dirk Johnson, "Colorado Klansman Refines Message for the 90s," *The New York Times*, February 23, 1992.

18. Eric Andrew Anderson, "Skinheads: From Britain to San Francisco via Punk Rock," pp. 58–96.
19. Ibid., pp. 97–101.
20. Richard Bullis, "Why, Yes, Dad, I'm a Skinhead," n.d. (ca. 1990, father tells story of his daughter), written communication to Center for Democratic Renewal; Kathy Dobie, "Long Day's Journey into White," *The Village Voice*, April 28, 1992.
21. "What Is a Skinhead?" leaflet, White Aryan Skinheads, Cincinnati, Ohio, n.d. (ca. 1987–1988).
22. William Pierce, *Hunter* (National Vanguard Books, 1989), p. 157.
23. William Pierce, letter, "Dear National Vanguard Reader," March 13, 1989.
24. "Affirmative Action: An Idea Whose Time Has Passed," *National Vanguard* 110, March–April 1989, pp. 8–10; The National Alliance tried it again in 1991 with a proxy vote against Israel: William Pierce, letter and resolution attachment to Robert E. Scannell, Corporate Vice President, AT&T, October 25, 1990; Robert E. Scannell, letter to Securities and Exchange Commission, December 6, 1990; "National Alliance Calls for AT&T Withdrawal from Israel," *IRRC News for Investors*, January 1991, p. 17.
25. "Affirmative Action: An Idea Whose Time Has Passed," p. 10.
26. Robert J. Hoy, "Skinheads: They're Young, They're Wild and Standing Up for America," *The Spotlight*, January 6–13, 1986, pp. 21–23; Gerry Gable, communication with author, February 1995, viz Hoy's photos of British skins.
27. Leonard Zeskind (unsigned), "Walking the Line Between Racist Violence and Electronic Wizardry: A Profile of Tom Metzger and the White Aryan Resistance," Center for Democratic Renewal, December 1987 (backgrounder documents shift in Metzger's thinking).
28. Louis Beam, letter beginning "Dear Tom," *WAR* 7, no. 6, p. 4.
29. Wyatt Clay Kaldenberg, *The Democratic Socialist: Voice of the New Aryan Left* newsletter 3, no. 3.
30. Wyatt Clay Kaldenberg, "Aryan Skinheads," *WAR '88* 7, no. 3, p. 5.
31. "Rock Against Communism" promotion, *WAR* 11, no. 4 (1983), p. 2.
32. "Return of the Warrior," *WAR* 7, no. 6, reprinted from *Heritage & Destiny 1981*.
33. "Aryan Festival '88," *WAR '88* 7, no. 4 (1988), p. 1; videotape of Oklahoma Fest distributed by White Aryan Resistance.
34. *Aryan Youth Movement–White Student Union*; Metzger published a dozen editions of this tabloid during the 1980s, and it became an entry point for young people into his organizational circles.
35. "W.A.R.'s Side of the Story," *WAR* 7, no. 6, pp. 2–3; Leonard Zeskind (unsigned), "White Supremacy Exploits Hot Television," *The Monitor*, May 1989.
36. William Pierce, letter beginning "Dear Tom," *WAR* 7, no. 6, p. 4.

23. German Unification and the Reemergence of Nationalism

1. Author, observation, February 12, 1990, Leipzig, Germany.
2. Bettina Muller and James Ridgeway, "Democracy Is So Difficult," *The Village Voice*, November 21, 1989; Jill Smolowe, "East Germany," *Time*, October 23, 1989 (New Forum); Ann Tusa, *The Last Division: A History of Berlin 1945–1989* (Reading, Mass.: Addison-Wesley, 1997), pp. 366–76.
3. Leonard Zeskind, "German Political Mix Includes Neo-Fascists," *Kansas City Jewish Chronicle*, March 9, 1990; author, observation.
4. Author, photos, interviews, and notes, February 1990; Leonard Zeskind, "German Political Mix Includes Neo-Fascists"; Graeme Atkinson (unsigned), "Nazis Campaign Openly," *Searchlight*, March 1990.
5. Author, observation, February 1990.
6. Author, observation of consumer goods in Berlin and Dresden, May 1990 (Johnny Cash was on the jukebox at a truck stop outside Leipzig); Serge Schmemann, "Two Germanys Unite After 45 Years With Jubilation and a Vow of Peace," *The New York Times*, October 3, 1990.
7. Eike Wunderlich, "German White Power: A Program for Cultural Hegemony," in *White Noise: Inside the International Nazi Skinhead Scene*, eds. Nick Lowles and Steve Silver (Il-

ford, UK: Searchlight Magazine Ltd, 1998) (skinheads in the East and West in the early 1980s); Ingo Hasselbach, *Führer-Ex: Memoirs of a Former Neo-Nazi* (New York: Random House, 1996), pp. 24–43 (East German skinheads emerge from local punk scene).

8. Paul Hockenos, *Free to Hate: The Rise of the Right in Post-Communist Eastern Europe* (New York: Routledge, 1993), p. 50; David Childs, "The Far Right in Germany Since 1945," in *Neo-Fascism in Europe*, eds. Luciano Cheles, Ronnie Ferguson, and Michalina Vaughn (London: Longman, 1991), p. 80 (for geographic breakdown).

9. Graeme Atkinson (unsigned), "The Meaning of Rostock," *Searchlight*, October 1992, pp. 12–21; Hockenos, *Free to Hate*, pp. 56–58 (for CDU adoption of Republikaner position); Graeme Atkinson (unsigned), "Neo-Nazi Violence in Germany Explodes!," *Searchlight*, November 1991, pp. 10–12.

10. Graeme Atkinson (unsigned), "100,000 March Against Fascist Terror," *Searchlight*, December 1991, p. 14, author, observation of Bertolt Brecht gravestone; author, observation of protest led by Beate Klarsfeld against immigrant deportations from Schoenefeld Airport.

11. Author, multiple conversations with Sonja Tichy in East Berlin and Michael Hahn and others in Germany during the period 1990 to 1995.

12. Michael Schmidt, *The New Reich: Violent Extremism in Unified Germany and Beyond*, trans. Daniel Hoch (New York: Pantheon Books, 1993), p. 122 (1988 statement by Franz Joseph Strauss of the Christian Social Union).

13. Ibid., p. 139 (quotes Eckard Fuhr, a columnist for the *Frankfurter Allgemeine*).

14. David A. Jodice, *United Germany and Jewish Concerns: Attitudes Toward Jews, Israel and the Holocaust* (New York: American Jewish Committee, 1991), pp. 4–5.

15. Ernst Nolte, James Knowlton and Truett Cates, trans., *Forever in the Shadow of Hitler?: Original Documents of the Historikerstreit, the Controversy Concerning the Singularity of the Holocaust* (Atlantic Highlands, N.J.: Humanities Press, 1993); the original German edition of the book was entitled, in German, *The Documentation of the Controversy Concerning the Singularity of the National-Socialist Annihilation of the Jews*; Nolte had preferred: *The Documentation of the Controversy Surrounding the Preconditions and the Character of the "Final Solution of the Jewish Question."*

16. Schmidt, *The New Reich*, pp. 133–38; the *Frankfurter Allgemeine* commissioned a poll during the Historikerstreit.

17. Ernst Nolte, "Between Historical Legend and Revisionism? The Third Reich in the Perspective of 1980," in *Forever in the Shadow of Hitler?*, pp. 13–14.

18. Ibid, pp. 13–15.

19. Ernst Nolte, interview with Ian B. Warren, *Journal of Historical Review*, January–February 1994, pp. 20–21.

20. Schmidt, *The New Reich*, quoting Rudolf Augstein, p. 144; author, visit to Sachsenhausen, 1991.

21. Tom Metzger, "Deutschland Skins," *WAR*.

22. Mark Weber, "Reviewing a Year of Progress," *The Journal of Historical Review* 10, no. 4, pp. 444–45.

23. John Roy Carlson II, personal communication to author.

24. Ernst Nolte, "The Past That Will Not Pass," in *Forever in the Shadow of Hitler?*, pp. 18–23.

25. James Knowlton and Truett Cates, in *Forever in the Shadow of Hitler?*, p. 3.

26. Ernst Nolte, in *Forever in the Shadow of Hitler?*, p. 8; Mark Weber, "A Prominent German Historian Tackles Taboos of Third Reich History," a review of the German language edition of Ernst Nolte's book *Points of Contention: Current and Future Controversies About National Socialism 1993, Journal of Historical Review*, January–February 1994.

27. Ernst Nolte, "Standing Things on Their Heads: Against Negative Nationalism in Interpreting History," in *Forever in the Shadow of Hitler?*, p. 149.

28. Mark Weber, "Institute for Historical Review Author Biographies," www.ihr.org/other/authorbios.html (accessed May 9, 2008).

29. John Roy Carlson II (Don Warren), "Initial Report and Impressions," (October 1990), personal communication to author.

30. "Faurisson, Toland, Irving, Leuchter Help Make IHR's Tenth Conference a Capital Success," *IHR Newsletter* 76 (November 1990), p. 6; Paul Grubach, "CN Writers Meet at Revisionist-IHR Conference," *The Christian News*, November 12, 1990, p. 18.

31. "Faurisson, Toland, Irving, Leuchter Help Make IHR's Tenth Conference a Capital Success," p. 3.
32. "Highlights of the Tenth International Revisionist Conference," Institute for Historical Review flyer.
33. John Roy Carlson II (Don Warren), "Initial Report and Impressions."
34. Vince Ryan, "Liberty Lobby Reports: Answers to Your Questions," *The Spotlight*, August 2, 1999, p. 4 (in 1993 the IHR journal had climbed to "7,770 subscribers and growing").
35. John Roy Carlson II (Don Warren), "Initial Report and Impressions."
36. Ibid.

24. The First Persian Gulf War and the Realignment of the Far Right

1. David Hudson, "Liberty Lobby Milestone: 35th Anniversary Washington Confab," *The Spotlight*, September 17, 1990; William Carmichael, "*Spotlight* Turns 15 Committed to Truth," *The Spotlight*, September 17, 1990; David Hudson, "BOP Meets, Conducts Business," *The Spotlight*, September 24, 1990; "Gritz Warns BOP Get Ready to Fight or Lose Freedom," *The Spotlight*, September 24, 1990; Felix, communication to author detailing the weekend of events, September 1990.
2. "President George Bush Announcing the War Against Iraq," January 16, 1991, www .historyplace.com/speeches/bush-war.htm.
3. William Carmichael, "Populist Institution's 35th Anniversary in Washington," *The Spotlight*, September 17, 1990, p. 13.
4. Stephen A. Koczak, "Shooting Imminent in Iraq: Israel Planning Preemptive Strike," *The Spotlight*, October 29, 1990, p. 1.
5. W. A. Carto, "Foreign Policy Must Have America as Focus," *The Spotlight*, October 15, 1990, p. 4.
6. Carto's ideas about culture distortion first published: E. L. Anderson, Ph.D. [Carto], "Cultural Dynamics I, II and III," *Right*, November 1959, March 1969, and June 1960.
7. *The Klansman*, Invisible Empire Knights of the Ku Klux Klan, publisher, January/February 1991.
8. "Is the U.S. Ready for War With Iraq?" *The Nationalist*, National Democratic Front newsletter 61 (December 1990).
9. Terre Rybovich, communication to author, January 16, 1991.
10. "STAND UP FOR AMERICA FIRST!" Populist Party of Florida, n.d.
11. Communication to Center for Democratic Renewal, "Populist Party Demonstration Anti–Gulf Intervention," November 10, 1990; "Protests Against Bush's War Held in Pennsylvania and New York," *The Populist Observer*, December 1990, p. 5.
12. Ibid.
13. "Populist Candidates Make Impact at the Ballot Box," *The Populist Observer*, December 1990.
14. William F. Buckley, Jr., "Pat Buchanan Part 2: In Search of Anti-Semitism," *National Review*, December 30, 1991, p. 31 (quotes Buchanan on war drums).
15. Ibid.
16. Patrick J. Buchanan, *Conservative Votes, Liberal Victories* (New York: Quadrangle/New York Times Book Co., 1975), pp. 48–71; Patrick J. Buchanan, *Right from the Beginning* (Boston: Little, Brown, 1988), pp. 80–102, 336–59; Patrick J. Buchanan, "Immigration Reform or Racial Purity?," *Washington Inquirer*, June 15, 1984.
17. Patrick J. Buchanan, "Immigration Reform or Racial Purity?"
18. Micah Sifry, "Anti-Semitism in America," *The Nation*, January 25, 1993, p. 94 (Treblinka diesel engines); Lucette Lagnado, "Pat Buchanan and The Émigré Nazis," *The Nation*, May 4, 1985 (Demjanjuk); Kenneth S. Stern, "Patrick Joseph Buchanan: Backgrounder" (American Jewish Committee, n.d.); "From Columnist to Candidate: Pat Buchanan's Religious War" (Anti-Defamation League, 1992); Mark Weber, "Reviewing a Year of Progress," *The Journal of Historical Review* 10, no. 4, pp. 444–45.
19. A. M. Rosenthal, "On My Mind Forgive Them Not," *The New York Times*, September 14, 1990; William F. Buckley, Jr., "The Pro-Buchanan Case: In Search of Anti-Semitism," *National Review*, December 30, 1991, p. 34.
20. William F. Buckley, Jr., "In Search of Anti-Semitism," p. 40.

21. Patrick J. Buchanan, "The 90s Are Still Up for Grabs," syndicated column appearing in *The Independent American* (Littleton, Col.), November 15, 1990, p. 1.

22. "Buchanan Registers a TKO Over Rosenthal," *The Populist Observer*, September/October 1990, p. 11.

23. Robert Blumetti, "Patrick J. Buchanan: The Personification of Populism," *The Populist Observer*, September/October 1990, p. 13.

24. Ibid.

25. "Buchanan Registers a TKO Over Rosenthal," *The Populist Observer*.

25. The Collapse of the Soviet Union and the Transformation of White Supremacy

1. "Soviet Union," *The 1992 Information Please Almanac* (Boston: Houghton Mifflin, 1992), pp. 253–56.

2. John B. Dunlop, *The Rise of Russia and the Fall of the Soviet Union* (Princeton, N.J.: Princeton University Press, 1993), pp. 123–85.

3. The process of unraveling continued long after the Soviet collapse was complete, lending credence to the notion that ethnic nationalism was not just a response to communism but had developed a dynamic of its own.

4. "Personal . . . From the Editor," *The Spotlight*, January 1 and 8, 1990, p. 2.

5. "Changing the Mask," *National Vanguard* 111 (June/July 1999), pp. 9–14.

6. Ibid.

7. William Pierce, "Dear Subscriber," letter, received July 17, 1990; William Pierce, "To My Fellow Thought Criminals," *National Vanguard* 111, pp. 2–4.

8. Eric Hobsbawm, *The Age of Extremes: A History of the World 1914–1991* (New York: Vintage, 1996), p. 256.

9. Michael Ignatieff, *Blood and Belonging: Journeys into the New Nationalism* (New York: Farrar, Straus and Giroux, 1993); Paul Hockenos, *Free to Hate: The Rise of the Right in Post-Communist Eastern Europe* (New York: Routledge, 1993).

10. Hobsbawm, *The Age of Extremes*, p. 255.

11. Francis Fukuyama, "The End of History?" *The National Interest*, Summer 1989; Francis Fukuyama, *The End of History and the Last Man* (New York: Free Press, 1992) (Hegelian extension of his core argument).

12. Samuel P. Huntington, *The Clash of Civilizations and the Remaking of World Order* (New York: Simon & Schuster, 1996), pp. 19–55, 301–21, for quote: 304–305.

13. Huntington, *The Clash of Civilizations*, pp. 19–55, 301–21.

14. Michael Hardt and Antonio Negri, *Empire* (Cambridge, Mass.: Harvard University Press, 2000), pp. 3–21, 69–113; Benjamin R. Barber, *Jihad versus McWorld: How Globalism and Tribalism Are Reshaping the World* (New York: Ballantine Books, 1996), pp. 219–35.

15. Louis Beam, "The Death of Anti-Communism," *The Seditionist* 11 (Fall 1991), p. 1.

16. Hobsbawm, *Age of Extremes*, p. 252: "Anti-communism was generally and viscerally popular in a country built on individualism and private enterprise."

17. Hobsbawm, *Age of Extremes*, p. 235; Hobsbawm cites Martin Walker, *The Cold War and the Making of the Modern World* (London: Fourth Estate, 1993), p. 55.

18. Louis Beam, "The Second Half of World War II Is Coming," *The Seditionist* 11 (Fall 1991), pp. 4–8.

19. Beam, "The Death of Anti-Communism," *The Seditionist* 11 (Fall 1991), p. 2.

20. Misha Glenny, *The Balkans: Nationalism, War, and the Great Powers, 1804–1999* (New York: Penguin Books, 2001).

21. Misha Glenny, *The Fall of Yugoslavia* (New York: Penguin Books, 1993), p. 19.

22. Chris Hedges, "Fascists Reborn as Croatia's Founding Fathers," *The New York Times*, April 12, 1997; Stephen Kinzer, "Pro-Nazi Legacy Lingers For Croatia," *The New York Times*, October 31, 1993; Franjo Tudjman, *Wastelands—Historical Truth*, originally published as: *Bespu'ca povjesne zbiljnosti* (Zagreb: Nakladni zavod Matice Hrvatske, 1989); English language excerpts available at www.srpska-mreza.com/library/facts/Tudjman.html; "Croatia's President Rejects 'Six Million' Story," *The Journal of Historical Review* 12, no. 2 (Summer 1992), pp. 240–43.

23. Michel Faci, "National Socialist Fight in Croatia!" *The New Order*, January/February 1993; "French Patriots Visit," *The Truth at Last* 360 (January 1994), (Faci talked to At-

lantans about his exploits in the former Yugoslavia); Gerhard (Gary) Lauck, "Dear National Socialist Comrade," letter, August 24, 1993 (Lauck returned from "between Croatian and Serbian postions"); Lauck distributed a videotape of Faci's "NS" military unit in Croatia.

24. Glenny, *The Balkans*, pp. 634–52.

25. Ibid., pp. 652–62.

26. Maureen Dowd, "Clinton Warns of Violent Nationalism," *The New York Times*, June 8, 1994.

27. This phenomenon was easier for Americans to see in Russia with Zhronovsky and in France with Le Pen than to see in their own country with Buchanan and America first nationalism.

26. Transatlantic Traffic

1. "Revisionist Rats Rally," *Searchlight*, April 1991; "Leuchter Laid Off in Munich," *Searchlight*, May 1991; Mark Weber, "Revisionists Meet in Munich Despite Conference Ban," *IHR Newsletter*, May 1991.

2. Mark Weber, "Revisionists Meet in Munich Despite Conference Ban," *IHR Newsletter*, May 1991.

3. Ibid.

4. Floyd Cochran, interview with author in Kansas City, August 20, 1992 (Cochran attended the wedding); "The Princes of the South Take Brides of the Princesses of the North," Aryan Nations, *Calling Our Nation* 63 (pictures from Kirk Lyons-Brenna Tate wedding); Kevin Sack, "Member's Racist Ties Split Confederate Legacy Group," *The New York Times*, November 8, 2001.

5. "Member Forms Legal Foundation," *National Alliance Bulletin*, November/December 1989; "Articles of Incorporation," Patriot's Defense Foundation, December 10, 1989.

6. Lee Hancock, "Law and Hate: Lawyer Finds Clientele on Right-Wing Political Fringe," *The Dallas Morning News*, February 18, 1990.

7. Kirk D. Lyons, "Dear Fellow Patriot," letter seeking donations, June 30, 1990 ("Remember that our primary mission here is to conduct legal warfare"); Kirk Lyons, "The Lawyer of the Right," *Volkstreue* fanzine, n.d. (translation from the German by M.H.).

8. Cover, photo of John Tyndall and Sam Dickson, credit Jimmie Lee, *Searchlight*, June 1991; "Atlanta Attorney Sponsors Tyndall Meeting," *The Monitor*, August 1991; "Nazi Godfather Jordan Accuses Tyndall of Election Sell-Out," *Searchlight*, May 1997 (cover photo of Tyndall in uniform without swastika).

9. John Tyndall, *The Eleventh Hour: A Call for British Rebirth* (London: Albion Press, n.d.), pp. 557–66; "British Neo-Nazi Barred Entry to North Carolina," photo of Tyndall in uniform before a swastika flag and a picture of Hitler, courtesy of *Searchlight, The Monitor* 20 (August 1990), p. 10.

10. "British National Party," *Searchlight*, January 1991, p. 12.

11. "The Education of John Tyndall," *Instauration*, November 1988, pp. 5–7 (*The Eleventh Hour* available from Dickson's Historical Review Press); "British Nationalists on Videocassette," *Instauration*, June 1987, p. 34.

12. Leonard Zeskind, "Briton Is Key Link to U.S. Neo-Nazis," *The Forward*, June 7, 1991.

13. John Tyndall, "Back to America," *Spearhead* 269 (July 1991), p. 4.

14. Articles of Incorporation of Howard Allen Enterprises, Inc., State of Florida, Humphrey Ireland, February 12, 1974; annual corporation registration, 1983, Humphrey Ireland and Mary Ireland, Melbourne, Florida, officers; Don Warren, communication to author after visit with Humphrey and Mary Ireland at their North Carolina home, March 31, 1993.

15. Tyndall, "Back to America," p. 7; "Thanks to Ed Fields and to Sam Dickson, who apart from his role in putting on the Atlanta meeting, also masterminded the entire tour."

16. Sam G. Dickson, "Dear Friend," letter on Anglo-American Forum letterhead, May 7, 1991.

17. Ibid.

18. Sam G. Dickson, "Dear Friend," letter with Atlanta Committee for Historical Review return address, May 21, 1990.

19. Nicole C. Crews, "White Power Leaders Map Plans," *Carolina Peacemaker*, May 23–29, 1991; Michael Collins Piper, "Populist Committee Officially Launched," *The Spotlight*, June 3, 1991; "First Amendment Alive: Tyndall, Fields Speak," *Populist Patriot*, newsletter

of the New Jersey Populist Party, May 1991; "Briton's John Tyndall Speaks in N.J., Populist Party Host Dynamic Orator," *The Post-Eagle*, June 12, 1991.

20. Tyndall, "Back to America," p. 5.

21. "Excerpts from John Tyndall's Address," *European-American Public Affairs Courier*, June 3, 1991, pp. 7–8.

27. The Duke Campaign(s) and the Louisiana Electorate

1. Eric Foner, *Reconstruction: America's Unfinished Revolution 1863–1877* (New York: Harper & Row, 1988), p. 551.

2. Foner, *Reconstruction*, pp. 575–83.

3. Lerone Bennett, Jr., *Before the Mayflower: A History of Black America*, 5th rev. ed. (New York: Penguin, 1987), pp. 250–52; Carrie Fleider, "Louisiana History," communication to author, August 9, 2001.

4. *The 1992 Information Please Almanac* (Boston: Houghton Mifflin Company, 1992), p. 749.

5. Leonard Zeskind, "For Duke, Just a Start?," *The New York Times*, October 9, 1990; the author owes a debt to Lance Hill, then of the Louisiana Coalition Against Racism and Nazism, for some of the ideas expressed.

6. "No Defeatism at Duke Election Night Party," and "Text of David Duke's Election Night Address," *European-American Public Affairs Courier*, December 1, 1991, pp. 1–6.

7. Bess Carrick, *Backlash: Race and the American Dream*, 1991, VHS format; Jason Berry, "White Lies: David Duke in the Media Mind," 1989, essay entered in the Wilson Center Media Studies Essay Competition (describes the many ways journalists tried to cover Duke).

8. "Weekly Update," Center for Democratic Renewal, January 16, 1990.

9. "Weekly Update," Center for Democratic Renewal, February 26, 1990.

10. Steve Gerstel, "Republican Senators Endorse Democratic Colleague," UPI, October 4, 1990; Alan Sayre, "Louisiana Primary," Associated Press, October 6, 1991.

11. Tyler Bridges and Jack Wardlaw, "Defeated Duke Still a Winner with La. Whites," *The Times-Picayune*, October 8, 1990.

12. Tyler Bridges, *The Rise of David Duke* (Jackson: University Press of Mississippi, 1994), p. 193.

13. Penni Crabtree, personal communication to author, January 31, 1991.

14. Iris Kelso, "For Louisiana Republicans, Tacks in the Catbird Seat," *The Times-Picayune*, May 16, 1991; Jack Wardlaw, "Roemer, Duke, Holloway triangle," *The Times-Picayune*, May 1991; Tyler Bridges, "Holloway GOP Pick for La. Governor," *The Times-Picayune*, June 16, 1991; Roberto Suro, "Duke Is in Runoff in Louisiana Race," *The New York Times*, October 20, 1991.

15. Penni Crabtree, personal communication to author about Duke "machine."

16. Tyler Bridges, "2 claim victory at GOP Caucus," *The Times-Picayune*, May 19, 1991.

17. "State Convention Rules Adopted by the State Central Committee of the Republican Party of Louisiana," May 11, 1991; 1991 Louisiana Republican State Convention twenty-page program booklet; "Instructions to Duke Delegates," n.d.

18. Penni Crabtree, "Into the Heart of Dukeness," *Details*, April 1992, pp. 22–26; Crabtree, personal communication to author.

19. Crabtree, "Into the Heart of Dukeness"; Evelyn Rich, communication to the Center for Democratic Renewal after attending the Institute for Historical Review conference, February 1986: "Duke is planning to employ a secretary. NAAWP has taken off in recent months and Duke, recognizing his shortcomings in the area of organization, wants someone to answer his mail in a more personal way."

20. Howie Farrell was the campaign manager, Kenny Knight organized the volunteers, the Shreveport office chief was David Touchstone, and Babs Wilson ran the office in Baton Rouge.

21. Penni Crabtree, in a communication to the author, emphasized the small NAAWP campaign office was unprepared for the volumes of mail Duke received.

22. Beth Bowman, "Young Republicans to Host Controversial Politician," *Current Sauce*, Northwestern State University, March 20, 1990; Associated Press, "Young Republicans Chapter Endorses Duke for Senate," March 31, 1991; Frank Main, "Racist Groups Grow on La. Campuses," *State-Times* (Baton Rouge), May 16, 1990.

23. Louisiana Coalition Against Racism and Nazism, in-depth telephone survey with 108 questions, July 1990, question 16.

24. Lance Hill, executive director of the Louisiana Coalition Against Racism and Nazism, emphasized on many occasions how Duke often pointed to his "controversial past" as proof of his true beliefs and leadership abilities.

25. David Duke debate with Edwin Edwards, *Meet the Press*, NBC, November 10, 1991, author videotape of the debate. Also see Tyler Bridges, *The Rise of David Duke*, p. 232.

26. Douglas D. Rose, "Six Explanations in Search of Support: David Duke's Senate Race," in Douglas D. Rose, ed., *The Emergence of David Duke and the Politics of Race* (Chapel Hill: The University of North Carolina Press, 1992), p. 157.

27. Marsha Shuler, "Duke's Religion Questioned by Some," *Baton Rouge Morning Advocate*, November 8, 1991.

28. William F. Buckley, "On the Right: Exit Dukeism?" *National Review*, December 16, 1991, p. 62.

29. Andrew W. Robertson, "All the Duke's Men," *National Review*, December 16, 1991, p. 45; Christopher Hitchens, "Minority Report," *The Nation*, December 16, 1991; Hitchens cited a *Times-Picayune* poll that revealed 14 percent of Duke voters did not believe he had changed; that would be 73,000 votes in 1991, and he drew over 150,000 in a subsequent congressional race.

30. Michael Barone and Grant Ujifusa, *Almanac of American Politics*, 1992 ed. (Washington, D.C.: National Journal, 1992), p. 500.

31. Ibid., p. 505.

32. Sara Diamond, *Roads to Dominion* (New York: Guilford Press, 1995), p. 271.

33. Lance Hill, "Questions About Duke's Environmentalism," *Dialogue*, October 1989.

34. "A Portrait of Louisiana's Voters," *The New York Times*, November 18, 1991.

35. Ibid.

36. Ibid.

37. "How 'It Can't Happen Here' Almost Happened in Louisiana: A Study of the David Duke Phenomenon in the 1990 Senate Race," Garin-Hart Strategic Research poll sponsored by the Center for National Policy, March 1991.

38. Rose, "Six Explanations in Search of Support," in *The Emergence of David Duke*, pp. 172–73.

39. Rose, *The Emergence of David Duke*; John C. Kuzenski, Charles S. Bullock III, Ronald Keith Gaddie, eds., *David Duke and the Politics of Race in the South* (Nashville: Vanderbilt University Press, 1995).

40. Stephen J. Caldas and John C. Kilburn, "A Parish Profile of the David Duke Vote: Sociodemographic, Economic and Voting Propensity Predictors," in *David Duke and the Politics of Race in the South*.

41. Rose, "Six Explanations in Search of Support," p. 178.

42. Michael Lind, *The Next American Nation: The New Nationalism & the Fourth American Revolution* (New York: Free Press, 1996), pp. 17–139.

43. Michael W. Giles and Melanie Buckner, "David Duke and the Electoral Politics of Racial Threat," in *David Duke and the Politics of Race in the South*.

44. Thomas B. Edsall, "Duke's Voter Appeal Holds Danger for Bush in '92," *The Washington Post*, November 17, 1991; Carl M. Cannon, "White On!" *Tropic* magazine insert for *Miami Herald*, February 9, 1992.

45. Rick Knox, "Duke Campaign: What Happened," *The Spotlight*, June 1, 1992; Scott Shepard, "David Duke Withdraws from Race for President," Cox News Service, published in *The Orange County Register*, April 23, 1992; Mathew Levie, "David Duke: Winning by Losing," *Chicago Tribune*, January 21, 1992; John Roberts, "Duke's S.C. Manager in Saluda," *Augusta Herald*, February 17, 1992.

28. Pat Buchanan Runs Through the Republican Presidential Primaries

1. Pat Buchanan, "Duke Challenges the Right," *From the Right*, October 25, 1991.

2. Pat Buchanan, "Duke's Challenge to the Right," *Washington Times*, October 23, 1991.

3. Monte Paulsen, "Buchanan Inc.," *The Nation*, November 22, 1999.

4. Jack W. Germond and Jules Witcover, *Mad as Hell: Revolt at the Ballot Box, 1992* (New York: Warner Books, 1993), p. 133.

5. Germond and Witcover, *Mad as Hell*, pp. 133, 395.

6. Ibid., p. 152 (final vote tally); Ben Smith III, "Challenger Asks Bush to Quit Race," *The Atlanta Journal-Constitution*, March 5, 1992; James M. Perry and David Rogers, "Buchanan's Strength in First Primary Is a Big Blow to Bush," *The Wall Street Journal*, February 19, 1992.

7. "What About Pat," Stirring *Instauration*, December 1991, p. 28.

8. Mark Sherman, "Duke Loses Bid for Ga. Primary," *The Atlanta Journal-Constitution*, January 22, 1992 (U.S. District Judge); "Court Denies Duke Georgia Ballot Slot," *Newsday*, February 24, 1992 (Supreme Court refusal).

9. "Duke Couldn't Duke it Out," *Valdosta Daily Times*, April 25, 1992; "Duke No Longer a Hazard," *Marietta Daily Journal*, April 27, 1992.

10. Rick Knox, "Duke Campaign: What Happened," *The Spotlight*, June 1, 1992, p. 6.

11. Peter Applebome, "Duke Plays to Empty Houses as Spotlight Trails Buchanan," *The New York Times*, March 6, 1992.

12. Peter Applebome, "Duke's Followers Lean to Buchanan," *The New York Times*, March 8, 1992.

13. "Current Candidates for President," *The Spotlight*, March 2, 1992.

14. Boyd Cathey, North Carolina state chair for Buchanan, "Do You Want to Help Pat Buchanan?," March 1992 (campaign advertisement listing state chairs); "Editorial Advisory Committee," *The Journal of Historical Review* 10 no. 2 (Summer 1990); "Boyd Cathey, Senior Editor," *Southern Partisan*, fourth quarter 1991, p. 2.

15. "The Excess of Anti-anti-semitism," *Southern Partisan*, fourth quarter 1991, p.10.

16. Leonard Zeskind, "White-Shoed Supremacy," *The Nation*, June 10, 1996, p. 21 (author interviewed Cathey in April 1996 for this article).

17. Associated Press, "Buchanan Aide Is Removed over Mixed-Marriage View," *The New York Times*, January 29, 1992; "Not Buchanan's Breed," *Newsday*, January 30, 1992.

18. Ibid.; "D'Alessio New Chairman in New Jersey," *The Populist Observer*, February 1992, p. 17.

19. "Individual Contributions," Selected List of Receipts and Expenditures, Buchanan for President, 1991–1992, Federal Election Commission.

20. Metzger had been working the immigration issue for years and regarded Buchanan as an interloper.

21. *Race and Reason*, community access cable TV program series, no. 115, May 23, 1992 (video of Metzger and Buchanan at the border).

22. "Excerpts From Report on Los Angeles Police," *The New York Times*, July 10, 1991; Annette Haddad, "LAPD Patrol Car Messages Reveal Racism," UPI, July 10, 1991; *The Christopher Commission Report: A Background Research Report*, People Against Racist Terror, Los Angeles.

23. Seth Mydans, "Brutality Issue Remains as Los Angeles Trial Nears," *The New York Times*, February 3, 1992.

24. Isabel Wilkerson, "Acquittal in Beating Raises Fears over Race Relations," *The New York Times*, May 1, 1992.

25. Seth Mydans, "11 Dead in Los Angeles Rioting," *The New York Times*, May 1, 1992.

26. Ted Appel, "Buchanan: Government Total Failure in Response," UPI, May 6, 1992.

27. Ronald Brownstein, "Buchanan Links Riot to Border Problem," *Los Angeles Times*, May 14, 1992.

28. "Buchanan Lashes Out at L.A. Mayor," *Los Angeles Times*, reprinted, *The Kansas City Star*, May 16, 1992.

29. Patrick J. Buchanan, "The War for the Soul of America," text of May 9, 1992, speech at Liberty University, *Human Events*, May 23, 1992.

30. Patrick Buchanan, "America First—A Foreign Policy for the Rest of Us," *From the Right* 2, no. 11 (September 1991).

31. Adam Clymer, "Messages of Warning to Bush and of Hope for Democrats," *The New York Times*, March 5, 1992 (exit polls by Voter Research and Surveys).

32. "Mr. Buchanan's Choice," *National Review*, March 2, 1992.

33. David Frum, *Dead Right* (New York: Basic Books, 1994), pp. 125–26 (Frum quotes Buchanan: "the conservative movement . . . had been hijacked"); Charles Krauthammer, "Buchanan's Agenda Control by '96 of the Paleo-Right," Washington Post Writers Group, November 22, 1991.

34. Samuel Francis, "The Buchanan Revolution II," in *Revolution from the Middle* (Raleigh, N.C.: Middle American Press, 1997), p. 141.

35. Samuel T. Francis, "The Front Line States: The Realities of Southern Africa," Heritage Foundation Background no. 78, Heritage Foundation, 1979; Samuel T. Francis, "Latin American Terrorism: The Cuban Connection," Heritage Foundation Background no. 104, Heritage Foundation, 1979; Samuel T. Francis, "Terrorism and Prevention," *Policy Review* 13 (Summer 1980); Nat Hentoff, "The Terrorists of Libel: The Consequences of Dissent," *Inquiry*, September 14, 1981; citations from Keith Hurt, *Samuel Todd Francis: A Bibliography*, n.d., communication to author.

36. "Roger Pearson," Biographies, Institute for the Study of Academic Racism, www.ferris.edu/isar/bios/Pearbib.htm (accessed November 23, 2004).

37. Samuel Francis, "Message from MARs," in Robert Whitaker, ed., *The New Right Papers* (New York: St. Martin's Press, 1982), p. 68.

38. E. Litwak, N. Hooyman, and D. Warren, "Ideological Complexity and Middle America Rationality," *Public Opinion Quarterly* 37 (Fall 1973); Don Warren, "Middle American Radicals," *The Nation*, August 17, 1974; Donald I. Warren, *The Radical Center: Middle Americans and the Politics of Alienation* (Notre Dame, Ind.: University of Notre Dame Press, 1976).

39. Francis, "Message from MARs."

40. Samuel Francis, "From Household to Nation: The Middle American Populism of Pat Buchanan," *Chronicles*, March 1996, p. 13.

41. Francis, "The Buchanan Revolution II," pp. 141–42.

42. Samuel Francis, "The Education of David Duke," *Chronicles*, February 1992.

43. Patrick J. Buchanan, text of speech, Republican National Convention, Houston, Texas, August 17, 1992 (available on Pat Buchanan's website, www.buchanan.org).

44. Germond and Witcover, *Mad as Hell*, pp. 410–11.

45. "Dear Friends," letter (cites polls), Institute for First Amendment Studies, September 1992.

46. Germond and Witcover, *Mad as Hell*, p. 413.

29. The Populist Party Goes with Bo Gritz

1. "Report on the Populist Party of NC Meeting 2/8/92," North Carolinians Against Religious and Racist Violence, communication to author, February 1992; Addie M. Winston, "Supremacists Plot Election Strategy," *Carolina Peacemaker*, February 12, 1992.

2. Kirk Lyons, "Speech at the Populist Party NC Meeting 2/18/92," transcript of tape recording.

3. Charles Tanner, Jr., communication to author, March 1993; Leonard Zeskind, notes from first-person observations.

4. Judy Thomas, "Hero or Huckster?: Bo Gritz Patriot Movement Leader," *The Kansas City Star*, March 14, 1999; James Pate, "Bo Knows Politics: Klansmen, Christics, Clowns and Gritz's Populist Party," *Soldier of Fortune*, September 1992.

5. Thomas, "Hero or Huckster?"; "Persian Gulf Tension Mounts: Marines Set Up as 'Bait,' Gritz Drops 'Bombshell' at D.C. Conference," *The Spotlight*, September 28, 1987.

6. James "Bo" Gritz, *Called to Serve: Profiles in Conspiracy from John F. Kennedy to George Bush* (Lazarus Publishing Company, 1991); James Ridgeway, "The Trial That Wasn't: Christic Struggles to Stay in Court," *The Village Voice*, January 10, 1989; Omar Barnet and M. Spenser Martin, "Questioning the Latest Conspiracy to Dismiss Conspiracy Theorists," *In These Times*, April 8–14, 1992; Sara Nelson, "Christic Institute Was Grossly Misrepresented in 'Bo' Gritz Story," *In These Times*, October 30–November 1, 1991.

7. Gritz, *Called to Serve*, pp. 609–12.

8. Bo Gritz, *Called to Serve*; Scriptures for America, audiotape no. C9113; Leonard Zeskind (unsigned), "Rambo Heads Populist Party," *The Monitor* 24 (December 1991), p. 19.

9. Bo Gritz, "Dear Willis," letter to Willis Carto, January 3, 1992 (Gritz distributed copies of the letter to Populist Party loyalists).

10. "Indictment," *United States of America v. Michael Lewis Lawrence, Daniel Roush, Forrest Hyde, Tina Christopher, Christopher Jones, Gregory Kennicutt*, U.S. District Court for Northern District of Oklahoma, Case no. 90CR 138B; Associated Press, "3 White Supremacists Are Convicted in Plot," *The New York Times*, October 20, 1992; *Connie Mansfield v. William Pierce*, U.S. District Court Western District of North Carolina Bryson City, Civil Action 2 95CV 62 (Church of the Creator member George Loeb was convicted on July 29, 1992, of murdering Harold Mansfield, suit pursued and won by Southern Poverty Law Center); Elinor Langer, *A Hundred Little Hitlers* (New York: Metropolitan Books, 2003).

11. Thom Robb, "Attention All Members of the Knights of the Ku Klux Klan," *White Patriot* 86, 1991.

12. Associated Press, "Aurora Neo-Nazi Hopes to Make Political Mark," *Rocky Mountain News*, December 1, 1991; Dirk Johnson, "Colorado Klansman Refines Message for the 90s," *The New York Times*, February 23, 1992.

13. "Sleepers," *Robb's Victory Report*, September 1, 1992.

14. Thom Robb, *Robb's Victory Report*, December 1, 1991 (reports on Ed Novak helping in Dubuque); Ken Peterson, interviews with Leonard Zeskind and Loretta Ross, November 2, 1992 (Robb's Wisconsin former state leader agreed to talk).

15. Robert J. Crawford, personal communication to author, July 1992.

16. "America First Coalition, Vote for 'Bo' Put America First," campaign brochure, Middleburg, Florida; "Contact List of Chairpersons for Each State," Bo Gritz National Presidential Campaign Committee, Middleburg, Florida, 1992.

17. Paul Richert, "Nomination of Gritz Highlights Populist Party's National Convention," *The Populist Observer*, June 1992, p. 18; personal communication to author, March 1993.

18. Kelly from the Federal Election Commission, phone conversation with author, October 31, 2001 (Gritz's campaign was funded from three registered campaign committees); Kelly from the Federal Election Commission, phone conversation with author, for 1992 vote totals; *The Populist Observer*, January 1993, p. 2 (counted 106,518 votes for Gritz).

19. Don Wassall, "Dear Populist Party Supporters," letter, January 5, 1993.

20. Howard Phillips, ed., *The Next Four Years: A Vision of Victory* (Franklin, Tenn.: Adroit Press, 1992) (see back cover for bio); Jerome L. Himmelstein, *To the Right: The Transformation of American Conservatism* (Berkeley: University of California Press, 1990), pp. 81–94.

21. Kelly from the Federal Election Commission, phone conversation with author, October 31, 2001 (U.S. Taxpayers Party spent $452,676 in 1992 campaign).

22. Pat Buchanan's 1992 campaign in the Republican Party primaries was important in this regard.

23. James Bo Gritz, "Rexburg Idaho Campaign," transcript of speech, March 1992.

30. The FBI Aims for Randy Weaver on Ruby Ridge

1. Francis X. Clines, "Theatrical Threshold at Hearing on the Deadly Shootout in Idaho," *The New York Times*, September 7, 1995; Leonard Zeskind, "Making a Martyr: Randy Weaver and Ruby Ridge in the Mind of America," *The Kansas City Jewish Chronicle*, May 31, 1996 (review of four-hour television mini-series *Ruby Ridge: An American Tragedy*).

2. Jess Walter, *Every Knee Shall Bow: The Truth & Tragedy of Ruby Ridge & The Randy Weaver Family* (New York: Regan Books, 1995), pp. 20–47; Donnelle Eller and Gwynne Skinner, "White Supremacy Group Has Waterloo Members," *The Northern Iowan*, November 8, 1985.

3. Randy Weaver, "Testimony," Hearing of the Senate Judiciary Committee, Terrorism, Technology and Government Information Subcommittee, Federal Raid in Idaho, September 6, 1985, Federal News Service transcript (Weaver said he had been at Aryan Nations camp multiple times).

4. Bill Morlin, "Weaver Wouldn't Spy for Feds," *The Spokesman Review*, September 13, 1992; Vicki Weaver, "To Aryan Nations & all our brethren of the Anglo Saxon Race," letter, June 12, 1990; *Massacre at Ruby Creek: The Randy Weaver Story* (Concerned Citizens of Idaho, n.d.), p. 166.

5. Walter, *Every Knee Shall Bow*, pp. 119–27.

6. Author, notes from August and September 1992.

7. James Corcoran, *Bitter Harvest* (New York: Viking, 1990), pp. 119–20 (Arthur Kirk); Symbionese Liberation Army events in 1974, www.pbs.org/wgbh/amex/guerrilla/peopleevents/e_kidnapping.html; MOVE bombing in 1985, www.libcom.org/library/move-bombing-1985.

8. Bill Rhoads, *Massacre at Ruby Creek*, videotape documentary of protesters and other events at the roadblock, n.d.; photos of protesters, *Massacre at Ruby Creek: The Randy Weaver Story*, pp. 30–40 (this publication collected many documents from the initial events).

9. Melanie Threlkeld, "5 Skinheads Arrested near Weaver's Cabin," *The Idaho Statesman*, August 26, 1992; Leonard Zeskind, "State of the Union," *Searchlight*, October 1992.

10. Mike Blair, "Confrontation in Idaho Harbinger for America," *The Spotlight*, September 7, 1992, p. 1; Tom Metzger, WAR Hotline telephone recording, August 24, 1992.

11. Pete Peters, *Special Message and Alert from Pastor Peters*, Scriptures for America, audiotape no. 552.

12. Peter J. Peters, "Dear Randy," letter faxed to Colonel Gritz, reproduced in: Peter J. Peters, "Concerning Innocent Bloodshed in the Land," September 1992; Pete Peters, *Special Message and Alert from Pastor Peters*, Scriptures for America, audiotape no. 552.

13. Bo Gritz and Jack McLamb, "S.A. Gene Glenn," August 28, 1992, *Massacre at Ruby Creek: The Randy Weaver Story*, p. 59.

14. Bo Gritz, "American Tragedy: Assault at Ruby Creek," August 31, 1992, press release on Bo Gritz for President letterhead; Melanie Threlkeld, "Weaver's Pal Surrenders," *The Idaho Statesman*, August 31, 1992; Associated Press, "Idaho Fugitive Gives Up After 11-day Standoff," *The Florida News*, September 1, 1992.

15. Bo Gritz, *For the People*, radio talk show with host Chuck Harder, August 31, 1992, KCMO-AM in Kansas City, transcript; William Rhoads, *Massacre at Ruby Creek*, film of Gritz with arm salute; Jane Ann Morrison, "Gritz Helps End Supremacist Standoff, Lands in Controversy: Candidate Denies Giving Nazi salute," *Las Vegas Review-Journal*, September 13, 1992.

16. Dan Popkey, "Populist Candidate Warns Rights Are Slipping Away," *The Idaho Statesman*, September 11, 1991.

17. Robert J. Crawford, communication to author, October 1992; Associated Press, "Candidate Gritz Brings Conspiracy Message to UM," *Great Falls Tribune*, September 19, 1992.

31. After the Shoot-out, the Militia

1. Louis R. Beam, Jr., acting director, "Wanted By Citizen Committee for Justice," September 1, 1992; Robert J. Crawford, personal communication to author, September 21, 1992.

2. Chris Temple, speech at Estes Park, Scriptures for America, audiotape no. RMR0.

3. Mark Thomas, telephone interviews with author, May 1996 and August 1997; Chris Temple, audiotape, presentation to class of Professor Rob Balch at the University of Montana, May 1997, Hitler and National Socialism from Temple's writings and speech before Balch class at University of Montana ("I am very much a national socialist"); Chris Temple, "Whither the Soviet Union?: A Coup Fails—Or Did It?" *The Jubilee*, July/August 1991.

4. Mike Mittlestadt, "Cortland Man Writes $3,000 in Bad Checks to Prove a Point," August 2, 1986; Chris Temple, Phoenix Financial Services, Polson, Montana, State Auditors Office Insurance, 1994.

5. Mike Weland, "Weaver Aftermath Draws Former Grand Dragon," *The Kootenai Valley Times*, September 30, 1992; Star Silva and Malcolm Hall, "Local Group to Examine Weaver Deaths," *Bonners Ferry Herald*, September 25, 1992; Robert Crawford (unsigned), "Recent Events in Bonners Ferry, Idaho," twenty-two-page background memo, Center for Democratic Renewal, March 23, 1993.

6. J. Todd Foster, "Ex-KKK Leader Criticizes Agents at Weaver Rally," *The Spokesman Review*, October 7, 1992.

7. Leonard Zeskind, "Armed and Dangerous: The NRA, Militias and White Supremacists Are Fostering a Network of Right Wing Warriors," *Rolling Stone*, November 2, 1995.

8. Pete Peters, "Preparatory for the October 1992 Meeting of Men of God," Scriptures for America, audiotape no. 556.

9. Louis Beam, speech at Estes Park, Scriptures for America, audiotape no. RMR05; Sheila Beam, "Affidavit," *Sheila M. Toohey v. Louis Ray Beam*, Idaho District Court First Judicial

District, case no. CV01-3900, August 8, 2001, p. 6 ("I have never shared Defendant's racist and anti-government philosophy"); Louis Beam, "Leaderless Resistance," reprinted in *Special Report on the Meeting of Christian Men Held in Estes Park Colorado October 23, 24, 25 1992*, Scriptures for America; Pete Peters, "Report on October 1992 Meeting," Scriptures for America, audiotape no. 557; Pete Peters, "Preparatory."

10. Kirk Lyons, speech at Estes Park, Scriptures for America, audiotape no. RMR03.
11. White Aryan Resistance chief Tom Metzger made much of this point.
12. Chris Temple, speech at Estes Park, Scriptures for America, audiotape no. RMR0.
13. Peter J. Peters, *A Scriptural Understanding of the Race Issue: God's Call for Repentance*, Scriptures for America, 1990 ("today we use the word minorities rather than aliens"); the word "strangers" was often used instead of "aliens."
14. Larry Pratt, speech at Estes Park, Scriptures for America, audiotape nos. RMR14 and RMR15.
15. Larry Pratt, *Armed People Victorious*, Gun Owners Foundation, 1990; Larry Pratt, "Introduction—Firearms: The Peoples Teeth," in Larry Pratt, ed., *Safeguarding Liberty: The Constitution and Citizen Militias* (Franklin, Tenn.: Legacy Communications, 1995), p. xiv.
16. Lawrence D. Pratt, "Dear Friend of the Family," Committee to Protect the Family Foundation, letter introducing Randall Terry letter, n.d.
17. Lawrence Pratt, "Greetings," Committee to Protect the Family Foundation letter, July 16, 1990.
18. Louis Beam, "1/4 Inch: The Randy Weaver Story," online n.d.
19. Kenneth S. Stern, *A Force upon the Plain: The American Militia Movement and the Politics of Hate* (New York: Simon & Schuster, 1996), p. 37.

32. Clinton's First Year and the Culture War

1. David Gunn, Sacred Heart Hospital Autopsy Protocol, MLA93-100, complaint no. 93-14390, G. D. Cumberland, M.D., forensic pathologist, March 12, 1993.
2. Michael Frederick Griffin, Pensacola Police Department Arrest Report, no. 128260, Steven A. Ordonia, badge no. 161, March 10, 1993.
3. Jeanie Russell Kasindorf, "A Call to Murder," *Redbook*, August 1993.
4. Michael Frederick Griffin, "Enlistee Evaluation Report[s]," U.S.S. *Whale*, period from January 1983 to April 1987, for Michael Frederick Griffin.
5. Monsanto Textiles Company Pensacola, Florida, Performance Appraisal for Michael Griffin, August 15, 1989.
6. "Ex Parte Order Enjoining Domestic Violence," Circuit Court, First Judicial Circuit Escambia County, Florida, 91-1564-ASP, April 8, 1991.
7. James Risen and Judy L. Thomas, *Wrath of Angels: The American Abortion War* (New York: Basic Books, 1998), p. 195 (quote taken from interview with Risen and Thomas, courtesy Judy Thomas).
8. David Mark Chalmers, *Hooded Americanism: The History of the Ku Klux Klan* (Durham, N.C.: Duke University Press, 1987), pp. 378–81.
9. *Peter Gunn Jr. v. John Burt*, amended complaint, Circuit Court of Escambia County, Florida, 95-391-CA.
10. Risen and Thomas, *Wrath of Angels*, pp. 342–43.
11. Dr. Edward Fields, letter to reader, *The Truth at Last*, December 1, 1993.
12. Tom Metzger, White American Resistance recorded phone message, reported in *The Hammer: Anti-Racist, Anti-Fascist News and Analysis* 8 (Fall 1984), p. 12.
13. "NAF Violence & Disruption Statistics," National Abortion Federation, December 31, 1997.
14. Risen and Thomas, *Wrath of Angels*, p. 338.
15. S. L. Gardiner, *Rolling Back Civil Rights: The Oregon Citizens' Alliance at Religious War*, Coalition for Human Dignity, Portland, Oregon, 1992; Timothy Egan, "Oregon Measure Asks State to Repress Homosexuality," *The New York Times*, August 16, 1992.
16. Coalition for Human Dignity, *The Dignity Report* 1, nos. 1–6, 1993.
17. Kevin McCullen, "Decision a Victory for 3 Cities' Laws," *Rocky Mountain News*, May 21, 1996.
18. *Romer v. Evans*, 517 U.S. 620 (1996).

19. Justice Kennedy, Opinion of the Court, *Romer v. Evans*, 517 U.S. 620 (1996); in dissent, Justice A. Scalia wrote: "In *Bowers v. Hardwick* [a previous case out of Georgia] we held that the Constitution does not prohibit what virtually all states had done from the founding of the Republic until very recent years—making homosexual conduct a crime. That holding is unassailable . . ."

20. Author, notes on videotaped focus group discussions sponsored by the Human Rights Project, Kansas City, 1992.

21. Ralph Reed, "Casting a Wider Net," *Policy Review*, Summer 1993, p. 31.

22. Samuel Francis, "Religious Wrongs," in Samuel T. Francis, *Revolution from the Middle* (Raleigh, N.C.: Middle American Press, 1997), pp. 209–10.

23. Ibid., p. 209.

24. Ibid., p. 208.

25. Ibid., pp. 210–11.

26. Ibid., pp. 205–11.

27. Ibid., p. 209.

28. Francis, "Culture and Power: Winning the Culture War," in *Revolution from the Middle*, p. 175.

33. Inferno at Waco and Randy Weaver Wins at Trial

1. *Report of the Department of the Treasury on the Bureau of Alcohol, Tobacco and Firearms Investigation of Vernon Wayne Howell also known as David Koresh*, September 1993, pp. 96–107, figures 33 and 34.

2. "ATF Stunned by Jubilee-Beam Counterattack," *The Jubilee* 6, no. 3 (November/December 1993); Kirk Lyons, interview with author, August 31, 1995; "Special Report on WACO for NRA Members," CAUSE Foundation (distributed at 1995 NRA convention); Leonard Zeskind, "Armed and Dangerous," *Rolling Stone*, November 10, 1995.

3. Colleen LeMay, "Allusion to Cult Standoff Puts Agent on the Defensive," *The Idaho Statesman*, June 4, 1993.

4. Kirk D. Lyons, "White-Collar Racists," *Sally Jessy Raphael*, March 18, 1993; Ben Stocking, "Hate Groups Have an Ally in Lawyer," *The News and Observer*, April 19, 1992.

5. Melanie Threlkeld, "Friends Call Weaver Close Religious Family," and *Statesman* staff, "Friends Say Weaver a Separatist, Not a White Supremacist," *The Idaho Statesman*, August 27, 1992.

6. Martin Johncox, "Weaver Pleads Innocent," *The Idaho Statesman*, September 2, 1992.

7. Martin Johncox, "US: Weaver Had 'Aryan' Plan," *The Idaho Statesman*, October 3, 1992.

8. Associated Press, "Defense Attorney: Feds Are Trying to Smear Weaver," September 30, 1992.

9. Timothy Egan, "U.S. Case Looks Weaker in Idaho Siege," *The New York Times*, June 23, 1993.

10. Dean Miller, "Supremacists Could Face Death Penalty," *The Spokesman Review*, October 7, 1992; Quane Kenyon, "Accounts of Mountaintop Shootout Differ," *Seattle Post-Intelligencer*, September 20, 1992; Dean Miller, "Aryan Leader Tells Jury About Weaver, Beliefs," *The Spokesman Review*, September 30, 1992; "2 Acquitted in U.S. Marshal's Slaying," *The New York Times*, July 9, 1993.

11. Colleen May, "Will Waco Repeat Results at Trial? Government Force Issue Will Take Spotlight Again When Branch Davidians Face Trial," and "How Weaver-Harris Standoff, Trial Unfolded," *The Idaho Statesman*, July 9, 1993.

34. A Suicide in North Carolina and the Birth of Resistance Records

1. Ben Klassen, "Will and Lucinda Williams," in Ben Klassen, *Trials, Tribulations and Triumphs* (Niceville, FL.: Church of the Creator, 1993), p. 215. At eight minutes after 8:00 on August 8, 1988, Will Williams married his girlfriend, Lucinda, at the COTC camp.

2. Ben Klassen, "Prelude," in Ben Klassen, *The Klassen Letters. Volume One: 1969–1976* (Otto, N.C.: Church of the Creator, 1988).

3. Ibid., p. 7.

4. Ben Klassen, *Nature's Eternal Religion* (Milwaukee: Milwaukee Church of the Creator, 1973), pp. 180 and 248–317; *Racial Loyalty*, August 1991.

5. Ron Word, "Sailor Slain," Associated Press, August 12, 1992; "In Memoriam," *Racial Loyalty*, March 1992, p. 3 (announces wife's death); William Pierce, letter to Ben Klassen, published in *Racial Loyalty*, May 1992, p. 4.

6. Rev. Brandon O'Rourke, P.M. [Pontifex Maximus], "RAHOWA! Six Years Later," *Racial Loyalty* no. 83 (January 1993); "New Leadership, New Location, New Challenges for the Church of the Creator," *Racial Loyalty* 84 (March 1993), p. 3; "Members, Supporters and Friends," letter insert in March tabloid, signed: Dr. Rick McCarty, Executive Director, COTC.

7. Klassen, *Trials, Tribulations and Triumphs*, pp. 308–12; Rick McCarty, "From the Desk of Dr. McCarty," *Racial Loyalty* 85 (1993), p. 10.

8. "Federal Grand Jury Indicts White Supremacists Plus One Additional Defendant," news release no. 97-181, U.S. Attorney Terre A. Bowers, July 29, 1993; Leonard Zeskind, "State of the Union," *Searchlight*, September 1993, p. 23; "Church of the Creator Founder Ben Klassen Commits Suicide," *Klanwatch Intelligence Report*, Southern Poverty Law Center, August 1993, p. 7; "Final Judgement," *Connie Mansfield v. the Church of the Creator*, Circuit Court for Escambia County, Florida, 94-345-CA, May 2, 1994.

9. Stephan Talty, "The Method of a Neo-Nazi Mogul," *The New York Times Magazine*, February 25, 1996.

10. *Under the Hammer: The Resistance Records Report*, Resistance Records, Autumn 1993.

11. Joseph Carl, "Jack London: An American Racialist," *Resistance* 6 (Spring 1996), pp. 20–24.

12. George Burdi, "Writer Identifies 'Skinheads' as Concerned Young People," *The Spotlight*, August 14, 1995, p. 18.

13. Eric Anderson, "Punk and the 'Symbolic Universe,'" in "Skinheads: From Britain to San Francisco," p. 59; Mark Hamm, *American Skinheads: The Criminology and Control of Hate Crime* (Westport, Conn.: Praeger, 1994), p. 85: "My hypothesis is that neo-Nazi skinheads emerge in a society not because of style, or rebellion. Instead, they emerge through the specific educational and behavioral management efforts orchestrated by adult racists."

14. Anderson, "Skinheads: From Britain to San Francisco," pp. 64, 97; George Burdi, interview with Southern Poverty Law Center, "Present at the Creation," *Intelligence Report*, Fall 2001.

35. Willis Carto Loses Control of the Institute for Historical Review

1. "Declaration of Michelle Matteau," October 17, 1993, *Legion for the Survival of Freedom v. Foundation to Defend the First Amendment*, Superior Court of the State of California, 719141.

2. "Declaration of Mark Weber," "Declaration of Sandra Lee Sisson," "Declaration of Thomas J. Marcellus," "Declaration of Theodore J. O'Keefe," "Declaration of William S. Hulsy," *Legion for the Survival of Freedom v. Foundation to Defend the First Amendment*, Superior Court of the State of California, 719141.

3. "Declaration of Thomas J. Marcellus," December 28, 1993, at point 47, *Legion for the Survival of Freedom v. Foundation to Defend the First Amendment*, Superior Court of the State of California, case no. 719141.

4. Ibid., at point 58.

5. Ibid., at points 41–46.

6. Ibid., at point 76.

7. Ibid., at point 14.

8. "Declaration of Thomas J. Marcellus," points 72–92; "Minutes of Special Board Meeting of Board of Directors of Legion for the Survival of Freedom, September 24, 1993"; Kerr later backed away from Weber and Marcellus: "Supplemental Declaration of Tom Kerr," December 29, 1993.

9. Sam Dickson, "Declaration of Sam Dickson," December 29, 1993; Tom Marcellus, letter to Sam Dickson, October 17, 1993.

10. Jean Farrel, letters to Willis Carto, August 31, 1983, and October 17, 1983, homepage.mac/lsf/litigation/farrel/831017jfeletter.html (accessed December 3, 2001).

11. "Complaint," *Legion for the Survival of Freedom, Inc. v. First Union National Bank and Joan Althaus*, Superior Court of North Carolina, Henderson County, May 16, 1986; "Plaintiff's Answers to Defendant's First Set of Interrogatories," December 4, 1986, *Legion for the*

Survival of Freedom, Inc. v. First Union National Bank and Joan Althaus, Superior Court of North Carolina, Henderson County, 86 CVS 463.

12. Tom Marcellus Declaration of December 28, 1993.

13. Last Will of Jean Farrel, Edison, January 16, 1984.

14. Willis A. Carto, "Dear Mr. Gibson," letters, October 7, 1985, October 19, 1985, November 1, 1985.

36. The Common Law Courts, Partners to the Militia

1. *The Kansas City Star*, January 28, 1994; "Agent Testifies He Urged ATF to Cancel Waco Raid: Superiors 'Not Truthful' About Warning," *The Washington Post*, January 29, 1994.

2. Second superseding indictment, *United States of America, Plaintiff v. Leroy M. Schweitzer, Daniel E. Petersen, Rodney O. Skurdal, Dale M. Jacobi, Richard E. Clark, John P. McGuire, Russell Landers, Dana Dudley a/k/a/ Dana Landers, William Stanton, Agnes Stanton, Ebert Stanton, Ralph Clark, Emmet Clark, Cheryl Petersen, Defendants*, U.S. District Court for the Billings Division of Montana, CR 96-117-BLG-JMB, November 22, 1996.

3. Clair Johnson, "People's Justice? Anti-Government Activity: A Special Report," *Billings Gazette*, March 27, 1994; Susan Hansen, "A Rule of Their Own," *The American Lawyer*, May 1996, pp. 59–61; David A. Neiwert, *In God's Country* (Pullman, Wash.: Washington State University Press, 1999), p. 102.

4. "Rule Ten: Our Posse Comitatus is under full protection of our supreme Law of the Land ex vi termini," Lawful Precept, In our Supreme Court in and for Justus Township, signed by William L. Stanton, April 27, 1994; Daniel Levitas, "Roots of Common Law: An Interview with an Expert on the Posse Comitatus, *Intelligence Report* 90 (Spring 1998).

5. Rodney Skurdal, "Edict," Common Law Affidavit in support for this Common Law, *Israel Appointing Power*, October 28, 1994.

6. *A Season of Discontent: Militias, Constitutionalists, and the Far Right in Montana, January Through May 1994* (Helena: Montana Human Rights Network, 1994); "'Freeman' in Jordan Threaten to Hang Local Sheriff," *Human Rights Network News*, Montana Human Rights Network 3, no. 2, June 1994; Devin Burghart and Robert Crawford, *Guns & Gavels: Common Law Courts, Militias & White Supremacy*, Coalition for Human Dignity, 1996; James Brooke, "Officials Say Montana 'Freeman' Collected $1.8 Million in Scheme," *The New York Times*, March 29, 1996.

7. Militia of Montana, "The Solution and the Plan to Re-establish Our Constitutional Form of Government," *Taking Aim* 2, no. 11 (January 1995): 4.

8. John Trochmann, "Declaration of John Ernest Trochmann," Republic of Montana State Sanders County, January 26, 1992.

9. U.S. Department of Commerce, Bureau of the Census, *County and City Data Book 1983*, 10th ed., p. 340.

10. Author, discussion with residents during visit to Noxon, Montana, October 25, 1988.

11. Floyd Cochran, interview with author, August 21–22, 1992; Neiwert, *In God's Country*, pp. 74–75.

12. Communication to author, November 1992; Neiwert, *In God's Country*, p. 68 (states Trochmann was at Estes Park, but this book mischaracterizes Beam's speech at Estes Park, which was not about Leaderless Resistance but about his travails when arrested in Mexico).

13. Marc Cooper, "Montana's Mother of All Militias," *The Nation*, May 22, 1995.

14. Dan Junas, "Letter to the Village Voice," distributed by e-mail, March 27, 1995; Daniel Junas, "Angry White Guys With Guns: The Rise of the Militias," *CovertAction Quarterly* (Spring 1995).

15. Aryan Nations, "In regards to John Trochmann's comments about the Aryan Nations," press release, April 5, 1995.

16. Leonard Zeskind (unsigned), "States 'Militias' and Gun Control," *Searchlight*, July 1994; Leonard Zeskind (unsigned), "Armed Militias Gain Strength," *Searchlight*, March 1995.

17. Bo Gritz, "The Colonel's Corner," *Center for Action Newsletter* 3, no. 2 (September 1993): 2–5; Bo Gritz, "SPIKE Training" brochure, February 1993; Jonathan Mozzochi, "Briefing on Center for Action 'Spike Seminar,' Including James 'Bo' Gritz and the Christian Patriot Association," Coalition for Human Dignity, February 28, 1993.

37. Birth of *American Renaissance*

1. Don Warren, transcript of phone communications with author, May 30, 1994 (Warren attended the conference, described Duke's exclusion, Weber's presence, and other activities); Leonard Zeskind, "White-Shoed Supremacy," *The Nation*, June 10, 1996; Samuel Taylor, "Atlanta Conference is a Great Success," *American Renaissance* newsletter, July 1994.

2. Sam G. Dickson, "Dawn's Early Light," 1994 American Renaissance Conference, transcription of audiotape no. T010; other speakers who emphasized these ideas of inherent biologically determined inequality included Dr. Michael Levin, "Policy Consequences of Racial Differences," audiotape no. T002.

3. Sam G. Dickson, "Dawn's Early Light," transcript p. 5.

4. Dr. Samuel T. Francis, "Inequality: Natural Political and Social," 1994 American Renaissance Conference, audiotape no. T003, transcript p. 8.

5. Rabbi Mayer Schiller, "Saving Our Civilization," 1994 American Renaissance Conference, audiotape no. T008, transcript; Ami Eden, "A Chasidic Spokesman Espouses Modernity and Racial Separation," *The Forward*, April 13, 2001; David Kerr, "A Conversation with Rabbi Mayer Schiller," www.ulsternation.org.uk, July 13, 2000 (published later in *Third Way* magazine); Ira Rifkin, "What Do Jewish Conservatives Want?," *The Jewish Advocate*, October 27, 1994; David Klinghoffer, "Toward Tradition's Parley Charts Rightward Course," *The Forward*, October 14, 1994.

6. Don Warren, transcript of phone communications with author, May 30, 1994 (Warren described conversations with Jared Taylor as well as an account of Taylor's leading role); IRS Form 990, 2002, lists Jared Taylor as president of New Century Foundation with an annual salary of $45,000.

7. Jared Taylor, *Shadows of the Rising Sun* (New York: William Morrow and Company, 1983). Title page includes personal background information.

8. Taylor, *Shadows of the Rising Sun*, p. 15 ("I would like to thank Mark Weber, who first urged me to write this book"); Jared Taylor, *Paved with Good Intentions: The Failure of Race Relations in Contemporary America* (New York: Carroll & Graf Publishers, Inc., 1992); "Jared Taylor," www.jaredtaylor.org, for stint with *PC* magazine.

9. "Who Speaks for Us?," *American Renaissance* newsletter, November 1990, "published monthly by the Jefferson Institute . . . Menlo Park, CA" (first issue).

10. "Who Speaks for Us," pp. 1–2.

11. Clint Bolick, "The Great Racial Divide," *The Wall Street Journal*, November 30, 1992.

12. Peter Brimelow, *National Review*, January 18, 1993, republished at www.vdare.com/pb/taylor_review.htm (accessed May 11, 2002).

13. Peter Brimelow, VDARE, www.vdare.com/pb/taylor_review.htm (accessed May 11, 2002).

14. Although American Renaissance conference attendees sometimes referred to Rich as Taylor's "wife," on December 6, 2006, she wrote an e-mail to the *Pittsburgh Post Gazette* reporter Dennis Roddy saying "I am not married to Jared." She also wrote that she did "proof read American Renaissance."

15. Evelyn Rich, Ph.D., "Ku Klux Klan Ideology, 1954–1988," dissertation, U.M.I. Dissertation Service, 1989.

16. Evelyn Rich, communication to the National Anti-Klan Network, "On Friday April 19 and Saturday April 20 1985, Duke and I visited Pierce at National Alliance Headquarters . . ."

17. Evelyn Rich, telephone conversation with author, April 24, 1986.

18. Evelyn Rich, report on the meeting between Duke and Pierce, April 19 and 20, 1985.

19. Rich note to National Anti-Klan Network, n.d.; later Evelyn Rich donated to Tulane University the contents of interviews conducted during research for her Ph.D. dissertation.

20. Don Warren, transcript of phone communications with author, May 30, 1994 (Warren described a conversation with Wayne Lutton, who made this claim).

21. Dr. Evelyn Fitch, "Attendees Raved about the Last IHR International Revisionist Conference," promotional page advertising the 10th International Revisionist Conference in 1990; Dr. Evelyn Fich, "Praise from Eleventh IHR Conference Attendees," Institute for Historical Review, n.d. [all spelling differences of the name are reflected in the original source material].

22. Dr. Evelyn Rich, "Praise from Eleventh IHR Conference Attendees."

23. "A Special Report on the IHR Controversy," *The Spotlight*, September 12, 1994: "Mark Weber . . . maintains regular contact with one Evelyn Rich . . . [who] is known to receive personal phone calls at home from Irwin Suall . . . chief of the ADL's international spy ring."

24. Ira Katznelson, *When Affirmative Action Was White: An Untold History of Racial Inequality in Twentieth-Century America* (New York: W.W. Norton & Company, 2005); Betsy Leondar-Wright, "White Affirmative Action," June 25, 2003, www.CommonDreams.org.

25. On the transformation of whiteness see: Theodore W. Allen, *The Invention of the White Race, Volume One: Racial Oppression and Social Control* (New York: Verso, 1994); Noel Ignatiev, *How the Irish Became White* (New York: Routledge, 1995); Grace Elizabeth Hale, *Making Whiteness: The Culture of Segregation in the South 1890–1940* (New York: Vintage Books, 1999); Matthew Frye Jacobson, *Whiteness of a Different Color: European Immigrants and the Alchemy of Race* (Cambridge: Harvard University Press, 1998).

26. Allan Chase, *The Legacy of Malthus: The Social Costs of the New Scientific Racism* (Urbana: University of Illinois Press, 1980), pp. 266–73.

27. Rich, "Ku Klux Klan Ideology, 1954–1988," p. 4: "Anti-Semitism provided the impetus for the growth of a revolutionary impulse." Rich's entire thesis develops around the change in the Klan's ideological disposition.

28. "Jared Taylor's Conference," *Instauration*, July 1994, p. 32; the May 1994 *Instauration* advertised the conference in advance, p. 31; the August 1994 issue published a second squib on it, p. 32.

29. Ian McKinney, April 5, 1996, "Stormfront: Infiltration." Nizkor file, p. 7.

30. Jared Taylor, "Teaching more millions to hate us," posted October 7, 2001, www.fpp.co.uk/online/01/10/WTC_Jared.html.

31. Communication to author, "Report on the *American Renaissance* Conference, 2002," Center for New Community; Leonard Zeskind, "American Renaissance Defends the 'West,' Nick Griffin Stumps the UA," *Searchlight*, May 2002.

32. Cat Lady, "The Most Rational Place on Earth," www.vanguardnewsnetwork.com, posted February 27, 2002 (report on the American Renaissance 2002 conference).

33. Sanford Griffith, "Weber Found His Guru in the African Desert," *The Spotlight*, February 12, 2001.

34. Wedding Invitation, "Nuptial Mass . . . Priscilla Marie and Mr. Mark Edward Weber," October 29, 1994, at St. James Roman Catholic Church; Mark Weber, "Letter to Donald Warren," November 20, 1994: "I was also happy with Taylor's performance. He was a superb best man, most notably as MC at our reception."

35. Don Warren, "A Narrative Summary of Key Events and Personalities at the 12th IHR Conference, 3–5 Sept. 1994," personal communication to author (includes background information on Priscilla Gray).

36. Mark Weber, "Letter to Donald Warren," November 20, 1994: "Fr. Tacelli did a fine job of officiating."

37. Taylor, *Shadows of the Rising Sun*, p. 15 ("I would like to thank Mark Weber, who first urged me to write this book"); Jared Taylor, "Letter to Don Warren," April 8, 1993.

38. Lawrence Auster, "Multiculturalism and the War Against White America: A Lecture . . . ," *American Renaissance*, August 1994, p. 4.

39. Dr. Wayne Lutton, "Immigration: The Silent Invasion," 1994 American Renaissance Conference, audiotape no. T007.

40. Wayne Lutton, correspondence with Don Warren.

41. Wayne Lutton and John Tanton, "About the Author," *The Immigration Invasion*, foreword by Senator Eugene McCarthy (Monterey, Va.: The Social Contract Press, 1994), first printing 200,000.

42. Wayne Lutton, "Soviet Naval Power Outstrips the West," parts 1 and 2, *Christian Crusade Weekly*, February 23, 1975, and March 2, 1975; Rep. Larry McDonald (R. Ga.), *Congressional Record*, vol. 121, pp. 22435–36 and pp. 23196–97. McDonald describes the author of these two articles as "Professor Wayne Lutton of American Christian College."

43. Wayne Lutton, "Today's Jews Descended from Khazars," review of book by Arthur Koestler, *American Mercury* 113 (Spring 1970); Wayne Lutton, "Facts About the Arab Boycott," *American Mercury* 114 (September 1978).

44. Jonathan Tilove, e-mail to author, April 12, 2006: "I also talked with Wayne Lutton while I was there and he denies that he wrote for the Journal of Historical Review."

45. Wayne Lutton, "The Surgeon General's Report on Acquired Immune Deficiency Syndrome," *National Review*, September 25, 1987; Wayne Lutton, "Nairobi to Vancouver: The World Council of Churches and the World, 1975–87" (book review), *National Review*, August 19, 1988; Lutton and Tanton, *The Immigration Invasion*.

46. "New EAC Members" (Editorial Advisory Committee), *IHR Newsletter* 30 (March 1985): 7: "Charles Lutton, whom you will recognize as a frequent contributor to the *Journal* . . ."; Charles Lutton, letter to Willis Carto in support of Keith Stimely, February 5, 1985 (reproduced from the original . . . Special Collections, Knight Library, University of Oregon); Charles Lutton, "Pearl Harbor: Fifty Years of Controversy," *Journal of Historical Review* 11, no. 4 (Winter 1991–1992): 431; Charles Lutton, "H.W.F. Saggs, The Might That Was Assyria," *Journal of Historical Review* 6, no. 2 (Summer 1985).

47. In the Noontide Press 1997 catalog, audiotape A025, "Axis Involvement with Arab Nationalists During World War Two," is listed on p. 31 with "Charles Lutton" the author-speaker; on the actual audiotape from the "1981 Int'l Revisionist Conference," the label of Tape T-25 lists the author as "Mr. Charles Sutton."

48. Ted O'Keefe, letter to Don Warren, August 13, 1991.

49. Wayne C. Lutton, letter to Don Warren, March 7, 1992; Wayne Lutton, letter to Don Warren, October 1, 1992 (letters provided by their recipient); Mark Weber, letter to Don Warren, April 19, 1995: "I was glad the other day to speak with Wayne Lutton, who is as busy as ever . . ."

50. New Century Foundation, IRS Form 990, 2002, "Wayne Lutton, Trustee 1."

38. Holocaust Denial: To the Moscow Station

1. "Spirited Twelfth IHR Conference Brings Together Leading Revisionist Scholars and Activists: Defying Powerful Adversaries, Institute Marks Progress," *The Journal of Historical Review* (November–December 1994): 2–8.

2. Ted O'Keefe, "Opening of Convention," and Mark Weber, "The Cultural Crisis of Our Age," First General Convention of the National Alliance, September 2–3, 1978, *National Alliance Bulletin*, June–July 1978; Fritz Berg, "Diesels, Gas Vans and Zyklon B," slide show and lecture, convention schedule, *National Alliance Bulletin*, July 1982.

3. Mark Weber, "Further Progress, New Challenges," 12th Int'l Revisionist Conference, Institute for Historical Review Tape A134.

4. Ibid.

5. Don Warren, "A Narrative Summary of Key Events and Personalities at the 12th IHR Conference, 3–5 September 1994," September 1994, communication to author.

6. "Spirited Twelfth IHR Conference Brings Together Leading Revisionist Scholars and Activists," *The Journal of Historical Review*; Don Warren, personal communication to author, March 19, 1994.

7. Frank Thompson, "IHR Pot Continues to Boil," *The Spotlight*, August 8, 1994; John Henry, "Tough Times Ahead for Conspirators," *The Spotlight*, January 9, 1995; Letters to the Editor, *The Barnes Review* 1 (October 1994).

8. Stanley R. Barrett, *Is God A Racist? The Right Wing in Canada* (Toronto: University of Toronto Press, 1987), pp. 156–70.

9. Christof Friedrich (Zundel) and Eric Thomson, *The Hitler We Loved & Why* (White Power Publications, 1977); Christof Friedrich (Zundel), "Four Books That Shook the World," *The Liberty Bell*, June 1976; Christof Friedrich (Zundel), "Who Is Behind Quebec Separatism," *The Liberty Bell*, January 1977; Christof Friedrich (Zundel), "What is Samisdat," *The Liberty Bell*, June 1977.

10. Michael A. Hoffman II, "Canada Ignores Civil Rights In Prosecution of Publisher," *The Spotlight*, April 22, 1985.

11. Author notes of Zundel videotapes: "Revisionism 101" and "Revisionism 102."

12. Deborah Lipstadt, *Denying the Holocaust: The Growing Assault of Truth and Memory* (New York: The Free Press, 1993), pp. 157–82; Martin A. Lee, *The Beast Reawakens* (New York: Little, Brown and Company, 1997), p. 342.

13. "Canada's Top Court Rules Holocaust 'Debunker' Legal," UPI, August 28, 1992; "Supreme Court of Canada: 1992 Zundel Judgement," Analysis, Section 181: "Its History, Purpose and Ambit," (available from Nizkor website).

14. Greg Raven, Introduction on Tape A140, Ernst Zundel, "New Historical Perspectives in Russia," 12th Int'l Revisionist Conference.

15. Ernst Zundel, "My Impressions of the New Russia: Is a 'National Socialist' Russia Emerging," *The Journal of Historical Review* (September/October 1995): 2; Serge Schmemann, "Nationalists Gain," *The New York Times*, December 13, 1993; Carey Goldberg, "Extremist's Triumph Frightens Supporters of Reform in Russia," *Los Angeles Times*, December 14, 1993.

16. Zundel, "My Impressions of the New Russia."

17. Zundel, "New Historical Perspectives in Russia," Tape A140; Zundel, "My Impressions of the New Russia"; Don Warren, communication to author.

18. Don Warren, communication to author.

19. Mark Weber, "Who Is Ernst Zundel, and Why Is He in Jail?," Institute for Historical Review, September 23, 2003; "Germany: Holocaust Denier Gets Five Years," *The New York Times*, February 16, 2007.

39. Elections 1994: An Anti-immigrant Voting Bloc Emerges

1. Sam Howe Verhover, "Republican Tide Brings New Look to Legislatures" and "State By State: The Balance of Power," *The New York Times*, November 12, 1994; Richard L. Berke, "Defections Among Men to G.O.P. Helped Ensure Rout of Democrats," *The New York Times*, November 11, 1994; Michael Barone and Grant Ujifusa, "The Restoration of the Constitutional Order and the Return to Tocquevillian America," *The Almanac of American Politics 1996*, National Journal, pp. xxiii–xxvi.

2. Jason F. Isaacson, "Republicans' Sweep of the 1994 Elections and Their Agenda in the New Congress," November 28, 1994, The American Jewish Committee.

3. "Portrait of the Electorate: Who Voted for Whom in the House," *The New York Times*, November 13, 1994, p. 15.

4. Helen Chenoweth (R. Idaho) was first elected to Congress in 1994 with the support of militia activists and opponents of conservation measures; Steve Stockman (R. Texas—10th Dist.) was first elected with the support of the Christian right and the gun lobby in 1994.

5. Jeffrey M. Peyton, "Pro-Family Surge Sways Elections," *Christian American* 5, 9 (November/December 1994); "Religious-Right Candidates Gain as G.O.P. Turnout Rises," *The New York Times*, November 12, 1994.

6. Richard L. Berke, "Defections Bare Fissure in G.O.P.," *The New York Times*, November 1, 1994; Kevin Phillips, "Under the Electoral Volcano," *The New York Times*, November 7, 1994; Isaacson, "Republicans' Sweep of the 1994 Elections and the Agenda in the New Congress." The split among Virginia Republicans over the Ollie North candidacy was particularly well known.

7. Michael Vlahos, "The New Wave: When Paradigms Collide," *National Review*, September 26, 1994, pp. 38–46.

8. "Races of the Week: Metcalf vs. Swift," *Human Events*, October 3, 1992; Metcalf lost his Washington State house seat in 1964, served in the state senate from 1966 to 1970, and won a state senate seat again in 1980.

9. "Fed Faces a Stiff Challenge," *The Spotlight*, January 3 and 10, 1983, p. 6; "State Senator Campaigning Against the Federal Reserve," *The Spotlight*, July 18, 1983; Jim Townsend, letter "To ROC Chairmen and Members," noted that Metcalf sponsored legislation in the Washington state house to file suit against the Federal Reserve Bank, n.d.; in 1984, Metcalf became a national cochairman of Redeem Our Country; he also published a newsletter entitled "Honest Money for America."

10. Robert Crawford, "Jack Metcalf: A Chenoweth at Heart? Banking Conspiracies & Native Americans Targeted," *The Dignity Report* 19, published by the Coalition for Human Dignity. Metcalf was a board member of two organizations opposed to Native Indian treaty rights, Salmon-Steelhead Preservation Action for Washington Now and United Property

Owners of Washington; Jack Metcalf, Congressional Record, May 13, 1999, p. H3155: "I urge my colleagues to join me in opposition to the renewal of [whaling] by the Makah Tribe of Northwest Washington State."

11. "Metcalf to Address New Party," *The Spotlight*, July 23, 1984, p. 29.
12. Jack Metcalf, speech at conference of Larry Humphreys Heritage Library, a Christian Identity establishment, September 1984, transcript made from videotape of his presentation.
13. Jim Simon, "Candidate Metcalf Assailed over Ties to Far Right Activist," *The Seattle Times*, October 29, 1994; "Jack Metcalf in the 2nd," *The Seattle Times*, November 1, 1994.
14. "Spotlight on People," *The Spotlight*, December 5, 1994, p. 20.
15. "Judge Blocks Enactment of New Immigration Law," Associated Press, published in *The Kansas City Star*, November 10, 1994; "CA's Anti-Immigrant Proposition 187 is Voided, Ending State's Five-Year Battle with ACLU, Rights Groups," ACLU press release, July 29, 1999.
16. Jane Adams, "Pro. 187—What's to Be Learned?," *Racefile: A Project of the Applied Research Center*, January–February 1995, pp. 20–21. Adams drew from a *Los Angeles Times* exit poll.
17. Michael Barone and Grant Ujifusa, *Almanac of American Politics 1996*, National Journal Inc., pp. 81–82.
18. Doug Brugge, "Pulling Up the Ladder: The Anti-Immigrant Backlash," In *Eyes Right! Challenging the Right Wing Backlash*, Chip Berlet, ed. (Boston: South End Press, 1995), p. 206.
19. Michael R. Alvarez and Tara L. Butterfield, "The Resurgence of Nativism in California? The Case of Proposition 187 and Illegal Immigration," *Social Science Quarterly* 81, no. 1 (March 2000): 167–79; M. V. Hood III and Irwin L. Morris, "Brother, Can You Spare a Dime? Racial/Ethnic Context and the Anglo Vote on Proposition 187," *Social Science Quarterly* 81, no. 1 (March 2000): 194–206; Caroline J. Tolbert and Robert E. Hero, "Race/Ethnicity and Direct Democracy: An Analysis of California's Illegal Immigration Initiative," *Journal of Politics* (1996): 58:806–18; Susan Welch and Lee Sigelman, "Getting to Know You? Latino-Anglo Social Contact," *Social Science Quarterly* 81, no. 1 (March 2000). It is important to note that there was diversity of opinion among these studies.
20. Hood III and Morris, "Brother, Can You Spare a Dime?" p. 203. Hood and Morris also cited a study by Jack Citron of "The Official English Movement" published in *Western Political Quarterly* 43 that supported similar results.
21. Alvarez and Butterfield, "The Resurgence of Nativism in California?," p. 168.
22. Ibid., pp. 174–77.
23. Tolbert and Hero, "Race/Ethnicity and Direct Democracy: An Analysis of California's Illegal Immigration Initiative."
24. Hood and Morris, "Brother, Can You Spare a Dime?," pp. 201–203.
25. Sam Francis, "Racialpolitik," in *Revolution from the Middle*, p. 216. In the same commentary Francis adds, "The vote for Proposition 187 goes far to relegitimize the racial aspect of American identity."
26. "Populist Tally 231,000 Votes in Chicago," *Populist Observer*, December 1994, p. 6; "Record Number of Populist Party Candidates in 1994," *Populist Observer*, September 1994, p. 6.

40. The Bell Curve: Legitimizing Scientific Racism
1. Seymour Martin Lipset and Earl Raab, *The Politics of Unreason: Right-Wing Extremism in America 1790–1970* (New York: Harper & Row Publishers), pp. 252, 265–66; Arnold Forster and Benjamin Epstein, *Danger on the Right: The Attitudes, Personnel and Influence of the Radical Right and Extreme Conservatives* (New York: Random House, 1964), pp. 248–49.
2. Revilo P. Oliver, "Dear Colonel Dall," letter, December 17, 1970.
3. Robert S. Griffin, *The Fame of a Dead Man's Deeds: An Up-Close Portrait of White Nationalist William Pierce*, pp. 137–38.
4. Since Oliver's death, collections of his writings have been posted on the Internet at www.stormfront.org/rpo/ and www.revilo-oliver.com.
5. Kirsten Kaiser Strom, speech, *The Revilo P. Oliver Memorial Symposium*, November 19, 1994.
6. Sam Dickson, letter of invitation to memorial, November 8, 1994.

7. Author, notes and transcription, *The Revilo P. Oliver Memorial Symposium*, Videotapes 1, 2, and 3, National Vanguard Books Item no. 625; memorial at Jumer's Castle Lodge, Urbana, Illinois, November 19, 1994.

8. Ibid., Tape 3.

9. Author, notes and transcription, *The Revilo P. Oliver Memorial Symposium*, David Duke, Tape 3.

10. Ibid.

11. Ibid.

12. Richard J. Herrnstein and Charles Murray, *The Bell Curve: Intelligence and Class Structure in American Life* (New York: The Free Press, 1994); Stefan Kuhl, *The Nazi Connection: Eugenics, American Racism and German National Socialism* (New York: Oxford University Press, 1994).

13. William Henry III, "Born Gay?," *Time*, July 26, 1993, pp. 36–41; "Debate: Is Homosexuality Biologically Influenced?," *Scientific American*, May 1994.

14. Robert Wright, "The Biology of Violence," *The New Yorker*, March 13, 1995, pp. 69–77.

15. Tom Morgenthau, "IQ: Is It Destiny," *Newsweek*, October 24, 1994, pp. 53–55.

16. "The Negro," *Encyclopaedia Britannica 1911*, reprinted in Russell Jacoby and Naomi Glauberman, *The Bell Curve Debate: History, Documents, Opinions* (New York: Times Books, 1995), p. 439.

17. www.google.com/search?hl=en&q=The+Bell+Curve+best+seller+list.

18. Tom W. Smith, "Public Opinion on Race and Affirmative Action, Table 7," National Opinion Research Center, University of Chicago, report prepared for the Southern Regional Council, December 1996.

19. Jason DeParle, "An Architect of the Reagan Vision Plunges into Inquiry on Race and IQ," *The New York Times*, November 30, 1990; Charles Murray, *Losing Ground: American Social Policy 1950–1980* (New York: Basic Books, 1984).

20. DeParle, "An Architect of the Reagan Vision Plunges into Inquiry on Race and IQ."

21. "In America IQ Is Not Destiny," unsigned editorial, *BusinessWeek*, October 31, 1994, reprinted in *The Bell Curve Debate: History, Documents, Opinions*.

22. "O Tempora, O Mores! Breakthrough on Race?," *American Renaissance*, December 1994, p. 8.

41. The Oklahoma City Bomb and Its Immediate Aftermath

1. "This Doesn't Happen Here," *Newsweek*, May 1, 1995; "Oklahoma Bombing Survivors Plan to Sue U.S.," *The New York Times*, March 20, 1997 (this article cites "more than 500 hurt"); Jo Thomas, "Bomb Trial Goes Swiftly," *The New York Times*, May 9, 1997 (this article cites 850 wounded, but the precise number of wounded victims was never established in court); Larry Mackey, "Closing Argument for the prosecution in the trial of Timothy McVeigh," *United States of America v. Timothy James McVeigh*, 96-CR-60, May 29, 1997 (cited evidence introduced during the trial of four thousand pounds of fertilizer purchased by McVeigh and Nichols, but the exact size of the bomb was never precisely established).

2. Larry B. Stammer and Carla Hall, "U.S. Muslims Feel Sting of Accusations," *The Los Angeles Times*, April 22, 1995 ("news reports said two men of 'Middle Eastern' appearance were being sought"); "Muslims Bury Baby, Decry Stereotypes," Associated Press, April 25, 1995 (mother miscarried after her home was stoned); Jorge Casuso, "Arabic Residents target of threats," *Santa Monica Outlook*, April 22, 1995.

3. A number of books were later written about the Oklahoma City bombing and its relationship to militia groups and other white nationalists, including: Levitas, *The Terrorist Next Door*; Richard A. Serrano, *One of Ours: Timothy McVeigh and the Oklahoma City Bombing* (New York: W. W. Norton & Company, 1998); Ken Stern, *A Force upon the Plain: The American Militia Movement and the Politics of Hate* (New York: Simon & Schuster, 1996); Stephen Jones and Peter Israel, *Others Unknown: Timothy McVeigh and the Oklahoma City Bombing Conspiracy* (New York: Public Affairs, 1998); Lou Michel and Dan Herbeck, *American Terrorist: Timothy McVeigh & the Oklahoma City Bombing* (New York: Regan Books, 2001); Mark S. Hamm, *In Bad Company: America's Terrorist Underground* (Boston: Northeastern University Press, 2002).

4. Todd S. Purdum, "Army Veteran Held in Oklahoma Bombing; Toll Hits 65 as Hope for Survivors Fades," David Johnston, "Just Before He Was to Be Freed, Prime Bombing Suspect Is Identified in Jail" (Perry, Oklahoma), and James Bennet, "With Helicopters Above, Agents Raid Michigan Farmhouse," *The New York Times*, April 22, 1995; Russell Watson et al., "Cleverness and Luck," *Newsweek*, May 1, 1995, pp. 30–32.

5. Serge F. Kovalski, "In a Mirror, Nichols Saw a Victim; Ex-Soldier, Ex-Salesman, Extremist Gravitated to Fringe Groups," *The Washington Post*, July 3, 1995; Levitas, *The Terrorist Next Door*, pp. 215–16; Richard Serrano, "McVeigh's Sister Describes His Rage at Government," *The Los Angeles Times*, May 6, 1997 (Jennifer McVeigh read from a letter her brother wrote: "We members of the citizen's militia . . . "); John Kiner, "Bomb Suspect Felt at Home Riding the Gun-Show Circuit," *The New York Times*, July 5, 1995; Terry L. Nichols, "Affidavit," March 16, 1994.

6. John Kifner, "Oklahoma Bomb Suspect: Unraveling of Frayed Life," *The New York Times*, December 31, 1995 (described McVeigh and *Turner Diaries*); "Come Clean, Janet," *The Spotlight*, April 7, 1997, p. 2, News You May Have Missed section; copy of postcard "Black Sunday" 1935 Oklahoma Dust Storm addressed to *The Spotlight*, stamped with a received date April (date indecipherable), 1995; "Conspiracy to Set-up Lobby Exposed," *The Spotlight*, July 21, 1997 (describes classified ad by "Tim Tuttle," one of McVeigh's aliases); James Ridgeway, "A Conspiratorial Gathering," *The Village Voice*, April 1, 1997 (includes discussion of postcard).

7. "The View From the Far Right," *Newsweek*, May 1, 1995, p. 36; "Special Issue: The Face of Terror," *Time*, May 1, 1995; "Militia Extremists," *Day One*, ABC News, April 27, 1995; "White Supremacist and Militia Groups Joining Forces," *Future Watch*, CNN, April 30, 1995; "Newspaper Editors Discuss Militias," *Weekend Show*, National Public Radio, April 30, 1995.

8. "Oklahoma Bombing Sets Stage for Social Engineering," *The Spotlight*, May 8, 1995; William Jasper interview with G. Vance Smith, "The Birch Society Battles On," *The New American*, August 19, 1996, pp. 16–19; Leonard Zeskind, "Armed and Dangerous: The NRA, Militias and White Supremacists are Fostering a Network of Right-Wing Warriors," *Rolling Stone*, November 2, 1995.

9. William L. Pierce, "American Dissident Voices," radio broadcast, April 29, 1995.

10. "Personal . . . From the Editor," *The Spotlight*, May 1, 1995; "Constitution at Risk," Vince Ryan, Liberty Lobby Reports, *The Spotlight*, May 8, 1995 ("The monstrous deed in Oklahoma").

11. Mike Blair, "Feds 'Fib' on Oklahoma City Bomb Says Ex-High Level FBI Official," *The Spotlight*, May 15, 1995 (high-tech bomb theory); Mike Blair, "New Facts Emerge in Oklahoma City Blast: Experts Nix Fertilizer," *The Spotlight*, June 5, 1995; Mike Blair, "All (Bad) Roads Lead to Arkansas in Oklahoma City Investigation," *The Spotlight*, July 10, 1995; Mike Blair, "Independent Investigators See Mideast Connection in Oklahoma City Bombing," *The Spotlight*, December 4, 1995.

12. Mike Blair, "Ex-Agent Claims Feds Employed 'Dupes' to Bomb Murrah Building," *The Spotlight*, November 11, 1996; "John Doe No. 2 Won't Go Away," *The New American*, November 11, 1996; "Federal Agencies Implicated in Oklahoma City Bombing," *The Free American*, June 1995; Mireya Navarro, "At Fair for Survivalists, Fallout from Oklahoma," *The New York Times*, June 12, 1995; Dan Yurman, "Militia Theories on John Doe #2: Real or Disinformation," Special to the Econet Western Lands Gopher Service, August 5, 1996; Jo Thomas, "Sightings of John Doe No. 2 In Blast Case, Mystery No. 1," *The New York Times*, December 3, 1995.

13. Notes, photos, literature, and audiotape collected, Committee of 1776 rally in Washington, D.C., June 4, 1995; Leonard Zeskind, "The Militias: From Oklahoma Tragedy to Washington Farce," *Searchlight*, July 1995, pp. 23–24.

14. Kirk Lyons, phone interview with author, August 31, 1995. Misty Ferguson's claims were later incorporated into a case pursued unsuccessfully by attorneys other than Lyons, United States Court of Appeals, 01-50154.

15. Notes and literature collected, "America 95, Constitution Restoration Rally, Freedom Expo," Kansas City area, June 10, 1995; Zeskind, "The Militias: From Oklahoma Tragedy to Washington Farce."

16. Author's notes, publications, tapes, and other materials collected, "For Peace of Mind in Our Changing World," Preparedness Expo, Orange County Convention Center, June 9–11, 1995.

17. Author's notes; Larry Pratt, "Gun Control: 2nd Amendment Under Fire," Panel at Expo, June 9, 1995; Zeskind, "Armed and Dangerous: The NRA, Militias and White Supremacists are Fostering a Network of Right-Wing Warriors."

18. Bo Gritz, interview with author, June 10, 1995; author's notes.

19. Bo Gritz, "Ark in a Time of Noah," Preparedness Expo speech, June 11, 1995.

20. Leslie Jorgensen, "A Tale of Terrorism: McVeigh Defense Enabled by White Supremacist, Militia Pro-gun Sources," *The Colorado Statesman* 97, no. 7; J. D. Cash, in a series of articles published in the *McCurtain Daily Gazette*, most actively pursued the holes.

21. Peter T. Kilborn, "Terror in Oklahoma: The Nichols Brothers; Seeking Clues Along a Highway," *The New York Times*, May 11, 1995; McVeigh's fingerprints were on the receipt for a fertilizer purchase, however.

22. "Leg lost in blast still a mystery," Associated Press, October 19, 1995; Mark Eddy, "Area Scientist Gets Call to ID Misidentified Leg from Bombing," *The Denver Post*, February 29, 1996; "Leg Is Matched to Woman Who Died in Bombing," Associated Press, February 24, 1996 ("death count was raised to 169").

23. Judy Thomas, "We Are Not Dangerous, Leader of Separatists Says," *The Kansas City Star*, March 17, 1996; Robert Millar, interview with James Ridgeway and author, March 1996, conducted on the grounds of Elohim City.

24. Judy Thomas, "We Are Not Dangerous, Leader of Separatists Says"; Howard Pankratz, "Records Hint at Link with Elohim City," *The Denver Post*, May 12, 1996.

25. Kirk Lyons, "Dear Supporter" letter, n.d., received March 1996; Robert Millar, interview with James Ridgeway and the author, March 1996 (confirmed McVeigh's call to Elohim City).

26. Markus Wallenberg, "Berlin-Oklahoma-Berlin," *Neues Deutschland*, February 3, 1996; Neil H. Payne, "The Story of Andi the German," *The Balance* (a publication of the CAUSE Foundation) 8, no. 1:3.

27. "Statement of Andreas Carl Strassmeir," *United States of America v. Timothy McVeigh*, CR-95-110, unsigned affidavit circulated after February 1996; Judy Thomas, "German Disavows Link to Oklahoma City Explosion," *The Kansas City Star*, March 1, 1996 (article based on the affidavit).

28. Andreas Strassmeir and David Holloway, interview with RLS, January 2, 1996; "The Story of Andi the German," *The Balance* 8, no. 1.

29. Search Warrant Recovery list, Public Storage Joplin, Missouri, Case ID 91A-KC-75819, February 13, 1996; Sharon Cohen, "'Bank Bandits' Motivated by Racism, Mission to Steal," *The Kansas City Star*, January 5, 1996; *United States of America v. Mark William Thomas, Peter Kevin Langan a/k/a "Commander Pedro," Scott Anthony Stedford a/k/a "Tudo," Kevin William McCarthy a/k/a "Blondie," Michael William Brescia a/k/a "Tim,"* United States District Court for the Eastern District of Pennsylvania, Indictment Date filed January 30, 1997; Michael Weber, "Guilty Verdict in Robberies by One Militia," *The New York Times*, February 11, 1997; Hamm, *In Bad Company: America's Terrorist Underground*.

30. Robert Ruth, "Shootout Was Brief, Violent, FBI Agents Testify," *The Columbus Dispatch*, July 31, 1996; Evidence Recovery Log for 1993 Ford XLT Pickup, Case ID 91A-SL-179944, February 12, 1996; Leonard Zeskind, "A Phineas Priest in Pink," *Searchlight*, January 1997, p. 23; Robert Ruth and Brent LaLonda, "Bank Bandit Found Hanged in Jail Cell," *The Columbus Dispatch*, July 13, 1996.

31. J. D. Cash, "FBI Says Strassmeir Was Government 'Operative,'" *McCurtain Sunday Gazette and Broken Bow News*, July 14, 1996; J. D. Cash, "Agents Probe OKC Bombing Links to Bank Robberies," *McCurtain Daily Gazette*, July 16, 1996; J. D. Cash, "German National Linked to Okla. City Bombing Suspect #2," *Media Bypass*, September 1996.

32. Robert Millar, interview with James Ridgeway conducted in Elohim City, March 1996; James Ridgeway and Leonard Zeskind, "The Fall Guy?," *The Village Voice*, April 9, 1996.

42. The Second Underground Collapses

1. James Brooke, "Freemen Farm Attracts the Fringe," *The New York Times*, April 28, 1996; "With Freemen Gone, a Surface Calm Descends," Associated Press, July 14, 1996.

2. "Federal, State and Local Law Enforcement Discuss Indictments and Arrest Status in Garfield County Case," United States Dept. of Justice, U.S. Attorney District of Montana, press release, March 26, 1996.

3. The debtor was one of those who had burst into the Garfield County Court that January day in 1994.

4. "Inventory Listing of All Items Seized at Search Warrant Site," Investigation no. 43572, July 2, 1996, U.S. District Court for Billings Division of Montana, CR 95–117.

5. News Advisory, U.S. Attorney District of Montana, March 25, 1996 (announcing arrest of Leroy Schweitzer and Daniel Peterson); Clair Johnson, "Leaders Accused of Threats Against Officials," *Billings Gazette*, March 27, 1996.

6. David Johnston, "F.B.I. Standoff With Militants Tests New Path," *The New York Times*, March 30, 1996.

7. Louis Sahagun and Richard Serrano, "FBI Found Rightists Key to Ending Montana Standoff; Surrender Strategy to Arrest 'Freemen' Without Violence Was to Seek Other Extremists' Help," *The Los Angeles Times*, June 15, 1996.

8. James "Bo" Gritz, "Between the Lines—A Case of Radical Extremes," fax from Vicci Gritz to Jim Dingman, May 20, 1996.

9. "Freemen Stand-Off Phase 1—Debriefing," *Taking Aim* newsletter, vol. 3, no. 3 (June 1996), Militia of Montana; David Perlmutt, "Freemen Negotiating Described," *Charlotte Observer*, June 18, 1996; Jack Horan, "Carolinas Men Help on Freemen; Leader Escorted on Trip to Meet Jailed Member," *Charlotte Observer*, June 12, 1996.

10. Perlmutt, "Freemen Negotiating Described."

11. "The Heat Is On: A Covert Attempt to Split Militia," *Taking Aim* newsletter, vol. 3, no. 1 (April 1996), p. 7.

12. Chris Temple, "Freemen Generate Mixed Reactions," *The Jubilee* 8, no. 5 (May/June 1996); Leonard Zeskind, "Justice vs. Justus: Montana Freemen Trial May Mark End of an Era," *Intelligence Report*, Spring 1998.

13. *Combating Terrorism: FBI's Use of Federal Funds for Counterterrorism Related Activities (FYs 1995–98)*, Government Accounting Office, November 1998, p. 2.

14. From ERRI Daily Intelligence Report, "Excerpts: Report on Domestic Terrorism," Monday, August 18, 1997, 3:230; *FBI Analysis of Terrorist Incidents in the United States 1983*, U.S. Department of Justice Federal Bureau of Investigation, prepared by Terrorist Research and Analytical Center Terrorism Section Criminal Investigation Division.

15. Ron Selden, "Cops Negotiate with Fugitive," *Missoulian*, August 27, 1993; Leonard Zeskind, "Oklahoma Indictments Issues," *Searchlight*, September 1995.

16. Ken Stern, *A Force upon the Plain*, p. 252.

17. Warrant for Arrest, *United States v. Ray Willie Lampley, Cecilia Lampley, Larry Wayne Crow, John Dare Baird*, U.S. District Court Eastern District of Oklahoma, Judge Richard Cornish, November 10, 1995; Leonard Zeskind, "New Bank Robbers Imitate Old Order," *Searchlight*, May 1996.

18. Leonard Zeskind, "Oklahoma Bombing Fails to Halt 'Christian Patriots.'" *Searchlight*, March 1997.

19. "Racial Slaying Prompts Probe," Associated Press, December 11, 1995; James Brooke, "For Most G.I.'s Only Few Hints of Hate Groups," *The New York Times*, December 21, 1995; Leonard Zeskind, "Skinhead Soldiers Arrested on Racist Murder Charges," *Searchlight*, February 1996.

20. Bill Morlin, "Indictment looms for Chevie Kehoe," *The Spokesman Review*, December 12, 1997.

21. "Indictment," *United States of America v. Chevie O'Brien Kehoe, Daniel Lewis Lee, Faron Earl Lovelace*, U.S. District Court, Eastern District of Arkansas; "Government's Motion to Amend Notice of Intent to Seek a Sentence of Death," *United States of America v. Chevie O'Brien Kehoe, Daniel Lewis Lee, Faron Earl Lovelace*, U.S. District Court, Eastern District of Arkansas, LR-CR-97-243, August 20, 1998; "Kehoe Republic, Trail of Death Follows White Supremacist Gang," *Intelligence Report*, Fall 1998.

22. Bill Morlin, "Terror Suspect a Nuclear Expert," *The Spokesman Review*, October 27, 1996; Kim Barker, "Bombing Suspects Held Without Bail: Judge Says Defendants Pose Risk if Released into Community," *The Spokesman Review*, October 17, 1996; "Bomb Suspect Was Nuclear Plant Worker," *Seattle Post-Intelligencer*, October 29, 1996 (Merrell worked on a nuclear submarine in the Navy and at an Arizona nuclear power plant).

23. James Brooke, "Bombing Arrests Further N. Idaho's Racist Reputation," *The New York Times News Service, Idaho Statesman*, October 27, 1996; "Declare ye among the nations" statement.

24. "Idolatry and Expiation at Baal-Peor," *The JPS Torah Commentary: Numbers*, commentary by Jacob Milgrom (Philadelphia: The Jewish Publication Society, 1990), p. 215.

25. Hoskins, "Phineas Priesthood," in *War Cycles, Peace Cycles* (Lynchburg: Virginia Publishing Company, 1985), pp. 33–34; Richard Kelly Hoskins, *Vigilantes of Christendom: The Story of the Phineas Priesthood* (Lynchburg: Virginia Publishing Company, 1990); Leonard Zeskind (unsigned), "Beckwith to Be Tried Again for 1963 Evers Murder: Is Beckwith a Phineas Priest?" *The Monitor*, December 1991, p. 10.

26. James P. Wickstrom, "Northeast Ohio Christian Posse Comitatus," January 1991.

27. "Klan History Rooted in American Spirit of Resistance," *The Klansman*, March–April 1991, published by the Invisible Empire Knights of the Ku Klux Klan.

28. "Suspect in Slaying of Evers Is Linked to Racist Group," *The New York Times*, October 30, 1991.

43. (Re)Birth of the Council of Conservative Citizens

1. Jerry Mitchell, "Carroll Has More Registered Voters Than People," *The Clarion-Ledger*, June 9, 1991; Jerry Mitchell, "Beckwith Eligible to Vote in Carroll County," *The Clarion-Ledger*, June 9, 1991. Mitchell also reported that Byron de la Beckwith was among those registered to vote in Mississippi while he was resident in a Tennessee jail. Beckwith was eventually convicted of the 1963 murder of civil rights leader Medgar Evers.

2. *County and City Data Book 1983: A Statistical Abstract Supplement*, U.S. Department of Commerce, Bureau of the Census, County population, education data, pp. 304–305.

3. "Black Hawk Rally in Mississippi," *Citizens Informer* 26 (Summer 1995): 7.

4. Peter Applebome, "Lott's Close Walk to the South's History of Segregation," *The New York Times*, December 13, 2002 (for Lott's vote on the King Holiday and the quote about Jefferson Davis); "A Partisan Conversation with Trent Lott," *Southern Partisan* 4, no. 4 (Fall 1984), Talking Points Memo Document Collection (www.talkingpointsmemo.com).

5. "Trent Lott Addresses Carroll County Citizens Council Banquet," *Citizens Informer*, May/June 1982, p. 5 ("The banquet concluded with President Brown presenting Congressman Lott with a plaque from the Council and a desk set of Confederate Flags for his office").

6. "Large Crowd Attends Meetings," *Citizens Informer* 23, no. 2 (Spring 1992).

7. "Trent Lott Addresses Carroll County Citizens Council Banquet," *Citizens Informer*, May–June 1982, p. 5, "Dignitaries introduced were . . . R. B. Patterson, founder; W. J. Simmons, Administrator . . . Honorable Leon Bramlett, unannounced candidate for governor . . . Circuit Judge Webb Franklin, candidate for Congress . . . State Senator Billy Lancaster . . . State Representatives Bunky Huggins, Mary Ann Stevens and Kenneth Williams. Special Guest introduced was Mrs. Ione Watson Lott, mother of Congressman Lott and a native of Carroll County . . . Senator Watson is the uncle of Congressman Lott"; "Additional Photos Taken at Carroll County Citizens Council Banquet," *Citizens Informer*, July/August 1982, p. 5 (among those pictured: William Lord, Jr., Rep. Trent Lott, State Rep. Mary Ann Stevens, State Sen. Arnie Watson); "Carroll County Citizens Council Honors McGregor," *Citizens Informer*, September/October 1982, p. 5 ("McGregor was president of the local council from 1966 through 1972 and was instrumental in laying the groundwork for Carroll Academy").

8. Tom P. Brady, *Black Monday*, published by Citizens Councils of America, July 23, 1954.

9. "Dear Judge" letter, January 27, 1957, attached to Western Union telegram from Brady confirming Carto's arrangements to speak at a council meeting in Fort Worth, Texas; Neil R. McMillen, *The Citizens' Council: Organized Resistance to the Second Reconstruction, 1954–64* (Urbana: University of Illinois Press, 1971), pp. 17, 265.

10. McMillen, *The Citizens' Council*, preface to the 1994 edition; "Council List," *Citizens Informer*, November/December 1980, pp. 3, 11 ("Regular Contributing Writers & Coordinators" include Gordon Lee Baum [MO] and Bill Lord, Jr. [AR MS]); "Gordon Lee Baum, Attorney at Law," advertisement, *Citizens Informer* 25, no. 3 (1992): 2; "Head of England's National Front Addresses Memphis Citizens Council," *Citizen Informer*, July/August 1979, p. 5.

11. "Sharks in the Mainstream," *Intelligence Report*, Southern Poverty Law Center, no. 93 (Winter 1999), pp. 21–26; Fred C. Jenning, ed., "Promotional letter," n.d., "The Citizens Informer is truly unique . . . Conservative Citizens Foundation, Council of Conservative Citizens, local chapters and Citizens Councils."

12. Jerry Mitchell, "Progress Cited in Racist Council's Demise," *The Clarion-Ledger*, January 24, 1994.

13. "Council's Growth Policy Working," *The Council Reporter* 4, no. 1 (Spring 1990).

14. "A Genuine Conservative Movement," *Citizens Informer*, Summer 1994, p. 3.

15. "Unity Meeting Savors Victory," *Citizens Informer* 25, Winter/Dec. 1994, p. 1 ("State Senator Mike Gunn gave the Mississippi report . . ."); "MISS ELECTED OFFICIALS Speaking at C of CC Seminar on April 11 . . . Sen. Mike Gunn," *Citizens Informer*, Spring 1992, p. 3; "William D. Lord Presenting C of CC Annual Certificate of Appreciation Awards to Members . . . Sen. MIKE GUNN (Miss.)," *Citizens Informer* 24, no. 2 (1993), p. 3.

16. "Sen. Gunn Receives the 'Outstanding Legislator' award," *Citizens Informer* 3, 1993, p. 6.

17. "Duke's Flier Jingled Like Cash, Not Racism, Gunn Says," *The Clarion-Ledger*, November 26, 1991; "Mike Gunn Running for Congress, 3rd District," *Citizens Informer*, Winter 1995/1996, p. 7 ("Sen. Gunn serves on the national CofCC Board of Directors").

18. Samuel Francis, "A Genuine Conservative Movement," *The Washington Times*, July 15, 1994, p. A21; Mac Gordon, "Pat Buchanan to Visit Jackson for Gunn Fund-raising Event," *The Clarion-Ledger*, April 7, 1995, p. 3B.

19. "South Carolina CofCC Keeps on Charging," *Citizens Informer* 26 (Summer 1995), p. 4 ("Along with state chairman Dr. William Carter . . ."); "CofCC Activities in North Carolina," *Citizens Informer* 26 (Summer 1995), p. 4 ("State chairman A. J. Barker advises . . ."); "Right Agenda for Victory Set," *Citizens Informer* 24, no. 3 (1993), p. 1 (". . . leading state figures, who gave stirring reports . . . Miss Hope Ann Lubrano, Louisiana").

20. Jared Taylor, "The Broader Context of Attacks on Our Flag," *Citizens Informer* 25 (Spring 1994), p. 9.

44. *The Washington Times* Fires Sam Francis

1. Samuel Francis, "Standing Alone Out of NWO Uniform," *The Washington Times*, September 29, 1995, p. A20.

2. Samuel Francis, "The Rise and Fall of a Paleoconservative at the *Washington Times* (Part I)," *Chronicles: A Magazine of American Culture*, April 1996, p. 35; Samuel Francis, "The Rise and Fall of a Paleoconservative at *The Washington Times* (Part II)," *Chronicles*, May 1996, p. 43.

3. Samuel Francis, *Revolution from the Middle* (Raleigh, N.C.: Middle American Press, 1997), "About the Author" ("In 1989 and 1990, he received the Distinguished Writers Award from the American Society of Newspaper Editors").

4. Samuel Francis, "All Those Things to Apologize For," *The Washington Times*, June 27, 1995, p. A23; reprinted in *Southern Partisan*, 1995, 3rd Quarter, as "Southern Baptist May Be on the Road to Liberalism"; Southern Baptist Convention, "Resolution on Racial Reconciliation on the 150th Anniversary of the Southern Baptist Convention," *SBCnet*, June 1995.

5. Dinesh D'Souza, "Racism: It's a White (and Black) Thing, The Superiority Complex and Other Dangerous Similarities," *The Washington Post*, September 24, 1995.

6. Francis, "The Rise and Fall of a Paleoconservative at *The Washington Times* (Part I)."

7. Paul Gottfried, *The Conservative Movement*, rev. ed. (Twayne Publishers, 1993), pp. 78–96; David Frum, *Dead Right* (New York: Basic Books, 1994), pp. 126–27.

8. Gottfried, *The Conservative Movement*, rev. ed., pp. 152–64; Frum, *Dead Right*, pp. 124–58 (Frum does not use the term "paleoconservatism," justifiably describing this phenomenon as "nationalism" instead).

9. Francis, "The Rise and Fall of a Paleoconservative at *The Washington Times* (Part I)," p. 35 ("there are limits to what you can and should say . . . none is more crucial for preserving liberal control . . . than its taboos on open discussion of race . . .").

10. Paul Richert, "Populist Party Holds Big Nat'l Convention; American Nationalist Union Formed," *The Nationalist Times*, pp. 3–5; Videotapes I & II of speeches given at Populist Party meeting on September 16, 1995.

11. "Fighting Back . . . and Winning," *Citizens Informer* 27 (Winter 1995/1996), p. 1.

12. Samuel Francis, "Roads to Revolution," *Chronicles*, August 1995, p. 9.

13. Monte Paulsen, "Buchanan Inc.," *The Nation*, November 22, 1999.

14. Monte Paulsen, "Milliken's $2 Million Aided Buchanan Group," *The State-Record* (Columbia, S.C.), March 13, 1996; Monte Paulsen, "Buchanan Inc., How Pat and Bay Built an Empire on Our Money," *The State-Record*, November 22, 1999.

15. Samuel Francis, "Culture and Power: Winning the Culture War," *Revolution from the Middle*, pp. 174–87 (essay taken from a speech at the American Cause conference, May 15, 1993); Samuel Francis, "Religious Wrong," *Revolution from the Middle*, pp. 205–12, (racial dispossession phrase on p. 211), essay originally published in *Chronicles*, December 1994.

45. Elections 1996: Pat Buchanan Roils the Republicans

1. Jonathan Mahler, "Buchanan's Breakout Stuns Party of Lincoln," *Forward*, February 23, 1996 ("Reeling from Patrick Buchanan's victory in the New Hampshire primary"); Ira Stoll, "Big Labor Balks at Buchanan Despite Blue-Collar Bravado," *Forward*, February 23, 1996; "Labor Leader Calls Buchanan Workers' Enemy," *The New York Times*, February 22, 1996.

2. "3,123,657 Vote," sum of primary election results taken state by state, *The Almanac of American Politics 2000*, Michael Barone and Grant Ujifsa, National Journal, 1999.

3. "Aide to Buchanan Steps Aside," *St. Louis Post-Dispatch*, February 16, 1996 (cites Pratt at St. Louis U.S. Taxpayers Party event in May 1995); Richard L. Berke, "Buchanan Aide Takes Leave Under Fire," *The New York Times*, February 16, 1996; Bob Herbert, "The Company They Keep," *The New York Times*, February 16, 1996.

4. Judy Thomas, "Buchanan Aide Visited Tribute to Doctor Killer," *The Kansas City Star*, February 27, 1996.

5. "Sen. Phil Gramm and his Korean wife Wendy . . . He divorced a White wife to marry an Asiatic," photo cutline, *The Truth at Last* 387 (formerly *The Thunderbolt*, edited by Ed Fields, Marietta, Georgia); "Sen. Gramm Blasts TTAL," *The Truth at Last* 389.

6. Douglas Frantz and Michael Janofsky, "Buchanan Drawing Extremist Support, and Problems Too," *The New York Times*, February 23, 1996.

7. Thomas Nord and Dave Roman, "Buchanan Campaign Fires Duval Coordinator," *Florida Times-Union*, Jacksonville, February 17, 1996.

8. James Ridgeway and Leonard Zeskind, "The Empire Strikes Back: As Dole Regains His Poise in the North, Buchanan Reverts to a Southern Strategy," *The Village Voice*, March 12, 1996 ("William Carter . . . was dismissed two weeks ago").

9. William Carter, "South Carolina Case Ends in Victory," *Citizens Informer*, Winter 1995–96; "South Carolina CofCC Continues to Grow," *Citizens Informer*, Winter 1995–96 ("S.C. CofCC state chairman Dr. Carter"); John Roberts, "Send Bush a Message, Duke Tells Receptive S.C. Crowd," *Augusta Chronicle*, March 6, 1992 (photo cutline "Duke flanked by S.C. campaign manager William Carter").

10. Katherine Q. Seelye, "Dole Says Buchanan Is Extreme in Outlook," *The New York Times*, February 24, 1996.

11. Dan Balz and Ann Devroy, "Dole Shifts Attack, Drops Extremist Tag," *The Washington Post*, February 23, 1996; Laurie Kellman and Ralph Z. Hallow, "Dole Rejects Call to Soften Line on Buchanan," *The Washington Times*, February 24, 1996.

12. Rabbi Daniel Lapin, "Buchanan's Lesson," opinion article faxed to the *Kansas City Jewish Chronicle* at Sun Publications, March 5, 1996.

13. "Special Buchanan Edition: Republican Voters Guide," *The Spotlight*, March 11, 1996; "Go Pat Go," editorial, *The Spotlight*, March 4, 1996.

14. Vince Ryan, "Pat: Form a New Party," Liberty Lobby Reports, *The Spotlight*, April 1, 1996, p. 17.

15. John R. Moore, "Buchanan Used, Abused Supporters," *The Spotlight*, July 6, 1998; Vince Ryan, "Populism Is Winning Worldwide," *The Spotlight*, March 8, 1999.

16. "New York dinner and rally . . . ," cutline under photo of Buchanan and Council of Conservative Citizens member Carmine Basciano, *Citizens Informer*, Summer 1995, p. 4; "Please join The Honorable Mary Cummins," Buchanan fund-raiser invitation, mailed June 6, 1995 (Fernando Vasquez, Chairman, Committee [*sic*] Robert Blumetti, Lena Harknett, Joseph Palau and Pedro Sequi); "Buchanan NY Campaign," *Citizens Informer*, Winter 1995–96.

17. "Mike Gunn Running for Congress, 3rd District," *Citizens Informer*, Winter 1995–96; Mac Gordon, "Pat Buchanan to Visit Jackson for Gunn Fund-raising Event," *The Clarion-Ledger*, April 7, 1995, p. 3B.

18. "AR Conference Is Huge Success," *American Renaissance* newsletter 7, no. 7 (July 1996); conference agenda, The Confederate Sentry; Donald Warren, "A Report and Observations of the American Renaissance Meeting in Louisville, KY. May 25–27, 1996," communication to author.

19. "The Second American Renaissance Conference: Favorable and unfavorable reports," *Instauration*, August 1996.

20. "After the Election: The Vote Under a Microscope," Portrait of the Electorate, *The New York Times*, November 10, 1996, p. 16.

21. Peter Mantius, "State Senator's Speech to Militia Cited," *The Atlanta Journal-Constitution*, October 30, 1996; at a March 1995 "Restore Our Liberty Convention," Glanton joined Posse Comitatus farmer Byron Dale, Arizona sheriff Richard Mack, Colorado state senator Charles Duke, and California state senator Don Rogers.

46. Carto Dispossessed

1. The case before this court was a formal appeal before Judge Maino of several previous decisions granting Weber et al. control of the legion.

2. *Legion for the Survival of Freedom, Inc., a Texas corporation (Plaintiff) v. Willis Carto aka Frank Tompkins aka E. L. Anderson, Ph.D.; Henry Fisher aka Henri Fischer; Liberty Lobby, Inc., a corporation; Vibet, Inc., a corporation; and DOES 1 through 50, inclusive (Defendants)*, Superior Court of the State of California for the County of San Diego, Civil no. N64581.

3. *Legion for the Survival of Freedom, Inc. Plaintiff and Respondent v. Willis Carto, Henry Fisher, Vibet, Inc., Liberty Lobby, Inc. et al. Defendant and Appellants*, Court of Appeal of the State of California, Fourth Appellant District, Division One, Reporter's transcript, October 28–29, 1996, and October 31, 1996, Barbara J. Schultz, CSR, RPR, CSR No. 8021, official reporter.

4. Thomas Musselman, "Opening Statement for Plaintiff," *Legion for the Survival of Freedom, Inc. Plaintiff and Respondent v. Willis Carto, Henry Fisher, Vibet, Inc., Liberty Lobby, Inc. et al. Defendant and Appellants*, transcript pp. 7–23.

5. Randall Waier, "Opening Statement for Defense," *Legion for the Survival of Freedom, Inc. Plaintiff and Respondent v. Willis Carto, Henry Fisher, Vibet, Inc., Liberty Lobby, Inc. et al. Defendant and Appellants*, transcript pp. 23–43.

6. *Liberty Lobby, Inc. Plaintiff v. National Review, Inc. Defendant*, Civil Action no. 79-3445, *National Review, Inc. v. Willis Carto and Robert Shaw, Defendants*, Civil Action no. 80-1067, U.S. District Court for the District of Columbia, vol. 7, October 18, 1985, and vol. 8, October 21, 1985, p. 1473.

7. *Liberty Lobby v. National Review*, p. 1414.

8. Ibid.

9. Ibid., p. 1438.

10. "Trial Coverage—IHR vs. Carto," Institute for Historical Review website article 961112trial.htm.

11. Randall Waier, *Legion for the Survival of Freedom, Inc. Plaintiff and Respondent v. Willis Carto, Henry Fisher, Vibet, Inc., Liberty Lobby, Inc. et al. Defendant and Appellants*, transcript p. 27.

12. Willis Carto, *Legion for the Survival of Freedom, Inc. Plaintiff and Respondent v. Willis Carto, Henry Fisher, Vibet, Inc., Liberty Lobby, Inc. et al. Defendant and Appellants*, transcript p. 677.

13. *Legion for the Survival of Freedom, Inc. Plaintiff and Respondent v. Willis Carto, Henry Fisher, Vibet, Inc., Liberty Lobby, Inc. et al. Defendant and Appellants*, transcript p. 78–88.

14. Ibid.

15. Randall Waier, "The evidence will show that all the organizations work together for a common scheme to promote revisionism, among other topics, to the same public." Ibid., p. 27.

16. Waier asked Carto about the past letters to Hulsey and McCloskey, in particular.

17. Thomas Marcellus, "Declaration of Thomas J. Marcellus," September 6, 1995; Thomas Marcellus, "Declaration of December 28, 1993; Question to Willis Carto," *Legion for the Survival of Freedom, Inc. Plaintiff and Respondent v. Willis Carto, Henry Fisher, Vibet, Inc., Liberty Lobby, Inc. et al. Defendant and Appellants*, transcript p. 352 (Vibet, a Bahamian corporation).

18. Brian Toohey, "Where the Missing Half-Million Went," *Australian National Times*, August 7, 1980; David Greason, "Whatever Happened to Henri Fischer's Stolen ALP Funds?," *Australia-Israel Review*, June 15, 1994; "IHR Update," no. 2, July 1995, Institute for Historical Review.

19. "Statement of Probable Cause," Affidavit of Investigator Larry Rooker, Costa Mesa police department: "On 3-10-95 I spoke to Det. Tim Carroll, San Diego Sheriff's Department . . . [he] provided the following . . . Willis Carto previously lived with Fischer at the Pine Heights Way estate for two or three years. During that time another man, Michael Brown, also lived there (Brown is the former bodyguard to Lincoln Rockwell . . . was convicted of possessing explosives . . . There were numerous complaints to the Sheriff's Department from neighbors . . .").

20. "Search Warrant for Willis Carto and Henry Fischer," issued by the City of Costa Mesa, Judge of the Municipal Court, March 17, 1995, "Statement of Probable Cause," affidavit of Investigator Larry Rooker, Costa Mesa police department.

21. Michael Collins Piper, "Liberty Lobby's West Coast H.Q. Hit, Multijurisdictional SWAT Raid," *The Spotlight*, April 10, 1995; Michael Collins Piper, "Usurpers, SWAT Raiders Face Massive Civil Lawsuit," *The Spotlight*, May 1, 1995.

22. *Legion for the Survival of Freedom, Inc. Plaintiff and Respondent v. Willis Carto, Henry Fisher, Vibet, Inc., Liberty Lobby, Inc. et al. Defendant and Appellants*, transcript pp. 775–76.

23. Ibid.

24. David Lee Preston, "Hitler's Swiss Connection," *The Philadelphia Inquirer*, January 5, 1997; Martin A. Lee, *The Beast Reawakens* (New York: Little, Brown and Company, 1997), p. 181.

25. Judge Rustin G. Maino, "State of Decision," November 14, 1996, *Legion for the Survival of Freedom, Inc. v. Willis Carto et al.*

26. Superior Court Judge Rustin G. Maino, "Dear Counsel" letter, November 13, 1996, re: *Legion for the Survival of Freedom, Inc. v. Willis Carto, et al.*, N64584.

47. Resistance Records: Buying and Selling in the Cyberworld

1. David Shepardson, Gary Heinlein, and Oralandar Brand-Williams, "White Supremacist Record Company in Oakland Raided in Tax-Fraud Probe," *The Detroit News*, April 10, 1997.

2. David Shepardson, "Police Want Skinheads' Bank Files," *The Detroit News*, April 11, 1997; David Shepardson, "White Separatists Vow Court Fight to Keep Files of Oakland County Company," *The Detroit News*, April 24, 1997.

3. Katja Lane, "Resistance Records Raided," Aryan News Agency, April 9, 1997; George Burdi, interviews and communications with author, December 2002; "Present at the Creation: A Key Architect of the International White Power Music Industry, Renouncing Racism, Recounts His Personal Odyssey," *Intelligence Report*, Fall 2001, pp. 32–37.

4. "Resistance Records Raid & Update," Resistance Records, January 1998; David Shepardson, "In Walled Lake: 'White Power' Music Company Is Back in Business," *The Detroit News*, May 23, 1997.

5. Devin Burghart, "Total War: White Power Music as Cultural Terrorism," and "Beyond Boots and Braces: The White Power Skinhead Music Scene in the United States," *Soundtracks to the White Revolution: White Supremacist Assaults on Youth Music Subcultures* (The

Center for New Community, 1999), pp. 9–22; communication from Minneapolis–St. Paul to author, June 1992.

6. Todd Blodgett, interview with Mark Potok and author, Washington, D.C., January 15, 2000.

7. Bodgett, interview; Willis Carto, letter to Jason Snow, "Receipt & Memorandum of Understanding," signed by Snow and Carto and stamp dated November 17, 1998.

8. Fred Blahut, "Dear Former Resistance Subscriber," letter: "You've Been Given a Six Month Subscription," *The Spotlight*, September 1998; Ashley C. L. Brown, "Memo to Willis Carto Re: Eric Fairburn," cc: Todd A. Blodgett and Jason Snow, September 7, 1998; Willis Carto, fax to Todd Blodgett, September 26, 1998.

9. Todd Blodgett, interview; Nick Lowles and Devin Burghart, "William Pierce in the Music Business," *Searchlight*, January 2000, pp. 4–5.

10. W.L.P. (William Luther Pierce), "Message from the Publisher," *Resistance* 10 (Spring 2000); Resistance Records LLC, Articles of Incorporation, District of Columbia, April 29, 1999; "The Music Connection," *National Alliance Bulletin*, July 1999; "New Acquisition," *National Alliance Bulletin*, October 1999; "Money, Music and the Doctor," *Intelligence Report*, Fall 1999, pp. 33–36.

11. Dan Schiller, *Digital Capitalism: Networking the Global Marketing System* (Cambridge, Mass.: The MIT Press, 1999), pp. 1–89;

12. Devin Burghart, "Cyberh@te: A Reappraisal," *The Dignity Report*, Coalition for Human Dignity, Fall 1996, pp. 12–16; Tara McKelvey, "Father and Son Team in Hate Site," *USA Today*, July 16, 2001.

13. In addition to Resistance Records, Panzerfaust Records, Nordland Records, Bound for Glory, Blood and Honor, and other music distributors emerged quickly with websites.

14. Peter Lewis, "Jewish Rights Group Urges Ban of All Hate Messages on Internet," *The New York Times*, January 10, 1996; "Hate Group Recruitment on the Internet," Research Report, Anti-Defamation League, 1995; David S. Hoffman, *The Web of Hate: Extremists Exploit the Internet* (New York: Anti-Defamation League, 1996); Kenneth S. Stern, *Hate and the Internet* (New York: The American Jewish Committee, 1999).

15. Devin Burghart (unsigned), "Creating a Killer: A Background Report on Benjamin 'August' Smith and the World Church of the Creator," The Center for New Community, July 1999.

16. John Markoff, "A Newer, Lonelier Crowd Emerges in Internet Study," *The New York Times*, February 16, 2000; Robert Kraut, Vicki Lundmark, Tridas Mukopadhyay, William Scherlis, "Internet Paradox: A Social Technology That Reduces Social Involvement and Psychological Well-Being?," *American Psychologist* 53, no. 9 (September 1998): 1017–31.

48. After the Oklahoma City Bomber(s) Are Tried, the Violence Continues

1. Joe Fields, "Patriots Meet at Palm Springs Despite Establishment Spasms," *The Spotlight*, May 29, 1995; Paul Hall, "So Where Was the ATF That Day?," *The Jubilee*, May/June 1995, vol. 7. no. 6 (this tabloid contained 12 pages of bomb coverage focused on possible government misdeeds); Jubilation '96, a Christian patriot conference organized by Identity-based newspaper, Lake Tahoe, Nevada, April 5–7 1996 (included speech on "OKC Bombing Cover-Up"); William F. Jasper, "ATF Informant Says Cover-Up," *The New American*, March 17, 1997; *The Spotlight*, as cited elsewhere in the notes, the John Birch Society's *The New American* magazine, and an Internet zine by an Alabama militia member called *John Doe Times* all regularly published versions of the "blame the government" conspiracies, and the talk pervaded militia meetings and preparedness expos as well.

2. "Petition for Writ of Mandamus of Petitioner Defendant, Timothy James McVeigh and Brief in Support," *Timothy James McVeigh v. Honorable Richard P. Matsch*, 96-CR-68-M, received March 25, 1997, by Patrick Fisher, clerk; Amber McLaughlin (for Stephan Jones firm), letters to Lawrence Myers (for *Media ByPass* magazine), February 16, 1996, and March 20, 1996, providing McVeigh phone records, a transcribed interview with potential witness, and handwriting samples, and reminding Myers of a signed non-disclosure agreement; Leslie Jorgensen, "A Dangerous Defense Campaign," *Colorado Statesman*, March 19, 1997 (Jorgensen reported well and regularly on the twists and turns of the Jones defense strategy); Gerry Gable, letter to author, January 13, 1996 (Gable met with Jones in London, Kelsey).

3. Jo Thomas, "U.S. Judge in Colorado to Hear Bombing Case," *The New York Times*, December 5, 1995.

4. Richard A. Serrano, *One of Ours: Timothy McVeigh and the Oklahoma City Bombing*, p. 256; Robert Nigh, interview with James Ridgeway and Leonard Zeskind, March 1996. Nigh mentioned defense expense records specifically.

5. Joseph H. Hatzler, "Opening statement for prosecution," *United States of America v. Timothy James McVeigh*, Criminal Action no. 96-CR-68, April 24, 1997, reporter's transcript; Serrano, *One of Ours*.

6. "FBI Expert to Testify in Okla," Associated Press, February 28, 1996; David Johnston, "F.B.I. Lab Practices Faulted in Oklahoma Bomb Inquiry," *The New York Times*, January 31, 1997; Jo Thomas, "A Tarnished Case: Flaws at F.B.I. Lab Offer Latest Setback to Prosecutors in Oklahoma City Bombing," *The New York Times*, April 17, 1997; Jo Thomas, "F.B.I. Handling of Evidence Is Attacked at Bomb Trial, Expert Defends Government's Procedure," *The New York Times*, May 21, 1997 (Linda Jones of the Forensics Explosives Laboratory in the British Ministry of Defense testified for the prosecution).

7. Lori Fortier, "Direct Testimony," April 29, 1997, Criminal Action no. 96-CR-68, April 24, 1997, reporter's transcript; Lori Fortier Cross Examination, April 30, 1997; Scott Cannon, "Friend Links McVeigh, Bombing," *The Kansas City Star*, April 30, 1997.

8. Jo Thomas, "Friend Says McVeigh Wanted Bombing to Start an 'Uprising,'" *The New York Times*, May 13, 1997; Richard Serrano, "U.S. Says It Has Key to Truck in Oklahoma Bombing Case," *The Los Angeles Times*, May 14, 1997; Scott Cannon, "Focus Shifts from Fortier to Truck," *The Kansas City Star*, May 14, 1997.

9. Jennifer McVeigh, "Testimony in the Timothy McVeigh Trial," May 5, 1997, unedited transcript provided by Court TV Online, www.courttv.com/archive/casefiles/oklahoma/transcripts; Jo Thomas, "McVeigh's Sister, Weeping, Testifies on Her Brother's Moves," *The New York Times*, May 7, 1997; Lou Michel and Dan Herbeck, *American Terrorist: Timothy McVeigh & the Oklahoma City Bombing* (New York: Regan Books, 2001), pp. 88–89 (according to this account, McVeigh joined a Klan group while he was in the army).

10. Stephen Jones and Peter Israel, *Others Unknown: Timothy McVeigh and the Oklahoma Bombing Conspiracy*, pp. 331–43.

11 James Ridgeway, "Terry Nichols's Posse," *The Village Voice*, October, 7, 1997; Sara Rimer and James Bennet, "Rejecting the Authority of the U.S. Government," *The New York Times*, April 24, 1995; Judy Thomas, "Women Say They Can't See Nichols as Deadly Bomber," *The Kansas City Star*, August 11, 1995.

12. Peter G. Chronis, "Tigar a Courtroom Legend," *The Sunday Denver Post*, September 28, 1997.

13. Michael Tigar, "Opening Statement," November 3, 1997, *United States of America v. Terry Lynn Nichols*, United States District Court for Colorado, Criminal Action no. 96-CR-68, www.courttv.com/archive/casefiles/oklahoma/transcripts; Kevin Murphy, "Lawyers Depict Two Sides of Nichols as Trial Begins," *The Kansas City Star*, November 4, 1997; John Kifner, "Case Against Nichols Is Thin, Lawyer Says," *The New York Times*, May 26, 1995.

14. Joan Millar, "Direct Testimony," December 10, 1997, *United States of America v. Terry Lynn Nichols*, trial transcript, www.courttv.com/archive/casefiles/oklahoma/transcripts.

15. Jo Thomas, "At Her Trial, Plot Suspect Reveals a Double Life," *The New York Times*, August 2, 1997.

16. Joan Millar, "Testimony," December 10, 1997; Carol Howe, "Testimony," December 10, 1997, *United States v. Nichols*, trial transcript.

17. Millar, "Testimony."

18. Howe, "Testimony."

19. During Nichols's trial, prosecutors presented evidence that Nichols's truck was seen at Geary Lake—the presumed bomb-manufacturing site—but they did not present evidence that Nichols himself had been seen there. And testimony on the process of mixing the bomb ingredients was not compelling.

20. Jo Thomas, "Nichols Guilty of Plotting Bomb Attack in Oklahoma, But Not of the Blast Itself," *The New York Times*, December 24, 1997; Sandy Shore, "Judge: Nichols Can Face Death," *Associated Press*, December 25, 1997; James Brooke, "A Few Determined

Holdouts Block Death Penalty Verdict for Nichols," *The New York Times*, January 11, 1998.

21. Rick Bragg, "As Execution Nears, FBI Blunder Does Not Change McVeigh Crimes," *The New York Times*, June 10, 2001; Rick Bragg, "McVeigh Dies for Oklahoma City Blast," *The New York Times*, June 12, 2001.

22. Leonard Zeskind, "Denver Skinhead Murder a Taste of Things to Come?," *Searchlight*, January 1998, p. 22.

23. Rick Bragg, "Abortion Clinic Bomb Was Intended to Kill, an Official Says," *The New York Times*, January 31, 1998 ("The bombing made history"); Jay Reeves, "Bombing at Alabama Abortion Clinic Kills Guard, Critically Injures Nurse," Associated Press, January 29, 1998.

24. David Johnston with Kevin Sack, "New Evidence Said to Link Olympic and Abortion Clinic Bombings," *The New York Times*, February 27, 1998; Kathy Scruggs and Ron Martz, "Bombings Linked, ATF Agent Says," *The Atlanta Journal-Constitution*, June 10, 1997.

25. Gina M. Smith and John Harmin, "Gray Truck Provides Lead in Bombing," *The Atlanta Journal-Constitution*, January 31, 1998; "Text of Letter From 'Army of God,'" Atlanta, Reuters News Service, February 2, 1998, 9:08 p.m.; James Risen and Judy L. Thomas, *Wrath of Angels: The American Abortion War*, pp. 366–70.

26. Eric Rudolph, "Lil," www.armyofgod.com/EricRudolphTil.html (describes Rudolph's life in the woods while he evaded capture); *United States of America v. Eric Robert Rudolph*, United States District Court for the Northern District of Alabama, Indictment no. CR-00-N-S.

27. Lawrence W. Myers, "Executing Judgement: Inside the Army of God (II)," *Media Bypass*, January 1999; "Running with Rudolph" (interview with Deborah Rudolph), Southern Poverty Law Center's *Intelligence Report* 104 (Winter 2001), pp. 35–39; Kevin Flynn and Gary Gerhardt, *The Silent Brotherhood*, p. 394 (for Gayman, The Order, and money); Eric Rudolph, "Full text of Eric Rudolph's written statement," www.armyofgod.com/EricRudolphstatement/html.

28. Nord Davis, Jr., letter to Ms. Davis-McCoy of North Carolinians Against Racist and Religious Violence, March 27, 1991; Nord Davis, Jr., *Desert Shield and the New World Order*, Northpoint Tactical Teams, n.d.; North Carolinians Against Racist and Religious Violence, "Memo to Concerned Media: Nord Davis and NCARRV's 1990 Report," March 6, 1991.

29. Eric Rudolph, "Full text of Eric Rudolph's written statement" (Rudolph says he rejects the Christian Identity belief system).

30. Jeffrey Gettleman, "Sympathy for Bombing Suspect May Cloud Search for Evidence," *The New York Times*, June 3, 2003; "Laura Blackly: Eric Rudolph Ain't No Hero," www.youtube.com/watch?v=-o0Aq5Hkjc4&feature=related.

31. Kathy Scruggs, "Possible Rudolph Sighting Reported," *The Atlanta Journal-Constitution*, August 18, 1998.

32. "5-Year Hunt for Bombing Suspect Ends," *The Kansas City Star*, June 1, 2003; "Rudolph Pleads Guilty to Bombings in Atlanta and Birmingham," news release, April 13, 2005, United States Attorney's Office, Northern District of Georgia.

33. *Terrorism in the United States 1997*, Counterterrorism Threat Assessment and Warning Unit, National Security Division, Federal Bureau of Investigation, Department of Justice.

49. The United States Congress and the Council of Conservative Citizens

1. House Resolution 35, "Condemning the racism and bigotry of the Council of Conservative Citizens," news release, contact Josh Rogin, February 2, 1999; "[Cong. Patrick] Kennedy Condemns Racism, Bigotry Espoused by Council of Conservative Citizens," press release, contact Larry Berman, February 19, 1999.

2. Thomas Edsall, "Resolution Targets Council of Conservative Citizens," *The Washington Post*, January 30, 1999.

3. Michael Barone and Grant Ujifusa, "Georgia Seventh District," *Almanac of American Politics 1996* (Washington, D.C.: National Journal, 1995).

4. "Remembering Larry McDonald: the distinguished congressman and chairman of the John Birch Society was an effective and implacable foe of Communism and international terror-

ism," *The New American*, September 8, 2003; "Klans Mourn Larry McDonald," *The Hammer* 5 (Winter 1984).

5. "CofCC National Conference in South Carolina June 5–6" (photo "with Rep. Bob Barr . . ."), *Citizens Informer* 29 (3rd Quarter 1998), p. 3.

6. Thomas Edsall, "Barr Spoke to White Supremacy Group," *The Washington Post*, December 11, 1998; Thomas Edsall, "Barr Rejects Racial Views of Group He Visited," *The Washington Post*, December 12, 1998.

7. Thomas Edsall, "Lott Renounces White 'Racialist' Group He Praised in 1992," *The Washington Post*, December 16, 1998; Colbert I. King, "Lott's Odd Friends," *The Washington Post*, December 19, 1998.

8. Jerry Mitchell, "Republicans Being Urged to Quit Organization by National Chairman," *The Clarion-Ledger*, January 22, 1999.

9. "RNC Member Quits Council of Conservative Citizens over Racism," Associated Press, February 28, 1999.

10. Juliet Eilperin, "GOP Blocks Effort to Cite Group as Racist, Measure Targeted Citizens Council," *The Washington Post*, March 24, 1999.

11. Editorial, "Watered-Down Racism Resolution," *The New York Times*, March 23, 1999.

12. Ishmael Reed, "Unequal Rights for Haters," Salon.com, January 23, 1999.

13. Peter Applebome, "Divisive Words: The Record, Lott's Walk Near the Incendiary Edge of Southern History," *The New York Times*, December 13, 2002; John Meacham, "The Past That Made Him—and May Undo Him: Race and the Rise of Trent Lott," *Newsweek*, December 23, 2002, pp. 23–37; Samuel Francis, "Lott May Have Unintentionally Said Something True," *Council of Conservative Citizens*, www.cofcc.org, December 13, 2002.

14. Leonard Zeskind, "American Renaissance Defends the 'West,'" *Searchlight*, April 2002; Lawrence W. Myers, "Gordon Lee Baum, 'Five Rules for Effective Cultural Activism,'" *Media Bypass*, January 1999, pp. 27–29.

15. "CofCC Conference in North Carolina November 14–15 Big Success," *Citizens Informer* 29 (Winter 1997–98), p. 3; communication to author, Council of Conservative Citizens' semi-annual conference, November 14–15, 1997, in Winston-Salem, N.C., transcript, part 2, January 9, 1998, pp. 20–29.

16. "The Alliance in the Media," *National Alliance Bulletin*, July 1999, p. 4; Brent Nelson, ed., "Issue Number One: Conservative Reactions to Multi-Cultural America," Occasional Papers of the Conservative Citizens' Foundation, 1997; Brent Nelson, ed., "Issue Number Two: Balkanization, Separatism or National Unity?," Occasional Papers of the Conservative Citizens' Foundation, 1998.

17. Frances Bell, "Put It Back on the Dome: Massive CofCC Rally Protests Lowering Confederate Flag in South Carolina," *Citizens Informer* 21 (July/August 2000), p. 1; "Alabama Immigration Rally," *Citizens Informer* 28 (Winter 1997–98), p. 5.

18. "Building Bridges to Europe," *Citizens Informer* 29 (3rd Quarter 1998), p. 4.

19. Robert Chiarella, "Council of Conservative Citizens Goes to France," *Citizens Informer* (1st Quarter 1999), p. 4.

20. Earl P. Holt III, "The Nuts and Bolts of Immigration Reform Rallies," *Citizens Informer* (January/February 2003).

21. Editorial Advisory Board, including: Virginia Abernethy, Ph.D., Wayne Lutton, Ph.D., Brent A. Nelson, Ph.D., *Citizens Informer* 21 (March/April 2001).

50. National Alliance Remakes Resistance Records

1. "European Festival Huge Success," *National Alliance Bulletin*, April 1999, pp. 1–5.

2. Clint O'Conner, "Sounds of Hate, Resistance Records, Local Neo-Nazi Uses Rock to Spew Racist Doctrine," *The Plain Dealer*, March 5, 2000.

3. Erich Gliebe interview, "Fighting for the Ultimate Cause," *Resistance Magazine* 9, Fall 1999, pp. 53–56.

4. "Message from the Publisher," *Resistance Magazine* 10, Winter 2000, p. 3.

5. "ZGram—September 7, 1996—Update on David Irving," E. Zundel, Internet, September 7, 1996; *David John Cawdell Irving and (1) Penguin Books Limited, (2) Deborah E. Lipstadt*, in the High Court of Justice Queens Bench Division, RWE1, National Alliance, pp. i–ii.

6. Jim Llewellyn, "David Duke Visit Ignites Melee at Lithuanian Hall," *Sun News*, May 22, 1997; David Duke photo, *Resistance Magazine* 9, Fall 1999, p. 36.

7. *Connie Mansfield, Personal Representative of the Estate of Harold Mansfield, on behalf of herself and the Estate v. William Pierce*, U.S. District Court for the Western District of North Carolina, Civil Action no. 2:95CV62, February 27, 1995; Ronald Smothers, "Verdict Means White Supremacist Must Pay Black Family," *The New York Times*, May 20, 1996.

8. "Expanding Radio Coverage," *National Alliance Bulletin*, November–December 1992, p. 2.

9. William Pierce, "Rising Graph," *National Alliance Bulletin*, July 1999, pp. 9–10.

10. William Blythe, "The Guru of White Hate," *Rolling Stone*, June 8, 2000, pp. 99–106, 140–42; "Iran Radio Interview," "Bismarck Radio," "Tampa TV Interview," *National Alliance Bulletin*, February 1999, p. 2.

11. "Confederate Memorial Ceremony," *National Alliance Bulletin*, April 1999, p. 5.

12. "National Membership Coordinator," *National Alliance Bulletin*, June 1999, p. 1.

13. "National Leadership Conference," *National Alliance Bulletin*, August 1999, p. 1.

14. "New Acquisition," *National Alliance Bulletin*, October 1999, pp. 1–3.

15. William Pierce letter to Eric Fairburn: "Todd is no longer involved in the management of Resistance Records," September 19, 1999.

16. "Fighting for the Ultimate Cause," *Resistance Magazine* 9, Fall 1999, pp. 53–56; Editorial, *Resistance Magazine* 10, Winter 2000, p. 2.

17. "Dear Resistance Reader," *Resistance Magazine* 11, Spring 2000, p. 2.

18. Ibid.

51. Liberty Lobby in Bankruptcy Court

1. Doug Luna, report to author re: July 1, 1999, hearing, e-mail sent July 2, 1999; "Motion of United States Trustee for the Appointment of a Chapter 11 Trustee," *Liberty Lobby, Inc, Debtor*, 98-1046, Chapter 11, United States Bankruptcy Court for the District of Columbia.

2. "Texas Court Rejects Carto's Bid to Take Control of Institute for Historical Review," Institute for Historical Review ("Harris County District Judge Harvey Brown rejected Carto's argument . . . lawsuit no. 94-40825 . . . Harris County 152nd Judicial County Court"); *Liberty Lobby, Inc. and Willis Carto Plaintiffs v. Mark Weber, Greg Raven, et al. Defendants*, United States District Court for the District of Columbia, 1:98CV00236, January 29, 1998, Complaint re: Civil RICO; "Liberty Lobby's 'Megasuit' Dismissed by DC Court," *Christian News*, May 17, 1999; "Another Judge Slaps Liberty Lobby," *The Spotlight*, May 3, 1999.

3. "LL 'Bankrupt' But Still Fighting," *The Spotlight*, June 1, 1998 ("On March 27 Maino issued an order giving a receiver . . . authority to seize mail addressed to 'Liberty Lobby' and 'Willis Carto'").

4. Ibid.

5. "'Fifth Amendment Willie' Has Another Bad Day in Court," *News About IHR*, February 27, 1998 (Legion describes Carto during a February 20 settlement conference); Willis Carto answered questions directly during a "Debtor Examination," N64584, June 21, 2001.

6. Blayne Hutzel, "Testimony at 341 Meeting of Creditors," United States Bankruptcy Court for the District of Columbia, 98-01046, June 19, 1998; Hutzel testified that the most recent printing of *The Spotlight* had been 81,000, of that 64,573 were paid subscribers (the numbers would drop further from there); Liberty Lobby, Inc., Cash Disbursements Summary Report Month Ended November 31, 1998, p. 4, Total Revenue, Year-to-Date $1,642,227; p. 5, Total Expenses, Year-to-Date $1,984,164.

7. Blayne Hutzel, "Testimony," 341 Meeting of Creditors, United States Bankruptcy Court for the District of Columbia, 98-01046, June 19, 1998.

8. Ibid.

9. "Motion of United States Trustee for the Appointment of a Chapter 11 Trustee," June 11, 1999, *In re: Liberty Lobby, Inc.*, United States Bankruptcy Court for the District of Columbia, 98-01046.

10. Paul Pearlstein, Attorney for the Debtor, Argument before Judge Martin Teel, July 1, 1999, *Liberty Lobby, Inc, Debtor*, 98-1046, Chapter 11, United States Bankruptcy Court for the District of Columbia; Douglas Luna, report to author.

11. Todd Blodgett, testimony, July 1, 1999, transcript by Johnson Transcription Service, July 1, 1999, *Liberty Lobby, Inc, Debtor*, 98-1046.

12. Judge Martin Teel, "Adjournment," *Liberty Lobby, Inc, Debtor*, 98-1046.

13. "Forbearance and Settlement Agreement and Mutual General Release," signed by Willis Carto, July 17, 1999, LaVonne Furr, July 26, 1999, Lewis Furr, July 26, 1999, Greg Raven for the Legion for the Survival of Freedom, August 2, 1999 (*Legion for the Survival of Freedom v. Willis Carto et al.*, California Superior Court, N64584).

14. Vince Ryan, "Good News for Liberty Lobby; Bad News for Our Enemies," *The Spotlight*, September 13, 1999, p. 7.

52. The Millennium Changes

1. Kenneth L. Woodward, "Prophecy—Millennial Visions: What the Bible Says About the End of the World," *Newsweek*, November 1, 1999, pp. 66–74.

2. Ibid., pp. 70–71.

3. Philip Lamy, "Millennialism in the Mass Media: The Case of Soldier of Fortune Magazine," *Journal for the Scientific Study of Religion* 31(4): 408–24 (postmodern secular millennialism); Philip Lamy, *Millennial Rage: Survivalists, White Supremacists, and the Doomsday Prophecy* (New York: Plenum Press, 1996); Chip Berlet, *Y2K and Millennial Pinball: How Y2K Shapes Survivalism in the U.S. Christian Right, Patriot and Armed Militia Movements, and Far Right*, January 26, 1999; Michael Barkun, ed., *Millennialism and Violence* (London: Frank Cass Publishers, 1996).

4. *Newsweek*, November 1, 1999, p. 4.

5. Leonard Zeskind (unsigned), "Y2K Is Not the End of the World Says Identity Preacher," *Searchlight*, October 1998, p. 23.

6. "Millennium Y2Kaos: Fears of Computer Bug Fueling the Far Right," *Intelligence Report*, Fall 1998. Many experts, including Barkun and the FBI's Blitzer, agree that extremists' fears and hopes surrounding Y2K have increased the danger of domestic terrorism. "It adds to apocalyptic fears," says Chip Berlet, who studies the far right for Cambridge-based Political Research Associates. "Therefore, it adds to the potential for violence."

7. *Project Megiddo*, Department of Justice, Federal Bureau of Investigation, 1999; Sam Francis, "FBI May Be the Real Danger," *The Spotlight*, December 6, 1999, p. 13.

8. Chip Berlet, e-mail communication, November 1, 1999 ("Why so late? . . . when apocalyptic violence tied to millennial expectation has been happening for years . . .").

9. Dan Boyer, "Conservatives Want Probe of FBI Terrorism Report," *The Washington Times*, November 19, 1999.

10. Sam Francis, "FBI May Be the Real Danger," *The Spotlight*, December 6, 1999, p. 13.

11. Michael Collins Piper, "Private Espionage Group Feeds FBI Apocalypse Report," *The Spotlight*, November 15, 1999, p. 1; "The Two Main Groups Targeted by the F.B.I.'s 'Project Megiddo,'" *America's Promise Newsletter*, November/December 1999, pp. 7–8.

12. *Project Megiddo*, FBI, pp. 4–5.

13. Ibid., p. 17.

14. "Millennium Y2Kaos."

15. George Petrisek, "Posse Leader: Y2K Will Bring Famine, Chaos," *Potter Leader-Enterprise*, Coudersport, Pennsylvania, Wednesday, August 12, 1998 (". . . James Wickstrom . . . warned that white Anglo-Saxon Lombards must be prepared to defend themselves . . .").

16. Bo Gritz, "The Colonel's Corner," *Center for Action Newsletter* 3, no. 2 (September 1993), pp. 2–5; event brochure: "SPIKE Training," author received February 1993.

17. Robert Crawford, Steven Gardiner, Jonathan Mozzochi, "Almost Heaven? Bo Gritz, SPIKE and the Christian Covenant Communities," *Coalition for Human Dignity (CHD)*, CHD Research Report, February 1994; Timothy Egan, "Idaho Community Built on Hatred and Fear," *The New York Times*, October 5, 1991.

18. Bo Gritz, "The Colonel's Corner," *Center for Action—SPIKE*, vol. 3, no. 8 (March 1994), pp. 1–3.

19. Conversation with author, "Preparedness Expo," Bartle Expo Hall, Kansas City, Missouri, April 16–18, 1999.

20. "Don't Be Fooled on Y2K," *The Spotlight* (News You May Have Missed), December 14, 1998, p. 2.

21. Andrew Arnold, "Doomsayers Cash In on Year 2000 Hysteria," *The Spotlight*, January 17, 2000, p. 9.
22. Special bulletin, "American Family Preparedness: Important Additional News and Views from *The Spotlight* on Your Constitutional Rights," Winter 1999 (*The Spotlight* twenty-page insert).
23. Pastor Peter J. Peters, "Y2K Millennium Bug: The Latest Fear Fad," *Scriptures for America Newsletter*, vol. 3, 1998; Zeskind, "Y2K Is Not the End of the World Says Identity Preacher."
24. Pastor Pete Peters, "A Special Message and Invitation," *Scriptures for America*, mailing insert and invitation to Peters's wedding on April 24, 1999, received March 25, 1999.
25. Pastor Peter J. Peters, "Y2K Millennium Bug."
26. Leonard Zeskind, *The Christian Identity Movement: Analyzing Its Theological Rationalization for Racist and Anti-Semitic Violence*, Center for Democratic Renewal, Published by the Division of Church and Society, National Council of Churches of Christ in the U.S.A., October 1986, pp. 21–25.
27. Michael Barkun, *Religion and the Racist Right: The Origins of the Christian Identity Movement* (Chapel Hill: University of North Carolina Press, 1994), pp. 110–12 ("for Identity, the ultimate disaster is not natural but demographic, and the harbor an obsessive concern with racial obliteration"), pp. 118–19 ("Identity's millenarian scenario is interwoven with [various instances of human action]").
28. "U.S. Summary 2000," United States Census Bureau, Census 2000, July 2002.
29. "By the Time She Retires, Will the U.S. Be an Overcrowded Country?," *Middle American News*, August 2003 (back page).
30. See also Jared Taylor, "Race and Nation." Text of 1996 speech at American Renaissance Conference in Jared Taylor, ed., *The Real American Dilemma: Race, Immigration, and the Future of America* (Oakton, Va.: New Century Foundation, 1988).
31. *Racial Attitudes of 18–29 Year Olds*, The Arthur Levitt Public Affairs Center at Hamilton College, August 1999, cosponsored by the NAACP and Zogby International, question no. 7, p. 5.

53. Elections 2000: The Neo-Confederate Resurgence

1. Leonard Zeskind, "Neo-Confederates Fight NAACP Boycott," *Searchlight*, February 2000; Joseph S. Stroud, "6,000 Attend Spirited Rally for Confederate Flag," *The State*, January 9, 2000; Jim Davenport, "6,000 Rally for Confederate Flag," Associated Press, January 8, 2000; Joseph S. Stroud, "As Legislators Return, S.C. Senator's 'Insult' Hardens Flag Debate," *The State*, January 11, 2000.
2. Leonard Zeskind, "Neo-Confederates Fight NAACP Boycott."
3. David Nordan, "Miller Vows to Strike Battle Flag," *Daily News*, May 29, 1992; "Flags That Have Flown over Georgia: The History of the Georgia State Flag," Georgia secretary of state Karen C. Handel, Georgia State Flag 2001–2003, sos.georgia.gov/museum; "Georgia Legislature Endorses New Flag," CNN.com, April 26, 2003; "Georgia Flag Facts," Camp 1399 Sons of Confederate Veterans, Warner Robins, Georgia.
4. "Big Pro-flag Rally Hilton Head Island, SC September 4th" and "South Carolina C of CC," *Citizens Informer* 25 (Summer 1994), p. 5. "State C of CC chairman Dr. William G. Carter."
5. Charles Hamel, "The Confederate Flag Battle: What Really Happened in South Carolina," *Southern Partisan*, 1st Quarter 2000.
6. Jared Taylor, "The Broader Context of Attacks on Our Flag," *Citizens Informer* 25 (Spring 1994), p. 9 (reprinted from "Confederate Crossroads newsletter John Hunt Morgan Camp SCV Louisville Ky April 1994").
7. J. Michael Martinez, "Confederate Symbols, the Courts, and the Political Question Doctrine," *Confederate Symbols in the Contemporary South* (Gainesville: University Press of Florida, 2000), pp. 321–35.
8. Leonard Zeskind, "Klan Bombs & Swastika Flags Mix in Nativist Movement," *Searchlight*, September 2005.
9. Pat Buchanan, "Battle Flag Issue Is Synthetic and Phony," *Citizens Informer* 25 (Summer 1994), p. 2.

54. Pat Buchanan and the Reform Party

1. "Reporters from *The Spotlight* and *The Baltimore Sun* Interviewed Pat Buchanan at the March 4 Reform Party Meeting in Greenbelt, Maryland," and "Liberty Lobby's Congressional Liaison," *The Spotlight*, April 3, 2000, p. 28; "Buchanan 2000: The People vs the Big Media, the Big Money & the Global Elite," tabloid reprint, Americans for Buchanan, April 10, 2000; Tom Stuckey, "Buchanan Wows Reform Party; Collects Eight Delegates," Associated Press, March 4, 2000.

2. Brigid Schulte and Ron Dzwonkowski, "United They Stand No Longer: Perot Movement Is Beset by Squabbling," *Detroit Free Press*, June 18, 1996, p. 4a.

3. Beverly Kidder, "The Wave of Reform: A History of the Reform Party," Reform Party 2000 convention document.

4. Mike Glover, "Reform Party Split Opens Complex Ballot Access Fight," Associated Press, August 25, 2000.

5. "How You Can Help Get Pat Nominated: Buchanan Supporters Must 'Go Reform' for Buchanan to Get Reform Party Nomination," *The Spotlight*, February 14, 2000; "America Needs Change at the Top," *The Spotlight*, February 14, 2000; Vince Ryan, "For Years Patriots Have Talked About 'Unifying Forces'—Here's the Man Who Can Do It," *The Spotlight*, January 31, 2000; Laurie Kellman, "Buchanan's Bid Called Quiet Coup," Associated Press, April 27, 2000.

6. John R. Moore, "Buchanan Used, Abused Supporters," *The Spotlight*, July 6, 1998, p. 21.

7. Christopher J. Petherick, "Buchanan Wants America's Sovereignty Restored," *The Spotlight*, February 7, 2001; "Liberty Lobby to Back Pat," *The Spotlight*, January 24, 2000; "Off and Running," *The Spotlight*, November 8, 1999.

8. Pat Buchanan, *Meet the Press* with Tim Russert, August 13, 2000, transcript from www.msnbc.com/news.

9. "Liberty Lobby's Congressional Liaison," p. 28.

10. "Editor-in-chief: Dr. Samuel Francis, Managing Editor: Chris Temple," *Citizens Informer* 31 (December 1999), p. 2.

11. Michael W. Masters, "Republican or Third Party?," *American Renaissance*, December 1999; *Citizen Informer*s for the year 2000 emphasized immigration and Confederate flag issues rather than presidential election alternatives.

12. Devin Burghart, *Party Crashers: White Nationalists and Election 2000*, report, Center for New Community, July 20, 2000, p. 10.

13. Ibid., pp. 9–11; "Support Pat Buchanan," fund-raiser at Holy Resurrection Serbian Orthodox Cathedral, Coalition for a Just Peace in the Balkans, June 30, 2000; Patrick J. Buchanan, "U.S. Should Stay Out of Bosnian Conflict," *Human Events*, May 15, 1993.

14. Burghart, *Party Crashers: White Nationalists and Election 2000*.

15. Mark Cotterill, "Pat Buchanan," *American Friends of the B.N.P. Members and Supporters Bulletin*, May–June 2000, p. 2.

16. Thomas Edsall, "Buchanan's Bid Transforms the Reform Party," *The Washington Post*, July 23, 2000, p. A4; Leonard Zeskind, "White Nationalists Just Love Buchanan," *Los Angeles Times*, July 30, 2000.

17. "Reform Leaders Vote to Drop Buchanan," Associated Press, July 30, 2000; Kellie B. Gormly, "Buchanan Removed from Ballot," Associated Press, July 30, 2000; Susan Parrott, "Hagelin Says Committee's Vote to Oust Buchanan Makes Him Sole Reform Party Candidate," Associated Press, July 31, 2000; Clayton Potts, "Buchanan Solidifies Hold on Party," *The Spotlight*, July 24, 2000.

18. Kellie B. Gormly, "Buchanan Removed from Ballot," Associated Press, July 30, 2000.

19. Clayton Potts, "Foes Try to Trip Up Buchanan," *The Spotlight*, August 14, 2000.

20. Devin Burghart, "Notes of Hagelin Press Conference, Westin Hotel, Long Beach, California," August 10, 2000, 9:00 a.m., communication to author; Devin Burghart, "Notes on Hagelin Party Convention Hall, Performing Arts Center," August 11, 2000, 3:30 p.m., communication to author.

21. Devin Burghart, "Notes of Buchanan Reform Party Convention Hall, Long Beach Convention Center," August 9, 2000, 2:00 p.m., communication to author; "Spotlight on People," *The Spotlight*, August 28, 2000, p. 20.

22. Warren Bates, "Retiree Hires Attorney to Help with Nativity Scene Battle," *Las Vegas Review Journal*, December 19, 1997.

23. Devin Burghart, "Notes on Buchanan Vice-President Announcement Press Conference Rainbow Harbor," August 11, 2000, 1:00 p.m., communication to author.

24. Peter Carlson, "Ezola Foster: Pat Buchanan's Far Right Hand," *The Washington Post*, September 13, 2000; "Buchanan Learns Running Mate Is Birch Member," Reuters, August 14, 2000; "Confederate Flag Stands for Heritage," Associated Press, October 25, 2000; Devin Burghart, "Ezola Foster's Reform Party Vice-Presidential Nomination Acceptance Speech," August 12, 2000.

25. Devin Burghart, "Notes on Ezola Foster Presentations," communication to author.

26. Devin Burghart, photos of Willis Carto and Joe Fields, Long Beach, communication with author.

27. Jared Taylor, "Ezola Foster for Vice President? A Disappointing Choice by Pat Buchanan," *American Renaissance*, October 2000.

28. Ibid.

29. Editorial, *The Spotlight*, December 4, 2000.

30. Tom Valentine, "Interview with Liberty Lobby Founder Willis A. Carto," *The Spotlight*, December 4, 2000.

31. Federal Election Commission, "2000 Presidential Popular Vote Summary for All Candidates Listed on at Least One State Ballot," update December 2001: Gore 50,999,897 (48.38 percent), Bush 50,456,002 (47.87 percent), Buchanan 448,895 (0.42 percent); John Nichols with research by David Deschamps, *Jews for Buchanan: Did You Hear the One About the Theft of the American Presidency?* (New York: New Press, 2001), pp. 86–87.

32. *George W. Bush et al. v. Albert Gore, Jr. et al.*, Supreme Court of the United States, 531 U.S.___2000, December 12, 2000.

33. Federal Election Commission, "2000 Presidential Popular Vote Summary for All Candidates Listed on at Least One State Ballot," update December 2001.

34. "Doctors Remove Buchanan's Gall Bladder," *The New York Times*, August 19, 2000.

35. Eun-Kyung Kim, "Will the Real Reform Party Nominee Stand? FEC to Decide," Associated Press, August 22, 2000; Chelyen Davis, "Reform Party Spat Back in U.S. Court," *Richmond Times Dispatch*, August 23, 2000; "Reform Factions Wage State-by-State Ballot Battle; Ballot-printing deadline: Some states hold a lottery to see if Hagelin or Buchanan get spot," *Telegraph Herald*, August 25, 2000; Scott Lindlaw, "Buchanan Wing Again Seeks Recognition as Presidential Nominee," Associated Press, September 5, 2000; "Reform Party Nomination Fight Moves to California Courts," *The Bulletin's Frontrunner*, September 6, 2000; Scott Lindlaw, "Judge Declines to Block Hagelin from Campaigning," Associated Press, September 7, 2000; Scott Lindlaw, "Return to Long Beach: Future of Reform Party May Rest in Court," Associated Press, September 7, 2000; "Buchanan Attorney Appeals Ballot Decision to Supreme Court," Associated Press, September 12, 2000; Amy Franklin, "Appeals Court Denies Buchanan's Appeal to Appear on Michigan Ballot," Associated Press, September 12, 2000; Matthew Daly, "Buchanan Files Suit to Win Place on Reform Party Line," Associated Press, September 13, 2000; "FEC Says Buchanan Should Get Federal Funds; Buchanan Heads to Bob Jones University," *The Bulletin's Frontrunner*, September 13, 2000; Richard A. Ryan, "Buchanan Vows Write-in Campaign: Reform Party Candidate's Lawyers Plan Lawsuit Alleging Voters Denied Voting Rights," *The Detroit News*, September 15, 2000; "Justices Block Reform Candidates: Pat Buchanan Heads for Federal Court to Argue for a Place on the State Ballot. His Rival from the Split Party Already Is On," *Grand Rapids Press*, September 16, 2000.

36. "The Coming Disappointment," unsigned editorial, *Citizens Informer*, January/February 2001.

37. Samuel Francis, "It's Race, Stupid," *American Renaissance*, January 2001.

38. Samuel Francis, "Rout of the Republicans," *Chronicles*, February 2001.

39. Federal Elections Commission, "Federal Elections Commission, 2000 Official Presidential General Election Results, updated December 2001": North Carolina—Buchanan 8,874; Bush 1,631,163; Gore 1,257,692. South Carolina—Buchanan 3,519; Bush 785,937; Gore 565,561.

40. "Proposed Statewide Amendment Number 2," Proposed Constitutional Amendments to Appear on Statewide Ballots, November 7, 2000, General Election, www.sos.state.al.us/election/2000/general/amendlang.htm.

41. Alabama General Election by Counties, Amendments 1–14, November 7, 2000.

42. Micah Altman and Philip A. Klinkner, "White Voting Versus Polling Results on Interracial Marriage: Measuring the Differences Between White Voting and Polling on Interracial Marriage," *Dubois Review Social Science on Race* 3(2), pp. 299–315.

55. The Liberty Lobby Fortress Crumbles

1. *The Spotlight*, July 9, 2001 ("You are holding in your hands the last edition . . .").

2. Judge Ruston G. Maino, "Decision," *Legion for the Survival of Freedom v. Carto, Fischer, Vibet, Furr, Furr and Liberty Lobby*, Superior Court of California, N64584, December 15, 2000 ("The Forbearance Agreement is hereby set aside and plaintiff may proceed to collect on the judgment"); "Judge Says: Seize Liberty Lobby," *The Spotlight*, December 31, 2000.

3. Judge Gladys Kessler, "Memorandum Order," filed September 10, 2001, *In Re: Liberty Lobby, Inc. Debtor*, United States District Court for the District of Columbia, Civil Action no. 01-1505 (GK) and Bankruptcy Case no. 01-1234 (describes Teel's order of June 29, 2001, and July 2, 2001, and denies Liberty Lobby's plea for a stay); Andrea Billups, "Liberty Lobby Goes Under, Ends *Spotlight* Publication," *The Washington Times*, July 10, 2001.

4. The transition and transformation cited here was movementwide, rather than just related to *The Spotlight*'s circulation figures, which had been slipping since President Reagan took office.

5. Sanford Griffith, "Insider Reveals New Facts About Weber & Cronies," *The Spotlight*, January 15, 2001; Sanford Griffith, "Conspirator Exposed," *The Spotlight*, January 22, 2001; Sanford Griffith, "Weber's Buddy: JDL Chief Irv Rubin," *The Spotlight*, January 29, 2001; Sanford Griffith, "Are You in Mark Weber's Secret File?," *The Spotlight*, February 5, 2001; Sanford Griffith, "Weber Found His Guru in the African Desert," *The Spotlight*, February 12, 2001; Sanford Griffith, "'Famous Historian' Might Get Fired," *The Spotlight*, February 19, 2001; Sanford Griffith, "Is Weber Sabotaging Revisionism?," *The Spotlight*, March 15, 2001; Mark Weber, "A Response to Recent *Spotlight* Attacks," April 3, 2001, homepage.mac/lsf/news/010403mwresponse.html (Weber described these attacks as "rubbish"); Mark Weber, interview with author, August 13, 2001, Weber denied the substance and the tenor of the attacks.

6. "Listing of cases between Willis Carto and the Legion for the Survival of Freedom (current as of 2/15/2001)," homepage.mac.com/lsf/litigation/cases.html; "The Willis A. Carto Information Site," homepage.mac.com/lsf/index2.html.

7. Rafael Medoff and Alex Grobman, *Holocaust Denial: A Global Survey—2007*, The David S. Wyman Institute for Holocaust Studies.

8. *David John Cawdell Irving v. Penguin Books Ltd. and Deborah E. Lipstadt*, in the High Court of Justice Queen's Bench Division; Deborah E. Lipstadt, *History on Trial: My Day in Court with David Irving* (New York: HarperCollins, 2005); "Holocaust Denier Irving Is Jailed," BBC News, February 20, 2006.

9. "13th IHR Conference: A Resounding Success," Institute for Historical Review, *Journal of Historical Review* 19, no. 3; "Thirteenth Conference Marks Revisionist Renaissance," Institute for Historical Review, *IHR Update*, July 2000.

10. "International Conference on Revisionism and Zionism Set for Beirut," *News from IHR*, December 26, 2000; David Saks, "Strong Objections to Beirut Holocaust Denial Conference," *The South African Jewish Report*, March 9, 2001; "Beirut 'Revisionism and Zionism' Conference Called Off," Institute for Historical Review, March 30, 2001; Leonard Zeskind, "Middle East Meets West in Beirut, Will Jürgen Graf Risk Leaving Iran," *Searchlight*, April 2001.

11. Daniel Schorr, "The Iranian Effort to Mount a Holocaust Denial Campaign Is Linked With the Israeli-Palestinian Crisis," *The Christian Science Monitor*, December 22, 2006; President George W. Bush, "Statement on Holocaust Denial Conference Sponsored by Iranian Regime," press release, December 12, 2006.

56. After September 11, 2001

1. "Bush's Remarks to Cabinet and Advisers," *The New York Times*, September 13, 2001, p. 16 (transcript of address).

2. Daniel Levitas, "The Radical Right After 9/11," *The Nation*, July 22/29, 2002, pp. 19–23; Debora MacKenzie, "Anthrax Preparation Indicates Home-grown Origin," *New Scientist (UW)*, October 1, 2001.

3. Adam Liptak, Neil A. Lewis, and Benjamin Weiser, "After September 11, a Legal Battle over Limits of Civil Liberty," *The New York Times*, August 4, 2002.

4. Leonard Zeskind, "One Year and Too Many Deaths Later," *Searchlight*, September 2002; James Ridgeway, "An Informed Citizenry, Telling Trend Takes Hold," *The Village Voice*, June 11–17, 2003.

5. Glenn A. Fine, Inspector General, U.S. Department of Justice, "Prepared Testimony Before the Senate Committee on the Judiciary," 2003 Federal News Service, Inc., June 25, 2003 (full report released June 2, 2003, titled "The September 11 Detainees: A Review of the Treatment of Aliens Held on Immigration Charges in Connection with the Investigation of the September 11 Attacks").

6. Joan McKinney, "Cooksey: Expect Racial Profiling," *Advocate Washington Bureau*, September 19, 2001 (quote from U.S. Rep. John Cooksey R-Monroe, Louisiana).

7. Levitas, "The Radical Right After 9/11"; Laurie Goodstein, "Falwell's Finger Pointing Inappropriate, Bush Says," *The New York Times*, September 15, 2001.

8. Ann Coulter, "This Is War, We Should Invade Their Countries," *National Review* (online), September 13, 2001; Jonah Goldberg, "L'Affaire Coulter: Goodbye to All That," *National Review* (online), October 1, 2001.

9. Richard A. Serrano, "Deluge of Hate Crimes After 9/11 Pours Through System Courts," *Los Angeles Times*, July 6, 2002; Jaxon van Derbeken, "American Nightmare: Sukhpal Singh Sodhi came to San Francisco to help his village in India . . . a year after his death, his family mourns again," *San Francisco Chronicle*, August 6, 2002.

10. Levitas, "The Radical Right After 9/11."

11. "Whirlwind: Around the country, the far right reacts to September's terror with anti-Semitic hatred, threats and conspiracy theories," *Intelligence Report*, Winter 2001, p. 18 (quote from Rocky Suhayda, Chairman of the American Nazi Party).

12. William Pierce, "Who Is Guilty?" *Free Speech*, National Alliance publication, vol. 7, no. 10, October 2001 (also broadcast via shortwave on September 22).

13. Graphic, *National Alliance Bulletin*, November 2001, p. 6.

14. Ibid.

15. William Pierce, "An Awakening," *American Dissident Voices*, December 1, 2001 (radio broadcast).

16. William Pierce, "New Opportunity," *National Alliance Bulletin*, November 2001, pp. 9–10.

17. Devin Burghart (unsigned), "Beyond a Dead Man's Deeds: The National Alliance After William Pierce," A Special Report by the Center for New Community, August 2002, p. 6; "New Building Started," *National Alliance Bulletin*, August 2001, p. 1.

18. "Internet Statistics," *National Alliance Bulletin*, October 2001, pp. 2–3 ("During the month there were 652,571 visits to our natvan.com website. That's an average of 21,051 per day").

19. "Report on National Alliance middle management leaders' briefing," sent to author, July 2001.

20. "Washington Protest," *National Alliance Bulletin*, July 2001, pp. 1–5.

21. "Anti-Terror Demonstration," *National Alliance Bulletin*, November 2001, pp. 1–2.

22. Ibid. Picture caption notes the "MOST CHALLENGING sign at the Israeli Embassy demonstration . . . Jewboy, Jewboy, What Ya' Gonna Do? What Ya' Gonna Do When WE Come for U"; Devin Burghart, photos, video and notes, communication to author, December 2001.

23. *Citizens Informer* 32, no. 6 (November/December 2001), p. 12 (photo caption notes "Speakers at the North Carolina CofCC November 10th anti-immigration protest in Conover, included . . . A. J. Barker"); "North Carolina," *Citizens Informer*, 33, no. 1 (January/February 2002), pp. 14, 16.

24. Jared Taylor, "Teaching More Millions to Hate Us," *Citizens Informer*, 32, no. 4 (July/August 2001), p. 3 (an editorial note introduces the article, stating it "does not necessarily

represent the editorial position of the *Citizens Informer*; it does, however, represent a view . . . that is too often silenced by the establishment media").

25. "Public Opinion Six Months Later; Nationhood, Internationalism Lifted," Pew Research for the People & the Press, March 7, 2002.

26. Robert D. Kaplan, "Looking the World in the Eye," *The Atlantic*, December 2001; Charles Krauthammer, "The Real New World Order: The American and the Islamic Challenge," *The Weekly Standard*, vol. 7, no. 9, November 12, 2001; David Brooks, "A Moment to Be Seized," *The Weekly Standard*, vol. 7, no. 17, January 14, 2002.

27. Andrew Kohut, "The 2004 Political Landscape: Evenly Divided and Increasingly Polarized," The Pew Research Center for the People & the Press, November 5, 2003, pp. 4–36.

28. Haider Rizvi, "Post-Katrina Poll Finds Americans Prioritizing Poverty over Terrorism," *Common Dreams News Center*, published on OneWorld.net, November 26, 2005 (conducted by "New California Media, a group representing more than 700 ethnic media organizations").

29. Samuel Francis, "How Do I Hate Thee? Let Me Count the Ways," *Chronicles*, January 2002, pp. 32–33; Philip Jenkins, "Thinking About the Fall of America," *Chronicles*, January 2002, pp. 49–50.

30. Francis, "How Do I Hate Thee? Let Me Count the Ways"; Samuel Francis, "The Tyrant's Lobby," *Chronicles*, February 2002, pp. 35–36.

57. The Anti-immigrant Movement Blossoms

1. "Council News: D.C., Virginia and Maryland," *Citizens Informer* 33, no. 1 (January/February 2002 ("The National Capital Region CofCC meeting on February 21, 2002"); communication to author, report on American Renaissance conference, "In Defense of Western Man," 2002 American Renaissance Conference, Herndon, Virginia, February 22–24, 2002.

2. Communication to author, report; The Cat Lady, "The Most Rational Place on Earth," *Vanguard News Network* (www.vanguardnewsnetwork.com), accessed February 27, 2002.

3. Patrick J. Buchanan, *The Death of the West: How Dying Populations and Immigrant Invasions Imperil Our Country and Civilization* (New York: St. Martin's Press, 2002), p. 5.

4. Ibid., pp. 11–24; communication to author, report.

5. Communication to author, report; The Cat Lady, "The Most Rational Place on Earth."

6. Devin Burghart, communication to author, September 2002.

7. Devin Burghart (unsigned), "Profile: Minuteman Civil Defense Corps (MCDC)," Building Democracy Initiative (www.buildingdemocracy.org), accessed September 4, 2007; Max Blumenthal, "Vigilante Injustice," Salon.com, May 22, 2003, accessed December 7, 2006.

8. Jeff Smith, "Protect Arizona Sounds OK Till You Add People," *Tucson Citizen*, July 7, 2004; Gill Donovan, "Arizona Bishops Oppose Proposition," *National Catholic Reporter Online*, October 29, 2004.

9. Secretary of State Jan Brewer, State of Arizona, Campaign Finance, Schedule E1, In-Kind Contributions, "Protect Arizona Now," June 30, 2004, report; Opinion (unsigned), "Support for Proposition 200 Has Its Deepest Roots Outside of Arizona," *Arizona Republic*, September 17, 2004.

10. Devin Burghart (unsigned), "Protect Arizona Now Selects White Supremacist Leader to Chair National Advisory Board," *Center for New Community*, Special Report, August 2004; Virginia Abernethy, "The Immigration Threat to Your Health and Your Pocket Book," *Citizens Informer* 33, no. 3 (May/June 2002), pp. 3, 12, 21: "Abernethy, Ph.D., is . . . on the Board of Directors of Carrying Capacity Network and a member of the *Citizens Informer* editorial advisory board." In addition, the Council News section features photos of "Lessons of 9-11" panel with Virginia Abernethy identified as panelist; "Too Much Immigration?," Carrying Capacity Network Advertisement, *Citizens Informer* 33, no.1 (January/February 2002), p. 8.

11. Burghart (unsigned), "Protect Arizona Now Selects White Supremacist Leader to Chair National Advisory Board."

12. "What FAIR Believes . . . One Unified American Community," Federation for American Immigration Reform, media press release, August 9, 2004.

13. Yvonne Wingett, "Protect Arizona Now Adviser Denies Racism Charge," *The Arizona Republic*, August 7, 2004.

14. "The Yes and No of Proposition 200—'The Immigration Initiative': Voters' Opinions About Proposition 200," *ThinkAZ*, August 2005.
15. Leonard Zeskind, "The New Nativism: The Alarming Overlap Between White Nationalists and Mainstream Anti-immigrant Forces," *The American Prospect*, November 2005, pp. A15–A18; John Hawkins, "An Interview with Congressman Tom Tancredo (R-CO)," *Right Wing News* (www.rightwingnews.com), accessed March 14, 2005.
16. Devin Burghart, Eric Ward, and Leonard Zeskind, "Nativism in the House: A Report on the House Immigration Reform Caucus," Center for New Community, Special Report, 2007; "About Us: Proposed Agenda for the 108th Congress," Congressional Immigration Reform Caucus (tancredo.house.gov), accessed August 24, 2005.
17. Devin Burghart, communication to author, July 15, 2005.

58. Willis Carto and William Pierce Leave the Main Stage

1. San Diego County Sheriff's Department, "Notice of Sheriff's Sale," *Legion for the Survival of Freedom (plaintiff) v. Willis Carto, et al. (defendant)*, February 20, 2002; "Carto Estate Auctioned for Pennies on the Dollar," March 20, 2002 (Legion says it paid $350,000 for the property and then turned around and offered it for sale).
2. Leonard Zeskind, "IHR Split Reveals Corporate Misdeeds," *Searchlight*, May 1994, p. 23; Leonard Zeskind, "Money Matters: Holocaust Denial Leaders Battle over Millions," *Intelligence Report*, Southern Poverty Law Center, Summer 1997; Leonard Zeskind, "Carto Loses Another Round," *Searchlight*, December 1997, p. 22; Leonard Zeskind, "Liberty Lobby Closes its Doors, *Spotlight* Ceases Publication," *Searchlight*, September 2001, pp. 32–33.
3. Willis Carto, "Debtor's Examination," June 21, 2001, *Legion for the Survival of Freedom v. Willis Carto*, N64584.
4. Attorneys for Willis A. and Elisabeth Carto, "Debtors' Schedules, Statement of Affairs, Attorney Compensation Disclosure . . . ," *In re Willis A. Carto and Elisabeth Carto*, United States Bankruptcy Court, Southern District of California, signed June 19, 1998 ("On May 19, 1998, Superior Court to be residence-owners in alter-ego capacity. Debtors deny this contention"); "Order Dismissing Case For Lack of Subject Matter Jurisdiction," *Hereford Corporation and Hans-Dirk Oldemeier, Plaintiffs v. Legion for the Survival of Freedom, Willis Carto and Elisabeth Carto*, United States District Court Southern District of California, 01CV2040 DTM (JFS), December 11, 2001.
5. "Carto Estate Auctioned for Pennies on the Dollar," March 20, 2002 ("It is thought to be worth in excess of $600,000"); "Notice of House for Sale, Hillside Hideaway," homepage.mac.com/lsf/personal/020227estate.html (this notice claimed the assessed value was $416,614).
6. *The Barnes Review* 9, no. 1 (January/February 2003); *American Free Press* 1, no. 1 (August 20, 2001); James P. Tucker, Jr., "OKC Cover-Up Exploding," *American Free Press*, May 16, 2004, www.americanfreepress.net.
7. "Dr. William L. Pierce Dies, Alliance Continues," *National Alliance Bulletin*, June 2002; Kevin Alfred Strom, "The Mission of the National Alliance," *National Alliance Bulletin*, June 2002.
8. Communication to author, August 2002.
9. *Beyond a Dead Man's Deeds: The National Alliance After William Pierce*, A Special Report by the Center for New Community, August 2002, p. 5.
10. Ibid.
11. David Cay Johnston, "William Pierce, 69, Neo-Nazi Leader, Dies," *The New York Times*, July 24, 2002.
12. Dennis Roddy, "Hate Was in His Blood but Not in His Genes," *Pittsburgh Post-Gazette*, August 28, 2002.
13. *Beyond a Dead Man's Deeds*, pp. 7–8.
14. "Erich Gliebe Chosen as National Alliance Chairman," *National Alliance Bulletin*, July 2002.

59. The Penultimate Moment

1. *Project Megiddo*, U.S. Department of Justice, Federal Bureau of Investigation ("National Alliance . . . Pierce is able to provide his followers with an ideological and practical framework for committing violent acts").
2. Devin Burghart, photos, video, and notes, communication to author, September 5, 2005; "Taxpayers Against Terrorism," *National Alliance Bulletin*, August 2002, pp. 4–6.
3. Billy Roper, "NA Attacked," National Alliance Membership e-mail (Members@Natvan .com), August 26, 2002.
4. Leonard Zeskind, "National Alliance Inches Toward a New Path," *Searchlight*, August 2004; Roger Williams, Kevin Alfred Strom, Rich Lindstrom, Robert Pate, et al., "Time for Leadership: Full Text of the Declaration of National Alliance Leaders and Members Demanding Honesty, Openness, Accountability, and Reorganization," April 22, 2005, www.nationalvanguard.org, accessed April 27, 2005.
5. David M. Pringle, "Demand an Audit," November 22, 2004, www.whitewire.net, accessed April 27, 2005.
6. David M. Pringle, "History Will Perform the Autopsy: It Is Time to Move On," February 2005, www.whitewire.net (accessed April 27, 2005).
7. Jayson Whitehead, "Strom Pleads Guilty to Child Porn," *Charlottesville News & Arts*, accessed September 9, 2008; "Strom Sentenced," www.nbc29.com, accessed September 9, 2008.
8. "Send Mail to: Tom Metzger . . . Warsaw, Indiana," *Aryan Update*, March 25, 2008.
9. "Final Decree of Divorce," *Sheila M. Toohey v. Louis Ray Beam*, U.S. District Court Idaho First Judicial District, CV 01-3900, November 10, 1997; Bill Morlin, "Judge Postpones Racist's Child Custody Hearing," *The Spokesman Review*, February 5, 2002.
10. "Got a Letter from Bruce Pierce," Free Your Mind Forum, www.freeyourmindproductions .com, accessed January 1, 2006.
11. David Lane, "Auto-biographical Portrait of the Life of David Lane & the 14 Word Motto" (St. Maries, Idaho: 14 Word Press, 1994) (Press established by David Lane. Publications include *Focus Fourteen*, described as the "Official Newsletter of 14 Word Press." The fourteen words were featured on the masthead: "We must secure the existence of our people and a future for White children"); David Lane, "If Federals Don't Succeed, They Will Try and Try Again," *The Spotlight*, June 5, 1995, p. 10; David Lane, "Vengeance Now!," *WAR* 13 (March 1994); David Eden Lane, "The Right WAY," *Calling Our Nation, Aryan Nations* 58, p. 6; "Warrior David Lane Died Today at Age 69," *Stormfront White Nationalist Community*, May 28, 2007 (www.stormfront.org), accessed May 30, 2007; Leonard Zeskind, "David Lane Dies in Prison," *Searchlight*, July 2007.
12. Stephen Stuebner, "True Gritz: Will the Real Bo Gritz Please Stand Up?," *Intelligence Report*, Fall 1998, pp. 10–15; Bob Fick, "Despairing Gritz Shoots Himself in the Chest," *Idaho Statesman*, September 22, 1998.
13. Anne Hall, "Back Home in Iowa, He's Got Memories," *Washington Post*, April 30, 2001.
14. Chris Temple, "Martha's Free—But I'm Not," *Chris Temple On Line*, March 6, 2005 (sentenced to six years in prison on July 21, 2004, U.S. District Court, Madison, Wisconsin).
15. "Trochmann Ousted from Militia, Starts New Group," *Montana Human Rights Network*, October 2006.
16. "About National Director Pastor Thomas Robb," The Official Website of The Knights Party, UWA (www.kkk.bz), accessed September 9, 2008 ("All three of [Robb's] grown children are active in the white rights movement").
17. Pete Peters, "From the Editor's Pen," *Scriptures for America*, vol. 5, 2006 ("Other items . . . allow us to improve our live video streaming and recording"); "Scripture for America 2006 Conferences & Vacations," *Scriptures for America*, vol. 4, 2006 (conferences from Waging Spiritual Warfare in Branson, MO, to Spiritual R&R in the Rocky Mountains of Colorado).
18. Tracy Rose, "The War Between the Sons: Members Fight for Control of Confederate Group," *Mountain Xpress*, Asheville, North Carolina, February 5, 2003; Kirk Lyons, "Kirk Lyons Responds to the Latest 'Hawks Smear Campaign' in Race for Army of Northern Virginia Commander," Lyons for ANV Commander press release, January 2002 (www.main.nc.us) (accessed September 11, 2005).

19. "Stormfront White Nationalist Community Statistics," *Stormfront.org* (www.stormfront.org), (accessed September 9, 2008) (members' statistics listed as 141,084 on September 8, 2008).

20. Wayne Lutton, "A Note from the Editor: Untimely Death of Samuel Francis Great Loss to National Debates," *The Social Contract*, 2005, p. 155.

60. The Future

1. "Voters Pass All 11 Bans on Gay Marriage," Associated Press, November 3, 2004; Leonard Zeskind, "The New Nativism," *The American Prospect*, November 2005.

2. "International European American Unity and Leadership Conference," May 28–30, program agenda brochure; "Untitled communication report detailing the event," to author, n.d. (the event site was the Airport Plaza Hotel); Leonard Zeskind, "Return of the Whiteist," *The Nation*, August 4, 2004, www.thenation.com/doc/20040816/zeskind.

3. "Congressman Duke? An Analysis of David Duke's Bid for the First Congressional District Seat," Southern Institute for Education and Research, January 25, 1999 (cites Duke's 11 percent vote in 1996 race); David Duke, "Victory! We Win Chairmanship of Largest Republican Parish in Louisiana!," *The David Duke Report* 36; Kevin McGill, untitled, Associated Press, May 2, 1999 (cites Duke vote at 19 percent); David Duke, "Anatomy of an Election," *The David Duke Report* 43.

4. David Duke, *My Awakening: A Path to Racial Understanding* (Covington, La.: Free Speech Press, 1998).

5. Postal Inspector William A. Bonney, "Ex-Klan Leader David Duke Sentenced to 15 Months for Mail and Tax Fraud," *U.S. Postal Inspection Service Bulletin*, October 2003, pp. 33–35, postalinspectors.usps.gov/radDocs/pubs/bull03_4; Alan Sayre, "Ex-Klan Leader David Duke Returns to U.S.," Associated Press, December 16, 2002 (cites Duke's attorney as claiming the investigation began with the discovery that Governor Mike Foster had paid Duke $100,000 for his contributors list); John McQuaid, "Duke's Decline," *The Times-Picayune*, April 13, 2003 (ex-girlfriend Christy Martin "approached authorities with evidence").

6. David Duke, letter, "I want to wish you and your family a meaningful and beautiful Christmas," December 10, 1998, reproduced in full as a graphic in Postal Inspector William A. Bonney, "Ex-Klan Leader David Duke Sentenced to 15 Months for Mail and Tax Fraud."

7. Postal Inspector William A. Bonney, "Ex-Klan Leader David Duke Sentenced to 15 Months for Mail and Tax Fraud."

8. Martin A. Lee, "Insatiable," *Intelligence Report* 109, Spring 2003; Leonard Zeskind, "David Duke: Playboynazisten," *Expo*, Stockholm, Nos. 3–4, 2005.

9. Richard Moore, "Israel 'Leading Terrorist Nation,'" November 13, 2002, www.gulf-daily-news/Articles.asp?Article=36963&Sn+BNEW (describes speech in Bahrain); communication to author, n.d. (Duke in Germany and France); John McQuaid, "Duke's Decline."

10. Betsy Blaney, "Duke Turns Himself In to Begin 15-Month Sentence in Big Spring Facility," Associated Press, April 15, 2003.

11. "Duke Released from Federal Prison in West Texas," Associated Press, April 9, 2004; David Duke, dickson-June 21, 2004 09:30.53.wma, audio broadcast file posted at the time, www.davidduke.com.

12. Sam Dickson, dickson-June 21, 2004 09:30.53.wma.

13. Ibid.

14. Ibid.

15. In addition to those factors taken into account by social scientists measuring public opinion, significant anecdotal data supports this observation. During David Duke's election races polling data continually undercounted his supporters.

ACKNOWLEDGMENTS

Acknowledgments cannot properly express my gratitude to the many people, some of whom are now deceased, who contributed to *Blood and Politics*.

Daniel Levitas generously shared his own research with me over the decades and pushed me down a path that led to this book. Ron Goldfarb, my literary agent, had faith in me to produce it. Denise Oswald demonstrated wisdom and patience while also wielding a green pencil as my editor. Kevin Goering, Jessica Ferri, Lisa Silverman, Thomas LeBien, Elizabeth Maples, Brian Gittis, and the others on the production team at Farrar, Straus and Giroux helped make it all happen. Elinor Langer read the entire manuscript with a sharp literary eye, convinced me to take out some of the jokes and most of the riddles, and taught me a few of the finer points of writing. Devin Burghart supported my effort in myriad ways, and his investigative and analytical skills were invaluable. Michael Hahn read the manuscript and saved me from myself at several crucial points.

Thanks to the Petra Foundation, which gave me one of its prized "unsung heroes" awards in 1992. The John D. and Catherine T. MacArthur Foundation made me a fellow in 1998. Jennifer Warburg often worked in tandem. Thanks also to Copaken, White, and Blitt. Without Celeste Phillips and Michael D. Sullivan this project may never have gotten started, and Celeste nursed it along the way.

In addition to those named above, reading and making substantial critical comments on chapters as they developed over the past fifteen years were: Jean Casella, Elaine Davenport, Lance Hill, Larry Powell, Bill Berkowitz, Jill Norgren, Chris Pyle, Juli Highfil, Brenda Vann, Lauren Miller, and Ruth Sacks. Lisa Woolery, Lisa Spaulding, Jim McDonald, and Elizabeth Lindquist served, in effect, as a focus group for the first full draft.

Others provided useful information and research: Robert J. Crawford, Charles L. Tanner, Jr., Elizabeth A. Rickey, Penni Crabtree, Scott Armstrong, Hylah Jacques, Ken Stern, Steven Gardiner, Keith Hurt, Mike Reynolds, Mark Potok, Sandi Dubowski, Marlene Hines, Ken Toole, Christine Kauffman, Travis McAdams, Clair Johnson, Donald I. Warren, Felix, Label Vitterman, Mark Alfonso and the staff and volunteers at the Center for Democratic Renewal, Robert Sweet, Elaine Cantrell, Renee Poe, Justin Massa, Martin Theriault, Randi-Lee Taylor, and Jonathan Mozzochi, who did double duty with a stint cleaning up the filing system.

Thanks to those who contributed to multiple office tasks over the years: Emilie Goodhart, Aaron Rittmaster, Larry Rittmaster, Ben Wilkins, Mike Enriquez, and Isabelle Fremerman.

Graeme Atkinson, Gerry Gable, Sonia Gable, Nick Lowles, and Steve Silver at *Searchlight* magazine have all assisted. Lynora Williams and Randall Williams first taught me the fundamentals of journalism. James Ridgeway kept asking "what is the story here?" as we worked together on the Oklahoma City bombing and other points of interest. The journalists Judy Thomas, Bill Morlin, Dennis Roddy, Jerry Mitchell, and Jim East acted in the most collegial fashion. Sonja Tichy, Carole Travis, Stew Albert, and Judy Albert provided emotional sustenance and shelter when it was needed. Librarians at special collections at Tulane University, the University of Oregon, Kansas University, the University of Iowa, and the Wisconsin State Historical Society were all gracious and granted access to important documents; my appreciation also to the staff at the Bloch Law School Library at the University of Missouri–Kansas City. Others helped in many ways.

Robert V. Crawford, Felix, Bob Jay, Marek Lumb, Dong Luna, and Label Vitterman are pseudonyms for sources cited in the notes.

David Goldstein taught me to do three-point speeches. Judy Hellman welcomed me to her family shtetl. To my immediate family, and particularly to Carol, not enough can be said to thank you for everything you have given.

INDEX